Toyota Land Cruiser Owners Workshop Manual

by J H Haynes
Member of the Guild of Motoring Writers
and Peter Ward

Models covered:

UK
All models fitted with the 4230 cc engine

USA
Covers FJ40, FJ43, FJ45 and FJ55 models fitted with the 236.7 cu in (3878 cc) and 258 cu in (4230 cc) engines

Covers petrol (gasoline) engines only

ISBN 0 85696 313 5

© Haynes Publishing Group 1977

All rights reserved. No part of this book may be reproduced or transmitted in any form or by any means, electronic or mechanical, including photocopying, recording or by any information storage or retrieval system, without permission in writing from the copyright holder.

Printed in England   (313 - 10C1)

ABCDE
FGHIJ
KLMNO

HAYNES PUBLISHING GROUP
SPARKFORD YEOVIL SOMERSET ENGLAND
distributed in the USA by
HAYNES PUBLICATIONS INC
861 LAWRENCE DRIVE
NEWBURY PARK
CALIFORNIA 91320
USA

Acknowledgements

Special thanks are due to Toyota Motor Sales Co, Ltd of Nagoya, Japan, and their UK concessionaires Toyota (GB) Ltd of Croydon, for the supply of technical information and certain illustrations. Toyota (GB) Ltd also supplied the FJ55 series Land Cruiser which is featured in the photographs. Castrol Limited supplied the lubrication data, and the Champion Sparking Plug Company supplied the photographs of various sparking plug conditions. The bodywork repair photographs used in this manual were provided by Lloyds Industries Limited who supply 'Turtle Wax', Dupli-color Holts,' and other Holts range products.

Special thanks are due to the Radstock Road Motor Company, Somer Garage, Radstock Road, Midsomer Norton, Bath, who kn kindly allowed us to photograph the Land-Cruiser Pick-up which appears on page 5.

Lastly, thanks are due to all those people at Sparkford who helped in the production of this manual. Particularly, these are, Brian Horsfall who did the mechanical work and Leon Martindale who took the photographs.

About this manual

Its aims

This manual is written especially for the practical owner who wishes to carry out the maintenance and repair of his vehicle without recourse to professional garage services. It is written in simple, everyday language so that even the inexperienced handyman can understand, and undertake, the tasks described. Wherever possible, the use of special tools has been avoided and detailed descriptions of alternative methods included.

Its arrangement

The book is divided into twelve Chapters. Each Chapter is divided into numbered Sections which are headed in **bold type** between horizontal lines. Each Section consists of serially numbered paragraphs.

It is freely illustrated, especially in those parts where there is a detailed sequence of operations to be carried out. The figures are numbered in sequence with decimal numbers according to their position in the Chapter, eg; Fig. 4.6 is the sixth illustration in Chapter 4. Photographs have a number in the caption which relates to a Section and paragraph number within the same Chapter.

Procedures, once described in the text, are not normally repeated. If it is necessary to refer to another Chapter the reference will be given in Chapter number and Section number.

There is an alphabetical index at the back of the manual as well as 'contents' listed at the front.

References to the 'left' or 'right' of the vehicle are in the sense of a person sitting in the driver's seat.

Points for the reader

Where appropriate, fault finding instructions are given at the end of Chapters. Accurate diagnosis of trouble depends on a careful, and above all, systematic approach. Please avoid the attitude 'if all else fails - read the handbook'. It is better and almost always quicker to say 'this could be one of several things so let's have a look at the *Haynes Manual* before trying anything'.

Whilst every care is taken to ensure that the information in this manual is correct - bearing in mind the changes in design and specification which are a continuous process, even within a model range - **no liability can be accepted by the authors and publishers for any loss, damage or injury caused by any errors in, or omissions from, the information given.**

Contents

Chapter	Page
Introductory sections	2 to 14
Acknowledgements	2
About this manual	2
Introduction to the Toyota Land Cruiser	6
Buying spare parts and vehicle identification numbers	6
Jacking and towing	7
Routine maintenance	8
Tools and working facilities	11
Chapter 1/Engine	15 to 38
Chapter 2/Cooling system	39 to 44
Chapter 3/Fuel, exhaust and emission control system	45 to 91
Chapter 4/Ignition system	92 to 103
Chapter 5/Clutch	104 to 111
Chapter 6/Transmission, transfer gear, power take-off and winch	112 to 141
Chapter 7/Propeller shaft	142 to 144
Chapter 8/Rear axle and suspension	145 to 152
Chapter 9/Front axle, front suspension and steering	153 to 164
Chapter 10/Brakes, wheels and tires	165 to 180
Chapter 11/Electrical system	181 to 243
Chapter 12/Bodywork and chassis	244 to 264
Metric conversion tables	265
Index	266 to 268

Land Cruiser Station Wagon (USA Specification)

Land Cruiser Pick-up (UK Specification)

Introduction to the Toyota Land Cruiser

The Land Cruiser models cover a wide range of applications. The FS40 series models are fairly basic utility-type vehicles, and are produced on a chassis with a wheelbase of 90 in/2285 mm (FJ40), 95.7 in/2430 mm (FJ43) and 116.1 in/2950 mm (FJ45). The range incorporates hardtop, canvas top, pick-up and wagon versions, as well as special application vehicles. FJ55 series is more luxuriously equipped, and is produced as a wagon version with a 106.3 in (2700 mm) wheelbase.

The engines on the models covered by this manual are the F series, 236.7 cu in, 6-cylinder for pre-1975 models and the 2F series, 258 cu in, 6-cylinder for 1975 models onwards. Drive to the axles is through a 3- or 4-speed manual transmission and transfer gear, and propeller shafts. The front and rear axles are attached to the ladder-type chassis frame by leaf springs.

Hydraulic brakes are used on all models, the later types having a tandem braking system. The parking brake is operated through a link and cable arrangement to the drum brake mounted on the transfer gear output shaft to the rear propeller shaft.

Buying spare parts

Spare parts are available from many sources; for example Toyota main dealers, other dealers and auto accessory shops, and motor factors. Our advice regarding spare part sources is as follows:

Officially appointed vehicle main dealers - This is the best source of parts which are peculiar to your vehicle and are otherwise not generally available (eg; complete cylinder heads, internal transmission components, badges, interior trim etc). It is also the only place at which you should buy parts if your vehicle is still under warranty. To be sure of obtaining the correct parts it will always be necessary to give the storeman your vehicle's engine and vehicle series numbers, and if possible, to take the 'old' part along for positive identification. Remember that many parts are available on a factory exchange scheme - any parts returned should always be clean! It obviously makes good sense to go straight to the specialists on your vehicle for this type of part, for they are best equipped to supply you.

Other dealers and auto accessory stores - These are often very good places to buy materials and components needed for the maintenance of your vehicle (eg; oil filters, spark plugs, bulbs, fan belts, oils and greases, touch-up paint, filler paste, etc). They also sell general accessories, usually have convenient opening hours, charge lower prices and can often be found not far from home.

Motor factors - Good factors will stock all of the more important components which wear out relatively quickly (eg; clutch components, pistons, valves, exhaust systems, brake cylinders/pipes/hoses/seals/shoes and pads etc). Motor factors will often provide new or reconditioned components on a part exchange basis - this can save a considerable amount of money.

Engine and vehicle serial numbers and information plates

The engine number is stamped on the right-hand side of the cylinder block above the starter motor (photo).

The vehicle serial number is stamped on the left main chassis member for FJ55 models and on the right main chassis member for FJ40 series models, just behind the front bumper.

Some models may also have a plate attached to the front seat frame, and an emission control label attached to the engine rocker cover (photos).

Location of the engine number

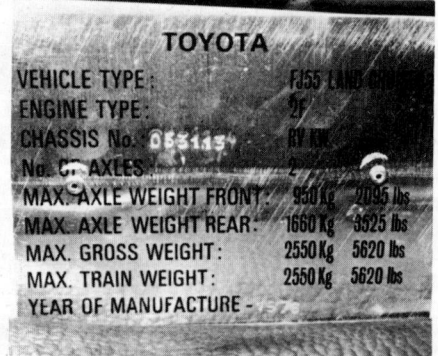
Vehicle loading plate attached to the front seat frame on some models

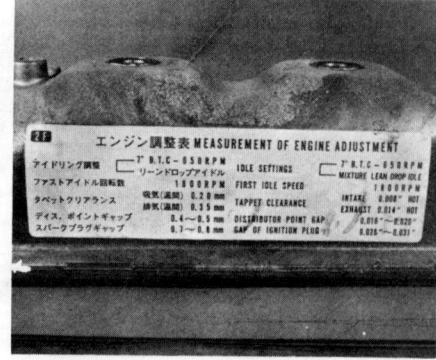
Typical emission control label

Jacking and towing

For wheel changing, the vehicle jack should be positioned beneath the front or rear axle at the appropriate side of the vehicle. Before the vehicle is raised, apply the parking brake.

When working beneath the vehicle, raise it using the jack beneath the axle or a chassis frame side member, then support the vehicle with suitable blocks or axle stands. If the brakes cannot be applied it is essential that the wheels which are on the ground are chocked for safety.

Note that the vehicle jack (and a tool bag) are normally stored beneath a front seat. The jack extension bars are normally stored behind the front seats or beneath the rear seat, whereas the jack handle is in the tool bag (photos).

In the event of the vehicle being towed, the front towing eye should be used. If the vehicle is being used for towing, the rear hook (if installed) or rear spring shackle may be used.

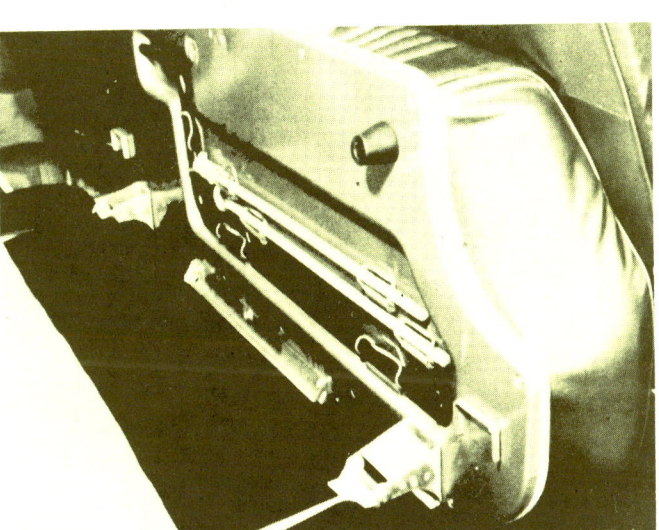
Jack bars and starting handle on FJ55 model

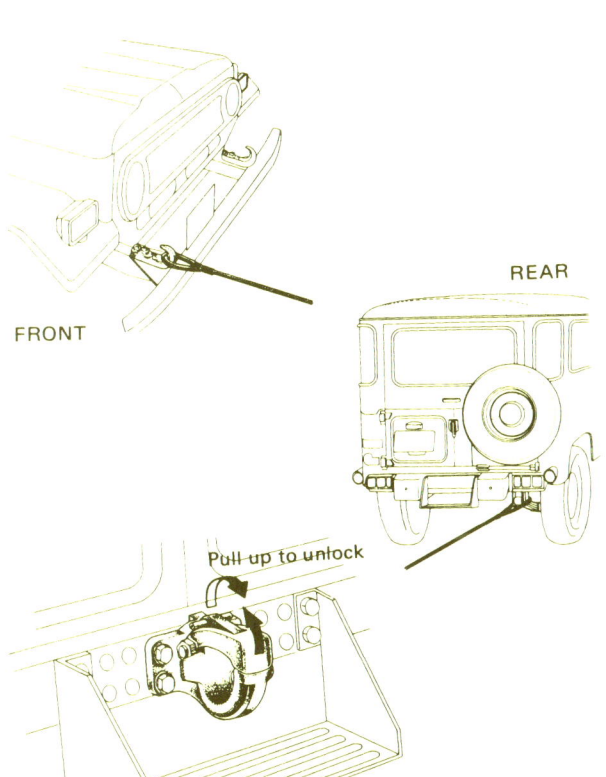
Typical towing points

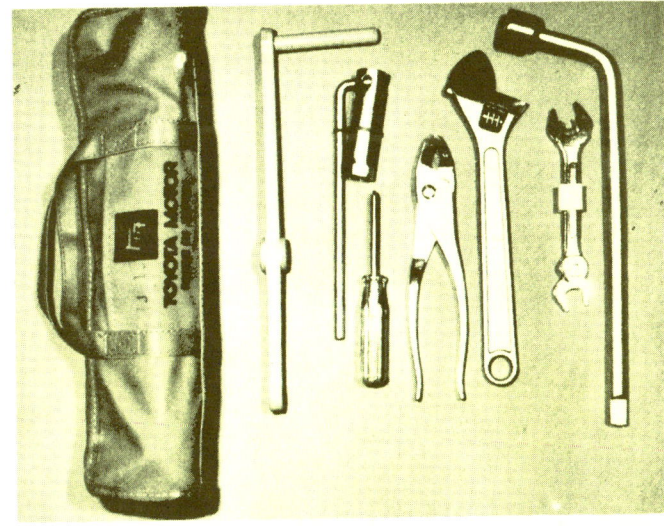
Contents of typical vehicle tool bag

Routine maintenance

Routine maintenance is essential for ensuring safety, and desirable for the purpose of getting the best in terms of performance and economy from any vehicle. In many instances, the largest element of maintenance is visual examination and a general sense of awareness. This may lead to repairs or renewals, but should help to avoid roadside breakdowns.

The maintenance summary is basically that recommended by the vehicle manufacturer, but in certain instances has been altered by the author where additional or more frequent checks are thought to be advisable.

It must be appreciated that not all maintenance tasks are applicable to all vehicles, and the owner should therefore ignore anything which is not applicable to his particular model.

Every 250 miles (400 km), weekly or before a long journey

Steering
Check tire pressures (when cold).
Examine tires for wear and damage.
Check steering for smooth and accurate operation.

Brakes
Check reservoir fluid level. If this has fallen noticeably, check for fluid leakage (photo).
Check for satisfactory brake operation.

Lights, wipers, horns, instruments
Check operation of all lights.
Check operation of windshield wipers and washers.
Top up reservoir if necessary (photo).
Check that horn operates.
Check that all instruments and gauges operate.

Engine compartment
Check engine oil level, and top up if necessary.
Check radiator coolant level.
Check battery electrolyte level.

Every 3000 miles (5000 km) or 3 months, whichever comes first

Change engine oil.
Lubricate all grease nipples (see lubrication chart for location).
Clean air cleaner element; renew oil in oil bath type.
Check brake pedal and parking brake free travel.
Check clutch fluid level (photo).

Every 6000 miles (10000 km) or 6 months, whichever comes first

Check transmission oil level.
Check transfer gear oil level.
Check front and rear axle oil levels.
Check winch oil level.
Lubricate steering knuckles (photo).
Renew engine oil filter. Smear engine oil on seal ring before installing (photo).
Check deflection of all drive belts (see Chapter 11, Section 8, and Chapter 12, Section 30).
Check distributor rotor, cap, points and points gap (except transistorized ignition).
Clean spark plugs (except transistorized ignition).
Check valve clearances.
Check ignition timing and operation of advance/retard mechanism (except transistorized ignition).
Check engine idle speed and mixture (except emission control models).
Check fuel pipes, hoses and connections for leaks and damage.
Check cooling system pipes, hoses and connections for leaks and damage.
Check clutch pedal free play.
Check front brake pads (disc brakes).
Check brake pipes, hoses and connections for leaks and damage.
Check for free play in steering linkage and ball joints (1 in/25 mm maximum permissible free play at rim of steering wheel).
Check for free play in front and rear suspension.
Check for free play in propeller shaft universal joints.
Check all nuts and bolts on chassis and body for tightness.

Every 12000 miles (20000 km) or 12 months, whichever comes first

Note: *Many of the items listed in this Section refer specifically to emission control models. Unless you have the necessary technical knowledge and equipment, these tasks should be carried out by your Toyota dealer or an emission control specialist.*

Check steering gear oil level.
Lubricate wheel bearings.
Renew engine coolant (systems without reservoir and long-life anti-freeze).
Check and renew PCV system valve and hoses.
Check brake linings and drums (including parking brake).
Check operation of brake booster.
Check steering geometry.
Check engine oil filler cap for satisfactory sealing.
Check serviceability of charcoal canister.
Check serviceability of fuel vapor check valve.
Check hoses and connections in fuel evaporative emission control system.
Check exhaust pipe and mountings.
Check torque tightness of cylinder head bolts (back off each bolt ¼ turn first).
Check torque tightness of rocker arm support bolts (back off each bolt ¼ turn first).
Check condition of vacuum fittings, hoses and connections.
Check condition of wiring harness connections.
Rotate exhaust gas heat control valve by hand; check that it rotates freely and returns under the action of the spring.
Check spark control modulation system (without checker).
Renew spark plugs.
Check condition of ignition system wiring, including resistance of spark plug wires.
Check condition of distributor cap and rotor.
Clean distributor breaker points (transistorized ignition).
Check ignition timing and dwell angle (transistorized ignition).
Check operation of hot air intake system.

Engine oil filler cap and dipstick (FILLER CAP, DIPSTICK)

Transmission and transfer filler and drain plugs (TRANSMISSION FILLER PLUG, TRANSFER FILLER PLUG, TRANSFER DRAIN PLUG, TRANSMISSION DRAIN PLUG)

Winch filler and level plugs (FILLER PLUG, LEVEL PLUG)

Power take-off drain plug (DRAIN PLUG for Power Take-off)

Brake fluid reservoir - typical for dual master cylinder

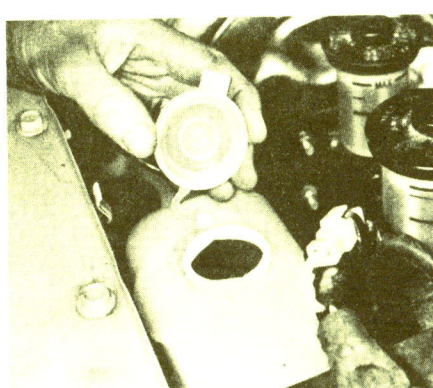

Windshield washer reservoir

Clutch fluid reservoir

Steering knuckle grease plug

Engine oil filter. This may need a chain wrench or similar item when unscrewing. When installing smear seal ring with engine oil and tighten by hand only. For the filter used on early F models engines see Fig. 1.19 in Chapter 1.

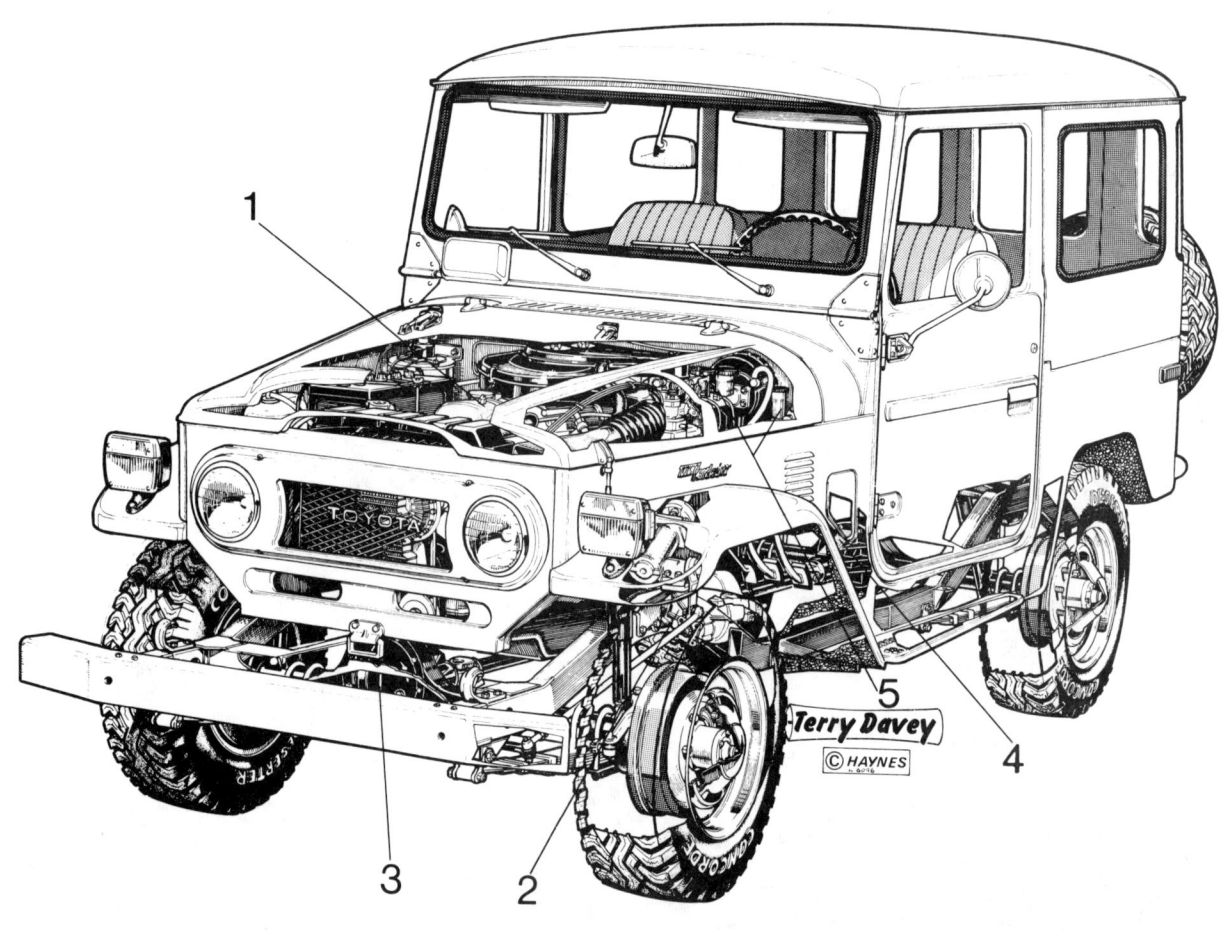

Recommended lubricants

Component	Castrol product
1 Engine	Castrol GTX
2 Transmission and transfer unit	Hypoy
3 Front axle	Hypoy B
4 Rear axle	Hypoy B
5 Hydraulic system	Castrol Girling Universal Clutch and Brake Fluid
Winch (standard)	Hypoy B

Note: The above recommendations are general: lubrication requirements vary from territory-to-territory. Consult the operators handbook supplied with your car.

Routine maintenance

Check engine idle speed and mixture (emission control models).
Check operation of throttle positioner system (without checker).
Check condition of air injection hoses and connections.
Check spark control modulator and throttle positioner systems using Toyota system checker.
Check operation of thermal reactor.
Check operation of power valve control system.
Check operation of high altitude compensation system.

Every 18000 miles (30000 km) or 18 months, whichever comes first

Renew air cleaner element.
Renew transmission oil.
Renew transfer gear oil.
Renew front and rear axle oil (photo).
Renew winch oil.
Add 30 cc of engine oil through filler plug of remote type brake servo.

Every 24000 miles (40000 km) or 24 months, whichever comes first

Note: *Many of the items listed in this Section refer specifically to emission control models. Unless you have the necessary technical knowledge and equipment, these tasks should be carried out by your Toyota dealer or an emission control specialist.*

Renew brake fluid.
Renew engine coolant (systems with reservoir and long-life anti-freeze).
Renew fuel filter.
Check resistance of spark plug wires (except transistorized ignition).
Renew all drive belts.
Renew PCV valve.
Renew fuel tank cap gasket and check condition.
Renew fuel vapor check valve.
Check engine compression pressure; this should be 115/150 lbf/in^2 (8.0/10.5 kgf/cm^2).
Renew distributor breaker points (transistorized ignition).
Check EGR system (without checker).
Check air pump, air by-pass valve and check valve.
Check EGR system using Toyota system checker.

Every 50000 miles (80000 km)

Renew charcoal canister.

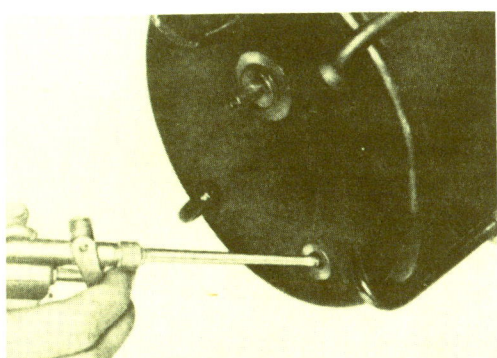
Adding engine oil to remote type brake servo

Front axle drain plug

Tools and working facilities

Introduction
A selection of good tools is a fundamental requirement for anyone contemplating the maintenance and repair of a motor vehicle. For the owner who does not possess any, their purchase will prove a considerable expense, offsetting some of the savings made by doing-it-yourself. However, provided that the tools purchased are of good quality, they will last for many years and prove an extremely worthwhile investment.

To help the average owner to decide which tools are needed to carry out the various tasks detailed in this manual, we have compiled three lists of tools under the following headings: Maintenance and minor repair, Repair and overhaul, and Special. The newcomer to practical mechanics should start off with the 'Maintenance and minor repair' tool kit and confine himself to the simpler jobs around the vehicle. Then, as his confidence and experience grows, he can undertake more difficult tasks, buying extra tools as, and when, they are needed. In this way, a 'Maintenance and minor repair' tool kit can be built-up into a 'Repair and overhaul' tool kit over a considerable period of time without any major cash outlays. The experienced do-it-yourselfer will have a tool kit good enough for most repair and overhaul procedures and will add tools from the 'Special' category when he feels the expense is justified by the amount of use these tools will be put to.

It is obviously not possible to cover the subject of tools fully here. For those who wish to learn more about tools and their use there is a book entitled 'How to Choose and Use Car Tools' available from the publishers of this manual.

Maintenance and minor repair tool kit
The tools given in this list should be considered as a minimum requirement if routine maintenance, servicing and minor repair operations are to be undertaken. We recommend the purchase of combination wrenches (ring one end, open-ended the other); although more expensive than open-ended ones, they do give the advantages of both types of wrench.

Combination wrenches - 10, 11, 13, 14, 17 mm
Adjustable wrench - 9 inch
Engine sump/gearbox/rear axle drain plug key (where applicable)
Spark plug wrench (with rubber insert)
Spark plug gap adjustment tool
Set of feeler gauges
Brake bleed nipple wrench
Screwdriver - 4 in. long x ¼ in. dia. (plain)
Screwdriver - 4 in. long x ¼ in. dia. (crosshead)
Combination pliers - 6 inch
Hacksaw, junior
Tyre pump
Tyre pressure gauge
Grease gun
Oil can
Fine emery cloth (1 sheet)
Wire brush (small)
Funnel (medium size)

Repair and overhaul tool kit
These tools are virtually essential for anyone undertaking any major repairs to a motor vehicle, and are additional to those given in the Basic

Tools and working facilities

list. Included in this list is a comprehensive set of sockets. Although these are expensive they will be found invaluable as they are so versatile particularly if various drives are included in the set. We recommend the ½ in square-drive type, as this can be used with most proprietary torque wrenches. If you cannot afford a socket set, even bought piecemeal, then inexpensive tubular box wrenches are a useful alternative.

The tools in this list will occasionally need to be supplemented by tools from the Special list.

Sockets (or box wrenches) to cover range 7 to 27 mm
Socket (or box wrench), 50 mm
Reversible ratchet drive (for use with sockets)
Extension piece, 10 inch (for use with sockets)
Universal joint (for use with sockets)
Torque wrench (for use with sockets)
'Mole' wrench - 8 inch
Ball pein hammer
Soft-faced hammer, plastic or rubber
Screwdriver - 6 in. long x 5/16 in. dia. (plain)
Screwdriver - 2 in. long x 5/16 in. square (plain)
Screwdriver - 1½ in. long x ¼ in. dia. (crosshead)
Screwdriver - 3 in. long x 1/8 in. dia. (electricians)
Pliers - electricians side cutters
Pliers - needle nosed
Pliers - circlip (internal and external)
Cold chisel - ½ inch
Scriber (this can be made by grinding the end of a broken hacksaw blade)
Scraper (this can be made by flattening and sharpening one end of a piece of copper pipe)
Centre punch
Pin punch
Hacksaw
Valve grinding tool
Steel rule/straight edge
Allen keys
Selection of files
Wire brush (large)
Axle stands
Jack (strong scissor, screw or hydraulic type)

Special tools

The tools in this list are those which are not used regularly, are expensive to buy, or which need to be used in accordance with their manufacturers instructions. Unless relatively difficult mechanical jobs are undertaken frequently, it will not be economic to buy many of these tools. Where this is the case, you could consider clubbing together with friends (or a motorists club) to make a joint purchase, or borrowing the tools against a deposit from a local garage or tool hire specialist.

The following list contains only those tools and instruments freely available to the public, and not those special tools produced by the vehicle manufacturer specifically for its dealer network. You will find occasional references to these manufacturers special tools in the text of this manual. Generally, an alternative method of doing the job without the vehicle manufacturers special tool is given. However, sometimes there is no alternative to using them. Where this is the case, and the relevant tool cannot be bought or borrowed, you will have to entrust the work to a franchised garage.

Valve spring compressor
Piston ring compressor
Ball joint separator
Universal hub/bearing puller
Impact screwdriver
Micrometer and/or vernier gauge
Dial gauge
Stroboscopic timing light
Dwell angle meter/tachometer
Universal electrical multi-meter
Cylinder compression gauge
Lifting tackle
Trolley jack
Light with extension lead

Buying tools

For practically all tools, a tool factor is the best source since he will have a very comprehensive range compared with the average garage or accessory shop. Having said that, accessory shops often offer excellent quality tools at discount prices, so it pays to shop around.

Remember, you don't have to buy the most expensive items on the shelf, but it is always advisable to steer clear of the very cheap tools. There are plenty of good tools around, at reasonable prices, so ask the proprietor or manager of the shop for advice before making a purchase.

Care and maintenance of tools

Having purchased a reasonable tool kit, it is necessary to keep the tools in a clean and serviceable condition. After use, always wipe off any dirt, grease and metal particles using a clean, dry cloth, before putting the tools away. Never leave them lying around after they have been used. A simple tool rack on the garage or workshop wall, for items such as screwdrivers and pliers is a good idea. Store all normal wrenches and sockets in a metal box. Any measuring instruments, gauges, meters, etc., must be carefully stored where they cannot be damaged or become rusty.

Take a little care when the tools are used. Hammer heads inevitably become marked and screwdrivers lose the keen edge on their blades from time-to-time. A little timely attention with emery cloth or a file will soon restore items like this to a good serviceable finish.

Working facilities

Not to be forgotten when discussing tools, is the workshop itself. If anything more than routine maintenance is to be carried out, some form of suitable working area becomes essential.

It is appreciated that many an owner mechanic is forced by circumstance to remove an engine or similar item, without the benefit of a garage or workshop. Having done this, any repairs should always be done under the cover of a roof.

Wherever possible, any dismantling should be done on a clean flat workbench or table at a suitable working height.

Any workbench needs a vise: one with a jaw opening of 4 in. (100 mm) is suitable for most jobs. As mentioned previously, some clean dry storage space is also required for tools, as well as the lubricants, cleaning fluids, touch-up paints and so on which soon become necessary.

Another item which may be required, and which has a much more general usage, is an electric drill with a chuck capacity of at least 5/16 in. (8 mm). This, together with a good range of twist drills, is virtually essential for installing accessories such as wing mirrors and reverse lights.

Last, but not least, always keep a supply of old newspapers and clean, lint-free rags available, and try to keep any working area as clean as possible.

Wrench jaw gap comparison table

Jaw gap (in.)	Wrench size
0.250	1/4 in. AF
0.275	7 mm AF
0.312	5/16 in. AF
0.315	8 mm AF
0.340	11/32 in. AF/1/8 in. Whitworth
0.354	9 mm AF
0.375	3/8 in. AF
0.393	10 mm AF
0.433	11 mm AF
0.437	7/16 in. AF
0.445	3/16 in. Whitworth/1/4 in. BSF
0.472	12 mm AF
0.500	1/2 in. AF
0.512	13 mm AF
0.525	1/4 in. Whitworth/5/16 in. BSF
0.551	14 mm AF
0.562	9/16 in. AF
0.590	15 mm AF
0.600	5/16 in. Whitworth/3/8 in. BSF
0.625	5/8 in. AF
0.629	16 mm AF
0.669	17 mm AF
0.687	11/16 in. AF
0.708	18 mm AF
0.710	3/8 in. Whitworth/7/16 in. BSF
0.748	19 mm AF
0.750	3/4 in. AF

0.812	13/16 in. AF	1.390	13/16 in. Whitworth/15/16 in. BSF
0.820	7/16 in. Whitworth/1/2 in. BSF	1.417	36 mm AF
0.866	22 mm AF	1.437	1 7/16 in. AF
0.875	7/8 in. AF	1.480	7/8 in. Whitworth/1 in. BSF
0.920	1/2 in. Whitworth/9/16 in. BSF	1.500	1 1/2 in. AF
0.937	15/16 in. AF	1.574	40 mm AF/15/16 in. Whitworth
0.944	24 mm AF	1.614	41 mm AF
1.000	1 in. AF	1.625	1 5/8 in. AF
1.010	9/16 in. Whitworth/5/8 in. BSF	1.670	1 in. Whitworth/1 1/8 in. BSF
1.023	26 mm AF	1.687	1 11/16 in. AF
1.062	1 1/16 in. AF/27 mm AF	1.811	46 mm AF
1.100	5/8 in. Whitworth/11/16 in. BSF	1.812	1 13/16 in. AF
1.125	1 1/8 in. AF	1.860	1 1/8 in. Whitworth/1 1/4 in. BSF
1.181	30 mm AF	1.875	1 7/8 in. AF
1.200	11/16 in. Whitworth/3/4 in. BSF	1.968	50 mm AF
1.250	1 1/4 in. AF	2.000	2 in. AF
1.259	32 mm AF	2.050	1 1/4 in. Whitworth/1 3/8 in. BSF
1.300	3/4 in. Whitworth/7/8 in. BSF	2.165	55 mm AF
1.312	1 5/16 in. AF	2.362	60 mm AF

Use of English

As this book has been written in England, it uses the appropriate English component names, phrases, and spelling. Some of these differ from those used in America. Normally, these cause no difficulty, but to make sure, a glossary is printed below. In ordering spare parts remember the parts list will probably use these words:

Glossary

English	American	English	American
Aerial	Antenna	Layshaft (of gearbox)	Counter shaft
Accelerator	Gas pedal	Leading shoe (of brake)	Primary shoe
Alternator	Generator (AC)	Locks	Latches
Anti-roll bar	Stabiliser or sway bar	Motorway	Freeway, turnpike etc.
Battery	Energizer	Number plate	Licence plate
Bodywork	Sheet metal	Paraffin	Kerosene
Bonnet (engine cover)	Hood	Petrol	Gasoline
Boot lid	Trunk lid	Petrol tank	Gas tank
Boot (luggage compartment)	Trunk	'Pinking'	'Pinging'
Bottom gear	1st gear	Propeller shaft	Driveshaft
Bulkhead	Firewall	Quarter light	Quarter window
Camfollower or tappet	Valve lifter or tappet	Retread	Recap
Carburettor	Carburetor	Reverse	Back-up
Catch	Latch	Rocker cover	Valve cover
Choke/venturi	Barrel	Roof rack	Car-top carrier
Circlip	Snap ring	Saloon	Sedan
Clearance	Lash	Seized	Frozen
Crownwheel	Ring gear (of differential)	Side indicator lights	Side marker lights
Disc (brake)	Rotor/disk	Side light	Parking light
Drop arm	Pitman arm	Silencer	Muffler
Drop head coupe	Convertible	Spanner	Wrench
Dynamo	Generator (DC)	Sill panel (beneath doors)	Rocker panel
Earth (electrical)	Ground	Split cotter (for valve spring cap)	Lock (for valve spring retainer)
Engineer's blue	Prussion blue	Split pin	Cotter pin
Estate car	Station wagon	Steering arm	Spindle arm
Exhaust manifold	Header	Sump	Oil pan
Fast back (Coupe)	Hard top	Tab washer	Tang; lock
Fault finding/diagnosis	Trouble shooting	Tailgate	Liftgate
Float chamber	Float bowl	Tappet	Valve lifter
Free-play	Lash	Thrust bearing	Throw-out bearing
Freewheel	Coast	Top gear	High
Gudgeon pin	Piston pin or wrist pin	Trackrod (of steering)	Tie-rod (or connecting rod)
Gearchange	Shift	Trailing shoe (of brake)	Secondary shoe
Gearbox	Transmission	Transmission	Whole drive line
Halfshaft	Axle-shaft	Tyre	Tire
Handbrake	Parking brake	Van	Panel wagon/van
Hood	Soft top	Vice	Vise
Hot spot	Heat riser	Wheel nut	Lug nut
Indicator	Turn signal	Windscreen	Windshield
Interior light	Dome lamp	Wing/mudguard	Fender

Miscellaneous points

An "Oil seal" is fitted to components lubricated by grease!

A "Damper" is a "Shock absorber", it damps out bouncing, and absorbs shocks of bump impact. Both names are correct, and both are used haphazardly.

Note that British drum brakes are different from the Bendix type that is common in America, so different descriptive names result. The shoe end furthest from the hydraulic wheel cylinder is on a pivot; interconnection between the shoes as on Bendix brakes is most uncommon. Therefore the phrase "Primary" or "Secondary" shoe does not apply. A shoe is said to be Leading or Trailing. A "Leading" shoe is one on which a point on the drum, as it rotates forward, reaches the shoe at the end worked by the hydraulic cylinder before the anchor end. The opposite is a trailing shoe, and this one has no self servo from the wrapping effect of the rotating drum.

Chapter 1 Engine

Contents

Camshaft, camshaft bearings and camshaft gear - examination and renovation ... 22	Lubrication system - general description ... 14
Camshaft, camshaft gear and timing gear cover - installation ... 37	Oil pan, oil strainer and oil pump - removal ... 8
Clutch housing - examination and renovation ... 28	Oil pump - dismantling, inspection and reassembly ... 15
Connecting rods and bearings - examination and renovation ... 19	Oil pump, oil strainer and oil pan - installation ... 38
Crankshaft and main bearings - examination and renovation ... 18	Pistons and connecting rods - dismantling ... 12
Crankshaft and main bearings - installation ... 35	Pistons and connecting rods - installation ... 36
Crankshaft and main bearings - removal ... 11	Pistons and connecting rods - removal ... 10
Cylinder bores - examination and renovation ... 20	Pistons, piston pins and piston rings - examination and renovation ... 21
Cylinder head - decarbonisation and examination ... 29	Pistons, piston rings and connecting rods - reassembly ... 32
Cylinder head - reassembly ... 33	Positive crankcase ventilation (PCV) system - description and servicing ... 16
Cylinder head and valve gear - dismantling ... 13	
Cylinder head and valve gear - installation ... 39	Rockers, rocker shaft, valve lifters and pushrods - examination and renovation ... 26
Cylinder head and valve gear - removal ... 7	The need for engine removal ... 2
Engine ancillaries - installation ... 41	Timing cover oil seal - renewal ... 30
Engine ancillaries - removal in preparation for engine dismantling ... 6	Timing gear cover, camshaft gear and camshaft - removal ... 9
Engine dismantling - general ... 4	Transmission, clutch and flywheel - removal ... 5
Engine - preparation for reassembly ... 31	Valve clearance - adjustment ... 40
Engine/transmission - removal and installation ... 3	Valve guides - examination and renovation ... 24
Examination and renovation - general ... 17	Valve rocker mechanism - reassembly ... 34
Fault diagnosis - engine ... 43	Valves and valve seats - examination and renovation ... 23
Flywheel and starter ring gear - examination and renovation ... 27	Valve springs - examination ... 25
General description ... 1	
Initial start-up after overhaul or major repair ... 42	

Specifications

Engine general

Engine type	...	6-cylinder, 4 cycle, overhead valve, water cooled
Firing order	...	1, 5, 3, 6, 2, 4 (No 1 nearest radiator)
Engine model	...	F - pre 1975
		2F - 1975 onwards

	F	2F
Bore	3.54 in (90 mm)	3.70 in (94 mm)
Stroke	4.00 in (101.6 mm)	4.00 in (101.6 mm)
Cubic capacity	236.7 cu in (3878 cc)	257.9 cu in (4230 cc)
Compression ratio	7.8 : 1	7.8 : 1
Engine oil capacity (total)	14 Imp pt/17 US pt/8.0 liter	
Valve clearances (hot)		
Intake	0.008 in (0.20 mm)	
Exhaust	0.014 in (0.35 mm)	

F model - fits, clearances and wear limits

Cylinder block

Cylinder bore diameter (standard)	3.5431/3.5450 in (89.995/90.045 mm)
Cylinder bore wear limit	0.008 in (0.2 mm)
Top surface, maximum out-of-true	0.006 in (0.15 mm)
Valve lifter bore diameter	
Standard	0.990/0.991 in (25.147/25.172 mm)
Oversize	0.992/0.993 in (25.197/25.222 mm)
Cylinder liner outside diameter	3.707/3.709 in (94.16/94.21 mm)
Cylinder liner inside diameter	3.703/3.705 in (94.06/94.10 mm)
Cylinder liner fitting tolerance	0.0024/0.0060 in (0.06/0.15 mm)

Chapter 1/Engine

Cylinder head
Gasket surface, maximum out-of-true	0.006 in (0.15 mm)
Intake valve seat contact width	0.055 in (1.4 mm)
Exhaust valve seat contact width	0.083 in (2.1 mm)
Valve seat contacting angle	45°

Pistons, piston rings and piston pins
Outer diameter (standard)	3.5415/3.5435 in (89.955/90.005 mm)
Oversize availability (mm)	0.25, 0.50, 0.75, 1.00, 1.50
Cylinder to piston oil clearance	0.0012/0.0020 in (0.03/0.05 mm)
Piston pin installing temperature	40/60°C (100/140°F)
Piston ring end gap	
No 1 compression ring	0.008/0.016 in (0.20/0.40 mm)
No 2 compression ring	0.006/0.014 in (0.15/0.35 mm)
No 1 oil ring	0.006/0.014 in (0.15/0.35 mm)
No 2 oil ring	0.006/0.014 in (0.15/0.35 mm)
Piston ring to groove clearance	
No 1 compression ring	0.0012/0.0028 in (0.03/0.07 mm)
No 2 compression ring	0.0008/0.0024 in (0.02/0.06 mm)
No 1 oil ring	0.0008/0.0024 in (0.02/0.06 mm)
No 2 oil ring	0.0008/0.0026 in (0.02/0.065 mm)

Connecting rods
Piston pin to bush clearance (standard)	0/0.00016 in (0/0.004 mm)
Piston pin to bush clearance (maximum)	0.002 in (0.05 mm)
Connecting rod thrust clearance (standard)	0.004/0.009 in (0.11/0.23 mm)
Connecting rod thrust clearance (maximum)	0.012 in (0.3 mm)
Bearing clearance (standard)	0.0008/0.0024 in (0.02/0.06 mm)
Bearing clearance (maximum)	0.004 in (0.1 mm)
Bearing undersizes (mm)	0.05, 0.25, 0.50, 0.75, 1.00

Crankshaft
Thrust clearance (standard)	0.0024/0.0065 in (0.06/0.16 mm)
Thrust clearance (maximum)	0.118 in (0.3 mm)
Journal oil clearance (standard)	0.0014/0.0018 in (0.035/0.045 mm)
Journal oil clearance (maximum)	0.004 in (0.1 mm)
Taper/out-of-round (maximum)	0.0012 in (0.03 mm)
Journal diameter (standard)	
Front	2.6366/2.6378 in (66.97/67.00 mm)
Second	2.6957/2.6969 in (68.47/68.50 mm)
Third	2.7547/2.7559 in (69.97/70.00 mm)
Rear	2.8138/2.8150 in (71.47/71.50 mm)
Bearing undersizes (mm)	0.25, 0.50, 0.75, 1.00 mm
Crankpin diameter (standard)	2.1252/2.1260 in (53.98/54.00 mm)

Camshaft
Thrust clearance (standard)	0.003/0.006 in (0.085/0.147 mm)
Thrust clearance (maximum)	0.008 in (0.2 mm)
Oil clearance (standard)	0.0010/0.0030 in (0.025/0.075 mm)
Oil clearance (maximum)	0.006 in (0.15 mm)
Taper/out-of-round (maximum)	0.002 in (0.05 mm)
Cam lobe height (standard)	
Intake	1.510/1.514 in (38.36/38.46 mm)
Exhaust	1.506/1.510 in (38.25/38.35 mm)
Cam lobe height (minimum)	
Intake	1.496 in (38.0 mm)
Exhaust	1.492 in (37.9 mm)
Camshaft journal diameter (standard)	
Front	1.8880/1.8888 in (47.955/47.975 mm)
Second	1.8289/1.8297 in (46.455/46.475 mm)
Third	1.7699/1.7707 in (44.955/44.975 mm)
Rear	1.7108/1.7116 in (43.455/43.475 mm)
Bearing undersizes (mm)	0.125, 0.25, 0.50 mm

Valves
Valve head diameter	
Intake	1.81 in (46.0 mm)
Exhaust	1.48 in (37.5 mm)
Valve head face angle	45°
Valve stem diameter	
Intake	0.3138/0.3144 in (7.970/7.985 mm)
Exhaust	0.3134/0.3140 in (7.960/7.975 mm)
Valve overall length	
Intake	4.902/4.925 in (124.5/125.1 mm)
Exhaust	4.909/4.933 in (124.7/125.3 mm)

Chapter 1/Engine

Valve head edge thickness limit
    Intake ... 0.031 in (0.8 mm)
    Exhaust ... 0.039 in (1.0 mm)
Valve correcting limit ... 0.02 in (0.5 mm)
Valve stem to bushing clearance (standard)
    Intake ... 0.0010/0.0024 in (0.025/0.060 mm)
    Exhaust ... 0.0014/0.0028 in (0.075/0.070 mm)
Valve stem to bushing clearance (maximum)
    Intake ... 0.004 in (0.10 mm)
    Exhaust ... 0.005 in (0.12 mm)

Valve guide bushes
Overall length
    Intake ... 2.13 in (54 mm)
    Exhaust ... 2.32 in (59 mm)
Protrusion from cylinder head ... 0.65/0.69 in (16.5/17.5 mm)
Finished inside diameter ... 0.315/0.316 in (8.01/8.03 mm)

Valve lifter
Outside diameter (standard) ... 0.9881/0.9894 in (25.097/25.128 mm)
Outside diameter (oversize) ... 0.9902/0.9913 in (25.147/25.178 mm)
Oil clearance (standard) ... 0.0007/0.0030 in (0.019/0.075 mm)
Oil clearance (maximum) ... 0.004 in (0.1 mm)

Valve springs
Free length ... 2.028 in (51.5 mm)
Installed length ... 1.693 in (43.0 mm)
Installed load ... 59.4/71.5 lb (27.0/32.5 kg)
Squareness limit ... 0.079 in (2.0 mm)

Valve rocker shaft and arms
Shaft outer diameter ... 0.7275/0.728 in (18.479/18.493 mm)
Arm inner diameter ... 0.7284/0.7292 in (18.500/18.521 mm)
Rocker shaft oil clearance (standard) ... 0.0003/0.0016 in (0.007/0.042 mm)
Rocker shaft oil clearance (maximum) ... 0.0039 in (0.10 mm)

Timing gears
Gear backlash (standard) ... 0.002/0.005 in (0.05/0.125 mm)
Gear backlash (maximum) ... 0.008 in (0.20 mm)
Timing gear runout limit ... 0.008 in (0.20 mm)

Flywheel
Runout limit ... 0.008 in (0.20 mm)

Manifold
Surface warpage limit ... 0.08 in (2.0 mm)

Oil pump
Type ... Gear
Driveshaft diameter ... 0.5506/0.5512 in (13.985/14.000 mm)
Driven shaft diameter ... 0.5496/0.5499 in (13.961/13.968 mm)
Drive shaft to body clearance ... 0.0006/0.0022 in (0.014/0.057 mm)
Driven shaft to gear clearance ... 0.0006/0.0016 in (0.014/0.042 mm)
Gear to cover clearance (standard) ... 0.0012/0.0035 in (0.03/0.09 mm)
Gear to cover clearance (maximum) ... 0.006 in (0.15 mm)
Gear tip clearance (maximum) ... 0.008 in (0.2 mm)
Gear tooth backlash (maximum) ... 0.037 in (0.95 mm)
Pump cover wear (maximum) ... 0.006 in (0.15 mm)

Oil pressure regulator
Opening pressure ... 44.3/50.0 psi (3.1 to 3.5 kg/cm^2) at 2400 rpm and 80°C/176°F

Oil filter
Type ... Paper element
Filter method ... Partial flow
Capacity ... 1.4 Imp pt/1.7 US pt/0.8 liter

2F model - fits, clearances and wear limits
Fits, clearances and wear limits for the 2F model engine are similar to those for the F model with the following exceptions

Cylinder head
Exhaust valve seat contact width ... 0.067 in (1.7 mm)

Camshaft
Bearing undersizes (mm) ... 0.25, 0.50

Cylinder block
Cylinder bore diameter (standard)	3.7008/3.7027 in (94.00/94.05 mm)

Pistons and piston rings
Piston diameter (standard)	3.6996/3.7016 in (93.97/94.02 mm)
(oversize 0.5 mm)	3.7189/3.7209 in (94.46/94.51 mm)
(oversize 1.00 mm)	3.7386/3.7405 in (94.96/95.01 mm)
(oversize 1.5 mm)	3.7583/3.7602 in (95.46/95.51 mm)
Piston clearance	0.0012/0.0020 in (0.03/0.05 mm)
Piston ring end gap (top and second)	0.0019/0.0150 in (0.20/0.38 mm)
Piston ring/groove clearance	
Top	0.0012/0.0024 in (0.03/0.06 mm)
Second	0.0008/0.0024 in (0.02/0.06 mm)
Piston pin to piston oil clearance	0.0003/0.0005 in (0.008/0.012 mm)

Connecting rods and bearings
Bearing undersizes (mm)	0.05, 0.25, 0.50

Crankshaft and bearings
Main journal oil clearance	0.0008/0.0017 in (0.020/0.044 mm)
Main journal undersize bearings	0.05, 0.25, 0.50 mm

Oil pressure regulator
Opening pressure	50.0/64 psi (3.5/4.5 kg/cm^2)

Oil filter
Filter method	Full flow

Torque wrench settings
	lb f ft	kg f m
Cylinder head	90	12.5
Main bearing cap: 1st, 2nd, 3rd	100	13.8
Main bearing cap: Rear	85	11.8
Oil pan	7	0.9
Oil pump	10	1.3
Rocker support		
10 mm	28	3.8
8 mm	18	2.5
Manifold (F model)	28	3.8
Manifold (2F model)	33	4.5
Flywheel	47	6.5
Crankshaft pulley	130	18
Camshaft thrust plate	10	1.3
Connecting rod bearing cap	45	6.2
Piston pin	45	6.2

1 General description

The engines used in the Land Cruisers are the Toyota F and 2F models. They are almost identical in design features, apart from the larger bore of the 2F model; this has brought the need for larger pistons which are of a modified type.

The engine is a conventional 6-cylinder, in-line, water cooled, overhead valve type. The cylinder block and head are cast iron, the latter housing wedge-shaped combustion chambers.

The counterbalanced crankshaft has four replaceable main bearings, the third bearing being used to take up end play.

Light alloy pistons are used for both engines, but the F model has two compression and two oil control rings, whereas the 2F model has two compression rings and one oil control ring.

The connecting rods are I-section forged steel, and are clamped to the piston pin by a bolt through the piston pin (small end) bearing housing.

The camshaft is geardriven from the front end of the crankshaft, and is mounted low down in the cylinder block. This drives the distributor and the oil pan mounted oil pump.

2 The need for engine removal

Something of a dilemma faces the owner who needs to carry out major repairs to his Land Cruiser engine. Due to the height of the engine compartment from the ground, and the total engine transmission weight, heavy lifting tackle will be required if the engine is to be removed. Conversely, it is not a good workshop practice to renew items such as crankshaft bearings with the engine installed, due to the possibility of dirt contamination. Therefore, the choice must remain with the owner, but it is considered preferable to remove the engine if items such as the crankshaft bearings require attention. Listed below are the items which can be attended to with the engine installed, followed by the items which will require engine removal. Note that it is not considered feasible to remove the engine without removing the transmission also, unless the transmission has already been removed.

Repair operations with the engine installed
Removal and installation of the cylinder head.
Removal and installation of the valve gear.
Removal and installation of the manifolds.
Removal and installation of the timing gear cover, timing gears and camshaft.
Removal and installation of the pistons and connecting rods.
Removal and installation of the oil pan and oil pump.
Renewal of the rear main oil seal (with transmission and flywheel removed).
Removal and installation of the flywheel.

Repair operations which require the engine to be removed
Removal and installation of the crankshaft and main bearings.

3 Engine/transmission - removal and installation

Note: Since there are many different vehicle specifications, it is impossible to give precise details of every step when disconnecting items such as those connected with the emission control system. We

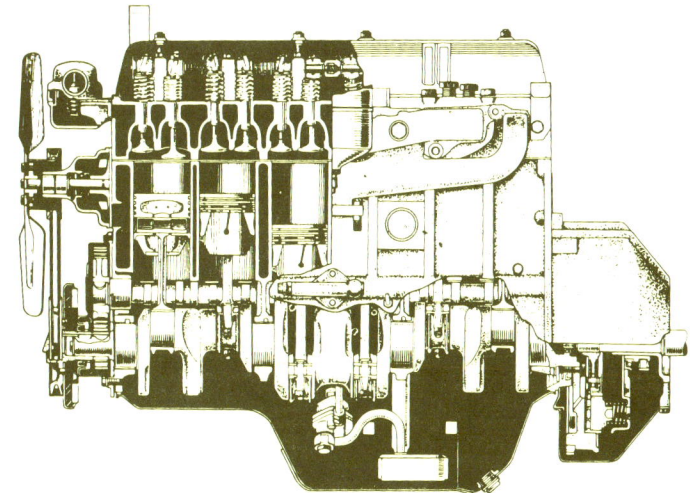

Fig. 1.1. Sectioned side view of F model engine

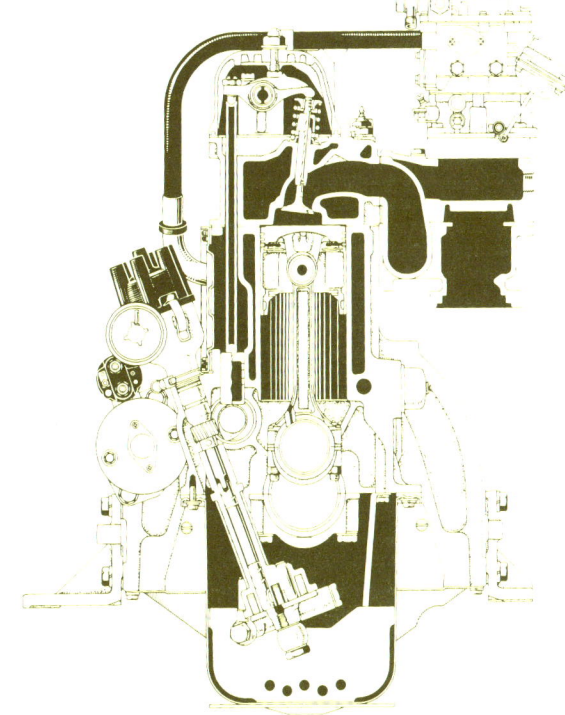

Fig. 1.2. Sectioned front view of 2F model engine

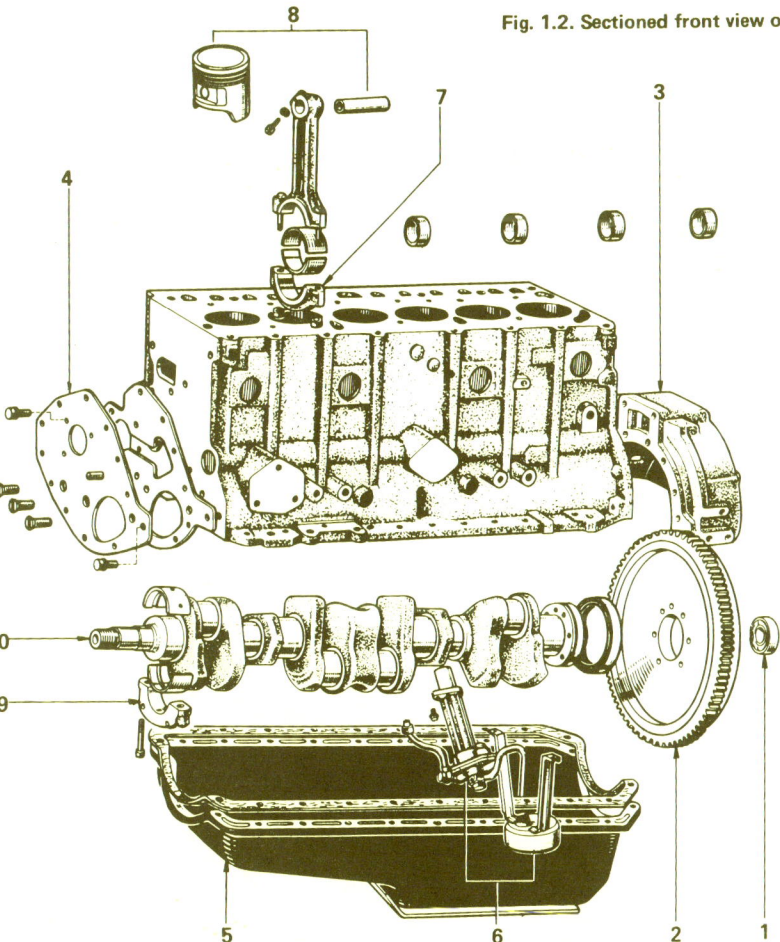

Fig. 1.3. Cylinder block and associated parts (2F model)

1 Input shaft bearing
2 Flywheel
3 Flywheel housing
4 Front end plate
5 Oil pan
6 Oil pump and strainer
7 Connecting rod cap
8 Piston and piston pin
9 Main bearing cap
10 Crankshaft

must therefore leave some of these details to the owner, but where there is likely to be confusion over the points of connection for the various electrical leads, hoses, etc., it is very important to tie labels to the leads or hoses, or alternatively make a sketch showing the connections. In some cases, it may be necessary to remove emission control items for access purposes, and we must again leave this to the individual owner. Where an air conditioning system is installed, it is most important that where any refrigerant lines need to be disconnected, the system is first depressurized by a qualified air conditioning specialist.

1 Initially mark the position of the engine compartment hood hinges to aid installation, then remove the hood (refer to Chapter 12 if necessary).
2 Drain the cooling system (radiator and engine block - refer to Chapter 2 if necessary).
3 Remove the radiator grille and the support rod for the hood. Note that on some models it may be necessary to detach the parking light leads as the lights are on the grille.
4 Detach the hood lock from the radiator support; remove the radiator support.
5 Disconnect the heater hose from the radiator pipe connection.
6 Disconnect the radiator top hose from the water outlet housing; disconnect the radiator lower hose from the water pump.
7 Remove the radiator (refer to Chapter 2 if necessary).
8 Remove the two heater supply hoses.
9 Disconnect the battery cables, and remove the battery from the vehicle.
10 Detach the electrical leads to the starter motor.
11 Disconnect the fuel hoses and remove the fuel filter.
12 Disconnect the feed wire to the ignition coil. It is also a good idea to remove the distributor cap as this often can be damaged during a removal procedure.
13 On column-shift models, detach both intermediate rods from the shifter shafts.
14 Remove the air cleaner assembly from the mountings on the engine; also detach the hoses, noting where they are connected to (refer to Chapter 3 if necessary).
15 Detach the alternator lead wires.
16 Remove the emission control system hoses and cables, as necessary, carefully noting to which item they should be connected. Further information will be found in Chapter 3. Also detach the brake servo hose (where applicable).
17 Disconnect the accelerator rod, throttle rod and choke rod from the carburetor.
18 On models with a vacuum controlled front wheel drive, remove the control unit hose from the intake manifold.
19 Disconnect the wires for the oil pressure gauge and temperature gauge sender units. Refer to Chapter 11 for their location.
20 Detach the exhaust downpipe from the manifold.
21 Disconnect the parking brake cable from the intermediate lever connection.
22 Disconnect the front and rear propeller shafts from the transfer drive flanges. Ensure that the installed position is marked to avoid altering the balance - refer to Chapter 7 if necessary. Where applicable, also disconnect the drive to the front winch - refer to Chapter 6 if necessary.
23 Remove the left and right cover plates (where applicable) from beneath the engine.
24 Remove the cover plate from beneath the transmission.
25 Remove the cotter pin then disconnect the high and low range shift rods from their respective inner levers.
26 Remove the high/low range shift link lever No 3, and the high/low shift rod.
27 Detach the clutch release fork spring, then remove the release cylinder from the engine bracket (refer to Chapter 5 if necessary).
28 On models with a vacuum controlled front wheel drive, remove the clamp screws and withdraw the vacuum lines from the transfer gear control unit diaphragm cylinder.
29 Remove the screws retaining the floor section around the transmission; lift the section out.
30 On models with a vacuum controlled front wheel drive, remove the front drive indicator switch.
31 Detach the leads from the reverse light switch and transfer switch (as applicable).
32 From beneath the vehicle, detach the speedometer drive from the transmission.
33 Remove the gearshift rod; on column change models also remove the gear selecting rod and the gear select outer lever. Where applicable, also remove the transfer gear shift rod.
34 Remove the nuts from the front and rear engine/transmission mountings.
35 Have a last check in the engine compartment to ensure that there are no hoses, cables, etc still attached, and that the way is clear for the engine/transmission to be lifted out.
36 Attach suitable lifting hooks onto the engine hangers, then take the weight on a suitable hoist or crane.
37 Place a suitable trolley jack beneath the transmission. If necessary, raise the jack a little to make sure that the mountings are free.
38 With the trolley jack supporting the transmission weight, carefully and slowly lift the engine upwards and forwards, until it is clear of the vehicle.
39 Place the engine on the floor or on a suitable workbench, then remove the external oil and grease using a water-soluble solvent. Take care that the water or solvent does not enter the alternator or carburetor (see next Section).
40 Installation of the engine and transmission is basically the reverse of the removal procedure. Do not forget to ensure that the engine (and transmission) are topped up with the correct grade and quantity of lubricant, and that the cooling system is filled. Check and adjust the clutch release fork play as described in Chapter 5. If the engine has been dismantled, also refer to Section 42.

4 Engine dismantling - general

1 It is best to mount the engine on a dismantling stand but if one is not available, then stand the engine on a strong bench so as to be at a comfortable working height.
2 During the dismantling process the greatest care should be taken to keep the exposed parts free from dirt. As an aid to achieving this, it is a sound scheme to thoroughly clean down the outside of the engine, removing all traces of oil and congealed dirt.
3 Use kerosene or a water soluble grease solvent. The latter compound will make the job much easier, as, after the solvent has been applied and allowed to stand for a time, a vigorous jet of water will wash off the solvent and all the grease and filth. If the dirt is thick and deeply embedded, work the solvent into it with a wire brush.
4 Finally wipe down the exterior of the engine with a cloth and only then, when it is quite clean should the dismantling process begin. As the engine is stripped, clean each part in a bath of kerosene or gasoline.
5 Never immerse parts which have internal oilways in kerosene (such as the crankshaft), but wipe them carefully with a gasoline soaked rag. Probe the oilways with a length of wire and if an air line is available, blow the oilways through to clean them.
6 Re-use of old engine gaskets is false economy and can give rise to oil and water leaks, if nothing worse. To avoid the possibility of trouble after the engine has been reassembled, always use new gaskets throughout.
7 Do not throw the old gaskets away as it sometimes happens that an immediate replacement cannot be found and the old gasket is then very useful as a template. Hang up the old gaskets as they are removed on a suitable hook or nail.
8 Wherever possible, replace nuts, bolts and washers finger-tight from wherever they were removed. This helps avoid later loss and muddle. If they cannot be replaced, lay them out in such a fashion that it is clear from where they came.

5 Transmission, clutch and flywheel - removal

1 Remove the flywheel side cover and the flywheel housing lower cover from the engine.
2 Remove the bolts retaining the transmission onto the clutch housing, then carefully withdraw the transmission and transfer. This is a heavy assembly and assistance will probably be necessary. Take care that the transmission weight is not taken by the input shaft as it is being removed.
3 Remove the clutch release bearing and hub from the clutch release fork, then remove the fork itself (refer to Chapter 5 if necessary).
4 If the same clutch cover is to be installed during reassembly, mark its installed position with respect to the flywheel.

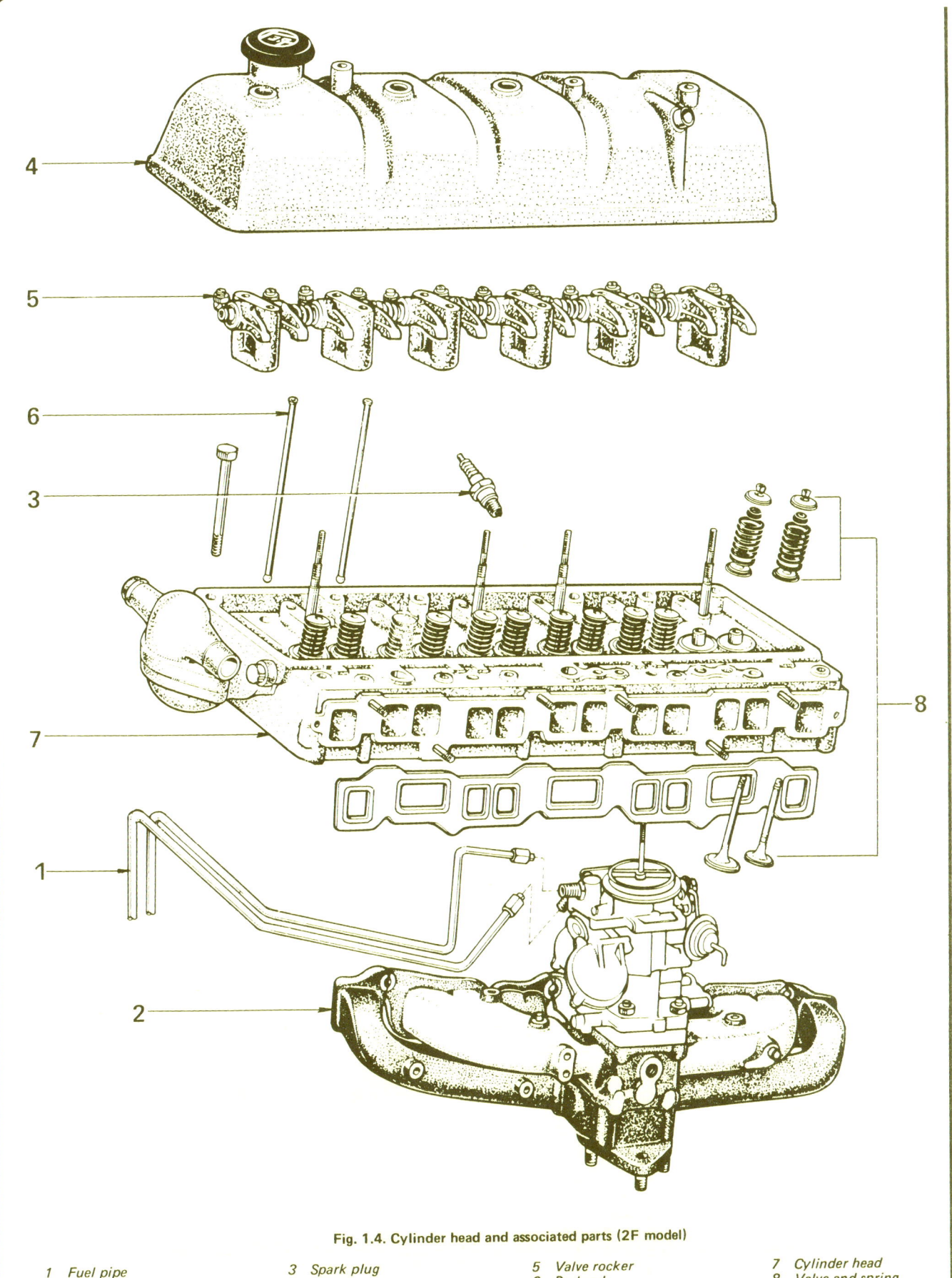

Fig. 1.4. Cylinder head and associated parts (2F model)

1 Fuel pipe
2 Manifold
3 Spark plug
4 Cylinder head cover
5 Valve rocker
6 Pushrod
7 Cylinder head
8 Valve and spring

5 Support the clutch hub with a suitable bar (eg: an old input shaft, tubular wrench, etc.), then progressively loosen the clutch cover bolts until the spring pressure on the release plate is released. Remove all the bolts, then withdraw the clutch and pull out the clutch hub supporting tool.
6 Remove the starter motor and the ground cable.
7 Fold back the washer tabs, then remove the flywheel retaining bolts. Withdraw the flywheel, taking care that it does not drop as it comes off the crankshaft spigot.

6 Engine ancillaries - removal in preparation for engine dismantling

1 Remove the retaining bolts and/or nuts, and take off the clutch housing.
2 With the engine suitably supported in an upright position, remove the oil pan drain plug and drain the oil into a container of suitable size.
3 Unscrew the oil filter from the engine.
4 Disconnect the starter solenoid wire from the ignition coil (where applicable).
5 Disconnect the vacuum pipe and fuel pipe(s) from the carburetor, then remove the carburetor (refer to Chapter 3 if necessary).
6 Loosen the alternator mountings, remove the V-belt and remove the alternator.
7 Where applicable, remove the air injection pump and/or air conditioning compressor.
8 Remove all the sender units, valves etc., which are attached to the cylinder block and head. Typically these will be:

Oil pressure sender
Water temperature sender
Anti-backfire valve
EGR valve
EGR gas cooler
Check valve
Air by-pass valve

9 Remove the water pump by-pass hose.
10 Remove the water pump and fan, and the V-belt adjusting bar (refer to Chapter 2 if necessary).
11 Remove the water outlet and water outlet housing from the cylinder head.
12 Remove the fuel pump pipe and the vacuum pipe to the distributor.
13 If not already removed, remove the spark plug and ignition coil HT leads.
14 Remove the distributor. Note its installed position with respect to the cylinder block; also, to simplify the installation procedure, check the position of the rotor when No 1 piston is at top-dead-center (tdc) on its firing stroke - refer to Chapter 4 for further information.
15 Remove the engine oil dipstick.
16 Detach the ignition coil from its mounting.
17 Remove the fuel pump (refer to Chapter 3 if necessary).
18 Where applicable, remove the oil filter inlet and outlet pipes, and remove the filter assembly from the manifold.
19 Remove the intake and exhaust manifolds and gaskets (refer to Chapter 3 if necessary).

7 Cylinder head and valve gear - removal

1 Remove the cylinder head rocker cover (four nuts and special seals) and the gasket. Be prepared for a little oil spillage at this point (photo).
2 Remove the rocker shaft oil delivery union, spring and oil connection sleeve from the valve rocker shafts (F model engines only).
3 Remove the rocker shaft support retaining nuts and bolts, then lift off the complete rocker mechanism.
4 Take out the valve rocker pushrods. Either label them or push them through holes in a wooden rack or piece of stiff cardboard so that they can be numbered for reinstallation in their original positions.
5 Remove the valve lifter cover (engine side cover) and gasket. Again, be prepared for a little oil spillage.
6 Take out the valve lifters and keep each one with its corresponding pushrod. Sometimes these can be difficult to remove, but if the engine is tilted on its side and struck with a soft faced mallet, it should remove them; alternatively a bar magnet can be used.

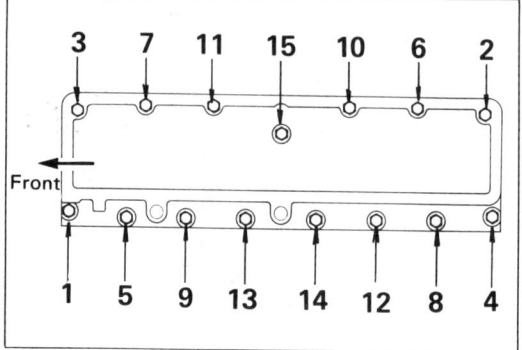

Fig. 1.5. Cylinder head bolt loosening sequence

Fig. 1.6. Using a screwdriver to free the cylinder head

Fig. 1.7. Removing the crankshaft pulley

Fig. 1.8. Checking timing gear backlash

Chapter 1/Engine

7.1 Rocker cover nut and seal

Fig. 1.9. Removing camshaft thrust plate bolts

Fig. 1.10. Checking connecting-rod thrust clearance

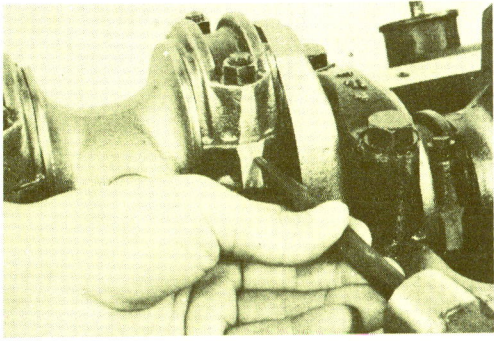

Fig. 1.11. Mark the connecting-rods and bearing caps

7 Remove the rocker shaft oil delivery union from the oil delivery pipe (F models).
8 Loosen the cylinder head bolts approximately ½ turn at a time in the order shown in Fig. 1.5. When each one has been loosened, remove them all.
9 The cylinder head can now be removed. Very often it will need some persuasion, but a blow along the edge using a soft faced mallet in two or three places will usually succeed. Alternatively, provided that care is taken, a screwdriver can be inserted in the notch - see Fig. 1.6.
10 Place the cylinder head on one side where it will not be damaged. Also remove the cylinder head gasket.

8 Oil pan, oil strainer and oil pump - removal

1 Tilt the engine on one side, and progressively loosen and remove the oil pan retaining bolts. Remove the oil pan and gasket. If the oil pan will not come off readily, insert a knife blade along the joint edge. Be prepared for a little oil spillage as it is removed.
2 Remove the oil strainer assembly (two bolts with tab washers).
3 Detach the oil pump outlet from the cylinder block.
4 Remove the oil pump retaining bolts (these are either wire locked or have tab washers), then pull out the pump assembly.
5 Where applicable, remove the oil filter adapter and gasket from the cylinder block.

9 Timing gear cover, camshaft gear and camshaft - removal

1 Using a suitable puller (see Fig. 1.7) draw off the crankshaft pulley.
2 Remove the retaining screws and spring washers and take off the timing gear cover. A knife blade can be inserted along the sealing edge if necessary.
3 Remove the oil slinger from the end of the crankshaft.
4 Now check the timing gear backlash (see Fig. 1.8). If this exceeds the specified amount it will be necessary to renew both timing gears.
5 Remove the two bolts retaining the camshaft thrust plate by working through the holes in the camshaft timing gear.
6 Draw out the camshaft and gear, taking care that the cam lobes do not strike the bearing edges or they may become chipped.
7 If major engine dismantling is being carried out, this is a convenient time to remove the crankcase end plate from the cylinder block; also remove the gasket.
8 At this point, the crankshaft timing gear can be removed if necessary, by using the same method adopted for the crankshaft pulley (paragraph 1). Also remove the Woodruff key to prevent it from being lost.

10 Pistons and connecting rods - removal

1 Using a feeler gauge, measure the thrust (side) clearance of each connecting rod. If this exceeds the specified limit, renew the connecting rod(s).
2 Using a center punch, mark the connecting rods and bearing caps to ensure that they are installed the correct way round.
3 Rotate the crankshaft as necessary for access to the connecting rod bearing cap nuts. Remove the nuts (on early models split cotter pins are used to retain them; later models use self-locking nuts which should be renewed during reassembly), and take off the bearing cap on one connecting rod at a time; noting which way the cap is installed on the connecting rod. Push the piston and connecting rod out of the bore using a hammer shaft. Temporarily install the bearing cap on the connecting rod and make sure that the bearing shells are not separated from the assembly. If not already marked, mark the piston, connecting rod, bearing cap and shells and keep all the parts together for that particular cylinder.
4 Repeat this procedure for the remaining five assemblies.

11 Crankshaft and main bearings - removal

1 Using a feeler gauge, measure the thrust (side) clearance of the

crankshaft at number 3 main bearing. If this exceeds the specified limit, a new bearing set will be required (even if otherwise satisfactory).
2 Remove the crankshaft main bearing cap bolts, one pair at a time, and take off the bearing cap and shell. If not already marked, mark the cap and shell so that they can be installed the same way round (where serviceable) in their original positions. **If shims are used beneath the bearing caps, ensure that these are not lost as they must be used in their original positions during reassembly.**
3 Lift out the crankshaft. This is heavy, and help from an assistant will be useful. Remove the shell bearings from the crankcase and ensure that they are kept with their mating caps and shells.
4 Remove the crankshaft rear oil seal.
5 At this point, the input shaft spigot bearing can be removed from the end of the crankshaft using a suitable claw-type extractor.

12 Pistons and connecting rods - dismantling

1 Each ring should be carefully sprung open to just permit it to ride over the lands in the piston body.
2 Once a ring is out of its groove, it is helpful to cut three ¼ in (6 mm) wide strips of tin and slip them under the ring at equidistant points. Using a twisting motion, this method of removal will prevent a ring from dropping into an already empty groove. Ensure that the piston rings are kept with the piston to which they belong.
3 Remove the piston pin bolt, then carefully push out the piston pin. (On early models the piston will need to be heated to 40/60°C (100/140°F) in hot water to enable the pin to be pushed out). Ensure that all associated parts remain with their correct piston/connecting rod assembly.

13 Cylinder head and valve gear - dismantling

1 Using a proprietary type of valve spring compressor, compress the valve spring and remove the valve spring locks (split collets).
2 Release the compressor and remove the spring retainer, spring, valve stem oil seal and spring seat.
3 Slide the valve out of the cylinder head. Keep all the associated parts of each valve together so that they can be installed in their original positions if still serviceable.
4 Remove the lock springs from each end of the valve rocker shaft and slide off the rocker arms, rocker shaft supports and springs. Keep all the parts in their correct order of installation - see Figs. 1.17 and 1.18.

14 Lubrication system - general description

1 Lubrication on the F model engine is by a force-feed gear type pump which directs oil in two different paths thru the engine. One oil path is thru the filter and back to the oil pan, whereas the other path is thru a drilling in the cylinder block, thru the crankshaft for lubrication of the crankshaft and connecting rod bearings, then via a tapping at number 3 main bearing to the camshaft and to the valve rocker gear.
2 On the 2F model engine, oil first passes thru the oil filter, but does not flow directly back to the oil pan. Instead, the oil flows thru the cylinder block and follows virtually the same path as that described for the F type engine in paragraph 1.

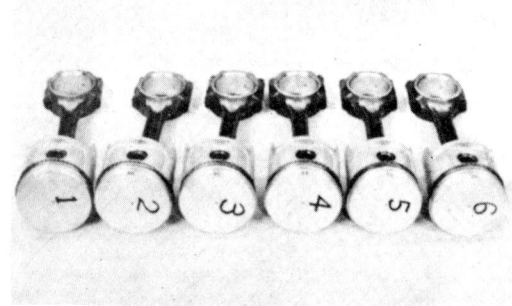

Fig. 1.12. Keep all the pistons and connecting-rods with their mating parts

Fig. 1.13. Checking crankshaft thrust clearance

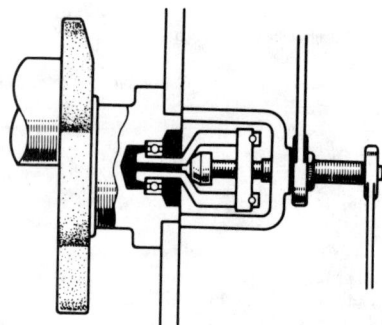

Fig. 1.14. Removing the input shaft spigot bearing

Fig. 1.15. Keep associated piston and connecting-rod parts together

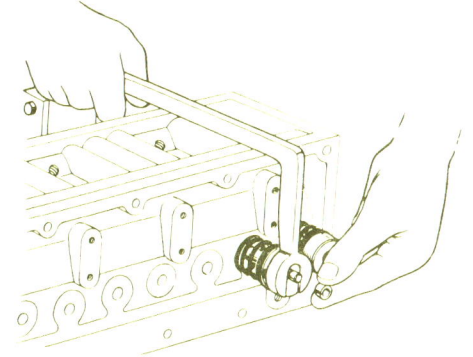
Fig. 1.16. Removing valve spring locks (split collets)

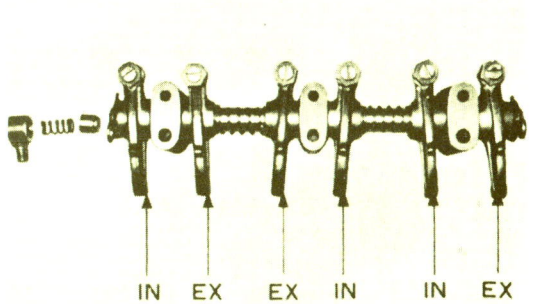
Fig. 1.17. F model valve mechanism (one half)

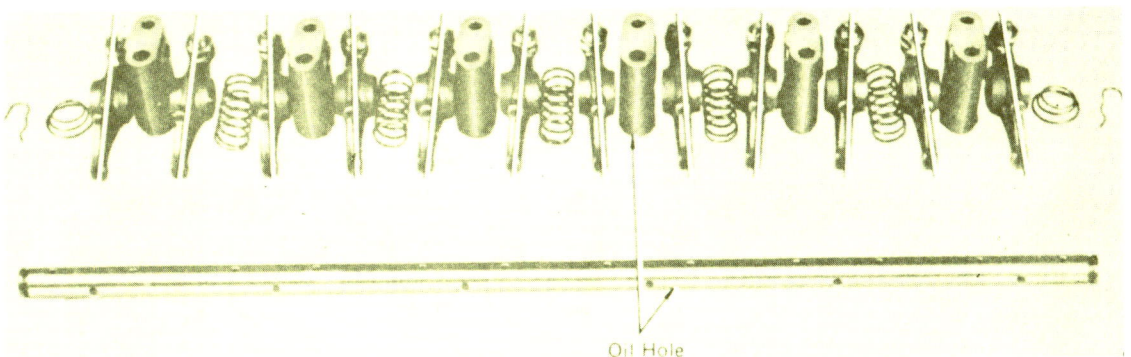
Fig. 1.18. 2F model valve mechanism

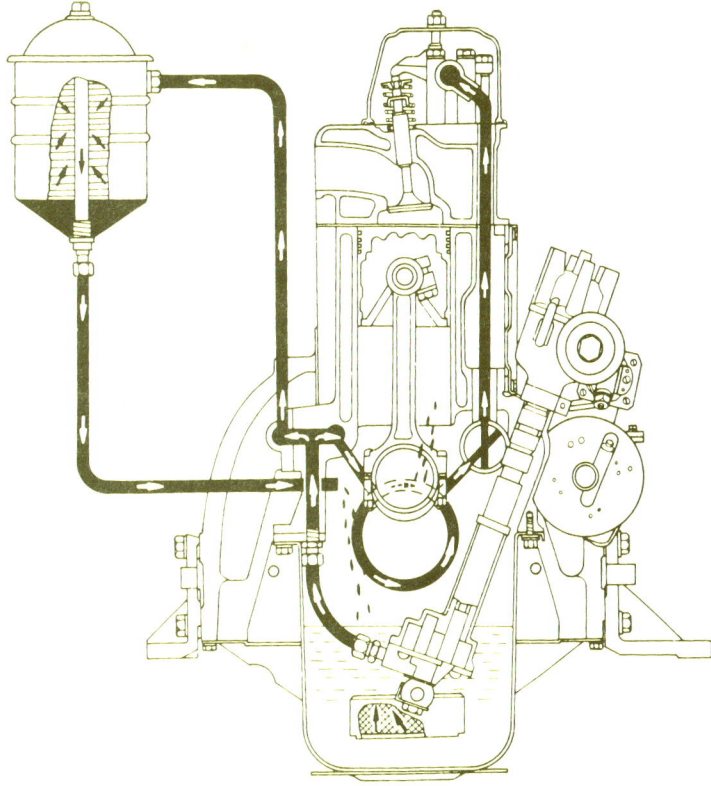
Fig. 1.19. Lubrication system - early F model engine. On later engines the oil filter was repositioned as in the 2F engine

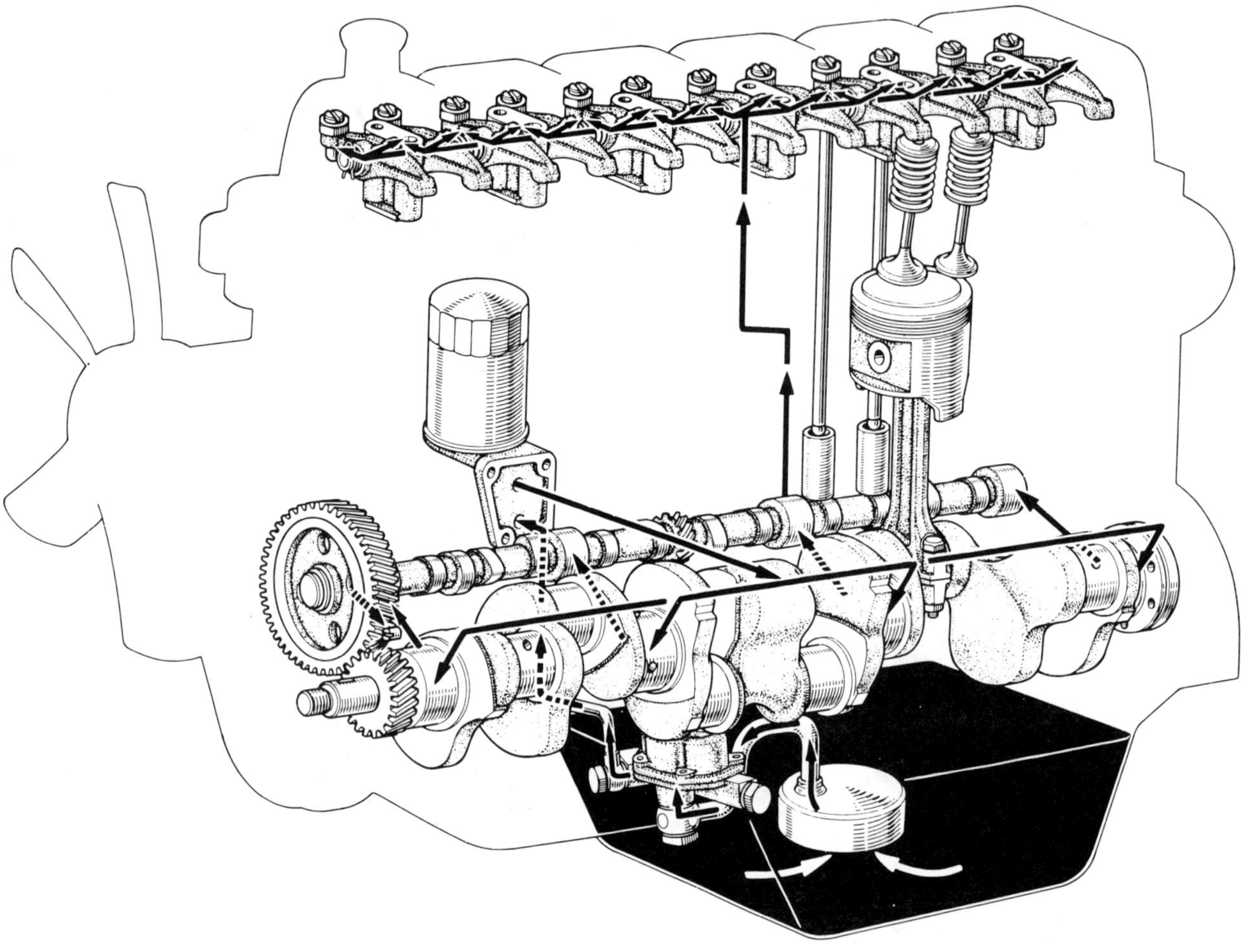

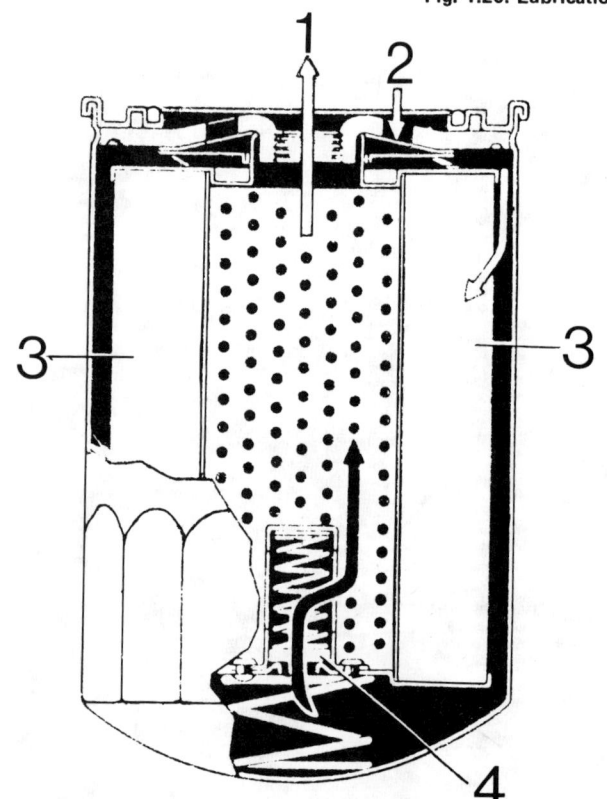

Fig. 1.20. Lubrication system 2F engine

Fig. 1.21. Oil filter (except early F models)

1 To oil circuit of engine
2 From oil pump
3 Element
4 Relief valve

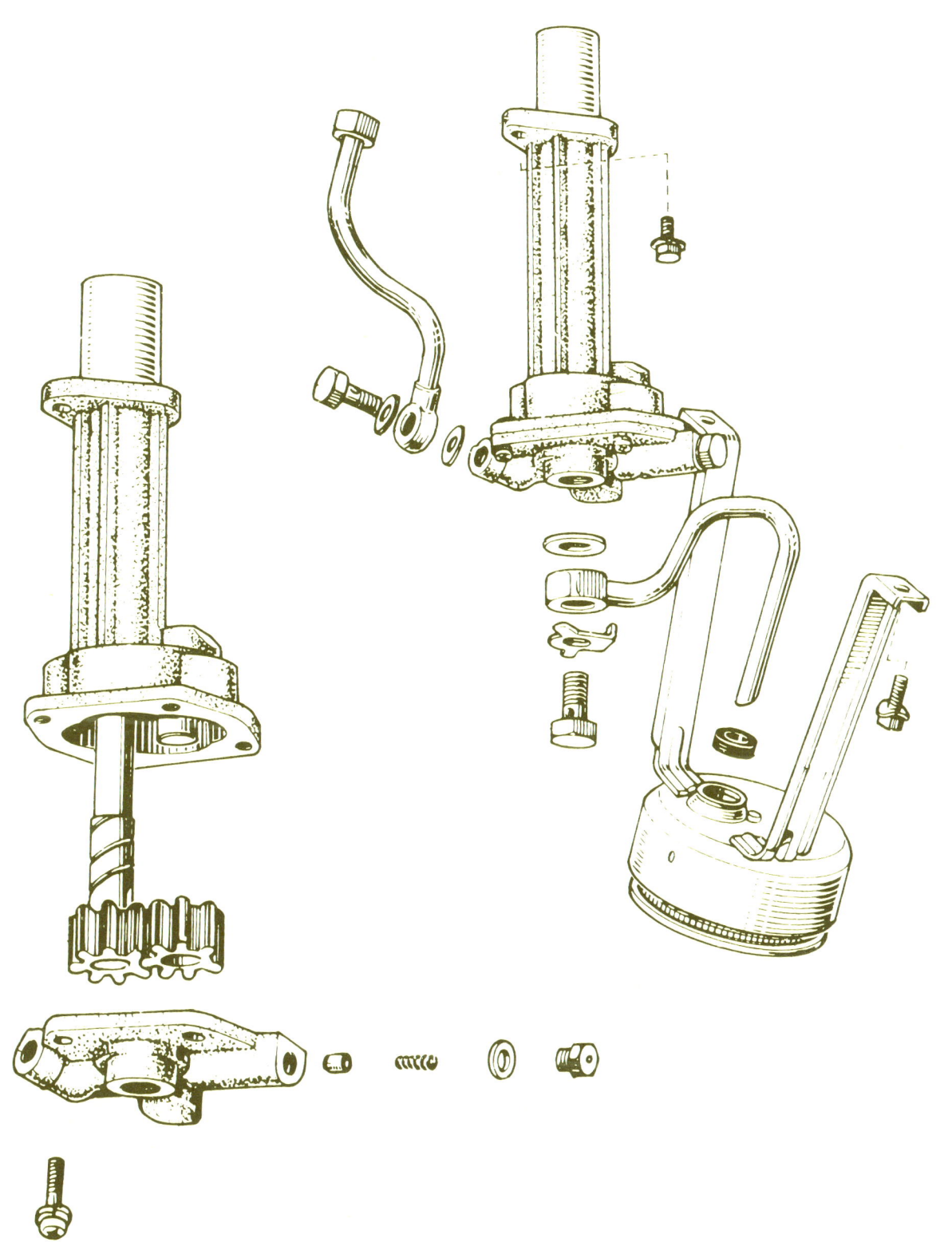

Fig. 1.22. Oil pump assembly

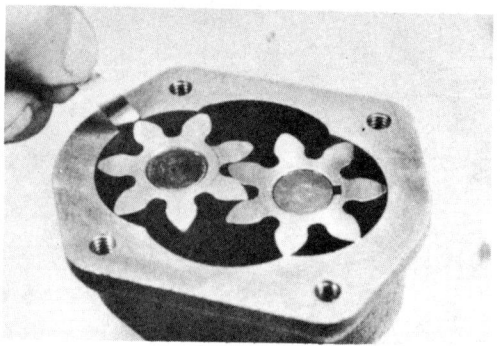

Fig. 1.23. Checking gear tip clearance

Fig. 1.24. Checking gear backlash

Fig. 1.25. Checking gear side clearance

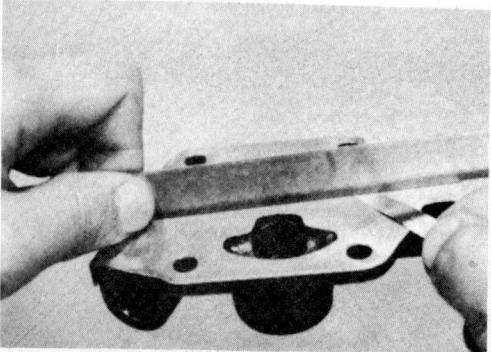

Fig. 1.26. Checking cover wear

15 Oil pump - dismantling, inspection and reassembly

1 Remove the oil pump cover; be prepared for some oil spillage as it is removed.
2 Slide out the driven gear and the drive gear together with the oil pump drive shaft.
3 Wash all the parts in kerosene, and dry carefully with a lint-free cloth.
4 Inspect all the parts for wear and damage; replace those parts which are outside the specified tolerances (see Figs. 1.22, 1.23, 1.24, and 1.25). Check the relief valve for wear and scoring; if damaged, renew the valve or pump assembly. Clean the oil strainer using kerosene and a stiff bristle brush; renew if damaged or corroded.
5 Assembly is basically the reverse of the dismantling procedure, but all parts should be liberally coated with engine oil. Ensure that the gears rotate freely after assembly.

16 Positive crankcase ventilation (PCV) system - description and servicing

1 The PCV system is installed to prevent blow-by gases which have leaked into the crankcase during the combustion process from escaping to atmosphere, by re-routing them from the crankcase and rocker cover into the intake manifold. At the same time, fresh air is drawn into the rocker cover to assist in the ventilation process. The PCV valve controls the blow-by gas in relation to the engine load. Although slight differences will be found in the vehicle according to the year of manufacture, the principle is shown in Fig. 1.27.
2 When idling or decelerating, the high vacuum in the intake manifold closes the PCV valve to limit the amount of blow-by gas to the manifold.
3 During normal vehicle operation, the lower intake manifold allows the valve to move to a mid-position of opening under the action of its spring, and therefore there is a relatively unrestricted path for the blow-by gases to the intake manifold (Fig. 1.28).
4 Under heavy load or acceleration, the intake manifold vacuum is very low and the PCV valve is fully open allowing the maximum amount of flow to the manifold. During very heavy acceleration conditions, the flow thru the valve may be partially restricted by the limiting factor of the valve seat area. In these cases, additional ventilation is provided by the hose from the rocker cover which allows air to pass through the air cleaner and into the engine.
5 When the engine is not running, or in the case of a backfire, the valve is fully closed by the action of its spring.
6 Servicing of the PCV system comprises checking the hoses and connections for deterioration and insecure fitting. Other items which will affect the system operation are leakage at the cylinder head gasket, oil filler cap, oil dipstick hole, timing cover and oil pan gasket.
7 If there is evidence of oil contamination in the air cleaner, this is a sign of the PCV valve sticking closed. This valve should be cleaned or renewed at the intervals given in the Routine Maintenance Section. It can be checked for serviceability by attaching a short length of hose to the crankcase side and checking for a free passage of air when blown through. With the hose on the manifold side it should not be possible to suck air through. Soak the valve in kerosene then shake dry in order to clean it. **Note:** A faulty PCV valve will affect the engine idle speed as well as giving poor fuel economy and acceleration.

17 Examination and renovation - general

1 With the engine completely stripped, clean every component in kerosene and dry carefully. Make sure that all oilways are then thoroughly cleaned out to remove all traces of kerosene.
2 Pay particular attention to the engine block. Scrape off all pieces of gasket or jointing compound, probe the oilways and waterways, examine the casting for cracks, and check the core plugs (freeze plugs) for security. Similarly ensure that the oilways in the crankshaft are unobstructed.
3 The individual components should be checked for wear or distortion as described in the following Sections.

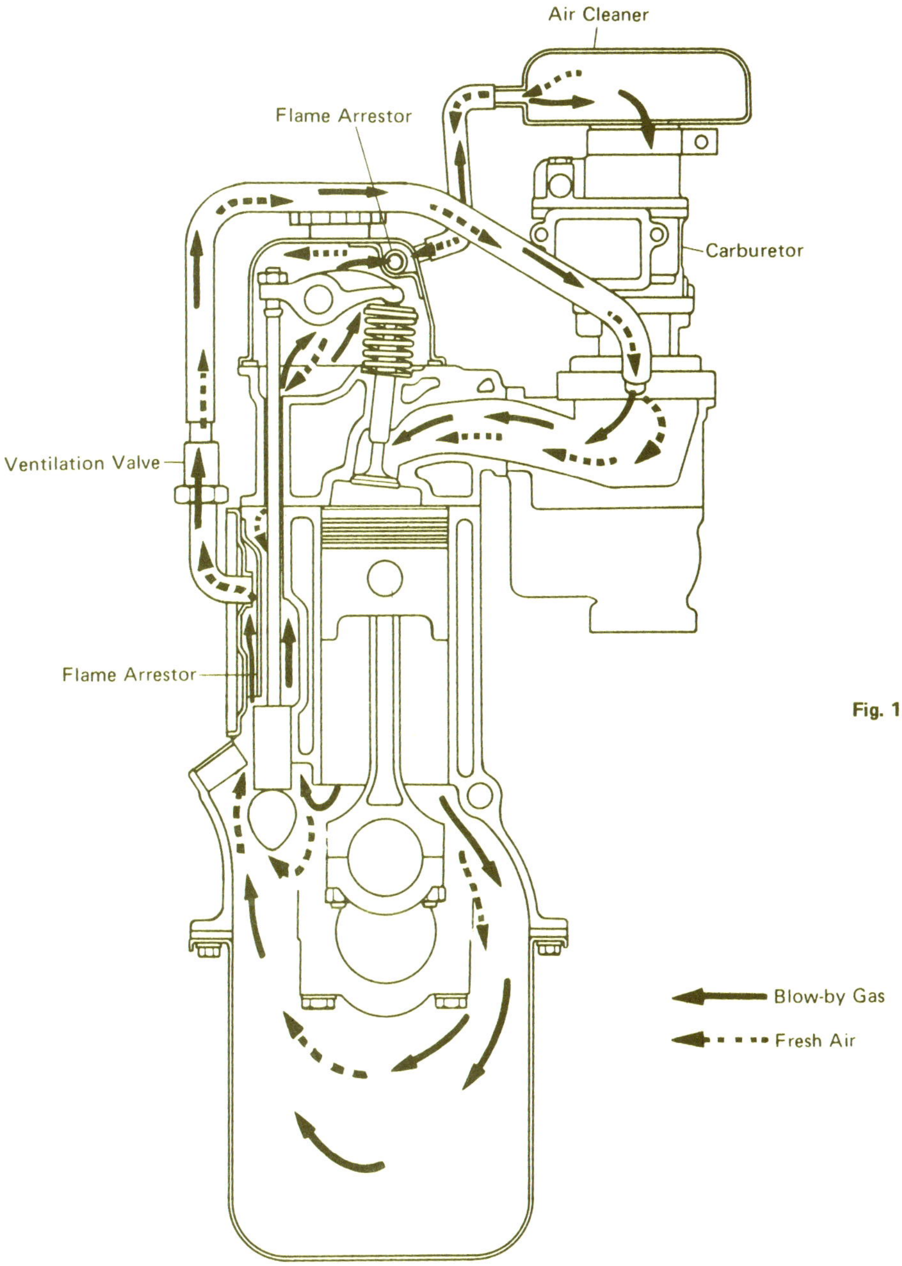

Fig. 1.27. PCV system - diagrammatic

⬅ Blow-by Gas
⬅ - - - Fresh Air

Fig. 1.28. PCV valve under normal running conditions

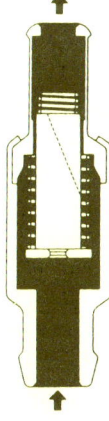

18 Crankshaft and main bearings - examination and renovation

1 Examine the crankpin and main journal surfaces for signs of scoring or scratches. Check the ovality of the crankpins at different positions with a micrometer. If more than specified out-of-round, the crankpin will have to be reground. It will also have to be reground if there are any scores or scratches present. Also check the journals in the same fashion.
2 If it is necessary to regrind the crankshaft and fit new bearings your local Toyota agent or automobile engineering works will be able to decide how much metal to grind off and the size of new bearing shells.
3 Full details of crankshaft regrinding tolerances and bearing undersizes are given in Specifications.
4 The main bearing clearances may be established by using a strip of Plastigage between the crankshaft journals and the main bearing/shell caps. Tighten the bearing cap bolts to a torque of 100 lb f ft (13.5 kgf m) for the front, second and third bearings, and 85 lb f ft (11.7 kgf m) for the rear bearing. Do not forget to use the shims beneath the caps if they were used during original assembly.
5 Examine the crankshaft timing gear for chipped or excessively worn teeth. Where applicable (even if the gear backlash was satisfactory - see Section 9), renew the gear; this will also mean that the camshaft gear will need renewing or considerable gear noise will result.

19 Connecting rods and bearings - examination and renovation

1 Connecting rod (big-end) bearing failure is indicated by a knocking from within the crankcase and a slight drop in oil pressure.
2 Examine the bearing surfaces for pitting and scoring. Renew the shells in accordance with the sizes given in Specifications. Where the crankshaft has been reground, the correct undersize shell bearing will be supplied by the repairer.
3 Should there be any suspicion that a connecting rod is bent or twisted or the small end bush no longer provides a good fit for the piston pin, then the complete connecting rod assembly should be exchanged for a reconditioned one.
4 Measurement of the connecting rod bearing clearances may be carried out in a similar manner to that described for the main bearings in the previous Section, but tighten the securing nuts on the cap bolts to 45 lb f ft (6.2 kgf m).

20 Cylinder bores - examination and renovation

1 The cylinder bores must be examined for taper, ovality, scoring and scratches. Start by carefully examining the top of the cylinder bores. If they are at all worn, a very slight ridge will be found on the thrust side. This marks the top of the piston ring travel. The owner will have a good indication of the bore wear prior to dismantling the engine, or removing the cylinder head. Excessive oil consumption, accompanied by blue smoke from the exhaust, is a sure sign of worn cylinder bores and piston rings.
2 Measure the bore diameter just under the ridge with a micrometer and compare it with the diameter at the bottom of the bore, which is not subject to wear. If the difference between the two measurements is more than 0.008 in (0.2 mm), it will be necessary to fit special pistons and rings, or to have the cylinders rebored and fit oversize pistons. If no micrometer is available remove the rings from a piston and place the piston in each bore in turn about ¾ in (18 mm) below the top of the bore. If a 0.0015 in (0.04 mm) feeler gauge slid between the piston and the cylinder wall requires more than a pull of between 2.2/5.5 lbf (1.0/2.5 kgf) to withdraw it, using a spring balance, then remedial action must be taken. Oversize pistons are available as listed in Specifications.
3 These are accurately machined to just below the indicated measurements so as to provide correct running clearances in bores bored out to the exact oversize dimensions.
4 If the bores are slightly worn but not so badly worn as to justify reboring them, special oil control rings and pistons can be installed, which will restore compression and stop the engine burning oil. Several different types are available and the manufacturer's instructions concerning their installation must be followed closely.
5 If new pistons are being installed and the bores have not been reground, it is essential to slightly roughen the hard glaze on the sides of the bores with fine glass paper so the new piston rings will have a chance to bed in properly.

21 Pistons, piston pins and piston rings - examination and renovation

1 Carefully remove the carbon from the piston ring grooves and piston crown.
2 Inspect the ring grooves for wear, burrs, nicks, etc., renewing as necessary.
3 Check the fit of the piston pin. At a temperature of 40/60°C (100/140°F) the piston pin should be capable of being moved under thumb pressure. (Immerse the piston in hot water for a few minutes to check this). Alternatively, check that with the connecting rod assembled to the piston pin and piston, there is no 'side-rock'. Renew the piston and piston pin if wear is evident.
4 Check the rings for wear and other obvious defects such as scoring.
5 With the rings installed on the piston, check the ring-to-groove clearance. If outside that given in the Specifications new rings and pistons should be obtained.
6 Install the rings into the bores about 1/3rd of the way down, and check the end gap using a feeler gauge. If outside that specified, where the bore is known to be satisfactory, it is permissible to dress the ends with a suitable file or carborundum stone. If the gap is excessive, new rings must be obtained.
7 When obtaining new rings for existing pistons, ensure that they are the correct size. Factory replacement pistons have the bore size marked on the head, but this may not be the case with replacements from other sources.

22 Camshaft, camshaft bearings and camshaft gear - examination and renovation

1 Carefully examine the camshaft journals for wear and damage. If evident, it is possible to have the camshaft reconditioned, but where this is necessary, it will also mean that the bearings in the block need attention also. This is obviously a job for the Toyota dealer or engine repair specialist.
2 Examine the cam lobes for wear, chipping or scoring; if evident a new camshaft should be obtained.
3 Examine the skew gear for wear and damage also: if evident this too will mean a new camshaft.
4 Check the camshaft/gear thrust plate clearance. If outside the specified limit, a new thrust plate must be installed which will mean removal of the gear (see next paragraph).
5 If the gear is chipped or excessively worn, a new one must be obtained (this will mean renewal of the crankshaft gear also, or considerable gear noise will result). The gear can be removed by removing the snap ring, supporting the thrust plate on a suitable spacer and carefully pressing out the camshaft.
6 Installation of the new gear is straightforward, but do not forget the Woodruff key (which should have stayed in the groove when the old gear was removed).

23 Valves and valve seats - examination and renovation

1 Examine the heads of the valves for pitting and burning, especially the heads of the exhaust valves. The valve seatings should be examined at the same time. If the pitting on valve and seat is very slight the marks can be removed by grinding the seats and valves together with coarse, and then fine, valve grinding paste. Also examine the valve stems for wear, renewing any which are outside the specified limit.
2 Where bad pitting has occurred to the valve seats it will be necessary to recut them and fit new valves. If the valve seats are so worn that they cannot be recut, then it will be necessary to fit new valve seat inserts. These latter two jobs should be entrusted to the local Toyota agent or automobile engineering works. In practice it is very seldom that the seats are so badly worn that they require renewal. Normally, it is the valve that is too badly worn for replacement, and the owner can easily purchase a new set of valves and match them to the seats by valve grinding.

Chapter 1/Engine 31

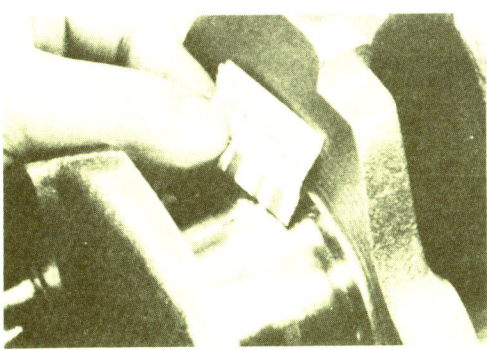

Fig. 1.29. Using 'Plastigage' to check bearing clearance

Fig. 1.30. Checking ring-to-groove clearance

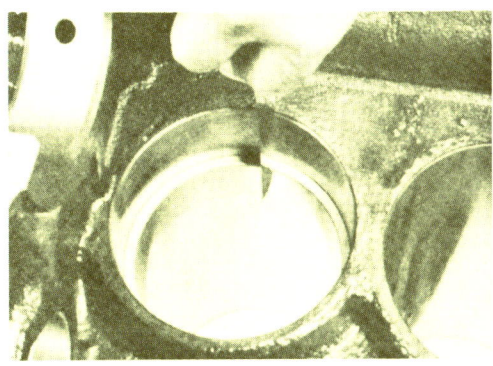

Fig. 1.31. Checking ring end-gap

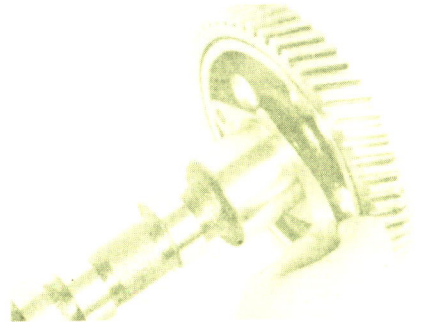

Fig. 1.32. Checking camshaft thrust clearance

3 Valve grinding is carried out as follows:
Smear a trace of coarse carborundum paste on the seat face and apply a suction grinder tool to the valve head. With a semi-rotary motion, grind the valve head to its seat, lifting the valve occasionally to redistribute the grinding paste. When a dull matt even surface finish is produced on both the valve seat and the valve, wipe off the paste and repeat the process with fine carborundum paste, lifting and turning the valve to redistribute the paste as before. A light spring placed under the valve head will greatly ease this operation. When a smooth unbroken ring of light grey matt finish is produced, on both valve and valve seat faces, the grinding operation is completed.

4 Scrape away all carbon from the valve head and the valve stem. Carefully clean away every trace of grinding compound, taking great care to leave none in the ports or in the valve guides. Clean the valves and valve seats with a kerosene soaked rag then with a clean rag, and finally if an air line is available, blow the valves, valve guides and valve ports clean.

24 Valve guides - examination and renovation

1 Test each valve in its guide for wear. After a considerable mileage, the valve guide bore may wear oval. This can best be tested by inserting a new valve in the guide and moving it from side to side. If the tip of the valve stem deflects by more than that given in the Specifications for valve stem to bushing clearances, new valve guides must be installed. This is a job for your local Toyota agent or automobile engineering works.

25 Valve springs - examination

1 During any major engine repair, particularly where valves are being renewed or reground, it is preferable to renew the valve springs also.
2 However, it is permissible to re-use springs, provided that it can be checked satisfactorily that they still meet their specified dimensions and load requirements.

26 Rockers, rocker shaft, valve lifters and pushrods - examination and renovation

1 Thoroughly clean the rocker shaft(s) and then check the shaft(s) for straightness by rolling on plate glass. It is most unlikely that it will deviate from normal, but if it does, purchase a new shaft. The surface of the shaft should be free from any worn ridges caused by the rocker arms. If any wear is present, renew the shaft.
2 Check the rocker arms for wear of the rocker bushes, for wear at the rocker arm face which bears on the valve stem, and for wear of the adjusting ball ended screws. Wear in the rocker arm bush can be checked by gripping the rocker arm tip and holding the rocker arm in place on the shaft, noting if there is any lateral rocker arm shake. If shake is present, and the arm is very loose on the shaft, a new bush or rocker arm must be fitted.

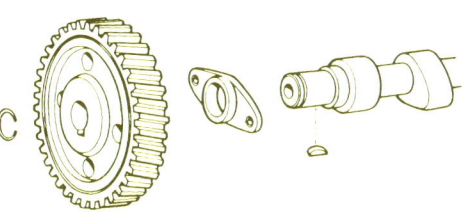

Fig. 1.33. Camshaft and gear

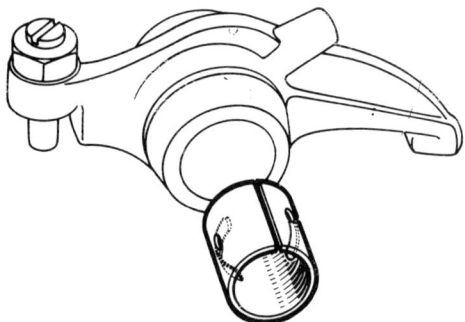

Fig. 1.34. Rocker arm and bush - note the oil holes which must be aligned with those in the arm

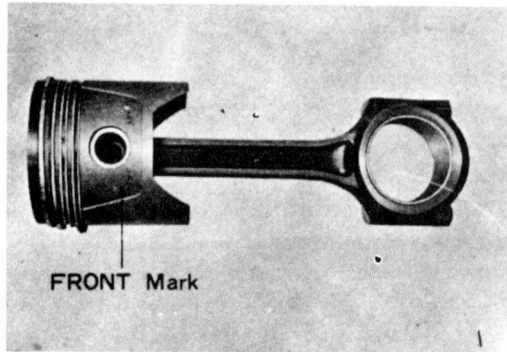

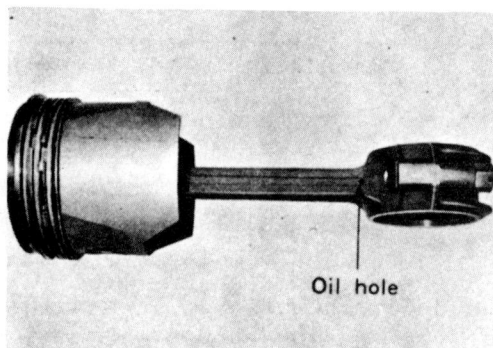

Fig. 1.35. F model piston 'front' marking and oil hole

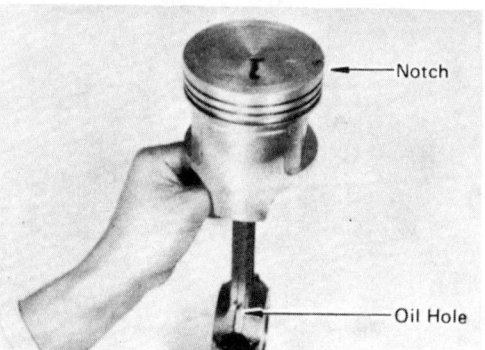

Fig. 1.36. 2F model piston notch and oil hole

3 Check the tip of the rocker arm where it bears on the valve head for cracking or serious wear on the case hardening. If none is present re-use the rocker arm. Check the lower half of the ball on the end of the rocker arm adjusting screw.

4 Check the pushrods for straightness by rolling them on the bench, renewing any that are bent. Also check for damage and indentation at the ends.

5 Check the valve lifters for scoring and pitting, and for wear, particularly on the rubbing surfaces. If new (oversize) lifters are required, the bores in the block will need to be machined; this is a job for the Toyota agent or automobile engineering workshop.

27 Flywheel and starter ring gear - examination and renovation

1 If the teeth on the flywheel starter ring are badly worn, or if some are missing then it will be necessary to remove the ring and fit a new one, or preferably exchange the flywheel for a reconditioned unit.

2 Either split the ring with a cold chisel after making a cut with a hacksaw blade between two teeth, or use a soft headed hammer (not steel) to knock the ring off, striking it evenly and alternately at equally spaced points. Take great care not to damage the flywheel during this process.

3 Heat the new ring in either an electric oven to about 392°F (200°C) or immerse in a pan of boiling oil.

4 Hold the ring at this temperature for five minutes and then quickly fit it to the flywheel so the chamfered portion of the teeth faces the transmission side of the flywheel.

5 The ring should be tapped gently down onto its register and left to cool naturally when the contraction of the metal on cooling will ensure that it is a secure and permanent fit. Great care must be taken not to overheat the ring, indicated by it turning light metallic blue, as if this happens the temper of the ring will be lost.

6 Examine the clutch plate contacting surface for scoring and cracks. Light scoring can be machined out, provided that the runout does not exceed that given in the Specifications. If the flywheel is unserviceable in any other way it must be renewed.

28 Clutch housing - examination and renovation

1 Examine the clutch housing for cracking and damaged screw threads. It may be possible to renew damaged screw threads by installing suitable thread inserts but other than this, a replacement will be required.

29 Cylinder head - decarbonising and examination

1 With the cylinder head removed, use a blunt scraper to remove all trace of carbon and deposits from the combustion spaces and ports. Scrape the cylinder head free from scale or old pieces of gasket or jointing compound. Clean the cylinder head by washing it in kerosene and take particular care to pull a piece of rag through the ports and cylinder head bolt holes. Any dirt remaining in these recesses may well drop onto the gasket or cylinder block mating surface as the cylinder head is lowered into position and could lead to a gasket leak after reassembly is complete.

2 With the cylinder head clean, test for distortion if a history of coolant leakage has been apparent. Carry out this test using a straight edge and feeler gauges or a piece of plate glass. If the surface shows any warping in excess of that permitted by the Specifications, the cylinder head will have to be resurfaced which is a job for a specialist.

3 Clean the pistons and top of the cylinder bores. If the pistons are still in the block then it is essential that great care is taken to ensure that no carbon gets into the cylinder bores as this could scratch the cylinder walls or cause damage to the piston and rings. To ensure this does not happen, first turn the crankshaft so that two of the pistons are at the top of their bores. Stuff rag into the other two bores or seal them off with paper and masking tape to prevent particles of carbon entering the cooling system and damaging the water pump.

4 Rotate the crankshaft and repeat the carbon removal operations on the remaining pistons and cylinder bores.

5 Thoroughly clean all particles of carbon from the bores and then inject a little light oil round the edges of the pistons to lubricate the piston rings.

30 Timing cover oil seal - renewal

1 Whenever a major engine overhaul is carried out, renew the timing cover oil seal as a matter of routine. Drive it out of its location using a piece of tubing as a drift.
2 Tap in the new seal squarely, making sure that the lips face the correct way. Refer to Section 35 for renewal of the crankshaft rear oil seal.

31 Engine - preparation for reassembly

1 To ensure maximum life with reliability from a rebuilt engine, not only must everything be correctly assembled but all components must be spotlessly clean and the correct spring or plain washers used where originally located. Always lubricate bearing and working surfaces with clean engine oil during reassembly of engine parts.
2 Before reassembly commences, renew any bolts or studs the threads of which are damaged or corroded.
3 As well as your normal tool kit, gather together clean rags, oil can, a torque wrench and a complete (overhaul) set of gaskets and oil seals.

32 Pistons, piston rings and connecting rods - reassembly

1 Assemble each piston, piston pin and connecting rod so that when installed the FRONT marking on the piston or the notch will be towards the front of the engine, and the oil hole in the connecting rod journal will be towards the camshaft. Ensure that the piston pin is centralized before tightening the piston pin bolt to the specified torque. Note that on F model engines, the piston should be heated to 40/60°C (100/140°F) for about 5 minutes before the piston pin is pushed in.
2 Install the piston rings to the piston grooves so that the identification markings are uppermost. Note that the rings for the F and 2F model pistons, and the pistons themselves, are considerably different. Ensure that the ring gaps are positioned as shown in Figs. 1.40 and 1.41.

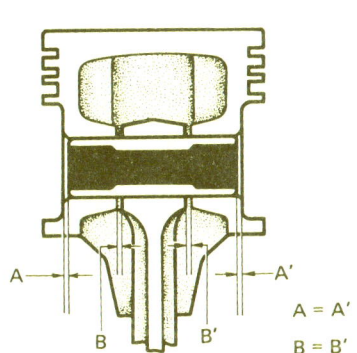

Fig. 1.37. Alignment of the piston pin, and connecting-rod

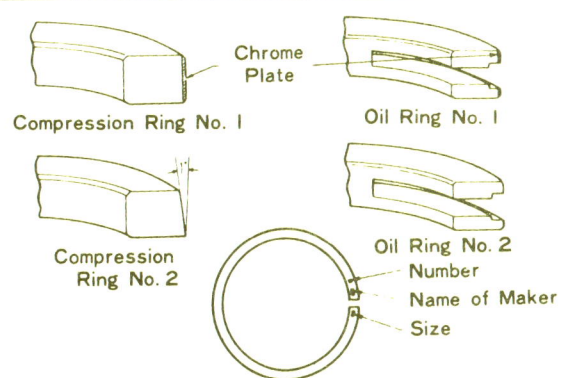

Fig. 1.38. F model piston ring markings

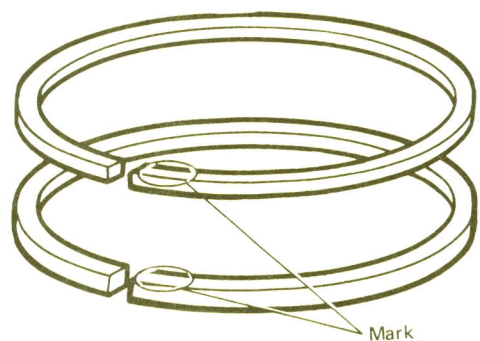

Fig. 1.39. 2F model piston ring markings

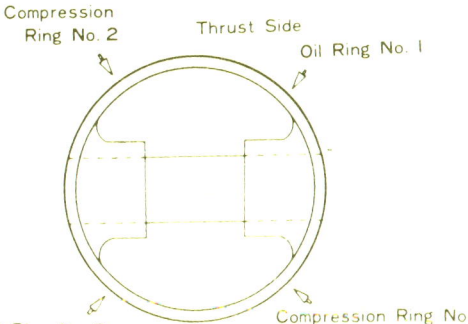

Fig. 1.40. F model ring gap position

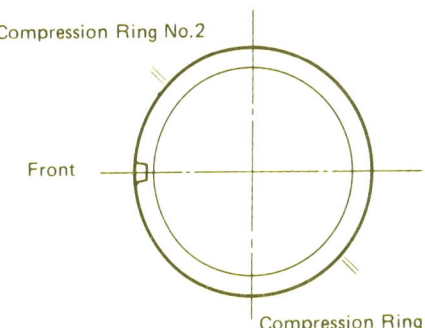

Fig. 1.41. 2F model ring gap position

Fig. 1.42. Installing a valve spring

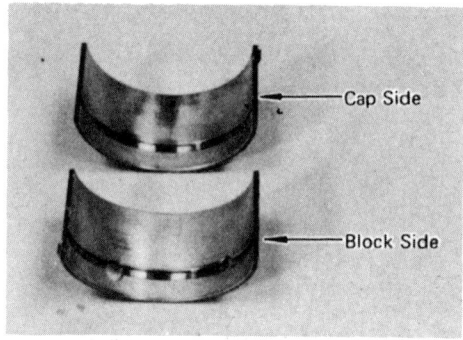

Fig. 1.43. No. 1 and No. 4 main bearing shells have oil holes for the block

Fig. 1.44. Install bearing caps in their original positions. Note the arrow mark which is towards the front

Fig. 1.45. Align the bearing cap marks for each connecting-rod

33 Cylinder head - reassembly

1 Smear the valve stems with engine oil then, working from one end of the cylinder head, insert an exhaust valve into its guide. Install the spring seat, spring, stem oil seal and spring retainers.
2 Using a proprietary spring compressor, compress the assembly and install the spring locks (split collets). Remove the compressor and tap the valve stem end with a mallet to ensure correct seating of the locks.
3 Repeat the procedure for the next (intake) valve then work progressively along the cylinder head.

34 Valve rocker mechanism - reassembly

1 Install the valve rocker arms, springs and arm supports onto the rocker shafts. Note that the F model and 2F model assemblies are different, and that the F model has two short shafts with the oil union in the middle; the open ends of the short shaft face the union. After assembly, install the lock springs to retain the components. The shaft(s) and rockers are shown in Figs. 1.17 and 1.18 - note the difference between the inlet and exhaust rockers.

35 Crankshaft and main bearings - installation

1 Ensure that the bearing housings in the block and caps are clean, and install new shells. Note that the shells for No 1 (front) and No 4 (rear) which fit into the block have oil holes.
2 Lubricate the shells with engine oil and install the crankshaft. At this point, also install the crankshaft rear oil seal; lubricate the seal lips with engine oil.
3 Lubricate the crankshaft journals with engine oil then install the bearing caps in their original positions (see Fig. 1.44). If shims were originally used beneath the caps, these must be used again. Do not forget that number 3 bearing is the thrust bearing; if this was renewed it will be necessary to re-establish the crankshaft endfloat (see Section 11). To prevent oil leakage, a non-setting gasket sealant should be applied to the contact surface of the front and rear bearing caps to prevent leakage.
4 Tighten the bearing caps progressively and evenly to the specified torque, checking that the crankshaft rotates freely (although perhaps stiffly) on completion.

36 Pistons and connecting rods - installation

1 Install the bearing shells to the connecting rods and bearing caps, and lubricate the rubbing surfaces with engine oil.
2 Lubricate the piston sides with engine oil then, after checking that the rings are correctly positioned (see Section 32), compress the rings of one piston with a proprietary piston ring clamp.
3 Insert the assembly into the correct bore, ensuring that it is the correct way round, pushing it down with a hammer shaft until it is in position on the crankpin. In doing this, the ring clamp will slide off and the rings will go in satisfactorily.

Fig. 1.46. Installing the crankcase endplate

Chapter 1/Engine

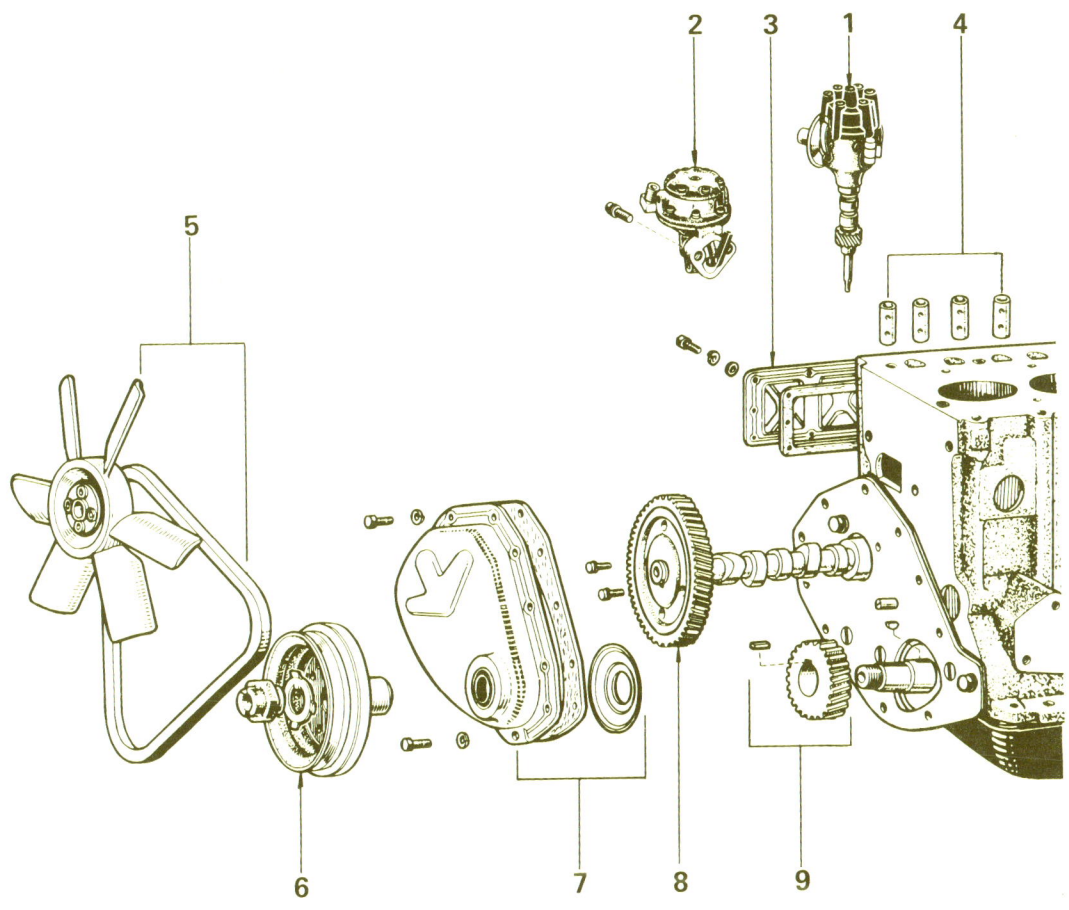

Fig. 1.47. Timing gear and associated parts

1 Distributor
2 Fuel pump
3 Valve lifter cover
4 Valve lifter
5 Fan and belt
6 Crankshaft pulley
7 Timing cover and oil slinger
8 Camshaft
9 Crankshaft timing gear

4 Install the appropriate bearing cap the correct way round and tighten the nuts progressively to the specified torque. Either use new self locking nuts or new cotter pins, according to the type installed.
5 Rotate the crankshaft as necessary, and repeat the procedure for the remaining assemblies.
6 Check that the crankshaft will still rotate after all the caps have been tightened.
7 Install the crankcase endplate, not forgetting to use a new gasket.
8 Install the crankshaft gear (where applicable) by carefully tapping it or using a suitable tubular drift. Do not forget to install the key.

37 Camshaft, camshaft gear and timing gear cover - installation

1 Lubricate the camshaft journals and lobes with engine oil, then carefully and squarely insert the shaft.
2 As the timing gear meshes with the crankshaft gear, ensure that the timing marks align (see Fig. 1.48). Tighten the thrust plate bolts to the specified torque.
3 Using a narrow feeler gauge, ensure that the timing gear backlash is within the specified limit. If this is not so, both gears should be renewed.
4 Using a dial gauge, check the runout of the timing gears. If this exceeds the specified amount, new gears must be obtained.

Fig. 1.48. Alignment of the timing marks

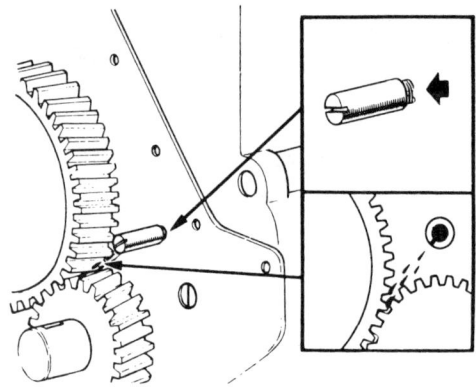

Fig. 1.49. Timing gear oil nozzle

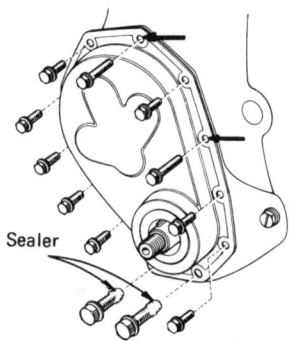

Fig. 1.50. Apply sealant to the bolts marked

Fig. 1.51. Apply sealant at the points marked

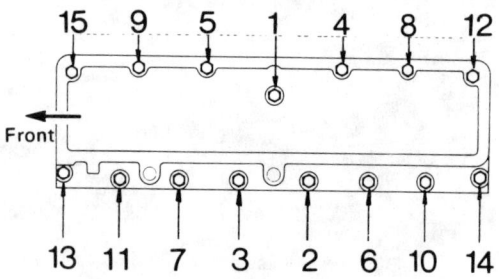

Fig. 1.52. Cylinder head tightening sequence

5 If the timing gear oil nozzle was removed, screw it in so that the nozzle points towards the gears, then lock it in two places by center punching.
6 Install the oil slinger onto the crankshaft, concave side outwards.
7 If the old oil seal has not been removed from the timing cover, pry it out with a screwdriver. Ensure that the cover is clean, then press in a new seal; lubricate the lips with engine oil.
8 Install the timing cover and a new gasket, using a non-setting sealant for the joint faces. Apply sealant to the bolts shown in Fig. 1.50, but do not fully tighten any of the bolts at this stage.
9 Check that the crankshaft key is in position then install the pulley. Tighten the nut to the specified torque.
10 Tighten the timing cover bolts.

38 Oil pump, oil strainer and oil pan - installation

1 Install the oil pump, tightening the bolts to the specified torque. Either use new tab washers, or wire lock the bolts, as applicable.
2 Install the oil strainer assembly.
3 Ensure that the oil pan and crankcase faces are clean, then position a new gasket on the crankcase. Apply a non-setting gasket sealant at the points shown in Fig. 1.51.
4 Install the oil pan, tightening the bolts progressively and evenly to the specified torque.
5 Install the oil pressure regulator using a new gasket.

39 Cylinder head and valve gear - installation

1 Ensure that the cylinder head and block mating surfaces are clean, then position a new gasket on the block. Ensure that the gasket holes align with the holes in the block.
2 Install the cylinder head (with the air cleaner support bracket, where applicable).
3 Install, and progressively tighten, the cylinder head bolts to the specified torque, in three stages. The tightening sequence is shown in Fig. 1.52.
4 Where applicable, install the oil delivery pipe.
5 Lubricate the valve lifters and pushrods, and install them in their respective bores.
6 Install the valve rocker gear onto the cylinder head. Where applicable, install the oil delivery union, spring and connecting sleeve. Tighten the rocker shaft support retaining bolts and nuts to the specified torque.

40 Valve clearance - adjustment

1 If this is being carried out during normal servicing with the engine installed, it will first of all be necessary to remove the air cleaner and rocker cover. Do not forget that this should be done after the engine has reached the normal operating temperature.
2 Each valve rocker pair should be checked/adjusted with the appropriate piston at top-dead-center (TDC) on its firing stroke. In this position both valves should be closed and there should be clearance between the rockers and pushrods. The correct clearances are given in the Specifications, and are obtained by loosening the nut of the adjusting screw then turning the screw until a feeler gauge of the correct size is a firm sliding fit between the end of the valve stem and the rocker (photo).
3 When the clearance is correct, tighten the locknut and recheck that it has not altered.
4 After checking/adjusting the rocker pair for the first cylinder, work progressively along the block. Do not forget that where this is being done during engine rebuild (ie: the engine is cold), the settings obtained are provisional only, and **MUST** be rechecked/adjusted after an initial warming-up run following installation.
5 An alternative way to check the valve rocker clearances when the engine is installed is to set the engine to No 1 cylinder at tdc on its firing stroke by aligning the timing mark with the pointer, when the distributor rotor is in the position shown in Fig. 1.53. Adjust 1, 2, 3, 5, 7 and 9 rockers in this position, then rotate the crankshaft through $360°$ and adjust 4, 6, 8, 10, 11 and 12 rockers.
6 On completion, install the rocker cover and a new gasket.

7 Where applicable, install the valve lifter cover (engine side cover) and a new gasket.

41 Engine ancillaries - installation

1 This procedure is basically the reverse of that set out in Section 6. However, particular attention should be paid to the following points.
  a) *Use a new gasket when installing the fuel pump.*
  b) *Use a new manifold gasket, and tighten to the specified torque.*
  c) *Use a new gasket when installing the carburetor.*
  d) *Use new gaskets for the water outlet housing and water pump assembly.*
  e) *When installing the oil filter, lubricate the seal ring with engine oil and install hand-tight only.*
  f) *Do not forget to install the input shaft spigot bearing in the end of the crankshaft.*
  g) *When installing the flywheel, use new tab washers and apply a non-setting gasket sealant to the bolt threads. Tighten the bolts to the specified torque.*
  h) *Where applicable, align the mating marks on the clutch cover and flywheel, and tighten the bolts to the specified torque. Note that it will be necessary to align the clutch correctly - for further information on this refer to Chapter 5.*
  j) *Install the distributor in its original position with the rotor correctly aligned. If the original position is not known, refer to the procedure given in Chapter 4.*
  k) *Install and adjust the V-belts - refer to Chapters 11 and 12 for the correct tension.*
  l) *Check/adjust the clutch lever height - refer to Chapter 5 for further information.*
  m) *Before installing the transmission, smear general purpose grease on the input shaft spigot and splines.*
  n) *Take care when connecting the various hoses and electrical wires to prevent mix-up.*

42 Initial start-up after overhaul or major repair

1 With the engine installed in the vehicle (see Section 3), have a last look round to ensure that all the hoses and wires have been connected, and that no tools or rags are left in the engine compartment.
2 Start the engine and check for any oil, water or fuel leaks; tighten any hose clips or bolts as necessary.
3 Run the engine at a fast idle to ensure that it is thoroughly warmed up. Check and adjust carburetor and ignition timing settings after a brief test run, then switch off the engine and recheck the valve rocker clearances as described in Section 40.
4 After about 600 miles (1000 km) of running, recheck the cylinder head and rocker arm support bolts for tightness (refer to the 12000 mile/2000 km Routine Maintenance checks). At this stage the engine oil should be renewed, and a new filter element installed also.

40.2 Valve clearance adjustment

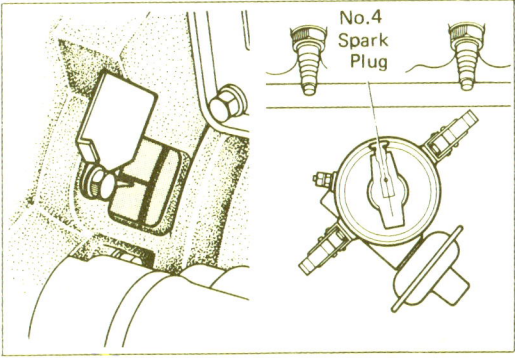

Fig. 1.53. Distributor rotor and timing mark position for first phase of valve rocker checking

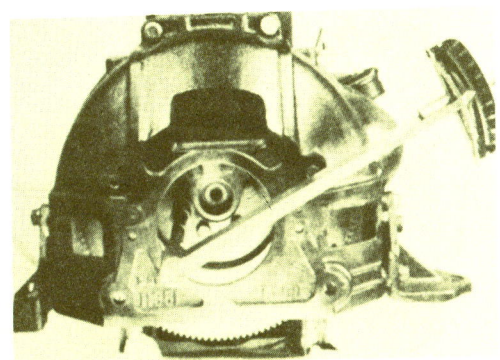

Fig. 1.54. Tightening the flywheel bolts

43 Fault diagnosis - engine

Symptom	Reason/s
Engine will not turn over when starter switch is operated	Flat battery. Bad battery connections. Bad connections at solenoid switch and/or starter motor. Defective starter motor.
Engine turns over normally but fails to start	No spark at plugs. No fuel reaching engine. Too much fuel reaching the engine (flooding).
Engine starts but runs unevenly and misfires	Ignition and/or fuel system faults. Incorrect valve clearances. Burnt out valves. Worn out piston rings.
Lack of power	Ignition and/or fuel system faults. Incorrect valve clearances. Burnt out valves. Worn out piston rings.
Excessive oil consumption	Oil leaks from crankshaft rear oil seal, timing cover gasket and oil seal, rocker cover gasket, oil filter gasket, oil pan gasket, oil pan plug washer. Worn piston rings or cylinder bores resulting in oil being burnt by engine. Worn valve guides and/or defective valve stem seals.
Excessive mechanical noise from engine	Wrong valve rocker clearances. Worn crankshaft bearings. Worn cylinders (piston slap). Slack or worn timing gears.

Note: *When investigating starting and uneven running faults do not be tempted into snap diagnosis. Start from the beginning of the check procedure and follow it through. It will take less time in the long run. Poor performance from an engine in terms of power and economy is not normally diagnosed quickly. In any event the ignition and fuel systems must be checked first before assuming any further investigation needs to be made.*

Chapter 2 Cooling system

Contents

Antifreeze and corrosion inhibiting mixtures ... 5	General description ... 1
Cooling system - draining ... 2	Radiator - removal and installation ... 6
Cooling system - filling ... 4	Temperature controlled cooling fan - general ... 11
Cooling system - flushing ... 3	Thermostat - removal, checking and installation ... 10
Electric cooling fan - general ... 12	Water pump - overhaul ... 9
Fault diagnosis - cooling system ... 13	Water pump - removal and installation ... 7
Fluid coupling - removal and installation ... 8	

Specifications

System type ... Pressurized with pump circulation and fan assistance

Thermostat
F model engine
Opening temperature ... 74.5/78.5°C (100/173°F)
Fully open ... 90°C (194°F)
Travel ... 0.39 in (10 mm)
2F model engine
Opening temperature ... 82°C (180°F)
Fully open ... 95°C (203°F)
Travel ... 0.31 in (8 mm)

Radiator type ... Corrugated pin and tube

Water pump type ... Centrifugal

Radiator pressure cap setting ... 12.8 psi (0.9 kgf/in^2)

Fanbelt tension ... Refer to Chapter 11, Section 8

Coolant capacity (approx) *
F model engine ... 35 US pt/29 Imp pt/16.7 litres
2F model engine ... 38 US pt/32 Imp pt/18 litres
* Actual quantity depends upon vehicle type and specification

Antifreeze ... Ethylene glycol type

1 General description

The cooling system is a pressurized, forced circulation type. The water pump is belt driven from the engine crankshaft, and forces water from the bottom of the radiator, through the cylinder block and head passages, and is returned through the water outlet to the radiator.

The system is pressurized to allow water temperatures in excess of the normal boiling point of the coolant to improve engine efficiency.

The thermostat restricts the flow of water to the radiator when the engine is cooled, to aid rapid warm-up.

On F model engines, the fan is directly driven from the water pump impeller shaft. On 2F model engines, a fluid coupling is used to allow a progressive degree of 'slip' as the engine speed increases; this reduces power loss from the engine. On 1977 USA and Canada models, a temperature controlled fluid coupling is used so that at low temperatures, a very reduced fan speed is obtained regardless of engine speed. This is accomplished by a bi-metal spring which opens or closes an oil passage within the coupling.

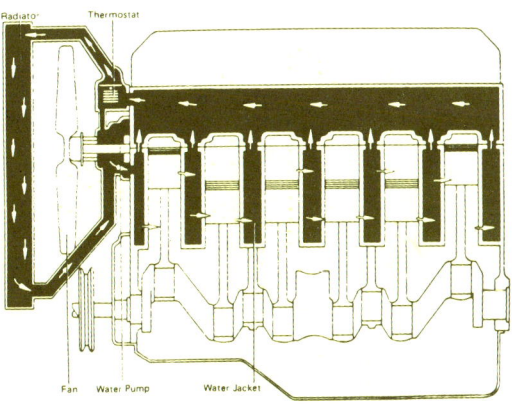

Fig. 2.1. Diagrammatic view of the cooling system

Also introduced for 1977 USA and Canada models was an electrically operated cooling fan which prevents hot air generated by the thermal reactor from affecting the carburetor, brake servo and engine compartment hoses. A thermal switch is mounted behind the carburetor to control the system.

2 Cooling system - draining

1 Place the vehicle on level ground. If the engine is hot, it is recommended that it is allowed to cool before draining commences.
2 Remove the radiator filler cap; if an expansion reservoir is installed, remove the expansion cap first. **Note: If the need arises for removing the radiator cap (systems without a reservoir) or reservoir cap (systems with a reservoir) when hot, extreme care must be taken to prevent scalding. Place a thick rag over the cap, and turn it slowly counter-clockwise to the detent until the hissing has stopped; then depress the cap, turn it further and remove it.**
3 Open the radiator drain tap or detach the bottom hose; also open the drain plug on the left side of the engine. If the coolant is to be used again, collect it in a container of suitable size (photo).

3 Cooling system - flushing

1 After some time the radiator and waterways in the engine may become restricted or even blocked with scale or sediment, which reduces the efficiency of the cooling system. When this condition occurs or the coolant appears rusty or dark in color the system should be flushed. In severe cases reverse flushing may be required as described later.
2 Unscrew fully the radiator and cylinder block drain taps.
3 Remove the radiator filler cap and place a hose in the filler neck. Allow water to run through the system until it emerges from both drain taps quite clear in color. **Do not flush a hot engine with cold water.**
4 In severe cases of contamination of the coolant or in the system, reverse flush by first removing the radiator cap and disconnecting the lower radiator hose at the radiator outlet pipe.
5 Remove the radiator as described in Section 6.
6 Invert the radiator and place a hose in the bottom outlet pipe. Continue flushing until clear water comes from the radiator top tank.
7 In cases of severe scalding or sedimentation, the use of a proprietary brand of flushing compound may be used, in which case the manufacturer's instructions should be followed.

4 Cooling system - filling

1 Tighten the radiator and engine block drain plugs, then pour in the coolant until it is up to the level of the filler neck of the radiator.
2 Run the engine at a fast idle speed for about ten minutes (until the thermostat opens), topping-up as necessary. The coolant level will probably drop sharply as air-locks are displaced, as well as when the thermostat opens.
3 When the level has finally ceased to fall, top-up up the radiator to 0.75 in (19 mm) below the filler neck (systems without a reservoir) or to the brim (systems with a reservoir). Where a reservoir is installed, top it up to just below the full mark (photo).
4 It is recommended that the level is checked again, when the engine has cooled, after a few miles of running. Where a reservoir is installed, only the reservoir level needs checking - unless it is empty, when the radiator level should be checked also.

5 Anti-freeze and corrosion inhibiting mixtures

1 It is recommended that the system is filled with an antifreeze mixture where climatic conditions warrant its use. The cooling system should be drained, flushed and refilled at the intervals stated in the Routine Maintenance Section. If the use of antifreeze mixture is not necessary because of favorable climatic conditions, never use ordinary water but always fill the system with a corrosion inhibiting mixture of recommended brand to protect the engine.
2 Before adding antifreeze to the system, check all hose connections and check the tightness of the cylinder head bolts as such solutions are searching. The cooling system should be drained and refilled with clean water as previously explained, before adding antifreeze.
3 The quantity of antifreeze which should be used for various levels of protection is given in the table below, expressed as a percentage of the system capacity.

Antifreeze volume	Protection to	Safe pump circulation
25%	−26°C (−15°F)	−12°C (10°F)
30%	−33°C (−28°F)	−16°C (3°F)
35%	−39°C (−38°F)	−20°C (−4°F)

4 Where the cooling system contains an antifreeze or corrosion inhibiting solution, any topping-up should be done with a solution made up in similar proportions to the original in order to avoid dilution.

6 Radiator - removal and installation

1 Drain the cooling system (refer to Section 2 if necessary).
2 Detach the radiator top and bottom hoses.
3 Remove the bolts retaining the radiator to the radiator support.
4 Taking care that the pins are not damaged, lift the radiator upwards and out of the engine compartment.
5 With the radiator removed, use an air blast to remove any congealed dirt, etc. which may restrict the air cooling path.
6 If the serviceability of the radiator is in doubt, it is a good policy to arrange for your Toyota garage to check the radiator cap, also, using a special pressure tester. Always renew a defective radiator cap.
7 Installation is the reverse of the removal procedure. On completion, refill the cooling system (refer to Section 4, if necessary).

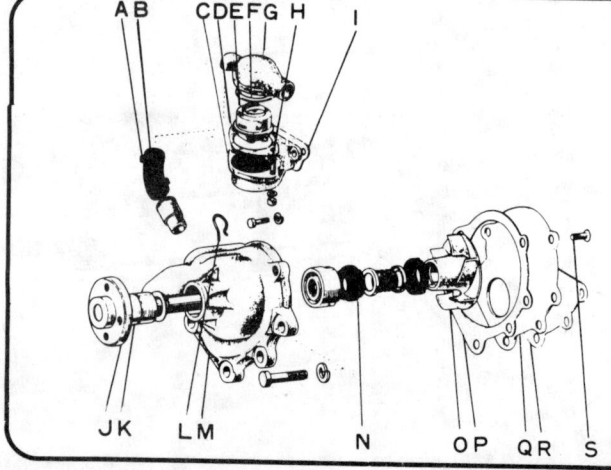

Fig. 2.2. Water pump and thermostat - exploded view

A Hose clip
B Bypass hose
C Water outler
D Gasket
E Thermostat
F Gasket
G Water outlet housing (thermostat cover)
H Stud bolt
I Gasket
J Pulley seat
K Water pump bearing
L Bearing retaining wire
M Water pump body
N Shaft seal
O Rotor
P Gasket
Q Seat plate
R Gasket
S Screw

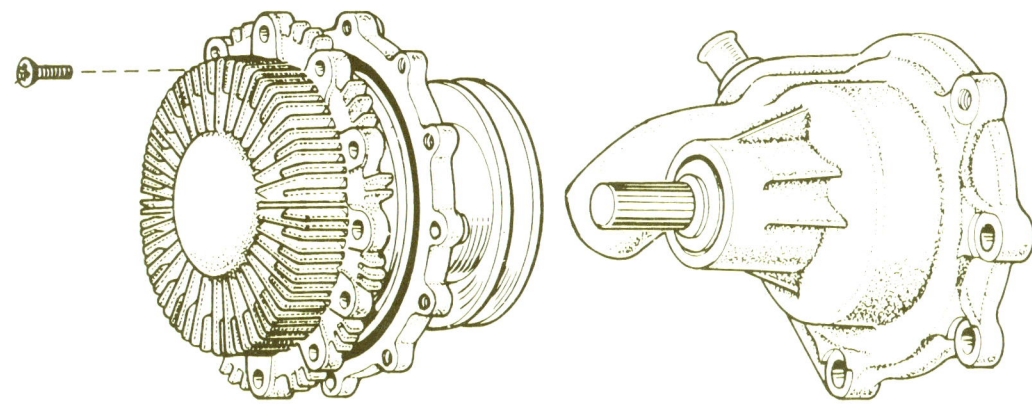

Fig. 2.3. Fluid coupling

Fig. 2.4. Removing pulley seat using special tool

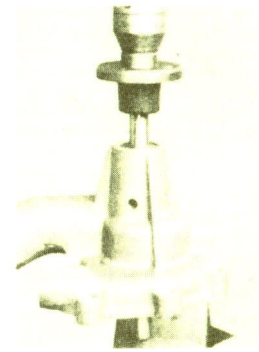

Fig. 2.5. Pulley seat installed depth (2F model)

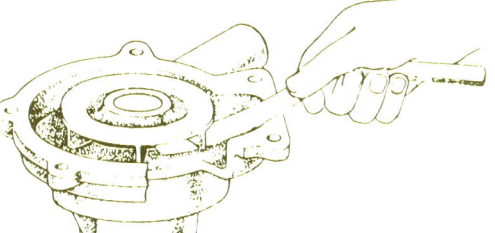

Fig. 2.6. Checking rotor blade-to-pump body clearance

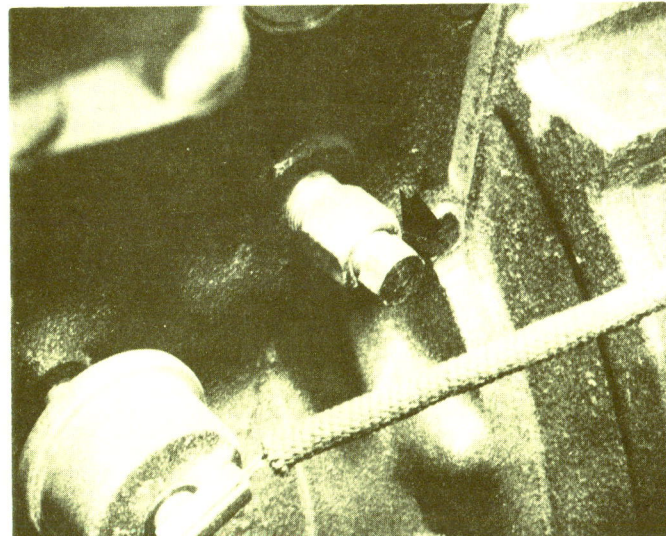

2.3 Engine block drain plug (arrowed)

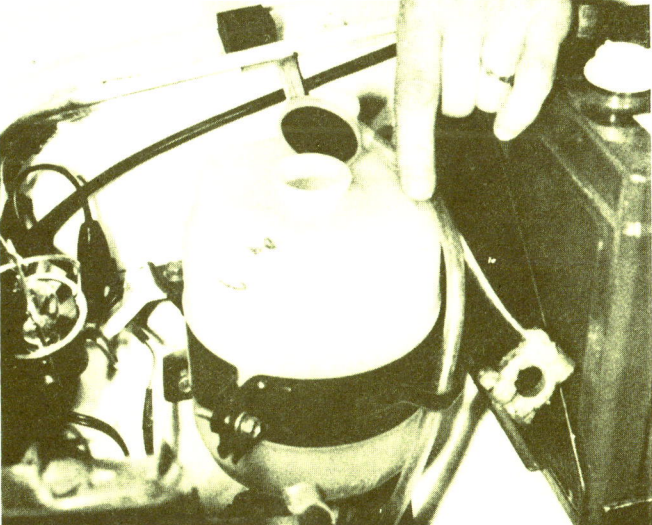

4.3 Expansion reservoir for cooling system

7 Water pump - removal and installation

Note: In addition to the information given below, it may be necessary to detach emission control items on some models.
1 Drain the cooling system (refer to Section 2, if necessary).
2 Remove the alternator adjusting link, fan, fan pulley (where applicable) and V-belt.
3 Detach the radiator lower hose and the water pump bypass hose.
4 Remove the retaining bolts, and detach the water pump assembly and gasket.
5 Installation is basically the reverse of the removal procedure, but always ensure that a new gasket is used and that the sealing faces are clean. A non-setting sealant is also recommended for the joint faces. Refill the cooling system on completion (refer to Section 4, if necessary).

8 Fluid coupling - removal and installation

1 Remove the water pump as described in Section 7.
2 Support the pulley on suitable blocks, then use a suitable tool to press out the pump assembly from the fluid coupling. **Note:** Once removed, the fluid coupling cannot be re-used.
3 When installing a replacement coupling, support the pump bearing shaft at the rotor end and press on the coupling. Take care that silicone oil is not lost from the coupling during this procedure.

9 Water pump - overhaul

1 Before commencing overhaul of a water pump, check with your Toyota dealer regarding the availability of spares, and the relative cost of obtaining an exchange assembly. If you decide to overhaul the pump, ensure that you have the necessary tools and equipment.
2 Release the pump seat and gasket.
3 Using a suitable puller (Toyota tool No 09235-60010 is available for this purpose), remove the pump pulley seat.
4 Using pliers, pull out the water pump bearing retaining wire.
5 Carefully support the pump body, and press out the bearing.
6 Take out the pump rotor and shaft seal.
7 Carefully clean all the parts; do not immerse the bearing in any cleaning solvent.
8 Carefully inspect all the parts for wear, corrosion and damage, renewing as necessary. It is recommended that seals and gaskets should always be renewed. If the bearing is in good condition it may be re-used, although it is preferable to install a new one if possible.
9 Commence installation by pressing in a new bearing, applying pressure on the outer race only. Install the bearing retaining wire.
10 Install the pulley seat, pressing it on until the end is flush with the bearing shaft (F model engine) or to the depth shown in Fig. 2.5 (2F model engine).
11 Assemble the shaft seal and seal thrust washer into the seal guide of the pump body, then press on the rotor using a suitable tubular tool.
12 Having pressed on the rotor, check that the rotor blade-to-pump body clearance is 0.012/0.027 in (0.3 to 0.7 mm).
13 Install the pump seat plate, using a new gasket, and tighten the retaining screws.
14 Before installing, check the pump rotor to ensure that it rotates freely.

10 Thermostat - removal, checking and installation

1 Partially drain the cooling system until the coolant level is below the thermostat housing height (refer to Section 2 if necessary).
2 Remove the two retaining screws, and take off the top cover. If necessary it may be tapped with a soft-faced hammer, or a knife blade inserted at the joint face if it is sticking.
3 Take out the thermostat.
4 The thermostat may be checked by immersing it in hot water alongside a thermometer. When the water is heated, the thermostat should commence opening, then be fully open, at the temperatures given in the Specifications. When cooled down, the thermostat should also close completely. Renew a thermostat which does not operate satisfactorily.
5 Installation is the reverse of the removal procedure, but ensure that the seating inside the cover, and the joint faces, are clean. Renew the gasket and/or sealing ring if either appears to have deteriorated. A non-setting jointing compound may be used on the gasket face (photo).
6 On completion, refill the cooling system (refer to Section 4, if necessary).

11 Temperature controlled cooling fan - general

1 A two-stage temperature controlled fluid coupling is used on 1977 USA and Canada models.
2 This is similar to the other fluid couplings used for later models except for the bi-metal controlled oil passage valve.
3 The coupling is designed to control the fan speed at two different levels according to the radiator through-air temperature.

12 Electric cooling fan - general

1 The electric cooling fan is designed to blow off the hot air generated in the thermal reactor which is installed on 1977 USA and Canada models.
2 When the ignition switch is ON, and the engine compartment temperature is above $176 \pm 9^{\circ}F$ ($80 \pm 5^{\circ}C$), a thermoswitch energizes the cooling fan relay which in turn operates the fan.
3 When the ignition is switched off, but the engine compartment temperature is still above the specified range, the fan remains on to dissipate the excessive heat.

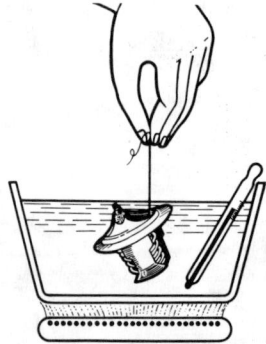

Fig. 2.7. Checking thermostat

Fig. 2.8. Temperature controlled cooling fan fluid coupling

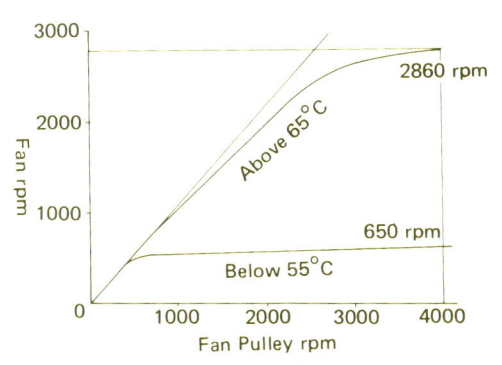

Fig. 2.9. Coupling performance graph

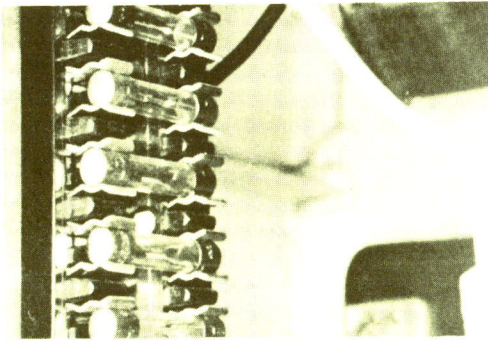

Fig. 2.10. Fuse locations for electric cooling fan circuit

Fuse	Circuit	Rating
1	*Engine*	*15A*
2	*Horn*	*20A*
3	*Cooling system*	*5A*

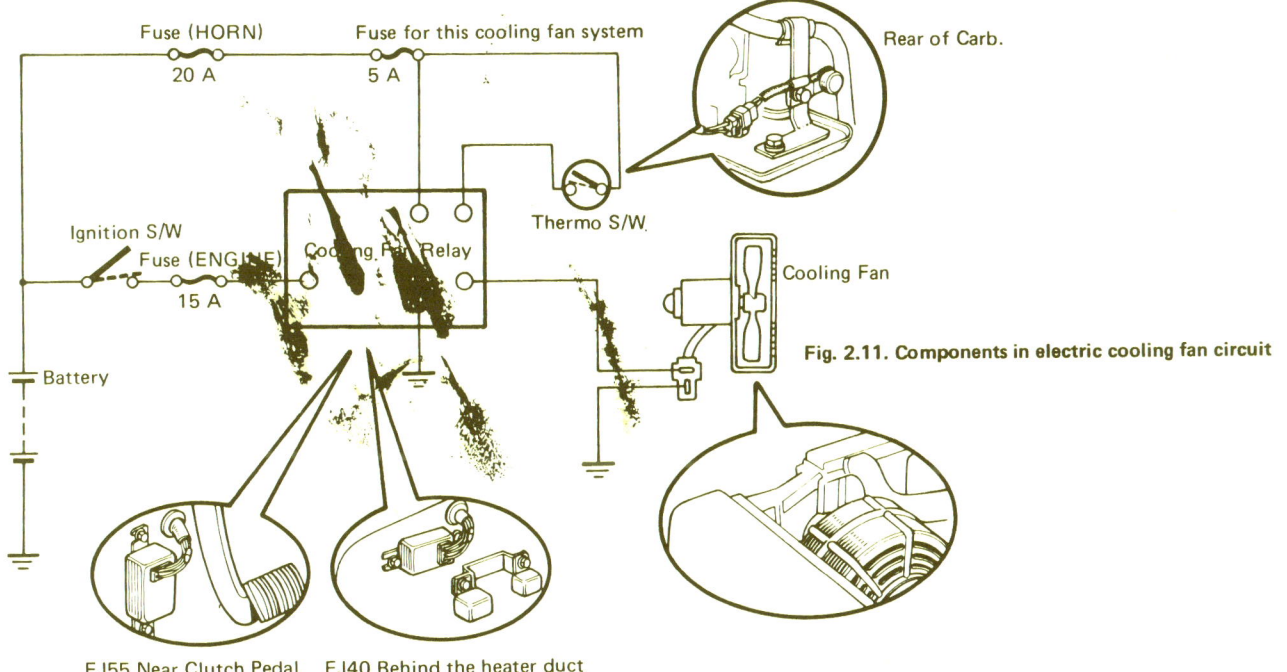

Fig. 2.11. Components in electric cooling fan circuit

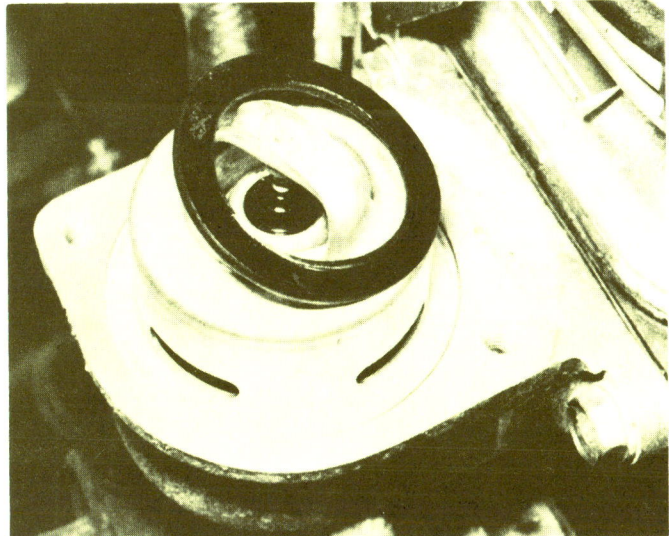

10.5a Ensure that the sealing ring ...

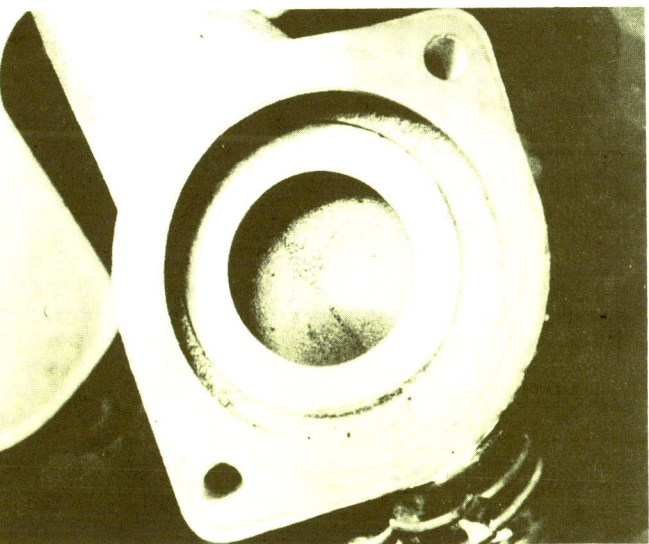

10.5b ... and the seating inside the cover are clean

13 Fault diagnosis - cooling system

Symptom	Reason/s
Overheating	Low coolant level
	Slack fanbelt
	Thermostat not operating.
	Radiator pressure cap faulty or of wrong type.
	Defective water pump.
	Cylinder head gasket blowing.
	Radiator core clogged.
	Binding brakes.
	Faulty fan fluid coupling.
Engine running too cool	Defective thermostat.
	Faulty water temperature gauge.
	Faulty fan coupling.
Loss of coolant	Leaking radiator or hoses.
	Cylinder head gasket leaking.
	Leaking cylinder block core plugs.
	Faulty radiator filler cap or wrong type.

Chapter 3 Fuel, exhaust and emission control systems

Contents

Accelerator linkage - removal and installation ... 14	Fuel evaporative emission control system ... 19
Air cleaner - general description ... 10	Fuel filter - removal, cleaning and installation ... 9
Air cleaner - removal and installation ... 12	Fuel pump - dismantling, inspection and reassembly ... 8
Air cleaner element - removal, cleaning and installation ... 11	Fuel pump - removal and installation ... 7
Air pump - servicing ... 23	Fuel tank - removal and installation ... 13
Carburetor - removal and installation ... 2	General description ... 1
Carburetor (single band, F engine) - dismantling, inspection, reassembly and preliminary adjustment ... 4	Heat control valve ... 28
	High altitude compensation system ... 29
Carburetor (two-barrel, F engine) - dismantling, inspection, reassembly and preliminary adjustment ... 3	Idle speed and mixture - adjustments ... 6
	Intake and exhaust manifolds ... 15
Carburetor (2 F engine) - dismantling, inspection, reassembly and preliminary adjustment ... 5	Manifold air injection system ... 22
	Power valve control system ... 25
Emission control systems - general ... 17	Spark control system ... 26
Engine modification system ... 18	Thermal reactor system ... 27
Exhaust gas recirculation ... 24	Throttle positioner ... 20
Exhaust system ... 16	Transmission controlled spark ... 21
Fault diagnosis - fuel system ... 30	

Specifications

Fuel pump
Type ... Mechanical, diaphragm type, driven from eccentric on camshaft
Pressure ... $3.4/4.8$ lbf/in^2 ($0.24/0.34$ mgf/cm^2)

Fuel tank
Capacity (pre 1974 models)
   FJ40 series models ... 18.5 US gal/15.4 Imp gal/70 litres
   FJ55 models ... 23.8 US gal/19.8 Imp gal/90 litres
Capacity (1974 models onwards)
   FJ40 series models ... 16.4 US gal/13.6 Imp gal/62 litres
   FJ55 models ... 21.7 US gal/18.0 Imp gal/82 litres

Fuel octane
Type ... Regular grade/90 octane (research method)

Air cleaner
Type ... Dry paper element or oil bath

Carburetor type
Type
   Early F engine ... Down draft, single barrel
   Later F engine ... Down draft, two-barrel
   2F engine ... Down draft, two-barrel
Specification
   No specifications are available for the single barrel carburetor

Later F engine	General markets	USA models
Air horn outer diameter	3.07 in (78.0 mm)	3.07 in (78.0 mm)
Main nozzle diameter		
Primary	0.11 in (2.8 mm)	.112 in (3.0 mm)
Secondary	0.11 in (2.8 mm)	.112 in (3.0 mm)
Venturi diameter		
Primary main	1.10 in (28.0 mm)	1.10 in (28.0 mm)
Primary small	0.69 x 0.35 in (17.5 x 9.0 mm)	0.69 x 0.35 in (17.5 x 9.0 mm)
Secondary main	1.22 in (31.0 mm)	1.22 in (31.0)
Secondary small	0.39 in (10.0 mm)	0.70 x 0.36 in (17.5 x 9 mm)

Throttle bore diameter		
Primary	1.50 in (38 mm)	1.50 in (38 mm)
Secondary	1.50 in (38 mm)	1.50 in (38 mm)
Main jet diameter		
Primary	0.0457 in (1.16 mm)	0.0465 in (1.18 mm)
Secondary	0.0787 in (2 mm)	0.0709 (1.8 mm)
Slow jet diameter		
Primary	0.019 in (0.5 mm)	0.019 in (0.5 mm)
Secondary	0.019 in (0.5 mm)	0.031 in (0.8 mm)
Economizer jet diameter	0.047 in (1.2 mm)	0.047 in (1.2 mm)
Pump jet diameter	0.019 in (0.5 mm)	0.019 in (0.5 mm)
Power jet diameter	0.035 in (0.9 mm)	0.027 in (0.7 mm)
Main air bleed diameter		
Primary	0.019 in (0.5 mm)	0.039 in (1 mm)
Secondary	0.019 in (0.5 mm)	0.039 in (1 mm)
Slow air bleed diameter		
Primary No 1	0.0335 in (0.85 mm)	0.035 in (0.9 mm)
Primary No 2	0.039 in (1 mm)	0.05 in (1.3 mm)
Secondary	0.039 in (1. mm)	0.039 in (1 mm)
Float level		
Raised position (from air horn fitting surface)	0.161 in (4.1 mm)	0.161 in (4.1 mm)
Lowered position (between needle valve push pin and float tab)	0.039 in (1 mm)	0.039 in (1 mm)
Fuel level (from body upper surface)	0.79 in (20 mm)	0.79 in (20 mm)
Accelerator pump stroke	0.31 in (8 mm)	0.31 in (8 mm)
High speed valve to bore clearance	0.039 in (1 mm)	0.039 in (1 mm)
Fast idle throttle valve opening	12°	12°
Mixture screw initial setting (for reference only)	Approx. 1¼ turns from fully seated	Approx. 1¼ turns from fully seated

* *For altitudes above 6600ft (2000m) use 0.0425 in (1.08 mm) main jet and 0.0315 in (0.8 mm) power jet*

2F engine (except 1977 USA and Canada)

Carburetor part number	19100-61010, 19100-61020, 19100-61030, 19100-61050	19100-61060, 19100-61070
Float raise position	0.295 in (7.5 mm)	0.295 in (7.5 mm)
Float lowered position	0.043 in (1.1 mm)	0.043 in (1.1 mm)
Primary throttle valve full open angle	90°	90°
Secondary throttle valve full open angle	90°	90°
Kick up	28° from bore	25° from bore
Fast idle	0.051 in (1.3 mm)	0.051 in (1.3 mm)
Choke breaker	38° from bore	38° from bore
Throttle positioner	0.031 in (0.8 mm)	0.031 in (0.8 mm)
Idle mixture screw initial setting (for reference only)	Approx. 1½ turns from fully seated	Approx. 1½ turns from fully seated
Accelerator pump stroke	0.374 in (9.5 mm)	0.374 in (9.5 mm)

2F engine, 1977 USA and Canada

Carburetor part number	21100-61022 (except Calif. and Canada)
	21100-61063 (California)
	21100-61073 (California)
	21100-61090 (High altitude)
	21100-61100 (Canada)
Float level	
Raised position	0.295 in (7.5 mm)
Lowered position	0.043 in (1.1 mm)
Throttle valve full open angle	90° from bore
Seco-touch angle	57°
Kick up	25° from bore
Fast idle	0.051 in (1.3 mm)
Throttle positioner	0.031 in (0.8 mm)
Accelerating pump stroke	0.374 in (9.5 mm)
Choke breaker	38° from bore
Idle mixture screw initial setting (for reference only)	Approx. 1½ turns from fully seated

Carburetor tune-up

F engine

Idle speed (general markets)	500 rpm
Idle speed (USA)	650 rpm
Manifold vacuum at idle speed	
General markets	18.1 in Hg (460 mm Hg)
USA markets	16.5 in Hg (420 mm Hg)

2F engine (except 1977 USA and Canada)

Idle speed	650 ± 50 rpm
Manifold vacuum at idle speed	16.5 in Hg (420 mm Hg)
Fast idle speed	1800 rpm
Throttle positioner setting speed	1200 rpm

Chapter 3/ Fuel, exhaust and emission control systems

2F engine, 1977 USA and Canada
Idle mixture setting speed ... 690 rpm
Idle speed ... 650 ± 50 rpm
Manifold vacuum at idle speed
   Except high altitude models ... Greater than 16.5 in Hg (420 mm Hg)
   High altitude models ... Greater than 12.6 in Hg (320 mm Hg)
Fast idle speed ... 1800 ± 200 rpm
   California and high altitude models: with EGR off and vacuum advance/retard out
   Other models: with spark control and EGR in normal condition
Throttle position setting speed
   California ... 1400 ± 100 rpm
   Except California and Canada ... 1200 ± 100 rpm

1 General description

1 The carburetor used on very early Land Cruisers is a single barrel type incorporating a vented float chamber, low speed system, high speed system, accelerator pump system and a choke/fast idle system.
2 Carburetors used on all later models are two-barrel types. In their main features, the carburetors are basically similar to the single barrel types, with an additional second barrel which permits greater volumes of mixtures to pass into the intake system at wider throttle openings.
3 The two-barrel carburetor used on the F engines has its secondary barrel butterfly valve linked mechanically to the primary valve linkage. At primary valve openings in excess of 50°, the secondary valve commences to open. To prevent over-rich mixtures during hard acceleration, an auxiliary high speed valve is incorporated upstream of the secondary valve; this opens when there is sufficient airflow thru the secondary barrel and closes under the action of a counter-weight at low airflows.
4 The two-barrel carburetor used on 2F engines has a different method of operation for the secondary valve but is otherwise generally similar to the early type. The secondary valve is operated by a diaphragm mechanism which senses the venturi throat pressure drop which occurs at high primary barrel airflows, and causes the secondary valve to open by an amount proportional to this pressure drop. USA carburetors also incorporate an auxiliary acceleration pump which provides an additionally rich mixture during very heavy acceleration.
5 The fuel pump used on all models is a mechanically operated diaphragm type which operates through a rocker arm from the engine camshaft. The pumps used on early engines have single inlet and outlet valves whereas those used on later ones have twin inlet and outlet valves.
6 Different types of air cleaner have been used but most of them use a dry paper element. However, on some models, an oil bath air cleaner is used. For further information see Section 10.
7 The exhaust system comprises a muffler (silencer), and the associated interconnecting pipes, mountings and clips.
8 A wide variety of emission control systems are in service, the details of which will be found in Section 17 onwards.

2 Carburetor - removal and installation

Note: Since there are numerous different vehicle specifications, it is only possible to give an outline procedure in this Section.
1 Remove the air cleaner (refer to Section 12, if necessary).
2 Detach the carburetor inlet and return pipes (photo).
3 Detach the electrical connections from the carburetor (eg: idle shut-off solenoid).
4 Detach the pneumatic connections from the carburetor (eg: distributor vacuum unit, throttle positioner diaphragm, EGR valve, etc). Note: It is recommended that labels are tied to the various pipes if there is any possibility of mix-up.
5 Detach the choke wire from the carburetor.
6 Detach the accelerator (and throttle, if applicable) linkage from the carburetor.
7 Remove the carburetor flange nuts and detach the assembly from the manifold.
8 Carefully remove all traces of gasket material from the carburetor and manifold flanges. Take great care that nothing falls into the intake manifold while the carburetor is removed.
9 Installation is the reverse of the removal procedure, but ensure that a new gasket is used.

3 Carburetor (two-barrel, F engine) - dismantling, inspection, reassembly and preliminary adjustment

1 Remove the pump arm securing screw and the connecting link snap ring; remove the arm and link.
2 Remove the choke wire clamp, solenoid valve and gasket from the air horn.
3 Remove the connecting link snap ring, connector and fast idle connector (Fig. 3.4).
4 Remove the retaining screws, and detach the air horn and gasket from the carburetor body.
5 Remove the pump plunger spring. If necessary, also remove the check ball retainer and ball.
6 Remove the gasket, stopper, discharge weight and ball (see Fig. 3.5).
7 Remove the securing screws and take out the primary main venturi and gasket. Similarly remove the secondary small venturi.
8 Using a suitable box wrench, remove the two slow jets.
9 Remove the power valve sub assembly. If necessary, also remove the power jet from the power valve.
10 Remove the main passage plug and primary main spare jet, then remove the main jet and gasket. Similarly, remove the secondary main jet.
11 If necessary, remove the level gauge clamp, glass and gasket.
12 Remove the two body screws and one flange screw, and separate the flange from the body.
13 Remove the screw, lever and washer (Fig. 3.7).
14 Remove the stop lever securing screw, high speed butterfly valve stop lever and spring.
15 Remove the mixture adjustment screw and spring.
16 To dismantle the high speed butterfly valve, remove the plate (two screws), retaining ring and shim, then slide the shaft from the body.
Note: The plate retaining screws are peened over, and this should be carefully removed by filing before they are unscrewed.

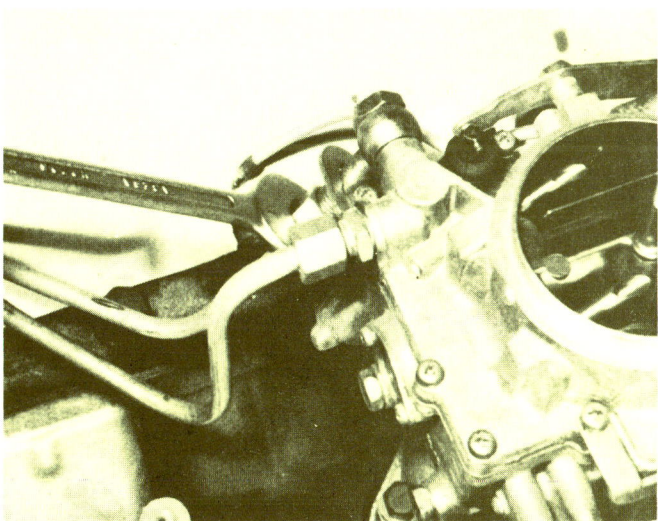

2.2 Detach fuel pipe(s) from carburetor

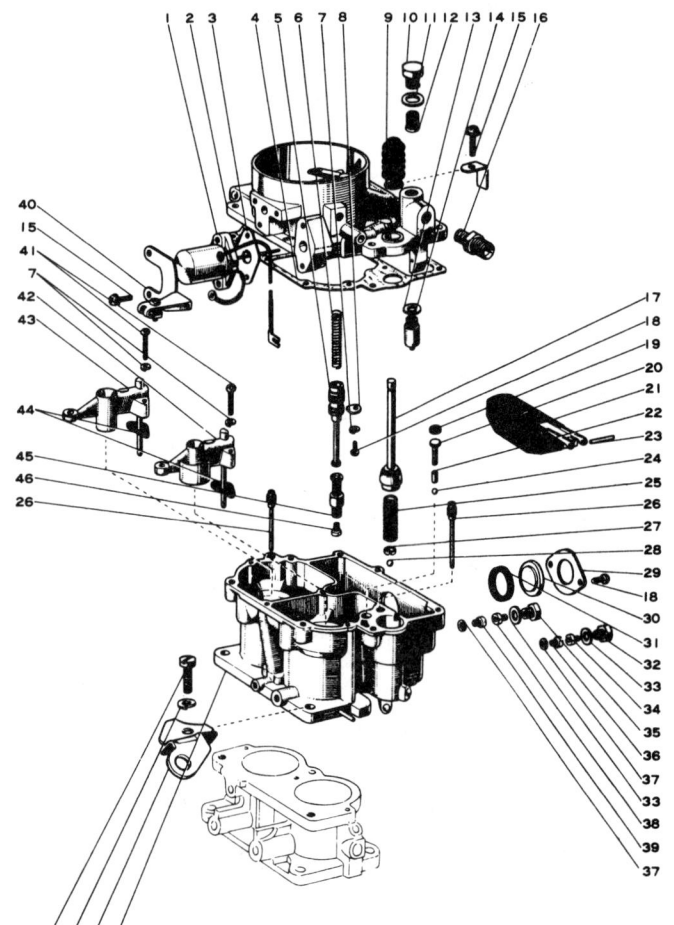

Fig. 3.1. Two-barrel, F engine carburetor - main components

1 Solenoid valve
2 Air horn
3 Gasket
4 Air horn gasket
5 Power piston
6 Power piston spring
7 Lock washer
8 Power piston stopper
9 Boot
10 Main passage plug
11 Strainer gasket
12 Strainer
13 Needle valve seat gasket
14 Needle valve subassembly
15 Screw
16 Fitting
17 Pump plunger
18 Screw
19 Gasket
20 Stopper
21 Float subassembly
22 Pump discharge weight
23 Float lever pin
24 Steel ball
25 Spring
26 Slow jet subassembly
27 Check ball retainer
28 Steel ball
29 Level gauge
30 Level gauge glass
31 Gasket
32 Main passage plug
33 Gasket
34 Primary main jet (spare)
35 Plug
36 Primary main jet
37 Gasket
38 Power jet (spare)
39 Secondary main jet
40 Choke wire clamp
41 Screw
42 Primary main venturi
43 Secondary small venturi
44 Venturi gasket
45 Power valve subassembly
46 Power jet
47 Bolt
48 Lock washer
49 Accelerator wire support
50 Carburetor body

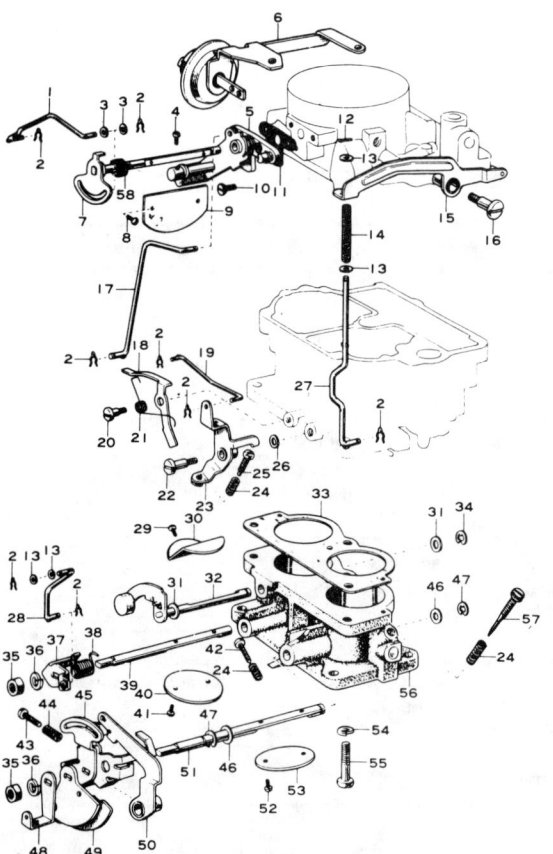

Fig. 3.2. Two-barrel, F engine carburetor - linkage (USA models)

1 Connecting link
2 Snap ring
3 Plate washer
4 Screw
5 Choke lever
6 Diaphragm subassembly
7 Choke shaft
8 Screw
9 Choke butterfly valve
10 Screw
11 Gasket
12 Cotter pin
13 Washer
14 Spring
15 Pump arm
16 Pump arm set screw
17 1st idle connector
18 High speed valve stop lever
19 Connector
20 Stop lever set screw
21 High speed valve stop lever spring
22 Screw
23 Lever
24 Idle adjust screw spring
25 Screw
26 Washer
27 Pump connecting link
28 Throttle shaft link
29 Screw
30 High speed butterfly valve
31 Shim
32 High speed shaft
33 Flange gasket
34 Retainer ring
35 Nut
36 Lock washer
37 Secondary throttle lever
38 Secondary throttle return spring
39 Secondary throttle shaft
40 Secondary throttle butterfly valve
41 Screw
42 Throttle adjusting screw
43 Screw
44 Spring
45 Primary throttle shaft arm
46 Primary throttle shaft shim
47 Retainer ring
48 Return spring arm
49 Throttle lever
50 1st idle adjusting lever
51 Primary throttle shaft
52 Screw
53 Primary throttle butterfly valve
54 Lock washer
55 Screw
56 Flange
57 Idle mixture adjusting screw
58 Choke valve relief spring

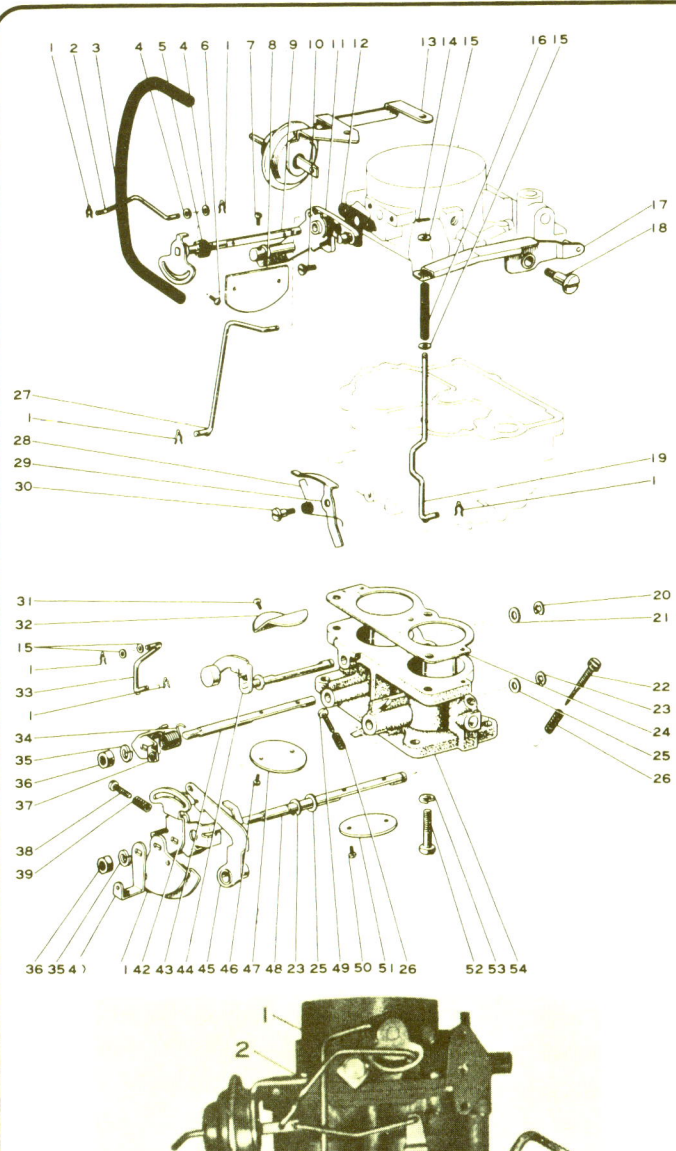

Fig. 3.3. Two-barrel, F engine carburetor - linkage (non USA models)

1 Snap ring
2 Connecting link
3 Pipe
4 Plate washer
5 Choke valve relief spring
6 Screw
7 Screw
8 Choke butterfly valve
9 Choke shaft
10 Screw
11 Choke lever
12 Case gasket
13 Diaphragm subassembly
14 Cotter pin
15 Washer
16 Spring
17 Pump arm
18 Pump arm set screw
19 Pump connecting link
20 Retainer ring
21 Shim
22 Idle mixture adjusting screw
23 Retainer ring
24 Flange gasket
25 Primary throttle shaft shim
26 Idle adjusting screw spring
27 1st idle connector
28 High speed valve stop lever spring
29 High speed valve stop lever
30 Stop lever set screw
31 Screw
32 High speed butterfly valve
33 Throttle shaft link
34 Secondary throttle return spring
35 Lock washer
36 Nut
37 Secondary throttle lever
38 Screw
39 Spring
40 Return spring arm
41 Throttle lever
42 Primary throttle shaft
43 Secondary throttle shaft
44 High speed shaft
45 1st idle adjusting lever
46 Screw
47 Secondary throttle butterfly valve
48 Primary throttle shaft
49 Throttle adjusting screw
50 Screw
51 Primary throttle butterfly valve
52 Screw
53 Lock washer
54 Flange

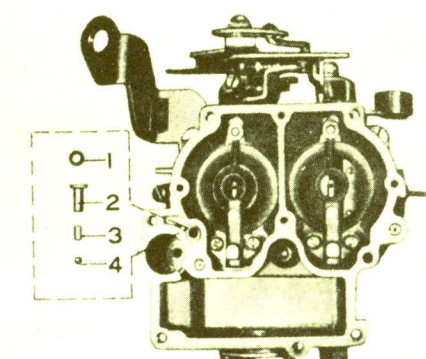

Fig. 3.5. Gasket (1), stopper (2), discharge weight (3) and ball (4)

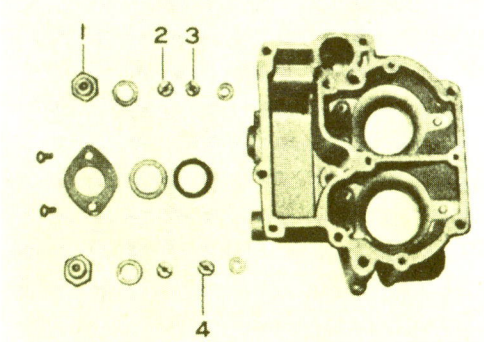

Fig. 3.4. Fast idle connector (1), connecting link (2) and connector (3)

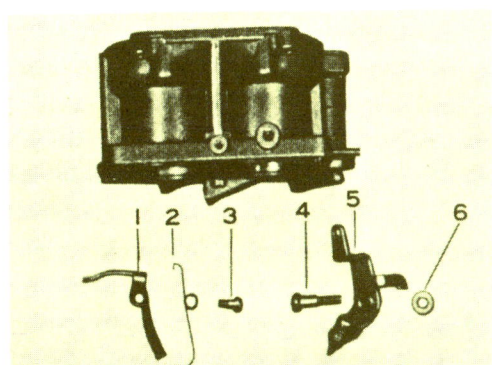

Fig. 3.6. Main passage plug (1), primary main spare jet (2), primary main jet (3) and secondary main jet (4)

Fig. 3.7. Stop lever (1), stop lever spring (2), securing screw (3), screw (4), lever (5) and washer (6)

17 To dismantle the secondary throttle butterfly valve mechanism, remove the snap ring and disconnect the link from the secondary throttle lever. Remove the throttle plate (see previous paragraph).
18 To dismantle the primary throttle butterfly valve, remove the plate retaining screws (see paragraph 16), then remove the plate, retainer ring and shim.
19 Slide out the shaft. If necessary, remove the nut so that the return spring arm, throttle lever, primary throttle shaft arm and fast idle adjusting lever can be removed.
20 Remove the pin so that the float and needle valve assembly can be removed. If necessary, remove the valve seat.
21 Remove the power piston stopper, and slide out the piston and spring. Remove the pump plunger and boot.
22 Remove the main passage plug and gasket, and take out the strainer.
23 If necessary, dismantle the choke valve. The procedure is basically as described earlier for the other butterfly valves.
24 Wash all the parts in clean gasoline and dry with compressed air. Blow through the jets and passages with compressed air to ensure that they are clear.
25 Inspect all the parts for corrosion, cracks, wear, damage and scoring etc., obtaining replacement parts as necessary. By sucking on the diaphragm assembly, check for a stroke of 0.32/0.39 in (8/10 mm).
26 Assembly is basically the reverse of the dismantling procedure, but the following should be noted:

  a) Use new gaskets and seals throughout during reassembly.
  b) Apply a trace of general purpose grease to all pivoting and sliding surfaces.
  c) Before fully tightening and peening any butterfly valve screws, ensure that the shaft operates smoothly and the butterfly opens and closes properly.
  d) To adjust the float, invert the air horn and measure the clearance between the upper surfaces of the float (ie the lower surface when inverted) and the air horn gasket surface. To obtain the specified clearance bend the central tab of the float lever. Having done this, raise the float and check that the specified clearance is obtained between the push-pin of the needle valve and the central tab. If necessary, bend the outer tabs of the float lever to obtain this clearance.
  e) Install the level gauge glass with the indent on the inside.
  f) Ensure that the pump discharge weight is installed with the countersink towards the ball.
  g) Ensure that the thicker throttle butterfly plate and longer screws are used on the secondary side.
  h) Adjust the primary throttle shaft by means of shims so that it is central in the bore. Shims are available in sizes of 0.004, 0.008, 0.012 and 0.024 in (0.1, 0.2, 0.3 and 0.6 mm).
  j) Ensure that the primary throttle valve is opened 50° before the secondary valve commences to open, and that when the primary valve is fully open the secondary valve is also fully open. Bend the throttle shaft link if necessary to obtain this.
  k) When installing the high speed valve, check for a thrust play of 0.016 in (0.4 mm). Adjust if necessary by using shims which are available in 0.004 and 0.008 in (0.1 and 0.2 mm) sizes.
  l) Using an unmarked twist drill shank, check that the clearance between the edge of the high speed valve and bore is 0.04 in (1.0 mm). A number 60 or 61 drill can be used for this check.

Adjustment

27 Bend the accelerator pump connecting link, if necessary, to obtain a pump stroke of 0.31 in (8 mm).
28 When the secondary throttle valve *just* commences to open, adjust the A part of the throttle arm to obtain a clearance of 0.016 to 0.026 in (0.4 to 0.7 mm) between the stop lever and the damper arm (Fig. 3.13).
29 To adjust the fast idle opening angle, position the throttle 4½° open (1½ turns of the throttle adjusting screw after it *just* contacts the throttle arm). Tighten the fast idle screw until it *just* contacts the fast idle lever then fully close the choke valve. Loosen the fast idle screw to obtain a clearance of 0.037 to 0.046 in (0.95 to 1.17 mm) between the throttle valve and flange wall. An unmarked twist drill shank within the number range of 63 to 56 can be used for this check.
30 On USA models, with the throttle positioner diaphragm open to atmosphere, turn the screw to *just* contact the throttle arm, then tighten the screw until a clearance of 0.026 to 0.034 in (0.66 to 0.86 mm) is obtained between the throttle valve and the flange wall. An unmarked twist drill shank within the number range of 71 to 65 can be used for this check. Adjust the stop lever and link to obtain a clearance of 0.078 to 0.118 in (2 to 3 mm) between the end of the throttle arm stopper and the screw. Ensure that the screw is not contacting the throttle arm when the diaphragm link rod is pushed by hand.
31 To adjust the choke pulling angle, fully close the choke valve by applying suction (130 ± 10 mm Hg) to the diaphragm. Adjust by bending the link to obtain a choke valve opening angle of 38°. Ensure that when the suction is released, the choke valve closes fully when the lever is pulled.
32 To adjust the reloader, bend the A portion of the fast idle lever to obtain a clearance between the high speed arm stopper and the fast idle lever of 0.020 to 0.039 in (0.5 to 1 mm) when the choke valve is fully closed. At an opening of 40° the high speed valve must rotate smoothly from fully closed to fully open; at an opening of 50°, the high speed valve should rotate about 20° only.
33 Screw the idle mixture screw out 1¼ turns from fully closed to obtain an approximate setting.
34 Tighten the throttle adjusting screw (idle speed screw) in ½ turn after it just contacts the throttle arm.

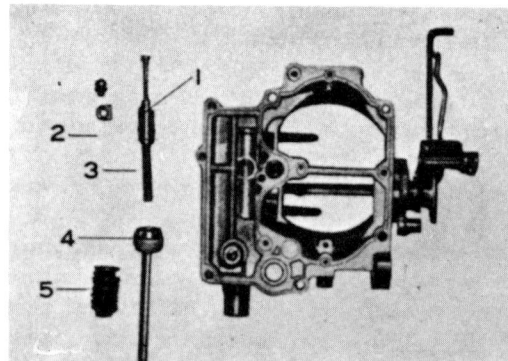

Fig. 3.8. Power piston (1), stopper (2), spring (3), plunger (4) and boot (5)

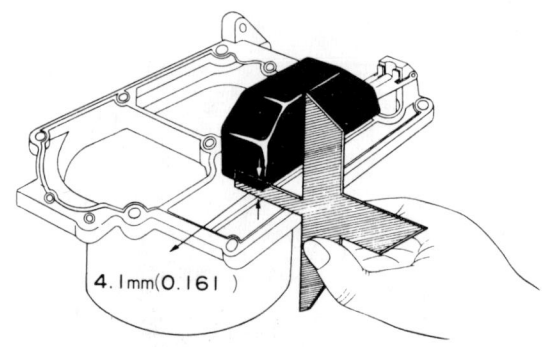

Fig. 3.9. Checking raised position of float

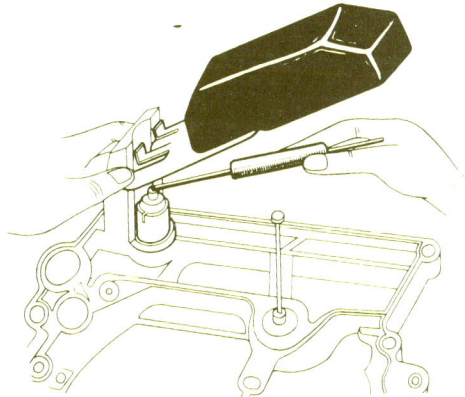

Fig. 3.10. Checking lowered position of float

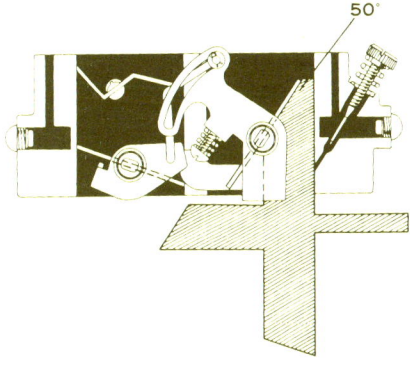

Fig. 3.11. Setting angle for primary/secondary throttle

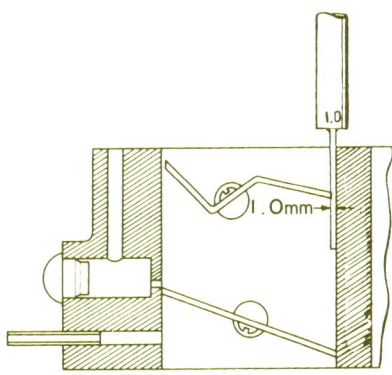

Fig. 3.12. Setting high speed valve

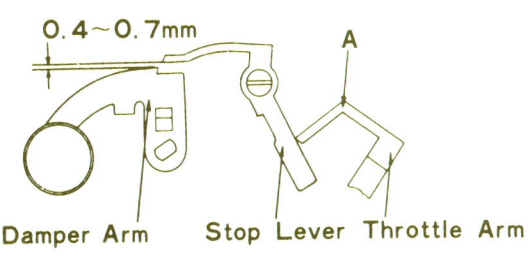

Fig. 3.13. Setting stop lever clearance

Fig. 3.14. Setting fast idle

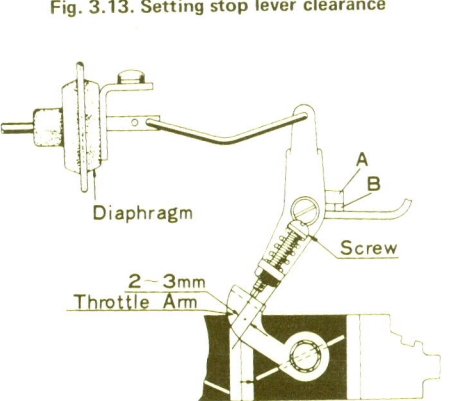

Fig. 3.15. Setting throttle positioner

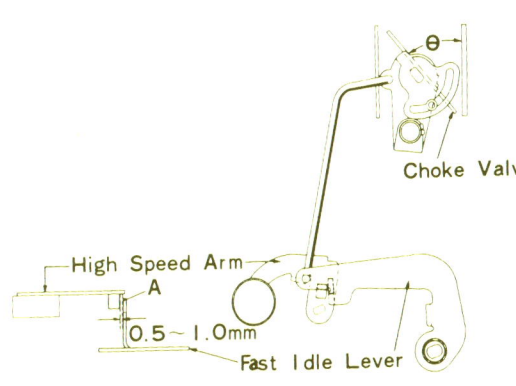

Fig. 3.16. Reloader adjustment

A Stop lever adjustment point   B Stop

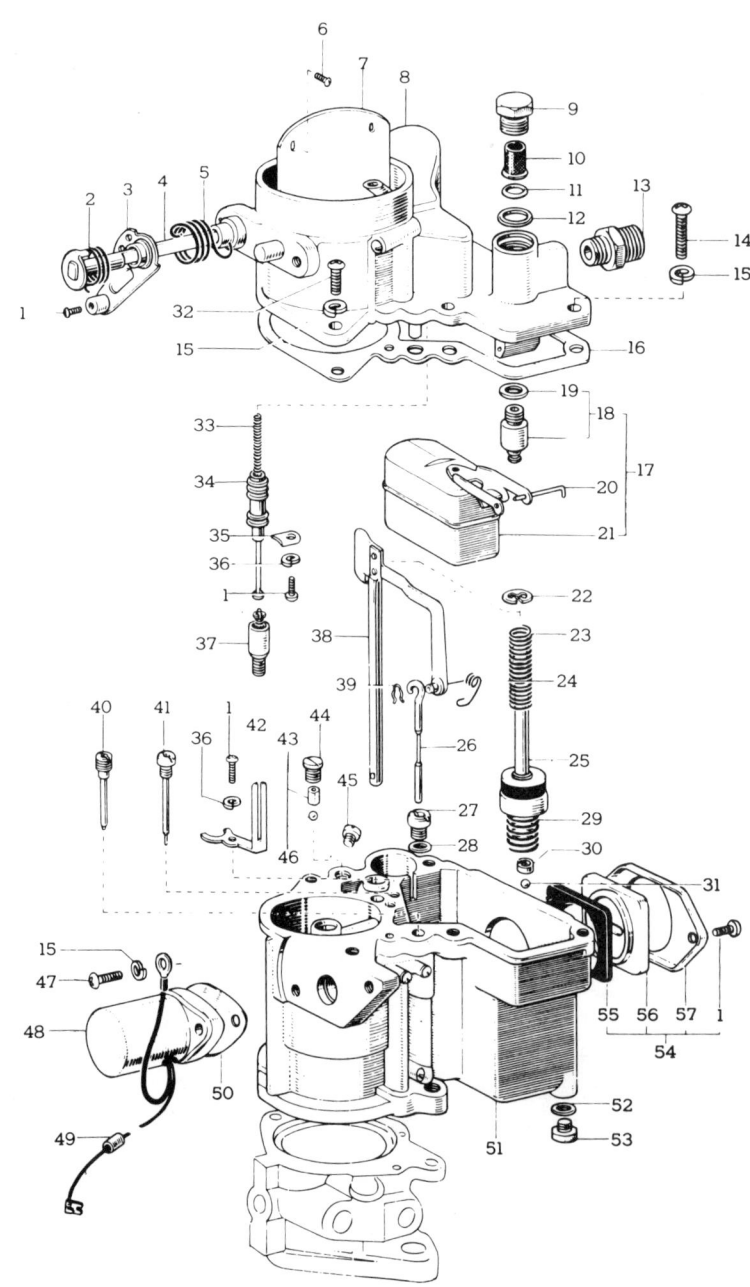

Fig. 3.17. Single barrel carburetor - exploded view of main components

1 Screw	16 Air horn gasket	31 Steel ball	45 Pump jet plug
2 Choke back spring	17 Float and needle sub-assy	32 Set screw	46 Steel ball
3 Choke lever	18 Needle valve sub-assy	33 Power piston spring	47 Set screw
4 Choke shaft sub-assy	19 Needle valve seat gasket	34 Power piston	48 Valve
5 Choke valve relief spring	20 Float lever pin	35 Power piston stop	49 Solenoid ring
6 Choke valve set screw	21 Float sub-assy	36 Spring washer	50 Gasket
7 Choke valve	22 Pump spring retainer	37 Power valve	51 Carburetor body
8 Air horn	23 Pump spring	38 Lifter rod	52 Pump jet screw gasket
9 Main passage plug	24 Step up rod spring*	39 Snap ring	53 Nut plug
10 Strainer	25 Pump plunger	40 Slow jet sub-assy	54 Carburetor level gauge sub-assy
11 Strainer cap	26 Step up rod	41 Main air bleeder sub-assy	
12 Inlet strainer gasket	27 Main jet	42 Guide	55 Level gauge gasket
13 Fitting	28 Main jet gasket	43 Pump discharge weight	56 Level gauge glass
14 Screw	29 Pump dumping spring	44 Plug	57 Level gauge clamp
15 Spring washer	30 Ball steel retainer		

* up to Engine No. F-257653 (April 1968).

4 Carburetor (single barrel, F engine) - dismantling, inspection, reassembly and preliminary adjustment

1 Remove the solenoid valve, fast idle connector and throttle lever spring.
2 Remove the air horn (five screws); remove the gasket.
3 Remove the throttle connecting link, then separate the main body from the flange (two screws).
4 Remove the float lever pin, then take out the float, push pin, spring and needle valve.
5 Unscrew the needle valve seat and gasket.
6 Remove the main passage plug and strainer.
7 Remove the power piston stopper then take out the power piston and spring.
8 Slide out the lifter rod together with the pump plunger and metering rod. Remove the spring and lifter rod guide.
9 Remove the snap ring, step-up rod spring and step-up rod from the lifter rod. Also remove the E-ring, pump plunger and spring.
10 Remove the main jet and power valve.
11 Remove the slow jet and main air bleeder.
12 Remove the screw plug and tip out the discharge weight ball.
13 Remove the idle mixture screw and spring.
14 Wash all the parts in clean gasoline and dry with compressed air. Blow through the jets and passages to ensure that they are clear.
15 Inspect all the parts for corrosion cracks, wear, damage and scoring etc. obtaining replacement parts as necessary.
16 Assembly is basically the reverse of the dismantling procedure, but the following should be noted:

   a) *Use new gaskets and seals throughout during assembly.*
   b) *Apply a trace of general purpose grease to all pivoting and sliding surfaces.*
   c) *Before fully tightening and peening any butterfly valve screws, ensure that the shaft operates smoothly and the butterfly opens and closes satisfactorily.*

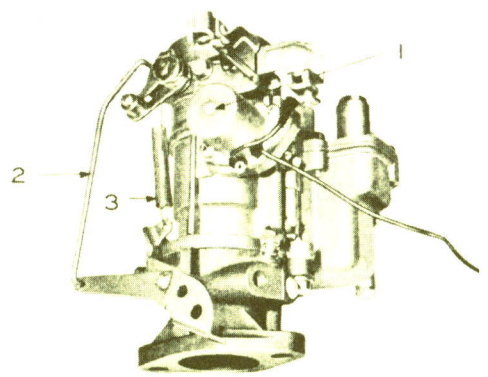

Fig. 3.18. Solenoid valve (1), fast idle connector (2) and spring (3)

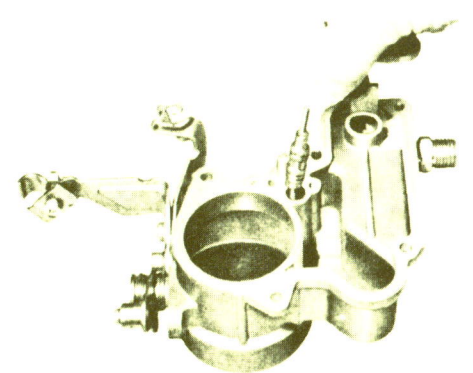

Fig. 3.19. Removing the power piston

Fig. 3.20. Lifter rod - component parts

Fig. 3.21. Main jet (1), power valve (2), slow jet (3), main air bleeder (4) and screw plug (5)

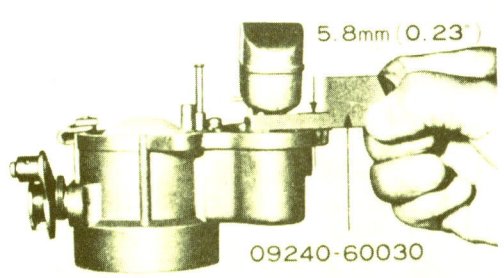

Fig. 3.22. Checking raised position of float

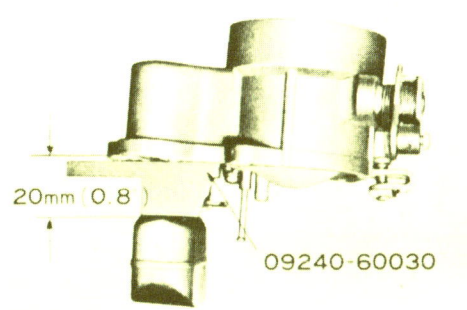

Fig. 3.23. Checking lowered position of float

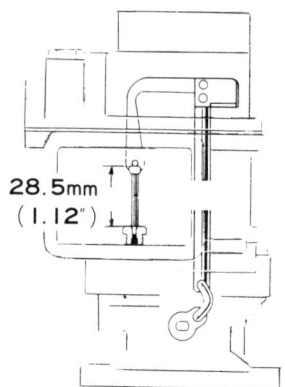

Fig. 3.24. Checking step-up - rod adjustment

d) To adjust the float, invert the air horn and adjust the clearance between the float surface and the air horn gasket surface to obtain a dimension of 0.23 in (5.8 mm) by bending the central tab of the float lever arm. Having done this, insert the assembly and allow the float to fall. Adjust the clearance, if necessary, between the air horn gasket surface and float to obtain a dimension of 0.8 in (20 mm) by bending the outer tabs of the float lever arm.
e) When assembling the throttle butterfly valve and shaft, close the valve completely and check the valve plate alignment with the slow port. It should be as shown in Fig. 3.24, otherwise renew the valve plate and shaft.

Adjustment

17 Before assembling the lifter rod and pump plunger to the carburetor body, remove the step-up rod from the lifter rod. After assembling the lifter rod and pump plunger, install the throttle connecting link.

18 Check the step-up rod height, and bend the throttle connecting link, if necessary, to adjust, to obtain a height of 1.12 in (28.5 mm). This check must be done by closing the throttle valve completely and not by operating the throttle adjusting screw.

19 When installing the idle speed adjusting screw, rotate it until it touches the flange, then screw it in until the butterfly plate is in the position shown in Fig. 3.25. This is approximately ¾ turn of the screw.

20 When installing the idle mixture screw, it should be approximately 1½ turns out from the fully closed position.

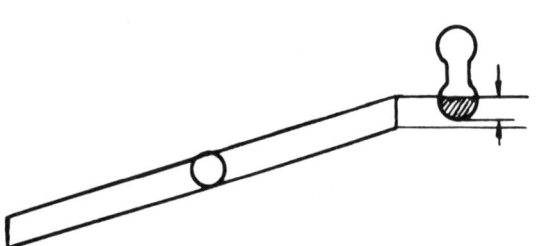

Fig. 3.25. Setting throttle butterfly plate

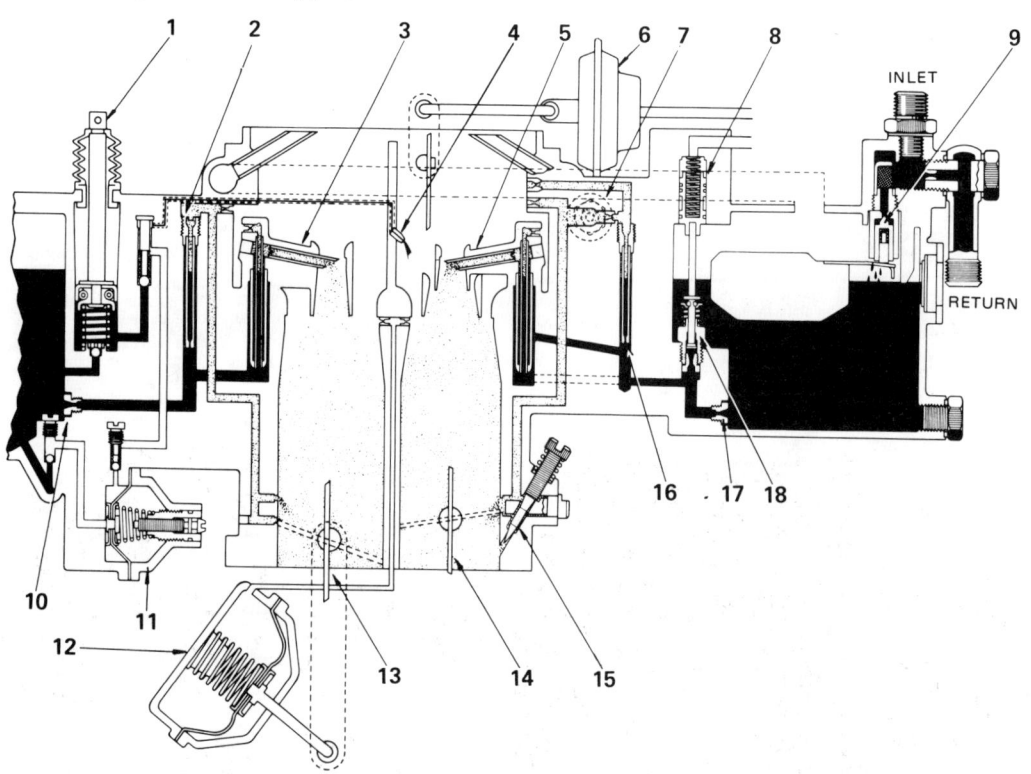

Fig. 3.26. Carburetor 2F engine - sectional view

1 Pump plunger	7 Solenoid valve	13 2nd throttle valve
2 2nd slow jet	8 Power piston	14 1st throttle valve
3 2nd main nozzle	9 Needle valve	15 Idle mixture adjusting screw
4 Pump jet	10 2nd main jet	16 1st slow jet
5 1st main nozzle	11 AAP *	17 1st main jet
6 Choke breaker	12 Diaphragm	18 Power valve

* The Auxiliary Acceleration Pump and associated parts are only used on USA models.

5 Carburetor (2F engine) - dismantling, inspection, reassembly and preliminary adjustment

1. Remove the pivot bolt and detach the pump arm (photo).
2. Disconnect the pump connecting link at its lower end.
3. Detach the choke breaker link.
4. Detach the fast idle connecting link.
5. Remove the pivot bolt and detach the choke breaker connecting link.
6. Remove the choke breaker from the carburetor.
7. Remove the retaining screws, and lift off the air horn and gasket.
8. Remove the float pin and take off the float (photo).
9. Remove the needle valve pin, spring, needle valve, valve seat and gasket.
10. Detach the pump plunger.
11. Remove the screw, washer and lockplate, and take out the power piston and spring.
12. Unscrew the solenoid valve.
13. Using a small file, remove the peening from the choke butterfly valve retaining screws. Remove the screws and take out the valve plate.
14. Remove the choke valve shaft after unhooking the return spring.
15. Remove the pump outlet ball and spring.
16. Remove the pump damping spring, followed by the pump inlet plug and ball.
17. Unscrew the slow jets.
18. On USA models, unscrew the plug and remove the AAP check ball and spring. Also remove the plug and ball from the bottom of the float well.
19. Remove the power valve.
20. Unscrew the plugs and washers, and the main jets and washers.
21. Remove the retaining screws, and lift out the two venturis and gaskets.
22. On USA models, remove the three screws and take off the AAP housing, gasket, spring and diaphragm. **On no account rotate the pre-set AAP adjusting screw.**
23. Remove the secondary throttle diaphragm assembly.
24. Wash all the parts in clean gasoline and dry with compressed air. Blow through the jets and passages to ensure that they are clear.
25. Inspect all the parts for corrosion, cracks, wear, damage, and scoring etc. obtaining replacement parts as necessary.
26. Assembly is basically the reverse of the dismantling procedure, but the following points should be noted:

   a) Use new gaskets and seals throughout during reassembly.
   b) Apply a trace of general purpose grease to all pivoting and sliding surfaces.
   c) Before fully tightening and peening any butterfly valve screws, ensure that the shaft operates smoothly, and the butterfly opens and closes properly.

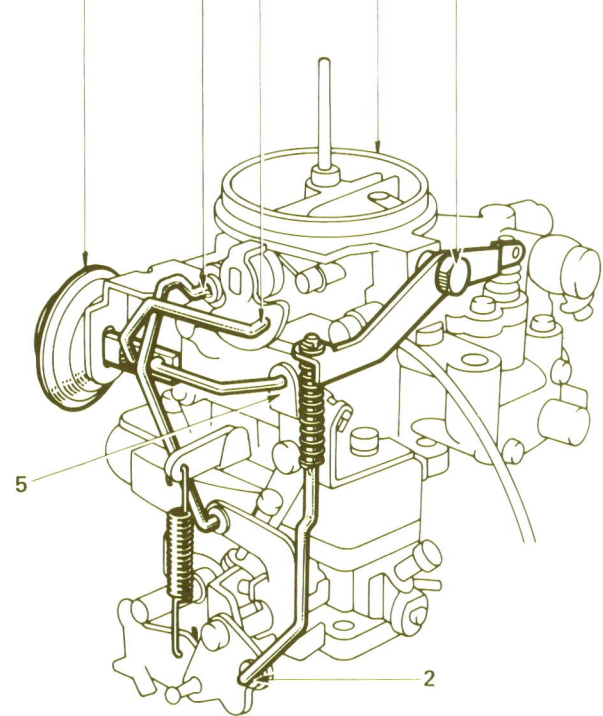

Fig. 3.27. Dismantling carburetor linkage

1. Pump arm
2. Pump connecting link
3. Choke breaker connecting link
4. Fast idle connecting link
5. Throttle positioner connecting link
6. Choke breaker
7. Air horn

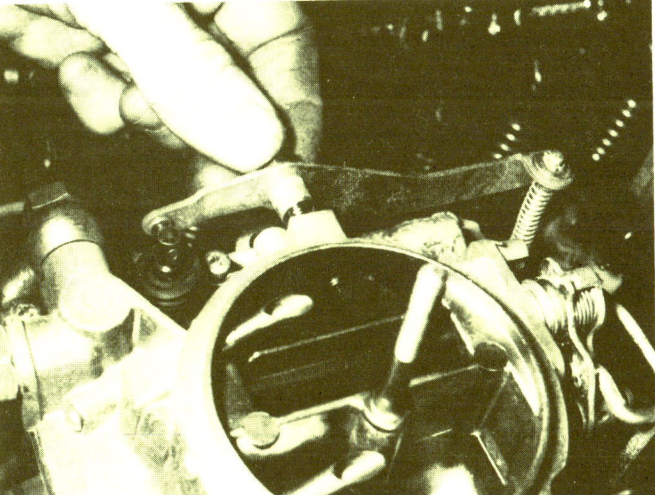

5.1 Removing the pivot bolt

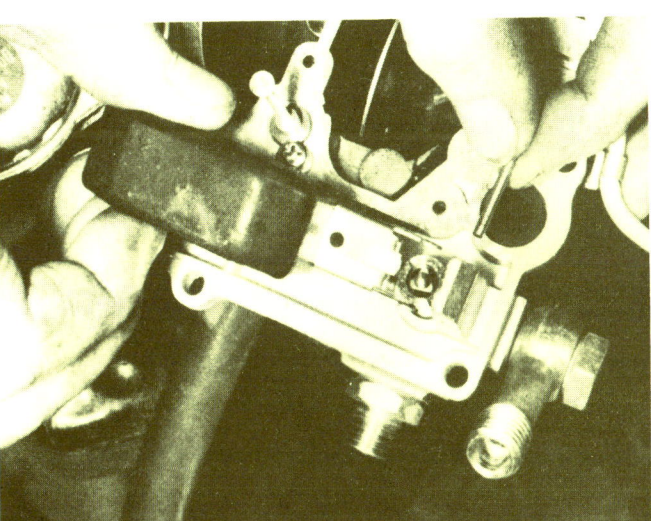

5.8 Removing the float pin

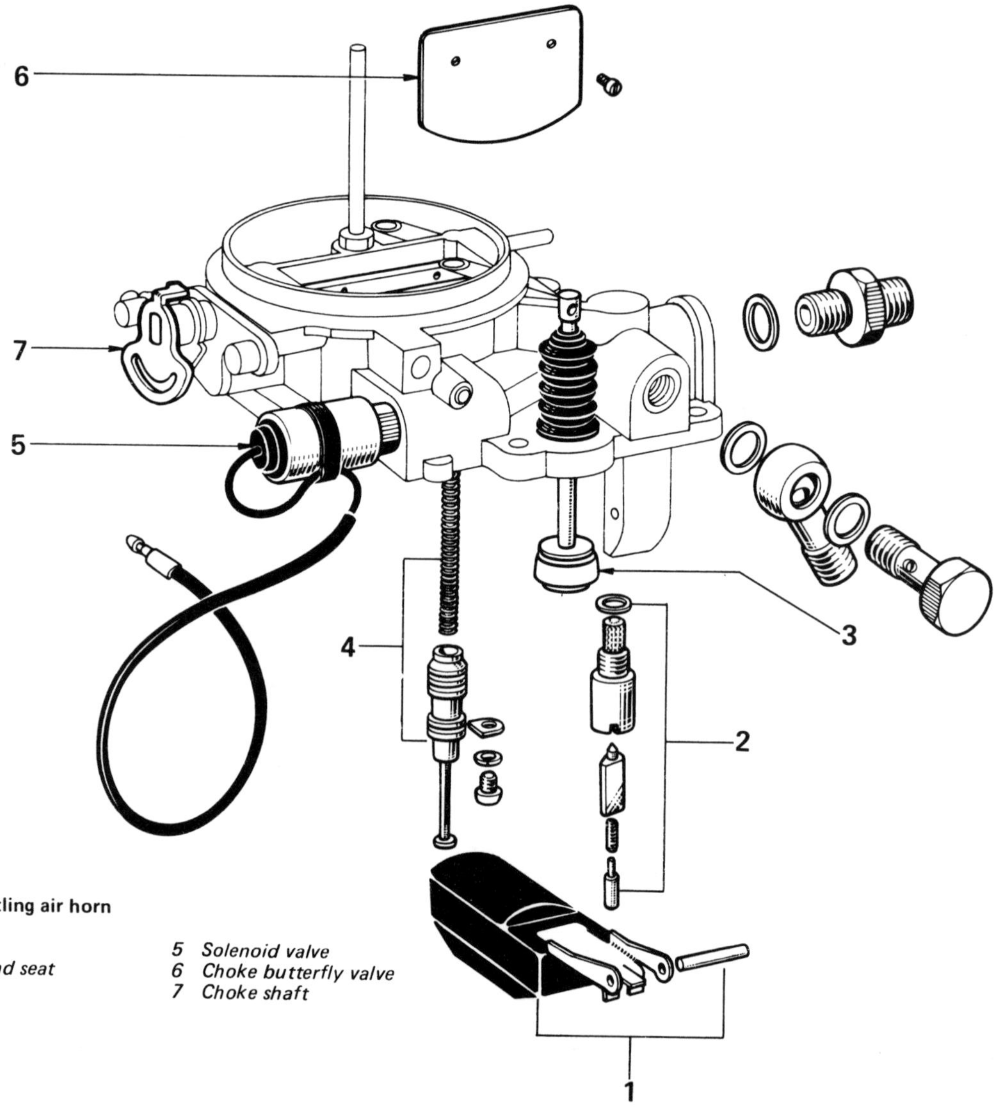

Fig. 3.28. Dismantling air horn

1 Float
2 Needle valve and seat
3 Pump plunger
4 Power piston
5 Solenoid valve
6 Choke butterfly valve
7 Choke shaft

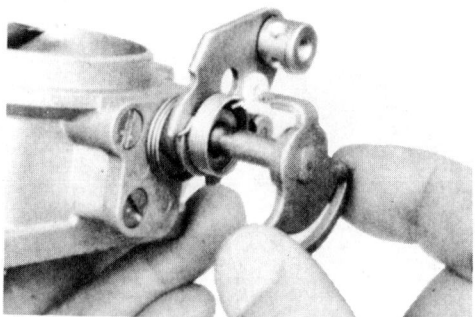

Fig. 3.29. Unhooking choke return spring

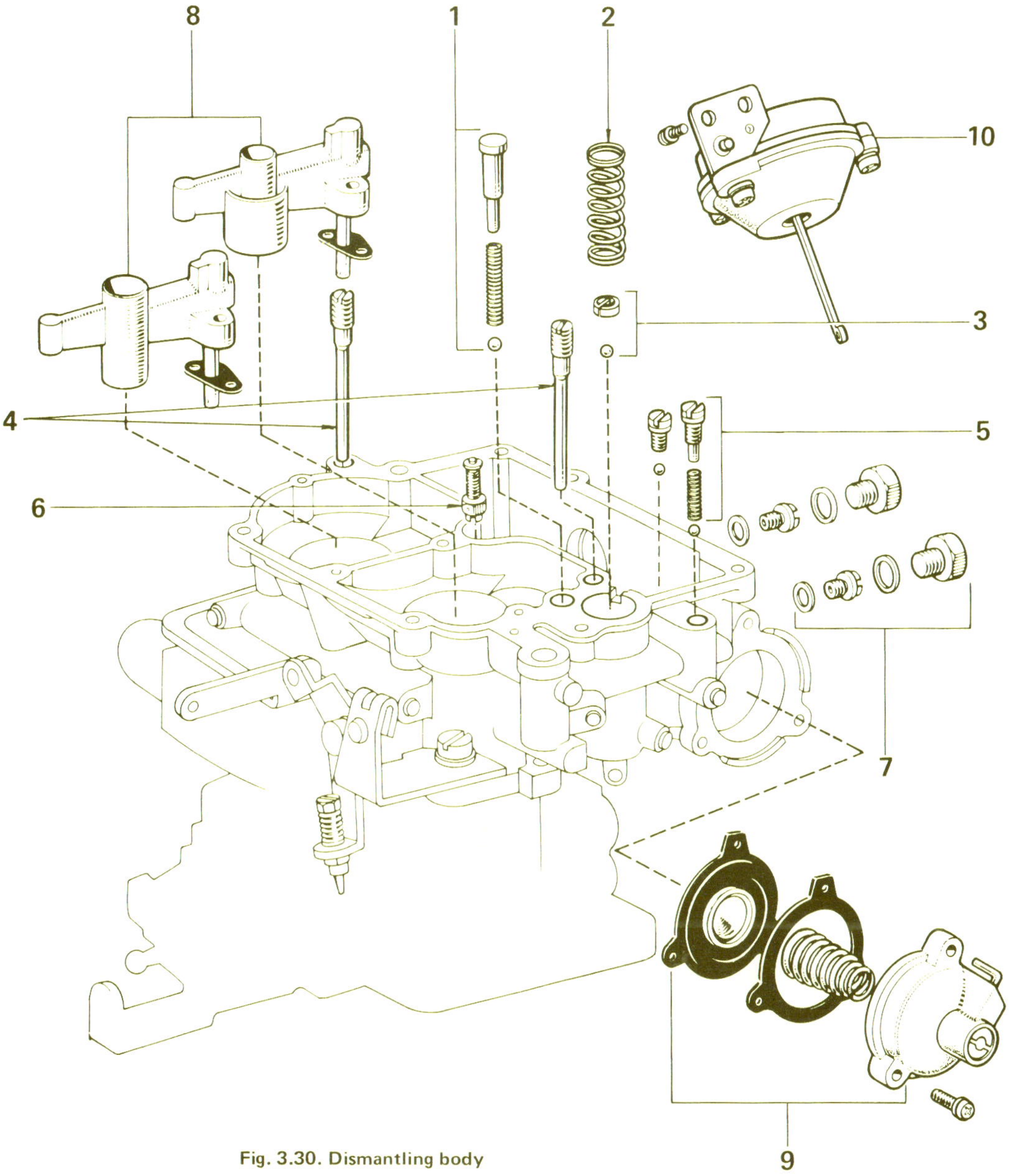

Fig. 3.30. Dismantling body

1. Pump outlet ball and spring
2. Pump damping spring
3. Pump inlet ball
4. Slow jet
5. AAP check ball (USA only)
6. Power valve
7. Main jet
8. Venturi
9. AAP diaphragm and housing (USA only)
10. Secondary diaphragm

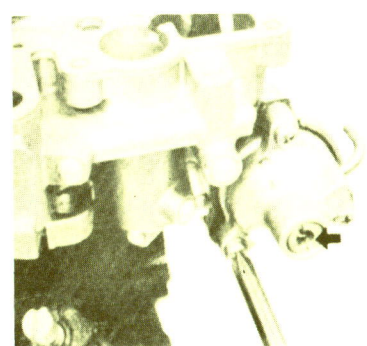

**Fig. 3.31. Removing AAP housing
DO NOT TOUCH THE ARROWED SCREW**

Fig. 3.32. Installed position of choke valve spring

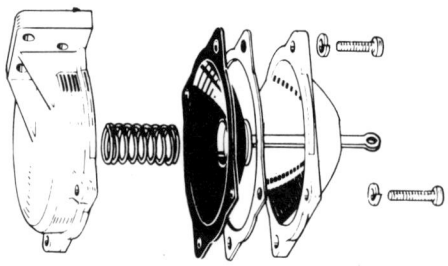

Fig. 3.33. Secondary diaphragm - assembly order

d) Insert the choke shaft and hook the spring end as shown in Fig. 3.32.
e) When installing the power valve piston, ensure that it operates smoothly.
f) To adjust the float level, invert the air horn and allow the float to fall under its own weight. Measure the clearance between the float and air horn; bend the central tab, if necessary, to obtain the specified clearance. Carefully raise the float to its full height, and check the clearance between the needle valve plunger and central tab. Bend the outer tabs if necessary to obtain the specified clearance (see also Figs. 3.9 and 3.10).
g) When installing the venturis, note that the primary is a triple type and the secondary is a double type.
h) When installing the slow jets, note that the longer or larger jet is on the secondary side.
j) When installing the main jets, note that the primary jet has a brass finish and the secondary jet has a chrome finish.
k) On USA carburetors, note that a small ball is used for the AAP and pump inlet, and a larger ball for the pump outlet.
l) On USA models, note that the AAP pump spring is installed with the small end towards the housing.
m) If the secondary diaphragm was dismantled, reassemble it as shown in Fig. 3.33.

Adjustment

27 With the butterfly valves fully open, check that they are parallel to the bore; bend the throttle lever stoppers if necessary to achieve this.
28 Check that when the primary valve is fully open, the secondary valve is open by the specified amount for kick-up. Adjust, if necessary, by bending the secondary throttle lever.

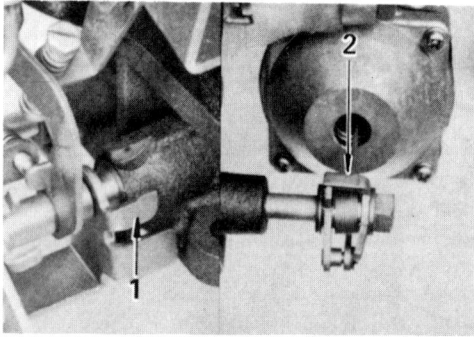

Fig. 3.34. Primary (1) and secondary (2) throttle lever stoppers

Fig. 3.35. Fast idle screw (1)

Fig. 3.36. Throttle positioner screw (1) and throttle lever tab (2)

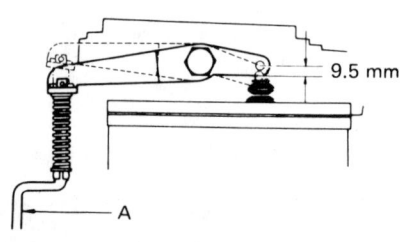

Fig. 3.37. Adjustment point (A) for accelerator pump

Chapter 3/Fuel, exhaust and emission control systems

29 To adjust the fast idle, fully close the choke valve, then check the clearance between the choke valve and bore. Turn the fast idle screw to obtain the specified clearance.
30 To check the choke breaker, push in the breaker rod to open the choke valve. Check for the specified choke breaker angle, and adjust, if necessary, by bending the choke breaker link.
31 To check the throttle positioner, screw in the adjusting screw until it contacts the throttle lever tab. Check the clearance between the throttle valve and bore, and adjust to the specified clearance, if necessary, by means of the adjusting screw (the unmarked shank of a number 68 twist drill may be used for this measurement).
32 Adjust the accelerator pump stroke, if necessary, to obtain that specified by bending the pump stroke rod.
33 To obtain an initial setting for the idle mixture screw, screw it out 1½ turns from the fully closed position.

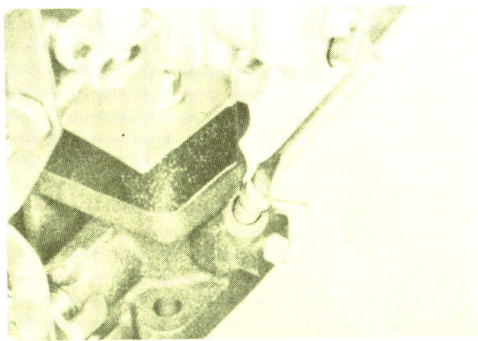

Fig. 3.38. Idle mixture screw setting

6 Idle speed and mixture - adjustments

Note: Before commencing any adjustments, ensure that valve clearances, distributor points gap/dwell angles, spark plugs and ignition timing are correctly set. Also ensure that the emission control and exhaust systems are fully serviceable and, unless otherwise stated, connected in the normal manner.

F engine
1 Having carried out the preliminary adjustment as described in Section 3 or 4, initially run the engine to bring it up to normal operating temperature.
2 Remove the intake manifold suction hole plug and connect a vacuum gauge.
3 Connect a tachometer to the ignition coil or distributor in accordance with the manufacturers instructions.
4 Run the engine at idle speed and check the fuel level at the gauge glass (sight glass) on the float chamber.
5 Turn the throttle valve adjusting screw (idle speed adjustments screw) to obtain the lowest speed at which the engine will run smoothly.
6 Turn the idle mixture adjusting screw in or out to obtain the highest steady vacuum at idle speed. (Note that a leaner mixture is obtained by turning the screw inwards, and vice versa).
7 Turn the throttle valve adjusting screw to obtain the highest vacuum reading, then readjust the mixture screw if necessary.
8 Set the engine idle speed and manifold vacuum to that given in the Specifications.
9 Stop the engine, then remove the air cleaner cover. Open the throttle valve fully and check that fuel flows from the discharge jet. Install the air cleaner on completion.

2F engine
10 Having carried out the preliminary adjustment as described in Section 5, initially run the engine to bring it up to normal operating temperature.
11 With the engine switched off, ensure that there is full travel of the choke and throttle butterfly valves when they are operated. Check that the fuel is up to the gauge level of the sight glass. With the air cleaner removed, check that fuel sprays from the accelerator pump discharge nozzle when the throttle valve is fully opened.
12 Connect a tachometer to the ignition coil or distributor is accordance with the manufacturers instructions.

Models produced for USA and ECE markets (2F engine)
13 Run the engine to obtain the fastest idle speed by adjusting the idle mixture screw.
14 Adjust the idle speed to that specified by means of the idle speed adjusting screw (throttle valve adjusting screw).
15 Make alternate adjustments as necessary until the maximum speed will not rise any further no matter what adjustment is made to the idle mixture screw. For this check an idle mixture speed of 690 rpm should be obtained for USA models, or 675 rpm for ECE models.
16 Finally set the initial idle speed by means of the idle mixture screw to obtain a speed of 650 ± 50 rpm.

Models for other markets (2F engine)
17 Remove the intake manifold suction hole plug and connect a vacuum gauge if one is available.
18 Run the engine and adjust the idle speed to 650 rpm by means of

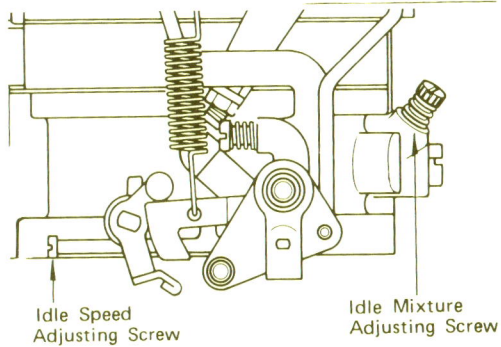

Fig. 3.39. Idle adjustment screws (2F engine carburetor shown)

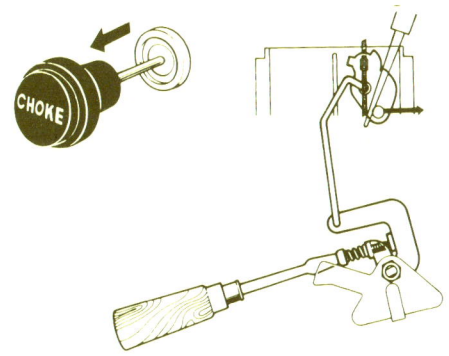

Fig. 3.40. Fast idle adjustment (2F engine carburetor shown)

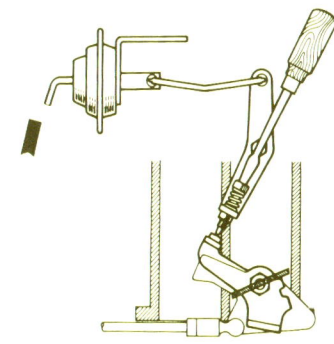

Fig. 3.41. Throttle positioner adjustment (2F engine carburetor shown)

Chapter 3/Fuel, exhaust and emission control systems

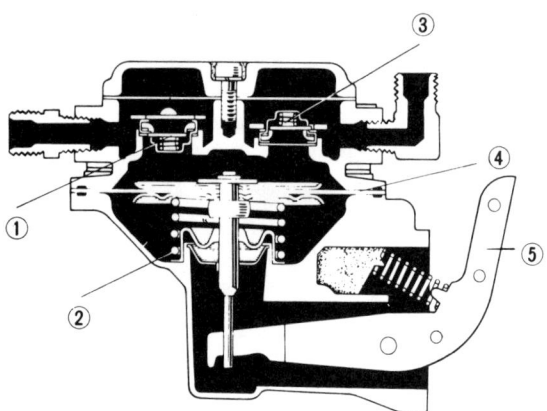

Fig. 3.42. Sectional view of fuel pump (F engine type)

1 Inlet valve
2 Diaphragm spring
3 Outlet valve
4 Diaphragm
5 Rocker arm

Fig. 3.43. Diaphragm tab position on later pumps

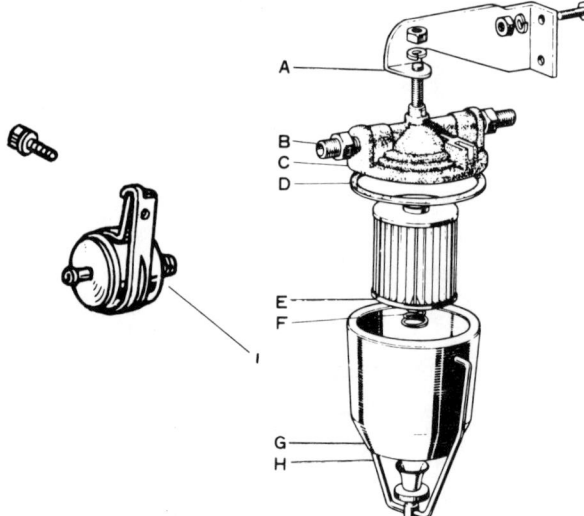

Fig. 3.44. Fuel filter

A Support
B Fitting
C Filter body
D Gasket
E Filter element ⎫
F Filter element spring ⎬ early type
G Filter bowl
H Filter bowl bail ⎭
I Filter assembly (later type)

the idle speed adjustment screw.
19 Adjust the idle speed or vacuum to obtain the highest value by means of the idle mixture adjustment screw.
20 Repeat the adjustments of paragraphs 18 and 19 to obtain the values given in the Specifications.

All models (2F engine)
21 Ensure that the engine idle speed returns to normal after being accelerated.
22 Stop the engine, remove the air cleaner, then pull the choke control to close the choke valve fully.
23 Open the choke valve with a screwdriver and start the engine. Set the fast idle speed to that specified by means of the fast idle adjusting screw.
24 With all idle speed adjustments correctly set and the engine warmed up detach the throttle positioner diaphragm hose.
25 Open the throttle slightly then release it, checking that the throttle positioner adjusting screw hooks onto the throttle valve lever.
26 Check that the throttle positioner idle speed is as specified or adjust, if necessary, by means of the adjusting screw.
27 Reconnect the throttle positioner hose, open the throttle valve slightly and check that the normal idle speed is obtained.

7 Fuel pump - removal and installation

1 Disconnect the fuel inlet and outlet pipes from the pump. To prevent fuel spillage it is recommended that the pipes are plugged.
2 Remove the mounting bolts, and detach the pump and gasket from the lower right side of the cylinder block (in front of the oil filter).
3 Installation is the reverse of the removal procedure, but ensure that a new gasket is used.

8 Fuel pump - dismantling, inspection and reassembly

1 Remove the securing screws and lift off the cover and gasket.
2 Scratch an alignment mark on the flange edges, then remove the securing screws and separate the two halves of the pump.
3 Press down and turn the diaphragm assembly to detach the pull rod from the rocker arm, then remove the diaphragm, spring, seal retainer (where applicable) and seal.
4 On early pumps, remove the retainers, and take out the inlet and outlet valve, and gaskets. (On later pumps the pairs of valves are staked in and should not be removed).
5 Although the rocker arm pivot can be drilled out for further dismantling, this is not recommended. If thought to be necessary, a replacement body assembly should be obtained.
6 Examine all the components for wear and damage, and obtain new parts as necessary. Note that the diaphragm assembly must be replaced as a complete item.
7 Reassembly is the reverse of the removal procedure. Do not use any sealant on the joint faces. Note the position of the diaphragm tab on later pumps, after assembly (Fig. 3.43).

9 Fuel filter - removal, cleaning and installation

1 On later models, an in-line filter is used, and is connected into the fuel delivery pipe to the fuel pump. It cannot be cleaned, and must be renewed at the intervals given in the Routine Maintenance Section. It is retained by a clip and screw, and the fuel hoses are pushed on and retained with clips (photo).
2 Early models have a bowl type filter which is attached to a bracket on the side of the engine.
3 To remove the filter element, unscrew the bail nut, and take off the bowl, spring, element and gasket.
4 Clean the parts in gasoline and renew any parts which are unserviceable.
5 Installation is the reverse of the removal procedure, but check for leaks as soon as possible with the engine running.

10 Air cleaner - general description

1 The air cleaner element is either a dry paper element type or an oil

bath type. The latter is likely to be found where the vehicle is operating in very dusty conditions.

2 Air cleaners used on models supplied for most markets from 1974 onwards have the Toyota automatic hot air intake system (HAI) incorporated in the air cleaner inlet duct.

3 The HAI system is designed to maintain the air drawn into the carburettor at a constant temperature to improve combustion efficiency. This is accomplished by the use of a wax temperature sensor inside the air cleaner, to sense engine temperature and operate a link and hot air valve. The hot air valve opens or closes to allow cold air, hot air or a mixture of both to be drawn into the carburetor in the correct proportions (photos).

4 On some models a manual hot air intake system is used. This system utilizes a valve on the air cleaner body so that during cold weather (below 50°F) air can be drawn from below the air cleaner where it is warmer. For temperature above 50°F, cold air is drawn in from the engine compartment.

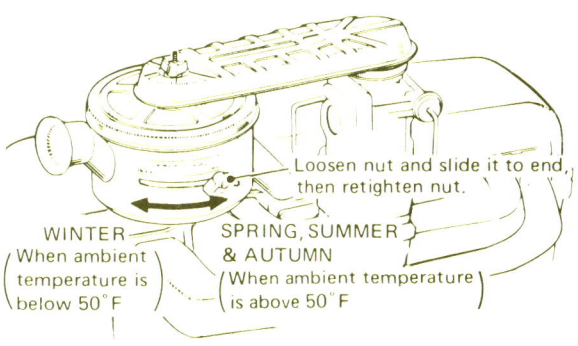

Fig. 3.45. Typical air cleaner with Summer/Winter settings

11 Air cleaner element - removal, cleaning and installation

Paper type

1 Remove the nut(s) and washer(s) retaining the air cleaner lid. Where applicable, spring back the clips also, and lift out the element (photos).
2 Tap the element sharply on a hard surface to remove excess dirt, then use a compressed air blast to remove the remaining dirt, blowing from the inside outwards.
3 If the air cleaner lid and case are reasonably clean, use a clean dry cloth to cover the carburetor inlet and use the air blast to remove the dirt.
4 If the lid and case are very dirty, remove the case (see next Section) and wash both in kerosene.
5 Dry with a lint free cloth then install by reversing the removal procedure. Never wash the element in kerosene; if badly soiled it must be renewed.

Oil bath type

6 Remove the nut and washer from the top of the casing, then carefully detach and lower the assembly away from the top part.
7 Remove the element and swill it in a bath of kerosene or gasoline to remove the dirt. Repeat the operation renewing the kerosene or gasoline, then take the element out and shake it dry.
8 Clean the case in a similar manner, but dry it inside completely with a lint-free cloth.
9 Add engine oil to the casing (approx. 0.6 litre/1.2 US pt/1.0 Imp pt) up to the level mark, then install the element.
10 Install the assembly to the engine by reversing the removal procedure.

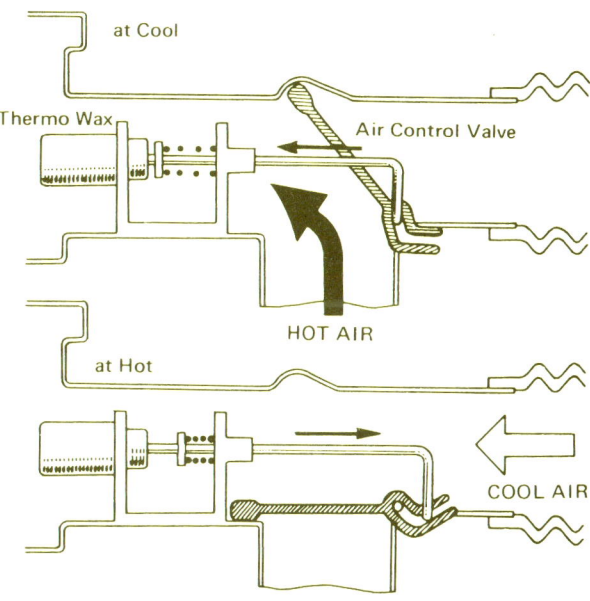

Fig. 3.46. Hot air intake system diagram

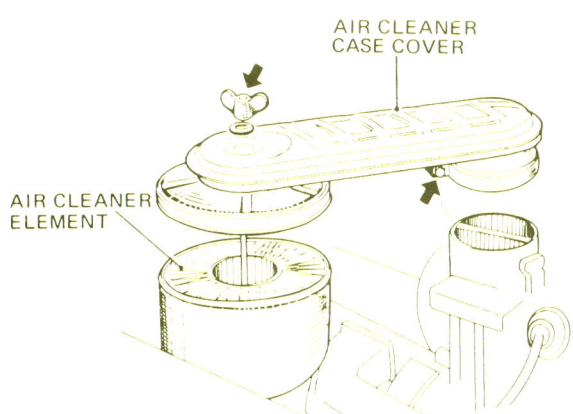

Fig. 3.47. Typical paper element air cleaner

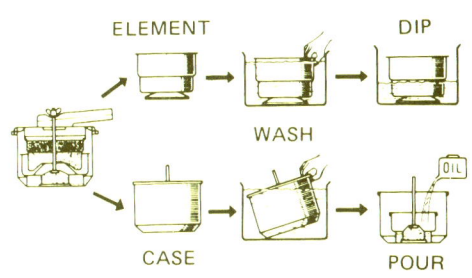

Fig. 3.48. Oil bath air cleaner - cleaning procedure

9.1 In-line fuel filter

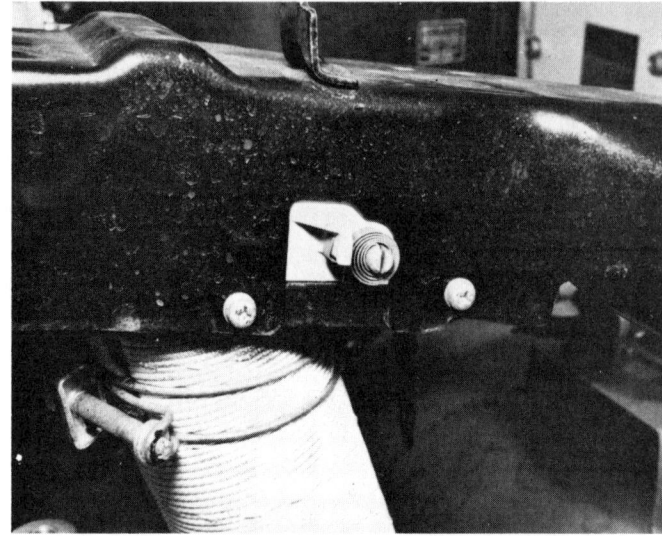

10.3a Hot air valve return spring ...

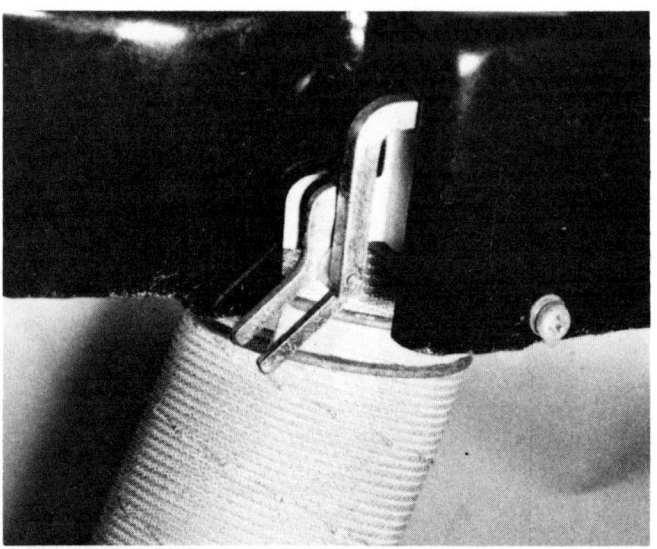

10.3b ... and link

11.1a Remove the nuts and washers ...

11.1b ... spring back the clips (where applicable) ...

11.1c ... and remove the lid

12 Air cleaner - removal and installation

1 Remove any breather and vacuum pipes from the air cleaner body.
2 It is preferable (but in most cases not essential) to remove the element (see previous Section).
3 Remove the air cleaner case retaining nuts and/or bolts. On some models a clip is used to secure the casing or intake duct to the carburetor. Remove this, if applicable.
4 Lift off the case (and intake duct, if applicable).
5 Installation is the reverse of the removal procedure. Note that special screws are used on some models to secure the casing intake duct to the vehicle frame; these screws have a small cut-out at the end. Where there is an intake pipe to a manifold heat store, ensure that this is connected correctly (photo).

13 Fuel tank - removal and installation

FJ40 series models

1 Detach the battery ground lead.
2 Remove the front seat on the right side of the vehicle.
3 Detach the wire from the tank sender unit.
4 Remove the drain plug from the tank and drain the contents into a suitable container.
5 Detach the fuel connection(s) from the tank. Where applicable, detach any emission control vent hoses (also see Section 18 and 19).
6 Remove the inlet pipe cover, then loosen the hose clip on the inlet pipe.
7 Remove the breather hose which runs alongside the inlet pipe.
8 Whilst supporting the tank on blocks, remove the bolts from the retaining bands.
9 Remove the bands and lower the tank, noting the position of any shims which may have been used.
10 If necessary, remove the screws and take out the sender unit.
11 Installation is the reverse of the removal procedure, but on completion check the whole system for fuel leaks.

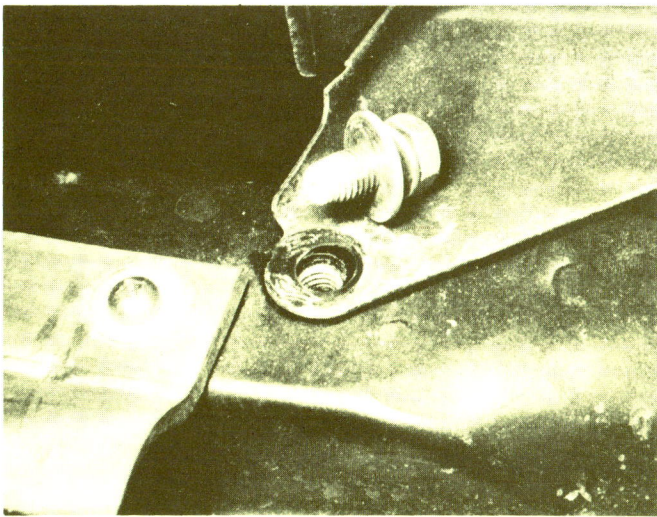

12.5 Special screw used for attachment to vehicle frame

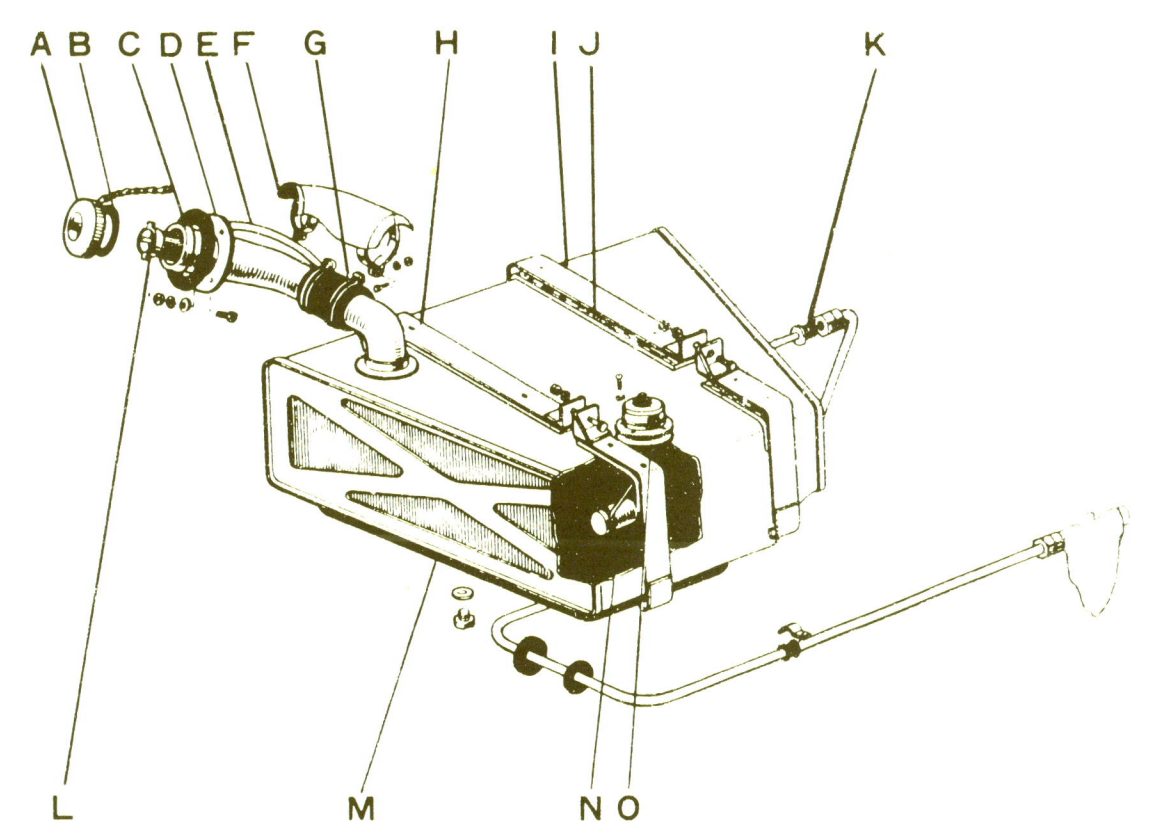

Fig. 3.49. Typical fuel tank for FJ40 series models

A Fuel tank cap	E Breather hose	I Fuel tank band	M Fuel tank
B Gasket	F Inlet pipe cover	J Band packing shim	N Sender unit
C Packing	G Inlet pipe joint	K Fuel suction tube	O Gasket
D Outer inlet pipe	H Fuel tank band	L Fuel strainer (optional)	

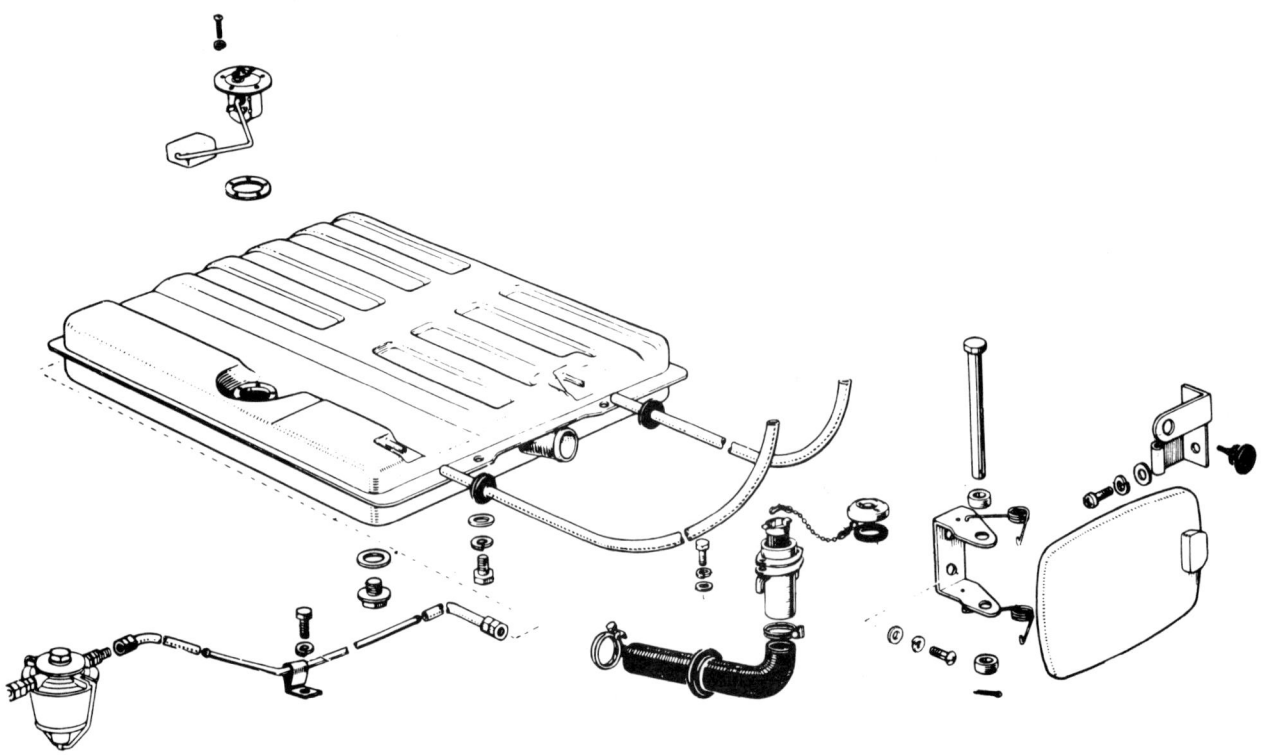

Fig. 3.50. Typical fuel tank for FJ55 models

FJ55 models
12 Detach the battery ground lead.
13 Remove the service hole cover (beneath the rear floor covering), and detach the wire from the sender unit.
14 Remove the drain plug from the tank and drain the contents into a suitable container.
15 Loosen the hose clip on the inlet pipe and detach the connection. Also detach the breather hose.
16 Detach the fuel connection(s) from the tank. Where applicable, detach any emission control vent hoses (also see Sections 18 and 19).
17 Remove the crossmember and spare-tire carrier from beneath the tank.
18 Remove the retaining bolts and, whilst supporting the tank, carefully lower it to the ground.
19 Installation is the reverse of the removal procedure, but on completion, check the whole system for fuel leaks.

14 Accelerator linkage - removal and installation

1 The accelerator linkage varies considerably on the different models, but removal is self-explanatory by reference to the accompanying illustrations.
2 After installing the linkage and/or cable, ensure that it operates freely. Adjust the cable end fitting to remove backlash, and check that for full travel of the pedal, there is full travel of the carburetor butterfly.

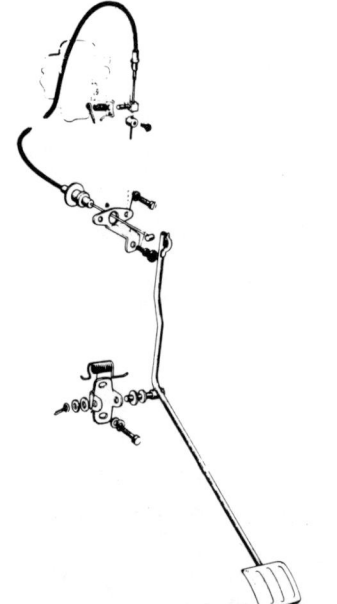

Fig. 3.51. Accelerator linkage - FJ40 series l.h.d.

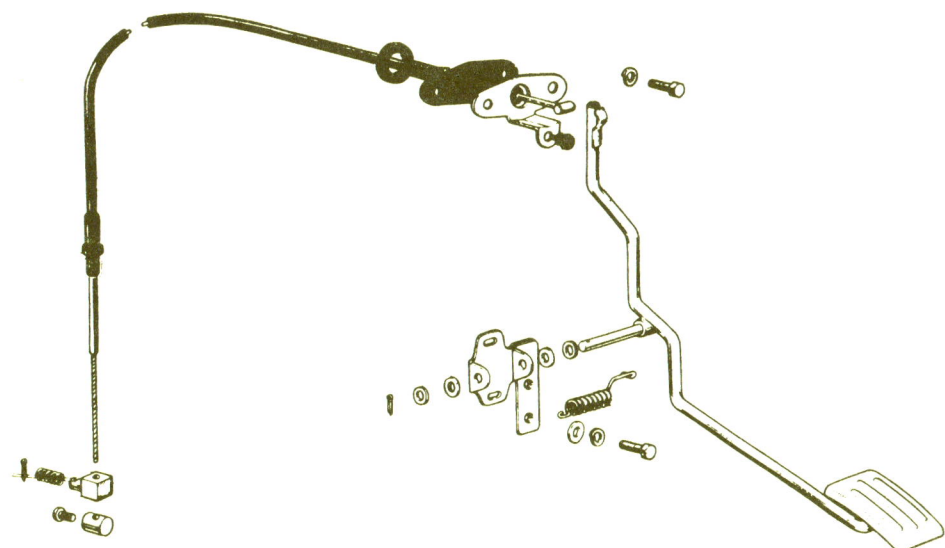

Fig. 3.52. Accelerator linkage - FJ55 series r.h.d.

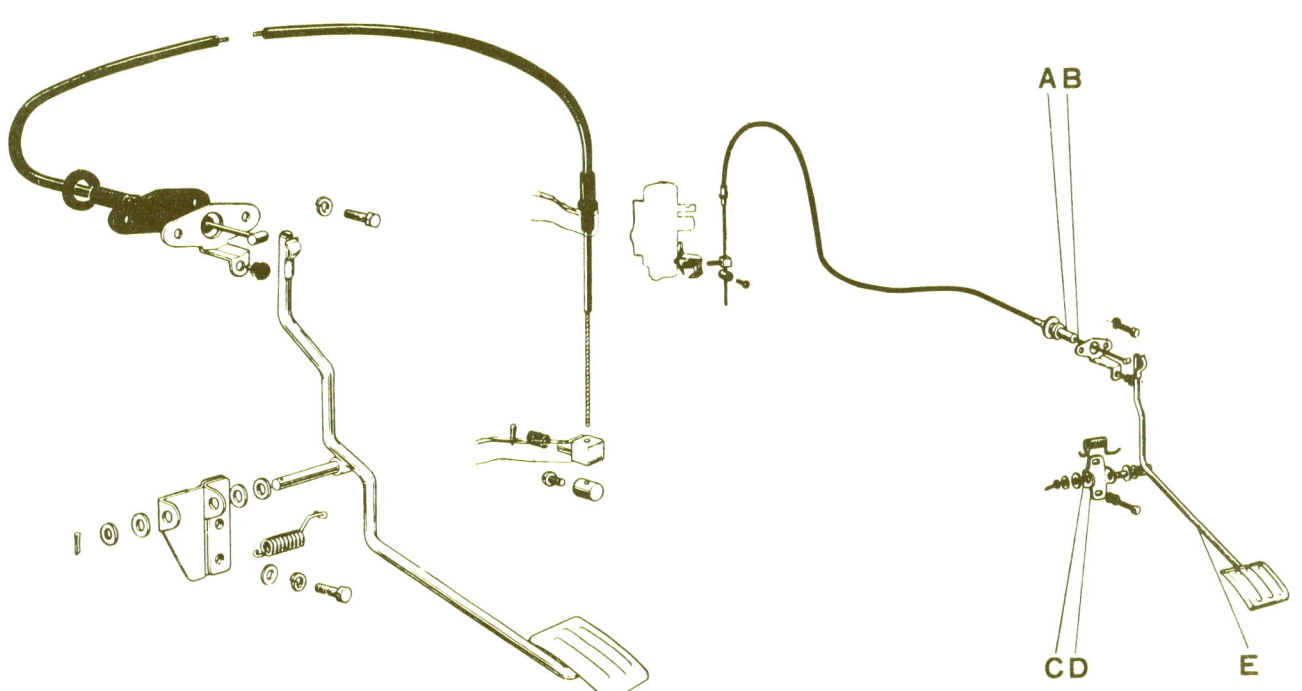

Fig. 3.53. Accelerator linkage - FJ55 series l.h.d.

Fig. 3.54. Accelerator linkage - FJ40 series r.h.d.

Chapter 3/Fuel, exhaust and emission control system

16.2 Typical exhaust hanger on later model

15 Intake and exhaust manifolds

1 The intake and exhaust manifolds are bolted together, and are attached to the left side of the cylinder head. Fig. 3.55 shows a typical arrangement. For information on the thermal reactor type of exhaust manifold, see Section 27. For details of the heat control valve used on later models, see Section 28.

2 There are no special instructions for removing the manifolds once the associated connections and ancillaries have been removed. These items will vary according to the vehicle model.

3 If a manifold is to be removed, both intake and exhaust manifolds must be removed together, then separated afterwards. Distortion on the cylinder head attachment face of up to 0.008 in (0.20 mm) is permissible.

4 The heat control valve should be checked to ensure that it is hooked onto the dowel pin (the coil should be wound just enough to hook its end onto the pin). A sticking valve should be freed using a mixture of penetrating oil and graphite.

16 Exhaust system

1 Typical exhaust arrangements are shown in the illustrations. There are no special instructions for removal and installation, but it is recommended that any joints and clamp bolts are lubricated with penetrating oil if they are to be removed.

2 On later models, it may be found that there are slight differences in the arrangements for suspending the various sections of the system (photo).

17 Emission control systems - general

1 A wide variety of emission control systems has been used on Land Cruiser models during the years in which they have been produced. It will be found that vehicles produced for one particular market for a given year can vary considerably from another basically similar vehicle produced for another market. Therefore, this Section has been compiled to include the most complicated systems likely to be found on vehicles during the various production years, and is generally applicable to models produced for the USA markets.

2 Servicing of the emission control system should be entrusted to a Toyota dealer due to the system complexities. It must also be understood that US Federal regulations do not permit interference with the system except by qualified service organisations.

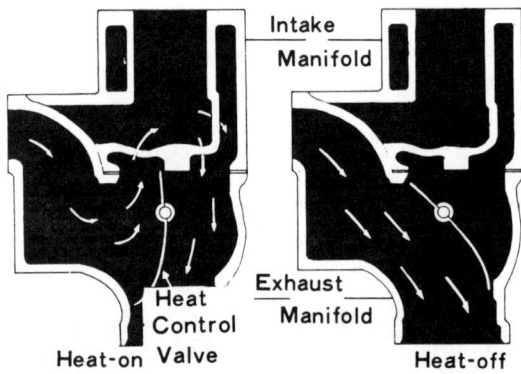

Fig. 3.55. Sectional view of heat control valve

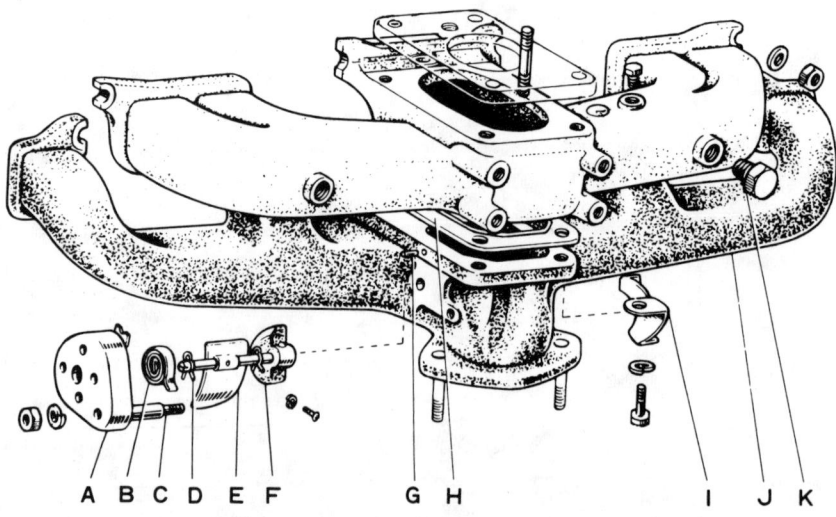

Fig. 3.56. Manifold arrangement - typical

- A Heat control bi-metal case
- B Heat control valve bi-metal coil
- C Case bolt
- D Retainer spring
- E Heat control valve
- F Shaft
- G Dowel pin
- H Gasket
- I Counter-weight stopper
- J Exhaust manifold
- K Taper screw plug

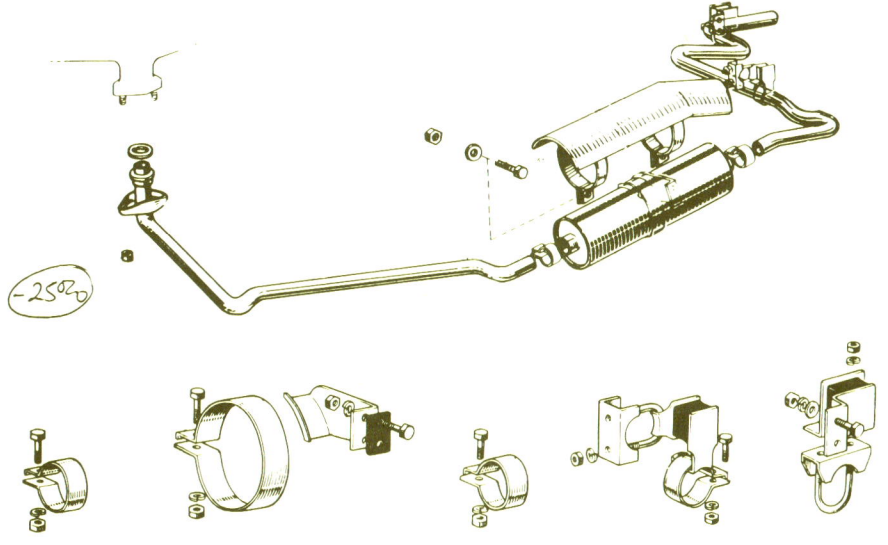

Fig. 3.57. Exhaust - typical for FJ40 series r.h.d.

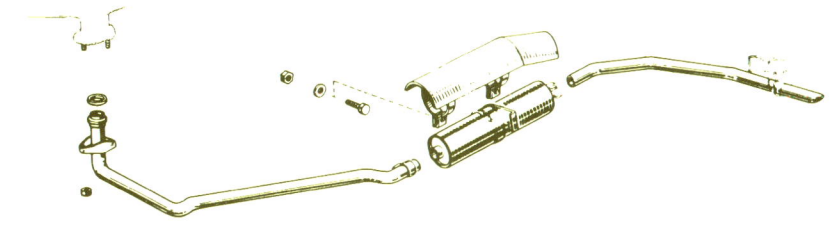

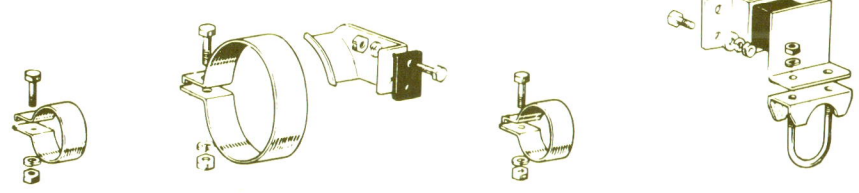

Fig. 3.58. Exhaust - typical for FJ40 series l.h.d.

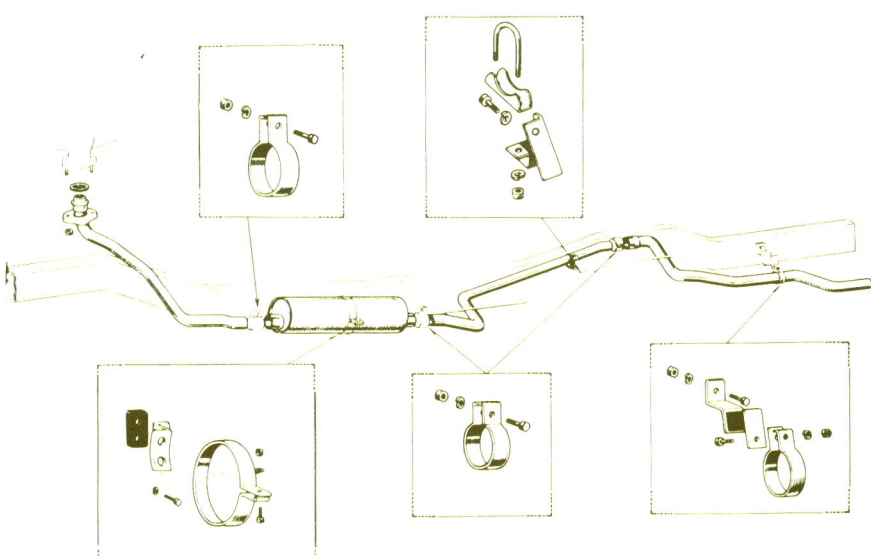

Fig. 3.59. Exhaust - typical for FJ55 series

18 Engine modification system

Description

1 The engine modification system comprises three main parts. These are the Improved Combustion System (ICS), Positive Crankcase Ventilation (PVC) System and Case Storage System (CSS).
2 The engine modification system applies to vehicles produced for the USA market up to 1973, except that the CSS applies to 1970 onwards for California models and 1971 onwards for other USA models.
3 The ICS comprises a modified carburetor, with a throttle positioner, a modified distributor with vacuum advance and retard, a speed detector, a speed marker (computor) and a vacuum switching valve. The system is designed to reduce the emission of unburnt hydrocarbons and carbon monoxide to safe levels.
4 During deceleration, the throttle positioner prevents the throttle from closing fully. The loss of engine braking effect is partially compensated for, by the loss of intake manifold vacuum being used to retard the ignition. At speeds below 14 mph the speed detector and speed marker operate the vacuum switching valve to allow the throttle to fully close.
5 The PCV system is described in Chapter 1.
6 The CSS is designed to reduce hydrocarbon emissions from the fuel system. It comprises a vacuum switching valve, fuel vapor storage case, air filter, thermal expansion tank and a modified fuel tank.
7 When the vehicle is stationary or running at less than 14 mph the vacuum switching valve is closed and vapor from the tank passes to the storage case. At speeds above 14 mph the vacuum switching valve is actuated by the speed marker and fuel vapors are drawn from the storage case and fuel tank into the intake manifold.

Inspection

8 To check the throttle positioner, run the engine up to normal operating temperature and check/adjust the idle speed. Detach the diaphragm vacuum hose and plug the vacuum line. Race the engine momentarily to set the throttle positioner then check the engine speed using a tachometer. Adjust, if necessary, then connect the vacuum hose and check that the engine idle speed now returns to normal. If this is not so, check the linkage, diaphragm, vacuum switching valve and speed marker for serviceability.
9 To check the distributor advance and retard unit, run the engine up to normal operating temperature and check/adjust the idle speed. Disconnect the hose from the C connection of the vacuum switching valve to the intake manifold and plug it. Disconnect the hose from the A connection of the vacuum switching valve and the distributor advance unit and connect it to the intake manifold. The engine speed should now decrease; if this does not occur, ensure that the hoses are in good condition. If these are satisfactory, the advance/retard unit is at fault.
10 To check the speed detector connect an AC voltmeter to the output wires and check for a voltage of 4.1 to 6.1 volts at a road speed of 37.5 mph (or at an engine speed of 637 rpm).
11 To renew the speed detector, detach the speedometer cable and disconnect the wires, then remove the detector from the transmission. Installation of a replacement is straightforward.
12 To check the speed marker, check whether the vacuum switching valve operates at speedometer readings of 10.5 to 15 mph. If this does not occur, check the system connections.
13 To renew the speed marker, detach the wires and remove the speed marker from the speedometer. Installation of a replacement is straightforward.
14 To check the ICS vacuum switching valve, detach the hoses and electrical leads. Using a flexible pipe check that air can be blown thru connection E to A, and B to C and D. Energize the valve from a 12 volt dc source and check that air can be blown thru connections E to C and D, and A to B. Renew a defective valve.
15 To check the CSS vacuum switching valve, connect a 12 volt dc source directly to the valve solenoid and disconnect the hose from the E connection. Run the engine and check that suction can be felt at the E connection. Renew a defective valve.

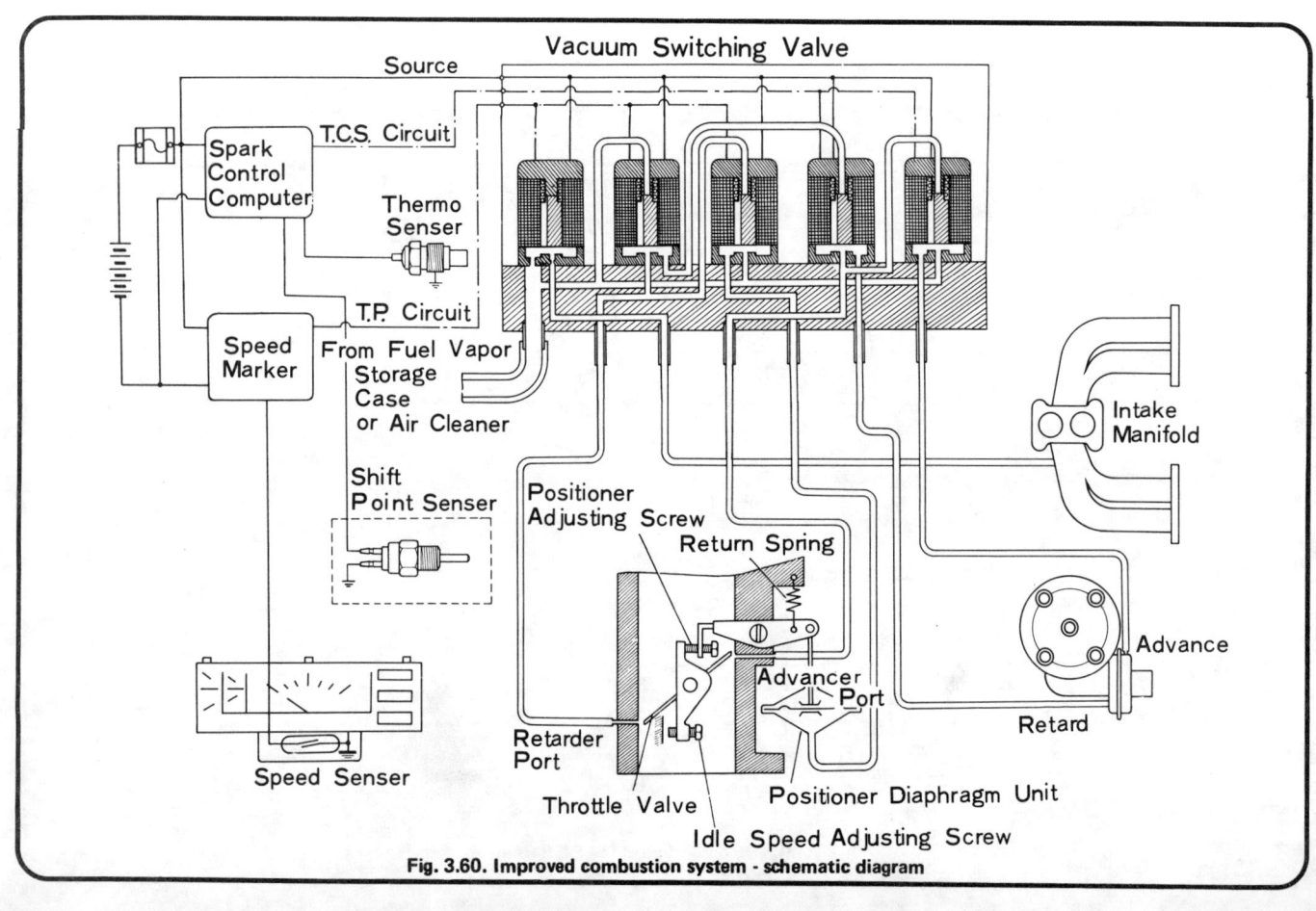

Fig. 3.60. Improved combustion system - schematic diagram

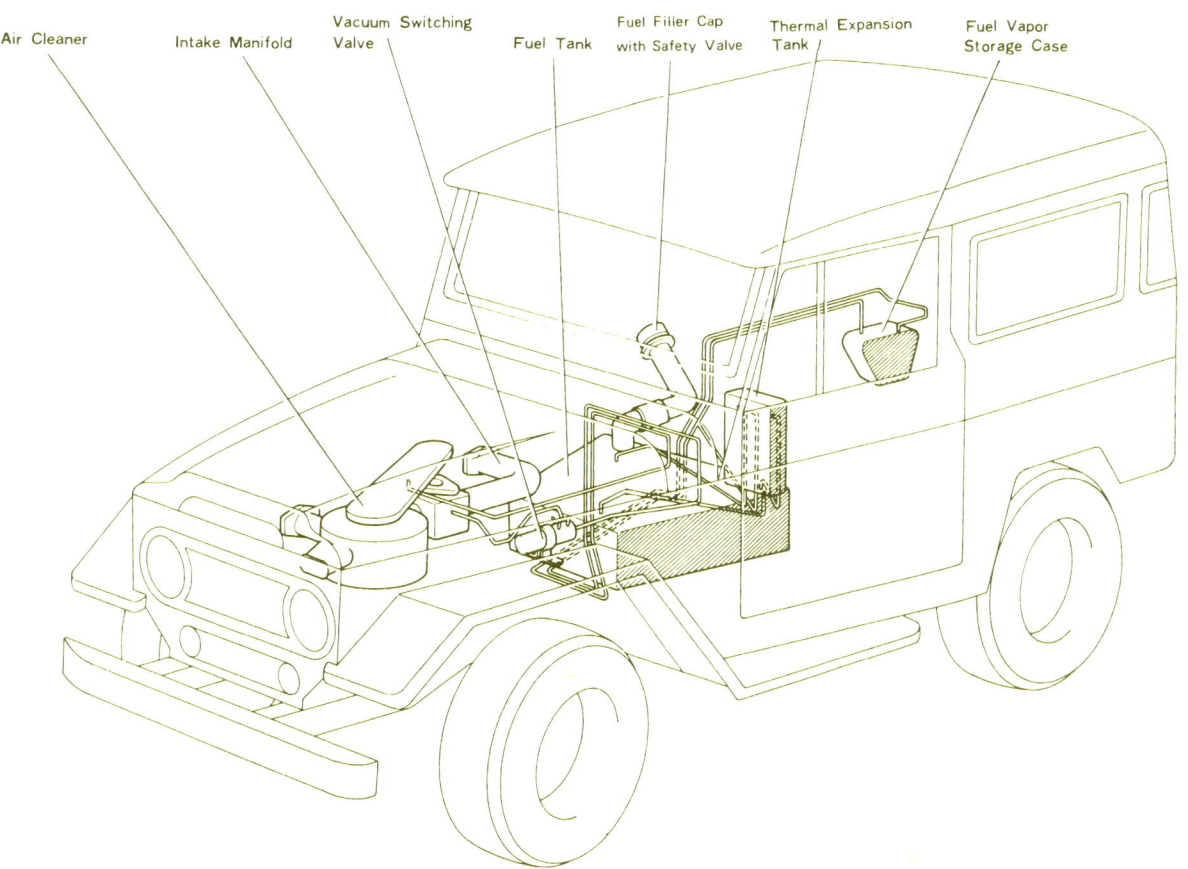

Fig. 3.61. Case storage system - FJ40 series models

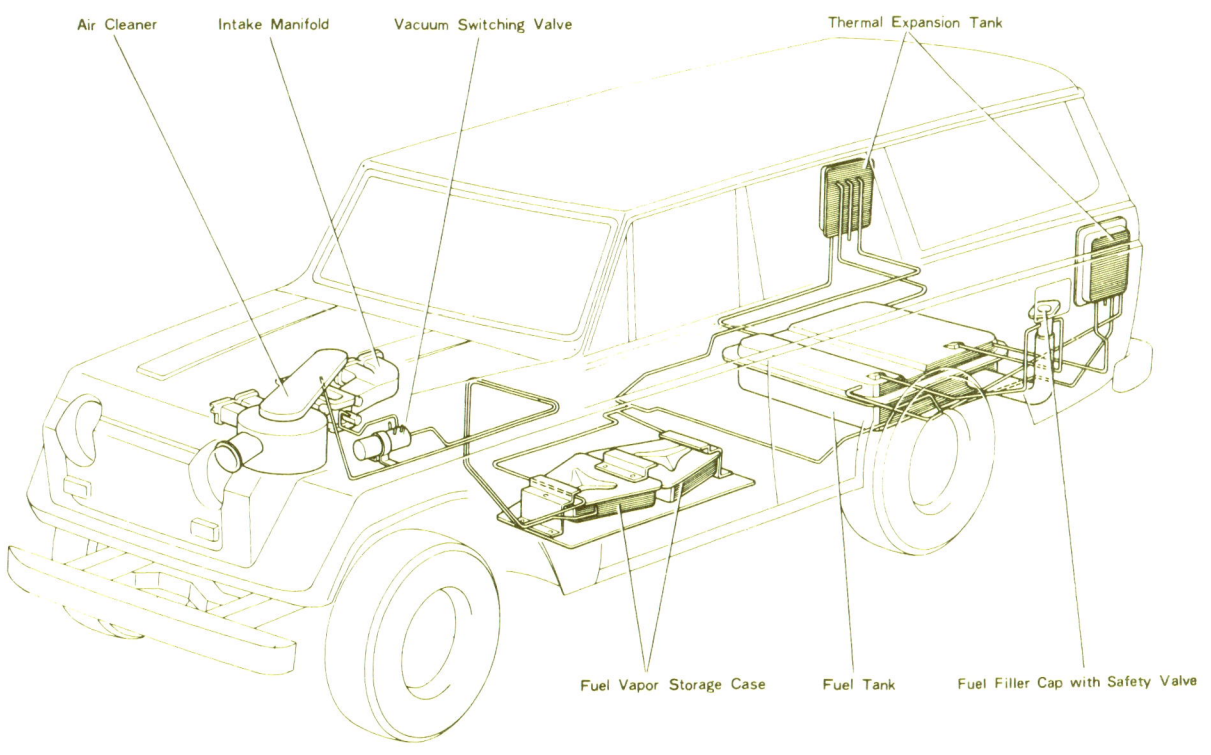

Fig. 3.62. Case storage system - FJ55 models

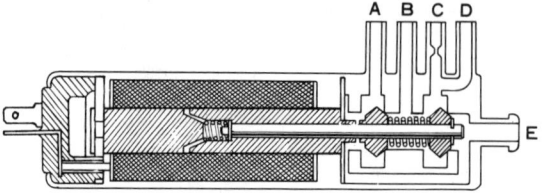

Fig. 3.63. Vacuum switch valve check - energized, showing connection number

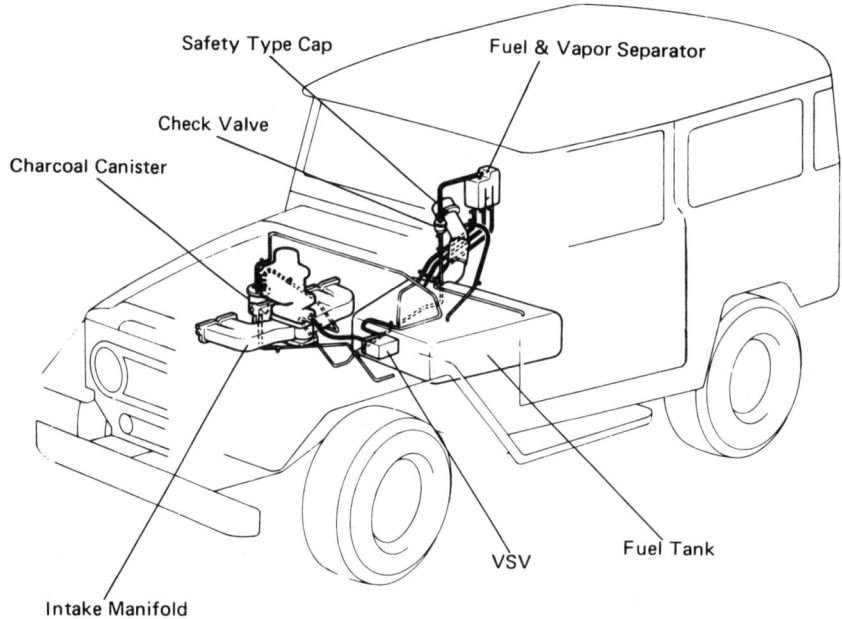

Fig. 3.64. EVAP system piping - FJ40 series models

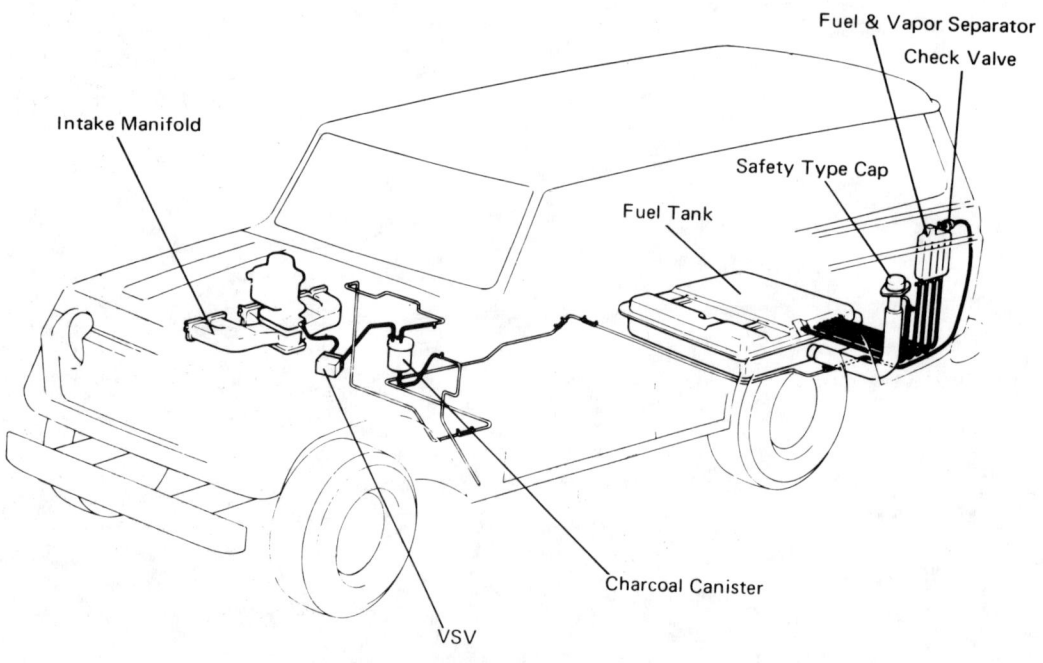

Fig. 3.65. EVAP system piping - FJ55 models

Chapter 3/Fuel, exhaust and emission control systems

19 Fuel evaporative emission control system

Description
1 The fuel evaporative emission control system (EVAP) is designed to feed evaporated hydrocarbons to the engine intake system. It is installed on all USA and ECE models from 1973 onwards.
2 When the vehicle is stationary or running at a low speed, signals from the speed sensor are passed to the computer which causes the vacuum switching valve (VSV) to de-energize. Thus, fuel vapors pass to the charcoal canister.
3 At higher engine speeds (above 9 ± 2 mph), the signal causes the VSV to energize and open the passage from the canister to the intake manifold where they are burned.
4 A safety type fuel tank cap is used to prevent the fuel vapors escaping to atmosphere.
5 A check valve, installed between the fuel and vapor separator and the canister remains closed until there is a vapor pressure build-up of 0.48 in Hg. Should there be a build-up of pressure on the canister side, the vapors are vented back to the tank when the pressure in the check valve reaches 0.60 in Hg.

Inspection
6 To check the charcoal canister, connect an air line to the A connection and plug the B connection with a finger. Blow air at 40 psi (3 kgf/cm^2) thru the unit and check for particles of activated carbon being blown thru, or resistance to airflow. If either is present the canister must be renewed.
7 Using a short flexible hose, check the check valve by ensuring that air can be blown thru (by mouth) in each direction. There should be a slight resistance before the valve opens. Renew a defective valve.
8 Visually examine the fuel tank cap for serviceability.

20 Throttle positioner

Description
1 A throttle positioner (TP) is used on all USA and ECE models from 1973 onwards and is similar to the one used in the Improved Combustion System except for 1977 (see Section 18) (photo).
2 The California and non-California 1977 models are similar to each other except for the addition of a vacuum transmitting valve (VTV) for California models. For medium and high speeds the vacuum switch-

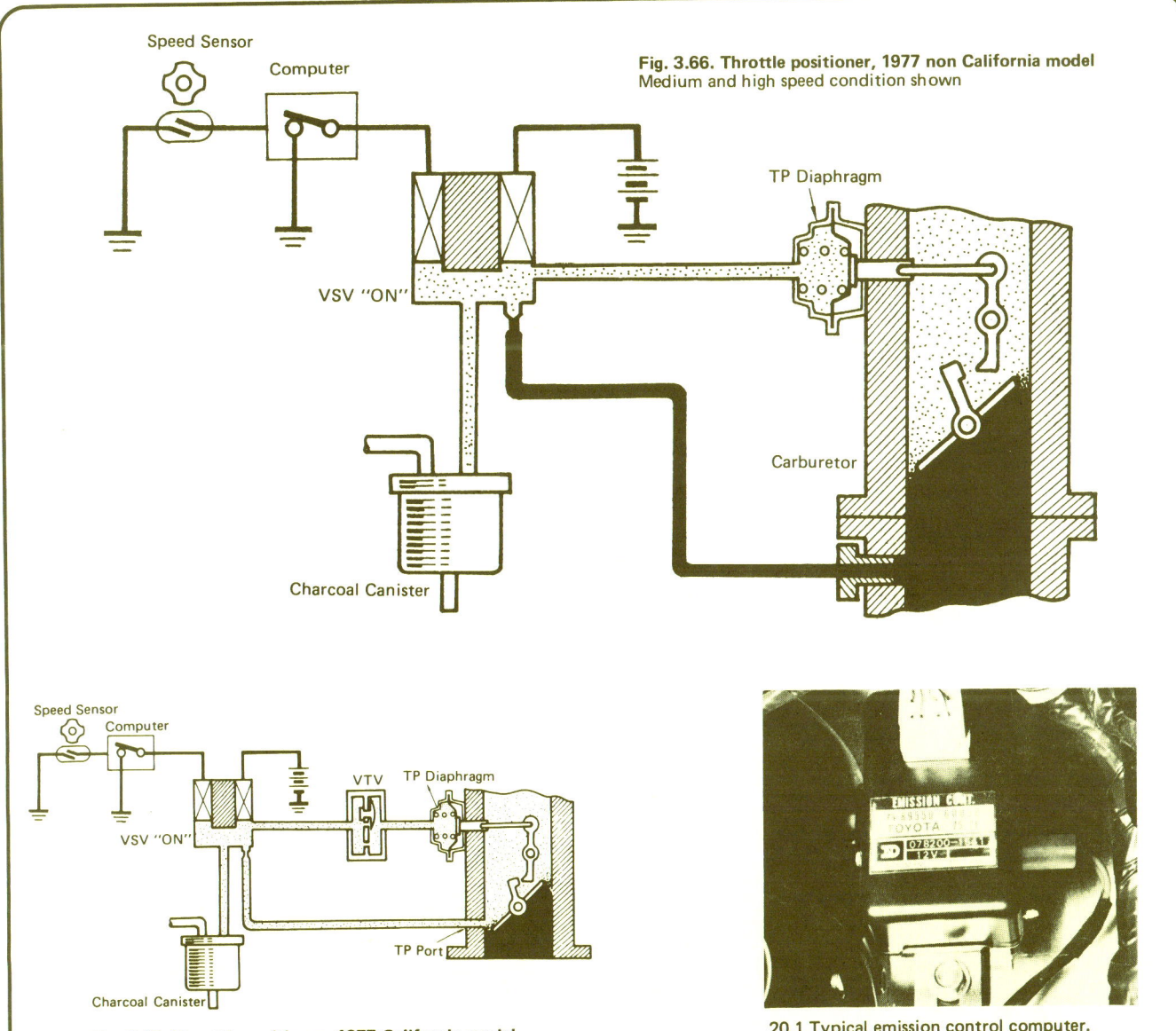

Fig. 3.66. Throttle positioner, 1977 non California model
Medium and high speed condition shown

Fig. 3.67. Throttle positioner, 1977 California model
Medium and high speed condition shown

20.1 Typical emission control computer. The installed position is usually beneath the dashpanel on the bulkhead

ing valve (VSV) is energized and open, and vents the TP to ambient rendering it ineffective. During deceleration the condition remains the same, which means that the throttle is prevented from closing fully until the engine speed falls below 14 to 20 mph (California) or 7 to 11 mph (non-California). Below this speed range the VSV is de-energized and closed, applying manifold suction to the diaphragm which allows the throttle to close fully. However, on California models, the VTV acts as a delaying device which allows a progressive throttle closing during the final stage of deceleration rather than letting the throttle snap closed.

Inspection and adjustment

3 Follow the procedure given for the throttle positioner in Section 18, but note that for 1977 California models when the vacuum hose is reconnected, there should be a slight delay before the engine speed falls to the normal idle speed.

21 Transmission controlled spark

Description

1 The transmission controlled spark (TCS) system is installed on all USA models from 1973 to 1976 (except California 1976). It is similar to the system incorporated into the Improved Combustion System (see Section 18), but additionally has a thermosensor for detecting coolant temperatures.
2 At engine coolant temperatures of 140 to 208°F (113 to 217°F for California) when the vehicle is accelerating in the range 13 to 41 mph, the speed sensor and thermosensor transmit a signal to the computor which energizes the vacuum switching valve (VSV). This opens the passage between the distributor retard diaphragm and carburetor, which retards the ignition. During deceleration a similar sequence occurs but at a speed range of 31 to 9 mph, (26 to 9 mph for California).

Inspection and adjustment

3 To check the thermo switch, the switch phial (only) should be immersed in water and the water heated to the temperature stated in the previous paragraph. The switch contacts should be open below the minimum stated temperature, closed during the temperature range, and open again above the maximum stated temperature.
4 To check the distributor retard unit, disconnect the vacuum line from the VSV then suck (by mouth) and check that the breaker plate moves.

22 Manifold air injection system

Description

1 The manifold air injection (AI) system blows compressed air into the hot gases discharged from the combustion chamber. This causes the hydrocarbons and carbon monoxide to burn to form carbon dioxide. It is installed on all USA models from 1973 onwards.
2 Clean air, drawn from the air cleaner, is compressed and passed to the air by-pass valve (ABV) or anti-afterburn valve (used on 1974 California models). From there it passes thru the check valve into the AI manifold then into the AI nozzles. A relief valve in the ABV or anti-afterburn valve prevents the system pressure from rising above a pre-determined level.
3 During sudden deceleration, the intake manifold vacuum causes the ABV to by-pass the air to atmosphere (or into the intake manifold on 1974 California models).

Inspection

4 The ABV can be checked by observation. With the engine idling, there should be no airflow from the ABV. During acceleration, air should flow from the ABV. Renew an ABV which does not operate satisfactorily.
5 To check an anti-afterburn valve, remove the intake manifold connection and check that when the engine is idling there is no discharge of air from the valve port. Momentarily race the engine and check that there is a discharge of air from the valve port for a short time. Renew a defective valve.
6 To check a check valve, ensure that air can be blown thru it towards the exhaust manifold side only.

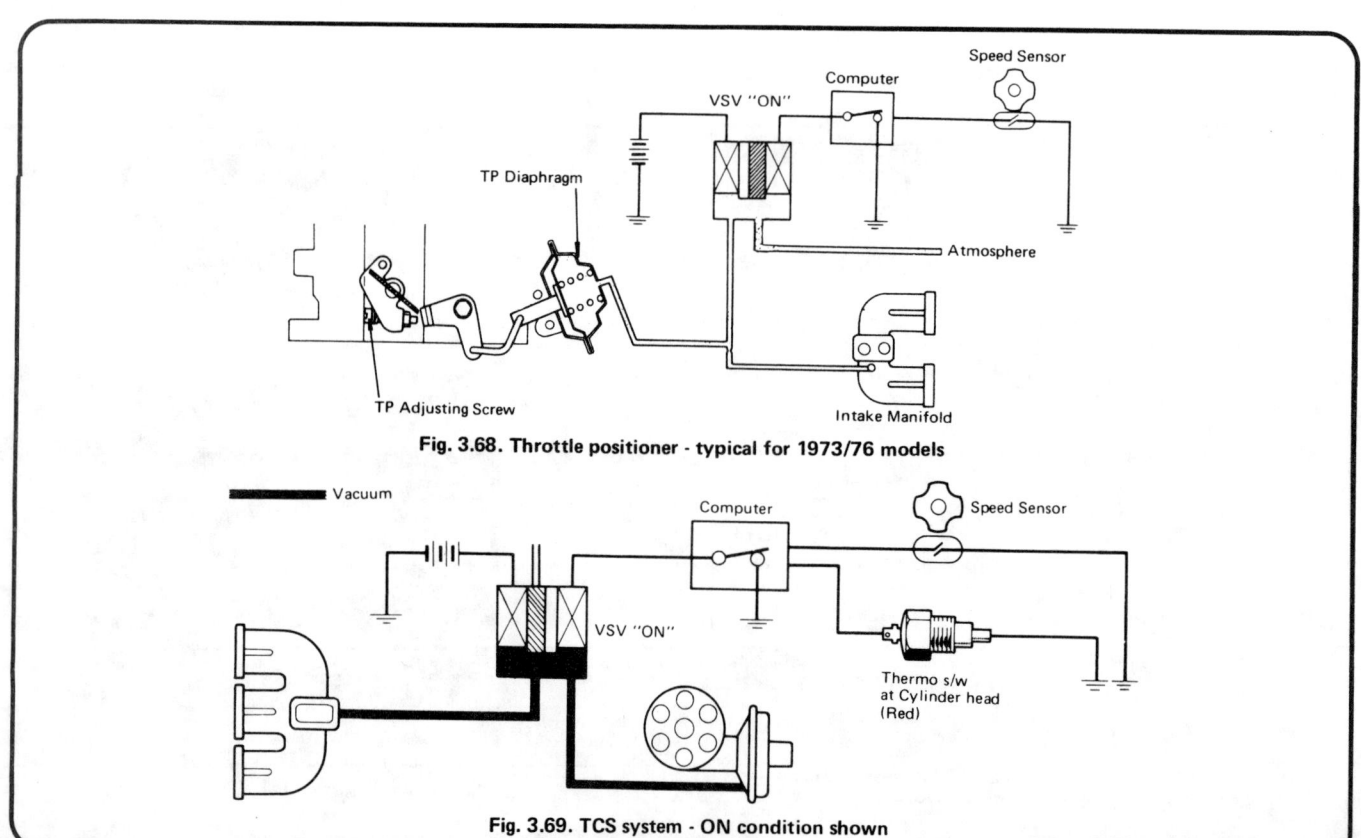

Fig. 3.68. Throttle positioner - typical for 1973/76 models

Fig. 3.69. TCS system - ON condition shown

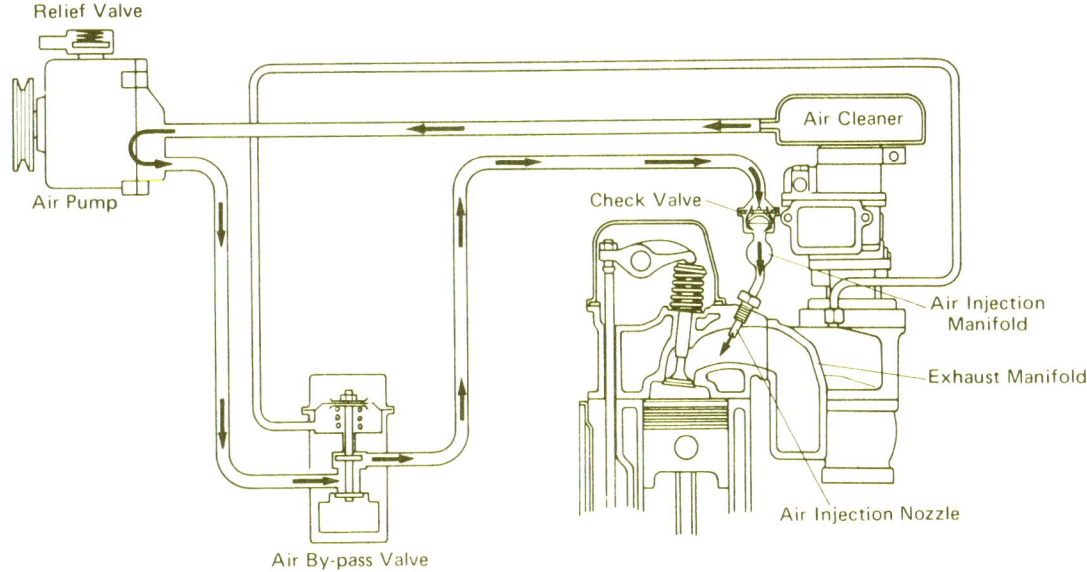

Fig. 3.70. AI system diagram (except 1974 California models)

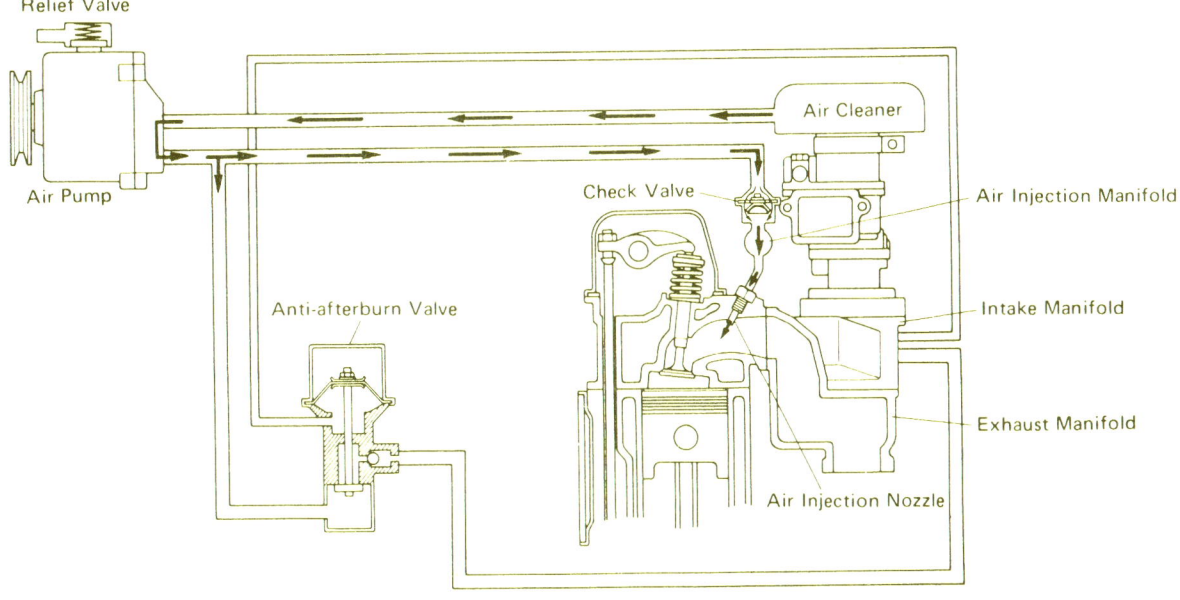

Fig. 3.71. AI system diagram (1974 California models)

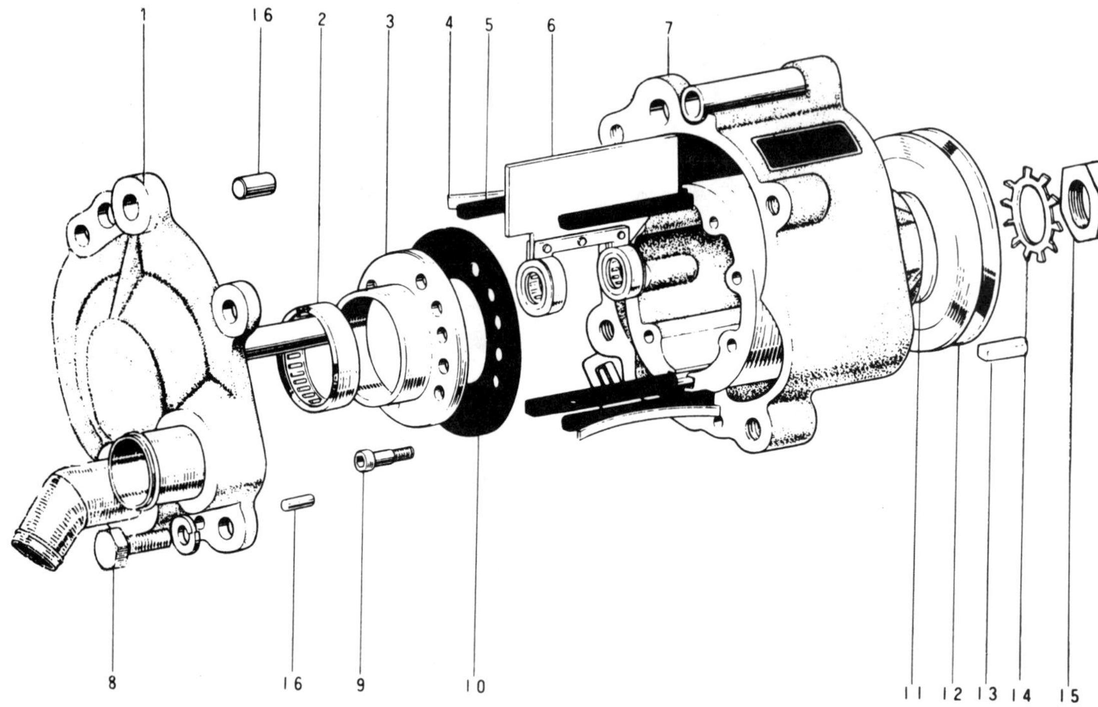

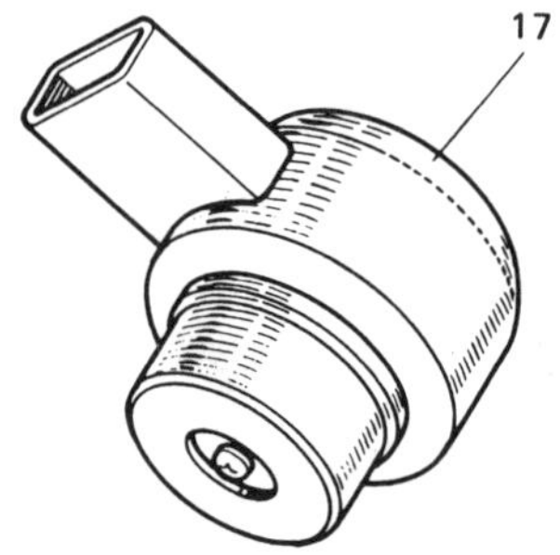

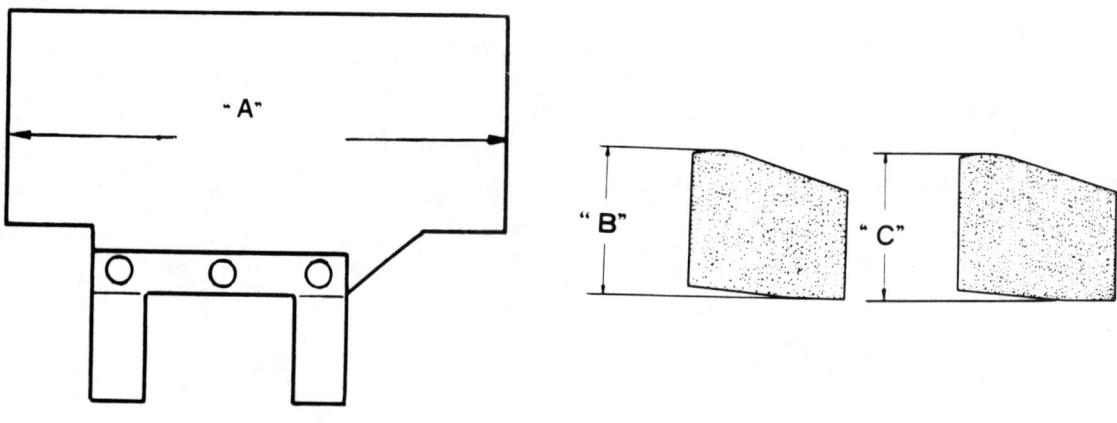

Fig. 3.72. Air pump - exploded view

1 Housing cover
2 Rear bearing
3 Rotor ring
4 Shoe spring
5 Carbon shoe
6 Vane
7 Rotor housing
8 Housing cover attaching bolt
9 Rotor ring screw
10 Rear seal
11 Pulley plate
12 Pulley
13 Key
14 Lock washer
15 Locknut
16 Dowel
17 Relief valve

Fig. 3.73. Air pump blade and carbon shoe dimensional wear diagram
For minimum dimensions see text

23 Air pump - servicing

1 The pump used for the manifold air injection system is of rotary, sliding blade type. It draws air from the 'clean' side of the air cleaner and will normally give a long trouble-free life. In the event of a fault developing, an exchange unit is recommended but where suitable tools are available it can be repaired.
2 Pry the relief valve from the top of the pump using two sharpened levers located beneath the valve housing rim.
3 Turn the pulley so that its keyway is at right angles to a line drawn through the centres of the two cover locating dowels.
4 Place the pump, pulley downwards and drive out the two dowels towards the pulley.
5 Remove the pump cover retaining bolts, and detach it from the pump housing by tapping it gently with a plastic faced hammer. Do not remove the pivot pin from the cover.
6 Hold the pulley still. This is best achieved by engaging a section of an old driving belt in the pulley and gripping the two ends of the belt as close to the pulley as possible in a vise. On no account grip any part of the air pump in the vise.
7 Using an Allen key, remove the socket screws from the rear rotor ring and detach the ring/bearing assembly and carbon seal.
8 Extract the blade assembly, carbon shoes and springs.
9 If necessary, the bearing can be pressed out from the rotor ring and a new one pressed in with its part number visible from the narrower diameter end of the ring.
10 The pulley must be removed with an extractor after unscrewing the securing nut (left hand thread). No further dismantling should be carried out.
11 Clean the internal surfaces of the pump and examine for wear. The pump blades should be at least 2.35 in (60 mm) in width and the carbon shoes in excess of the minimum dimensions shown in Fig. 3.73, (dimensions B and C), otherwise renew them.
12 Check that the rear seal has not worn below a thickness of 0.016 in (0.4 mm) otherwise renew it.
13 Check that the shoe spring deflection, at the highest point of its curvature when the spring is standing free on a flat surface, is not less than 0.12 in (3 mm) otherwise renew it.
14 Reassembly is a reversal of dismantling but observe the following points. Lubricate all roller bearings with general purpose grease. Position each blade assembly so that it aligns with the centre of the

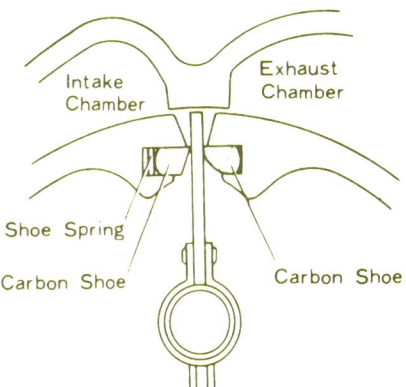

Fig. 3.74. Installation diagram for air pump blades and shoes

division in the rotor housing which divides the air intake chamber from the exhaust chamber. Fit the carbon shoes so that the deeper one (white mark on its end) is installed in the deeper recess but having its colored end mark towards the pump cover. The shoe springs are located in the deeper recess with their convex surface in contact with the carbon shoe. Tighten the rotor ring socket screws in diametrically opposite sequence to a torque of no more than 4 lbf ft (0.55 kgf m).
15 Finally, install the pump cover, insert four securing bolts finger tight and drive in the dowels from the cover end. Tighten the cover bolts to a torque of 10 lbf ft (1.4 kgf m). The new blades may squeak for the first 100 miles (160 km) until they have bedded in.

24 Exhaust gas recirculation

Description
1 The exhaust gas recirculation (EGR) system was introduced for 1974 California models, then used on all subsequent models. The system has been modified thru-out the years of production but its function has remained unaltered. It is designed to introduce a small amount of exhaust gas into the engine intake system to lower the combustion temperature and thereby reduce nitrogen oxide emissions.

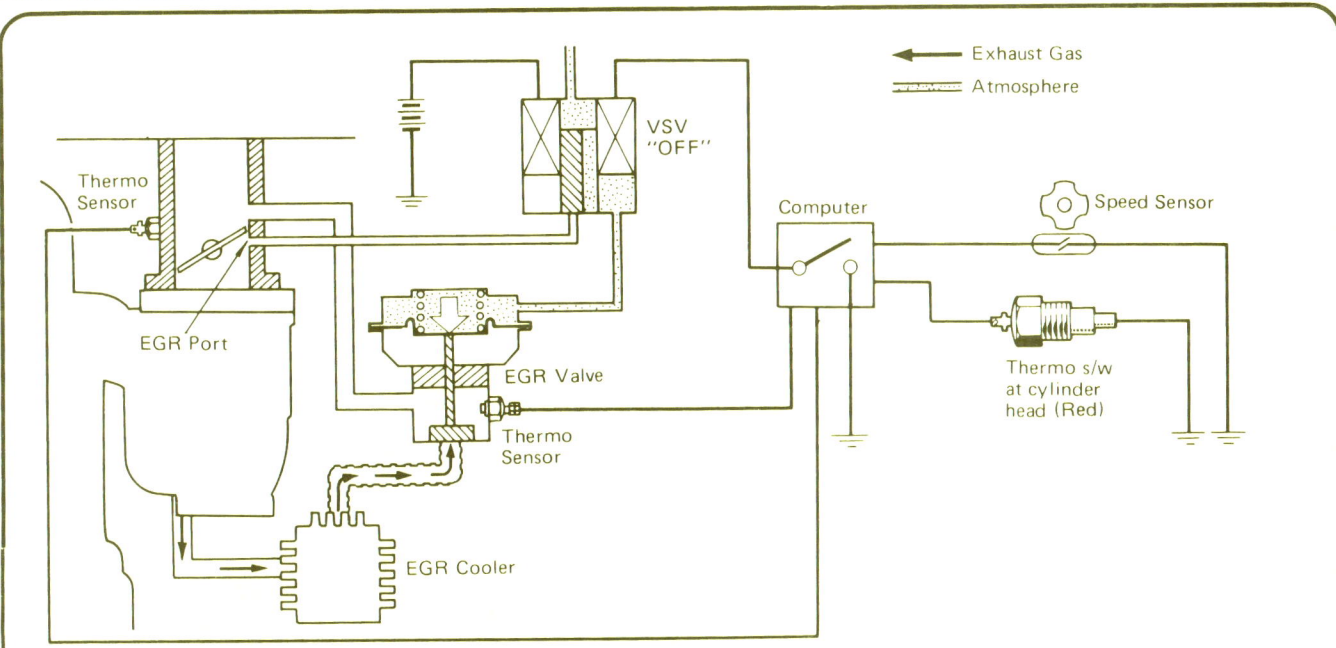

Fig. 3.75. EGR system diagram, 1975 and 1976 models - OFF condition shown (1974 California model is similar except for the EGR cooler and carburetor thermosensor)

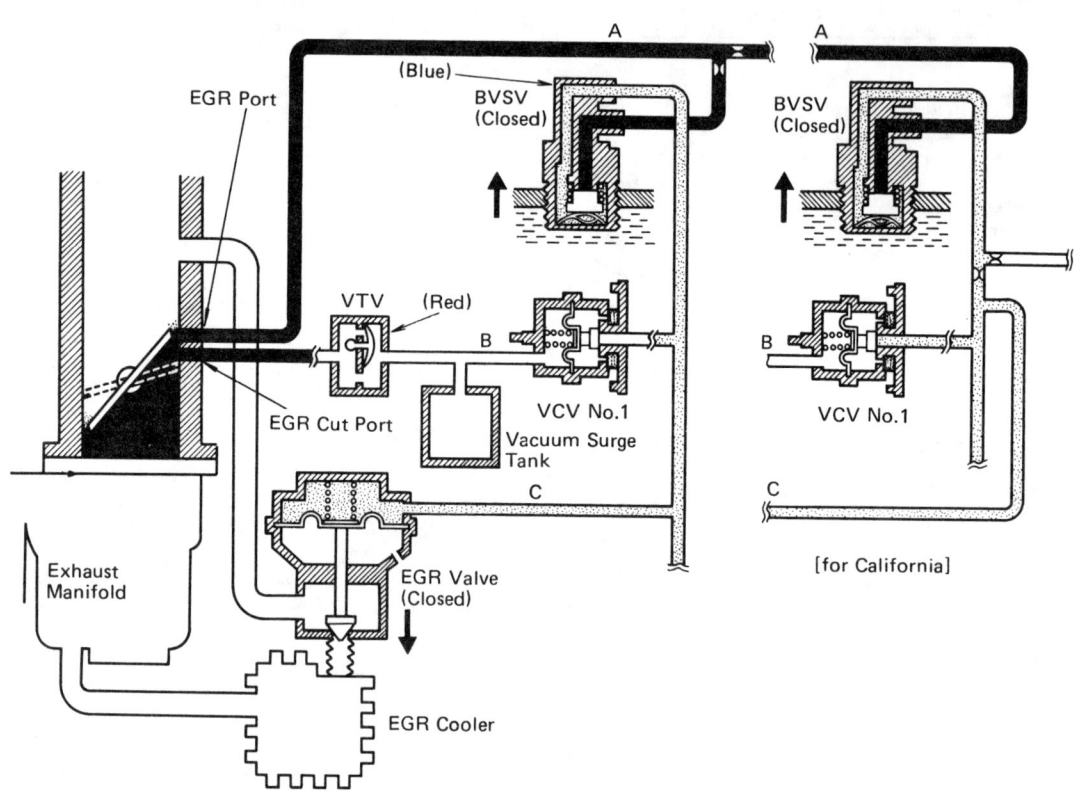

Fig. 3.76. EGR system diagram, 1977 models - OFF condition shown

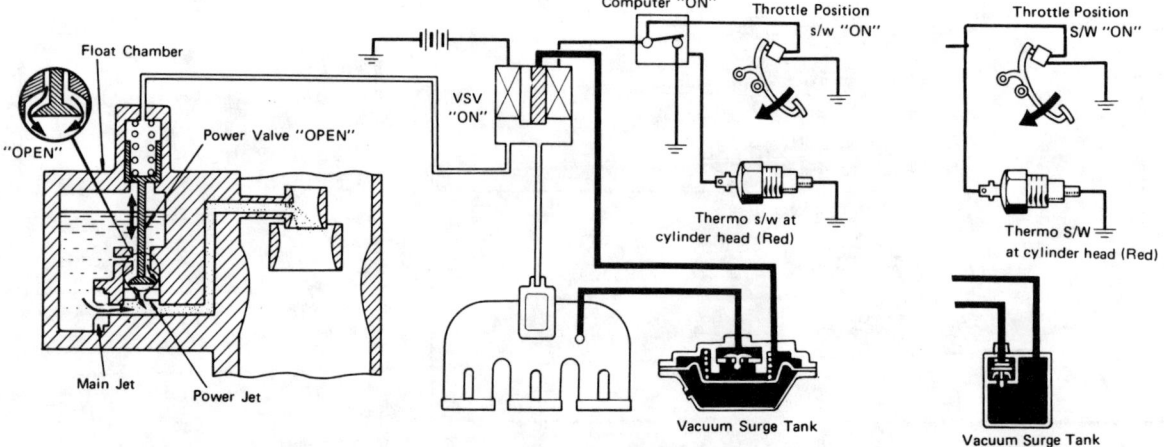

Fig. 3.77. Power valve control system, 1975 model - ON condition shown
Inset - Differences for 1976/77 models

Chapter 3/Fuel, exhaust and emission control systems

2 The conditions which affect the system operation are engine coolant temperature, vehicle speed, EGR gas temperature, carburetor temperature (some models) and throttle valve opening (some models).
3 After 25,000 miles of operation, an EGR warning light will illuminate when the ignition is switched on. This is an indication that the system should be serviced by a Toyota dealer.
4 Apart from periodically checking the hoses and electrical connections it is not considered advisable to carry out any maintenance work on the various systems.

25 Power valve control system

Description
1 The power valve control system is used on most 1975 thru 1977 models for the USA, to further reduce emissions of carbon monoxide. A slightly modified vacuum surge tank is used for 1976/77 models, and the thermoswitch signals are not fed thru the computer.
2 At coolant temperatures below 122°F, or when the throttle is fully opened, the vacuum switching valve (VSV) will energize and allow intake manifold vacuum to act on the power valve in the carburetor float chamber. Since the manifold is nearly at atmospheric pressure the power valve will open under spring action and provide a rich mixture.

3 At coolant temperatures above 122°F, provided that the accelerator is not fully depressed, the VSV will be de-energized and the vacuum in the surge tank will act on the power valve causing it to close. This prevents an excessively rich mixture.
4 The purpose of the surge tank is to store the manifold vacuum, and the internal check prevents loss of vacuum during conditions of low manifold vacuum.

Inspection
5 A continuity tester can be used to check the operation of the throttle position switch. There should be continuity when the switch is depressed, and an open circuit when the switch is released.

26 Spark control system

Description
1 The spark control system (SC) is designed to delay the spark advance for a given time to reduce nitrogen oxide and hydrocarbon emissions. It is incorporated for the first time on 1977 USA models (1976 California models).
2 Three different systems are in service; one system is for general US markets, the second is for California markets, and the third is for high altitude markets.

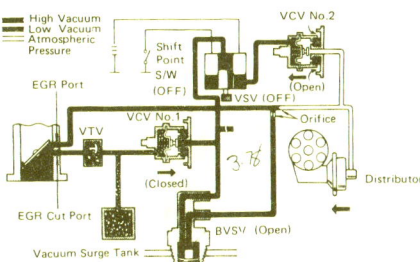

Fig. 3.78. Spark control system (except California and high altitude models) - hot engine condition with delayed spark shown

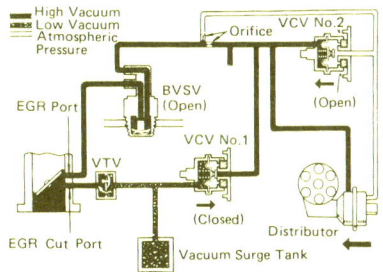

Fig. 3.79. Spark control system (California) - hot engine condition with delayed spark shown

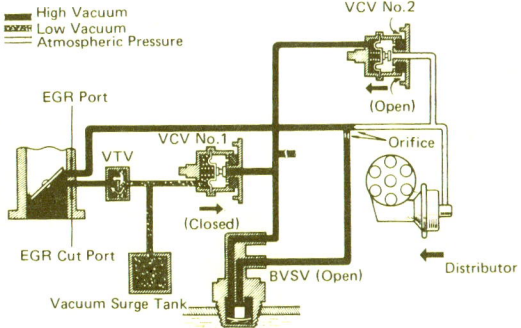

Fig. 3.80. Spark control system (high altitude) - hot engine condition with delayed spark shown

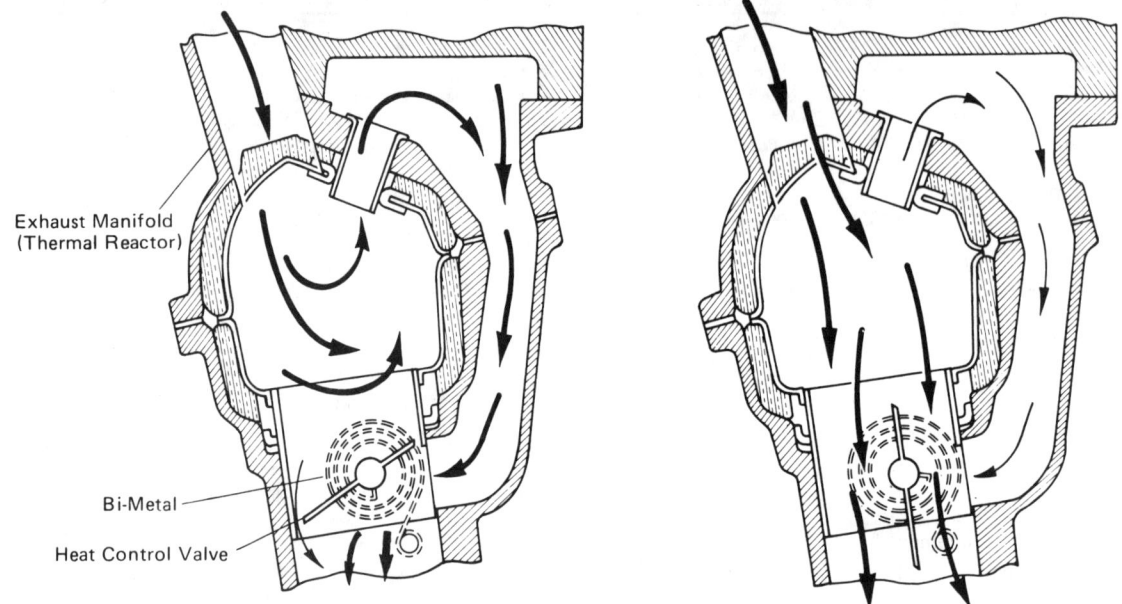

Fig. 3.81. Sectional view of thermal reactor showing gas flow

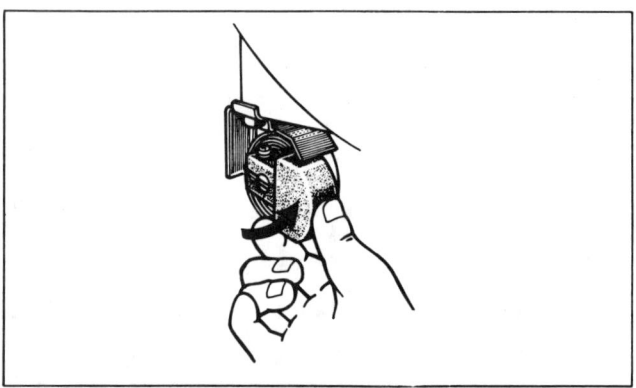

Fig. 3.82. Checking heat control valve

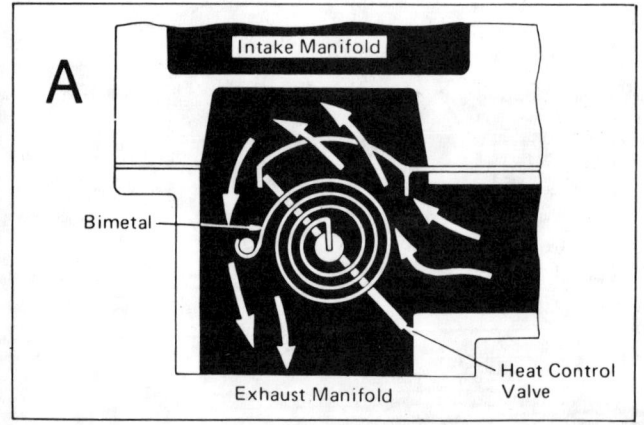
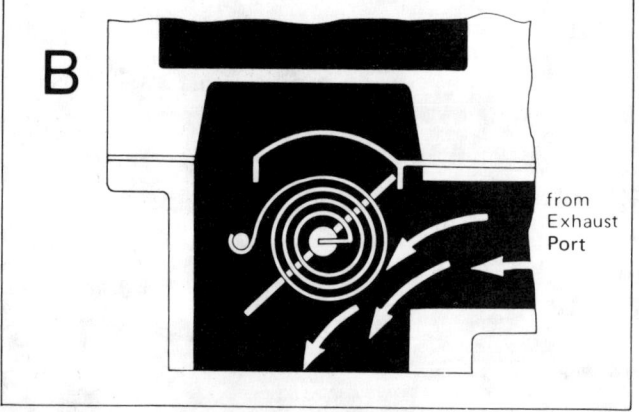

Fig. 3.83. Heat control valve

A Cold engine   B Hot engine

Inspection
3 Because of the complexity of the system, it is not considered practicable to check the system components, other than to check the security of the vacuum connections (and electrical connections, where applicable).

27 Thermal reactor system

Description
1 This system is used on 1977 California models.in place of the exhaust manifold system. It is designed to maintain the exhaust gases at a high temperature for a longer time to further increase the mixture efficiency of exhaust gas and secondary air. The system is an addition to the air injection system.

Inspection
2 Check that the heat control valve turns smoothly by hand and returns under spring action.
3 The thermal reactor can be dismantled, if necessary, by removing the three bolts and two nuts to remove the intake manifold.
4 Assembly is the reverse of the dismantling procedure, but tighten the nuts and bolts to a torque of 26 lbf ft (3.7 kgf m). Ensure that warpage of the cylinder head contact face does not exceed 0.08 in (2 mm), then install on the cylinder head. Tighten the nuts and bolts to a torque of 43 lbf ft (6 kgf m).

28 Heat control valve

Description
1 The heat control valve is used on 1977 non-California USA models. It is mounted on the exhaust manifold and is used to heat the intake manifold fuel vapor during warm-up conditions to improve combustion. Although it has a different purpose, it acts in a similar way to that used on the thermal reactor for California models (see previous Section).

29 High altitude compensation system

Description
1 The high altitude compensation (HAC) system is used to compensate for the over-rich mixtures which tend to occur at higher altitudes due to the lower density of the air.
2 The system operates by allowing additional air to be metered into the low speed circuit of the carburetor at altitudes above 4,000 ft (1,220 m).

Inspection
3 Periodically check the security of the vacuum connections.

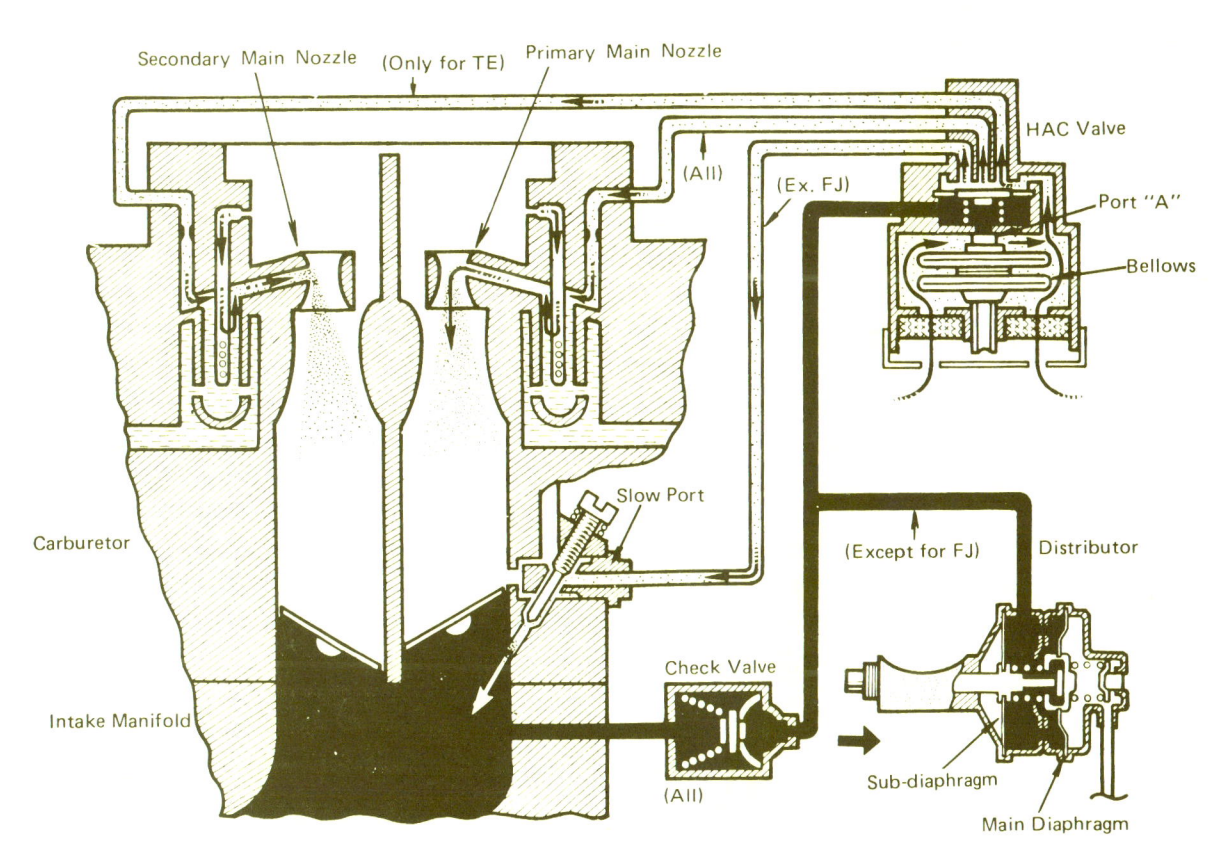

Fig. 3.84. High altitude compensation system - high altitude condition shown
Note: This is a general diagram for Toyota systems. References to models other than FJ should be ignored

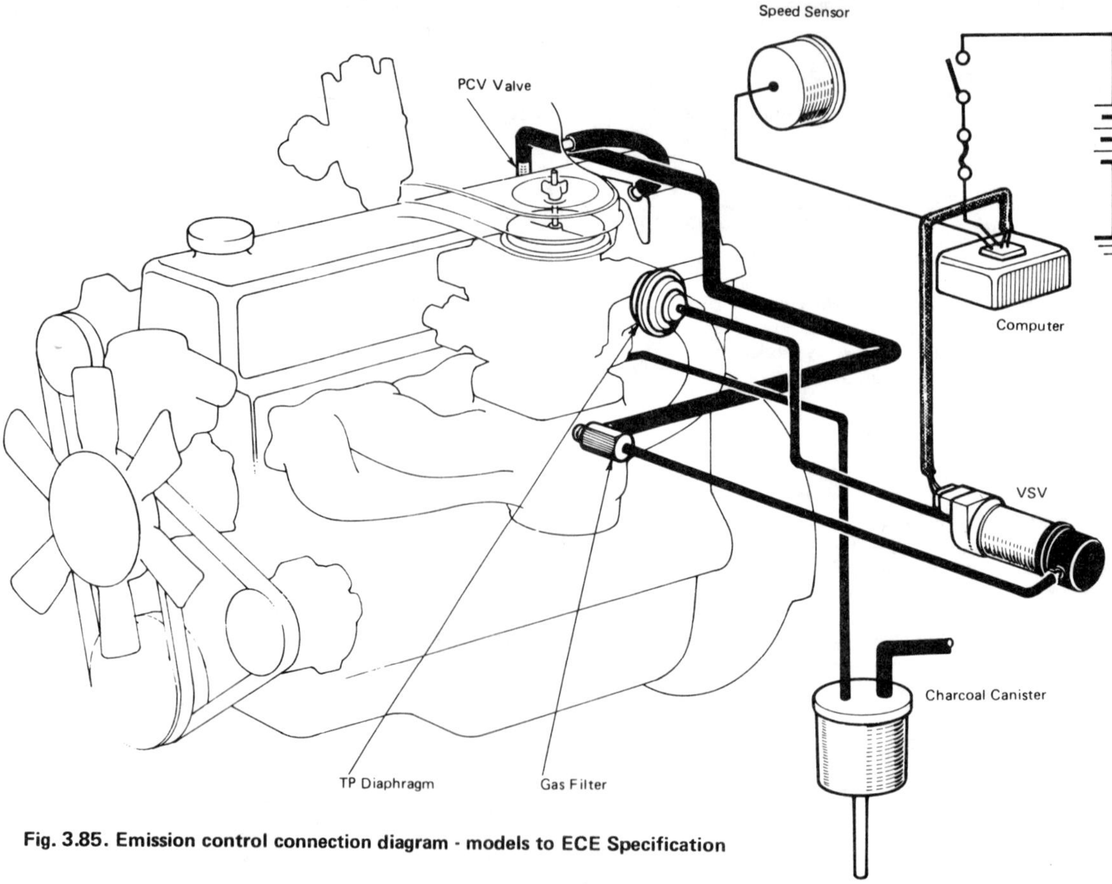

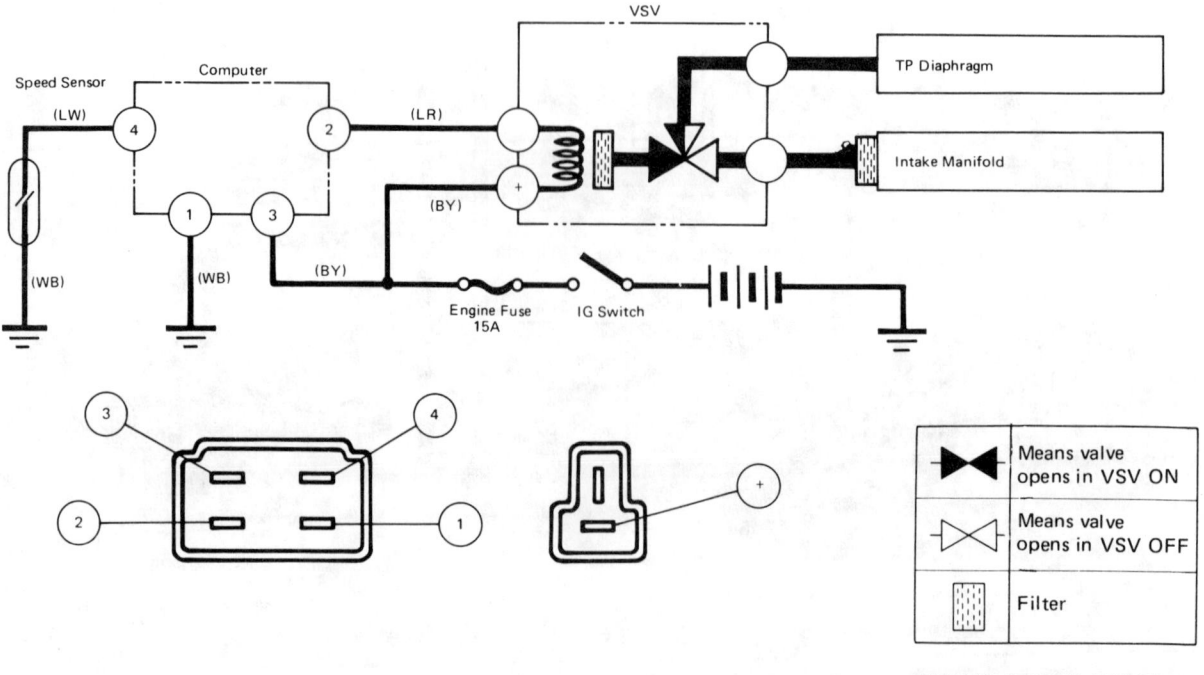

Fig. 3.85. Emission control connection diagram - models to ECE Specification

WIRING COLOR CODES

(R) ..... red (W) ..... white
(L) ..... light purple
(B) ..... black (Y) ..... yellow
Example
(BY) is for black and yellow line

Fig. 3.86. Emission control schematic diagram - models to ECE Specification

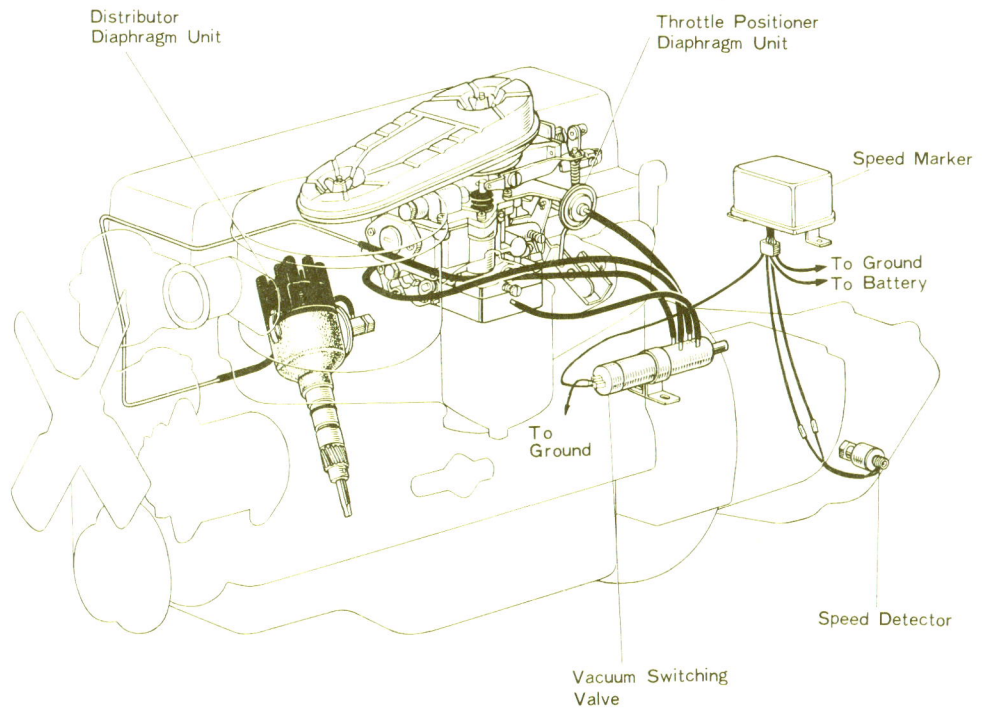

Fig. 3.87. Engine modification system connection diagram - pre-1972 USA models

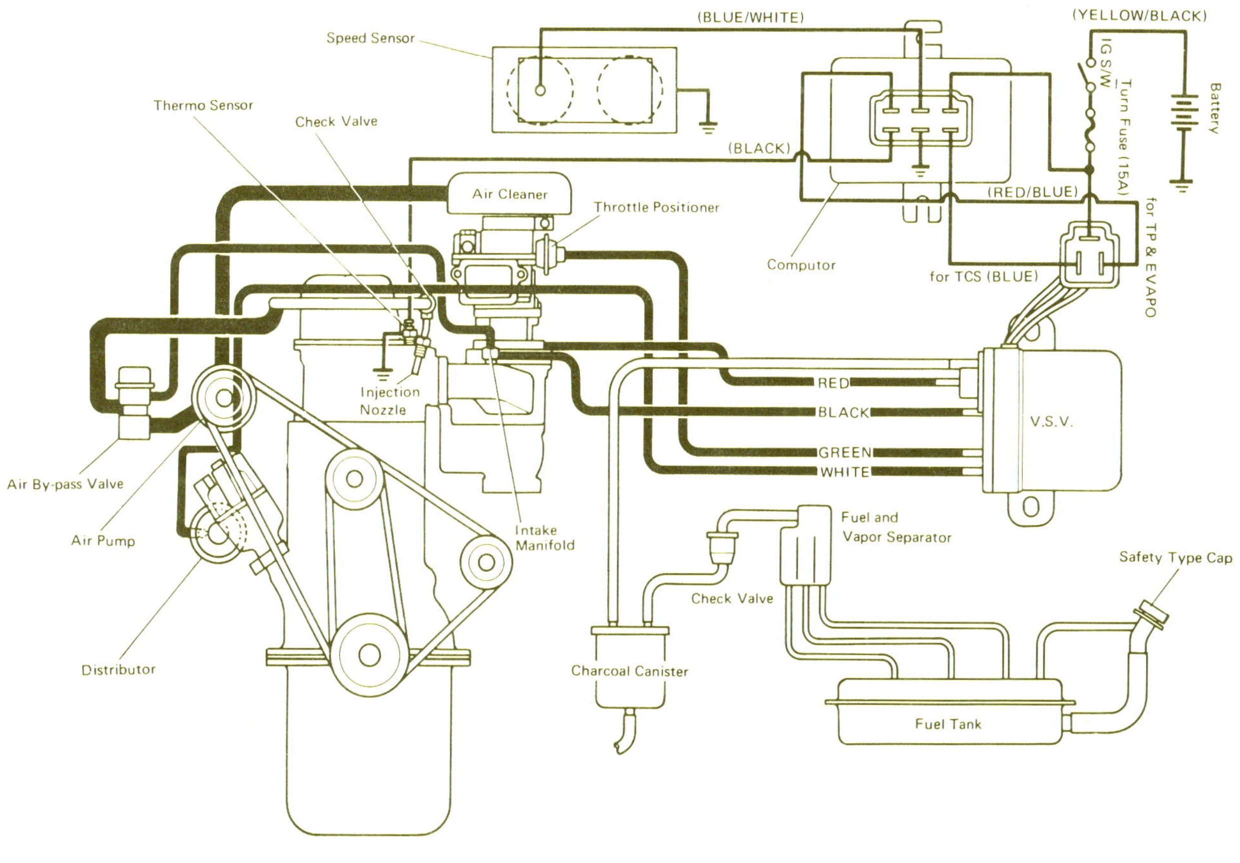

Fig. 3.88. Emission control connection diagram - 1972/73 USA models

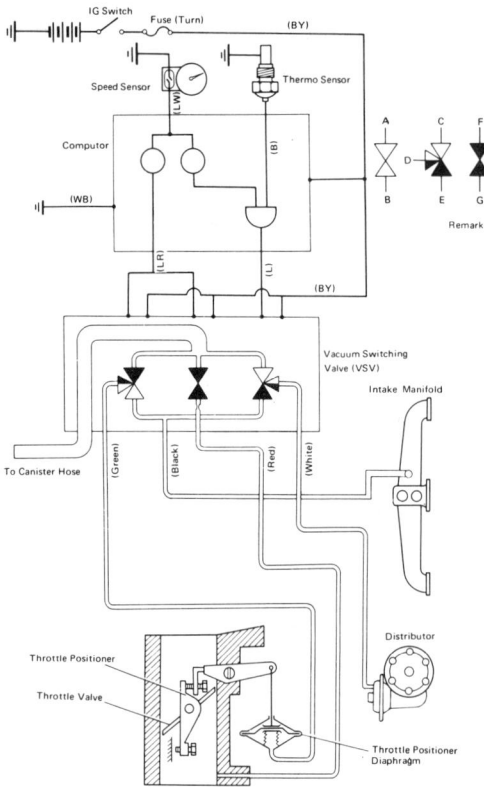

Fig. 3.89. Emission control schematic diagram - 1972/73 USA models

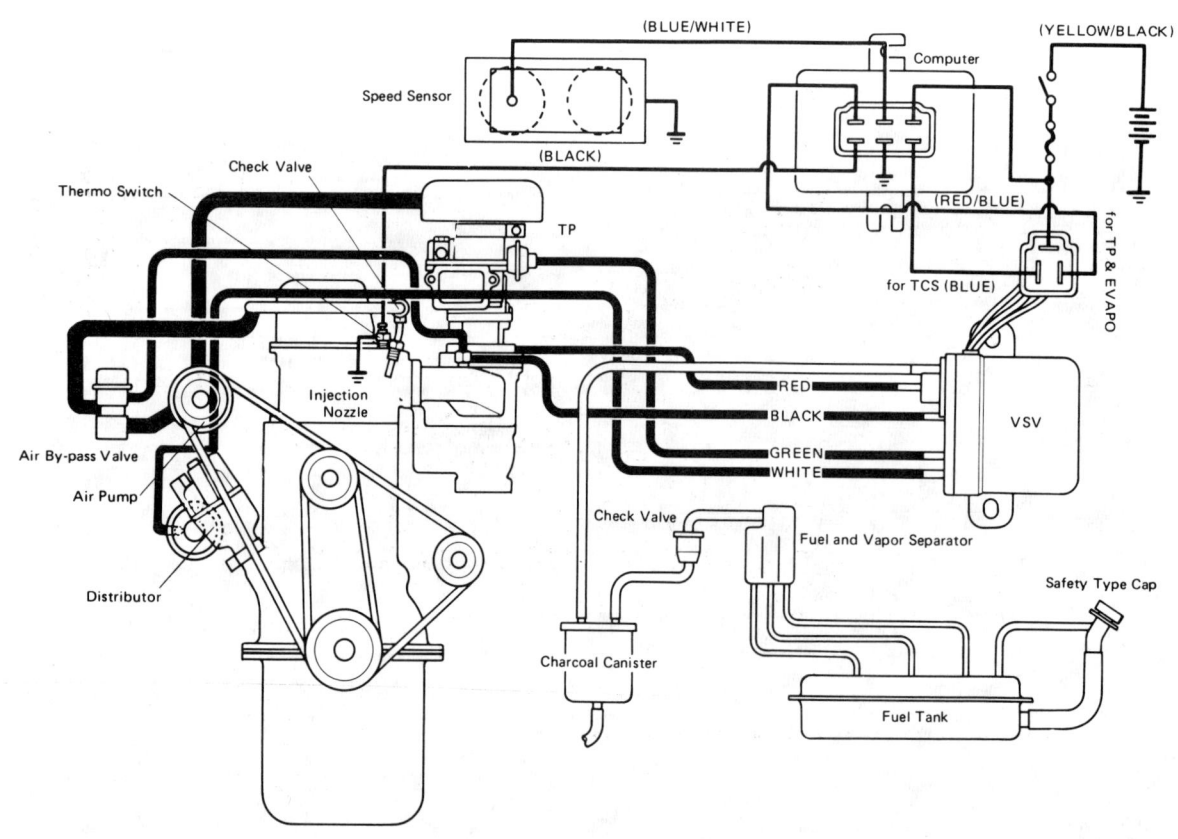

Fig. 3.90. Emission control connection diagram - 1974 USA models, except California

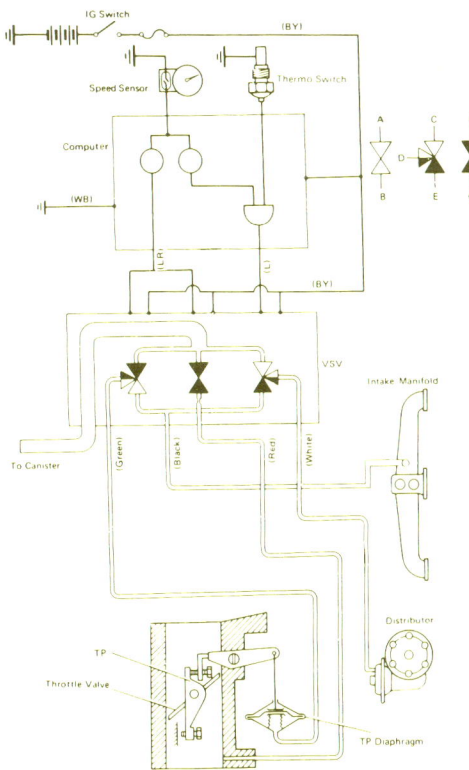

Fig. 3.91. Emission control schematic diagram - 1974 USA models, except California

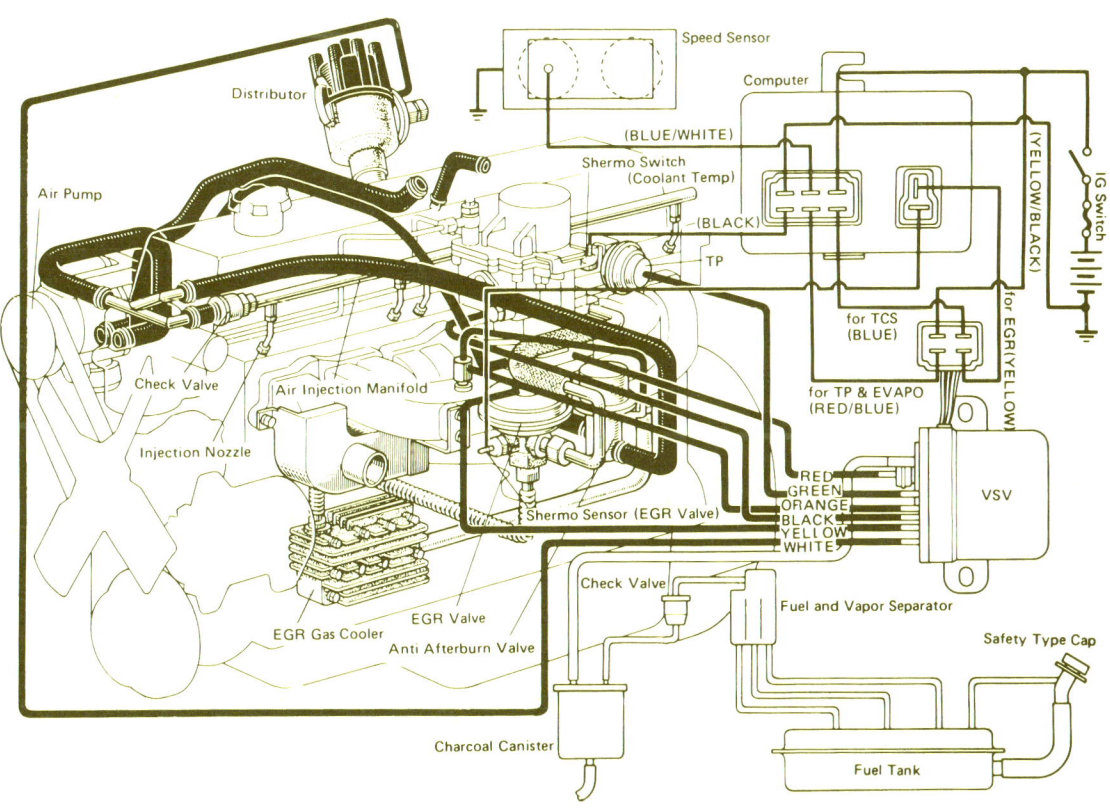

Fig. 3.92. Emission control connection diagram - 1974 California models

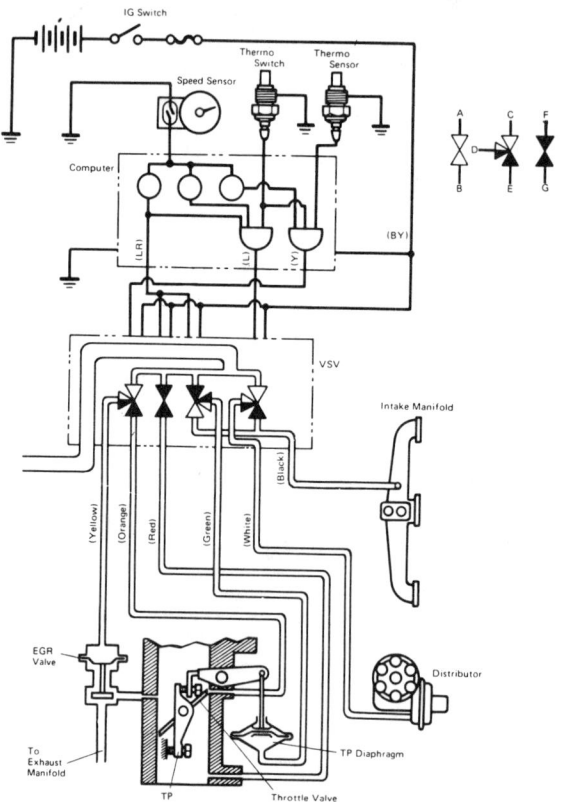

Fig. 3.93. Emission control schematic diagram - 1974 California models

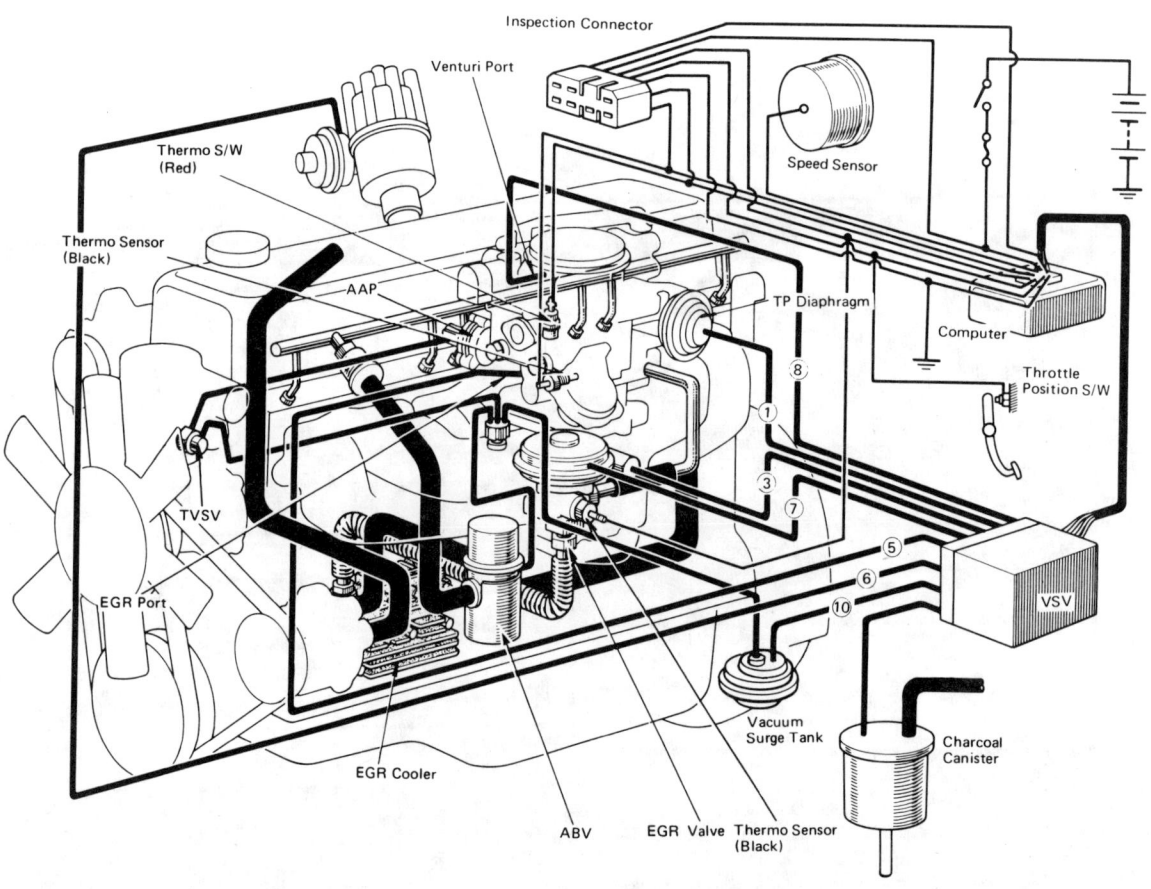

Fig. 3.94. Emission control connection diagram - 1975 USA models, except California

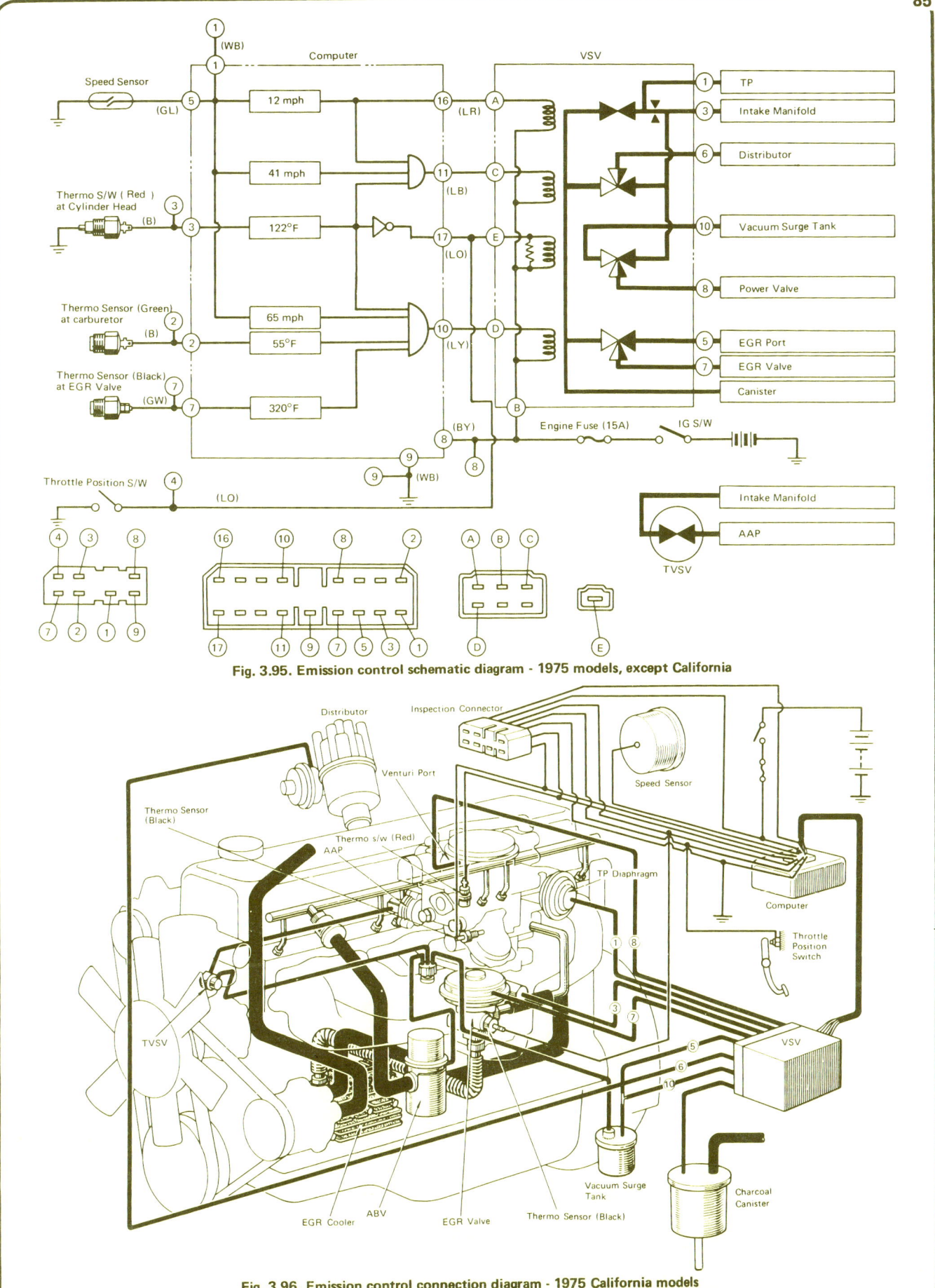

Fig. 3.95. Emission control schematic diagram - 1975 models, except California

Fig. 3.96. Emission control connection diagram - 1975 California models

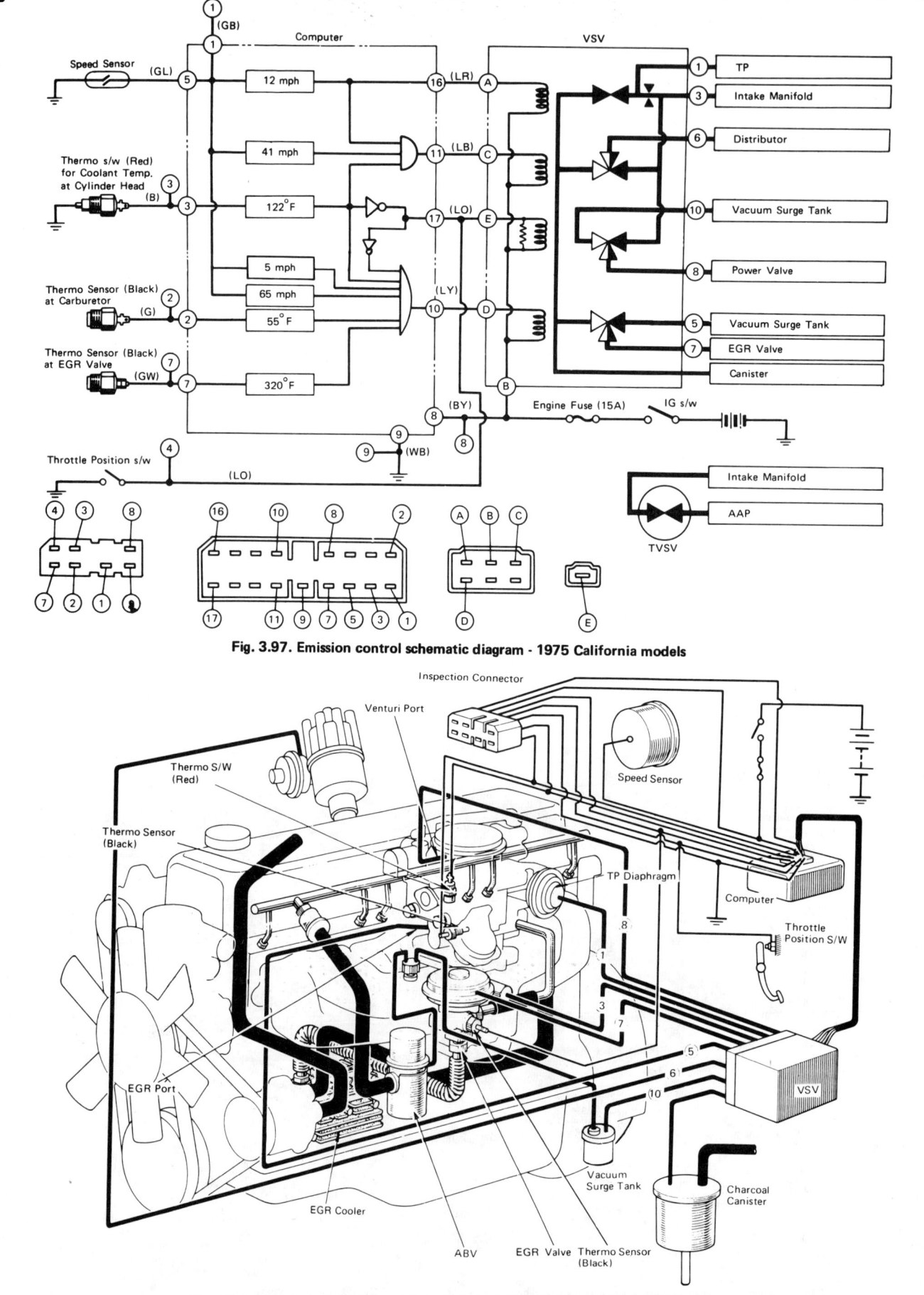

Fig. 3.97. Emission control schematic diagram - 1975 California models

Fig. 3.98. Emission control connection diagram - 1976 USA models, except California

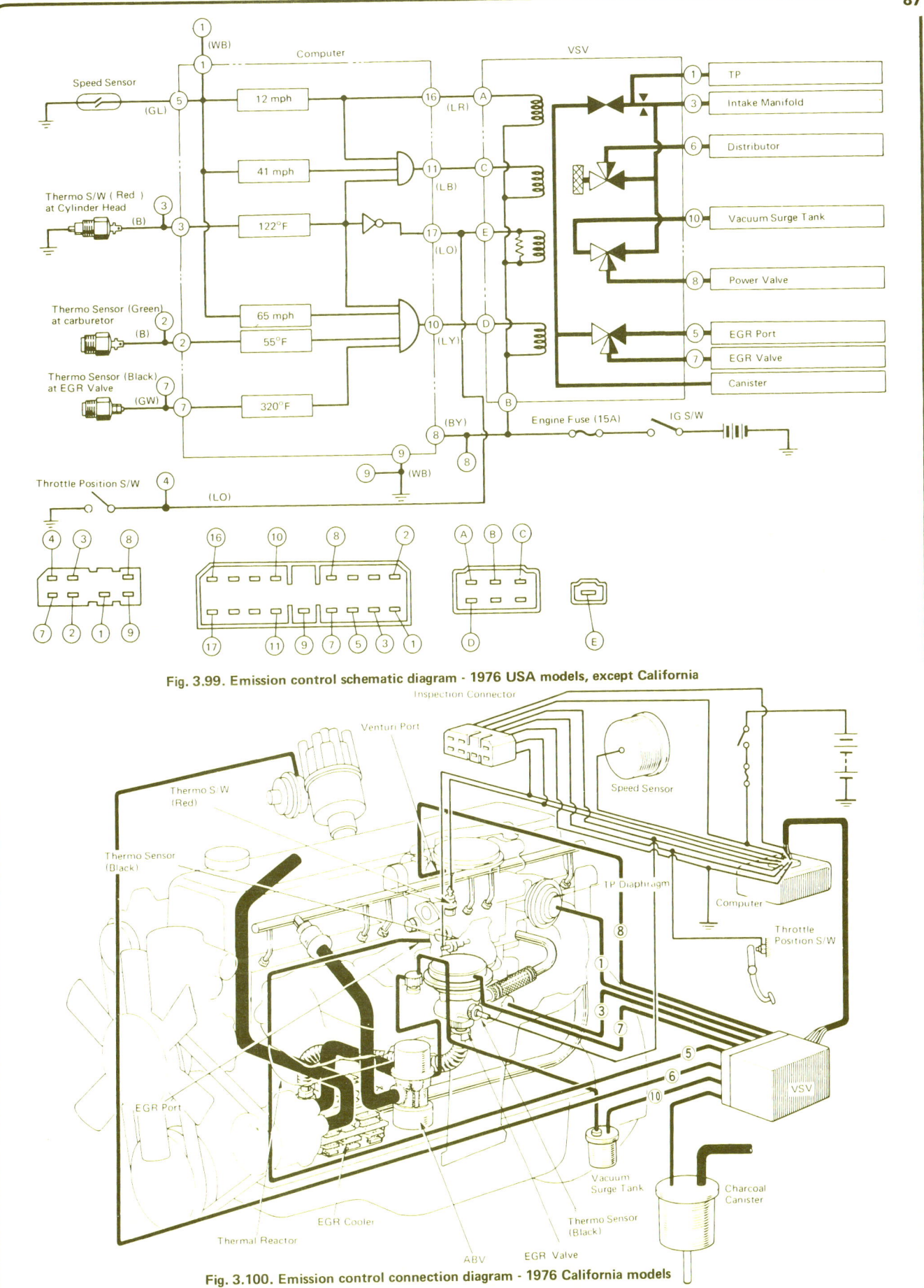

Fig. 3.99. Emission control schematic diagram - 1976 USA models, except California

Fig. 3.100. Emission control connection diagram - 1976 California models

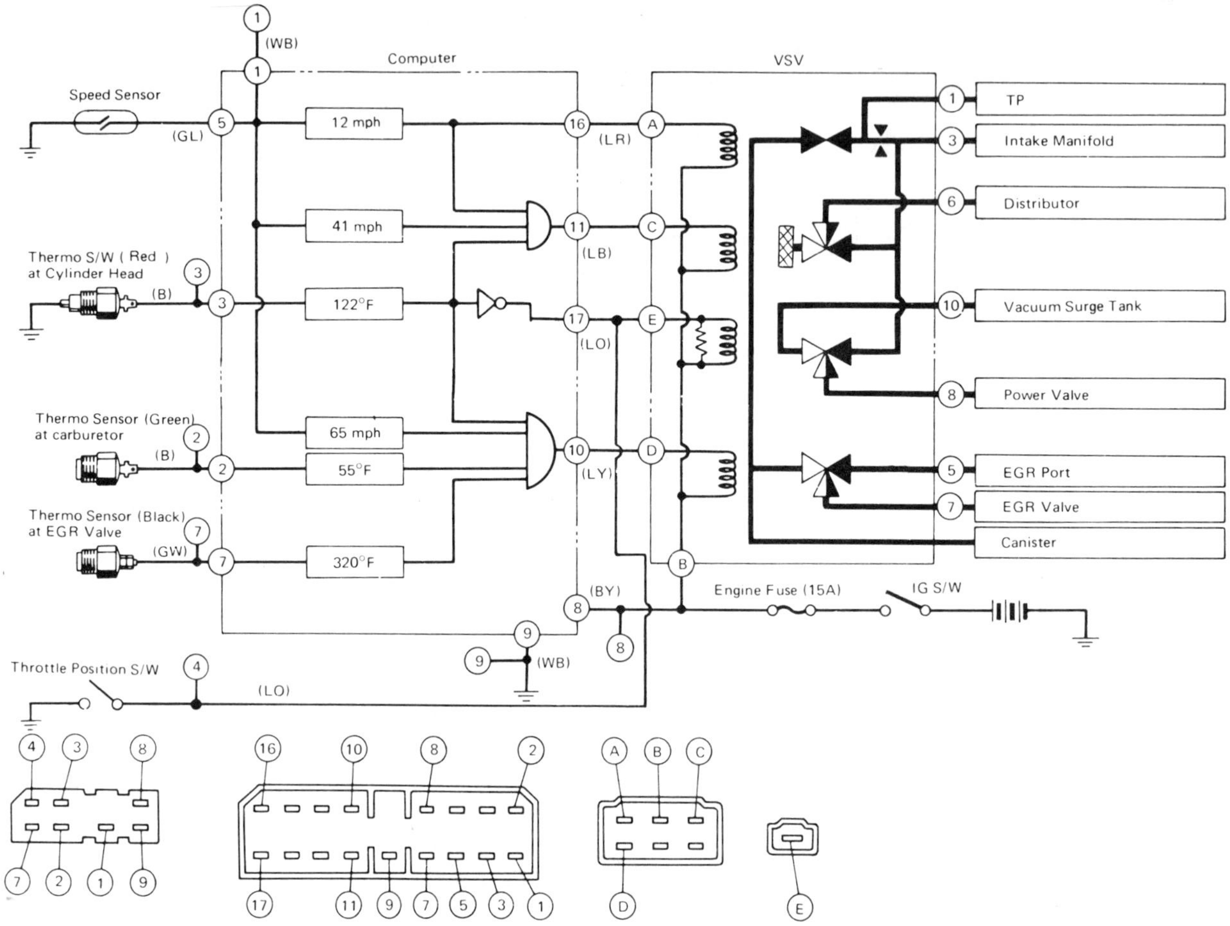

Fig. 3.101. Emission control schematic diagram - 1976 California models

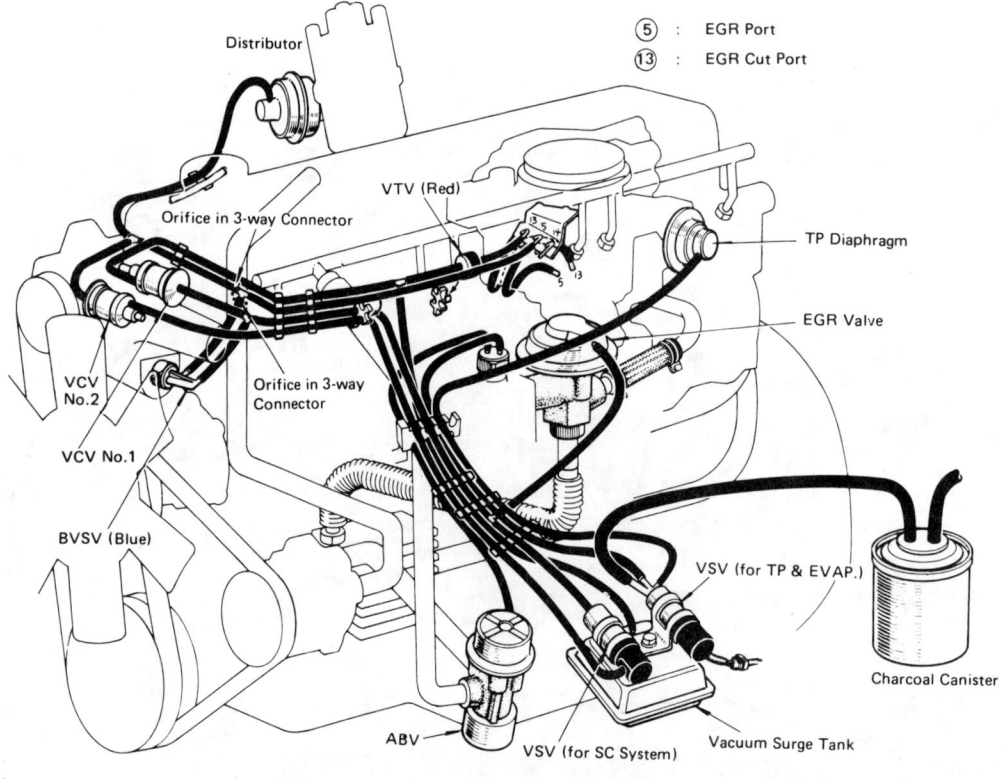

Fig. 3.102. Emission control connection diagram - 1977 USA models, except California

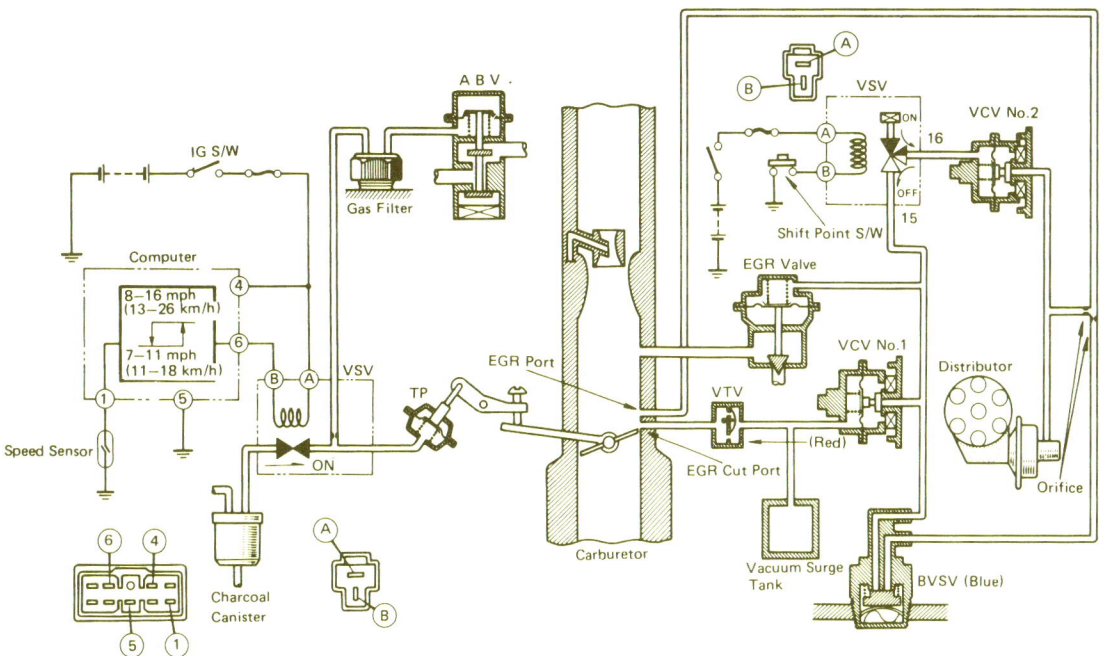

Fig. 3.103. Emission control schematic diagram - 1977 USA models, except California

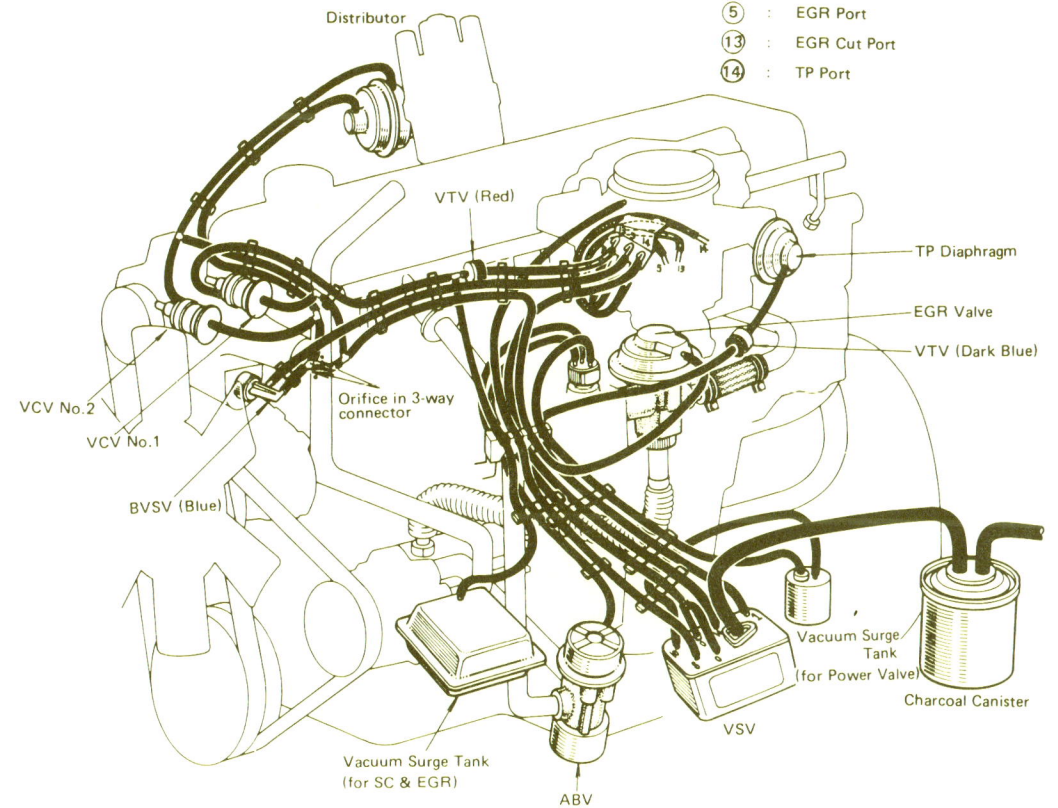

Fig. 3.104. Emission control connection diagram - 1977 California models

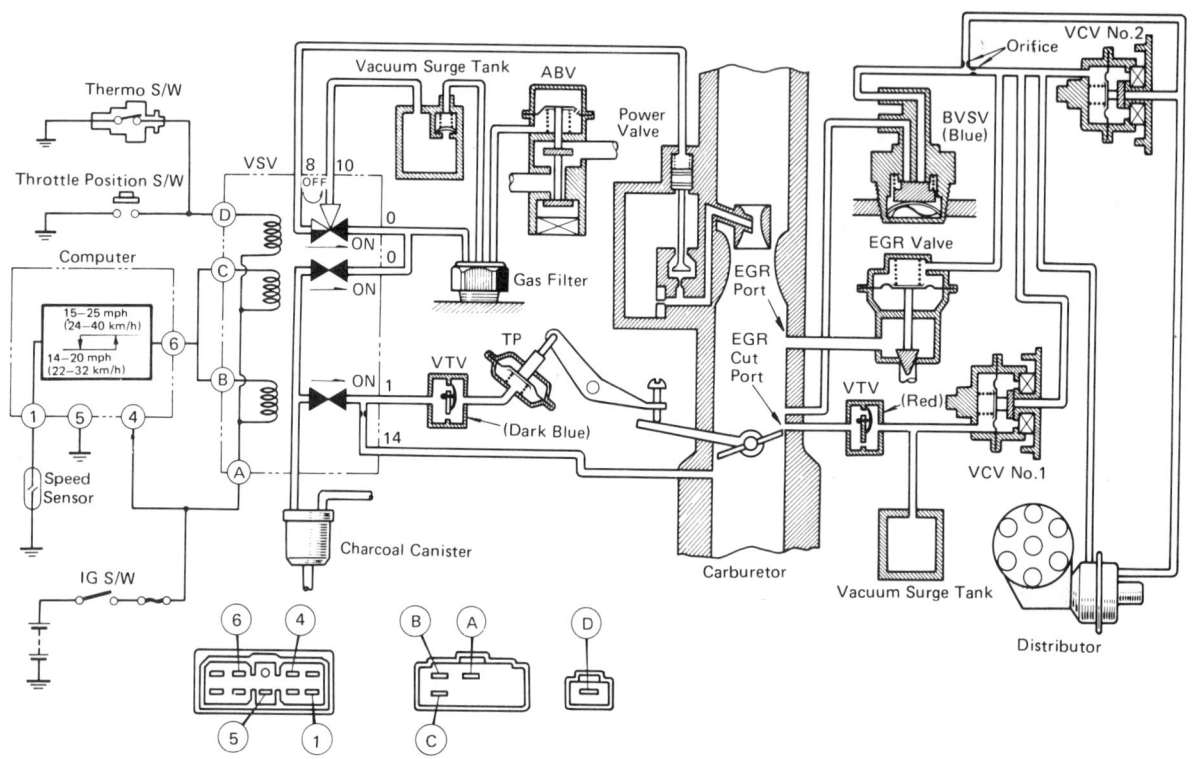

Fig. 3.105. Emission control schematic diagram - 1977 California models

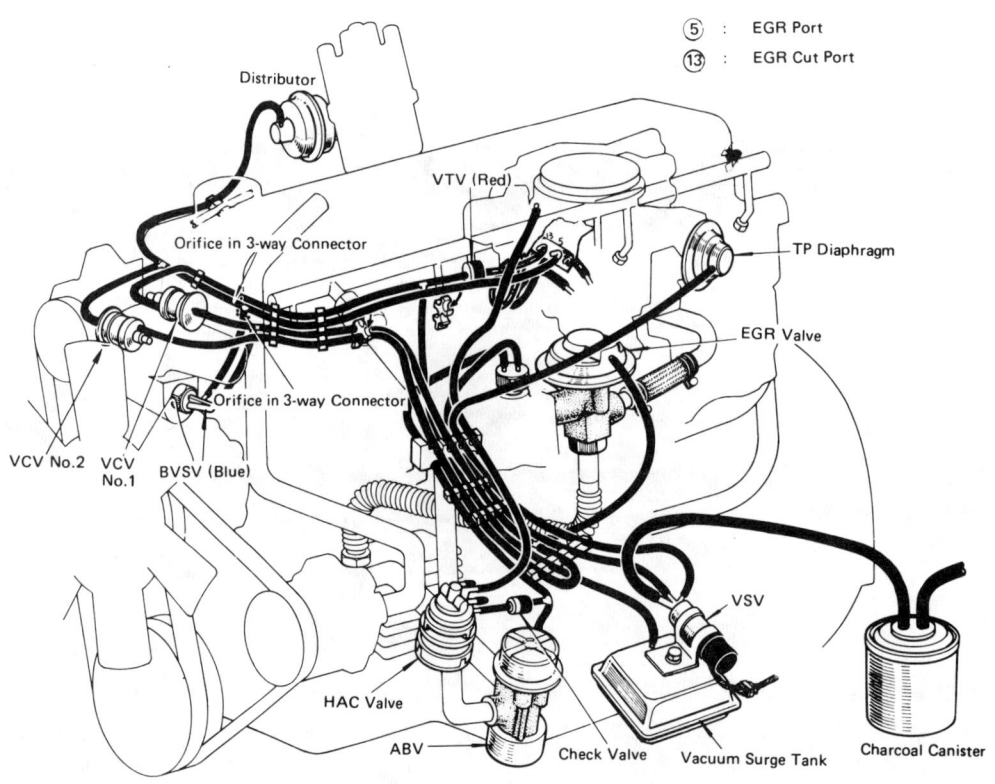

Fig. 3.106. Emission control connection diagram - 1977 high altitude models

Chapter 3/Fuel, exhaust and emission control systems

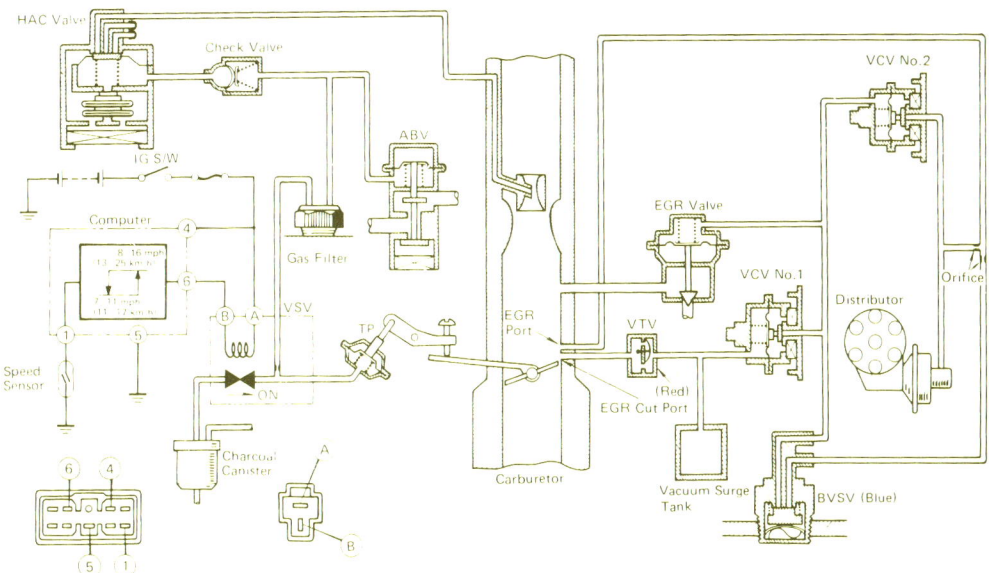

Fig. 3.107. Emission control schematic diagram - 1977 high altitude models

30 Fault diagnosis - fuel system

Unsatisfactory engine performance and excessive fuel consumption are not necessarily the fault of the fuel system or carburetor. In fact they more commonly occur as a result of faults in the emission control system or ignition system. Because of the complexities and interdependence of the components in the emission control system, it is difficult to give a satisfactory diagnostic procedure; however, the checks and adjustments given in this Section are fairly straightforward and should always be carried out when problems occur. Fault finding and servicing of the ignition system should always be carried out before attending to problems which are leading to excessive fuel consumption, erratic or unsatisfactory performance, etc.

The table below assumes that the associated systems are correct.

Symptom	Reason/s	Remedy
Smell of petrol when engine is stopped	Leaking fuel lines or unions Leaking fuel tank	Repair or renew as necessary. Fill fuel tank to capacity and examine carefully at seams, unions, and filler pipe connections. Repair as necessary.
Smell of petrol when engine is idling	Leaking fuel line unions between pump and carburetor Overflow of fuel from float bowl due to wrong level setting or ineffective needle valve or punctured float	Check line and unions and tighten or repair. Check fuel level setting and condition of float and needle valve, and renew if necessary.
Excessive fuel consumption for reasons not covered by leaks or float bowl faults	Worn jets Sticking choke mechanism Accelerator pump incorrectly set	Renew jets. Check correct movement and operation of choke plate. Check and adjust as necessary.
Difficult starting, uneven running, lack of power, cutting out	One or more jets blocked or restricted Float bowl fuel level too low or needle sticking Fuel pump not delivering sufficient fuel Intake manifold gaskets leaking, or manifold fractured Check valve sticking PCV valve stuck open	Dismantle and clean carburetor. Dismantle and check fuel level and needle. Check pump delivery and clean or repair as required. Check tightness of mounting nuts and inspect manifold. Check and replace as necessary. Check and clean as necessary.
Engine will not idle	PCV valve sticking Idle solenoid sticking closed Incorrect idle settings	Check and clean as necessary. Check and replace as necessary. Check and adjust as necessary.
Dieseling (running-on)	Idle solenoid sticking open	Check and replace as necessary.
Engine will not run	Fuel pump inoperative	Check and repair as necessary.

Chapter 4 Ignition system

Contents

Condenser (capacitor) - removal, testing and installation ... 4	Ignition system - fault finding ... 10
Contact breaker points - adjustments ... 2	Ignition system - fault symptoms ... 11
Contact breaker points - removal and installation ... 3	Ignition timing - checking and adjustments ... 6
Distributor - dismantling, inspection and reassembly ... 7	Semi-transistorized ignition unit ... 8
Distributor - removal and installation ... 5	Spark plugs and leads ... 9
General description ... 1	

Specifications

System type ... Battery, coil and contact breaker. Electronic ignition system used on later USA models, commencing with 1974 California models onwards.

Firing order ... 1, 5, 3, 6, 2, 4 (No. 1 cylinder nearest radiator)

Ignition timing
USA models (F engine) ... 7° BTDC at 650 rpm
Other models (F engine) ... 7° BTDC at 500 rpm
All models with 2 F engine ... 7° BTDC at 650 rpm

Distributor
Breaker points gap ... 0.018 in (0.45 mm)
Dwell angle ... 39 to 43°
Condenser capacity (not applicable to electronic ignition) ... 0.22 mfd

Spark plugs
Type (F engine) ... Denso W17ES
NGK B5ES
Type (2 F engine, USA - electronic ignition) ... Denso W14EX
NGK BP5EZ
Type (2 F engine, other markets) ... Denso W14ED
NGK B5ES
Electrode gap
USA models (2 F engine) ... 0.039 in (1.0 mm)
Other models ... 0.031 in (0.8 mm)

Torque wrench setting

	lb f ft	kg f m
Spark plug ...	13	1.8

1 General description

Two different types of ignition system are used on Land Cruiser models. These are conventional contact breaker type and a semi-transistorized system introduced in 1974 for California models.

Conventional type

The ignition system comprises the following components:
The battery which provides a current to the coil.
The ignition/starter switch.
The coil which acts as a transformer to step up the 12 volt battery voltage to many thousands of volts, sufficient to jump the spark plug gaps.
The distributor which comprises, contact breaker, condenser, rotor arm, distributor cap with brush, and centrifugal and vacuum advance and retard mechanism, and is driven by the oil pump drive shaft at half crankshaft speed.
The spark plugs which are the medium to ignite the compressed mixture in the combustion chambers.
Low and high tension wires connecting the various components.
When the ignition is switched on, a current flows from the battery to the ignition switch, through the coil primary winding to the moving contact breaker inside the distributor cap and to earth when the contact breaker points are in the closed position. During this period of points closure, the current flows thru the primary winding of the coil and magnetises the laminated iron core which in turn creates a magnetic field thru the coil primary and secondary windings.
Each time the points open due to the rotation of the distributor cam, the current flow thru the primary winding of the coil is interrupted. This causes the induction of a very high voltage (25000 volts) in the

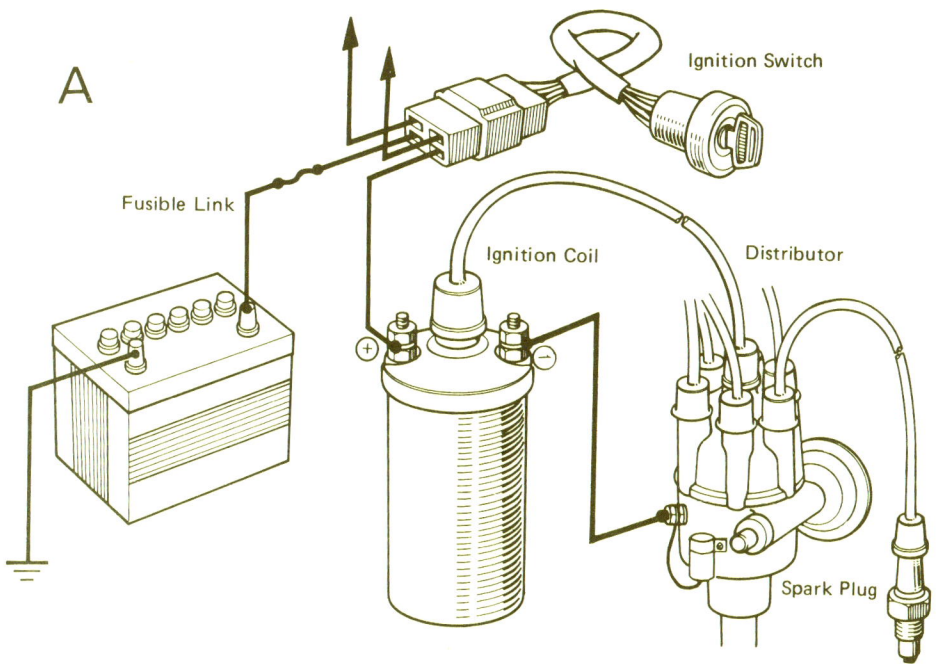
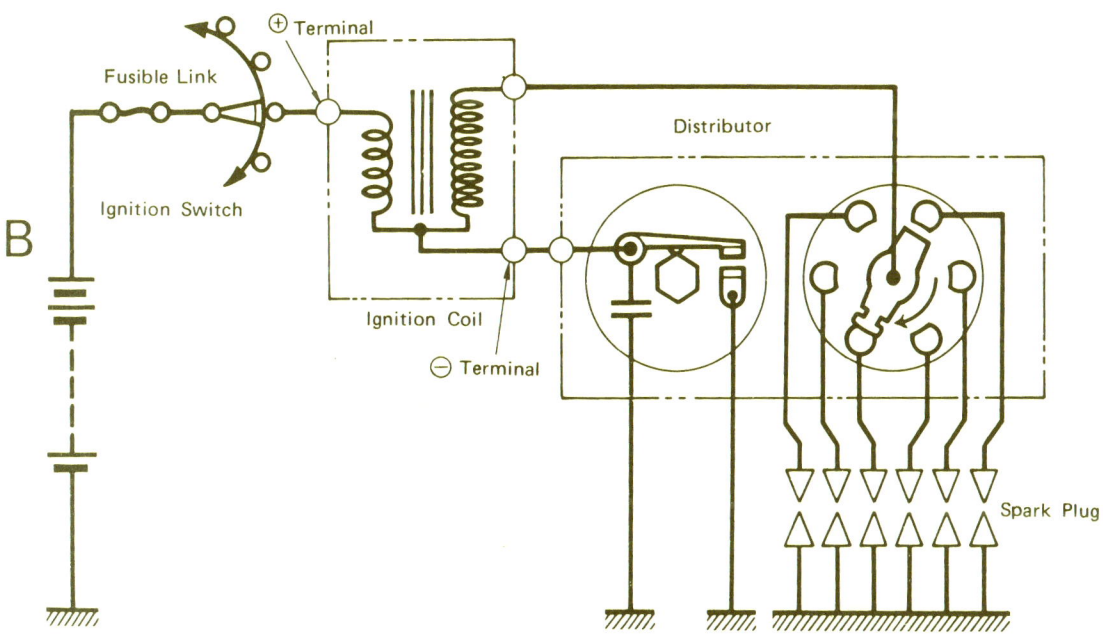

Fig. 4.1. 'Conventional' ignition system

A Component layout   B Circuit diagram

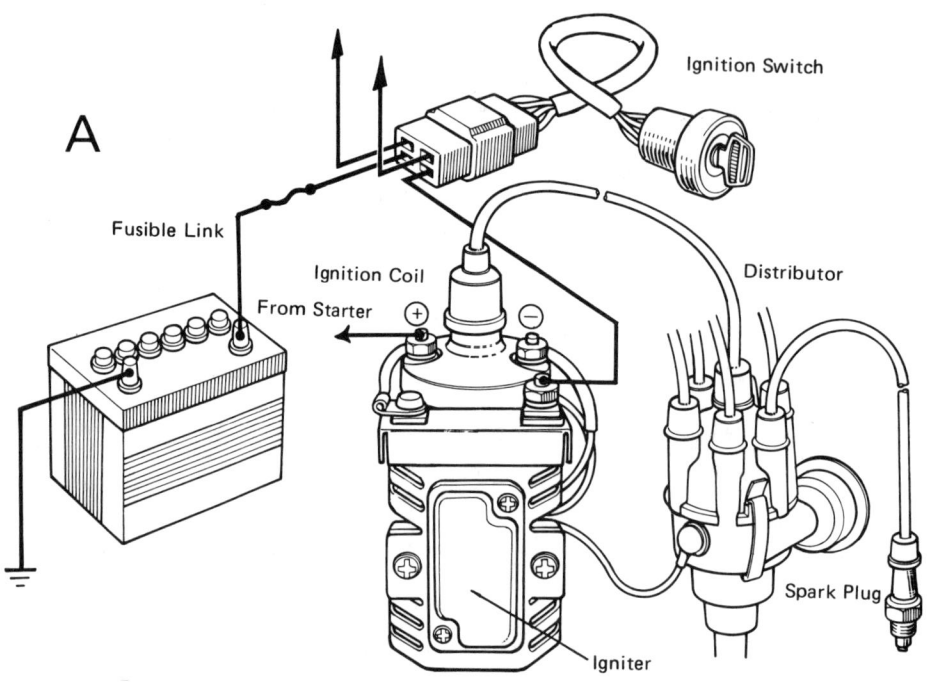
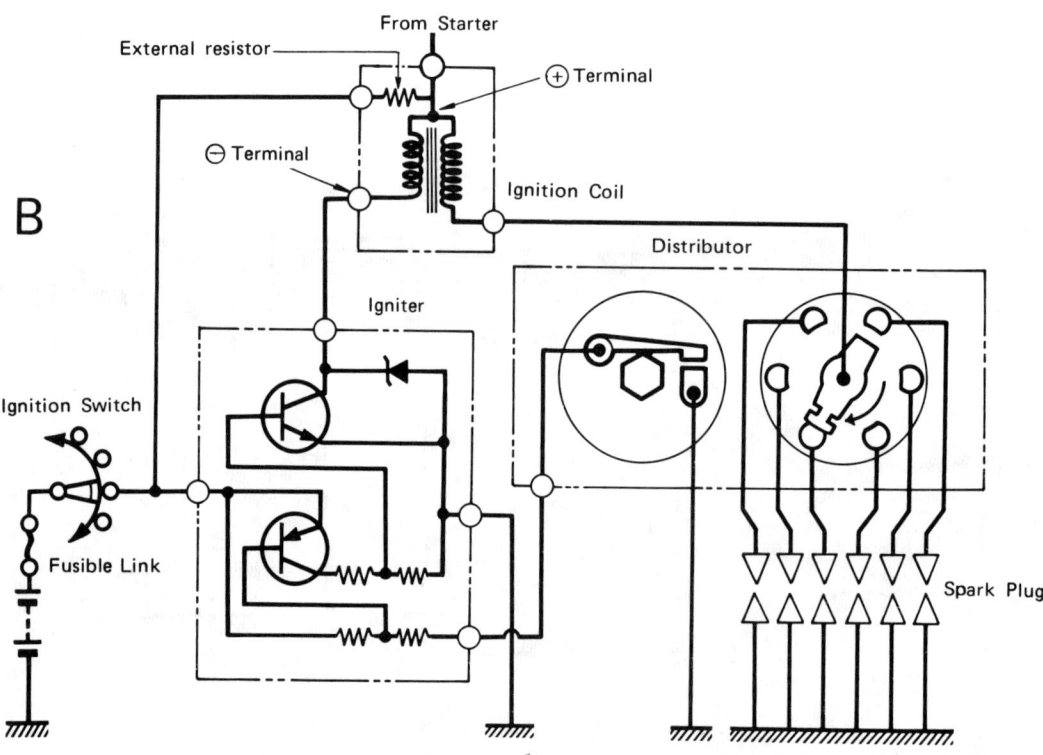

Fig. 4.2. Semi-transistorized ignition system

A Component layout
B Circuit diagram

coil secondary winding. This HT (high tension) current is distributed to the spark plugs in correct firing order sequence by the rotor arm and by means of the cap brush and HT leads.

A condenser is fitted to the distributor, and is connected between the moving contact breaker and ground. It prevents excessive arcing and pitting of the contact breaker points, and also assists in the rapid breakdown of the coil magnetic field.

The actual point of ignition of the fuel/air mixture which occurs a few degrees before TDC is determined by correct static setting of the ignition timing as described in Section 6. The ignition is advanced to meet varying operating conditions by the centrifugal counterweights fitted in the base of the distributor body and by vacuum from the inlet manifold operating thru a capsule linked to the movable distributor baseplate.

Slight variations of the static ignition setting may be made by means of the vernier adjuster to compensate for different fuel qualities.

Semi-transistorized type

In the semi-transistorized ignition circuit, the contact breaker part of the circuit is modified by the deletion of the condenser which is normally connected in parallel with the contact breaker points. Instead, an electronic switching circuit (igniter) is incorporated, which helps to prolong the life of the points and produces an improved spark during starting and slow running conditions.

When the contact breaker points are closed current flows in the path shown in heavy lines in Fig. 4.3; this flows thru the ignition coil primary winding in the same way as with the 'conventional' system.

When the contact breaker points open, no current flows thru the igniter and the coil primary current is switched off. This induces a high coil secondary voltage in a similar manner to that in the 'conventional' system.

In the event of failure of the semi-transistorized system an emergency measure can be taken to prevent the vehicle from being immobilized. This requires a 0.22 mfd condenser being connected to the distributor body terminal and earth, the distributor body terminal being connected to the ignition coil - terminal, and the original igniter terminations being disconnected completely.

Note where a semi-transistorized ignition system is installed it is essential that any tachometer correction is made to the ignition coil - terminal instead of the distributor body terminal. If this is not done, the engine may misfire.

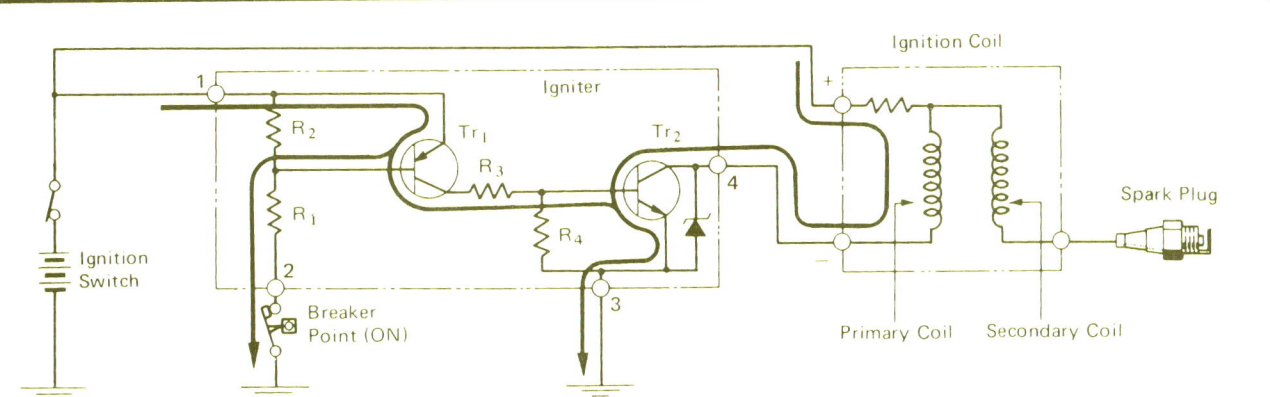

Fig. 4.3. Semi-transistorized ignition system - current flow diagram with points closed

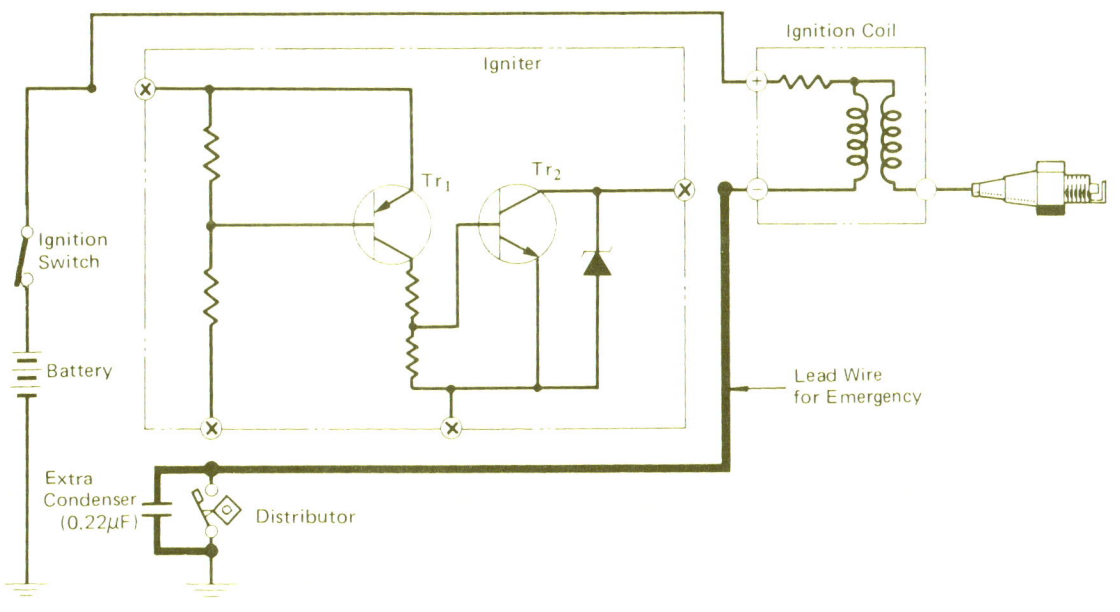

Fig. 4.4. Circuit connections for bypassing semi-transistorized system igniter in the event of failure

2 Contact breaker points - adjustment

1 Pull off the HT leads from the spark plugs and mark them 1 to 6 for easy identification.
2 Spring back the distributor cover securing clips and lift the cover to one side. Withdraw the rotor and the dustproof cover.
3 Using the cranking handle, rotate the engine in its normal direction of rotation until the heel of the movable contact breaker arm is on one of the six high points of the cam. Removal of the spark plugs will make turning the engine easier.
4 Examine the contact faces of the (now open) points, and if they are pitted or burned, they must be removed and dressed as described in the next Section.
5 If the points are in good order, check the gap by inserting a feeler gauge of the specified thickness. Insert the feeler blade in a vertical position and if the gap is correct, it will just fall by its own weight. If the gap is incorrect, adjust the fixed contact arm by loosening the retaining screw slightly and moving it, as necessary, by means of a screwdriver blade inserted in the cut-out in the contact arm.
6 When the gap is correct, tighten the contact arm screw, remove the feeler blade, install the dustproof cover, rotor arm and distributor cap. Reconnect the HT leads. Note: Wherever possible it is recommended that a proprietary dwell angle meter is used for setting the points gap. This should be used in accordance with the manufacturer's instructions.

3 Contact breaker points - removal and installation

1 Carry out operations 1 and 2 of the preceding section.
2 Detach the spring retaining clip from the top of the contact breaker arm pivot post.
3 Unscrew the nuts on the LT terminal on the outside of the distributor body just enough to enable the contact arm lead and spade terminal to be withdrawn, then lift the movable arm from the baseplate.
4 Remove the securing screw and lift the fixed contact breaker arm from the baseplate.
5 Examine the points. After a period of operation, one contact face should have a pip and the other a crater caused by arcing. This is a normal condition which should be removed by dressing the faces squarely on an oilstone.
6 Excessive pitting of the contact points may be caused by operation with an incorrect gap, the voltage regulator setting too high, faulty or wrong type of condenser, distributor baseplate or battery.
7 Where contact breaker points are so badly worn or the pitting so deep that excessive rubbing would be required to eliminate it, then they should be renewed.
8 Wipe the faces of the points with gasoline or alcohol before installing and smear the high points of the cam with petroleum jelly. Apply a drop of engine oil to the pivot points of the contacts and mechanism, to the lubrication pad on top of the cam, and to the lubricator on the distributor body (if installed).
9 Install the rotor, cap and HT leads.

4 Condenser (capacitor) - removal, testing and installation

1 The condenser ensures that with the contact breaker points open, the sparking between them is not so excessive as to cause severe pitting. The condenser is fitted in parallel and its failure will automatically cause failure of the ignition system as the points will be prevented from interrupting the low tension circuit. It is not used with the semi-transistorized ignition system.
2 Testing for an unserviceable condenser may be effected by switching on the ignition and separating the contact points by hand. If this action is accompanied by a blue flash then condenser failure is indicated. Difficult starting, missing of the engine after several miles running or badly pitted points are other indications of a faulty condenser.
3 The surest test is by substitution of a new unit.
4 To remove the condenser, unscrew its retaining screw and detach its lead from the LT terminal on the distributor body.
5 Installation is the reverse of the removal procedure.

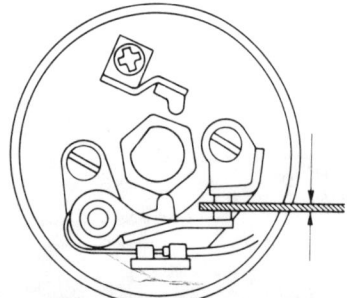

Fig. 4.5. Contact breaker points gap check

2.5a Checking the points gap

2.5b Adjusting points gap

5 Distributor - removal and installation

1 Disconnect the LT wire from the distributor body and the vacuum line from the advance/retard unit.
2 Pull off the HT leads from the spark plugs and mark them 1 to 6 for easy identification. Also remove the ignition coil HT lead.
3 Release the clips and take off the distributor cap.
4 Rotate the engine crankshaft so that the timing mark on the flywheel appears in the inspection window. This is 7° before top dead centre (TDC). Now align the distributor up with the rotor, in its installed attitude, and check that the rotor is pointing towards No. 1 spark plug segment in the cap. If it is pointing towards No. 6 segment, rotate the crankshaft thru 360° (photo).
5 Mark the installed position of the distributor body on the block, and the rotor with respect to the distributor body, for easy installation.
6 Remove the distributor clamp bolts and lift the distributor out.
7 Installation is the reverse of the removal procedure, but it is most important that the original position of installation is retained. Note the position of the slot on the oil pump shaft (see Fig. 4.6).
8 If this position has been lost (for example if the crankshaft was rotated with the distributor removed), set to No. 1 or No. 6 piston at 7° BTDC as described in paragraph 4. Whichever of the two pistons is reaching TDC as the crankshaft is rotated will have the valves of that cylinder closed. This can be checked by feeling the cylinder compression with the spark plugs removed from these cylinders, or by removing the rocker cover and checking which of the two cylinders has its valve rockers 'rocking' (ie; clearance is evident at both valve/rocker contact faces). If necessary, rotate the crankshaft thru 360° so that No. 1 piston is on its compression stroke or its valves rockers are 'rocking'.
9 Using this method, set No. 1 piston to 7° BTDC then align the distributor body above its location hole so that it is approximately as shown in photo 2.5.
10 Position the rotor so that it is approximately aligned with No. 1 spark plug segment in the distributor cap, then rotate it approximately 30° counterclockwise.
11 Install the distributor in this position, noting that the rotor moves clockwise as the gear engages. Adjust the final position if necessary before tightening the clamp bolts.
12 Finally check the ignition timing as described in Section 6.

6 Ignition timing - checking and adjustment

1 If the ignition timing point has been lost completely, it will be necessary to check that the distributor is installed in the correct position with regard to the crankshaft. This is dealt with in Section 5.
2 To check the static ignition timing, first check the distributor points gap and/or dwell angle as previously described (Section 2).
3 Rotate the crankshaft to get No. 1 piston at 7° BTDC as described in paragraph 4, of Section 5.
4 Connect a 12v bulb of 5 watts maximum rating between a ground point on the engine and the terminal on the distributor body.
5 Switch on the ignition. If the timing is correctly set the bulb should have just illuminated at this point, but it will be necessary to rotate the crankshaft slightly less than 1 revolution to check it (this will, in effect, time the engine on No. 6 cylinder, but this is not important).
6 Check the point at which the bulb *just* illuminates; this should be as the timing mark aligns with the pointer. If the bulb illuminates before the mark on the flywheel reaches the pointer, the ignition is too far advanced, and the distributor must be turned clockwise a little to correct it. On distributors with a micrometer adjustment (octane selector), this check should be done with the adjuster set at the 'standard' line. If the bulb illuminates after the mark on the flywheel reaches the pointer, the ignition is too far retarded and the distributor must be turned counter-clockwise a little.
7 After any adjustment, tighten the distributor clamp bolts and recheck the setting.
8 Having checked the static setting, the timing should be set dynamically with the engine running at idle speed using a stroboscopic lamp in accordance with the manufacturer's instructions. It may be necessary to reposition the distributor very slightly now, or, where applicable, to alter the octane selector slightly. (One graduation of the adjuster scale is equal to 5.2° of distributor advance or retard). No variation in timing should be obtained whether the distributor vacuum line is connected or not at idle speed.
9 With the engine idling and the vacuum line disconnected, check that the timing point varies with throttle opening. This checks that the centrifugal advance is functioning.
10 With the engine idling, detach the vacuum hose and apply suction (by mouth) to the distributor diaphragm. For USA models (retard diaphragm, suction pipe on distributor side of diaphragm), the timing should now retard; for other models (advance diaphragm, suction pipe on outer side of diaphragm) the ignition should advance.
11 It may be found that minor adjustment is necessary to prevent 'pinging' from the engine when laboring or when a low octane fuel is used; in this event, retard the ignition slightly (octane selector moved towards R mark on distributor). Where higher octane fuels are used it may be found possible to advance the ignition slightly (octane selector moved towards A mark on distributor).

7 Distributor - dismantling, inspection and reassembly

Note: The procedure given in this Section is basically that for the 'conventional' distributor. The semi-transistorized ignition system distributor is very similar except that a different breaker plate and diaphragm unit are used. Also the breaker plate carries a damping

5.4 The engine timing marks on the flywheel housing. Note the plate which covers the inspection window

Fig. 4.6. Oil pump driveshaft position

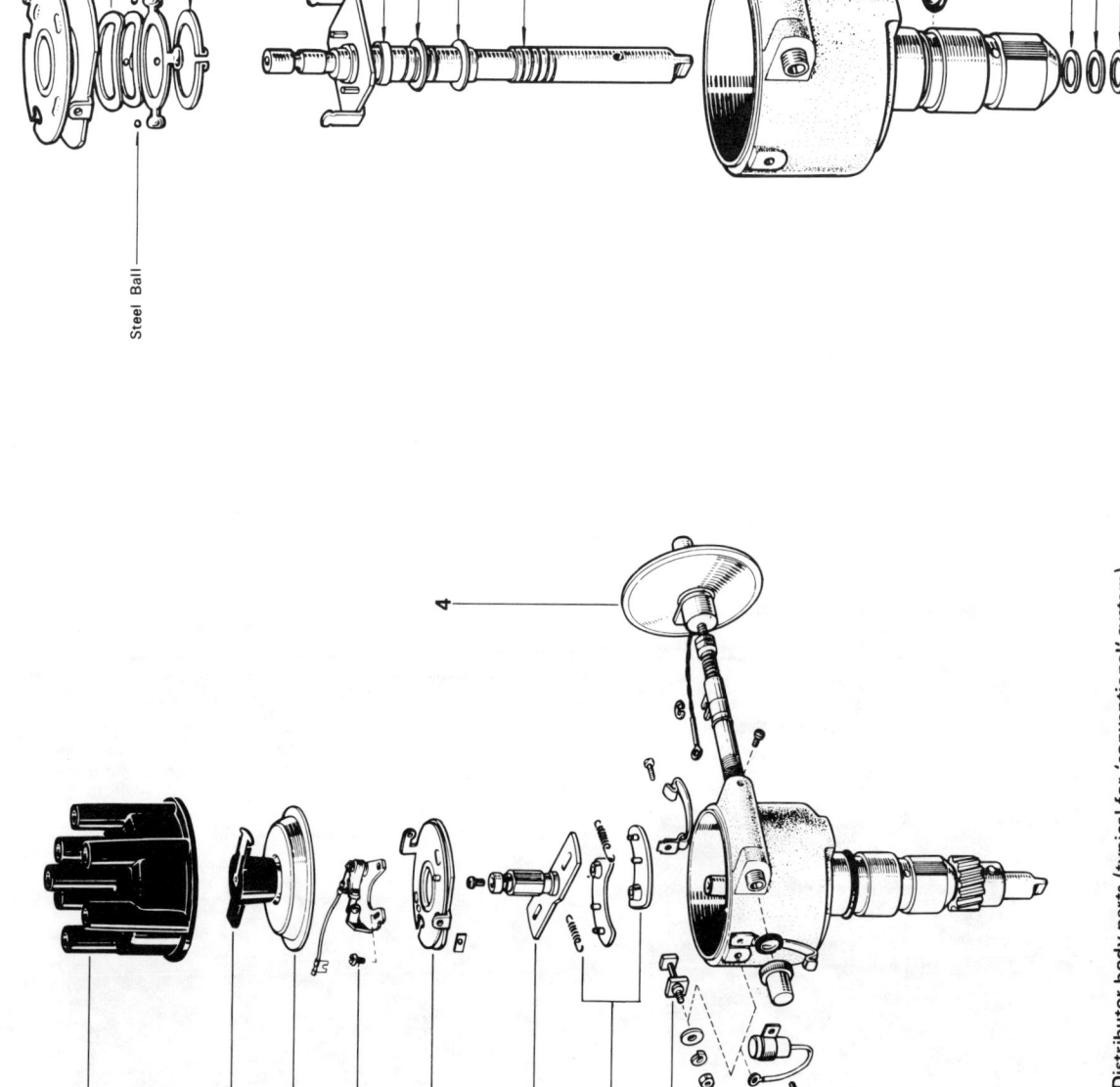

Fig. 4.7. Distributor body parts (typical for 'conventional' system)

1 Cap, rotor and cover
2 Terminal and condenser
3 Breaker points
4 Diaphragm unit (advance)
5 Breaker plate
6 Cam
7 Springs and weights

Note: On some models the condenser is mounted on the breaker plate, not on the body

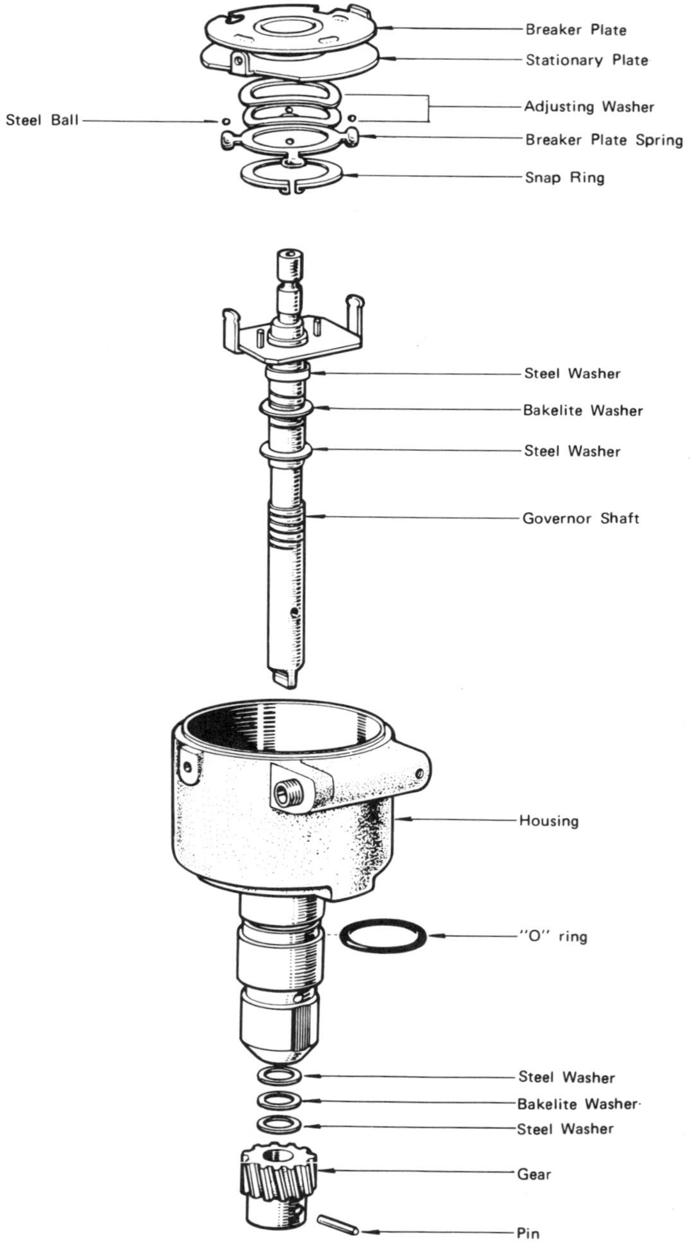

Fig. 4.8. Distributor rotating parts (typical for 'conventional' system)

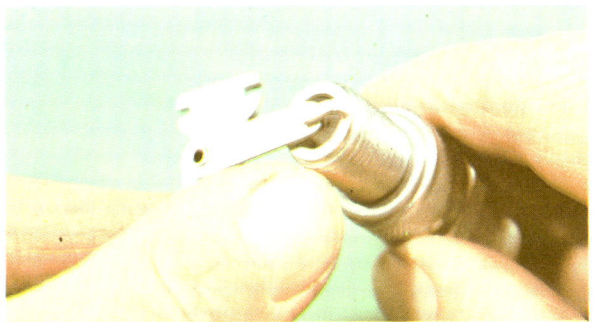

Measuring plug gap. A feeler gauge of the correct size (see ignition system specifications) should have a slight 'drag' when slid between the electrodes. Adjust gap if necessary

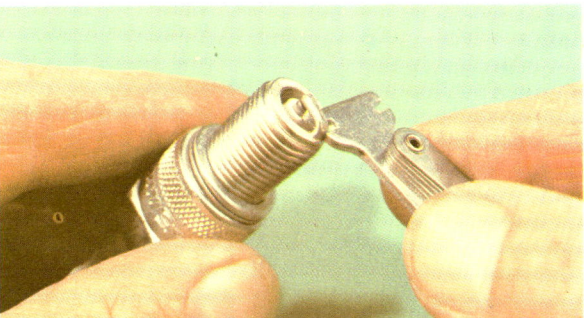

Adjusting plug gap. The plug gap is adjusted by bending the earth electrode inwards, or outwards, as necessary until the correct clearance is obtained. Note the use of the correct tool

Normal. Grey-brown deposits lightly coated core nose. Gap increasing by around 0.001 in (0.025 mm) per 1000 miles (1600 km). Plugs ideally suited to engine and engine in good condition

Carbon fouling. Dry, black, sooty deposits. Will cause weak spark and eventually misfire. Fault: over-rich fuel mixture. Check: carburettor mixture settings, float level and jet sizes; choke operation and cleanliness of air filter. Plugs can be re-used after cleaning

Oil fouling. Wet, oily deposits. Will cause weak spark and eventually misfire. Fault: worn bores/piston rings or valve guides; sometimes occurs (temporarily) during running-in period. Plugs can be re-used after thorough cleaning

Overheating. Electrodes have glazed appearance, core nose very white - few deposits. Fault: plug overheating. Check: plug value, ignition timing, fuel octane rating (too low) and fuel mixture (too weak). Discard plugs and cure fault immediately

Electrode damage. Electrodes burned away; core nose has burned, glazed appearance. Fault: initial pre-ignition. Check: as for 'Overheating' but may be more severe. Discard plugs and remedy fault before piston or valve damage occurs

Split core nose (may appear initially as a crack). Damage is self-evident, but cracks will only show after cleaning. Fault: pre-ignition or wrong gap-setting technique. Check: ignition timing, cooling system, fuel octane rating (too low) and fuel mixture (too weak). Discard plugs, rectify fault immediately

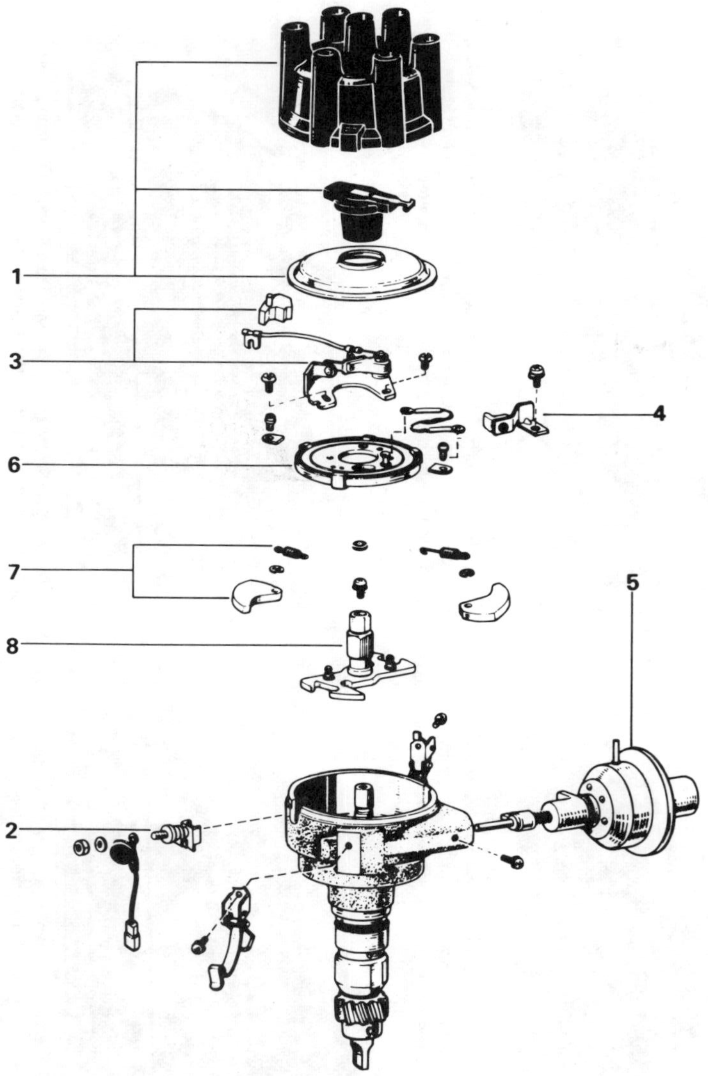

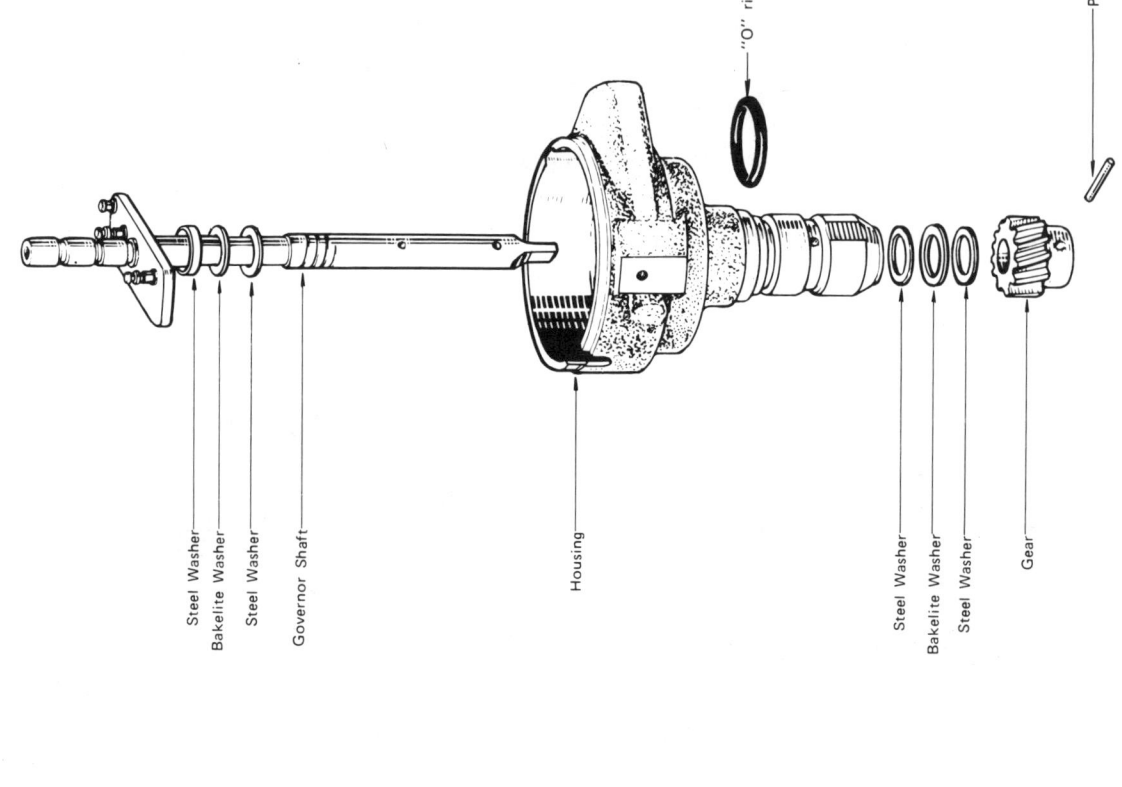

Fig. 4.10. Distributor rotating parts (typical for semi-transistorized systems)

Fig. 4.9. Distributor body parts (typical for semi-transistorized system)

1 Cap, rotor and cover
2 Terminal
3 Breaker points and cover
4 Damping spring
5 Diaphragm unit (retard)
6 Breaker plate
7 Springs and weights
8 Cam

spring. When spare parts are required, ensure that they are correct for the type of distributor being serviced.

1 Remove the distributor from the engine as described in Section 5.
2 Remove the cap, rotor arm and dust proof cover.
3 Remove the contact breaker arms as described in Section 3. Unscrew the cap from the vernier adjuster.
4 Remove the vacuum diaphragm unit by withdrawing the retaining screws and the circlip.
5 Remove the distributor cap retaining spring clips, the externally mounted condenser and the LT terminal.
6 Remove the contact breaker arm mounting plate and the baseplate.
7 Pick out the rubber cap from the top of the distributor shaft; unscrew and remove the central cam screw and remove the cam.
8 Remove the counter weights and springs.
9 Carefully drill out the peened end of the pin which secures the spiral gear and the spacer collar at the bottom end of the distributor shaft. Drive out the pin and retain the shaft washers.
10 Withdraw the shaft upwards thru the body.
11 Check for wear between the shaft and the body. If evident it will be more economical to exchange the complete distributor unit for a reconditioned one rather than attempt to repair the old unit.
12 Check the fit of the counter weights on their pivot posts. The maximum clearance is 0.008 in (0.2 mm).
13 Examine the distributor cap for cracks and for burned or eroded contacts. Check the carbon brush in the centre of the cap interior, if it has worn below 0.28 in (7 mm) in length, renew it.
14 Separate the contact breaker swivel plate from the baseplate. Do this by removing the circlip and carefully detaching the small components. Do not lose the rolling balls. Renew any items which are worn or distorted.
15 Check the teeth on the spiral gear and renew the gear if they are worn or chipped.
16 Lubricate the shaft with clean engine oil and insert it into the distributor body.
17 Install thrust washers, spacer and spiral gear. Insert a new pin but do not peen the end until the shaft end float has been checked. The correct end float should be between 0.006 and 0.020 in (0.15 and 0.5 mm). Test with feeler blades inserted between the end of the distributor body and the face of the washer. If the endfloat is incorrect, remove the pin and substitute the adjusting washer for one of different thickness. If the endfloat is within the specified tolerance, rivet the ends of the pin. Note that the plastic washer must be located between the steel washers.
18 Smear the recommended grease onto the sliding surface of the baseplate and reassemble the sliding plate and components to it. Gently pull the two plates apart using screwdrivers inserted at opposite sides and measure the clearance between them. This should not exceed 0.008 in (0.2 mm), if it does remove one of the adjusting washers. When correctly installed, the sliding plate should move smoothly on the baseplate with an applied force of not more than 500 grams (1.1 lb).
19 Install the counter weight and springs. Oil the counter weight pivot holes.
20 Smear grease on the upper end of the distributor shaft, fit the cam to it and tighten the cam central retaining screw. Fill the recess in the top of the cam above the screw with recommended grease and seal with the rubber cap. Note that on the semi-transistorized distributor, the cam '15' mark must be aligned with the stopper.
21 Install the baseplate assembly into the distributor body and secure it with the screws which retain the distributor cap clips in position.
22 Install the vacuum diaphragm unit and the condenser and the contact breaker arms. On semi-transistorized distributors, adjust the damping spring gap to 0.004/0.016 in (0.1/0.4 mm).
23 Install the LT terminal to the distributor body and connect the condenser and contact breaker arms to it.
24 Set the octane selector to the 'standard' position then screw on the cap. Renew the O-ring on the lower body.
25 Install the distributor to the engine block

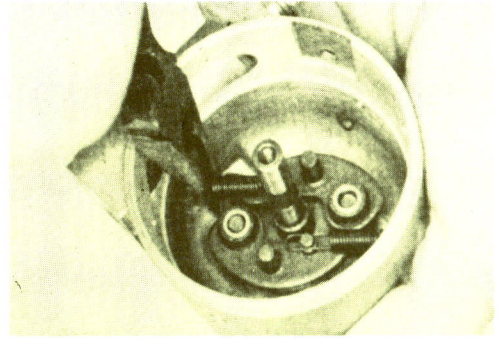

Fig. 4.11. Installing governor weights (conventional distributor)

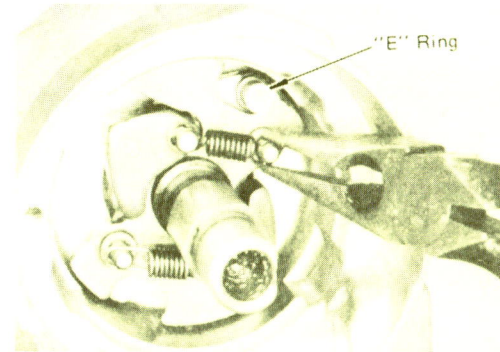

Fig. 4.12. Installing governor weights (semi-transistorized distributor)

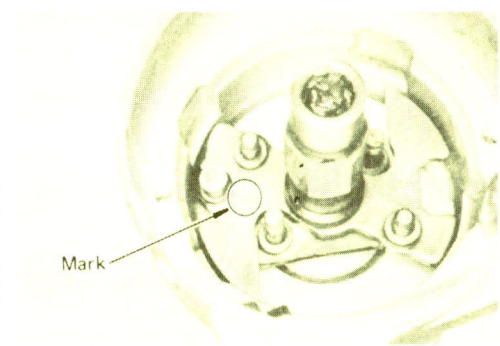

Fig. 4.13. Align the '15' mark with the stopper (semi-transistorized distributor)

8 Semi-transistorized ignition unit

1 This unit requires no maintenance apart from being kept clean and dry externally. In the event of malfunction, it can be by-passed as described in Section 1. If an internal fault occurs it should be repaired by a Toyota dealer, or an exchange unit obtained.

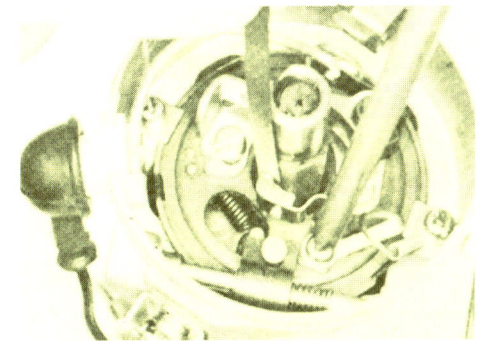

Fig. 4.14. Adjusting damping spring gap (semi-transistorized distributor)

9 Spark plugs and leads

The correct functioning of the spark plugs is vital for the correct running and efficiency of the engine. The plugs fitted as standard are listed in the Specification page.

2 At the intervals stated in Routine Maintenance the plugs should be removed, examined, cleaned and, if worn excessively, replaced. The condition of the spark plug will also tell much about the overall condition of the engine.

3 If the insulator nose of the spark plug is clean and white, with no deposits, this is indicative of a weak mixture, or too hot a plug. (A hot plug transfers heat away from the electrode slowly - a cold plug transfers it away quickly).

4 If the top and insulator nose is covered with hard black looking deposits, then this is indicative that the mixture is too rich. Should the plug be black and oily, then it is likely that the engine is fairly worn, as well as the mixture being too rich.

5 If the insulator nose is covered with light tan to greyish brown deposits, then the mixture is correct and it is likely that the engine is in good condition.

6 If there are any traces of long brown tapering stains on the outside of the white portion of the plug, then the plug will have to be renewed, as this shows that there is a faulty joint between the plug body and the insulator, the compression is being allowed to leak away.

7 Plugs should be cleaned by a sand blasting machine, which will free them from carbon more thoroughly than cleaning by hand. The machine will also test the condition of the plugs under compression. Any plug that fails to spark at the recommended pressure should be renewed.

8 The spark plug gap is of considerable importance, as, if it is too large or too small the size of the spark and its efficiency will be seriously impaired. The spark plug gap should be set to the gap given in the Specifications.

9 To set it, measure the gap with a feeler gauge, and then bend open, or close the outer plug electrode until the correct gap is achieved. The centre electrode should never be bent as this may crack the insulation and cause plug failure.

10 The HT leads to the coil and sparking plugs are of internal resistance, carbon core type. They are used in the interest of eliminating interference caused by the ignition system and have a resistance not exceeding 25 K ohms. They are much more easily damaged than copper cored cable and they should be pulled from the spark plug terminals by gripping the metal end fitting at the end of the cable. Occasionally wipe the external surfaces of the leads free from oil and dirt using a fuel moistened cloth.

11 Always check the connection of the HT leads to the spark plugs is in the correct firing order sequence 1, 5, 3, 6, 2, 4.

10 Ignition system - fault finding

Failures of the ignition system will either be due to faults in the HT or LT circuits. Initial checks should be made by observing the security of spark plug terminals, switch terminals, coil and battery connection. More detailed investigation and the explanation and remedial action in respect of symptoms of ignition malfunction in a 'conventional' system are described in the next Section.

If a fault develops in a semi-transistorized ignition system, the procedure in the following Section can be followed as far as is practicable, but the easiest way of eliminating the igniter unit is to disconnect it and connect a 0.22 mfd across the distributor breaker points - see Section 1.

11 Ignition system - fault symptoms

Engine fails to start

1 If the engine fails to start and the car was running normally when it was last used, first check there is fuel in the tank. If the engine turns over normally on the starter motor and the battery is evidently well charged, then the fault may be in either the high or low tension circuits. First check the HT circuit. Note: If the battery is known to be fully charged; the ignition light comes on, and the starter motor fails to turn the engine check the tightness of the leads on the battery terminals and also the secureness of the earth lead to its connection to the body. It is quite common for the leads to have worked loose, even if they look and feel secure. If one of the battery terminal posts gets very hot when trying to work the starter motor this is a sure indication of a faulty connection to that terminal.

2 One of the commonest reasons for bad starting is wet or damp spark plug leads and distributor. Remove the distributor cap. If condensation is visible internally, dry the cap with a rag and also wipe over the leads. Install the cap.

3 If the engine still fails to start, check that current is reaching the plugs, by disconnecting each plug lead in turn at the spark plug end, and hold the end of the cable about 3/16th inch (4 mm) away from the cylinder block. Spin the engine on the starter motor.

4 Sparking between the end of the cable and the block should be fairly strong with a regular blue spark. (Hold the lead with rubber to avoid electric shocks). If current is reaching the plugs, then remove them, and clean and regap them. The engine should now start.

5 If there is no spark at the plug leads take off the HT lead from the centre of the distributor cap and hold it to the block as before. Spin the engine on the starter once more. A rapid succession of blue sparks between the end of the lead and the block indicates that the distributor cap is cracked, the rotor arm faulty, or the carbon brush in the top of the distributor cap is not making good contact with the spring on the rotor arm. Possibly the points are in bad condition. Clean and reset them as described in Section 2.

6 If there are no sparks from the end of the lead from the coil, check the connections at the coil end of the lead. If it is in order start checking the low tension circuit.

7 Use a 12v voltmeter or a 12v bulb and two lengths of wire. With the ignition switch on and the points open, test between the low tension wire to the coil (it is marked +) and earth. No reading indicates a break in the supply from the ignition switch. Check the connections at the switch to see if any are loose. Refit them and the engine should run. A reading shows a faulty coil or condenser, or broken lead between the coil and the distributor.

8 Take the condenser wire off the points assembly and with the points open, test between the moving point and earth. If there now is a reading, then the fault is in the condenser. Install a new one and the fault is cleared.

9 With no reading from the moving point to earth, take a reading between earth and the — terminal of the coil. A reading here shows a broken wire which will need to be replaced between the coil and distributor. No reading confirms that the coil has failed and must be replaced, after which the engine will run once more. Remember to install the condenser wire to the points assembly. For these tests it is sufficient to separate the points with a piece of dry paper while testing with the points open.

Engine misfires

10 If the engine misfires regularly run it at a fast idling speed. Pull off each of the plug caps in turn and listen to the note of the engine. Hold the plug cap in a dry cloth or with a rubber glove as additional protection against a shock from the HT supply.

11 No difference in engine running will be noticed when the lead from the defective circuit is removed. Removing the lead from one of the good cylinders will accentuate the misfire.

12 Remove the plug lead from the end of the defective plug and hold it about 3/16th inch (4 mm) away from the block. Restart the engine. If the sparking is fairly strong and regular the fault must lie in the spark plug.

13 The plug may be loose, the insulation may be cracked, or the points may have burnt away giving too wide a gap for the spark to jump. Worse still, one of the points may have broken off. Either renew the plug, or clean it, reset the gap, and then test it.

14 If there is no spark at the end of the plug lead, or if it is weak and intermittent, check the ignition lead from the distributor to the plug. If the insulation is cracked or perished, renew the lead. Check the connections at the distributor cap.

15 If there is still no spark, examine the distributor cap carefully for tracking. This can be recognised by a very thin black line running between two or more contacts, or between a contact and some other part of the distributor. These lines are paths which now conduct electricity across the cap thus letting it run to earth. The only answer is a new distributor cap.

16 Apart from the ignition timing being incorrect, other causes of misfiring have already been dealt with under the section dealing with the failure of the engine to start. To recap - these are that:

a) The coil may be faulty giving intermittent misfire.
b) There may be a damaged wire or loose connection in the low tension circuit.
c) The condenser may be faulty.
d) There may be a mechanical fault in the distributor (broken driving spindle or contact breaker spring).

17 If the ignition timing is too far retarded, it should be noted that the engine will tend to overheat, and there will be a quite noticeable drop in power. If the engine is overheating and the power is down, and the ignition timing is correct, then the carburetor should be checked, as it is likely that this is where the fault lies.

Chapter 5 Clutch

Contents

Clutch - inspection and renovation ... 10	Clutch release cylinder - removal and installation ... 6
Clutch - installation ... 12	Clutch slip - diagnosis and cure ... 15
Clutch assembly - removal ... 9	Clutch spin - diagnosis and cure ... 16
Clutch faults ... 13	Clutch squeal - diagnosis and cure ... 14
Clutch judder - diagnosis and cure ... 17	General description ... 1
Clutch pedal - removal and installation ... 2	Hydraulic system - bleeding ... 8
Clutch pedal and release fork - adjustment ... 3	Master cylinder - dismantling and reassembly ... 5
Clutch release bearing - renewal ... 11	Master cylinder - removal and installation ... 4
Clutch release cylinder - dismantling and reassembly ... 7	

Specifications

Type ... Single dry plate, coil spring or diaphragm spring, hydraulically operated

Clutch pedal height
Pre-1975 models
FJ40 series, with brake servo ... 8.6 in (220 mm)
FJ40 series, without brake servo ... 7.6 in (192 mm)
FJ55 with brake servo ... 7.3 in (185 mm)
FJ55 without brake servo ... 6.9 in (175 mm)
1975 models onwards
FJ40 series, with brake servo ... 8.5 in (215 mm)
FJ40 series, without brake servo ... 7.8 in (198 mm)
FJ55 with brake servo ... 7.3 in (185 mm)
FJ55 without brake servo ... 6.8 in (172 mm)

Clutch pedal free play
Pre-1975 models ... 0.04/0.27 in (1/7 mm)
1975 models onwards ... 0.02/0.12 in (0.5/3 mm)

Release fork tip play
Pre-1975 models ... 0.16/0.24 in (4/6 mm)
1975 models onwards ... 0.12/0.16 in (3/4 mm)

Clutch plate minimum thickness ... 0.012 in (0.3 mm) clearance above rivet heads

Clutch disc run-out, maximum ... 0.04 in (1.0 mm)

Clutch fluid specification ... DOT 3 or SAE J1703

Torque wrench settings | lb f ft | kg f m
Clutch release lever yoke bolts ... 27 | 3.7
Clutch cover retaining bolts ... 14 | 1.9

1 General description

1 All models in the range are fitted with a single dry plate type clutch. Operation is by means of a pendant foot pedal and hydraulic circuit. Prior to 1975 a coil spring and release lever assembly was used, but after this a diaphragm spring clutch was used. The assembly is bolted by means of its cover to the rear face of the flywheel.
2 The driven plate (friction disc) is free to slide along the transmission input shaft, and it is held in place between the flywheel and pressure plate faces by the pressure exerted by the coil springs and release levers or the diaphragm spring. The friction lining material is riveted to the driven plate which incorporates a rubber cushioned hub designed to absorb transmission rotational shocks and to assist in ensuring smooth take-offs.
3 Depressing the clutch pedal pushes the release bearing forward to bear against the release levers and the fingers of the diaphragm spring. This action causes the pressure plate to move rearwards to disengage the pressure plate from the driven plate.
4 When the clutch pedal is released, the release levers or diaphragm

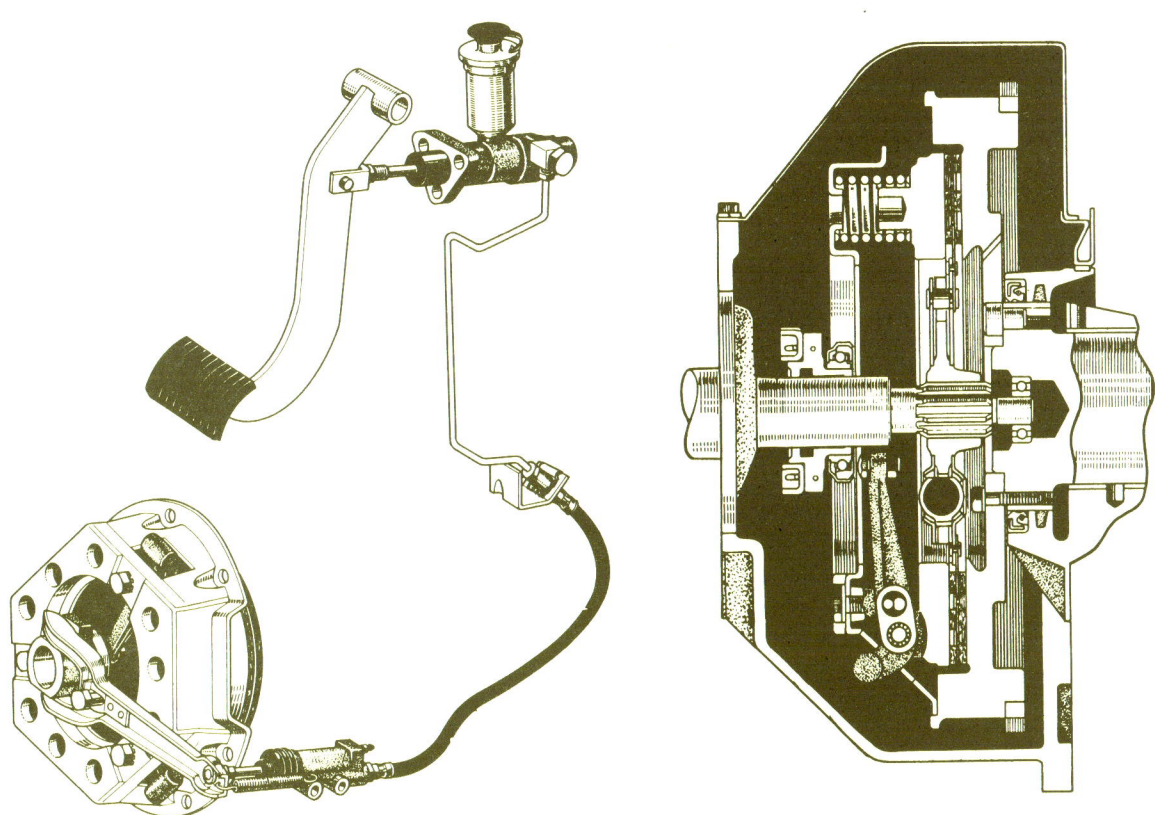

Fig. 5.1. Clutch system layout - early type coil spring clutch shown

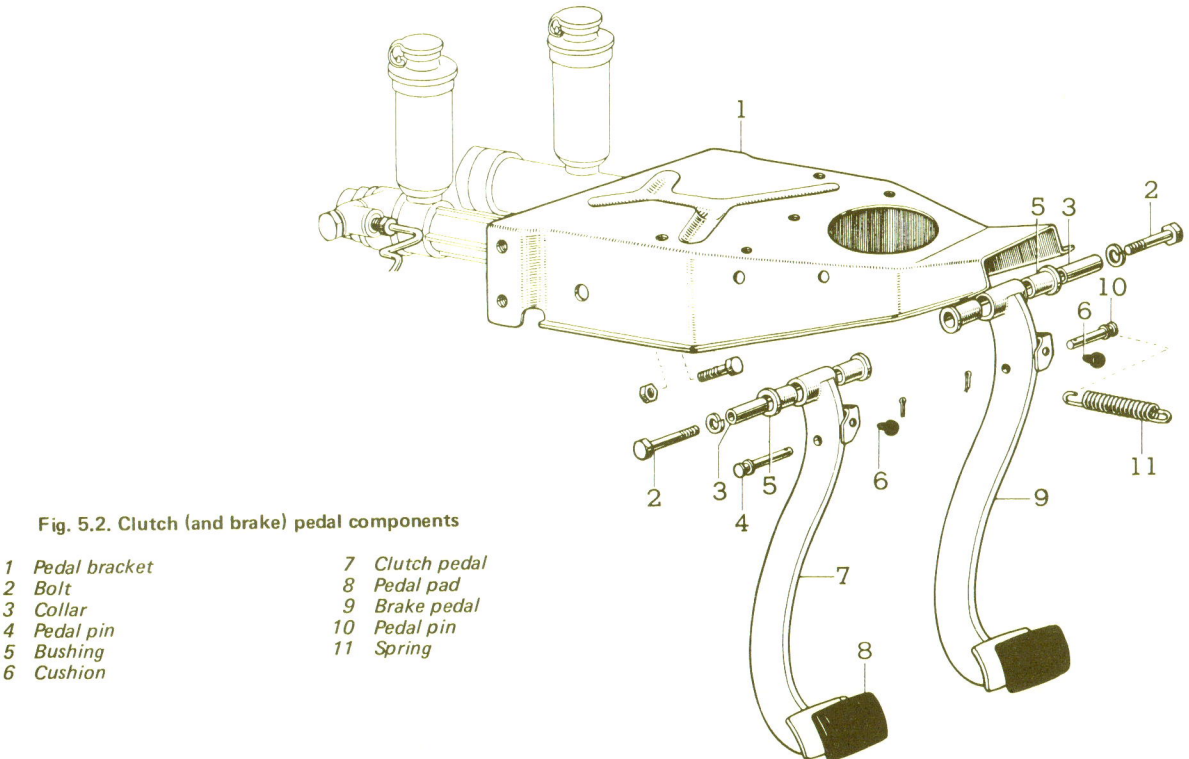

Fig. 5.2. Clutch (and brake) pedal components

1 Pedal bracket
2 Bolt
3 Collar
4 Pedal pin
5 Bushing
6 Cushion
7 Clutch pedal
8 Pedal pad
9 Brake pedal
10 Pedal pin
11 Spring

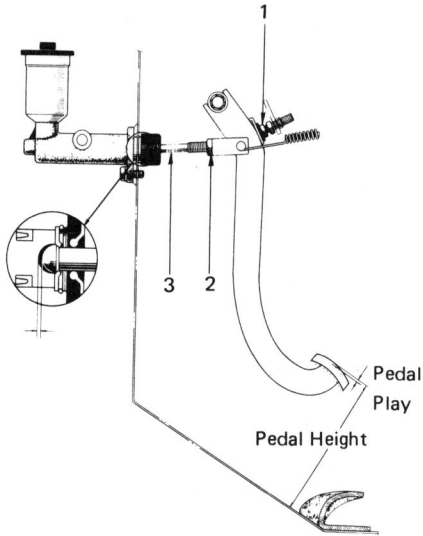

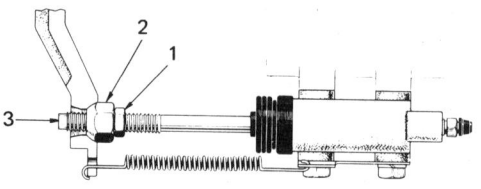

Fig. 5.3. Adjustment points for the clutch pedal - typical

1 Stop bolt
2 Locknut
3 Pushrod

Fig. 5.4. Release fork tip play adjustment - typical

1 Locknut
2 Pushrod nut
3 Pushrod

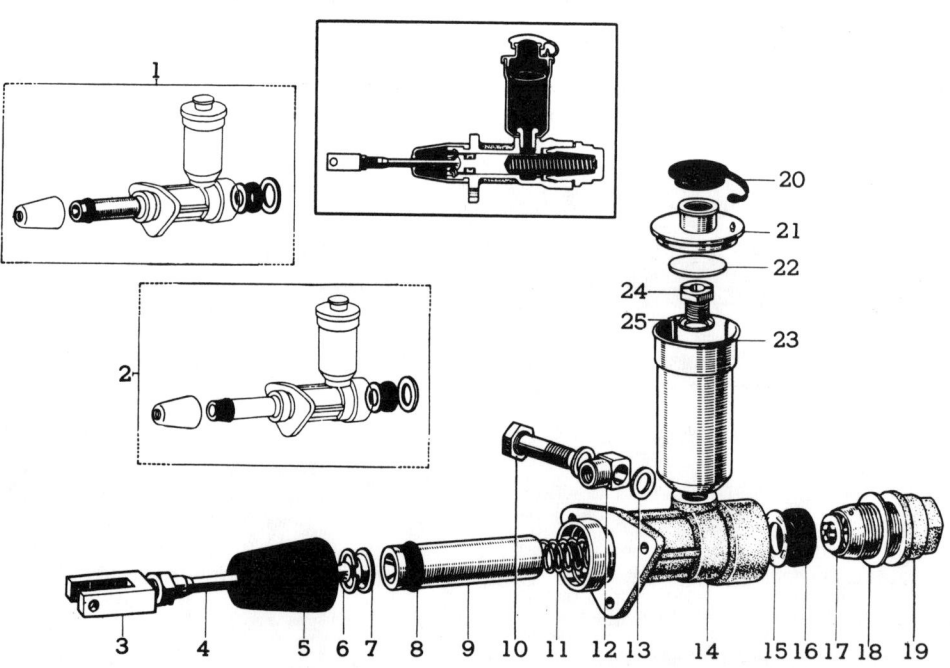

Fig. 5.5. Early type master cylinder - exploded view

1 Clutch master cylinder kit
2 Clutch master cylinder piston cup kit
3 Push rod clevis
4 Push rod
5 Boot
6 Snap ring
7 Piston stop plate
8 Cylinder cup
9 Piston
10 Union bolt
11 Return spring
12 Union
13 Gasket
14 Cylinder body
15 Piston cup spacer
16 Cylinder cup
17 Spring seat
18 Gasket
19 Cap
20 Reservoir filler cap
21 Reservoir cap
22 Float
23 Reservoir
24 Reservoir bolt
25 Washer

spring force the pressure plate into contact with the friction linings of the driven plate and at the same time pushes the driven plate fractionally forward on its splines to ensure full engagement with the flywheel. The driven plate is now firmly sandwiched between the pressure plate and the flywheel and so the drive is taken up.

2 Clutch pedal - removal and installation

1 Remove the clutch pedal tension spring.
2 Remove the cotter pin and the master cylinder pushrod clevis pin.
3 Remove the pedal bracket bolt and take off the pedal.
4 Remove the collar and bushings from the pedal.
5 Examine the bushings and shaft collars for wear, obtaining replacement parts as necessary.
6 Installation is the reverse of the removal procedure, but smear the bushings and pivots with general purpose grease prior to assembly. On completion adjust the pedal as described in the following Section.

3 Clutch pedal and release fork - adjustment

1 Adjust the clutch pedal height by first loosening, the locknut on the pushrod, then positioning the stop bolt as necessary. The correct height is given in the Specifications.
2 Having adjusted the height, rotate the pushrod to obtain the specified pedal free play.
3 Having adjusted the pedal free play, adjust the play at the release fork tip by loosening the locknut, then either rotating the pushrod as the pushrod nut is held, or rotating the pushrod nut, as applicable. The correct release fork tip play is given in the Specifications.

4 Master cylinder - removal and installation

1 Detach the master cylinder pushrod from the clutch pedal.
2 Plug the master cylinder to prevent excessive fluid loss, then remove the union bolt from the cylinder and detach the hydraulic line.
3 Remove the master cylinder retaining bolts to free the cylinder from the bulkhead. Take care that the fluid does not spill as it damages paintwork.
4 Installation is the reverse of the removal procedure, but on completion top-up and bleed the system as described in Section 8, and check the adjustment as described in Section 3.

5 Master cylinder - dismantling and reassembly

Note: *The procedure given in this Section is basically for the earlier type of master cylinder. (Fig. 5.5). The slight differences in procedure for the later type of cylinder can be noted from Fig. 5.6, which shows the parts in order of dismantling.*
1 Remove the reservoir cap, drain the contents and remove the float.
2 Remove the bolt and detach the reservoir from the cylinder body.
3 Remove the boot, then remove the snap ring so that the pushrod and associated parts may be removed.
4 Remove the piston and return spring from the cylinder, then remove the cylinder cup from the piston.
5 With the cylinder held in a vise, unscrew the cylinder cap, and remove the cup and spacer.
6 Wash all the parts in clean hydraulic fluid or alcohol. Examine the piston surface and cylinder bore for scoring and scratches; if evident these parts must be renewed.
7 Discard the rubber cups and obtain the appropriate repair kit.
8 Reassembly is now the reverse of the dismantling procedure. Lubricate the cups with brake fluid or rubber lubricant during assembly; if rubber lubricant is used, check after assembly is complete, that it is only remaining on the seal edges of the cups.

6 Clutch release cylinder - removal and installation

1 To prevent excessive fluid loss, first plug the master cylinder reservoir.
2 Unhook the clutch release fork spring, then remove the nut so that

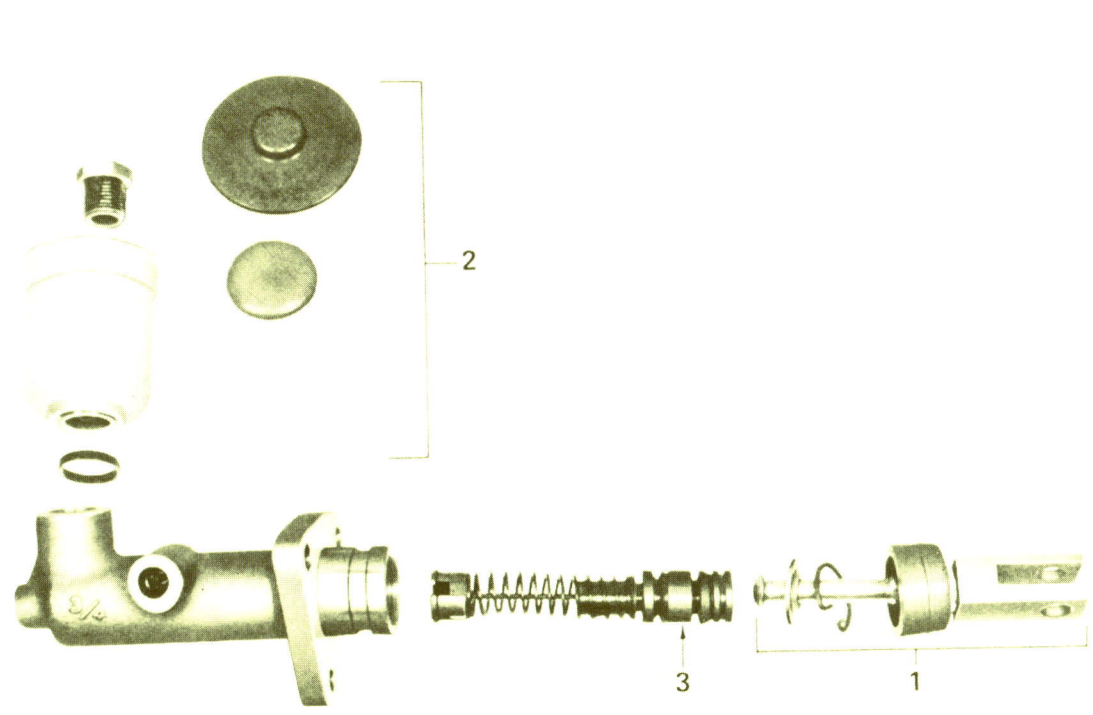

Fig. 5.6. Later type master cylinder components

1 Pushrod, rubber boot and snap-ring
2 Reservoir assembly
3 Piston assembly

the high and low shift link lever can be detached from the link lever shaft.
3 Detach the flexible hose and pull out the clip.
4 Remove the retaining bolts and detach the release cylinder from the engine mounting rear bracket.
5 Installation is the reverse of the removal procedure, but on completion top-up and bleed the system as described in Section 8, and check the adjustment as described in Section 3.

7 Clutch release cylinder - dismantling and reassembly

Note: The procedure given in this Section is basically for the earlier type of release cylinder (Fig. 5.8). The slight differences in procedure for the later type of cylinder can be noted from Fig. 5.9, which shows the parts in order of dismantling.
1 Depress the pushrod two or three times to eject any fluid from the cylinder, then pull out the pushrod assembly and rubber boot.
2 Eject the piston by applying air pressure to the fluid inlet port or by tapping the end of the cylinder on a hardwood surface. If necessary, unscrew the bleed nipple.
3 Wash all the parts in clean hydraulic fluid or alcohol. Examine the piston surfaces and cylinder bore for scoring and scratches; if evident, these parts must be removed.
4 Discard the rubber cups and obtain the appropriate repair kit.
5 Reassembly is now the reverse of the dismantling procedure. Lubricate the cups with brake fluid or rubber lubricant during assembly if rubber lubricant is used, check after assembly is complete that it is only remaining on the seal edges of the caps (and in the piston groove, where applicable).

8 Hydraulic system - bleeding

1 Gather together a clean glass jar, a length of rubber or plastic tubing which fits tightly over the bleed nipple on the release cylinder, a tin of hydraulic fluid and someone to help.

2 Check that the master cylinder is full. If it is not, fill it and cover the bottom two inches of the jar with hydraulic fluid.
3 Remove the rubber dust cap from the bleed nipple on the release cylinder, and with a suitable wrench open the bleed nipple approximately three quarters of a turn.
4 Place one end of the tube securely over the nipple and insert the other end in the jar so that the end of the tubing is below the fluid level.
5 The assistant should now depress the pedal and hold it down. Close the bleed screw and allow the pedal to return to its normal position.
6 Continue this procedure until clean hydraulic fluid without any traces of air bubbles emerges from the end of the tubing. Ensure that the reservoir level is checked frequently so that there is no danger of air entering the system again.
7 When no more air bubbles appear, tighten the bleed nipple on the downstroke of the pedal.
8 On completion, install the bleed nipple dust cap. Ensure that the reservoir fluid level is correct, and install the cap. Discard the fluid in the jar since it has almost certainly deteriorated in quality and its re-use could contaminate the system.

9 Clutch assembly - removal

1 Remove the transmission and transfer; refer to Chapter 6, if necessary. Also remove the clutch housing.
2 Detach the clutch release cylinder from its mounting point. If necessary, refer to Section 6, but note that it is not necessary to detach the hydraulic line.
3 Scribe or centre-punch index marks on the clutch cover and flywheel to ensure correct installation (if the original cover is to be re-used), then progressively loosen the clutch cover retaining bolts.
4 Remove the bolts and carefully lift the cover away from the flywheel. Take care that the clutch disc (friction plate) does not drop out as it is being removed. If the disc is to be re-used, take care that it is not contaminated with oil or grease.

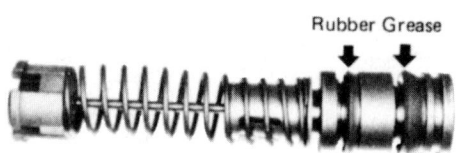

Fig. 5.7. Apply rubber lubricant to the points shown if available. Alternatively use hydraulic fluid

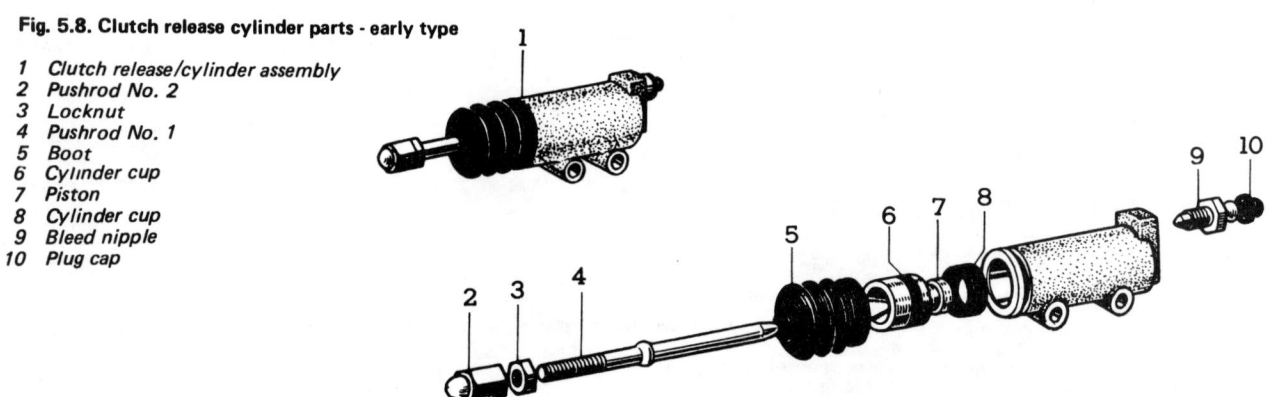

Fig. 5.8. Clutch release cylinder parts - early type

1 Clutch release/cylinder assembly
2 Pushrod No. 2
3 Locknut
4 Pushrod No. 1
5 Boot
6 Cylinder cup
7 Piston
8 Cylinder cup
9 Bleed nipple
10 Plug cap

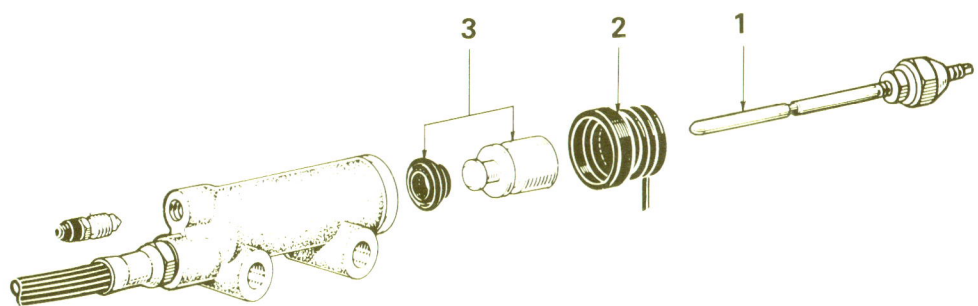

Fig. 5.9. Clutch release cylinder parts - later type

1 Pushrod assembly
2 Boot
3 Piston assembly

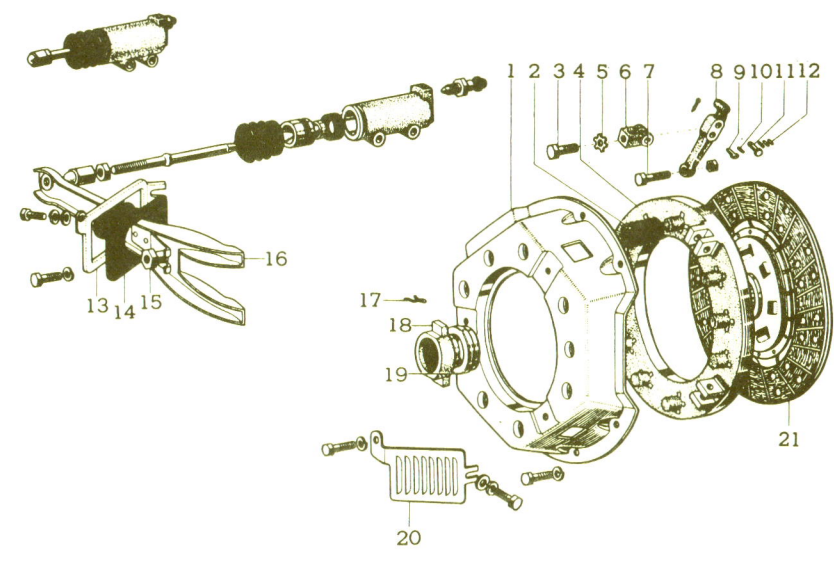

Fig. 5.10. Clutch components - early type

1 Clutch cover	7 Adjusting bolt	12 Pin roller	17 Bearing hub clip
2 Spring	8 Release lever	13 Boot plate	18 Bearing hub
3 Bolt	9 Lever pin	14 Boot	19 Bearing
4 Pressure plate	10 Roller	15 Release fork ball	20 Cover plate
5 Washer	11 Pressure plate pin	16 Release fork	21 Clutch disc (friction plate)
6 Release lever yoke			

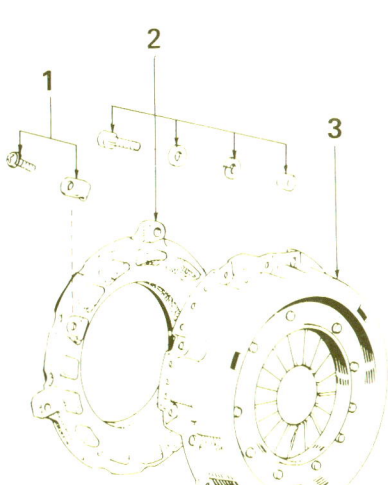

Fig. 5.11. Clutch components - later type

1 Retracting pin
2 Pressure plate and bolts
3 Clutch cover assembly

10 Clutch - inspection and renovation

1 Examine the clutch disc friction linings for wear and loose rivets, and the disc itself for run-out. If either of these is outside the specified limit, the clutch plate must be renewed.
2 Where a diaphragm clutch is installed, examine the cover assembly for damage, and for security of assembly. If necessary, the pressure plate can be removed; it is not recommended that the individual parts of the cover are renewed if wear or damage is evident, but that a complete new cover is obtained. Assuming that damage has not occured to the cover assembly, the most likely point of wear is the diaphragm spring fingers.
3 Where a coil spring clutch is installed, the cover can be dismantled for inspection by using a wood block on top of the cover to compress the spring while the release lever yoke bolts are removed. Release the pressure slowly to avoid the springs flying out. If necessary, the pressure plate pins and rollers can be removed also.
4 With the coil spring clutch, examine the release lever, springs and associated parts for wear and damage, renewing as necessary.
5 While the clutch is removed, check the machined face of the flywheel for searing which, if evident, will mean that the flywheel must be removed and re-machined.
6 Also check the input shaft pilot bearing in the end of the crankshaft. If this is showing signs of wear or corrosion, it must be removed and a replacement installed.
7 During any major clutch repair, it is false economy not to renew the release bearing. This procedure will be found in the following Section.

11 Clutch release bearing - renewal

1 Remove the release bearing hub clips, then remove the bearing and hub.
2 If necessary, remove the release arm from its pivot bolt.
3 Using a distance piece of suitable diameter, press the hub from the bearing inner track, and press on a new one. Ensure that the pressure ring of the bearing is towards the friction plate when assembled.
4 Installation of the bearing is the reverse of the removal procedure. It is recommended that the lever pivot bolt dowel head is smeared with a general purpose grease prior to the lever being installed.

12 Clutch - installation

1 Installation of the clutch is basically the reverse of the removal procedure (see Sections 9 and 10). However, there is one very important thing which must be done, and that is to centralize the clutch disc; also ensure that the disc is the correct way round (Fig. 5.12).

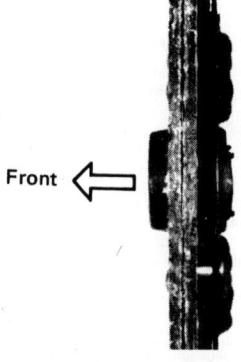

Fig. 5.12. Note which way round the friction plate is installed

2 This is done by installing the clutch assembly loosely (in its original installed position if the same parts are being used again), then inserting a round bar or screwdriver thru the clutch hub splined hole, to align it with the pilot bearing.
3 Now progressively, in a diagonal pattern, tighten the clutch cover bolts to the specified torque.
4 The clutch housing can now be installed. With the diaphragm type clutch, ensure that the spring fingers are a uniform distance from the cover rear face to within 0.04 in (1 mm). With the coil spring clutch, adjust the release lever height so that each is 2.93 in (74.5 mm) from the cover rear face; the levers should be a uniform distance from the face to within 0.02 in (0.5 mm).
5 Smear some general purpose grease on the transmission input shaft splines, then install the transmission.
6 Carry out the clutch adjustment described in Section 3.

13 Clutch faults

There are four main faults to which the clutch and release mechanism are prone. They may occur by themselves or in conjunction with any of the other faults. They are clutch squeal, slip, spin and judder.

14 Clutch squeal - diagnosis and cure

1 If, on taking up the drive or when changing gear, the clutch squeals, this is a sure indication of a badly worn clutch release bearing.
2 As well as regular wear due to normal use, wear of the clutch release bearing is much accentuated if the clutch is ridden, or held down for long periods in gear, with the engine running. To minimise wear of this component the vehicle should always be taken out of gear at traffic lights and for similar hold-ups.
3 The clutch release bearing is not an expensive item, but difficult to get at.

15 Clutch slip - diagnosis and cure

1 Clutch slip is a self-evident condition which occurs when the clutch friction plate is badly worn, oil or grease having got into the flywheel or pressure plate faces, or the pressure plate itself is faulty.
2 The reason for clutch slip is that, due to one of the faults listed above, there is either insufficient pressure from the pressure plate, or insufficient friction from the friction plate to ensure solid drive.
3 If small amounts of oil get into the clutch, they will be burnt off under the heat of clutch engagement, and in the process, gradually darkening the linings. Excessive oil on the clutch will burn off leaving a carbon deposit which can cause quite bad slip, or fierceness, spin and judder.
4 If clutch slip is suspected, and confirmation of this condition is required, there are several tests which can be made.
5 With the engine in second or third gear, and pulling lightly up a moderate incline, sudden depression of the accelerator pedal may cause the engine to increase its speed without any increase in road speed. Easing off on the accelerator will then give a definite drop in engine speed without the vehicle slowing.
6 In extreme cases of clutch slip, the engine will race under normal acceleration conditions.

16 Clutch spin - diagnosis and cure

1 Clutch spin is a condition which occurs when the release arm travel is excessive, there is an obstruction in the clutch either on the primary gear splines, or in the operating lever itself, or the oil may have partially burnt off the clutch linings and have left a resinous deposit which is causing the clutch disc to stick to the pressure plate or flywheel.
2 The reason for clutch spin is that due to any, or a combination of, the faults just listed, the clutch pressure plate is not completely freeing from the centre plate even with the clutch pedal fully depressed.
3 If clutch spin is suspected, the condition can be confirmed by extreme difficulty in engaging first gear from rest, difficulty in

changing gear, and very sudden take-up of the clutch drive at the fully depressed end of the clutch pedal travel as the clutch is released.
4 Check that the clutch pedal free movement is correctly adjusted and, if in order, then the fault lies internally in the clutch. It will then be necessary to remove the clutch for examination, and to check the transmission input shaft.

17 Clutch judder - diagnosis and cure

1 Clutch judder is a self-evident condition which occurs when the transmission or engine mountings are loose or too flexible, when there is oil on the faces of the clutch friction plate, or when the clutch pressure plate has been incorrectly adjusted during assembly.
2 The reason for clutch judder is that due to one of the faults just listed, the clutch pressure plate is not freeing smoothly from the friction disc, and is snatching.
3 Clutch judder normally occurs when the clutch pedal is released in first or reverse gears, and the whole vehicle shudders as it moves backwards or forwards.

Chapter 6 Transmission, transfer gear, power take-off and winch

Contents

Column shift linkage - adjustment ... 16	Front winch - removal and installation ... 26
Driveshaft - removal and installation ... 25	General description ... 1
Fault diagnosis - front winch and power take-off ... 29	Power take-off - dismantling, inspection and reassembly ... 24
Fault diagnosis - transmission and transfer ... 28	Power take-off - removal and installation ... 23
Four-speed transmission - dismantling into major assemblies ... 5	Transfer front drive vacuum control lines and electrical connections 22
Four-speed transmission (F engine) - reassembly ... 13	Transfer front drive vacuum control system - description ... 18
Four-speed transmission (2F engine) - reassembly ... 14	Transfer front drive vacuum control system - dismantling, inspection and reassembly ... 20
Four-speed transmission countershaft assembly (F engine) - dismantling ... 7	Transfer front drive vacuum control system - removal and installation ... 19
Four-speed transmission countershaft assembly (F engine) - reassembly ... 11	Transfer gear - dismantling, inspection and reassembly ... 17
Four-speed transmission output shaft - dismantling ... 6	Transfer shift linkage ... 21
Four-speed transmission output shaft (F engine) - reassembly ... 9	Transmission components - inspection ... 8
Four-speed transmission output shaft (2F engine) - reassembly ... 10	Transmission and transfer - removal and installation ... 2
Four-speed transmission top cover - dismantling, inspection and reassembly ... 15	Transmission and transfer - separation and reconnection ... 3
Front winch - dismantling, inspection and reassembly ... 27	Three-speed transmission - dismantling ... 4
	Three-speed transmission - reassembly ... 12

Specifications

Transmission type ...	Three- or four-speed transmission with transfer gear
Transfer gear type ...	Two-speed, helical sliding gear with front drive selection

Gear ratios

Three-speed ...	1st	2.757 : 1
	2nd	1.691 : 1
	3rd	1.000 : 1
	Reverse	3.676 : 1
Four-speed, USA and Canada with F2 engine (Type H42) ...	1st	3.555 : 1
	2nd	2.292 : 1
	3rd	1.410 : 1
	4th	1.000 : 1
	Reverse	4.271 : 1
Four-speed, other markets with F2 engine (Type H41) ...	1st	4.925 : 1
	2nd	2.643 : 1
	3rd	1.519 : 1
	4th	1.000 : 1
	Reverse	4.925 : 1
Four-speed with F1 engine ...	1st	5.299 : 1
	2nd	2.843 : 1
	3rd	1.634 : 1
	4th	1.000 : 1
	Reverse	5.299 : 1

Transfer gear ratios:		
Three-speed ...	High	1.000 : 1
	Low	2.313 : 1
Four-speed ...	High	1.000 : 1
	Low	1.992 : 1

Transmission, transfer and power take-off lubricant type ...	SAE 90 EP gear oil

Lubricant capacities (approximate)

Three-speed transmission ...	3.6 US pt/3.0 Imp pt/1.7 liters
Four-speed transmission ...	6.6 US pt/5.4 Imp pt/3.1 liters
Transfer gear ...	3.6 US pt/3.0 Imp pt/1.7 liters

Chapter 6/Transmission, transfer gear, power take-off and winch 113

Transfer gear with power take-off	4.4 US pt/3.8 Imp pt/4.2 liters
Winch	1.2 US pt/1.0 Imp pt/0.6 liter

Fits, clearances and wear limits

Four-speed transmission (F2 engine)

3rd gear thrust clearance	0.005/0.014 in (0.13/0.35 mm)
3rd gear oil clearance	0.0028/0.0047 in (0.07/0.12 mm)
2nd gear thrust clearance	0.007/0.014 in (0.18/0.35 mm)
Reverse idler gear oil clearance (max.)	0.0063 in (0.16 mm)
3rd and 4th synchro rings clearance (min.)	0.032 in (0.8 mm)
Hub sleeve and shift forks clearance (max.)	0.032 in (0.8 mm)
Reverse idler gear slot and shift arm shoe clearances (max.)	0.028 in (0.7 mm)
Synchro ring No. 1 dimension (max.)	1st 0.110 in (2.8 mm)
	2nd 0.071 in (1.8 mm)
Reverse shift arm shoe thickness (limit)	0.319 in (8.0 mm)
Selective snap-ring thicknesses:	
Input shaft bearing	0.1303/0.1346 in (3.31/3.42 mm)
	0.1260/0.1303 in (3.20/3.31 mm)
Output shaft (front)	0.0945/0.0965 in (2.40/2.45 mm)
	0.0965/0.0984 in (2.45/2.50 mm)
	0.0984/0.1004 in (2.50/2.55 mm)
	0.1004/0.1024 in (2.55/2.60 mm)
	0.1024/0.1043 in (2.60/2.65 mm)
	0.1043/0.1063 in (2.65/2.70 mm)
Countershaft (front)	0.0807/0.0827 in (2.05/2.10 mm)
	0.0846/0.0866 in (2.15/2.20 mm)
	0.0886/0.0906 in (2.25/2.30 mm)

Four-speed transmission (F engine)

Forward gears to output shaft clearance	0.003/0.005 in (0.08/0.121 mm)
Reverse idler to idler shaft clearance	0.0045/0.006 in (0.115/0.153 mm)
Input shaft to No. 2 synchro ring clearance	0.038/0.063 in (0.97/1.59 mm)
3rd gear to No. 2 synchro ring clearance	0.034/0.067 in (0.87/1.69 mm)
No. 1 synchro ring to 2nd synchro outer ring clearance	0.004/0.020 in (0.1/0.5 mm)
No. 1 synchro ring to 1st synchro outer ring clearance	0.004/0.020 in (0.1/0.5 mm)
Shift fork to sleeve clearance	0.0039/0.0118 in (0.10/0.30 mm)
Output shaft 2nd gear thrust clearance	0.004/0.012 in (0.1/0.3 mm)
Synchro ring No. 2 thrust clearance	0/0.008 in (0/0.2 mm)
Selective snap-ring thicknesses:	
Output shaft 2nd gear	0.0984 in (2.5 mm)
	0.1024 in (2.6 mm)
Synchro ring No. 2	0.0945 in (2.4 mm)
	0.0984 in (2.5 mm)

Three-speed transmission (F2 engine)

2nd gear thrust clearance	0.0032/0.016 in (0.08/0.4 mm)
Countergear thrust clearance	0.002/0.016 in (0.05/0.4 mm)
2nd gear oil clearance (max.)	0.0035 in (0.09 mm)
2nd and 3rd synchro ring (min.)	0.032 in (0.8 mm)
Hub sleeve and shift forks (max.)	0.032 in (0.8 mm)
Selective snap-ring and thrust washer thicknesses:	
Input shaft bearing	0.0957/0.1012 in (2.43/2.57 mm)
	0.0906/0.0953 in (2.30/2.42 mm)
Output shaft (front)	0.0925/0.0945 in (2.35/2.40 mm)
	0.0886/0.0906 in (2.25/2.30 mm)
Countergear thrust washer	0.0571/0.0591 in (1.45/1.50 mm)
	0.0591/0.0610 in (1.50/1.55 mm)
	0.0610/0.0630 in (1.55/1.60 mm)

Three-speed transmission (F engine)

Synchro ring to gear cone clearance	0.039/0.073 in (1.00/1.85 mm)
2nd and 3rd shift to clutch hub sleeve clearance	0.0059/0.0118 in (0.15/0.30 mm)
1st/reverse shift fork to 1st/reverse gear clearance	0.0039/0.0118 in (0.10/0.30 mm)
2nd gear thrust clearance	0.0031/0.009 in (0.08/0.23 mm)
Countergear thrust clearance	0.002/0.008 in (0.05/0.20 mm)
Selective snap-ring thicknesses:	
Input shaft bearing	0.0957/0.1024 in (2.43/2.60 mm)
	0.0905/0.0953 in (2.30/2.42 mm)
Countergear thrust washer	0.0578/0.0590 in (1.45/1.50 mm)
	0.0590/0.0610 in (1.50/1.55 mm)
	0.0610/0.0630 in (1.55/1.60 mm)
2nd gear thrust clearance snap-ring	0.0957/0.1024 in (2.43/2.60 mm)
	0.0905/0.0953 in (2.30/2.42 mm)

Transfer gear

Idler gear thrust clearance	0.004/0.016 in (0.1/0.4 mm)

Output gears oil clearance	0.00138/0.004 in (0.035/0.09 mm)
Hub sleeve and shift fork clearance (max.)	0.04 in (1.0 mm)
Transfer output shaft bearing preload:	
New bearing	2.6/9.0 lb (1.2/4.1 kg)
Original bearing	More than 1.04 lb (0.47 kg)
Spacer and shim thicknesses:	
Idler gear thrust spacer	0.047/0.051 in (1.2/1.3 mm)
	0.051/0.055 in (1.3/1.4 mm)
	0.055/0.059 in (1.4/1.5 mm)
	0.059/0.063 in (1.5/1.6 mm)
	0.063/0.067 in (1.6/1.7 mm)
	0.067/0.071 in (1.7/1.8 mm)
Output shaft bearing shim	0.0039 in (0.10 mm)
	0.0059 in (0.15 mm)
	0.0079 in (0.20 mm)
	0.0098 in (0.25 mm)

Front winch

Worn bearing preload adjusting shims	0.009 in (0.228 mm)
	0.020 in (0.5 mm)

Torque wrench settings

	lb f ft	kg f m
Transmission case/case cover four-speed	26	3.7
Transmission case/transfer case	47	6.5
Transmission case/clutch housing	47	6.5
Transmission output shaft nut (four-speed)	90	12.5
Transmission output shaft nut (three-speed)	105	14.5
Transfer output front shaft nut	90	12.5
Parking brake drum nut	90	12.5
Power take-off universal joint flange nut	14	1.9
Winch bearing retainer to gear case	18	2.5

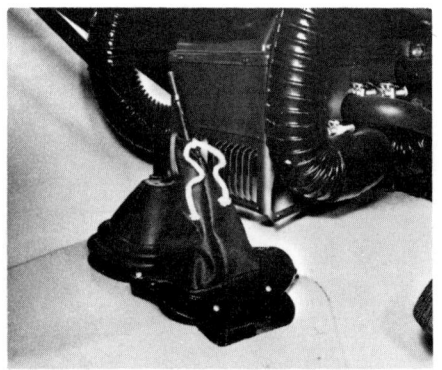

2.9 Remove the shift lever knobs and boots

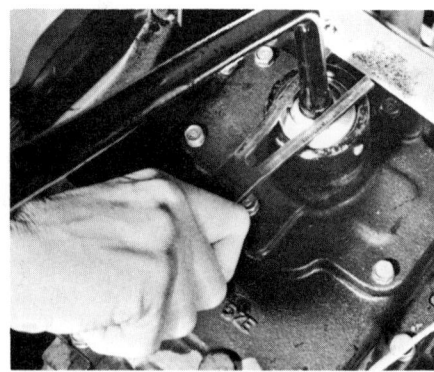

2.11a Tool used for removing gearshift lever

2.11b Removing the gearshift lever

2.16 Speedometer cable attachment

2.18 Removing the flywheel housing cover plate

Chapter 6/Transmission, transfer gear, power take-off and winch

1 General description

Land Cruiser models utilize either a three speed manual transmission with synchromesh on 2nd and top gears, or a four speed transmission with synchromesh on all forward ratios. The three speed transmission is supplied with a column shift linkage for some models, but all other variants have a direct floorshift mechanism.

A transfer gear assembly is attached to the transmission, and it is from this that the vehicle drive is obtained. Two types of control are used, one being a direct-coupled control for selection of high gear, (two-wheel drive (H2), high gear, four-wheel drive (H4) or low gear, four-wheel drive (L4)), the other being a vacuum control which utilizes intake manifold vacuum; the latter system has the same selections and uses a floor mounted lever for high/low selections and a dash-mounted control knob for engaging the four-wheel drive. A neutral position is provided for both systems, and is used when the power take-off (eg winch) is in operation.

The power take-off (where installed) is attached to the transfer gear. It comprises straight cut gears with sliding mesh action, and drives the front worm-gear winch thru a driveshaft with Hookes-type universal joints.

2 Transmission and transfer - removal and installation

1 Place the vehicle over an inspection pit, or raise it and support it on suitable axle stands to provide working room beneath.
2 Remove the cover plate from beneath the transmission.
3 Detach the front and rear propeller shafts; refer to Chapter 7 for further information.
4 Drain the transmission and transfer lubricant into a container of suitable size.
5 On FJ40 series models, drain the contents of the fuel tank into a container of suitable size.
6 On FJ40 series models, remove the pipe clip from the right-hand side of the transmission floor cover plate.
7 On FJ40 series models, remove the fuel tank cover plate and the fuel tank itself; refer to Chapter 3 for further information.
8 On FJ40 series models, remove the front seats, seat frames and console box.
9 Remove the shift lever knobs and boots (photo).
10 Remove the bolts and take out the transmission floor cover plate.
11 *Floor-shift models:* Make up a tool from a piece of 1/8 in (3 mm) steel plate as shown in the photograph, then press and turn clockwise at the base of the gearshift lever to remove it. Cover the hole in the transmission to prevent dirt from entering (photos).
12 *Column shift models:* Remove the rod pins and cotter pins, and detach the intermediate rods.
13 *Vacuum operated transfer:* Disconnect the vacuum hoses and electrical connections, noting the points to which they are normally attached.
14 Detach the electrical leads from the transmission, noting the points to which they are normally attached.
15 Remove the pin, and detach the high/low gearshift rod from the transfer high and low shift inner lever on the transfer.
16 From beneath the vehicle, detach the speedometer cable and remove the parking brake cable complete; refer to Chapter 10 for information on the parking brake cable (photo).
17 Where applicable, remove the power take-off driveshaft and shift lever; refer to Section 23 for further information.
18 Remove the cover plate from beneath the flywheel housing (photo).

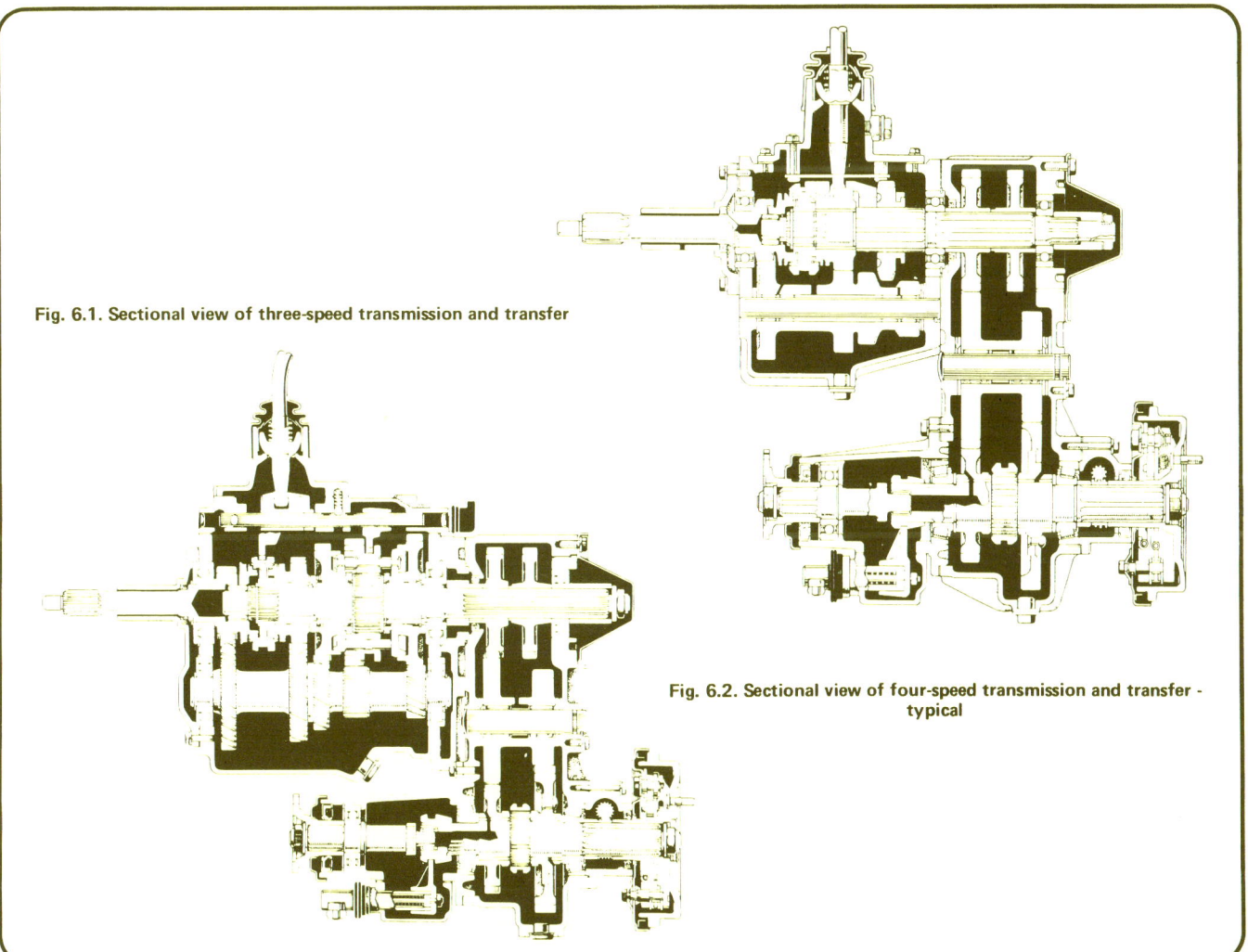

Fig. 6.1. Sectional view of three-speed transmission and transfer

Fig. 6.2. Sectional view of four-speed transmission and transfer - typical

Fig. 6.3. Supporting the transmission when removing the retaining bolts

19 It is now necessary to support the transmission weight. For reasons of accessibility, this is best done using a hoist or crane and ropes, with the jib over the vehicle or passed thru a front door. Alternatively, the transmission must be supported using a trolley jack with suitable wooden packs.
20 Remove the bolts securing the transmission to the clutch housing, then carefully ease the assembly rearwards. Lower it to the floor so that it can be moved to a suitable work place for cleaning.
21 Use a water-soluble solvent, if available, or kerosene, clean the grease and dirt from the exterior of the transmission. Take great care that solvents or water do not contaminate the electrical and/or vacuum connections, and that no foreign matter enters the transmission or transfer.
22 Installation of the transmission and transfer is basically the reverse of the removal procedure. Do not forget to add the transmission and transfer oil. Where applicable, adjust the shift linkage; for further information refer to Sections 16 and 21.

3 Transmission and transfer - separation and reconnection

1 On direct drive models, remove the shift lever guide.
2 Remove the cotter pin and lock bolt, and detach the shift lever and rod. Take care that the link lever shoe is not lost.
3 Unscrew the back-up light switch, and remove the gasket.

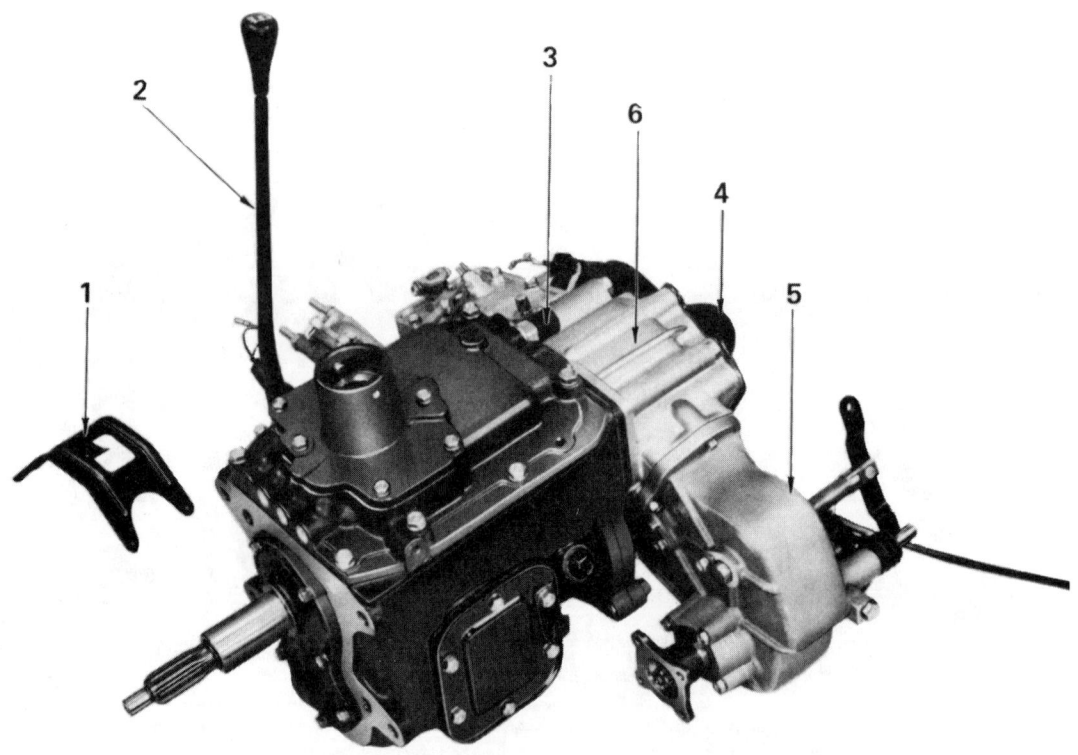

Fig. 6.4. Transmission and transfer ready for separation

1 Shift lever guide (direct drive only)
2 Lever and rod
3 Back up light switch
4 Case cover No. 2
5 Power take-off (or cover)
6 Transfer

Chapter 6/Transmission, transfer gear, power take-off and winch

4 On four-speed transmission, remove the top cover assembly and gasket. On all transmissions remove the transfer case cover No. 2 and gasket from the rear of the transfer.

5 Where applicable, detach the power take-off from the transfer case; refer to Section 23 for further information. Alternatively remove the power take-off cover plate.

6 Remove the parking brake drum assembly nut from the transmission. To prevent the front drive shaft from turning, select front drive then use a suitable bar held between two bolts in the front drive flange, while the brake drum nut is removed. Refer to Chapter 10 for further information, if necessary.

7 Fold back the lock washer tab then, whilst preventing the transfer input gear from rotating by wedging it with a hardwood block, remove the nut from the transmission output shaft. Remove the shaft spacer.

8 Remove the five bolts and spring washers securing the transfer to the transmission.

9 With luck, the transfer will separate easily, but if it is reluctant to do so, it will mean that a puller of the type shown in Fig. 6.8 will have to be made up. With this device, the load is taken on the end of the transmission output shaft as the transfer is drawn away from the transmission. **Take great care that the power take-off gears do not fall out as the transfer is drawn away.**

10 Reconnection of the transfer to the transmission is basically the reverse of the separation procedure, but take care that the transfer input and power take-off drive gears are installed the correct way round. A special tubular tool (Toyota part No. 09323 - 60010) is available to hold these gears in line while the transfer is being aligned for installation, but if this tool is used, the transfer rear bearing must be removed to enable it to be used. Note that on transfers which are used with a four-speed transmission, they have a stopper (item 11 in Fig. 6.6) which is positioned between the input gear and the transmission output shaft casing rear bearing; the stopper shoulder is towards the bearing. Always use a new gasket and a non-setting jointing compound for the joint face.

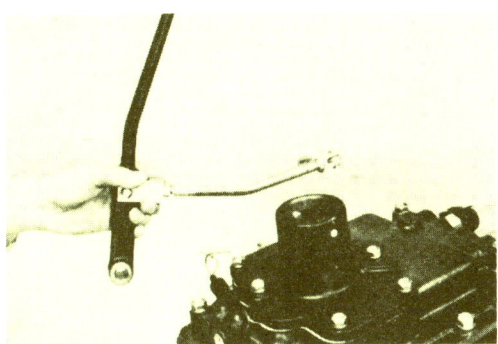

Fig. 6.5. Remove the shift lever and rod

Fig. 6.6. Removing the output shaft nut

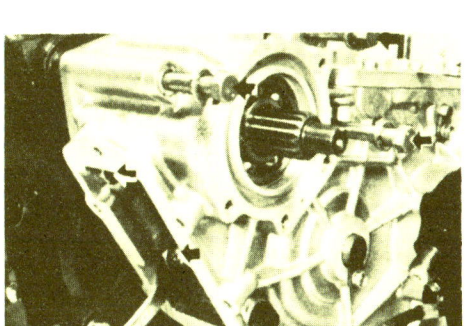

Fig. 6.7. Transfer retaining bolts arrowed

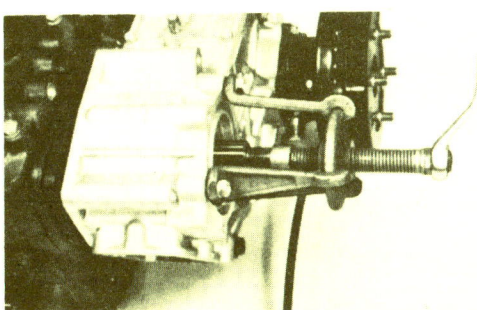

Fig. 6.8. Separating the transfer from the transmission using a puller

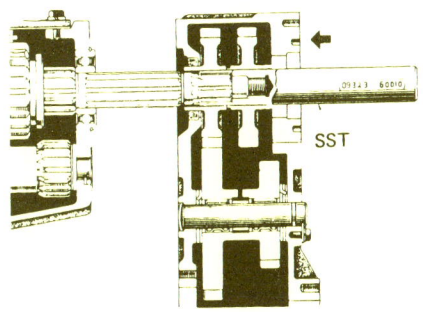

Fig. 6.9. Using the special tool when installing the transfer

4 Three-speed transmission - dismantling

1 Place the transmission on a suitable workbench, then remove the bolt and take out the gear select outer lever (where applicable).
2 Remove the transmission case cover (eight bolts and washers), and its gasket.
3 Remove the input shaft bearing retainer (four bolts and washers), and its gasket.
4 Carefully drive out the shift fork shaft towards the front of the casing using a brass or aluminium drift. Take care not to lose the shift fork lock balls and the straight pin.
5 Take out the reverse/1st shift fork, followed by the 2nd/3rd shift fork. Remove the shift fork lock balls and springs.
6 Drive out the countershaft (layshaft), using a brass or aluminium drift, towards the rear of the casing. Remove the woodruff key from the rear of the countershaft; leave the countergear in the casing for the time being.
7 The input shaft and bearing must now be removed from the casing. If a slide hammer is available, a suitable adaptor can be made to attach it to the input shaft end (Toyota tool No. 09910 - 00013 is available for this purpose); alternatively a brass or aluminium drift can be used on the outer race of the input shaft bearing to carefully drive it forward out of the casing.
8 Using a brass or aluminium drift, carefully tap the output shaft rearward to remove the bearing from the casing.
9 Using a universal extractor, draw the bearing off the rear of the output shaft.
10 Carefully draw the output shaft from the casing, complete with gears and synchro assembly.
11 Remove the snap-ring from the front end of the output shaft and slide the clutch hub No. 2, sleeve, synchro ring, 2nd gear and 1st/reverse gear from the output shaft.
12 Remove the countergear and tube, the bearing rollers and washers, and the side thrust washers. Note which way round the thrust washers are installed, and take care that the rollers are not lost from the countergear.
13 Remove the washers, bearing rollers and tube from the countergear.
14 Drive out the reverse idler gear towards the rear using a brass or aluminium drift. Remove the woodruff key from the shaft.
15 Take out the reverse idler gear, bearing rollers and thrust washers from the casing.

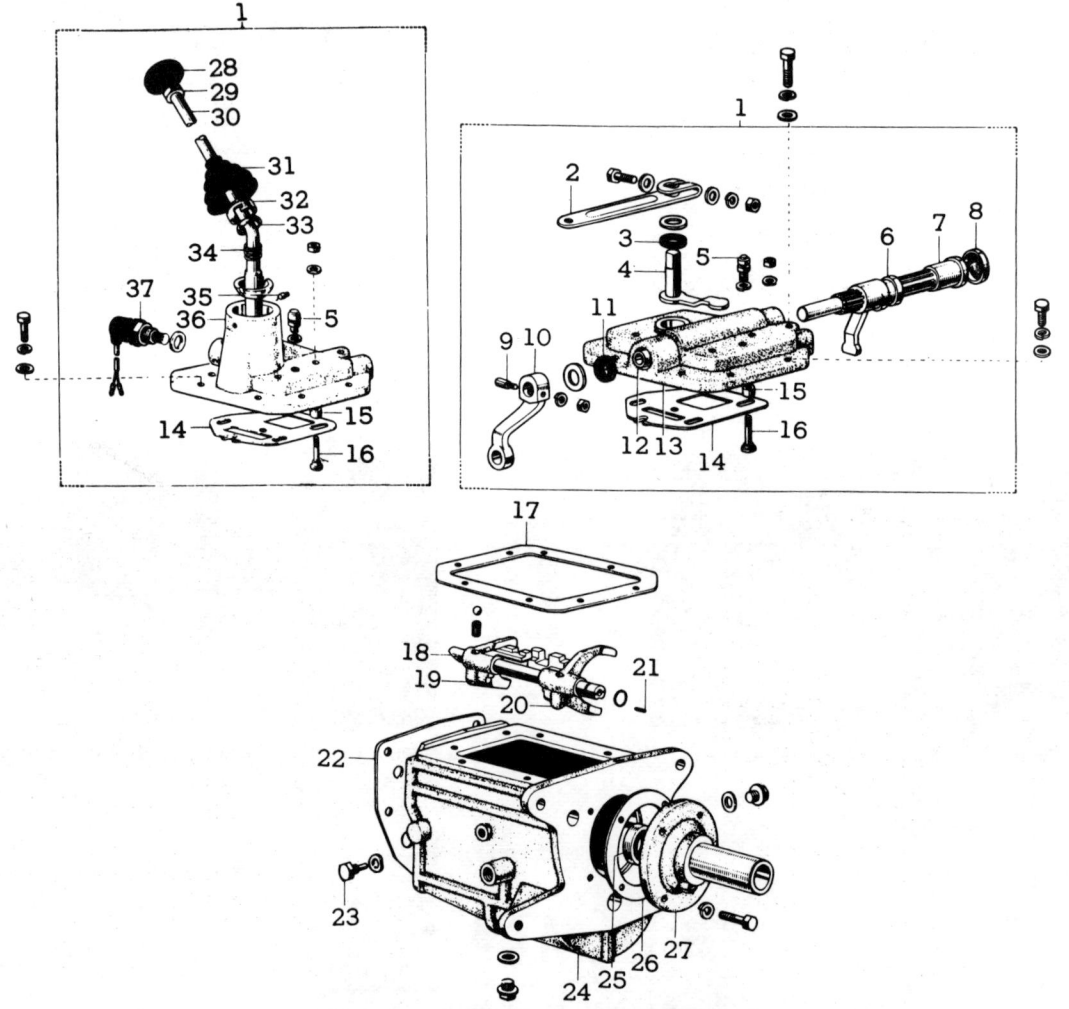

Fig. 6.10. Three-speed transmission case and cover

1 Transmission case cover assembly	10 Outer shift lever	19 Reverse/first shift fork	28 Shift lever knob
2 Gear select outer lever	11 Oil seal	20 Second/third shift fork	29 Nut
3 Oil seal	12 Bushing	21 Straight pin	30 Shift lever
4 Select lever shaft	13 Transmission case cover	22 Gasket	31 Boot
5 Breather plug	14 Shift iner-lock plate	23 Shift fork stopper	32 Cap
6 Sliding shift lever	15 Spacer	24 Transmission case	33 Spring seat
7 Shift lever shaft	16 Inter-lock plate set bolt	25 Oil seal	34 Spring
8 Plug	17 Case cover gasket	26 Gasket	35 Dowel pin
9 Lever lock pin	18 Shift fork shaft	27 Front bearing retainer	36 Transmisstion case cover
			37 Back-up light switch

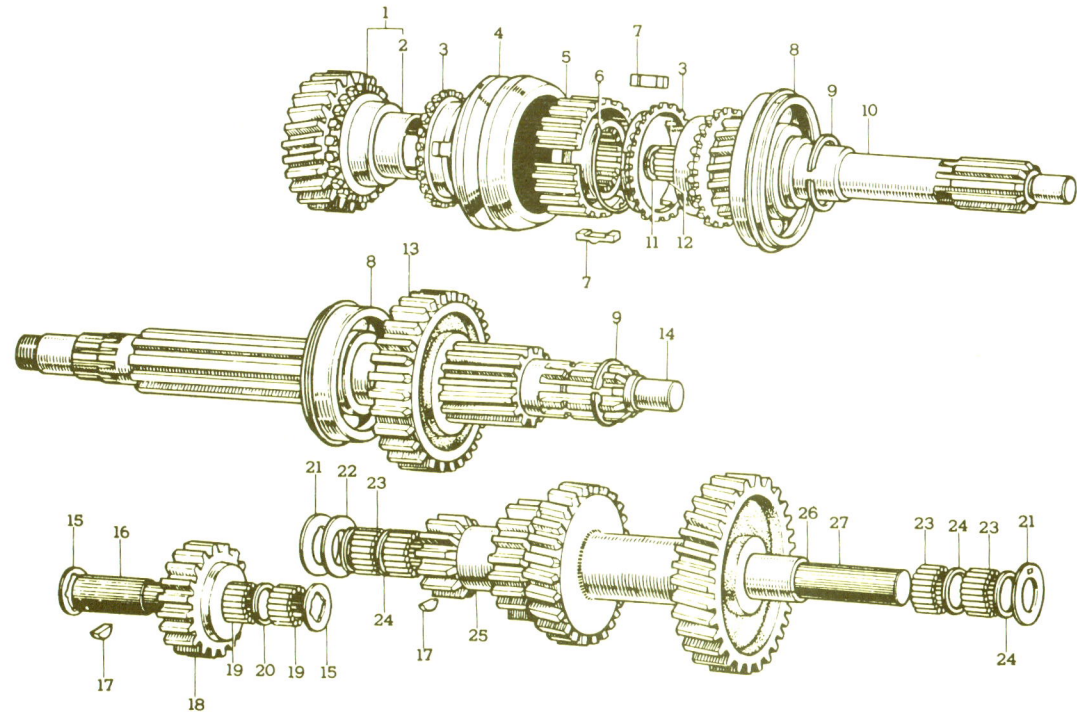

Fig. 6.11. Three-speed transmission gears and shafts

1 Second gear
2 Second gear bushing
3 Synchronizer ring No. 2
4 Clutch hub sleeve
5 Clutch hub No. 2
6 Shifting key spring
7 Shifting key No. 2
8 Bearing
9 Snap-ring
10 Input shaft
11 Snap-ring
12 Bearing roller
13 First/reverse gear
14 Output shaft
15 Reverse idler thrust washer
16 Reverse idler shaft
17 Woodruff key
18 Reverse idler
19 Bearing roller
20 Washer
21 Countergear case side thrust washer
22 Countergear side thrust washer
23 Bearing roller
24 Washer
25 Countershaft drive gear
26 Countershaft tube
27 Countershaft

Fig. 6.12. Remove gear select outer lever (column shift)

Fig. 6.13. Straight pin in shift fork shaft

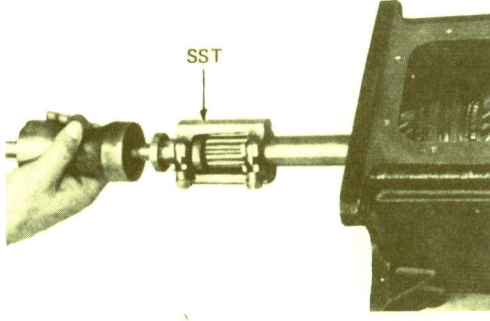

Fig. 6.14. Removing input shaft with special tool (sst)

5 Four-speed transmission - dismantling into major assemblies

1 Remove the transmission rear bearing retainer and its gasket.
2 Remove the transmission front bearing retainer and its gasket.
3 The input shaft and bearing must now be removed from the casing, but first align the cut-out on the synchro gear with the countergear. If a slide hammer is available, a suitable adaptor can be made to attach it to the input shaft end (Toyota tool No. 09910 - 00013 is available for this purpose); alternatively a brass or aluminium drift can be used on the outer race of the input shaft bearing to carefully drive it forward out of the casing. Take care that the needle bearing rollers are not lost as the input shaft is removed (Fig. 6.17).
4 Remove the snap-ring from the output shaft rear bearing, then use a suitable puller to draw the bearing out of the casing. If a puller is not available, use two screwdrivers in the snap-ring groove and carefully lever the bearing from the casing.
5 Lift the output shaft and gears from the casing, but hold them tightly together to prevent them from accidentally separating. Lay the shaft on one side for attention later.
6 On transmission used with type F engines, straighten the lockwasher tabs on the front end of the countershaft, remove the two bolts and take off the retainer plate.
7 On transmission used with type 2F engines, remove the small snap-ring from the countergear shaft at the front end.
8 Remove the large snap-ring from the countergear shaft front bearing and draw the bearing from the casing using a suitable puller. If a puller is not available, use two screwdrivers in the snap-ring groove and carefully lever the bearing from the casing.
9 Remove the snap-ring from the countershaft rear bearing.
10 Using a suitable puller, remove the countershaft rear bearing from the casing, inserting the puller claws through the service holes in the casing. If a puller cannot be used, it will be necessary to drive out the bearing from inside the casing using a brass or aluminium drift.
11 Take out the countergear assembly from the casing.
12 Remove the shift arm pivot and reverse shift arm.
13 Either draw or drive the reverse idle shaft out of the casing in a rearward direction.

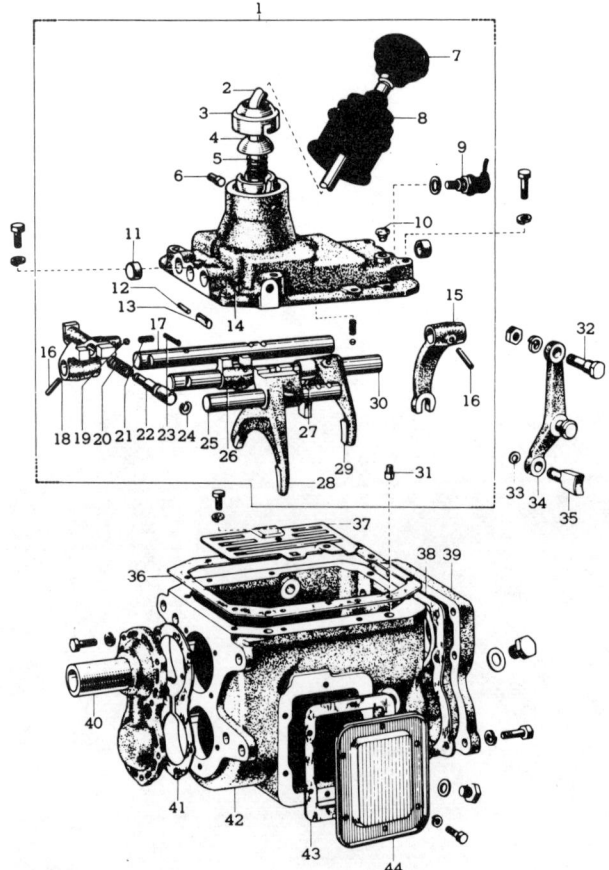

Fig. 6.15. Four-speed transmission case and cover (F engine type)

1 Tranmission case cover assembly	12 Straight pin	23 Cotter pin
2 Shift lever	13 Roller	24 C-washer
3 Cap	14 Screw plug	25 Third/fourth shift fork shaft
4 Spring seat	15 Reverse shift fork	26 First/second shift head
5 Spring	16 Slotted spring pin	27 Spacer
6 Dowel pin	17 Reverse shift fork shaft	28 Third/fourth shift fork
7 Knob	18 Reverse shift head	29 First/second shift fork
8 Boot	19 Lock ball	30 First/second shift fork shaft
9 Back up lamp switch	20 Spring	31 Dowel pin
10 Breather plug	21 Spring	32 Shift arm pivot
11 Plug	22 Reverse shift return plunger	33 Shaft snap-ring

34 Reverse shift arm
35 Shift arm shoe
36 Cover gasket
37 Oil filter plate (some models)
38 Gasket
39 Rear bearing retainer
40 Front bearing retainer
41 Gasket
42 Transmission case
43 Gasket
44 Power take-off cover

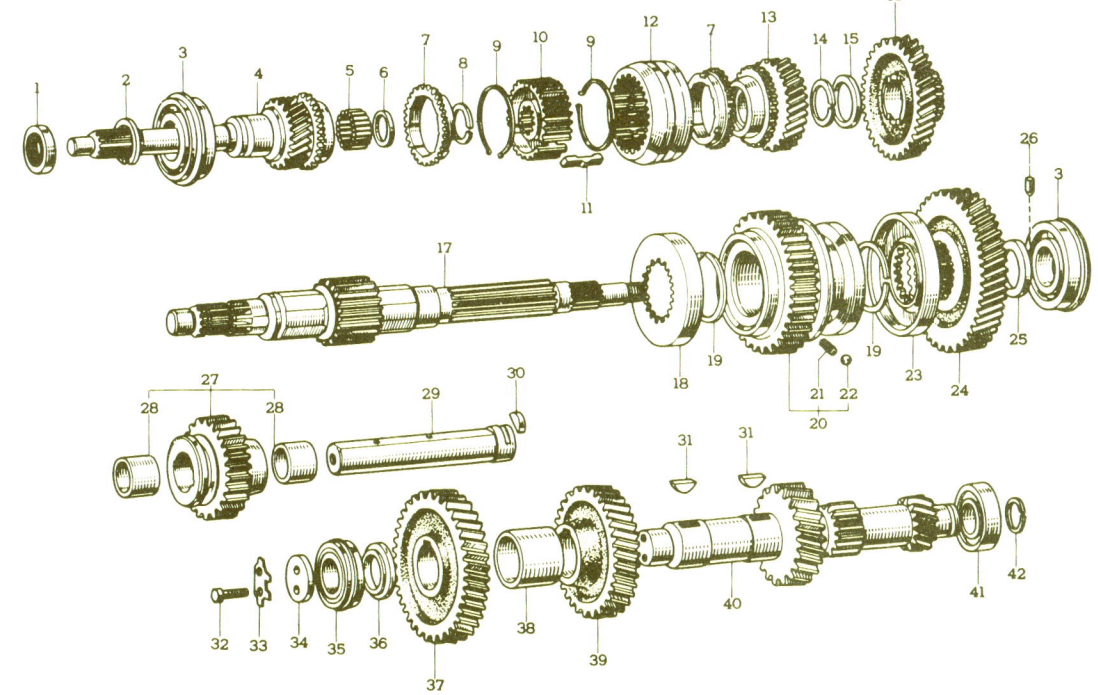

Fig. 6.16. Four-speed transmission gears and shaft (F engine type)

1 Oil seal	12 Hub sleeve	22 Lock ball	33 Lock washer
2 Snap-ring	13 Third gear	23 First synchronizer outer ring	34 Lock plate
3 Bearing	14 Shaft snap-ring	24 First gear	35 Bearing
4 Input shaft	15 Second gear thrust washer	25 First gear thrust washer	36 Front bearing spacer
5 Bearing roller	16 Second gear	26 Straight pin	37 Countershaft drive gear
6 Bearing spacer	17 Output shaft	27 Reverse idler gear	38 Spacer
7 Synchronizer ring No. 2	18 Second synchronizer outer ring	28 Bushing	39 Countershaft third gear
8 Shaft snap-ring		29 Reverse idler shaft	40 Countershaft
9 Shifting key spring	19 Shaft snap-ring	30 Woodruff key	41 Bearing
10 Clutch hub No. 2	20 Synchronizer ring No. 1	31 Woodruff key	42 Snap-ring
11 Shifting key No. 2	21 Spring	32 Bolt	

Fig. 6.17. Driving out the input shaft bearing

Fig. 6.18. Removing the output shaft and gears

Fig. 6.19. Removing a casing bearing - typical

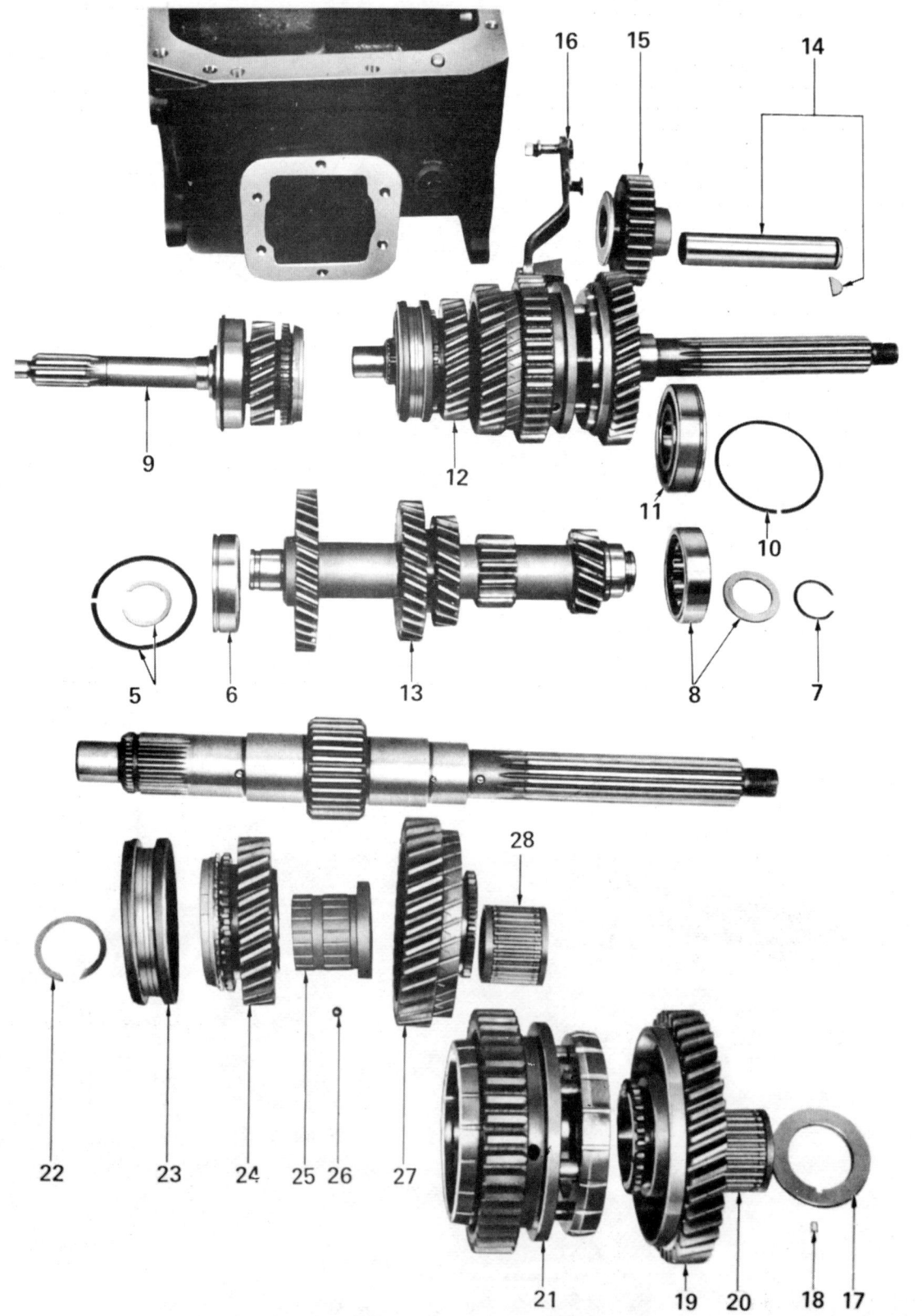

Fig. 6.20. Four-speed transmission (2F engine) gears and shafts

5 Snap-rings	12 Output shaft	18 Pin	23 Clutch Hub No. 2, sleeve and synchronizer ring
6 Bearing	13 Countershaft	19 First gear	
7 Snap-ring	14 Reverse idle gear shaft	20 Bearing	24 Third gear
8 Bearing	15 Reverse idle gear	21 Synchronizer Ring No. 1 subassembly	25 Bushing
9 Input shaft	16 Reverse shift arm		26 Ball
10 Snap-ring	17 Thrust washer	22 Snap-ring	27 Second gear
11 Bearing			28 Bearing

Items 1 to 4 not illustrated

6 Four-speed transmission output shaft - dismantling

1 Slide the thrust washer and 1st gear rearward from the output shaft. Remove the straight pin; where applicable also remove the needle bearing assembly.
2 Remove the snap-ring at the front end of the output shaft. Take off the clutch hub and sleeve, synchro ring and 3rd gear.
3 Where applicable, remove the snap-ring, and slide off the 2nd gear and thrust washer. Alternatively, remove the bushing and take out the steel ball from the drilling in the output shaft, then remove the 2nd gear and needle bearing assembly.
4 Remove the remaining synchro assembly, from the output shaft.

7 Four-speed transmission countershaft assembly (F engine) - dismantling

On transmissions used with type F engines, the drive gear and woodruff key, spacer, and third gear and woodruff key can be pressed off the countershaft sssembly.

8 Transmission components - inspection

1 Clean all the transmission components in kerosene, and dry carefully with a lint-free cloth.
2 Check all gears for wear and chipping of the teeth. Where it is found that one gear needs renewal, the appropriate mating gear should also be renewed if possible to reduce gear noise and improve life.
3 Check for wear and roughness on the synchro ring contacting surface, renewing as necessary.
4 Check for wear on the gear bearings and bushings, renewing as necessary.
5 Check the synchro rings for external tooth wear and damage. Check the contacting surface for signs of uneven wear. Place the synchro ring onto the respective gear core and check for specified clearance according to the particular transmission.
6 Check the shift keys and springs for wear, distortion and damage, replacing parts only as a complete set.
7 Examine all casing bearings and backings, for wear and noise when running. The bearings may be lubricated with a drop or two of transmission oil when checking. If the input shaft bearing needs renewal, remove the snap-ring and draw the bearing off using a universal puller.
8 Examine the bearing rollers for pitting and corrosion, replacing only as a complete set.
9 Check the shaft splines for wear and damage, particularly on bearing surfaces and oil seal contacting surfaces. Renew the shaft if damaged.
10 Examine the case assembly for damage such as cracks, or burrs on gasket surfaces.
11 Oil seals should be renewed as a matter of course. These can be pried from their locations and the new ones pressed in, once it has been established that the housings are clean. Lubricate the seal lip with transmission oil before installing the assembly to the transmission.
12 Check the shift fork to groove clearance, renewing parts as necessary if outside that specified. Also check for general damage of the forks, levers and shafts.
13 Inspect the splines of the clutch hubs and sleeves for wear and damage, renewing parts only as a complete set.
14 Inspect the reverse shift arm components for wear and damage.

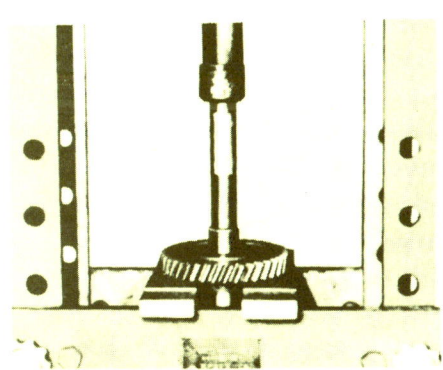

Fig. 6.21. Pressing off countershaft gear (F type transmission)

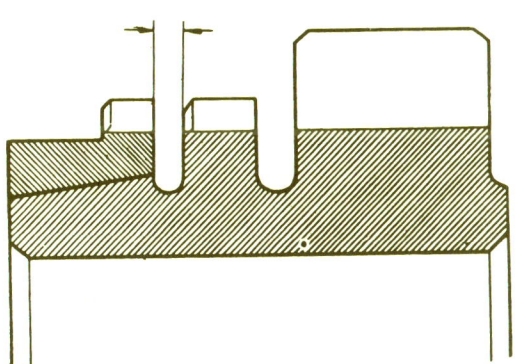

Fig. 6.22. Synchro ring to gear clearance measurement

Fig. 6.23. Measuring gear to bush oil clearance (A minus B)

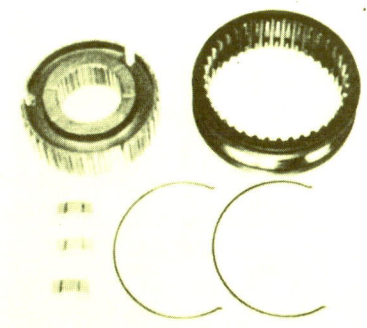

Fig. 6.24. Synchro components

Fig. 6.25. Checking shift fork to groove clearance

Fig. 6.26. Check the input shaft at the points arrowed

Fig. 6.27. Checking points for the reverse shift arm

1 Shoe
2 Shoe mounting
3 Pivot mounting
4 Pivot

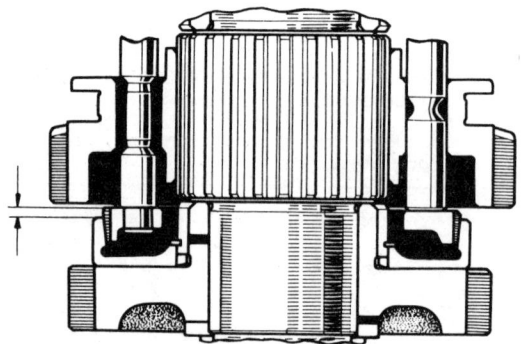

Fig. 6.28. Synchro ring clearance checking point

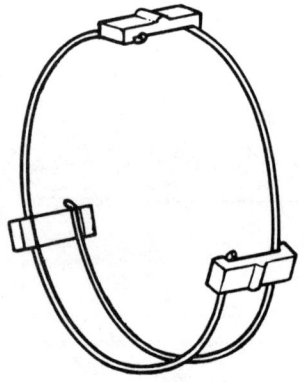

Fig. 6.29. Synchro spring arrangement

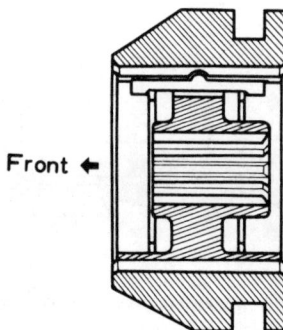

Fig. 6.30. Installed attitude of clutch hub and sleeve.

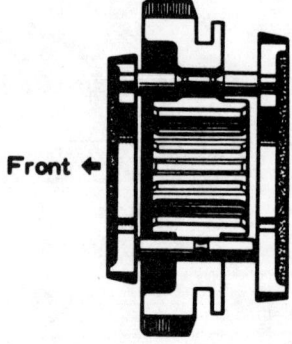

Fig. 6.31. Installed attitude of synchro unit

Fig. 6.32. Installing the ball and bush

9 Four-speed transmission output shaft (F engine) - reassembly

1 Slide the 2nd gear onto the shaft with the synchro outer ring to the rear, then install the 2nd gear thrust washer.
2 Select and install a snap-ring to provide the specified 2nd gear thrust clearance.
3 Slide on the 3rd gear with the synchro ring core towards the front of the shaft.
4 Assemble the synchro unit by installing the two shift key springs onto the clutch hub; place the three shift keys into the hub key slots. Install the springs so that they are as shown in Fig. 6.29.
5 Install the hub sleeve onto the clutch hub. After assembling the synchro unit, ensure that the hub moves freely.
6 Install the synchro ring No. 2, then slide the assembled clutch hub sleeve onto the output shaft. Ensure that it is in the direction shown in Fig. 6.30.
7 Select and install a snap-ring to obtain the specified synchro ring No. 2 thrust clearance.
8 Slide the synchro ring No. 1 assembly (reverse gear) onto the output shaft, in the direction shown in Fig. 6.31. After installation, check that the synchro ring moves smoothly.
9 Finally, install the 1st gear onto the output shaft.

10 Four-speed transmission output shaft (2 F engine) - reassembly

1 Install the needle roller assembly onto the front end of the output shaft, followed by the 2nd gear.
2 Place the steel ball in the hole, then install the bushing so that the groove aligns with the ball.
3 Install the 3rd gear and synchro ring.
4 Install the clutch hub No. 2 and sleeve, then select and install a snap-ring which will reduce the endfloat to a minimum. At this point also check that the 2nd and 3rd gear thrust clearances are within the specified limits.
5 Assemble the synchro unit as described in paragraphs 4 and 5 of Section 9.
6 Install the synchro ring No. 2, then slide the assembled synchro unit onto the output shaft. Ensure that it faces the direction shown in Fig. 6.34.
7 Install the needle roller assembly and 1st gear.
8 Install the shaft pin followed by the thrust washer, aligning the cut-out with the pin.

11 Four-speed transmission countershaft assembly (F engine) - reassembly

1 Place the woodruff key in the countershaft groove adjacent to 2nd gear.
2 Press on the 3rd gear, aligning the keyway with the key so that the hub is away from the 2nd gear.
3 Slide the spacer onto the shaft and install the second woodruff key.
4 Press on the drive gear, aligning the keyway with the key, so that the hub is towards the 3rd gear.

12 Three-speed transmission - reassembly

1 Smear a little general purpose grease into the reverse idler gear bore, then install the bearing rollers and washer.
2 Stick the thrust washers to the idler gear using grease, check that the rollers are all in position (held by the grease), then drive in the idler shaft from the rear. Retain the shaft with the woodruff key.
3 Smear general purpose grease in the bore of the countergear and install the tube.
4 Install the bearing rollers and washers into the bore of the countergear, using grease to retain them as for the reverse idler gear. Wherever possible, install a dummy countershaft into the countergear bore to retain the rollers in position; if one is not available take care that the rollers are pressed evenly against the bore of the countergear.
5 Place the countergear, the gear thrust washer and the casing side thrust washer into the transmission case. If necessary, the thrust washers can be held in position using grease.

Fig. 6.33. Checking 2nd and 3rd gear thrust clearances after selecting and installing snap-ring

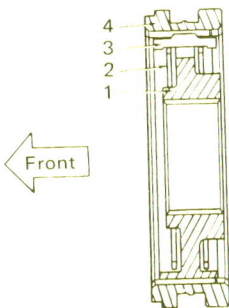

Fig. 6.34. Direction of installing clutch hub and sleeve

1 Hub
2 Sleeve
3 Shift keys
4 Key springs

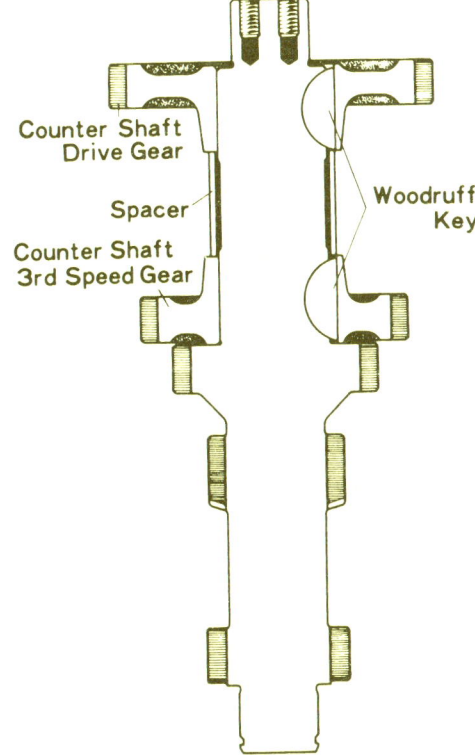

Fig. 6.35. Countershaft arrangement (F engine)

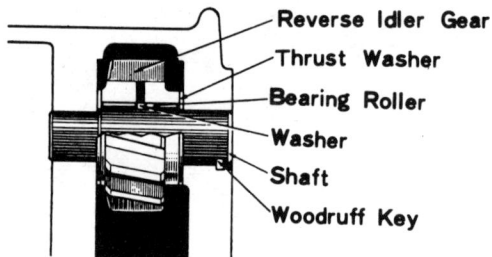

Fig. 6.36. Reverse idler gear arrangement

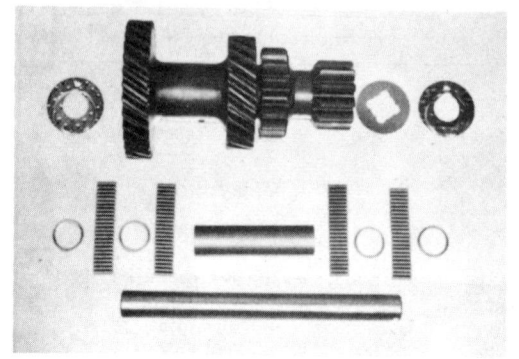

Fig. 6.37. Countergear and associated parts

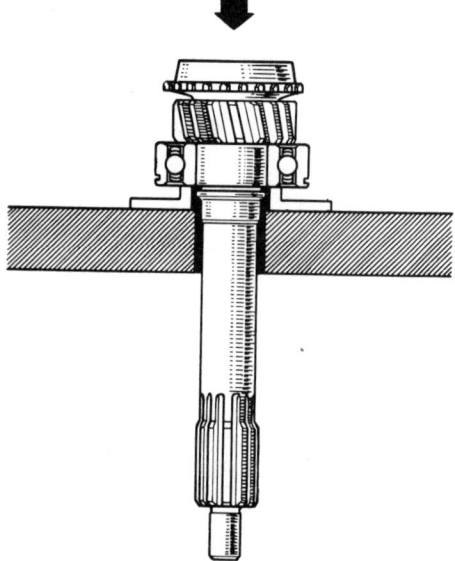

Fig. 6.38. Pressing on input shaft bearing

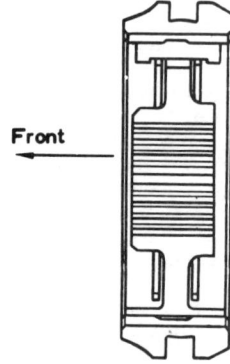

Fig. 6.39. Direction of installing synchro assembly

Fig. 6.40. Measuring 2nd gear thrust clearance

Fig. 6.41. Installing shift fork shaft

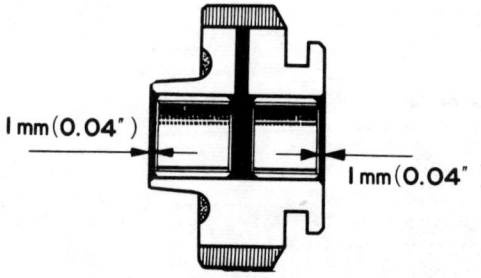

Fig. 6.42. Reverse idler gear bushings installation

6 If the input shaft bearing was removed, install the bearing on the shaft by carefully pressing it on by the inner race. Select a suitable snap-ring to obtain the minimum amount of thrust play on the shaft.
7 Smear some general purpose grease in the counterbore of the input shaft, then install the needle bearing and retain it with the snap-ring.
8 Install the input shaft, pressing on the outer race of the bearing to retain it.
9 Carefully lift the countergear into position and push in the countershaft. If a dummy shaft has been used this will be straightforward; if a dummy countershaft has not been used, check that the thrust washers and needle rollers are in position and very carefully push in the shaft. Take great care as the end of the shaft passes the rollers so that no parts are displaced.
10 Secure the countershaft with the woodruff key.
11 Measure the countershaft thrust clearance using a feeler gauge; if outside that specified, select and fit a new side thrust washer at the rear end of the shaft to bring it into the tolerance.
12 Assemble the synchro units by installing the shift key springs onto the clutch hub and placing shifting keys into the clutch tube hub slots. Ensure that the springs are aligned as shown in Fig. 6.29 and that the synchro unit is as shown in Fig. 6.39.
13 Slide the clutch hub sleeve onto the clutch hub.
14 Assemble the 2nd gear, synchro ring No. 2 and the assembled synchro unit onto the output shaft, then measure the 2nd gear thrust clearance. If outside the specified limit, select a new snap-ring for the front end of the mainshaft. Install the shaft snap-ring.
15 Slide the 1st/reverse gear onto the output shaft.
16 Place the output shaft assembly and synchro ring No. 2 into the casing. Select 3rd gear with the hub sleeve to ensure that the input shaft will enter.
17 Install the output shaft bearing over the shaft and into the casing, tapping it in on the outer race only.
18 At this stage, liberally lubricate the gears with transmission oil, checking that everything operates and rotates freely.
19 Put the 1st/reverse and 2nd/3rd shift forks in position.
20 Install the shift fork lock springs and balls into the shift fork holes. While pressing down on the balls with a screwdriver, drive in the shaft. Install a new O-ring on the shaft and lock the shaft with the straight pin.
21 Install the front bearing retainer and gasket, using a non-setting gasket sealant. Ensure that the oil hole (where applicable) is at the bottom.
22 Install the transmission case cover and gasket, ensuring that the shift lever engages correctly.
23 Where applicable, install the gear select outer lever, and retain it with the bolt.

13 Four-speed transmission (F engine) - reassembly

1 If the reverse idler gear bushings were removed they should be installed with their open ends 90° apart. Press them into the depth shown in Fig. 6.42.
2 Install the reverse idler gear, with the fork groove towards the front, and carefully drive in the shaft and woodruff key. Ensure that the key aligns with the slot in the casing.
3 Install the reverse shift arm and pivot, tightening finger-tight only.
4 Make-up three gauges using stiff card as shown in Fig. 6.43.
5 Install gauge B into the reverse idler shift groove (in reverse position) then rotate the shift pivot to obtain a dimension of 4.49 in (114 mm) between the outer rear end of the casing and the front of the gear. Tighten the pivot nut securely.
6 Using gauge A on the reverse shift arm pin and gauge C in the gear shift groove, check the neutral position which should be 2.71 in (69 mm) from the front end of the gear to the outer rear end of the casing. If necessary, re-adjust the shift arm pivot.
7 Position the assembled countershaft into the casing, then install the rear bearing by pressing or tapping on the outer race only. Install the countershaft snap-ring.
8 Install the front bearing spacer onto the countershaft with the shoulder forward.
9 Press on the front bearing until the snap-ring contacts the front of the casing, pressing on the outer race only.
10 Install the retainer plate and lockwasher on the front end of the crankshaft, and tighten the retaining bolts. Check for free rotation of

the shaft then fold up the washer tabs.
11 Carefully install the assembled output shaft into the casing.
12 Place the 1st gear thrust washer on the shaft, aligning the thrust washer slot with the straight pin on the shaft.
13 Align the shaft and gears in the casing. Install the rear bearing, carefully tapping it in on the outer race only.
14 Install the rear bearing retainer using a new gasket.
15 If the input shaft bearing was removed press on a replacement. Make sure that load is only applied to the bearing inner race.
16 Smear some general purpose grease into the rear end counterbore of the input shaft and put the eighteen rollers evenly in position.
17 Install the input shaft into the casing, position the spacer on the nose of the output shaft and bring the two shafts into alignment. Check that the synchro ring No. 2 has its keyways aligned with the shifting keys.
18 Install the front bearing retainer, using a new gasket.
19 At this point, generously lubricate the gears with transmission oil, and check that all parts rotate or slide correctly.

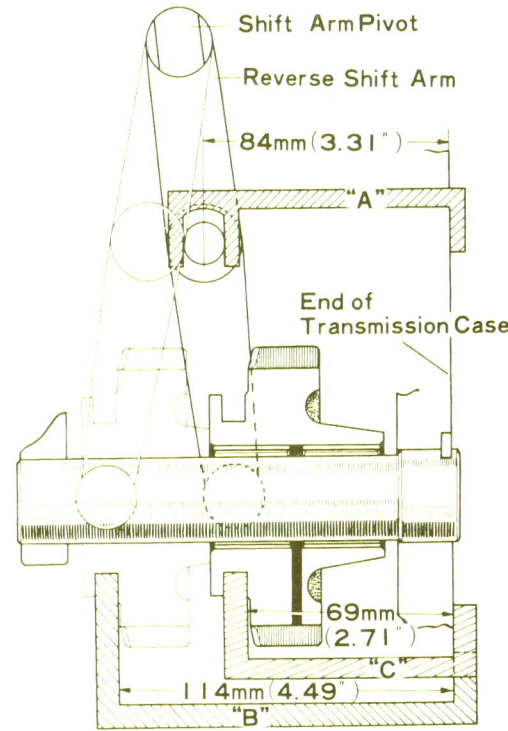

Fig. 6.43. Gauges for setting up reverse shift arm

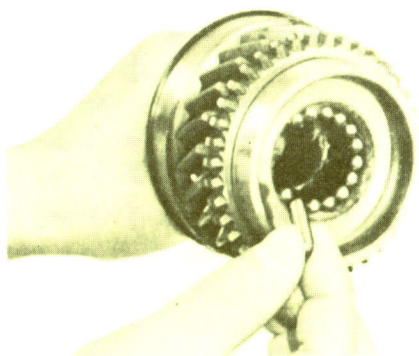

Fig. 6.44. Installing input shaft rollers

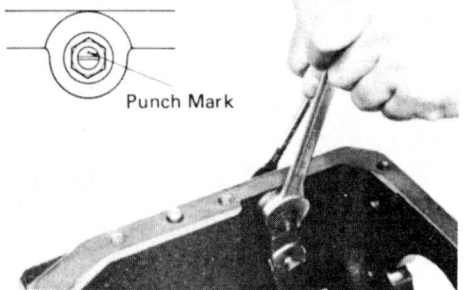

Fig. 6.45. Punch mark on reverse arm pivot

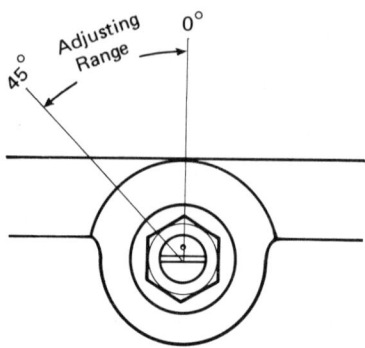

Fig. 6.46. Reposition pivot, if necessary, over the range shown

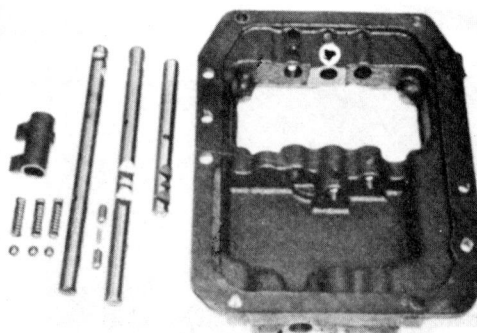

Fig. 6.47. Case cover parts

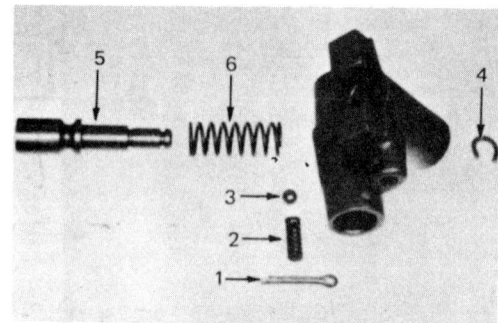

Fig. 6.48. Reverse shift head parts

1 Cotter pin 4 C-washer
2 Spring 5 Plunger
3 Ball 6 Spring

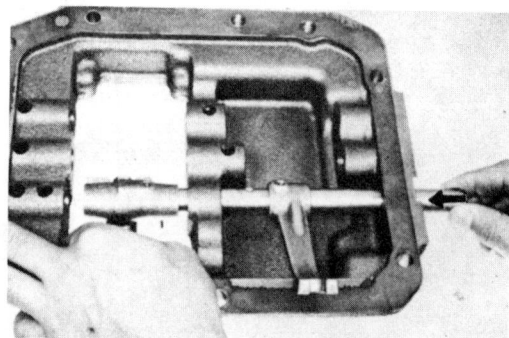

Fig. 6.49. Installing the reverse shift shaft

Fig. 6.50. Installing an interlock pin

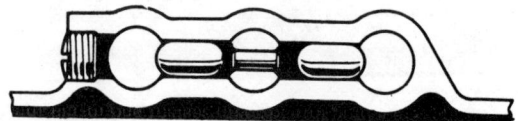

Fig. 6.51. Interlock pin arrangement

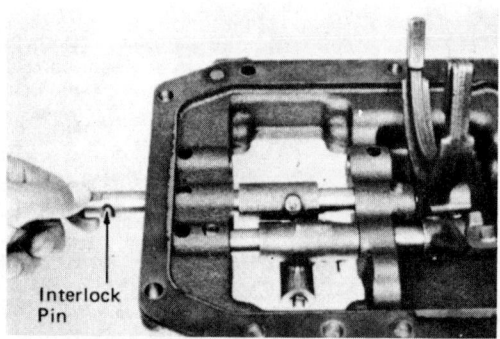

Fig. 6.52. Installing 1st/2nd shaft interlock pin

14 Four-speed transmission (2 F engine) - reassembly

1 This transmission is similar to the F engine transmission as described in Section 15. However, the following points should be noted:

a) When installing the reverse shift arm pivot, a punch mark on the pivot should always be installed in the uppermost position.
b) When installing the countershaft front bearing select a snap-ring for the shaft which will eliminate end-play.
c) Install the top cover before reconnecting the transmission to the transfer, and check that all gears can be selected correctly. Check that reverse gear can be selected without any grating noise. If necessary, the reverse shift link pivot can be repositioned over the range shown in Fig. 6.46 to correct this.

15 Four-speed transmission top cover - dismantling, inspection and reassembly

1 Move the 3rd/4th shift fork to the neutral position, then drive out the spring pin with a suitable punch. Carefully drive out the shaft with a brass or aluminium drift, collect the shift fork, lock ball and spring.
2 Move the 1st/2nd shift fork to the neutral position, then drive out the spring pins from the 1st/2nd shift fork and the 1st/2nd shift head.
3 Remove the plug at the rear end of the cover, then drive out the shaft, complete with the plug at the front end, with a brass or aluminium drift.
4 Remove the shift fork, shift head, lock ball and spring. Remove the pin at the front end of the 1st/2nd shift fork shaft.
5 With neutral selected, drive out the spring pins from the reverse shift fork and the reverse shift head.
6 Take out the reverse shift fork, shift head, lock ball and spring.
7 Remove the two interlock pins in the cover. If necessary, remove the taper screw plug and push them out with a long drift.
8 Remove the cotter pin, and take out the reverse shift head spring and lock ball.
9 Remove the C-washer, and pull out the reverse shift return plunger and spring from the reverse shift head.
10 Examine the shafts and shift head for wear and damage on the sliding surfaces. Check the balls and springs for corrosion, wear and damage. Check the shift forks and grooves as described in Section 8.
11 Install the spring and reverse shift return plunger into the shift head and secure them with the C-washer.
12 Install the ball and spring, and retain them with the cotter pin.
13 Place the reverse shift head and shift fork onto the cover. Install the fork lock spring and ball, then install the shaft thru the cover from the front end. Push the fork lock ball down with a screwdriver as the shaft passes thru the shaft head.
14 Align the holes and drive the spring pins into the reverse shift fork and shift head. This is done in the neutral position.
15 Smear the interlock pin with grease and install it in the interlock hole of the cover.
16 Install the 1st/2nd shift head and fork, and the lock spring and ball, following the same procedure as for the reverse shift components. Install the straight pin in the hole in the 1st/2nd shaft, then assemble the shift (and spacer on transmissions used with F engines) from the front of the cover. Push down the ball with a screwdriver as the shaft passes thru.
17 Drive in the spring pin to secure the shift head and shift fork in the neutral position.
18 Smear the second interlock pin with grease and install it into the interlock hole in the cover.
19 Install the fork lock spring and ball, then assemble the 3rd/4th shift fork and shaft. Drive in the spring pin to retain the fork in the neutral position.
20 Check for smooth operation of the shift forks, then smear a non-setting gasket sealant onto new expansion plugs and drive them in so that they are approximately 0.075 in (2 mm) below the cover surface. Smear the screw plug threads with sealant and install them.

16 Column shift linkage - adjustment

1 Detach the adjustable length rods at their adjustable ends.
2 Place the shift lever and the transmission levers in the neutral position.
3 Adjust the length of the shift rods so that they can be connected without moving the shift lever or the transmission levers.
4 Lock the adjustments, then reconnect the shift rods.
5 If necessary, a slight further adjustment may be made if road testing indicates that it is necessary.

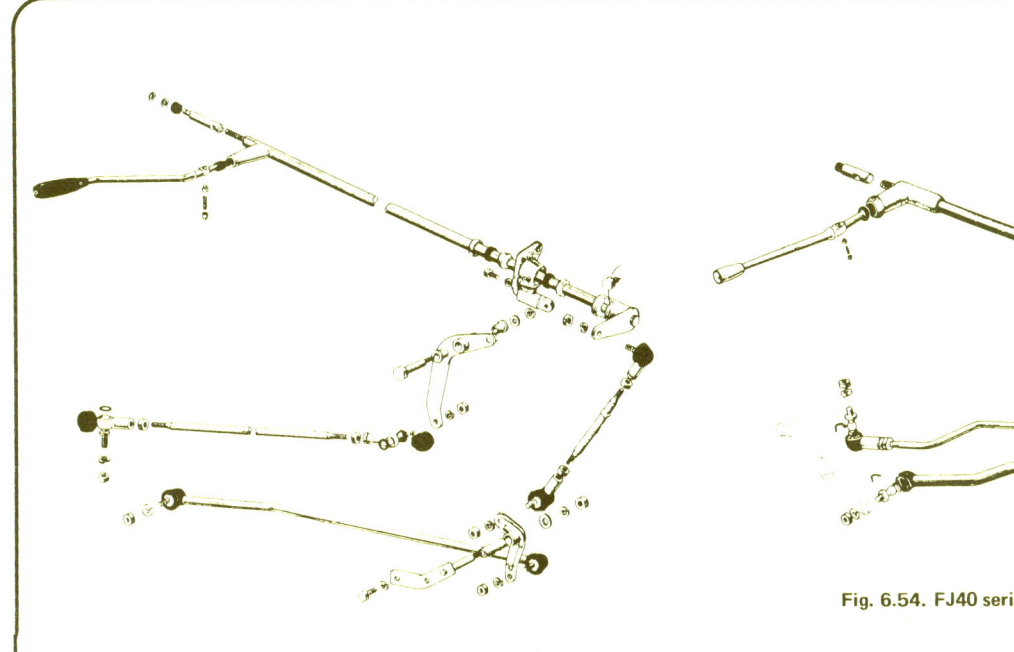

Fig. 6.53. FJ55 series column shift linkage

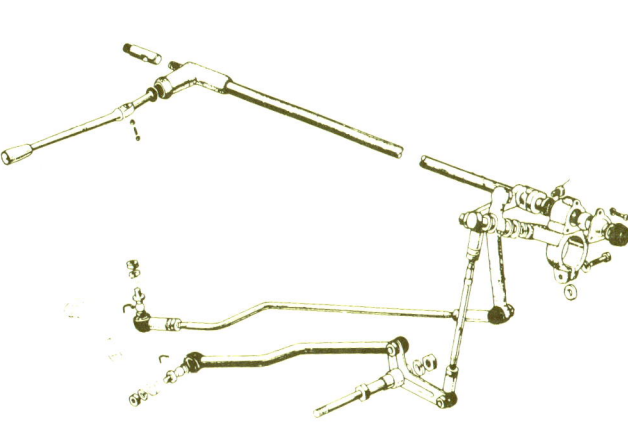

Fig. 6.54. FJ40 series column shift linkage

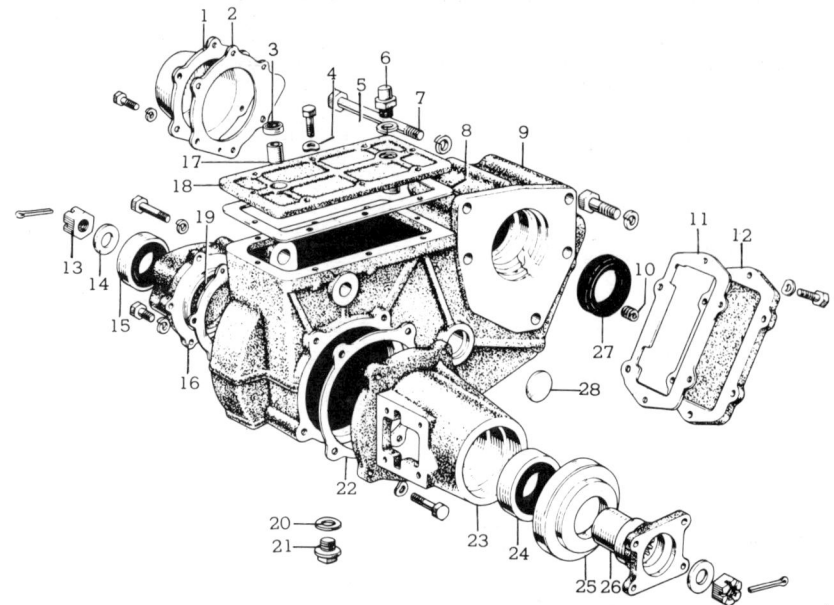

Fig. 6.55. Transfer case and cover

1 Transfer case cover No. 2
2 Gasket
3 Oil seal
4 Wave washer
5 Lock washer
6 Breather plug
7 Bolt
8 Gasket
9 Transfer case
10 Spring
11 Gasket
12 Power take-off cover
13 Retaining nut
14 Washer
15 Oil seal
16 Output shaft bearing rear retainer
17 Bushing
18 Cover
19 Gasket
20 Gasket
21 Plug
22 Gasket
23 Extension housing
24 Oil seal
25 Dust deflector
26 Joint flange
27 Oil seal
28 Expansion plug

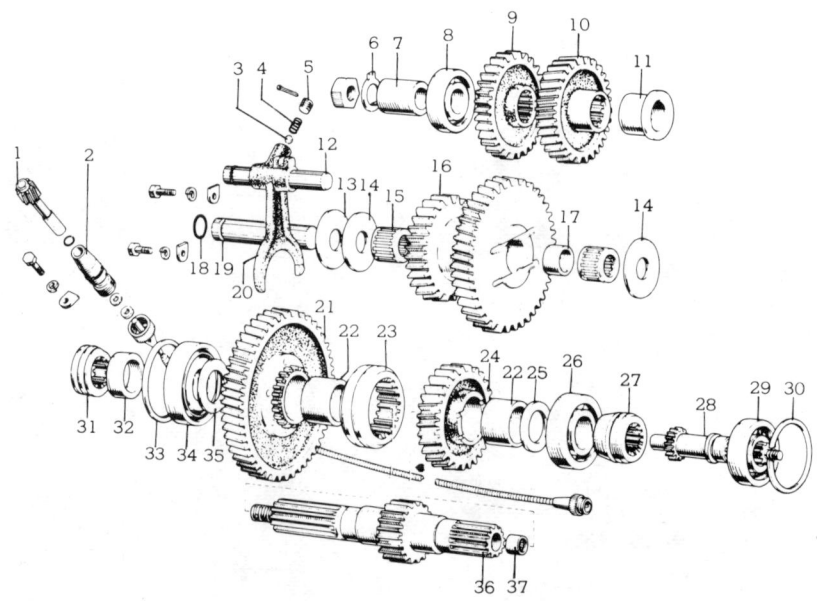

Fig. 6.56. Transfer shafts and gears

1 Speedometer driven gear
2 Speedometer shaft sleeve
3 Shift fork lock ball
4 Spring
5 Screw plug
6 Lock washer
7 Input shaft spacer
8 Bearing
9 Power take-off drive gear
10 Transfer input gear
11 Input gear stopper (four-speed T/M)
12 Transfer high/low shift fork shaft
13 Idler gear spacer
14 Washer
15 Needle roller bearing
16 Transfer idler gear
17 Spacer
18 O-ring
19 Idler gear shaft
20 High/low shift fork
21 Low speed output gear
22 Bushing
23 High/low clutch sleeve
24 High speed output gear
25 Washer
26 Bearing
27 Front drive clutch sleeve
28 Transfer output front shaft
29 Bearing
30 Hole snap-ring
31 Speedometer drive gear
32 Spacer
33 Adjusting shim
34 Bearing
35 Washer
36 Output shaft
37 Needle roller bearing

17 Transfer gear - dismantling, inspection and reassembly

1 Remove the cotter pin, or relieve the nut stacking, and unscrew the parking brake drum retaining nut.
2 Pull the brake drum off the transfer output shaft, then detach the parking brake plate assembly from the output shaft rear bearing retainer.
3 Remove the speedometer sleeve lockplate, followed by the shaft sleeve assembly, from the rear bearing retainer.
4 Remove the rear bearing retainer and its gasket.
5 Slide the speedometer drive gear and spacer off the transfer output shaft.
6 Remove the diaphragm cylinder, or shift shaft guide, and the front drive fork assembly and gasket from the transfer extension housing.
7 Remove the cotter pin, or relieve the nut stacking, and unscrew the front driveshaft flange nut. Prevent the flange from rotating by passing two bolts thru the flange holes and using a bar for leverage.
8 Remove the extension housing and gasket together with the internal parts.
9 Remove the front driveshaft flange, then drive out the front shaft and clutch sleeve towards the rear.
10 Pry out the oil seal from the extension housing.
11 Remove the snap-ring and use a suitable tubular drift to press out the front bearing. Apply pressure to the bearing outer race only.
12 Remove the transfer case cover assembly and gasket.
13 Remove the cotter pin and unscrew the screw plug from the shift fork. Invert the casing and tip out the ball and spring.
14 Remove the lock plate and drive out the shift fork shaft towards the rear using a brass or aluminium drift; remove the shift fork.
15 Whilst preventing the low speed gear from moving forward by wedging it against the case with a screwdriver or suitable spacer, remove the shaft together with the high speed gear and the high and low clutch sleeve. Also remove the low speed gear from the case.
16 Carefully drive or press the output shaft out of the gear, taking care that the shaft and gear are not damaged in doing so.
17 Measure the idler gear thrust clearance, and if outside the specified limit, obtain a new thrust washer for use during reassembly.
18 Using a suitable extractor screwed into the end of the idler shaft, draw the shaft out of the casing.
19 Remove the bearings, spacer and thrust washers, carefully noting their installed positions.
20 Clean all the transfer components in kerosene, and dry carefully with a lint-free cloth.
21 Check all the gears for wear and chipping of the teeth. Where it is found that one gear needs renewal, the appropriate mating gear should also be renewed to reduce gear noise and improve operating life.
22 Check for wear on the gear bearings and bushings, renewing as necessary.
23 Check all casing bearings and bushings for wear and noise when running. The bearings may be lubricated with a drop or two of transmission oil when checking.
24 Check the shaft splines for wear and damage and, particularly, on bearing surfaces and oil seal contacting faces. Renew the shaft if damaged.
25 Examine the case assembly for damage such as cracks, or burrs on gasket faces.
26 Oil seals should be renewed as a matter of course. These can be pried from their locations and new ones pressed in once it has been extablished that the housings are clean. Lubricate the seal lip with transmission oil before installing shaft(s).
27 Check the shift fork for groove clearance, renewing parts as necessary if outside that specified. Also check for general damage to the fork and shaft.
28 Inspect the splines of the clutch hub and sleeve for wear and damage, renewing parts only as a complete set.
29 Check the speedometer driven and drive gears for damage, renewing as necessary.
30 Commence reassembly by installing the bearing spacer and two needle roller bearings into the transfer idler gear.
31 Place the idler gear and the two idler gear spacers and washer in position in the casing. Install a new O-ring onto the shaft then drive it in from the rear.
32 Recheck the thrust clearance (see paragraph 17) to ensure that it is correct.

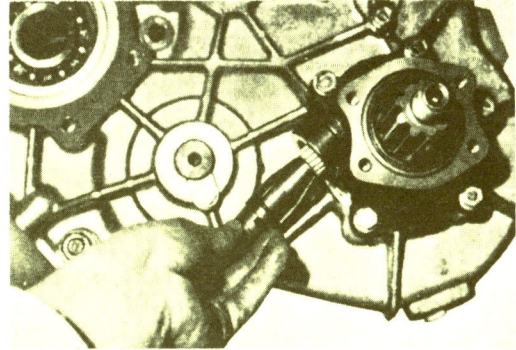

Fig. 6.57. Removing speedometer shaft sleeve

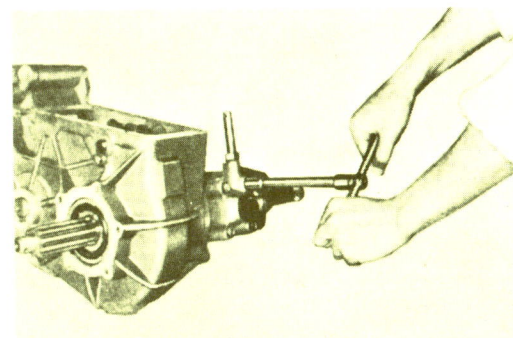

Fig. 6.58. Removing the shift shaft guide

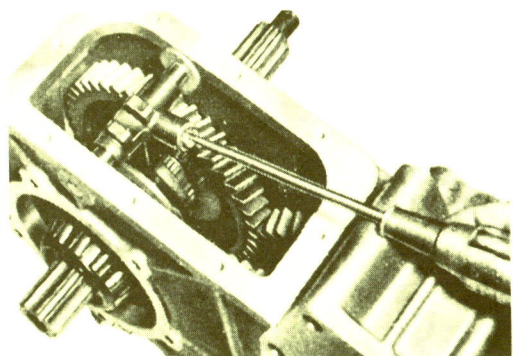

Fig. 6.59. Removing the screw plug for access to the ball and spring

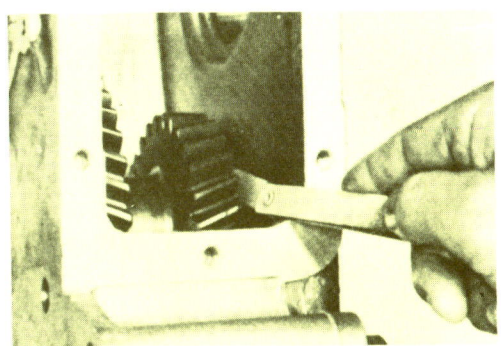

Fig. 6.60. Measuring idler gear thrust clearance

33 Secure the transfer idler shaft with the lock plate.
34 Slide the high speed gear onto the output shaft, then install the washer and press on the bearing. Drive on the bearing using the inner race only and using a suitable tubular spacer.
35 Place the low speed gear and high/low clutch sleeve in position in the casing, then install the output shaft, gear and bearing.
36 Install the washer and rear bearing on the output shaft using a suitable tubular spacer on the inner race only.
37 Carefully press in the front and rear bearing cups (outer races) in the casing.
38 On the extension housing, install the front shaft bearing and retain it with the snap-ring.
39 If not previously installed, install the oil seal and lubricate the lip with transmission oil.
40 Install the output front shaft into the extension housing and install the joint flange. Install the washer and tighten the nut to the specified torque. Install the cotter pin or stake the nut, as applicable.
41 Using a rear gasket and a non-setting gasket sealant, install the extension housing assembly and front drive clutch sleeve onto the casing, and secure with the bolts. **Note: Ensure that the tapered side of the clutch sleeve is towards the rear.**
42 Slide the spacer and speedometer gear onto the output shaft.
43 Place the bearing adjuster shim in position on the output shaft rear bearing cup, then install the bearing retainer using a new gasket with non-setting gasket sealant.
44 Install the parking brake and tighten the retaining nut to the specified torque. Do not install the cotter pin or stake the nuts.
45 Using a spring balance and cord, check the bearing pre-load with the high/low clutch sleeve in neutral and the front drive disengaged. If necessary, remove the parking brake assembly and select a new shim to obtain the correct bearing pre-load.
46 Remove the parking brake drum, then install the high/low shift fork and shift fork shaft. Do not forget the shaft O-ring. Secure the shift fork shaft with the lockplate.
47 Insert the shift fork lock ball and spring into the shift fork, and screw in the straight plug. Lock the plug with the cotter pin.
48 Assemble the high/low inner lever, and the outer lever.
49 Install the case cover and gasket.
50 Install the speedometer shaft sleeve and driven gear into the rear bearing retainer and secure with the lock plate.
51 Install the parking brake assembly and the brake drum. Tighten the nut to the specified torque and install the cotter pin or stake the nut, as applicable.

18 Transfer front drive vacuum control system - description

1 This system is available as an option from September 1972 onwards and has been developed to provide an easier shift.
2 The front drive is engaged by pulling a dash mounted switch knob, and disengaged by pushing it. When the shift lever is moved to 'Low', the front drive engages automatically without using the dash mounted switch.
3 The operation of the system is explained diagrammatically in the accompanying illustrations (Fig. 6.64).

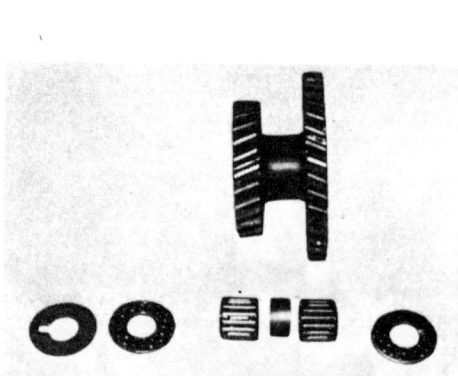

Fig. 6.61. Idler gear component layout

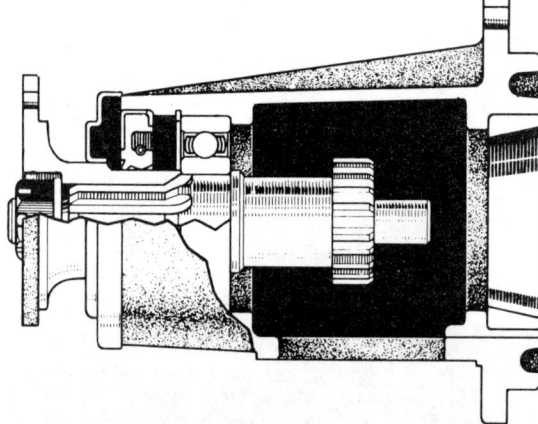

Fig. 6.62. Transfer extension housing assembly

Fig. 6.63. Direction of installing clutch sleeve

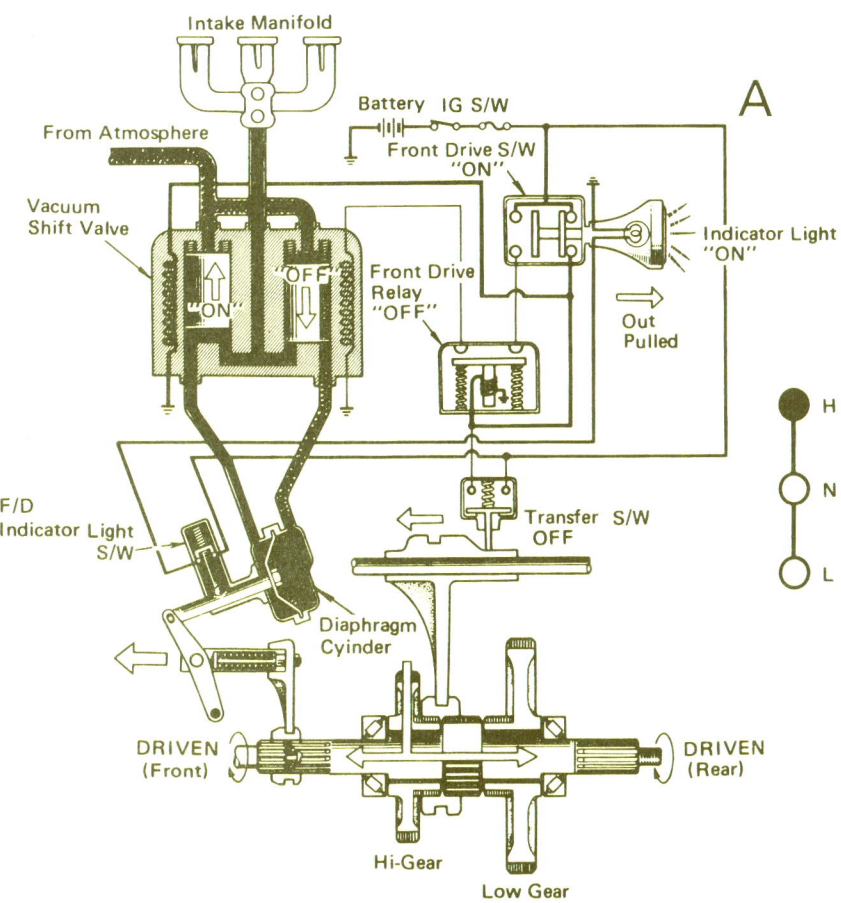
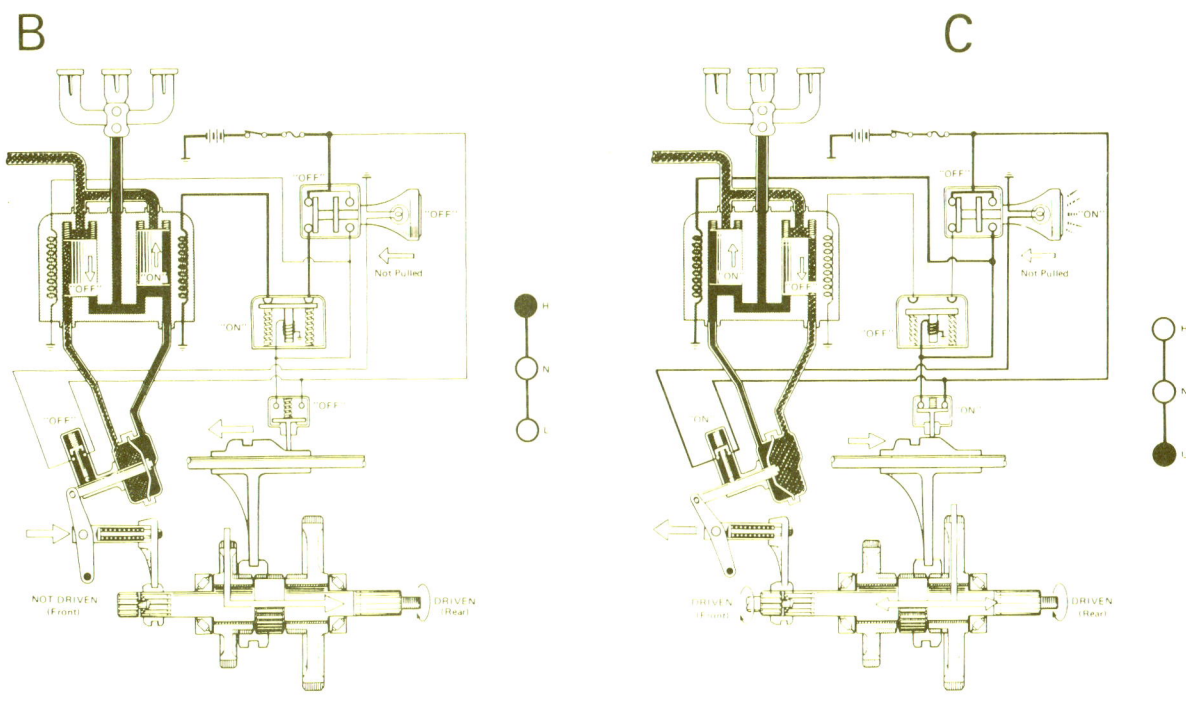

Fig. 6.64. Front drive vacuum control system - schematic diagram

A System switch 'ON' B System switch 'OFF' C Low range selected

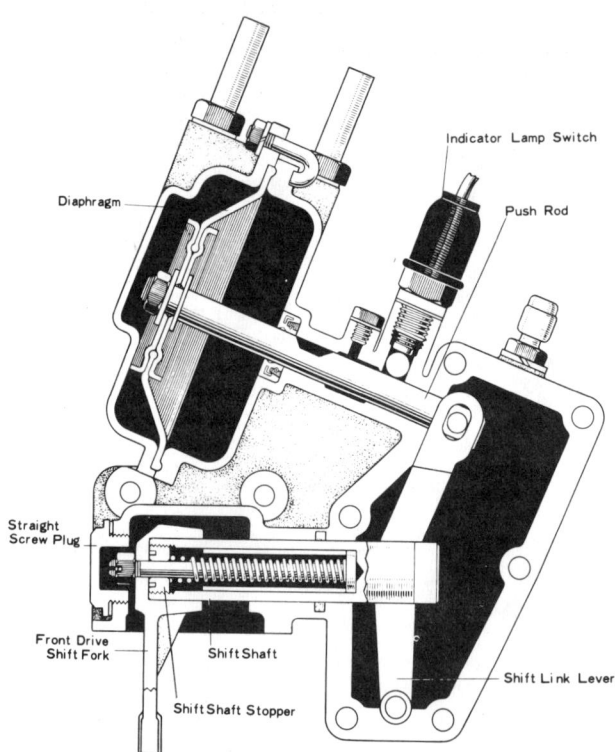

Fig. 6.65. Sectional view of vacuum unit

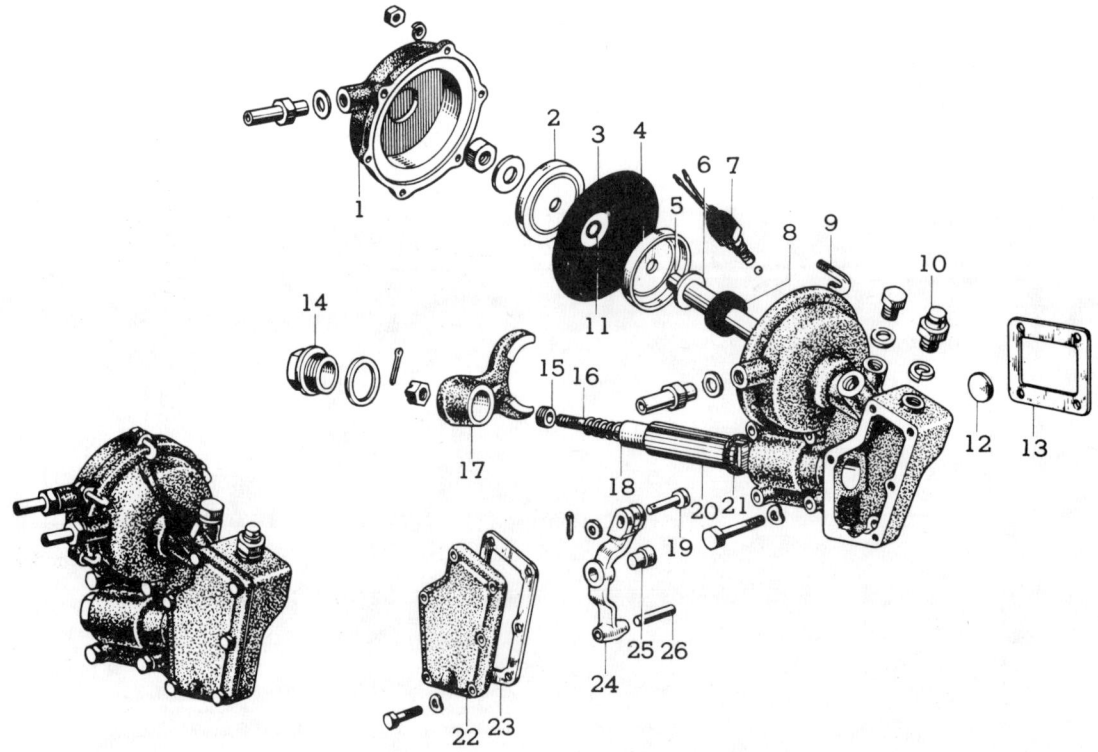

Fig. 6.66. Vacuum unit - exploded view

1 Diaphragm cylinder body cover	6 Washer	13 Gasket	20 Front drive shift shaft
2 Diaphragm plate	7 Front drive indicator switch	14 Screw plug	21 Dust seal
3 Diaphragm	8 Oil seal	15 Stopper	22 Diaphragm cylinder cover
4 Diaphragm plate	9 Bolt	16 Bolt	23 Gasket
5 Pushrod	10 Breather plug	17 Shift fork	24 Shift link lever
	11 O-ring	18 Spacer	25 Link lever shoe
	12 Expansion plug	19 Pin	26 Straight pin

19 Transfer front drive vacuum control system - removal and installation

1 Remove the cover plate from beneath the transmission.
2 Drain the transfer gear lubricant into a container of suitable size.
3 Remove the cotter pin and detach the high/low shift rod No. 3 from the transfer high/low shift outer lever.
4 Loosen the hose clips and disconnect the vacuum hoses cylinder body and cover unions.
5 Detach the front drive indicator switch wiring.
6 Remove the bolts and detach the front drive fork assembly from the transfer extension housing.
7 Installation is basically the reverse of the removal procedure. However, when installing the diaphragm cylinder and transfer front drive fork assembly, apply a non-setting sealant to the gasket surfaces. Top up the transfer with the correct grade and quantity of oil; finally check the system operation during a road test.

20 Transfer front drive vacuum control system - dismantling, inspection and reassembly

1 Remove the front drive indicator light switch and steel ball from the diaphragm cylinder body.
2 Remove the cylinder body cover.
3 Remove the diaphragm cylinder cover and gasket.
4 Remove the straight pin from the shift link lever; also remove the cotter pin and washer.
5 Remove the pushrod pin, and take out the shift link lever.
6 Slide the pushrod and diaphragm out of the cylinder body.
7 Remove the screw plug and washer, then remove the cotter pin and nut from the pushrod bolt.
8 Remove the front drive shift fork from the shift shaft, then slide the shift shaft out of the cylinder body.
9 Unscrew the shift shaft stopper using a peg wrench or similar tool, and take out the pushrod bolt, spring and spacer.
10 Remove the diaphragm nut, diaphragm plates, diaphragm and washer from the diaphragm pushrod.
11 Wash all the metal parts in kerosene and dry thoroughly. Wipe clean the diaphragm and oil seal, and renew if worn or otherwise damaged. Check the fit of the pushrod in the diaphragm cylinder body, renewing parts as necessary. Check for excessive wear in the front drive shift shaft groove and on the lever shoe, renewing parts as necessary.
12 Reassembly is basically the reverse of the dismantling procedure, but the following should be noted:

   a) Ensure that the slot in the diaphragm pushrod is towards the indicator lamp switch side.
   b) After assembling the front drive shift shaft, lock the stopper in two places by center punching.
   c) Apply a little general purpose grease to all pivoting and sliding surfaces.

21 Transfer shift linkage

1 The component parts of the different types of shift linkage are shown in Figs. 6.67, 6.68, 6.69 and 6.70.
2 If dismantling is required, it should be carried out by detaching components in numerical order as shown in the illustrations.

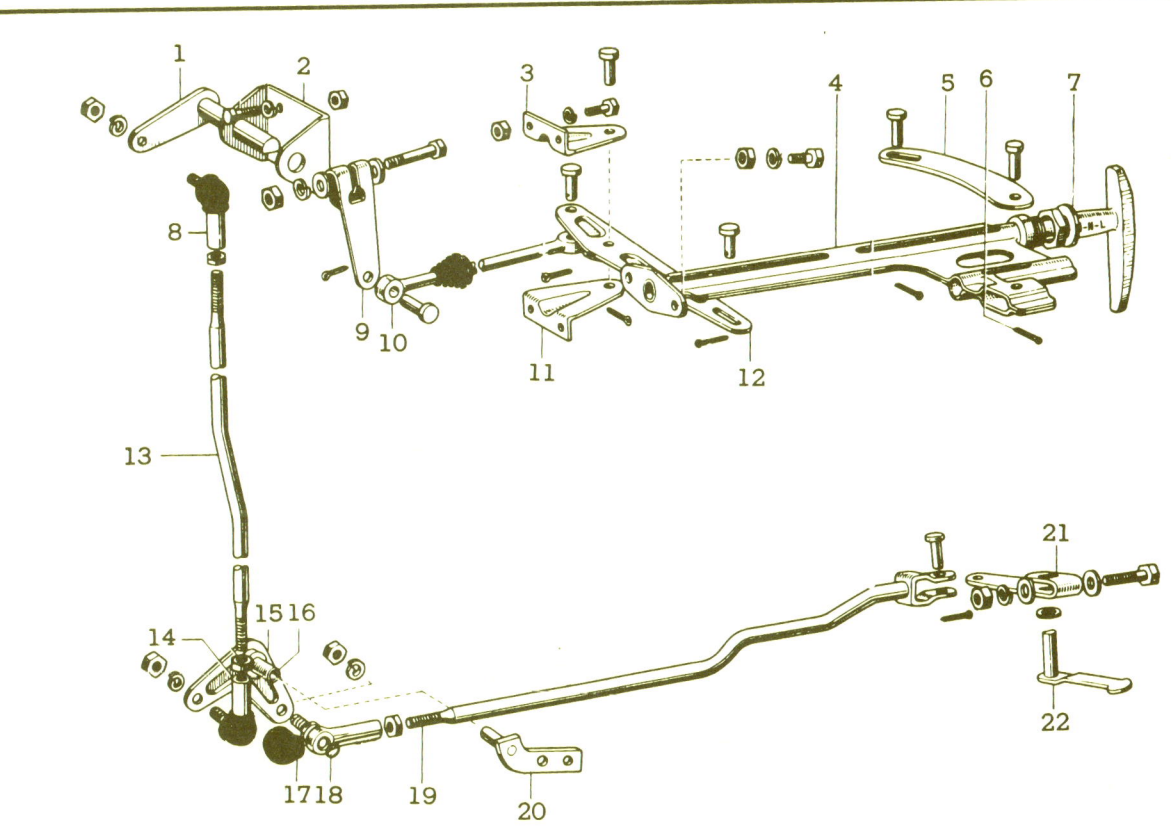

Fig. 6.67. Direct shift transfer linkage - early type

1 High/low shift link lever	7 High/low shift lever	12 Front drive guide lever No. 2	17 Dust seal
2 Shift link bracket	8 Connecting rod end No. 1	13 High/low shift rod No. 2	18 Snap-ring
3 Shift link bracket No. 1	9 Shift link lever No. 1	14 Connecting rod end No. 2	19 High/low shift rod No. 3
4 Shift lever guide	10 High/low shift rod No. 1	15 Shifting bell crank	20 Link-lever support
5 Front drive guide lever No. 1	11 Shift link bracket No. 1	16 Bell crank bushing	21 Transfer high/low shift lever
6 Cotter pin			22 Shift inner lever

Fig. 6.68. Direct shift transfer linkage - later type

1 Shift lever knob
2 Shift lever
3 Shift lever guide
4 High/low shift rod No. 3
5 High/low shift link lever
6 High/low shift rod No. 1
7 Shift lever pin No. 1
8 Support shaft
9 Shift lever pin No. 2
10 Support shaft
11 Shift link lever
12 Link lever shoe
13 Shift shaft guide assembly
14 Pin
15 Shift fork
16 Shift shaft guide
17 Shift shaft
18 Grease nipple

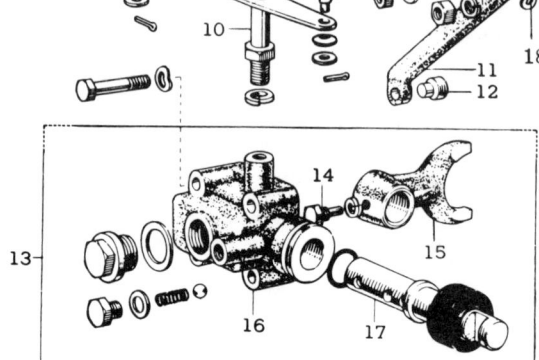

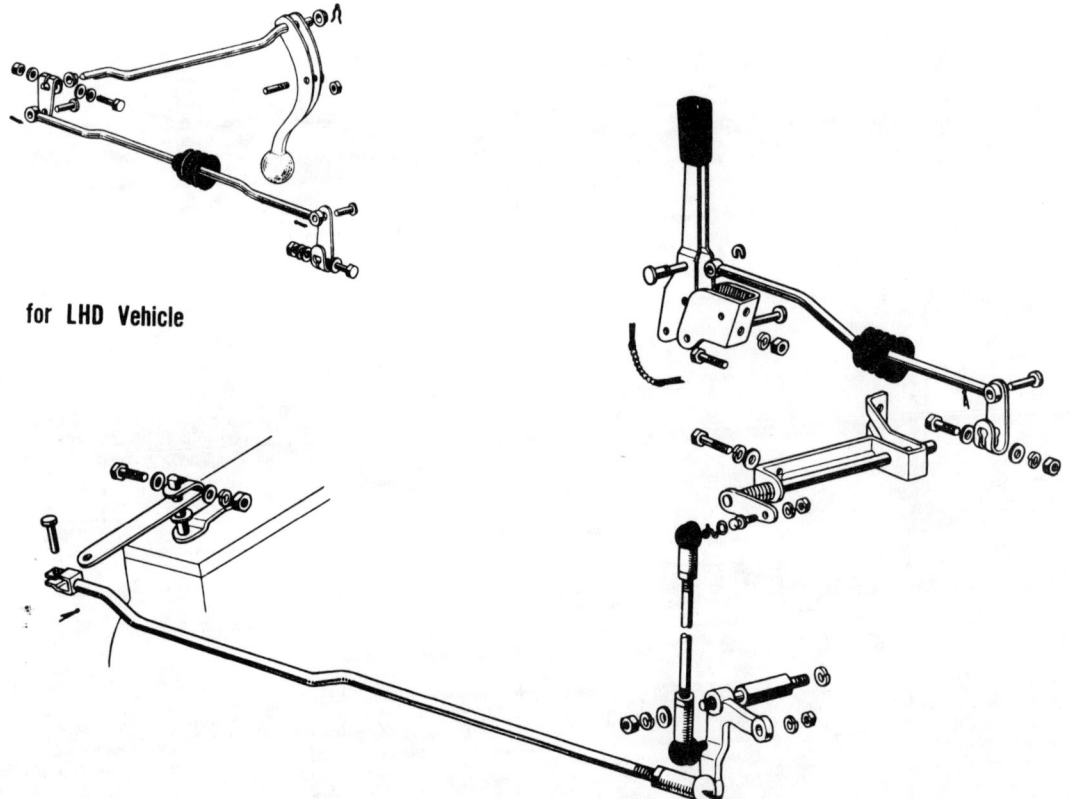

Fig. 6.69. Vacuum shift transfer linkage - early FJ40 series

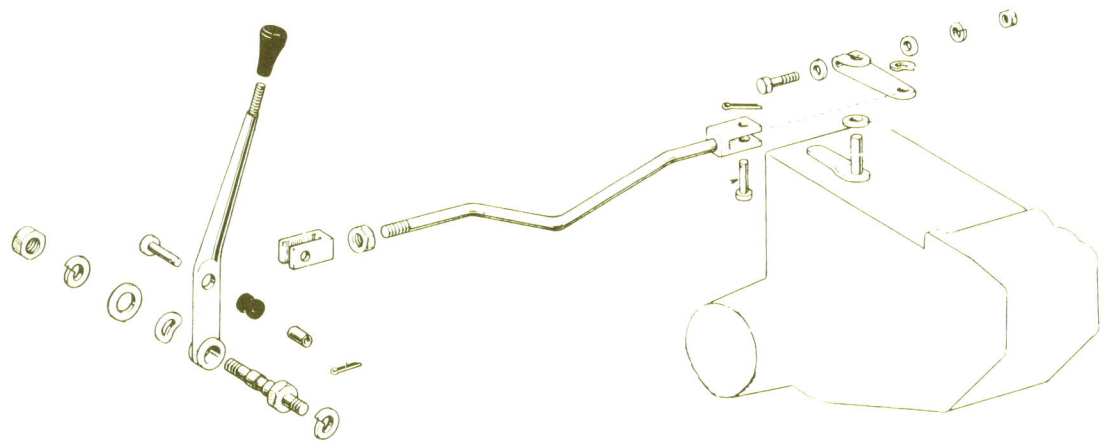

Fig. 6.70. Vacuum shift transfer linkage - later type

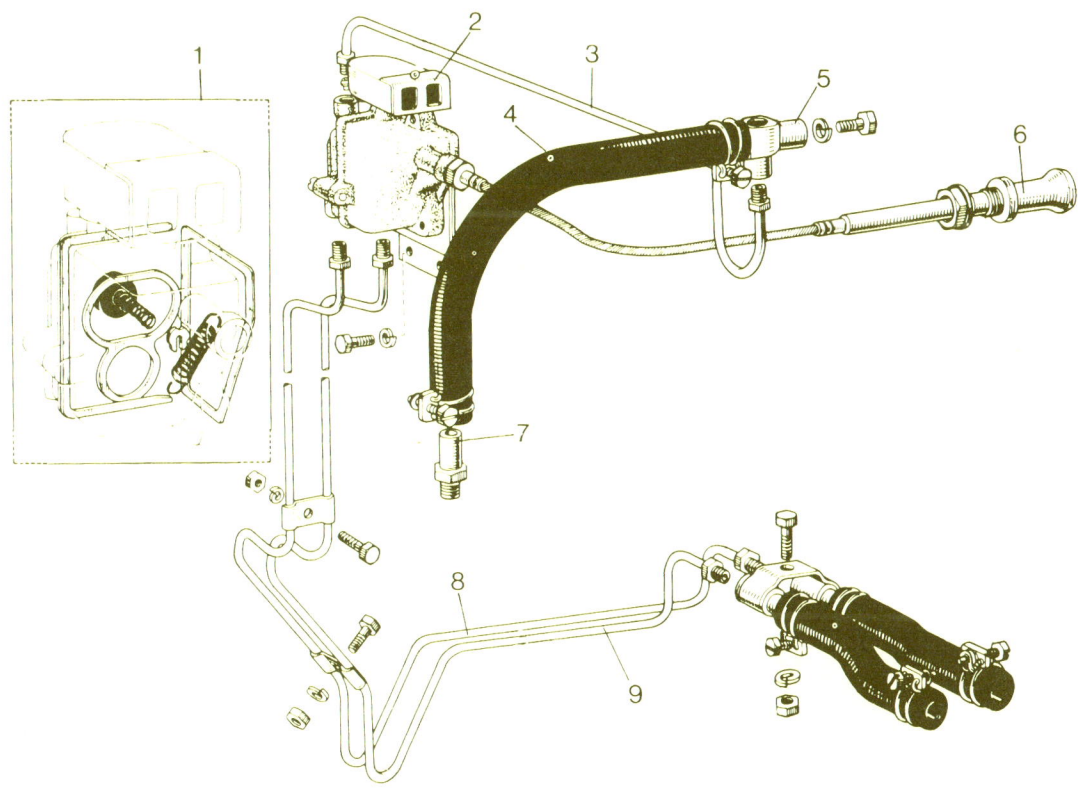

Fig. 6.71. Vacuum line connections - typical

1 Vacuum shift valve repair kit
2 Vacuum shift valve
3 Vacuum tube No. 3
4 Vacuum hose
5 Check valve
6 Vacuum shift valve control
7 Union
8 Vacuum tube No. 1
9 Vacuum tube No. 2

22 Transfer front drive vacuum lines and electrical connections

1 The correct operation of the vacuum unit depends upon the vacuum lines and electrical connections being correctly installed and in good condition.
2 Periodically, these should be inspected for serviceability. If the vacuum lines are to be detached, refer to Fig. 6.71 which shows a typical arrangement.

23 Power take-off - removal and installation

1 Raise the vehicle to a suitable working height and place it on axle stands; alternatively run it over an inspection pit.
2 Remove the transmission lower cover plate.
3 Drain the transfer gear and power take-off lubricant into containers of suitable size.
4 Detach the driveshaft at the power take-off (see Section 25).
5 Remove the power take-off from the transfer gear.
6 Detach the power take-off shift link lever.
7 Installation is the reverse of the removal procedure. Use a new gasket when installing; do not forget to add the correct type and quantity of gear oil on completion.

24 Power take-off - dismantling, inspection and reassembly

1 Remove the input gear shaft lockplate and pull the shaft out of the casing. If it proves difficult to remove, it can be driven rearward to remove the expansion plug, then driven forward using a brass or aluminium drift.
2 Take out the spacer and input gear, together with the bearing.
3 Renew the reverse idler shaft lock plate and drive the shaft rearward from the case. Remove the idler gear and spacer.
4 Remove the lock bolt on the base, then remove the spring and shift fork lock ball.
5 Remove the fork shaft lock bolt then pull the fork and boot out of the case. Now remove the shift fork.
6 Remove the joint flange retaining nuts and take off both joint flanges.
7 Remove the bearing retainers, oil seals and gaskets, then remove the shaft Woodruff keys.
8 Whilst retaining the output gear with the hand, drive the output shaft and rear bearing out of the casing to the rear.
9 Remove the output gear and spacer, then drive out the bearing using a brass or aluminium drift.
10 Clean all the parts in kerosene, and dry with a lint-free cloth.
11 Check the gear teeth, shaft splines, bearings, casing, shift fork, bushings, etc, as generally described in Section 8 or 17, renewing parts as necessary.
12 Commence reassembly by positioning the output gear into the casing with the shift fork groove to the rear, then install the shaft.
13 Place the spacer on the forward side of the output shaft. Whilst holding the shaft in position, install the front bearing so that the snap-ring contacts the casing.
14 Install the Woodruff key, followed by the front bearing retainer and a new gasket. Use a non-setting sealant on the gasket faces.
15 Install the front universal joint flange, and temporarily tighten the nut.
16 Press on the output shaft rear bearing, then install the Woodruff key.
17 Install the rear bearing retainer and gasket, using a non-setting sealant on the gasket face.
18 Install the universal joint flange and tighten the nut. Also, tighten the front flange retaining nut fully.
19 Lubricate the gears with transmission oil and check that they operate smoothly. If end play exists, renew the shaft bearings. Install the flange nut cotter pins, or stake the nuts, as appropriate.
20 Place the shift fork in the groove of the output gear, with the flange towards the front.
21 Slide the shift shaft into the casing and thru the shift fork. Align the fork lock bolt hole with the fork shaft, and install the lock bolt and washer.

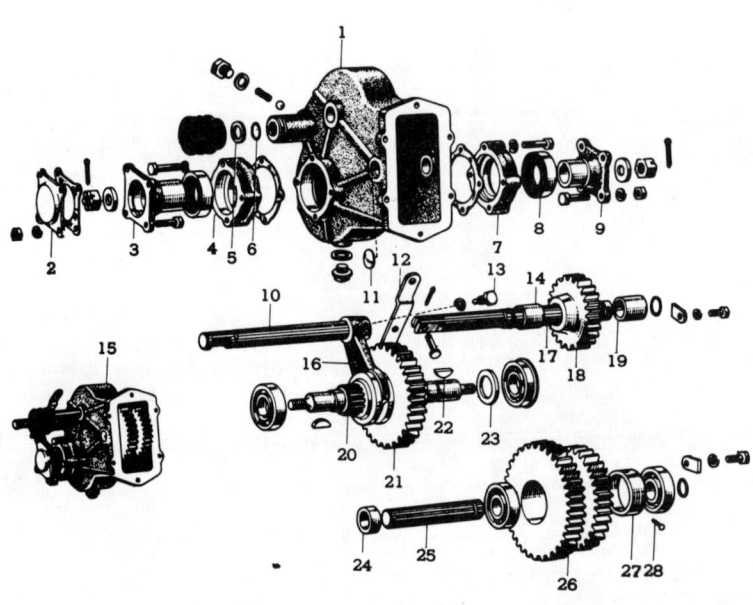

Fig. 6.72. Power take-off exploded view

1 Power take-off cover	8 Oil retainer	15 Power take-off assembly	22 Woodruff key
2 Retainer cap	9 Universal joint flange	16 Shift fork No. 1	23 Spacer
3 Universal joint flange	10 Fork shaft No. 1	17 Reverse idler shaft	24 Spacer
4 Bearing retainer	11 Expansion plug	18 Reverse idler gear	25 Input gear shaft
5 Dust seal	12 Shift link lever	19 Bushing	26 Input gear
6 O-ring	13 Lock bolt	20 Output shaft	27 Bearing spacer
7 Bearing retainer	14 Reverse idler gear spacer	21 Output gear	28 Rivet

22 Place the lock ball and spring into the drilling in the casing and tighten the lock bolt and gasket. Install the shaft dust boot.
23 Place the reverse idle gear and spacer in the casing, with the gear hub to the rear; ensure that the spacer is between the gear hub and case.
24 Install the 'O' rings in the groove of the reverse idle shaft, then install the shaft from the rear of the casing. Align the groove with the front end of the shaft, then install the lock plate.
25 Place the input gear into the casing, smaller gear to the front, and mesh the reverse idler gear. Install the spacer.
26 Install the 'O' ring in the input gear shaft groove, then drive the shaft into the casing from the front. Install the shaft lockplate.
27 If the expansion plug was removed, install a new one using a non-setting gasket sealant. Peen the center of the plug to secure it.
28 Install the shift link lever, lubricate the remaining gears with transmission oil, and check that everything operates smoothly.

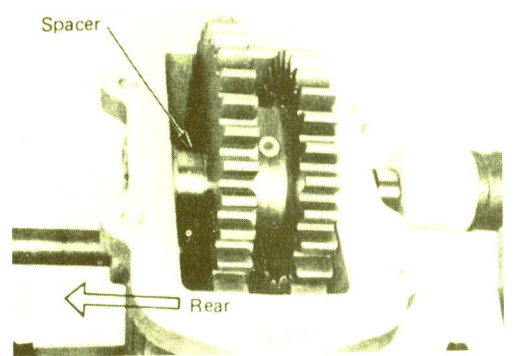

Fig. 6.73. Position of spacer in casing

25 Driveshaft - removal and installation

Note: If the driveshaft is to be dismantled, refer to Fig. 6.74 which shows the parts. For renewal of the universal joint, refer to the procedure given in Chapter 7, but note that the bearing snap-rings are outboard of the yoke rather than inboard.
1 Raise the vehicle to a suitable working height and place it on axle stands; alternatively run it over an inspection pit.
2 Remove the transmission and engine lower cover plates.
3 Remove the bolts retaining the universal joint flange yoke to the input shaft. Pull the No 2 driveshaft out of the No 1 shaft.
4 Remove the winch as described in Section 26.
5 Remove the universal joint yoke at the front of the No 1 driveshaft.
6 Remove the Woodruff key at the rear end of the No 1 driveshaft, then remove the bolt retaining the pillow block body to the bracket.
7 Withdraw the shaft and pillow block body, then remove the pillow block body from the shaft.
8 Installation is the reverse of the removal procedure, but ensure that the universal joints are aligned as shown in Fig. 6.75. Finally, lubricate the joint grease nipples with general purpose grease.

26 Front winch - removal and installation

1 Remove the cotter pin and straight pin at the front end of the No. 1 driveshaft, and disconnect the shaft from the winch worm.
2 Remove the bolts securing the front and rear base members to the vehicle frame and bumper.
3 Drain the winch lubricant into a container of suitable size, and remove the assembly from the vehicle.
4 Installation is the reverse of the removal procedure. On completion add the correct grade and quantity of lubricant.

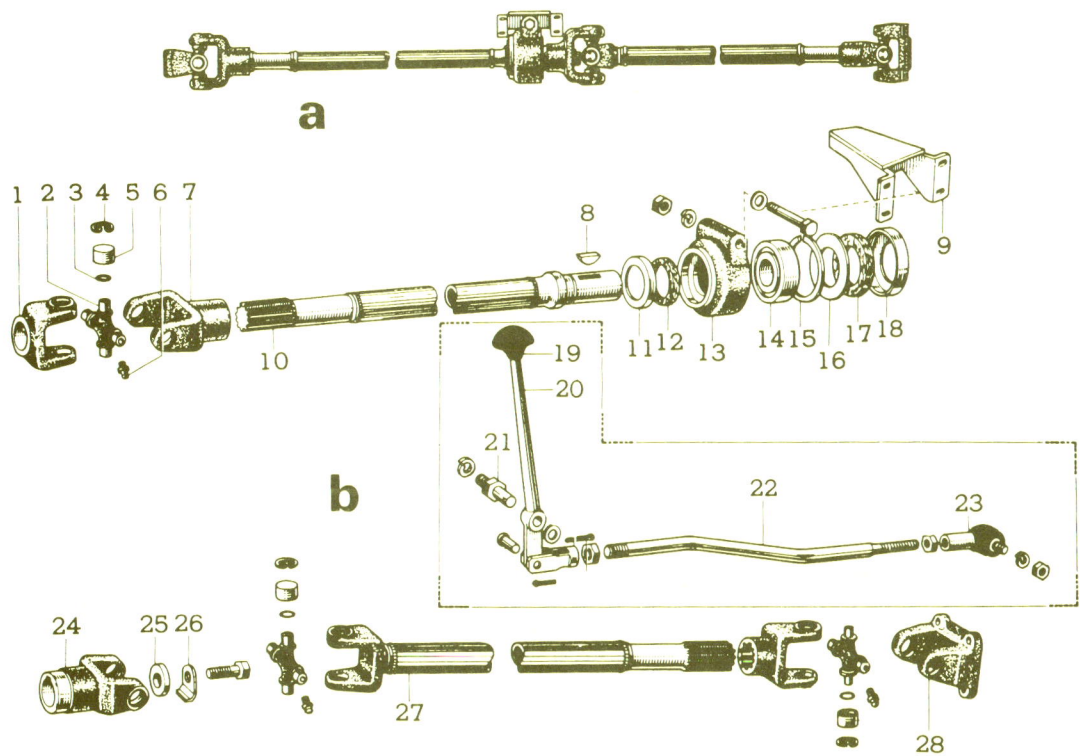

Fig. 6.74. Driveshaft universal joint alignment (a) Front drive shaft - exploded view (b)

1 Universal joint yoke	8 Woodruff key	15 Snap-ring	22 Shift rod
2 Universal joint spider	9 Pillow block bracket	16 Seal washer	23 Connecting rod end
3 O-ring	10 Front drive shaft No. 1	17 Seal	24 Sleeve yoke
4 Snap-ring	11 Seal retainer No. 2	18 Seal retainer No. 1	25 Washer
5 Spider bearing	12 Dust seal	19 Knob	26 Lock plate
6 Grease fitting	13 Pillow block body No. 2	20 Shift lever	27 Front drive shaft No. 2
7 Sleeve yoke	14 Bearing	21 Support shaft	28 Universal joint flange yoke

27 Front winch - dismantling, inspection and reassembly

1 Remove the front and rear base members and roller bracket support.
2 Drive out the winch clutch lever securing pin, and detach the clutch lever, clutch lower lever and brake shoe.
3 Remove the end bracket and the clutch feather key spacer from the worm gear shaft.
4 Slide the clutch off the worm gear shaft, then remove the two clutch keys and feather key spacer.
5 Slide the drum assembly off the worm gear shaft, then remove the gear case cover and gasket.
6 Remove the worm bearing retainers and shims from both sides of the winch gear case, then remove the worm and bearings.
7 Drive the shaft and worm gear out of the gear case.
8 Press the shaft out of the worm gear.
9 Check the gear teeth, bearings, casing, clutch etc. as generally described in Section 8 or 17, renewing parts as necessary.
10 Commence reassembly by adjusting the worm bearing pre-load. Note that during reassembly the bushings, bearings, clutch mechanism and the inside of the drum should be smeared with a general purpose grease.
11 Install the worm gear and bearings into the case, then install the bearing retainers and shims, and tighten the bolts to the specified torque.
12 Rotate the worm and check for gear backlash, end-play and tight spots when turning. There should be no tightness or end-play. The bearing pre-load may be adjusted by re-selecting the shims if necessary, but the same total shim thickness should be used at each side.
13 After adjustment, remove the bearing retainers, shims and worm from the gearcase.
14 Place the sliding key in the worm gear shaft end groove, then press on the gear.
15 Re-install the worm and bearings in the case, and install the retainers and shims selected at paragraph 12.
16 Install the case cover using a new gasket and a non-setting jointing compound.
17 Slide the drum assembly onto the shaft.
18 Install the feather key spacer, indented side towards the outside, aligning the indents with the grooves on the shaft.
19 Install the clutch keys. **Note:** New keys must be used if the original ones are damaged in any way.
20 Install the clutch, and the feather key spacer with the indented side towards the clutch.
21 Install the end bracket. Install the torsion spring onto the clutch lower lever shaft, then assemble the lower lever, brake shoe and clutch lever onto the end bracket.
22 Align the holes in the lower lever shaft and clutch lever, and drive in the pin.
23 Assemble the front and rear base members, and the roller bracket supports onto the end bracket and gearcase.
24 Shift the winch clutch lever in the disengaged position and check that the brake shoe plate contacts the drum and locks it securely. Renew the brake plate if necessary.

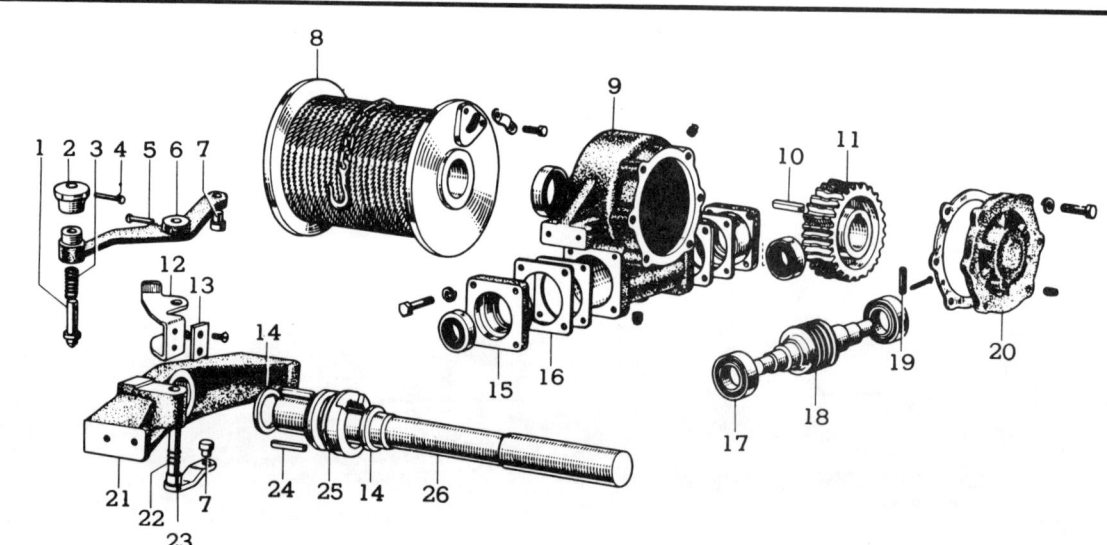

Fig. 6.76. Winch - exploded view

1	Lever shift lock pin	8	Drum	14	Feather key spacer	20 Gear case cover
2	Clutch lever knob	9	Gear case	15	Worm bearing retainer	21 End bracket
3	Spring	10	Sliding key	16	Shim	22 Spring
4	Pin	11	Worm gear	17	Worm bearing	23 Clutch lower lever
5	Pin	12	Brake shoe	18	Worm	24 Clutch key
6	Clutch lever	13	Brake plate	19	Straight pin	25 Clutch
7	Head pin					26 Worm gear shaft

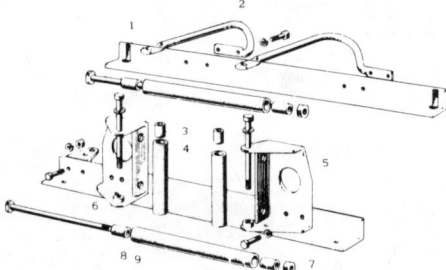

Fig. 6.77. Winch member and bracket

1 Rear base member
2 Roller bracket support
3 Spacer
4 Wire guide roller
5 Winch roller bracket No. 2
6 Winch roller bracket No. 1
7 Front base member
8 Bushing
9 Wire guide roller

28 Fault diagnosis - transmission and transfer

Fault	Possible cause
Ineffective synchromesh on one or more gears	Worn synchro units.
Jumps out of one or more gears	Weak detent springs. Worn selector forks. Worn engagement dogs. Worn synchro hubs.
Whining, roughness, vibration allied to other faults	Bearing failure and/or overall wear.
Noisy and difficult gear shift	Clutch not operating correctly.
Sloppy and impositive gear selection	Overall wear throughout the selector mechanism.
Difficult transfer shift	High/low clutch sleeve splines damaged. Fault in vacuum shift mechanism or hoses.

29 Fault diagnosis - front winch and power take-off

Fault	Possible cause
Difficult engagement of drive	Worn selector fork or linkage.
Winch does not operate	Broken shear pin (straight pin) at front end of driveshaft.

Chapter 7 Propeller shafts

Contents

General description ... 1	Propeller shaft (front or rear) - removal and installation ... 2
Propeller shaft - fault diagnosis ... 4	Universal joints - inspection, dismantling and reassembly ... 3

Specifications

Propeller shafts
Type ... Twin shafts with sliding sleeves and universal joints

Universal joints
Type ... Needle roller
Bearing cup snap-ring sizes:
  Pre-1975 ... 0.057 in (1.45 mm)
  0.059 in (1.50 mm)
  0.061 in (1.55 mm)

  1975 onwards ... 0.058/0.06 in (1.48/1.53 mm)
  0.06/0.062 in (1.53/1.58 mm)
  0.062/0.064 in (1.58/1.63 mm)

Torque wrench settings

	lb f ft	kg f m
Flange nuts (up to Chassis No 12552)	14	1.9
Flange nuts (from Chassis No 12552)	35	4.8

1 General description

1 The drive from the transfer gear to the front and rear axles is thru two propeller shafts. The shafts are similar in design; they have a Hookes-type universal joint at each end, and a sliding sleeve to compensate for up-and-down/fore-and-aft movement of the axles due to the deflection of the springs.

2 The universal joints comprise a four-way trunnion (or spider). each leg of which runs in a needle roller bearing race which fits into the bearing yoke. The joints are renewable, but the use of selective thickness snap-rings is required to eliminate end play of the spider within the yoke to 0.002 in (0.05 mm).

3 Grease nipples are provided on the universal joint spiders and on the splined shafts for lubrication in service (photo).

4 Although the procedures described in this Chapter are specifically for the main vehicle propeller shaft, the same basic principles apply to the steering intermediate shaft joints used on FJ55 models (see Chapter 9), and to the front winch driveshaft joints (see Chapter 6). However, with these shafts, the snap-rings are outboard of the joints, whereas the snap-rings on the propeller shaft are inboard of the joints (except on some early models).

2 Propeller shaft (front or rear) - removal and installation

1 Raise the vehicle to a suitable working height for access to the propeller shaft and universal joints. Ensure that the vehicle is well supported, and that the road wheels remaining on the ground are chocked, for safety reasons. It can be advantageous for one of the axle wheels to be off the ground so that the wheel can be rotated to provide improved access to the joint retaining bolts.

2 Mark the position of the joint flanges relative to each other so that they may be installed in the same relative positions. If the joints are to be dismantled, also mark the installed position of the spider in the yoke.

3 Remove the bolts retaining the joint flange yoke to the differential then detach the shaft. Provided that care is taken it is alright for the shaft to hang down without support.

4 Remove the bolts retaining the universal joint yoke to the transfer joint flange; support the shaft then withdraw it.

5 Installation of the propeller shaft is the reverse of the removal procedure, but ensure that the mating marks are aligned. If a new shaft has been used, ensure that the shaft is installed in the relationship shown in Fig. 7.2.

6 If the rear propeller shaft has to be detached for attention to the parking brake, it may be detached at the front end only, then a suitable lever used to pry the front section of the shaft rearwards. However, this is fairly difficult, and the complete removal of the shaft is really considered worthwhile.

3 Universal joints - inspection, dismantling, and reassembly

1 Preliminary inspection of the universal joints can be carried out with the propeller shaft installed.

2 Grasp each side of the universal joint, and with a twisting action, determine whether there is any play or slackness in the joint. Also try an up-and-down rocking motion for the same purpose. If there is any sign whatsoever of play, the joints need renewal.

3 Remove the propeller shaft as described in Section 2.

4 Dot punch adjacent edges of the yokes so that they will be refitted in their original positions. Remove the snap-rings.

5 The bearing cups may be removed by one of two methods. Either

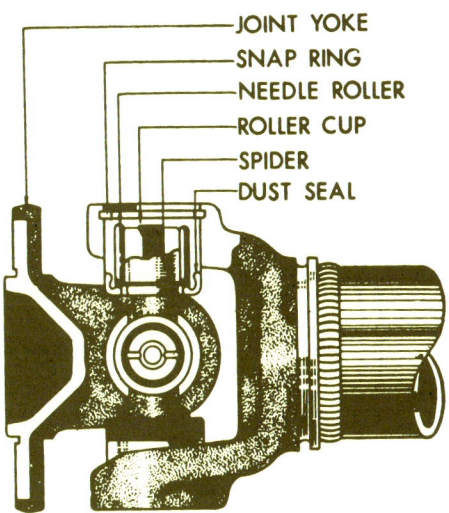

Fig. 7.1. Sectional view of early type universal joint with snap-ring outboard of the joint. This is typical of the front winch driveshaft joints and FJ55 steering intermediate shaft joints.

- JOINT YOKE
- SNAP RING
- NEEDLE ROLLER
- ROLLER CUP
- SPIDER
- DUST SEAL

1.1. Propeller shaft grease nipples

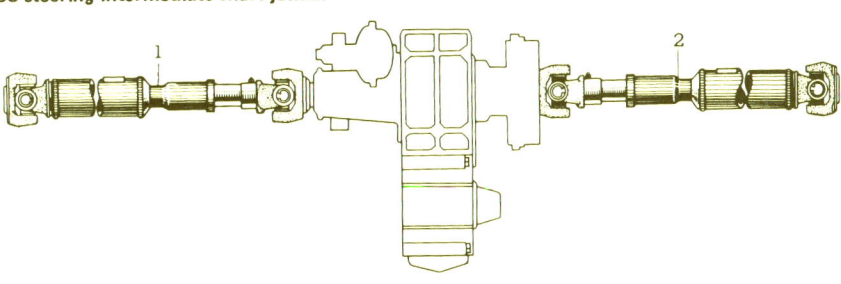

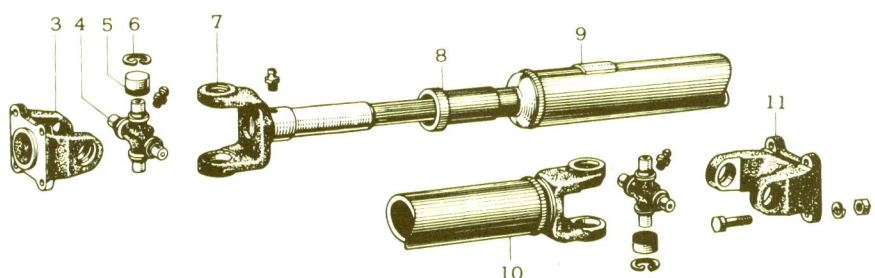

Fig. 7.2 Driveshaft arangement

1	Front driveshaft	4	Spider	7	Sliding yoke	10	Front driveshaft
2	Rear driveshaft	5	Bearing	8	Sliding shaft dust cover	11	Universal joint flange yoke
3	Universal joint flange yoke	6	Snap-ring	9	Balance weight		

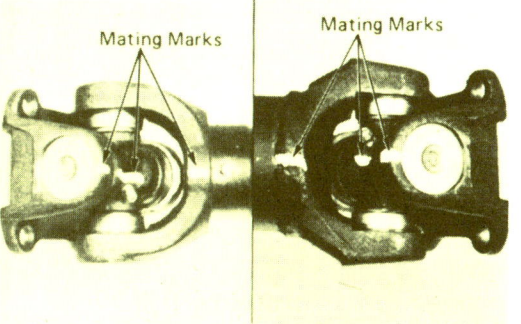

Fig. 7.3. Mating marks on the yokes and spider

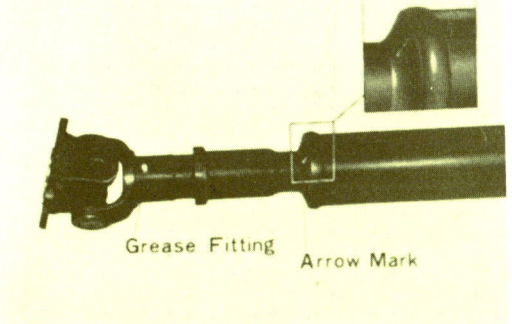

Fig. 7.4. Alignment mark for the grease nipple

hit the yoke (supported in the hand) adjacent to the bearing cup hole with a wooden or plastic mallet until the cup begins to emerge, or press the cup out in a vise, using an old bearing cup on one side and tubular spacer on the other to receive the ejected cup. With both methods, pull the cups out of their seats, once they have emerged far enough to be able to grip them with a self-locking wrench.

6 Inspect the holes in the yokes for elongation. Evidence of this is only likely in the event of previous neglect or abuse in which case the yokes must be renewed. On some yokes a drill mark may be found near the bearing cup hole. This indicates that an oversize bearing hole exists and the appropriate red-marked oversize bearing cup must be used.

7 Obtain the appropriate repair kit for each joint. This will comprise spider, bearing cups, needle bearings and seals.

8 Locate the spider within the yoke; check that the 'O' ring seals are in position and that the dot punch marks mate.

9 Fill the bearing cup 1/3rd full with grease, and check that the needle bearings are correctly held in position (with grease) around the inside of the cup.

10 Using a vise and an old bearing cup, press the new bearing cup into the yoke, at the same time holding the spider in alignment so that the cup will slide on. Ensure that the grease nipple on the sliding yoke and the arrow mark on the shaft are aligned (see Fig. 7.4).

11 Repeat the operations for the remaining three bearings of each universal joint.

12 Insert new snap-rings **which must be of the same thickness for each opposite pair of bearing cups** and must be selected from the sizes listed in the Specifications to ensure an axial end-play of not more than 0.002 in (0.05 mm).

4 Propeller shaft - fault diagnosis

Symptom	Reason/s
Vibration	Worn universal joints. Propeller shaft bent. Loose drive flange bolts. Propeller shaft out of balance. Transfer shaft out of balance. Parking brake drum loose.
Knocking during starting, gear changing or at the moment of deceleration	Worn universal joints. Worn splines on shafts. Loose drive flange bolts. Parking brake drum loose.

Chapter 8 Rear axle and suspension

Contents

Axleshafts (fully floating axle) - removal and installation ... 3	Hub (fully-floating axle) - removal and installation ... 4
Axleshafts, bearings and oil seals (semi-floating axle) - removal and installation ... 2	Pinion oil seal - renewal ... 7
	Rear axle - removal and installation ... 8
Differential carrier - removal and installation ... 6	Rear shock absorber - removal and installation ... 10
Fault diagnosis - rear axle and suspension ... 11	Rear suspension - removal and installation ... 9
General description ... 1	Rear wheel bearing (fully-floating axle) - adjustment ... 5

Specifications

Axle
Type ... Hypoid, semi- or fully-floating

Differential ratio ... 3.7 : 1 or 4.11 : 1

Axle lubricant type ... SAE 90EP Gear oil

Axle lubricant quantity ... 2.6 US qts/2.2 Imp qts (2.5 liters)

Rear suspension type ... Leaf spring

Damper type ... Telescopic, hydraulic, double-acting

Torque wrench settings

	lb f ft	kg f m
Hub lock nut (fully-floating axle)	65	9
Axleshaft nuts (fully-floating axle)	25	3.4
Filler and drain plugs	58	8
Differential pinion shaft pin	14	1.9
Differential carrier retaining nuts	35	4.8
Companion flange nut	160	22
Spring shackle nuts	47	6.5
Spring bracket pin nuts	47	6.5
U-bolt nuts	60	8.3
Shock absorber retaining nuts	32	4.5

1 General description

Most Land Cruiser models use a semi-floating hypoid type rear axle which is attached to the chassis thru leaf springs. Later models with a higher load capacity may use a fully-floating axle which differs principally in the fact that the outer end of the axleshaft runs in a hub with twin taper roller bearings instead of in a single roller bearing.

Operations on the rear axle should be limited to those described in this Chapter. Where a fault has developed in the differential, it is recommended that a factory reconditioned unit is installed since repair requires special tools and knowledge if it is to be carried out properly.

2 Axleshafts, bearings and oil seals (semi-floating axle) - removal and installation

1 Jack-up on the rear axle housing and support it on suitable stands. Chock the front roadwheels and remove the appropriate rear roadwheel.
2 Remove the brake drum.
3 Drain the axle oil into a suitable container.
4 Remove the nuts and washers and take off the differential housing cover.
5 Remove the differential pinion shaft pin.
6 Pull the pinion shaft out of the differential case and remove the shaft spacer.
7 Remove the lock ring from the end of the axleshaft; this will be made easier if the shaft can be pushed in towards the differential.
8 Withdraw the axleshaft from the housing.
9 Using an internal puller, draw out the bearing and oil seal from the housing. (If only the oil seal is to be renewed, this can be prised out with a small screwdriver).
10 Examine the axleshaft for wear and damage, particularly to the splines. Clean the bearing (if removed) in kerosene or similar, and dry it with an air blast or by shaking it and using a lint-free cloth. Examine for scoring, rough running and signs of overheating (a bluish color). To remove the inner race, grind a groove, then use a hammer and chisel to remove it from the axleshaft.
11 Installation is basically the reverse of the removal procedure. Press the bearing into the axle casing using a suitable mandrel on the outer

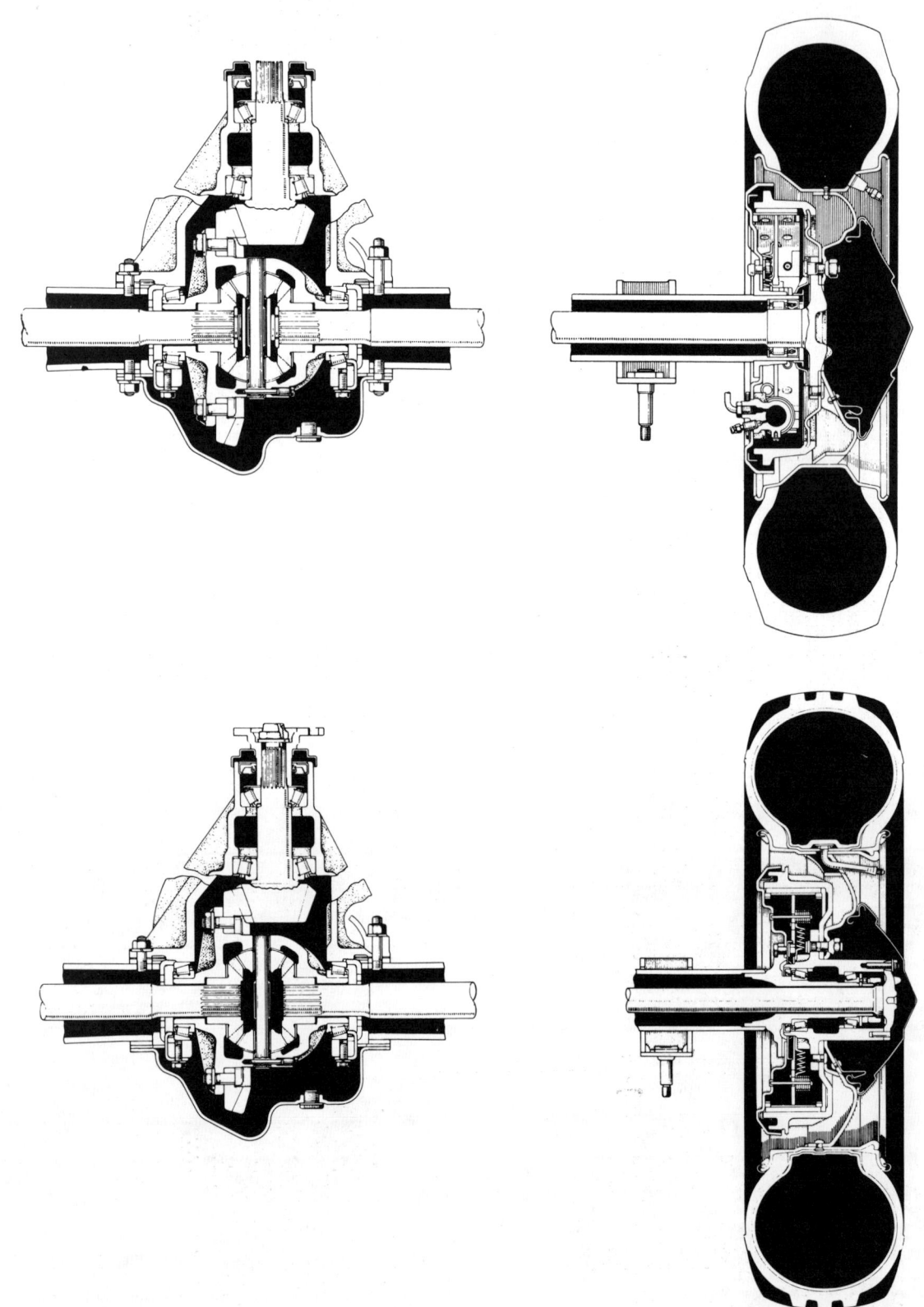

Fig. 8.1. Sectional view showing semi-floating axle (top) and fully-floating axle (bottom)

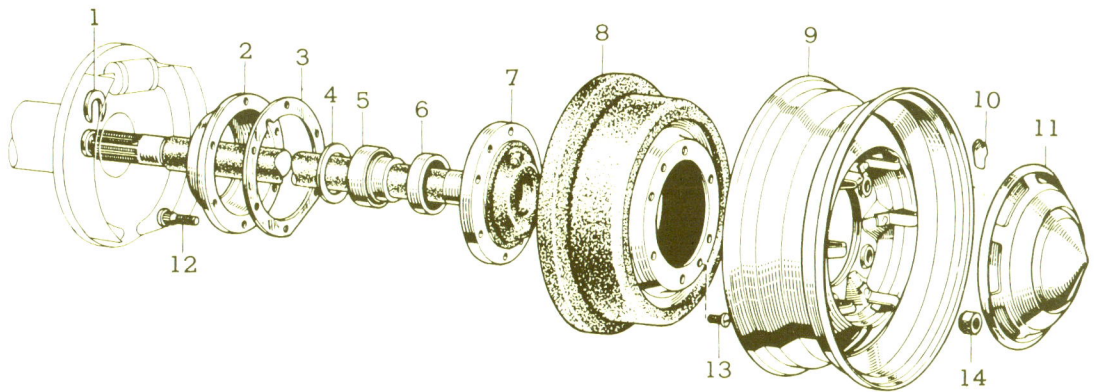

Fig. 8.2. Semi-floating axleshaft components

1 Rear axleshaft lock
2 Brake drum oil deflector
3 Gasket
4 Washer
5 Bearing
6 Oil seal
7 Rear axleshaft
8 Brake drum
9 Disc wheel
10 Balance weight
11 Wheel cap
12 Hub bolt
13 Drum set bolt
14 Hub nut

Fig. 8.3. Removing differential shaft pin

Fig. 8.4. Removing pinion shaft and spacer

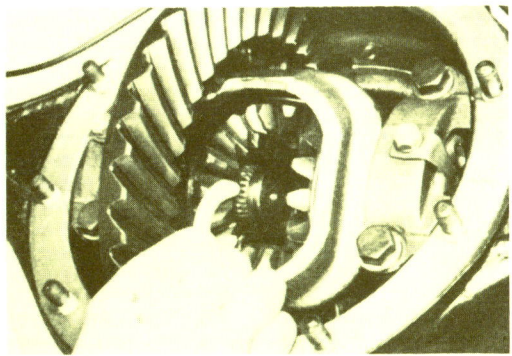

Fig. 8.5. Removing axleshaft lock ring

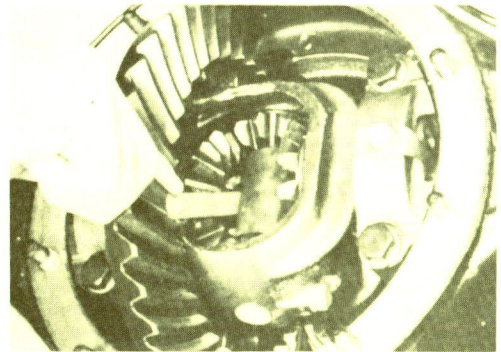

Fig. 8.6. Checking axleshaft/pinion shaft clearance

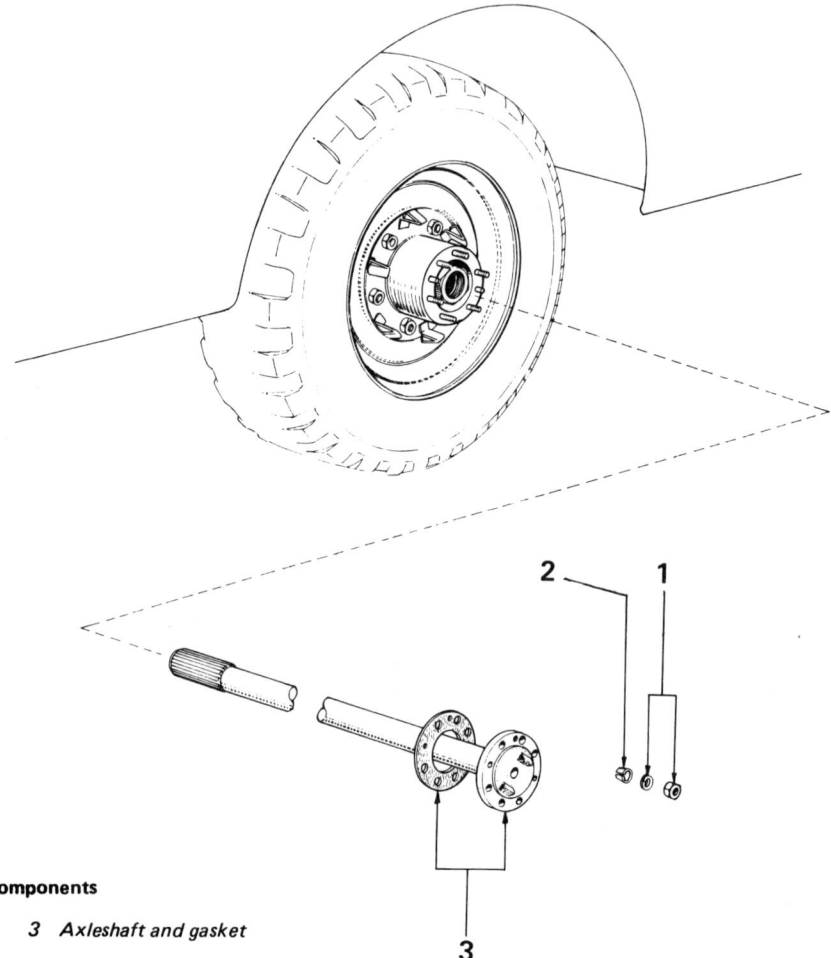

Fig. 8.7. Fully-floating axleshaft components

1 Nut and washer
2 Cone washer
3 Axleshaft and gasket

race. Heat the inner race to around 300°F (150°C) and press it into position on the shaft. The new oil seal should be lubricated with axle oil and pushed into position with the lips towards the differential.
12 After installing the axle shaft and lock ring, measure the clearance between the shaft end and the pinion shaft spacer, if outside the range 0.0024/0.0181 in (0.06 to 0.46 mm), it will be necessary for a new spacer to be installed. These are available in thicknesses of 1.173 in (29.8 mm), 1.189 in (30.2 mm) and 1.204 in (30.6 mm).
13 On completion, top-up the differential housing with the appropriate grade and quantity of oil. **Note:** It is recommended that a non-setting sealant is used on the differential housing gasket joint.

3 Axleshafts (fully-floating axle) - removal and installation

1 Remove the rear hub cap (where applicable).
2 Remove the retaining nuts and washers from the axleshaft flange.
3 Drive a screwdriver or small chisel into the slot in each cone washer to release it, then remove them from the studs.
4 Screw a suitable bolt into the threaded picking hole(s) in the axleshaft flange. This will break the gasket seal and allow the shaft to be withdrawn.
5 Installation of the shaft is the reverse of the removal procedure, but if there is any doubt about the condition of the flange gasket or the oil seal which is an integral part of the outer adjustment nut, new items must be used.

4 Hub (fully-floating axle) - removal and installation

1 Jack-up the car on the rear axle housing and support it on suitable stands. Chock the front roadwheels and remove the appropriate rear roadwheel.
2 Remove the brake drum.

3 Using a suitable tubular box wrench, remove the bearing outer adjusting nut.
4 Remove the slot headed screw, and unscrew the bearing inner adjusting nut. Remove the locking washer.
5 Remove the hub assembly from the axle.
6 Clean the hub, axle housing and bearing parts using kerosene and dry thoroughly. Examine the bearing parts for wear, scoring and corrosion, renewing as necessary. If any part of a bearing appears to be unserviceable, the whole bearing must be renewed. Bearing races can be driven in and out of the hub using a suitable drift.
7 Installation of the hub is basically the reverse of the removal procedure. Work a little general purpose grease into the bearing roller assemblies, and pack the recess between the bearings with the same type of grease. Press in a new oil seal carefully and squarely, lubricating the seal lips with the grease. Before installing the axleshaft, the hub bearing must be adjusted - see next Section.

5 Rear wheel bearing (fully-floating axle) - adjustment

1 This procedure is similar to that described for the front wheel bearing in Chapter 9 once the axleshaft has been removed, except that a different arrangement is used for locking the adjusting nuts - see Fig. 8.9.

6 Differential carrier - removal and installation

1 Initially proceed as described in Sections 2 or 3 to remove (or partially withdraw) the axleshafts. Do not mix up the left and right shafts.
2 Detach the propeller shaft from the axle companion flange (refer to Chapter 7 if necessary).
3 Remove the retaining nuts and spring washer, and draw the complete

Chapter 8/Rear axle and suspension

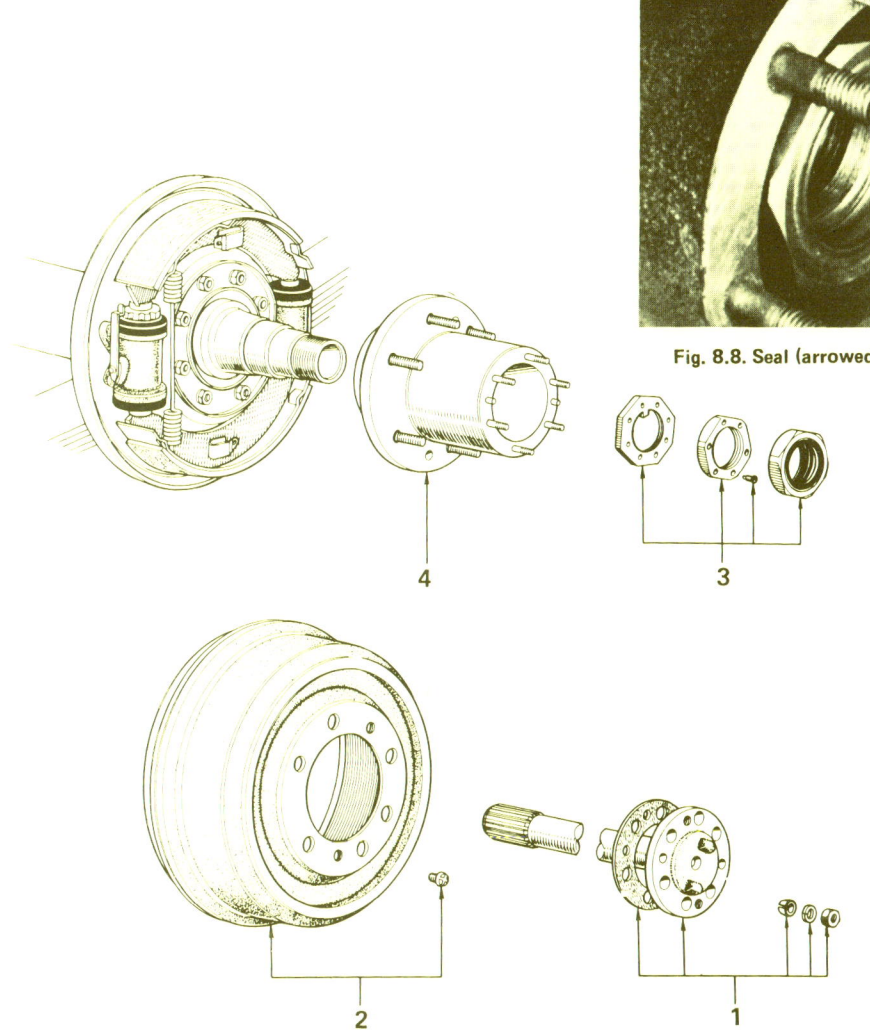

Fig. 8.8. Seal (arrowed) in outer adjustment nut

Fig. 8.9. Hub (fully-floating axle) - major parts

1 Axleshaft   2 Brake drum   3 Adjusting nuts and washer   4 Hub assembly

differential carrier forward and away from the axle.
4 Installation is the reverse of the removal procedure; it is recommended that a non-setting sealant is used for the gasket joints. Do not forget to check the axleshaft/pinion shaft spacer clearance as described in Section 2 for semi-floating axles.

7 Pinion oil seal - renewal

1 Jack-up the rear of the vehicle and support the axle on suitable stands.
2 Detach the propeller shaft from the axle companion flange (refer to Chapter 7 if necessary).
3 Hold the companion flange still by bolting a suitable steel bar to two of the flange holes, then remove the flange nut. Note that early models use a nut and split cotter pin whereas later models use a self-locking nut.
4 Tap or pull off the flange.
5 Carefully tap off the dust deflector, ensuring that it is not damaged.
6 Using a small screwdriver, pry out the oil seal.
7 Ensure that the sealing faces are clean, then lubricate a new seal with axle oil and carefully press it into position.
8 Install the dust deflector and companion flange by following the reverse of the removal procedure. Use a new self-locking nut or split pin as appropriate, tightening the nut to the specified torque.

Fig. 8.10. Pack hub with grease in recess shown

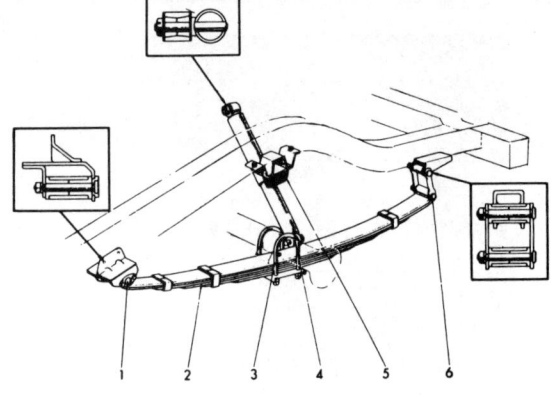

Fig. 8.11. Typical rear suspension arrangements

Top — FJ40, FJ43
1 Hanger and shackle pin
2 Rear spring
3 U-bolt
4 Rear shockabsorber
5 Rubber cushion
6 Hanger and shackle pin

Middle — FJ45
1 Hanger and shackle pin
2 Rear shockabsorber
3 Rear spring
4 U-bolt
5 Rubber cushion
6 Cushion stopper
7 Hanger and shackle pin

Bottom — FJ55
1 Rear stabilizer bar
2 Shockabsorber
3 Stabilizer link
4 Spring bumper
5 Spring bracket
6 Spring shackle
7 Stabilizer bushing
8 Spring U-bolt seat
9 U-bolt
10 Spring bracket pin

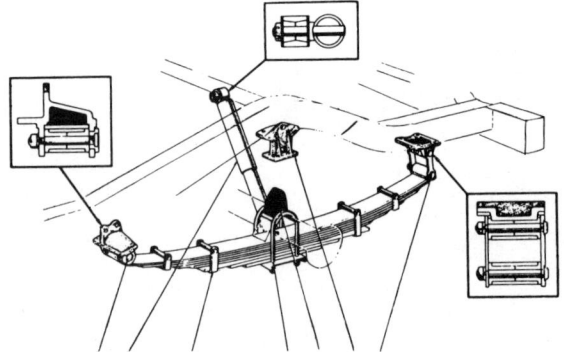

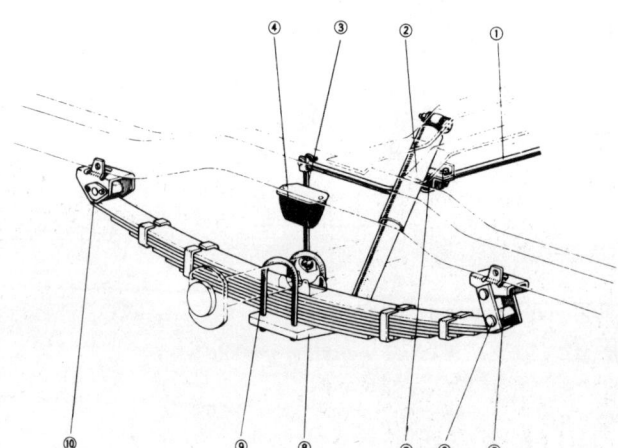

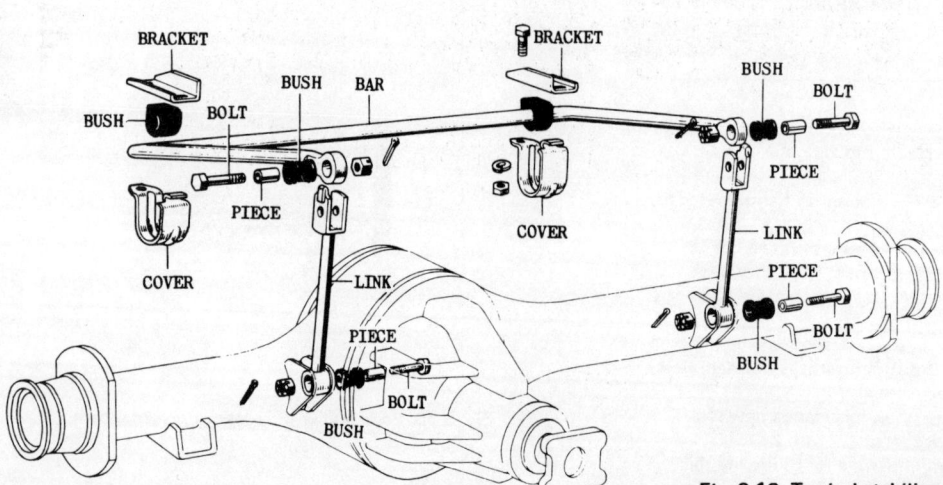

Fig. 8.12. Typical stabilizer bar attachments on FJ55 models

8 Rear axle - removal and installation

1 Jack-up the rear of the vehicle and support the chassis sidemembers on suitable stands. Chock the front roadwheels and remove both rear roadwheels.
2 Drain the axle oil into a suitable container.
3 Detach the propeller shaft from the axle companion flange (refer to Chapter 7 if necessary).
4 Where applicable, detach the stabilizer bar from the rear axle. Fig. 8.12 shows the typical arrangement.
5 Detach the brake lines from the rear of the brake backplates. Plug the ends to prevent excessive loss of fluid.
6 Support the axle weight with suitable jacks or stands, then detach the shock absorbers at their lower mountings.
7 Detach the rear springs at their shackles and bracket pin, (see Section 9 if necessary), and manoeuver the axle from beneath the vehicle. During this operation it may be necessary to raise or lower the axle supports to facilitate detachment of the springs.
8 With the axle removed, the U-bolts can be removed and the springs detached.
9 Installation is basically the reverse of the removal procedure, but do not tighten the nuts on the shackles and spring bracket pin until the vehicle weight is on the spring. Do not forget to bleed the brakes, as described in Chapter 10, on completion.

9 Rear suspension - removal and installation

1 Jack-up the rear of the vehicle and support the chassis sidemembers on suitable stands. Chock the front roadwheels and remove both rear roadwheels.
2 Support the axle weight on suitable jacks or stands.
3 Remove the cotter pin and nut, and detach the shock absorber from the pivot pin on the axle housing.
4 Where applicable, remove the cotter pins and nuts, and detach the lower ends of the stabilizer bar links from the axle housing. The bracket covers can now be withdrawn and the stabilizer bar (and links) removed (photo).
5 Remove the nuts from the U-bolts. Take off the spring seats and withdraw the U-bolts upwards.
6 Adjust the axle height to just take the weight off the spring shackle inner plate.
7 Pry the spring shackle with a suitable bar, then remove the shackle and rubber bushings.
8 Remove the two bolts retaining the spring bracket pin to the bracket. Drive out the pin to release the spring assembly.
9 Remove the cotter pin and nut at the upper end of the shock absorber, so that it can be released complete with its bushings.
10 Installation is the reverse of the removal procedure, but do not tighten the nuts on the shackles and spring bracket pin until the vehicle weight is on the spring.

10 Rear shock absorber - removal and installation

1 Jack-up on the rear axle housing and support it on suitable stands. Chock the front roadwheels; for improved accessibility remove the rear roadwheel.
2 Remove the cotter pin and nut, and detach the shock absorber from the pivot pin on the axle housing.
3 Remove the cotter pin and nut at the upper end of the shock absorber, so that it can be released complete with its bushings (photo).
4 To test a shock absorber, grip the lower mounting in a vise with the unit in a vertical position. Extend and contract the shock absorber over its full range of travel about ten times; if there is not a positive resistance to travel in both directions, the unit must be renewed. Renewal is also necessary if there is any sign of oil leakage around the piston rod or shock absorber body.
5 Installation of the shock absorber is the reverse of the removal procedure.

9.4 Stabilizer bar attachment and link

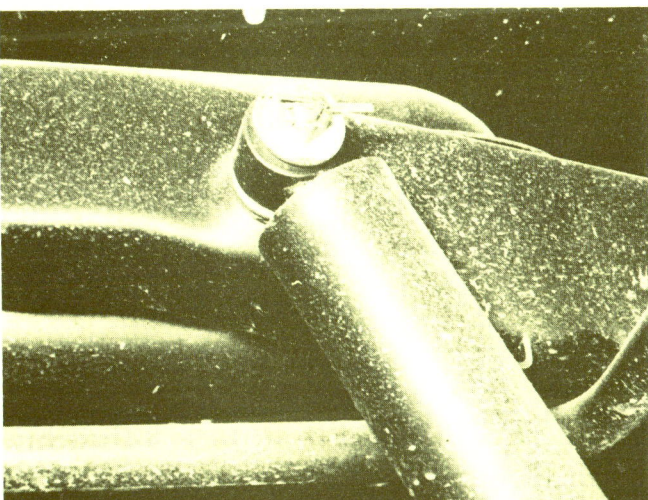

10.3 Upper attachment of the shock absorber

Fault Diagnosis overleaf

11 Fault diagnosis - rear axle and suspension

Symptom	Reason/s
Noisy differential	
a) During normal running	Lack of oil. Damaged or worn gears. Incorrect adjustment.
b) During deceleration	Incorrect adjustment. Damaged drive pinion bearings.
c) During turning of vehicle	Worn axleshaft bearing. Worn differential gears.
Noisy rear hub	Worn axleshaft bearing. Buckled roadwheel. Bent axleshaft.
Excessive pitching and rolling on corners	Defective shock absorber. Broken, worn or loose spring.
Vehicle leans to one side	Broken, worn or loose spring.

Chapter 9 Front axle, front suspension and steering

Contents

Axleshaft and steering knuckle - removal and installation ... 2	Front wheel bearing - adjustment ... 4
Differential carrier - removal and installation ... 9	General description ... 1
Fault diagnosis - front axle, front suspension and steering ... 16	Pinion oil seal - renewal ... 10
Freewheel bearing - adjustment ... 5	Steering gear - removal and installation ... 13
Front axle constant velocity joint - overhaul ... 3	Steering intermediate shaft - dismantling and reassembly ... 12
Front axle - removal and installation ... 7	Steering linkage - removal, dismantling, reassembly and installation ... 14
Front shock absorber - removal and installation ... 6	
Front spring - removal and installation ... 8	Steering wheel and mainshaft - removal, dismantling, reassembly and installation ... 11
Front wheel alignment ... 15	

Specifications

Axle type	Hypoid, fully floating
Differential ratio	3.7 : 1 or 4.1 : 1
Driveshaft joint type	Ball or constant velocity joint
Axle lubricant type	SAE 90EP gear oil
Axle lubricant quantity	2.6 US qts/2.2 Imp qts (2.5 liters)
Front suspension type	Leaf spring
Damper type	Telescopic, hydraulic, double acting
Steering gear type	Worm and sector
Steering swivel type	Taper roller bearings
Steering gear lubricant type	SAE 90 gear oil
Steering gear lubricant quantity	0.6 US qt/0.5 Imp qt (0.6 liters)

Steering and suspension geometry

Toe-in	0.12 to 0.20 in (3 to 5 mm)
Castor angle	1º
Camber angle	1º
Steering swivel (king pins) angle	9º 30'

Torque wrench settings

	lb f ft	kg f m
Steering knuckle arm/steering knuckle	49	6.7
Steering knuckle/knuckle spindle/bashing plate	13.5	1.9
Axle hub/free-wheel hub body	21.7	3.0
Axle hub/axle outer shaft flange	22.8	3.2
Steering knuckle spindle/lock nut	65	9.0
Steering gear housing and cover	27	3.7
Steering gear housing bracket	34	4.7
Sector shaft/pitman arm	130	18

Chapter 9/Front axle, front suspension and steering

1 General description

The Land Cruiser models use a fully floating hypoid type front axle which is attached to the chassis through leaf springs.

Drive to the front wheels is through twin driveshafts which have either a ball joint or constant velocity joint at the steering swivel ends. The steering swivels run in taper roller bearings, and carry the front hubs which also incorporate taper roller bearings.

The steering gear is a worm and sector type which connects with the front wheels through a pitman arm, drag link, center arm (relay lever), relay rod, tie-rod and steering knuckles.

Free-wheel front hubs are available on some later models. These permit the wheels to be disengaged from the drive shafts when using two-wheel drive, to reduce friction and rotational losses.

Operations on the front axle should be limited to those described in this Chapter. Where a fault has developed in the differential, it is recommended that a factory reconditioned unit is installed since repair requires special tools and knowledge if it is to be carried out properly.

2 Axleshaft and steering knuckle - removal and installation

Note: Ideally, this operation requires the use of special tools and equipment to ensure that the steering knuckle is correctly adjusted in the axle housing. If excessive vibration and premature wear are occurring in the axleshaft, it is recommended that the adjustment is checked by your Toyota dealer, if these symptoms are not occurring, the procedure described is satisfactory provided that due care is taken.

1 Jack-up the front of the vehicle and support the axle on suitable stands. Chock the rear roadwheels and remove the appropriate front roadwheel.
2 Remove the outer hub flange grease cap and snap-ring.
3 Remove the six flange bolts, then screw two bolts into the tapped holes to draw off the flange; also remove the gasket.
4 Where applicable, remove the two screws and take off the brake drum.
5 Fold back the lock washer tabs. Using a suitable tubular box wrench, remove the front wheel bearing adjusting nuts.

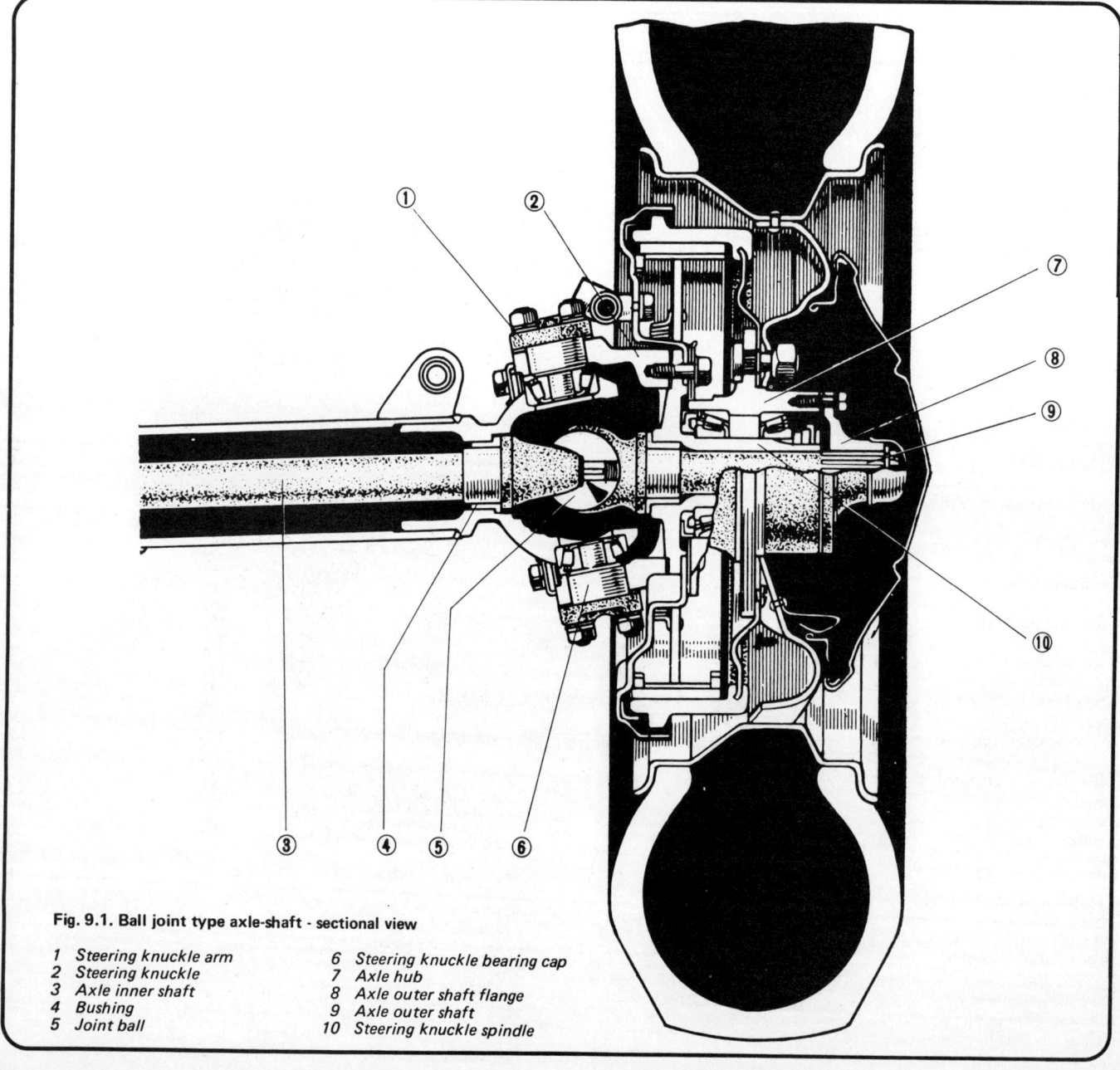

Fig. 9.1. Ball joint type axle-shaft - sectional view

1 Steering knuckle arm
2 Steering knuckle
3 Axle inner shaft
4 Bushing
5 Joint ball
6 Steering knuckle bearing cap
7 Axle hub
8 Axle outer shaft flange
9 Axle outer shaft
10 Steering knuckle spindle

Chapter 9/Front axle, front suspension and steering

6 Pull off the front hub complete with claw washer, bearings and oil seal.
7 Break the locking wire and remove the brake backing plate bolts. The brake backing plate can now be removed and tied to the steering or suspension linkage to prevent strain on the hose. If necessary the steering wheel can be turned to facilitate this step.
8 Tap the steering knuckle spindle with a soft mallet or drift to remove it. Take care where a ball joint axleshaft is used as the outer shaft and joint ball will also come out. Also remove the gasket.
9 On models with a ball joint axleshaft, slide the inner axleshaft out of the axle housing. On models with a constant velocity joint axleshaft, remove the complete axleshaft assembly from the housing; this will need to be turned so that the flat part of the outer shaft is at the top.
10 Remove the oil seal covers for the steering knuckle.
11 Remove the nuts which secure the steering knuckle arm to the steering knuckle.
12 Remove the dowels from the steering knuckle arm by striking their sides or driving a screwdriver into their slots.
13 Using a small drift and hammer, carefully tap the knuckle arm thru the center of the knuckle upper bearing, working from inside the knuckle. During this operation take care that the knuckle adjusting shims (installed between the knuckle arm and knuckle) are not lost. Record the thickness and position of the shims for use during reassembly.
14 Using the same procedure as in paragraphs 12 and 13, remove the steering knuckle bearing cap retaining nuts.
15 Remove the steering knuckle bearing cap using a small drift and hammer as described in paragraph 12. Record the thickness and position of the shims for use during reassembly.
16 Taking care that the bearings do not drop out, remove the knuckle and bearings from the axle housing.
17 Remove the outer and inner knuckle oil seals from the housing.
18 Pry the oil seal from the front hub using a screwdriver, then remove the hub bearing.
19 Clean all the parts in kerosene and allow them to dry. Inspect for worn or damaged parts, renewing as necessary. Where a ball joint is used, also check that there is no excessive wear or scoring on the inner and outer shaft machined surfaces. The diameter should be 1.2586 to 1.2595 in (31.970 to 31.991 mm). Where a constant velocity joint is used, check the joint for smooth operation; if necessary, repair it as described in the following Section.
20 Where necessary, bushings can be carefully drawn or driven out, and replacements installed.

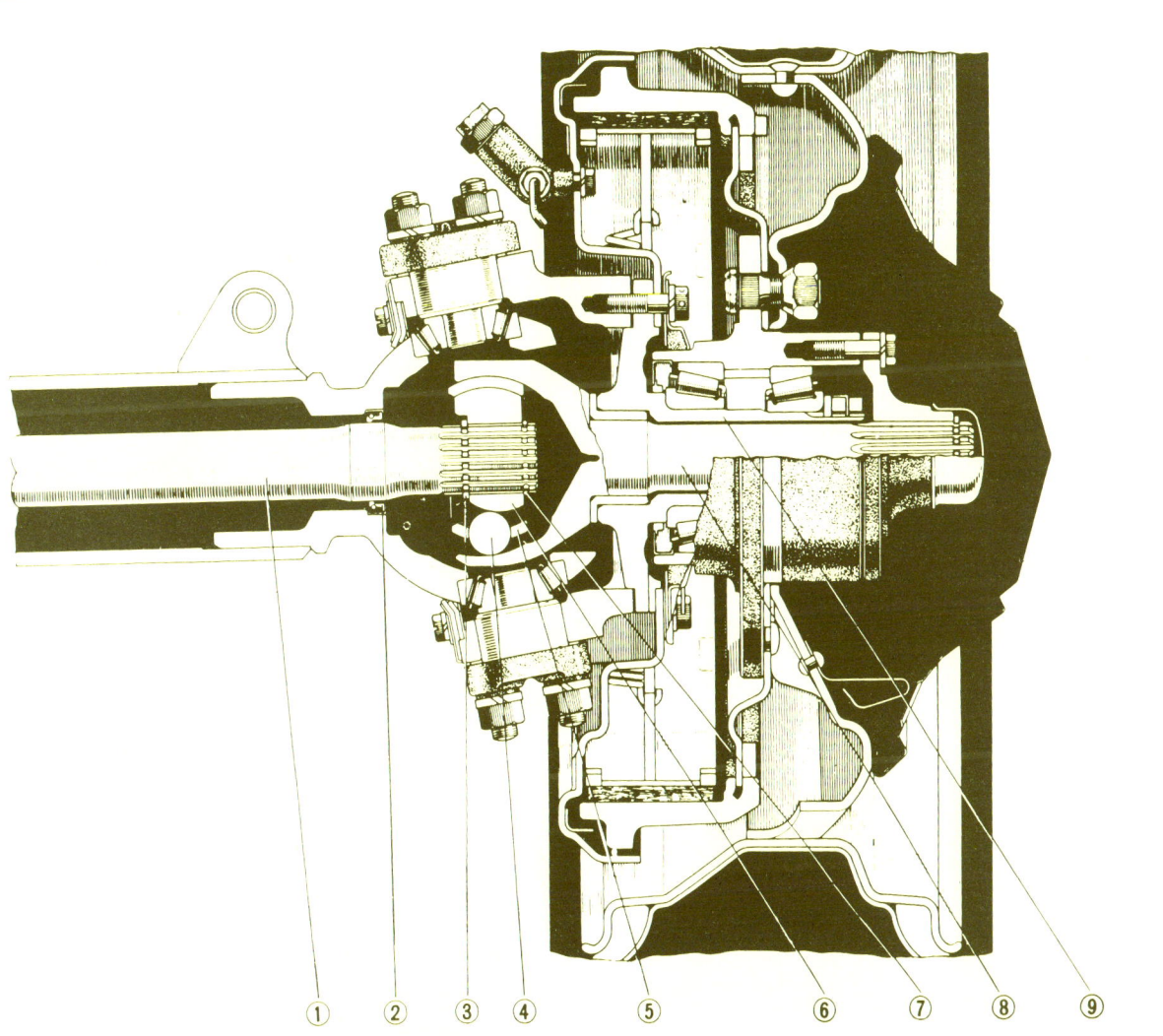

Fig. 9.2. Constant velocity joint type axle-shaft - sectional view

1 Axle inner shaft
2 Oil seal
3 Shaft snap-ring
4 Bearing ball
5 Joint cage
6 Joint inner race
7 Shaft snap-ring (inner)
8 Axle outer shaft
9 Steering knuckle spindle

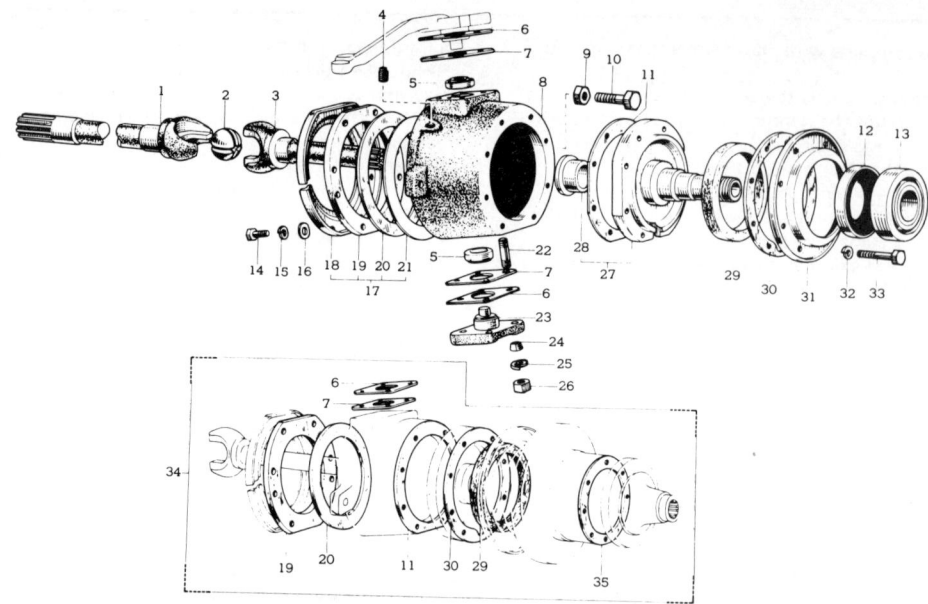

Fig. 9.3. Exploded view of ball joint type axle-shaft

1 Axle inner shaft	9 Nut	18 Oil seal cover	27 Steering knuckle spindle
2 Drive joint ball	10 Bolt	19 Outer oil seal	28 Knuckle spindle bushing
3 Axle outer shaft	11 Gasket	20 Inner oil seal	29 Dust seal
4 Plug	12 Oil seal	21 Oil seal inner ring	30 Oil retainer gasket
5 Steering knuckle bearing	13 Axle hub inner bearing	22 Stud bolt	31 Oil retainer
6 Steering knuckle adjusting shim No. 1	14 Bolt	23 Steering knuckle bearing cap	32 Lock washer
7 Steering knuckle adjusting shim No. 2	15 Lock washer	24 Dowel	33 Bolt
	16 Washer	25 Lockwasher	34 Axle gasket kit
8 Steering knuckle	17 Steering knuckle oil seal set	26 Nut	35 Flange gasket

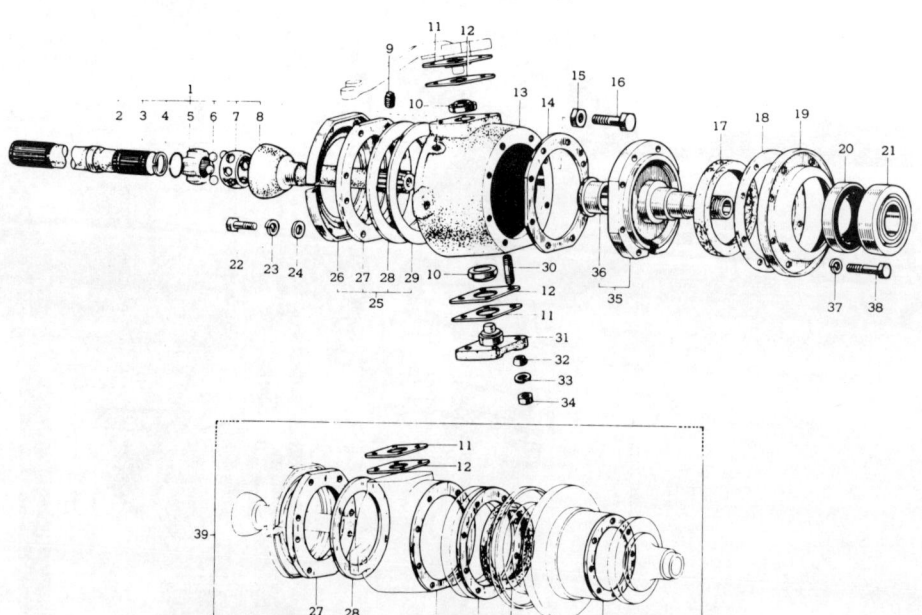

Fig. 9.4. Exploded view of constant velocity joint type axle-shaft

1 Drive shaft assembly	11 Adjusting shim No. 1	21 Hub inner bearing	31 Steering knuckle bearing cap
2 Axle inner shaft	12 Adjusting shim No. 2	22 Bolt	32 Dowel
3 Shaft snap-ring	13 Steering knuckle	23 Lock washer	33 Lock washer
4 Shaft snap-ring	14 Gasket	24 Washer	34 Nut
5 Joint inner race	15 Lock nut	25 Oil seal set	35 Steering knuckle spindle
6 Ball	16 Bolt	26 Oil seal cover	36 Bushing
7 Joint cage	17 Dust seal	27 Outer oil seal	37 Lock washer
8 Axle outer shaft	18 Oil retainer gasket	28 Inner oil seal	38 Bolt
9 Plug	19 Oil retainer gasket	29 Oil seal inner ring	39 Axle gasket kit
10 Steering knuckle bearing	20 Oil seal	30 Stud bolt	40 Flange gasket

21 Reassembly and installation are basically the reverse of the removal procedures. Renew all oil seals and gaskets, and lubricate all rubbing surfaces with a general purpose grease. Particular attention should be paid to the following points:

  a) With the steering knuckle assembled into the axle housing, attach a spring scale to the knuckle arm and check that a right-angled pull of 3.9 to 5 lb (1.8 to 2.3 kg) is required to move it in either direction. If necessary, the bearing preload can be adjusted by adding or substracting the same amount of shims from both the upper and lower knuckle bearings Caution: Failure to adjust the bearings properly will result in premature wear and excessive vibration from the joint, particularly when cornering.
  b) Where a ball joint is used, install the inner axle (complete with spacer) until the splines on the shaft are fully meshed with the differential side gears. The steering knuckle should then be filled ¾ full with a general purpose grease, and the joint ball installed.
  c) Install the axle assembly into position in the axle housing until the splines on the shaft end mesh with the differential side gears. Next, fill the knuckle housing ¾ full with a general purpose grease, and complete the assembly.
  d) When installing the snap-ring on the end of the outer shaft, install a bolt into the shaft and so that it can be drawn outwards. This will ensure that the snap-ring seats correctly.
  e) On completion, adjust the wheel bearing as described in Section 4, and adjust the toe-in as described in Section 15. If the brake line was disconnected for any reason, the brakes must be bled as described in Chapter 10.

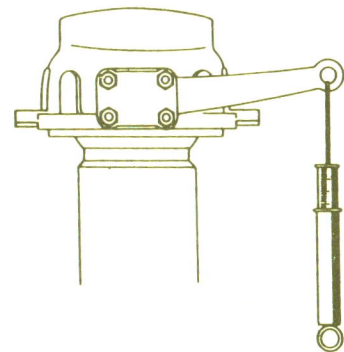

Fig. 9.5. Using a spring balance to check the knuckle arm preload

3 Front axle constant velocity joint - overhaul

1 Remove the axleshaft as described in the previous Section.
2 Secure the inner shaft in a vise, then using a brass or aluminium drift drive the outer shaft and joint inner race off the inner shaft. This operation will cause the inner snap-ring to shear.
3 Push downward on one side of the joint inner race and remove the nearest ball. In a similar manner the remaining balls can be removed.
4 Turn the cage and inner race in the housing so that they can be removed thru the large opening in the housing
5 Now turn the inner race in the cage so that it can be removed when aligned with the cage large opening.
6 Clean all the parts in kerosene and dry them with a lint-free cloth. Examine for wear and damage, and obtain new parts as necessary.
7 Lubricate all the parts with a general purpose grease, then commence assembly by installing the inner race into the cage, flat end towards the joint cage narrower side.
8 Assemble the cage and inner race into the axleshaft housing with the protrusions on the inner race facing outward. The balls can now be installed one by one.
9 Install new snap-rings into the grooves at the end of the shaft.
10 With the inner snap-ring compressed, fit the inner shaft into the joint inner race until the outer shaft snap-ring contacts the inner race. The inner snap-ring will now lock into place.
11 Finally, check the joint for smooth operation before commencing installation as described in the previous Section.

Fig. 9.6. Driving off the outer shaft

Fig. 9.7. Removing the cage and inner race

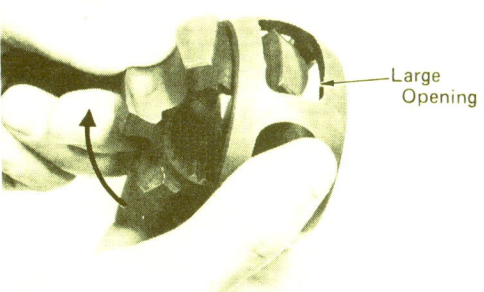

Fig. 9.8. Removing the inner race

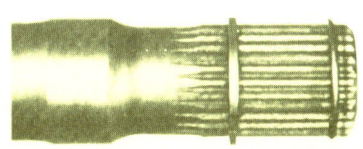

Fig. 9.9. Shaft snap-rings in position

4 Front wheel bearing - adjustment

1 Jack-up the front of the vehicle and support the axle on a suitable stand. Chock the rear roadwheels and remove the appropriate front roadwheel.
2 Rotate the brake drum to ensure that the brakes are not binding.
3 Remove the outer hub flange grease cap and snap-ring.
4 Remove the six flange bolts, then screw two bolts into the tapped holes to draw off the flange; also remove the gasket.
5 Fold back the lockwasher tabs. Using a suitable tubular box wrench, remove the outer of the two adjusting nuts. Also remove the lockwasher.
6 Whilst rotating the brake drum, firmly tighten the inner adjusting nut to ensure that the bearings are fully seated.
7 Loosen the adjusting nut by 1/8 to 1/6 of a turn, then install the lockwasher and tighten the outer adjusting nut. Fold up the lockwasher tab(s).
8 Install the flange using a new gasket.
9 When installing the snap-ring on the outer end of the shaft, install a bolt into the shaft end so that it can be drawn outwards. This will ensure that the snap-ring seats correctly.
10 Ensure that the brake drum still rotates freely, then install the grease cap followed by the roadwheel.

5 Free-wheel front hubs - removal, dismantling, reassembly and installation

1 Jack-up the front of the vehicle and support the axle on suitable stands. Chock the rear roadwheels and remove the appropriate front roadwheel.
2 Rotate the hub control to the free position, and remove the retaining bolts from the cover assembly.
3 Remove the cover assembly and gasket, then remove the snap-ring from the end of the outer driveshaft.
4 Remove the nuts and washers from the hub retaining bolts, then use a small chisel or screwdriver, driven into the slots in the core washers, to free them. The hub can now be pulled off.
5 To dismantle the hub, remove the large snap-ring so that the inner member and associated parts can be removed.
6 Next, remove the smaller snap-ring so that the hub ring end spacer can be removed.
7 Remove the compression spring, follower, tension spring and clutch.
8 Remove the snap-ring, cover and handle from the body assembly. Take care that the ball and spring are not lost.
9 Remove the ball and spring, from the handle, and take off the O-ring.
10 Clean all the parts in kerosene, and dry them with a lint-free cloth. Check that the outside diameter of the inner member is not more than 0.012 in (0.3 mm) smaller than the inside diameter of the free-wheel hub ring. Check for general wear, damage and corrosion, and renew parts accordingly.
11 Reassembly is essentially the reverse of the dismantling procedure, but ensure that all parts are lubricated with a general purpose grease. When assembling the tension spring into the clutch, ensure that the spring end is aligned in the initial groove. Also ensure that the free-wheel hub ring is installed in the correct direction (see Fig. 9.14).
12 Set the handle and clutch to the free position, then temporarily install the cover assembly to the body assembly to ensure that it operates smoothly.
13 Installation is now the reverse of the removal procedure but ensure that the sliding surfaces are liberally lubricated with general purpose grease. Do not forget to use a new gasket when installing the cover assembly. When installing the snap-ring on the outer end of the shaft, install a bolt into the shaft end so that it can be drawn outwards. This will ensure that the snap-ring seats correctly.

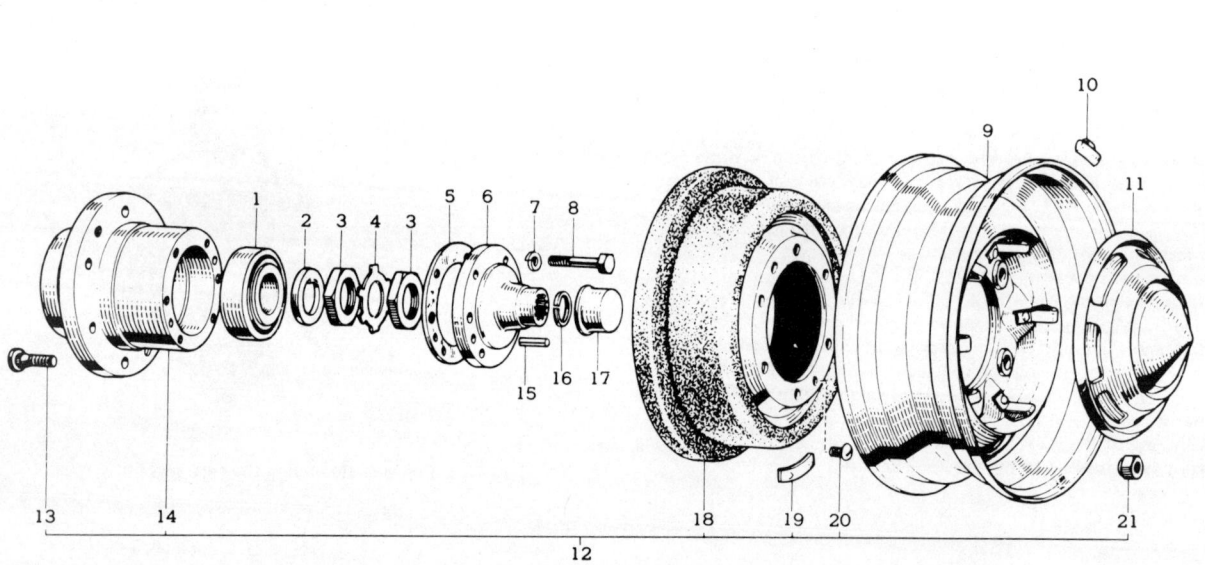

Fig. 9.10. Front wheel bearing - exploded view (typical)

1 Hub outer bearing
2 Claw washer
3 Front wheel adjusting nut
4 Lock washer
5 Flange gasket
6 Outer shaft flange
7 Lock washer
8 Bolt
9 Wheel
10 Balance weight
11 Hub cap
12 Hub and brake drum assembly
13 Hub bolt
14 Hub
15 Straight pin
16 Shaft snap-ring
17 Outer shaft flange cap
18 Brake drum
19 Balance piece
20 Brake drum screw
21 Hub nut

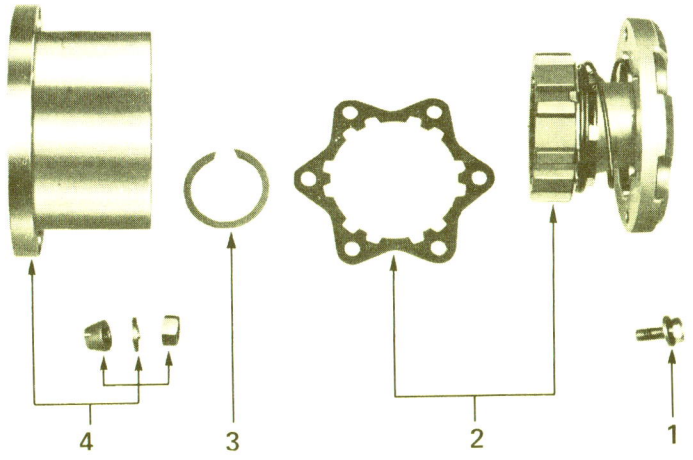

Fig. 9.11. Free-wheel hub - remove parts in numerical order

1 Cover assembly bolts
2 Cover assembly and gasket
3 Snap-ring
4 Free-wheel hub, nuts, spring washer and cone washer

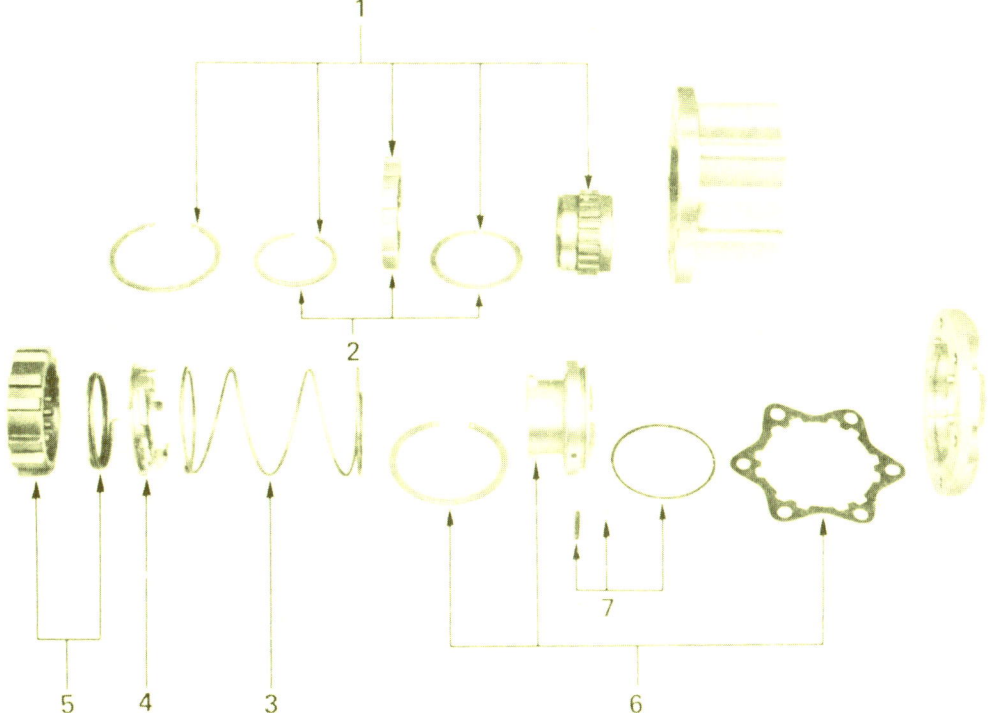

Fig. 9.12. Free-wheel hub - dismantle in numerical order

1 Snap-ring and inner member
2 Snap-ring, free-wheel hub ring and spacer
3 Compression spring
4 Follower
5 Tension spring and clutch
6 Snap-ring, handle and cover
7 'O' ring, spring and ball

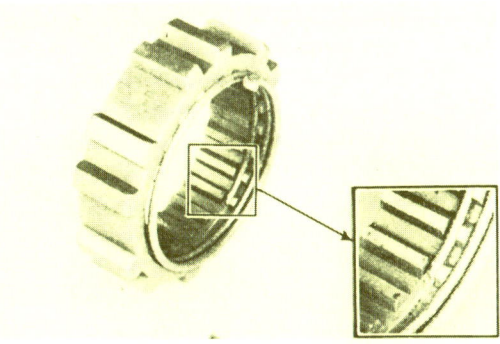

Fig. 9.13. Tension spring in initial groove

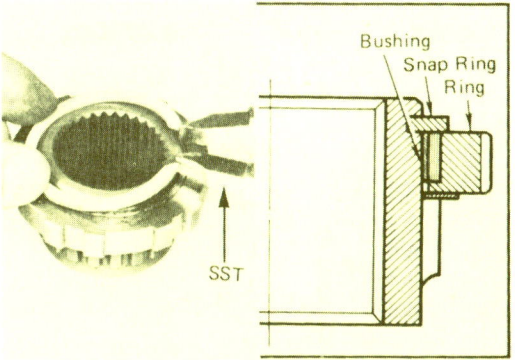

Fig. 9.14. Snap-ring installation

Chapter 9/Front axle, front suspension and steering

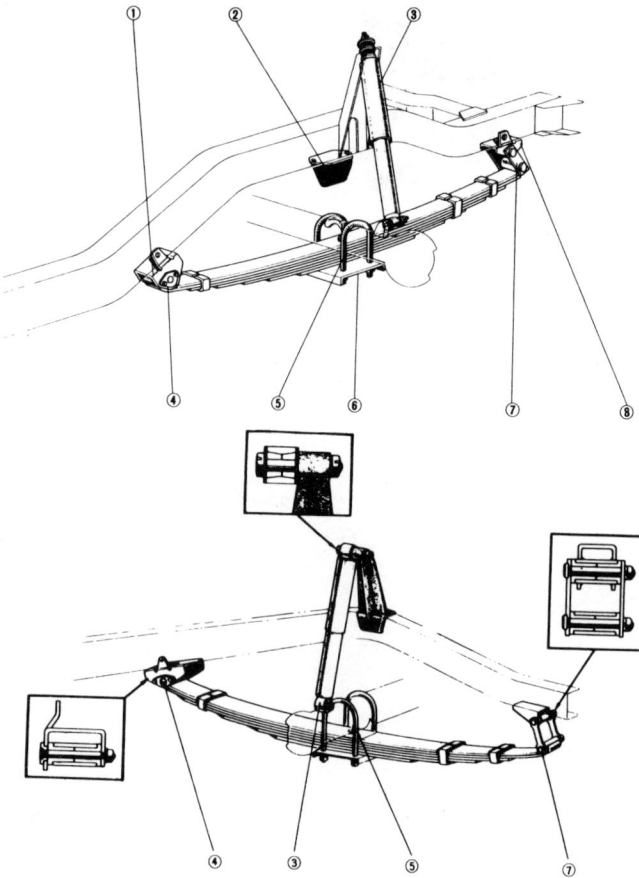

6 Front shock absorber - removal and installation

1 Jack-up the front of the vehicle and support the axle on suitable stands. Chock the rear roadwheels; for improved accessibility remove the front roadwheel.
2 At the shock absorber upper mounting, remove the nuts, cushion and cushion retainer so that the shock absorber can be detached.
3 Remove the cotter pin and nut at the lower mounting so that the shock absorber can be removed.
4 To test a shock absorber, grip the lower mounting in a vise with the unit in a vertical position. Extend and contract the shock absorber over its full range of travel about ten times; if there is not a positive resistance to travel in both directions; the unit must be renewed. Renewal is also necessary if there is any sign of oil leakage around the piston rod or shock absorber body.

7 Front axle - removal and installation

1 Raise the front of the vehicle to a suitable height and support the bodyframe side members on suitable stands or blocks. Chock the rear wheels for safety.
2 Remove the front roadwheels.
3 Support the axle weight on suitable jacks or stands.
4 Disconnect the brake hoses from the wheel cylinders. Plug the hose ends to prevent loss of fluid.
5' Disconnect the tie-rod end at each steering knuckle arm, and the relay rod at the steering center arm. For further information see Section 14. Remove the relay rod and tie-rod.
6 Detach the propeller shaft from the axle companion flange.
7 Remove the steering knuckles, axle shafts, driveshafts, and ball joints as described in Section 2.
8 Remove the four nuts so that the spring U-bolts can be removed.
9 Detach the lower shock absorber mounting, then lower the axle jacks so that the axle can be withdrawn.
10 Installation is the reverse of the removal procedure.

Fig. 9.15. Front shock absorber and spring mountings

Upper	FJ55 series	Lower	FJ40 series
1	Spring brakcet	5	U-bolt
2	Front spring bump stop	6	U-bolt seat
3	Shock absorber	7	Spring shackle
4	Spring bracket pin	8	Spring bracket

8 Front spring - removal and installation

1 Remove the shock absorber as described in Section 6.
2 Support the bodyframe sidemembers on suitable stands or jacks. Support the axle so that its weight is just taken up.
3 Remove the nuts so that the spring U-bolts can be removed.
4 Remove the nuts so that the spring shackle inner plate can be taken off.
5 Using a suitable pry bar, remove the spring shackle and rubber bushings.
6 Remove the two bolts to release the spring bracket pin from the spring bracket.
7 Carefully drive out the spring bracket pin to release the spring, then remove the spring rubber bush.
8 Installation is the reverse of the removal procedure, but do not tighten the nuts on the shackles and spring bracket until the vehicle weight is on the spring.

9 Differential carrier - removal and installation

1 Detach the propeller shaft from the axle companion flange (refer to Chapter 7 if necessary).
2 Withdraw the axle shafts as described in Section 2.
3 Remove the retaining nuts and spring washers, and draw the complete differential carrier rearward and away from the axle. Collect the axle oil in a suitable container.
4 Installation is the reverse of the removal procedure; it is recommended that a non-setting sealant is used for gasket joints. On completion, top up the differential housing with the appropriate grade and quantity of oil.

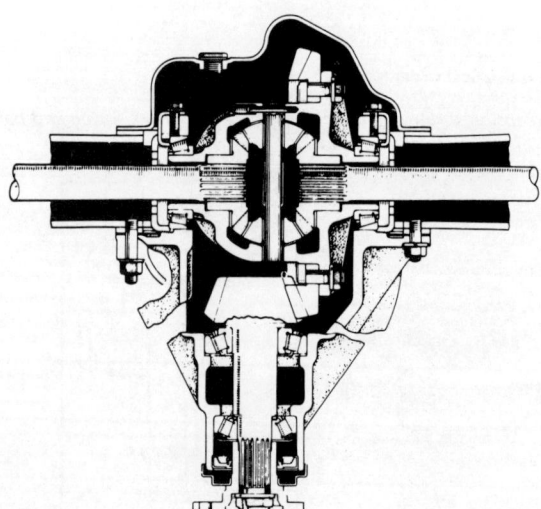

Fig. 9.16. Sectional view of front axle differential

10 Pinion oil seal - renewal

Renewal of the oil seal is a similar operation to that described for the rear axle in Chapter 8.

Chapter 9/Front axle, front suspension and steering

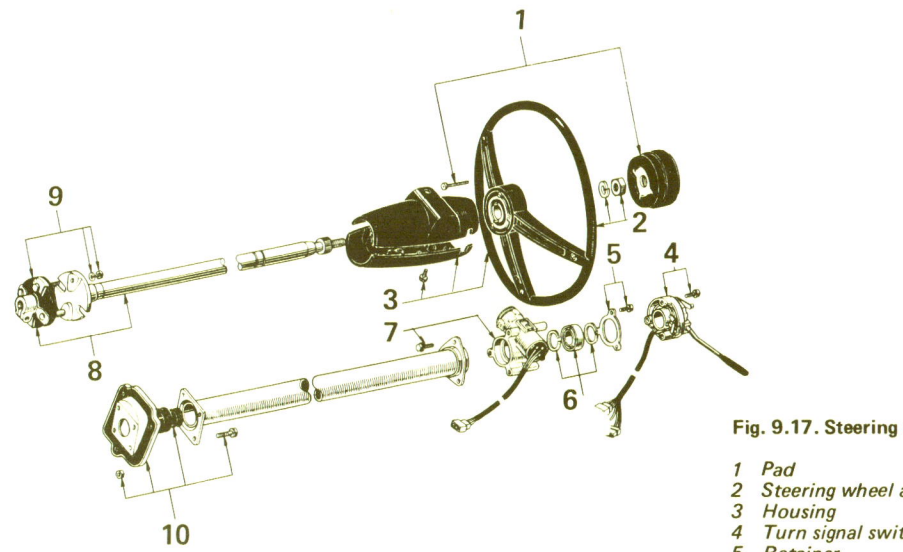

Fig. 9.17. Steering column - late model FJ40 series shown

1 Pad
2 Steering wheel assembly
3 Housing
4 Turn signal switch
5 Retainer
6 Bearing
7 Upper bracket assembly
8 Shaft and coupling
9 Coupling
10 Hole cover and seal

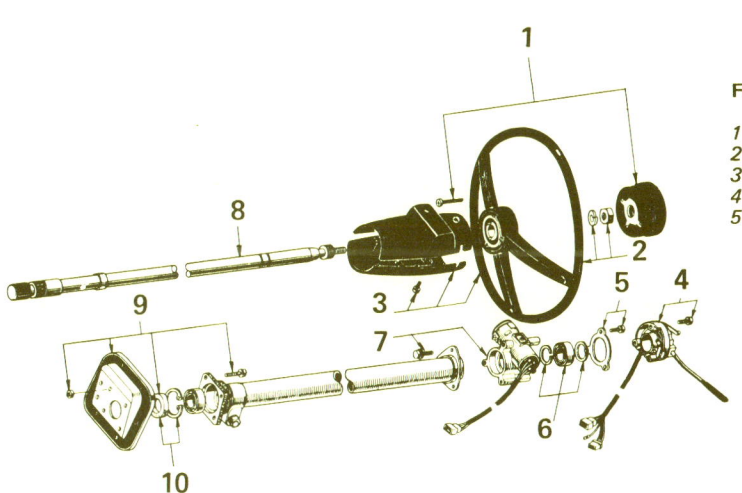

Fig. 9.18A. Steering column - late model FJ55 series shown

1 Pad
2 Steering wheel assembly
3 Housing
4 Turn signal switch
5 Retainer
6 Bearing
7 Upper bracket assembly
8 Shaft
9 Hole cover
10 Bearing

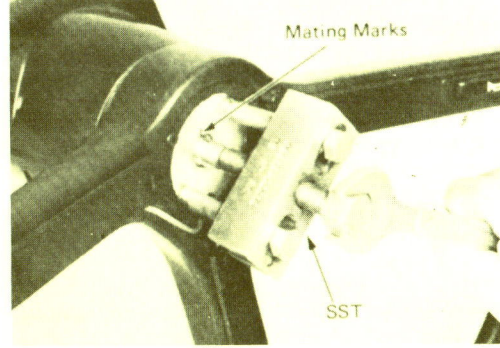

Fig. 9.18B. Removing the steering wheel using an extractor

11 Steering wheel and mainshaft - removal, dismantling, reassembly and installation

1 Index mark the steering gear, couplings and mainshaft (FJ40 series vehicles) or yoke and mainshaft (FJ55 series vehicles) to ensure correct reassembly.
2 Remove the hole cover bolts and washers from the toe-board.
3 Detach the upper bracket and electrical lead connectors.
4 Withdraw the complete steering wheel and mainshaft from the vehicle.
5 From behind the steering wheel remove the pad retaining screws, take off the pad.
6 Remove the nut and spring washer, then index mark the steering wheel and shaft to ensure correct reassembly.
7 Make up a suitable extractor as shown in Fig. 9.18 b so that the steering wheel can be pulled off.
8 The remainder of the assembly can be dismantled, if necessary, by reference to Figs 9.17 and 9.18, which show the parts in the order of dismantling.
9 Inspect all the parts for wear and damage, and obtain new parts as necessary.
10 Assembly and installation are the reverse of the removal procedure. Pack grease into the upper bearing, and ensure that the mating marks are correctly aligned.

Chapter 9/Front axle, front suspension and steering

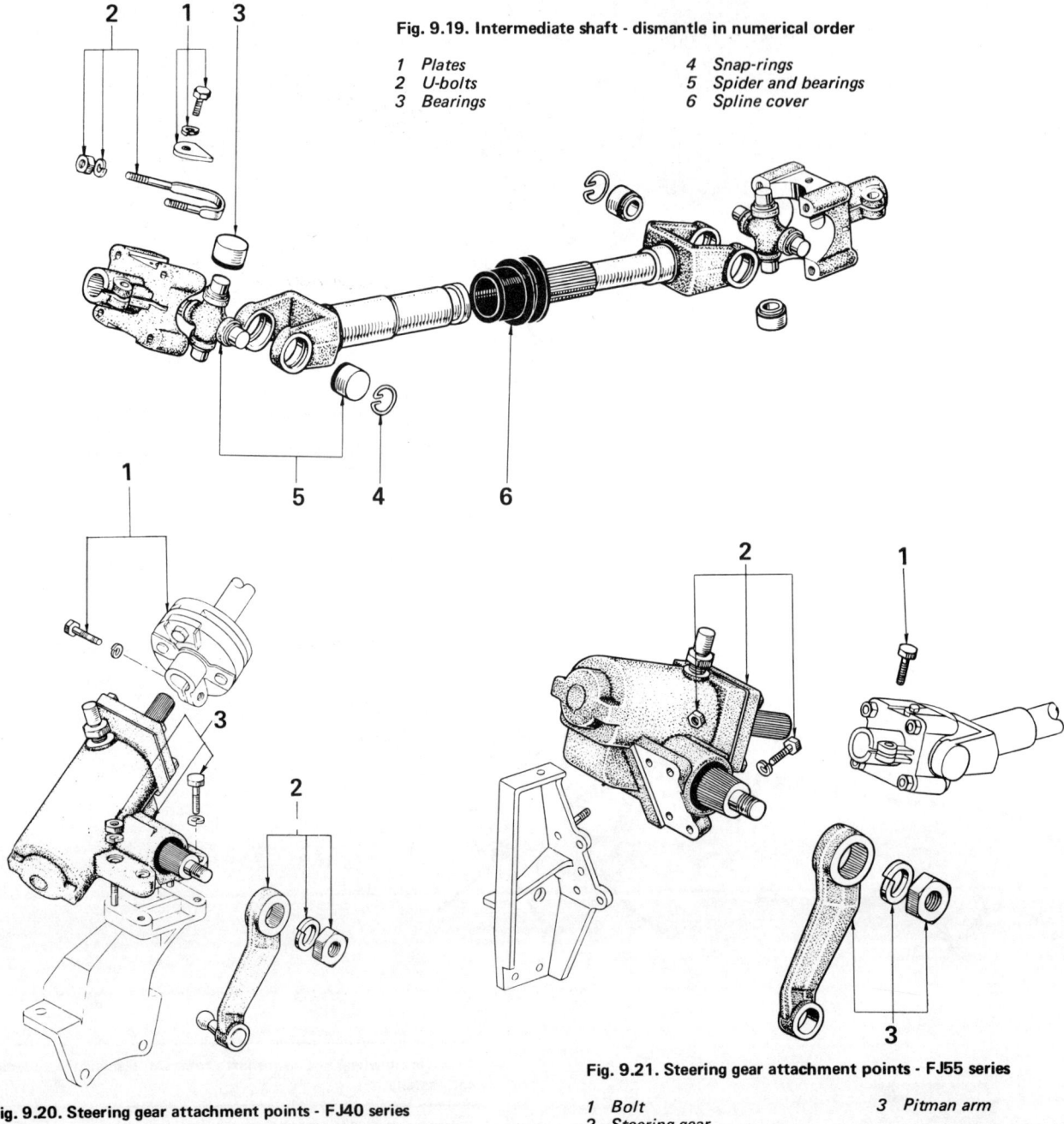

Fig. 9.19. Intermediate shaft - dismantle in numerical order

1 Plates
2 U-bolts
3 Bearings
4 Snap-rings
5 Spider and bearings
6 Spline cover

Fig. 9.20. Steering gear attachment points - FJ40 series

1 Main shaft
2 Pitman arm
3 Steering gear

Fig. 9.21. Steering gear attachment points - FJ55 series

1 Bolt
2 Steering gear
3 Pitman arm

12 Steering intermediate shaft - dismantling and reassembly

1 Index mark the installed position of the universal joint housings to ensure correct reassembly.
2 Remove the pinch bolt from each coupling so that the halves of the shaft can be slid towards each other and detached.
3 Remove the locking plates and U-bolt nuts to release one pair of bearings from each end.
4 Remove the snap-rings, spiders and remaining pairs of bearings. Further information on the techniques involved will be found in Chapter 7, since these bearings are essentially the same as those used for propeller shafts, except for the location of the snap-rings (photo).
5 During reassembly, select snap-rings of a thickness which will provide minimum thrust clearance in the joint spider. These are available in sizes of 0.0424 in (1.2 mm), 0.0492 in (1.25 mm) and 0.0512 in (1.3 mm). When coupling together the two shaft halves, ensure that they are in the relationship shown in the illustration.

13 Steering gear - removal and installation

Note: It is not recommended that any overhaul of the steering gear is attempted since special tools and equipment are required. This job should be entrusted to a Toyota dealer, or an exchange assembly obtained.

1 On FJ 40 series vehicles, remove the steering wheel and mainshaft as described in Section 11. On FJ 55 series vehicles, index mark the installed position of the pinch bolt, remove the bolt and slide back the lower end of the intermediate shaft.
2 Remove the nut and washer from the pitman arm, then index mark the installed position of the pitman arm on the sector shaft.
3 Using a suitable extractor or split wedges, remove the pitman arm. Provided that care is taken it should be possible to drive the taper of a cold chisel between the pitman arm and the steering gear housing to achieve the same result.
4 Remove the bolts and washers, and nuts and washers, and detach the

Chapter 9/Front axle, front suspension and steering

12.4 Intermediate shaft coupling

13.5 Steering gear filler plug. Note the breather cap which is used on some models

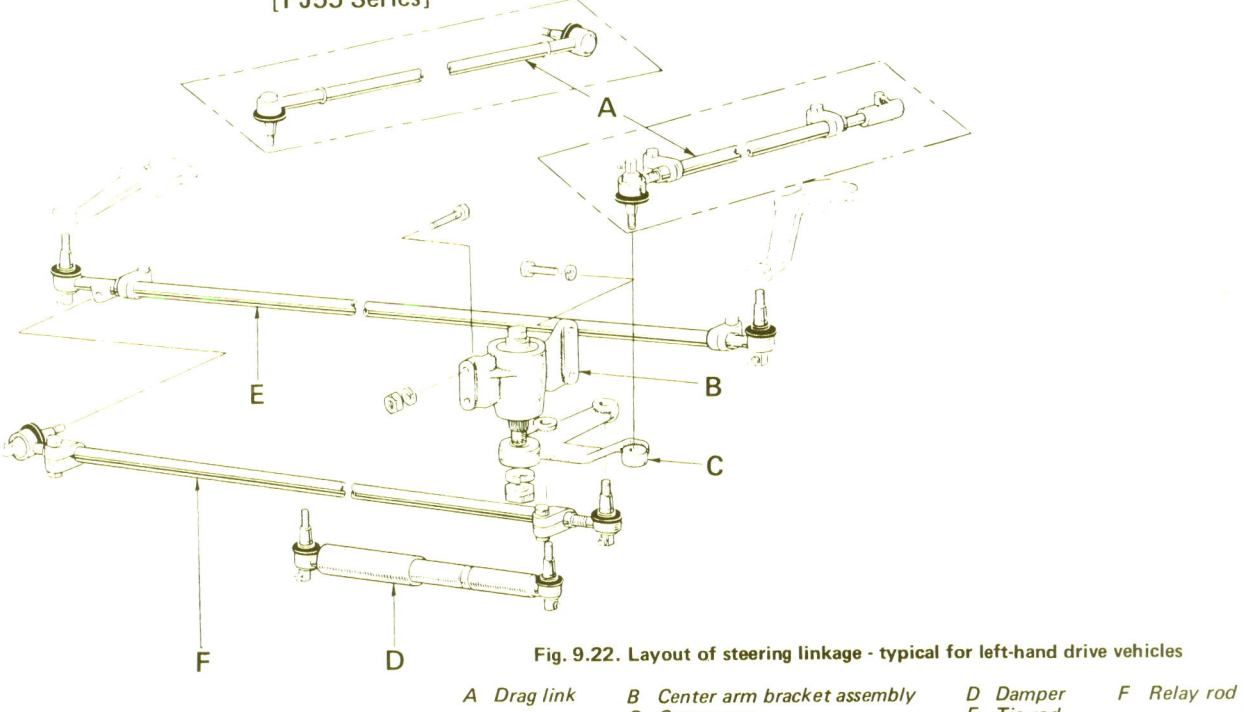

Fig. 9.22. Layout of steering linkage - typical for left-hand drive vehicles

A Drag link
B Center arm bracket assembly
C Center arm
D Damper
E Tie rod
F Relay rod

steering gear from its mounting.

5 Installation of the steering gear is the reverse of the removal procedure, but care must be taken to align the mating marks. Add gear oil as necessary so that it is just below the level of the filler plug hole (photo).

14 Steering linkage - removal, dismantling, reassembly and installation

1 After a long period of service, wear can be expected in the various ball joints and pivots of the steering linkage. The various items of linkage are shown in Fig. 9.14. Although this is for left-hand drive vehicles, right-hand drive models are the opposite way round.
2 To remove ball joints, first remove the cotter pin and retaining nut, then use a proprietary ball joint separator or split wedges to extract the ball joint taper from the mating eye. Provided that care is taken, the same result can be achieved by driving in the taper of a cold chisel.

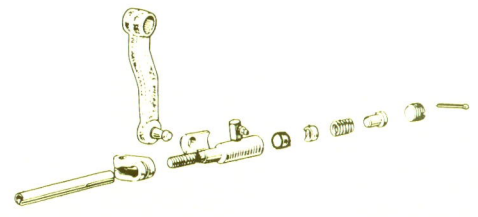

Fig. 9.23. Exploded view of FJ40 series drag link ball joint at Pitman arm end

3 Installation of replacement ball joints is straightforward, but since they have to be removed from the appropriate rod or link, it is essential that they are install again in their relative positions. For the steering relay rod, the correct distance between ball joint centers is 32.56 in (827 mm); for the tie-rod, the correct distance between ball joint centers is 47.44 in (1205 mm); for the drag link or FJ 40 series vehicles, the correct distance between ball joint centers is 33.66 in (855 mm).

4 A different type of ball joint is used at the pitman arm end of the drag link on FJ40 series vehicles. Dismantling is straightforward after the cotter pin and screwed plug have been removed.

5 If wear exists in the center arm bracket assembly, remove the nut and washer and withdraw the center arm as described in Section 13 for the pitman arm. The assembly can then be removed and dismantled as necessary, and replacement parts installed. When reassembling, a liberal coating of general purpose grease should be applied.

15 Front wheel alignment

1 Accurate front wheel alignment is essential for good steering and tire wear. Before considering the steering angles, check that the tires are correctly inflated, that the front wheels are not buckled, the hub bearings are not worn or incorrectly adjusted, and that the steering linkage is in good order, without slackness or wear at the joints.

2 Wheel alignment consists of four factors:

Camber, which is the angle at which the front wheels are set from the vertical when viewed from the front of the car. Positive camber is the amount (in degrees) that the wheels are fitted outwards at the top from the vertical.

Castor, is the angle between the steering axis and a vertical line when viewed from each side of the car. Positive castor is when the steering axis is inclined rearward.

King pin inclination, is the angle, when viewed from the front of the car, between the vertical and an imaginary line drawn between the upper and lower steering swivels.

Toe-in, is the amount by which the distance between the front of the road wheels (measured at hub height) is less than the diametrically opposite distance measured between the rear of the front road wheels.

3 Camber, castor and king pin inclination cannot be altered as they are design characteristics of the axle. If these are to be checked special gauges are required, and the job must be entrusted to a Toyota dealer.

4 Front wheel tracking (toe-in) may be checked and adjusted by carrying out the following operations.

5 Place the vehicle on level ground with the wheels in the straight ahead position.

6 Obtain or make a toe-in gauge. One may be easily made from

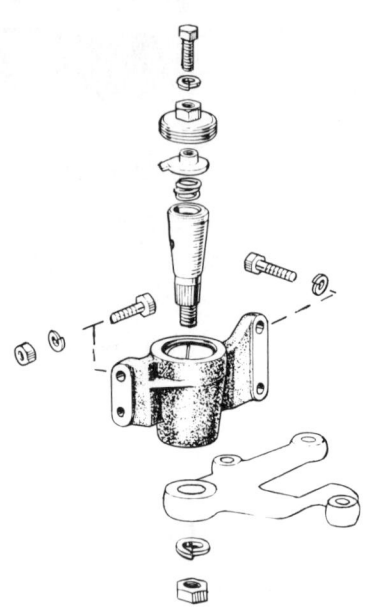

Fig. 9.24. Exploded view of center arm bracket assembly

tubing, cranked to clear the underside of the vehicle, having an adjustable nut and setscrew at one end.

7 With the gauge, measure the distance between the two inner wheel rims at hub height at the front of the wheel.

8 Rotate the road wheel thru 180° (half a turn) and measure the distance between the inner wheel rims at hub height at the rear of the wheel. This measurement should be greater by between 0.12 and 0.20 in (3.0 and 5.0 mm). This represents the correct toe-in of the front wheels.

9 Where the toe-in is found to be incorrect, slacken the tie-rod clamp bolts and rotate the rod. It is a good plan to first measure between the ball joint centers in case it has been adjusted unevenly by a previous owner. When adjustment is correct, tighten the clamp bolts ensuring that the clamp openings are in alignment with the slots in the tie rod tubes and that the track rod ends are positioned in the centers of their arcs of travel.

16 Fault diagnosis - front axle, front suspension and steering

Symptom	Cause
Heavy steering	Low tire pressure. Incorrect front wheel alignment. Lack of lubrication. Defective steering knuckle bearing or incorrect pre-load. Steering gear incorrectly adjusted. Defective balljoints.
Steering shimming	Incorrect tire pressures. Incorrect front wheel alignment Wheels and tires out of balance. Loose or damaged wheel. Defective wheel bearing. Loose steering gear mounting. Play in steering linkage. Defective steering damper.
Steering pulls to one side	Uneven tire pressures. Defective front spring. Defective shock absorbers. Damaged frame or axle. Wheel bearing incorrectly adjusted.

Chapter 10 Brakes, wheels and tires

Contents

Bleeding the hydraulic system ... 3	Fault diagnosis - brakes ... 18
Brakes - adjustment ... 2	Fault diagnosis - tires ... 19
Brake servo (booster) - general description ... 6	General description ... 1
Brake servo (early type) - removal, overhaul and installation ... 7	Hydraulic lines - inspection, removal and installation ... 14
Brake servo (later types, single and dual master cylinders) - removal and installation ... 8	Parking brake linkage and cables - removal and installation ... 16
	Parking brake shoes - removal and installation ... 15
Disc brakes - pad renewal ... 11	Single master cylinder - removal, overhaul and installation ... 4
Disc brake calipers - overhaul ... 13	Tandem master cylinder - removal, overhaul and installation ... 5
Drum brake wheel cylinders - overhaul ... 12	Twin-leading shoe brakes - shoe renewal ... 10
Dual twin-leading shoe brakes - shoe renewal ... 9	Wheels and tires ... 17

Specifications

Brake system type ... Hydraulic; drum front and rear *or* discs at front and drums at rear. Vacuum servo and/or dual braking system installed according to specification.

Parking brake (handbrake) ... Lever and cable operated to single drum brakes on transfer gear.

Detailed specifications of the brakes are not included due to the numerous types which have been used. For specific information on any particular model, consult your Toyota dealer.

Brake pedal height (from toeboard)
FJ40 series, 1968/71 ...	7.48 in (190 mm)
FJ55 series, 1968/71 ...	6.69 in (170 mm)
FJ40 series, 1972/74 ...	9.65 in (245 mm)
FJ55 series, 1972/74 ...	6.69 in (170 mm)
FJ40 series, with servo, 1975 onwards ...	8.46 in (215 mm)
FJ40 series, without servo, 1975 onwards ...	7.80 in (198 mm)
FJ55 series, with servo, 1975 onwards ...	7.28 in (185 mm)
FJ55 series, without servo, 1975 onwards ...	6.77 in (172 mm)

Minimum brake lining thickness ... 0.06 in (1.5 mm)

Minimum brake pad thickness ... 0.04 in (1.0 mm)

Minimum brake disc thickness ... 0.74 in (19 mm)

Maximum brake disc runout ... 0.005 in (0.12 in)

Brake fluid specification ... DOT 3 or SAE J1703

Maximum brake drum diameter
Dual twin-leading shoe front brakes, and rear brakes on FJ45 models and FJ55 fire truck models ...	11.70 in (297 mm)
All other brake drums ...	11.50 in (292 mm)

Wheels
Type ... Pressed steel disc

Tires
Type ... Tire type varies according to vehicle specification and application (see pressures overleaf)

Chapter 10/Brakes, wheels and tires

Pressures

	Tire size	Front kgf/cm² (lbf/in²) Under 80 km/h (50 mph)	Front kgf/cm² (lbf/in²) Above 80 km/h (50 mph)	Front kgf/cm² (lbf/in²) Under 80 km/h (50 mph)	Front kgf/cm² (lbf/in²) Above 80 km/h (50 mph)
FJ40 models	7.60-15 6PR	1.8 (26)	2.1 (30)	2.1 (30)	2.4 (34)
	7.00-15 6PR LT	1.8 (26)	2.0 (28)	2.4 (34)	2.8 (40)
	7.00-15 8PR LT	2.4 (34)	2.4 (34)	2.4 (34)	2.4 (34)
	7.00-16 6PR LT	1.8 (26)	2.0 (28)	2.2 (31)	2.6 (27)
	7.50-16 6PR LT	1.8 (26)	2.0 (28)	1.8 (26)	2.0 (28)
	9.00-15 6PR	1.2 (17)	—	1.8 (26)	—
FJ43 models	7.00-15 6PR LT	1.8 (26)	2.2 (31)	2.6 (37)	3.0 (43)
	7.00-15 8PR LT	2.4 (34)	2.4 (34)	2.6 (37)	3.0 (43)
	7.00-16 6PR LT	1.8 (26)	2.2 (31)	2.4 (34)	2.8 (30)
	7.50-16 6PR LT	1.8 (26)	2.2 (31)	2.4 (34)	2.8 (40)
	9.00-15 6PR	1.2 (17)	—	2.0 (28)	—
FJ45 models	7.00-16 6PR LT	1.8 (26)	2.2 (31)	—	—
	7.00-16 8PR LT	2.4 (34)	2.4 (34)	4.0 (57)	4.3 (61)
	7.50-16 6PR LT	1.8 (26)	2.2 (31)	—	—
	7.50-16 6PR LT	2.3 (34)	2.4 (34)	3.3 (46)	3.8 (53)
	9.00-15 6PR	1.3 (19)	—	2.3 (33)	—
FJ55 models	7.00-15 6PR LT	1.8 (26)	2.2 (31)	3.0 (43)	3.3 (46)
	7.00-16 6PR LT	1.8 (26)	2.2 (31)	2.8 (40)	3.3 (46)
	7.50-16 6PR LT	1.8 (26)	2.2 (31)	2.6 (37)	3.0 (43)
	9.00-15 6PR	1.4 (20)	—	2.3 (33)	—

The above tire pressures are typical. For further information consult your tire dealer or Toyota agent. Where 9.00-15 6PR tires are used, vehicle speed must be limited to 50 km/h (30 mph).

Torque wrench settings

	lb f ft	kg f m
Master cylinder reservoir bolt	11.5	1.6
Parking brake drum nut on transfer output shaft	100	14
Brake disc/hub	35	4.8
Brake caliper/steering knuckle	65	9.0
Brake servo (booster) valve fitting	32	4.5

1 General description

Hydraulic brakes are used on all models, but with the differing vehicle specifications which are available, several different types of system may be encountered. Most models have drum brakes all round, although some later models may have disc brakes at the front. Single and dual braking systems are employed, and alternative types of vacuum servo may be used on some versions.

The parking brake operates through a lever and cable to a drum arrangement mounted on the transmission transfer assembly.

All early models have front brakes with twin-leading shoes; these brakes use two wheel cylinders, each with one piston. All rear brakes and the front drum brakes used on later models have dual twin-leading shoes; these brakes use two wheel cylinders, each with two pistons. An alternative arrangement on some later models is the use of disc front brakes.

2 Brakes - adjustment

Brake pedal

1 For models with a brake servo, initially loosen the stop light adjustment nuts, then adjust the brake pedal height to the specified amount by rotating the pushrod. Adjust the stop light switch so that the lights operate as soon as the pedal is depressed.
2 For models without a brake servo, loosen the pushrod adjusting nut, then adjust the pedal height to the specified amount by repositioning the stop light switch.
3 After setting the pedal height, check for a freeplay of 0.12 to 0.23 in (3 to 6 mm) where a brake servo is fitted. If this cannot be obtained there is excessive play in the pedal pivots or a fault in the servo. Where no brake servo is fitted, adjust the pedal freeplay to 0.12 to 0.23 in (3. to 6 mm) for models with front disc brakes or dual two-leading shoes, or 0.02 in (0.5 mm) for models with two-leading shoes, by rotating the pushrod.

Brake shoes

4 Where excessive brake pedal travel is evident the drum brake shoes must be adjusted. This adjustment is carried out as described in the following paragraphs.
5 Raise the appropriate roadwheel and check that it rotates freely. If the rear brakes are being adjusted, the parking brake must be released, so for safety chock the wheels which are still on the ground.
6 Remove the adjuster hole plugs from the brake backplate.
7 Using a suitable tool (a short screwdriver can be used) rotate the adjusters through the backplate holes so that the tool tip moves in a direction from the wheel center towards the rim. In this way, expand the shoes to firmly contact the drum (photo).
8 Depress the brake pedal two or three times to center the shoes, then recheck that the shoes are contacting the drum.
9 Now turn back the adjusters five notches and check that the drum rotates freely. If necessary, the adjuster may be turned back one extra notch, but if the shoes are still dragging against the drum, uneven wear is indicated and the drum should be removed for investigation.
10 Install the plugs in the adjuster holes, then repeat the adjustment for the remaining brakes.

Parking brake

11 Release the parking brake lever, then jack-up the rear of the vehicle and support the axle on suitable stands. Chock the front wheels for safety.
12 Turn the adjuster on the rear of the brake drum until the shoes are fully expanded, then back it off one notch.
13 Operate then release, the handbrake. If the drum is found to be rubbing, back off the adjuster one extra notch.
14 After this adjustment, the parking brake lever should have a travel of 6 to 9 notches (pre 1975 models) or 7 to 12 notches (1975 models onwards). If necessary, adjustment can be made at the turnbuckle or cable end nut, as appropriate.

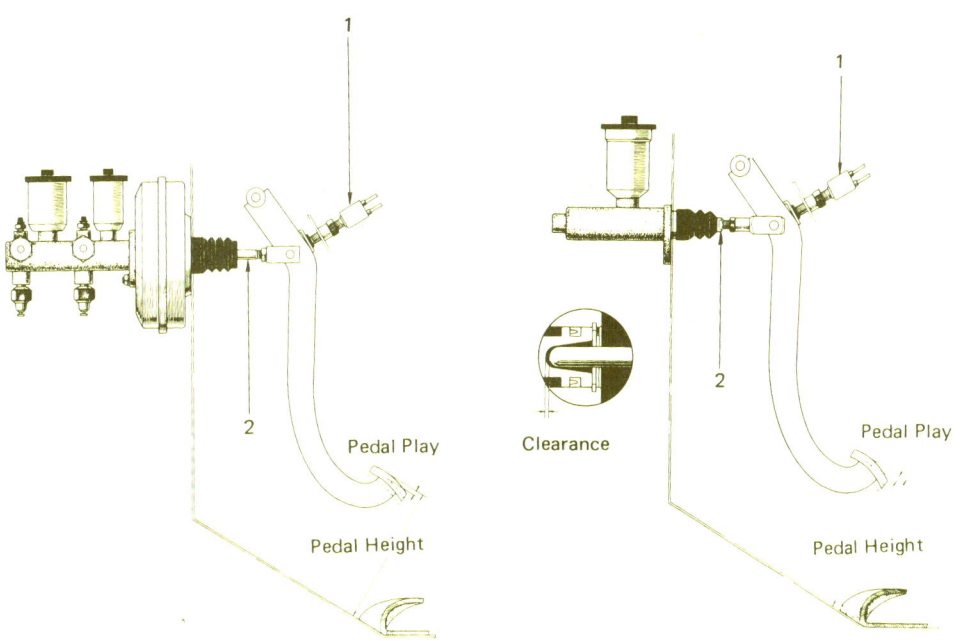

Fig. 10.1. Brake pedal adjustments - typical

Left — servo type
1 Stoplight switch
2 Pushrod

Right — non-servo type
1 Stoplight switch
2 Pushrod

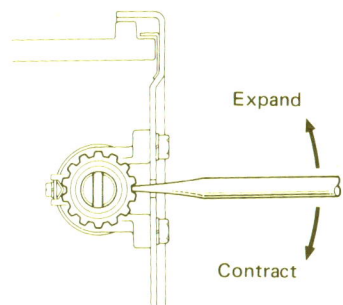

Fig. 10.2. Brake adjustment

2.7 Drum brake adjustment

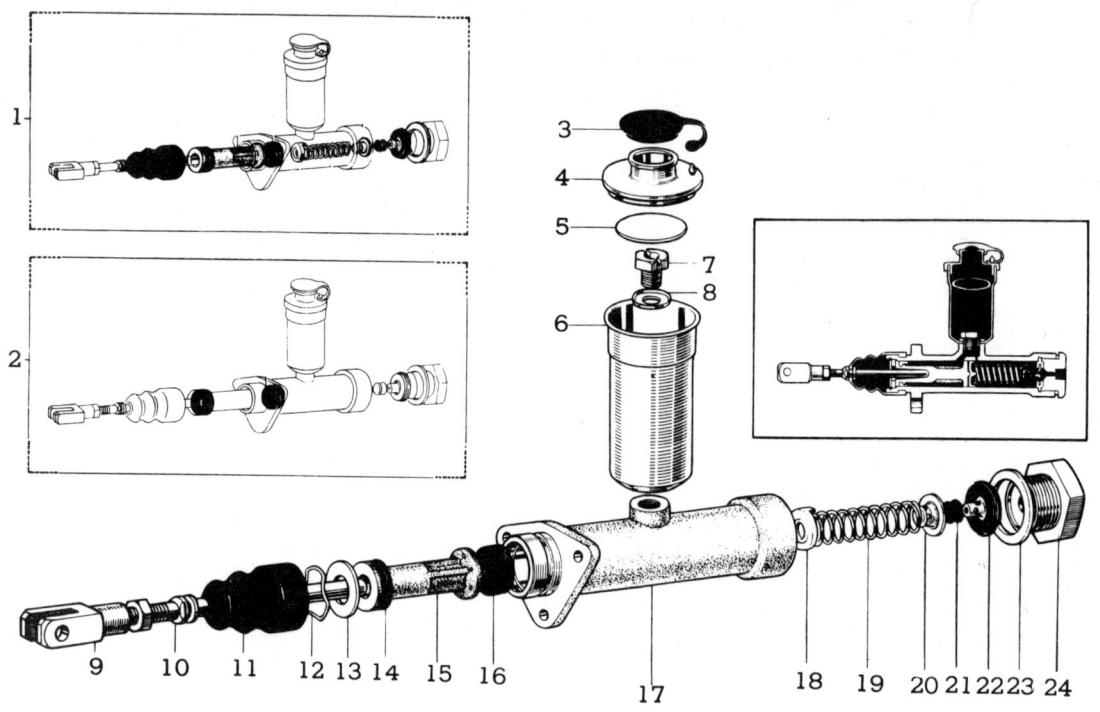

Fig. 10.3. Single master cylinder (early type) - exploded view

1. Master cylinder repair kit
2. Master cylinder piston cup repair kit
3. Reservoir filler cap
4. Reservoir cap
5. Float
6. Reservoir
7. Reservoir set bolt
8. Washer
9. Pushrod clevis
10. Master cylinder pushrod
11. Boot
12. Snap-ring
13. Washer
14. Cylinder cup
15. Piston
16. Cylinder cup
17. Master cylinder body
18. Return spring retainer
19. Piston return spring
20. Outlet check valve seat
21. Outlet check valve
22. Seat gasket
23. Gasket
24. Plug

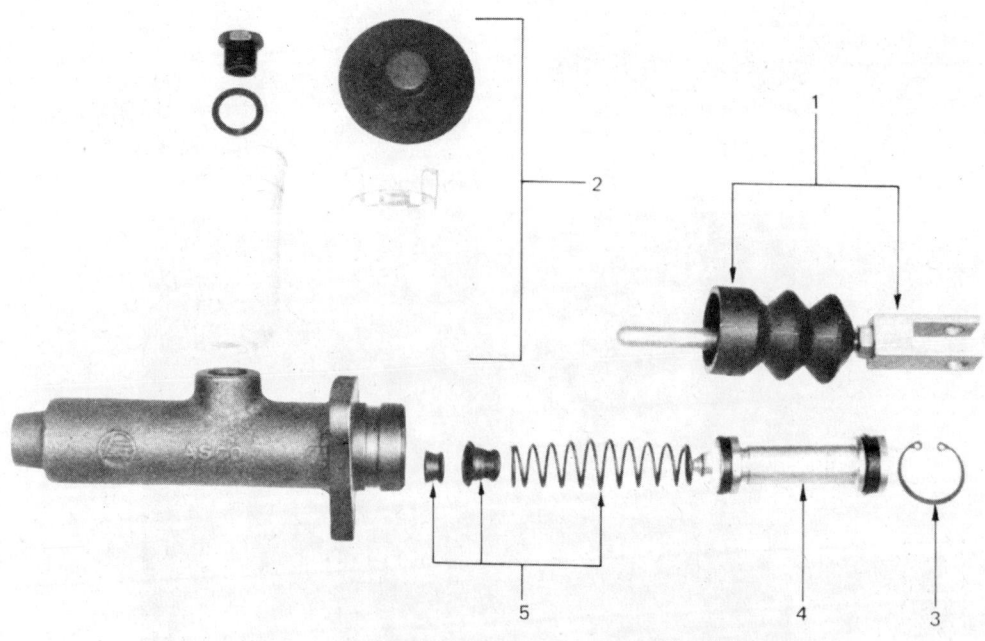

Fig. 10.4. Single master cylinder (later type) - exploded view

1. Pushrod and boot
2. Reservoir
3. Snap ring
4. Piston
5. Spring and seat

3 Bleeding the hydraulic system

1 If any part of the brake hydraulic system has been disconnected, it will be necessary to bleed the system of air as described in the following paragraphs.
2 Use only clean fluid (which has remained unshaken for 24 hours and has been stored in an airtight container) for topping-up the master cylinder reservoir(s) during the following operations. Keep the reservoir(s) well topped-up during the whole of the bleeding operation otherwise air will be drawn into the system and the whole sequence of bleeding will have to start over again.
3 Where applicable, depress the foot brake pedal several times and 'destroy' the vacuum effect in the servo unit.
4 Fit a rubber or plastic bleed tube to the nipple(s) on the master cylinder, and immerse the free end of the tube in a jar containing sufficient clean hydraulic fluid to keep the end of the tube covered. If the master cylinder does not have a bleed nipple(s), commence the bleeding operation at the wheel cylinder further from the master cylinder. Note: If there is a bleed nipple on the brake servo (where fitted) this should be bled before the wheel cylinders are bled (photos).
5 Unscrew the nipple ½ turn, and, with the help of an assistant, watch the fluid being expelled from the end of the tube while the brake pedal is depressed firmly to the full extent of its travel. Give both long and slow and short sharp strokes of the brake pedal until air bubbles cease to emerge from the tube. It is essential during bleeding operations to keep the end of the tube in the jar covered with fluid and to keep the master cylinder reservoir(s) filled to a high level.
6 After each stroke of the brake pedal allow it to fly back to its stop with the foot completely removed.
7 Tighten the nipple when the foot pedal is fully depressed using a suitable wrench. Remove the bleed tube and install the rubber dust cap. Where applicable, repeat the procedure for the other master cylinder bleed nipples.
8 Repeat the bleeding procedure at the wheel cylinder further from the master cylinder (or next furthest, if this has already been done), then work progressively towards the nearest one.
9 Take care that brake fluid does not contact the vehicle paintwork during the operation, and on completion top-up the reservoir fluid level as necessary.

4 Single master cylinder - removal, overhaul and installation

1 Place a polythene film over the brake reservoir filler install the cap, to prevent excessive loss of brake fluid, then detach the hydraulic line from the cylinder.
2 Remove the mounting bolts and take off the master cylinder.
3 Drain the reservoir contents, then remove the set bolt and washer to detach the reservoir from the cylinder body.
4 Remove the rubber boot and take out the snap-ring from the end of the cylinder.
5 Remove the internal parts. On early cylinders, the plug can be removed from the forward end of the cylinder, and the associated parts removed. Refer to Figs. 10. 3 and 10.4 which show the different types of cylinder.
6 Discard all the rubber parts, and clean the remaining parts in alcohol or clean brake fluid. Check the piston and cylinder bore for wear, scoring and corrosion, and renew parts as necessary. The maximum permissible piston-to-bore clearance is 0.006 in (0.15 mm). If damaged, a new spring should be obtained.
7 Lubricate all the internal parts with clean brake fluid, then reassemble the cylinder by following the reverse of the dismantling procedure.
8 Installation of the cylinder is straightforward. After topping-up the fluid level, bleed the brakes as described in Section 3, then check the pedal adjustment as described in Section 2.

5 Tandem master cylinder - removal, overhaul and installation

1 Plug the reservoir inlets to prevent excessive loss of brake fluid, then detach the hydraulic lines from the master cylinder. Also remove the leads from the pressure switches.
2 Remove the mounting bolts and take off the master cylinder.
3 Drain the reservoir contents, then remove the bolts and take off the two reservoirs.
4 Unscrew the pressure switches from the cylinder body.
5 Unscrew the plugs from the cylinder body, and take out the check valves and springs. Do not lose the washers from the plugs.
6 Unscrew the stop bolt from the cylinder body.
7 At the pushrod end, remove the boot, then take out the snap-ring which retains the moving parts.
8 Take out the No 1 piston, spring, No 2 piston, spring and piston stopper.
9 Discard all the rubber parts, and clean the remaining parts in alcohol or clean brake fluid. Check the pistons and cylinder bore for wear, scoring and corrosion, and renew parts as necessary. If damaged, new springs should be obtained.
10 Lubricate all the internal parts with clean brake fluid, then reassemble the cylinder by following the reverse of the dismantling sequence. When installing the stop bolt, ensure that both pistons are pressed fully in; also ensure that the boot is installed with the 'UP' mark to the top of the cylinder. When installing the small check valves, ensure that the bakelite piece is at the top.
11 Installation of the cylinder is straightforward. After topping-up the fluid level, bleed the brakes as described in Section 3, then check the pedal adjustment as described in Section 2.

3.4a Master cylinder bleed nipples (arrowed)

3.4b Brake bleed nipples (arrowed)

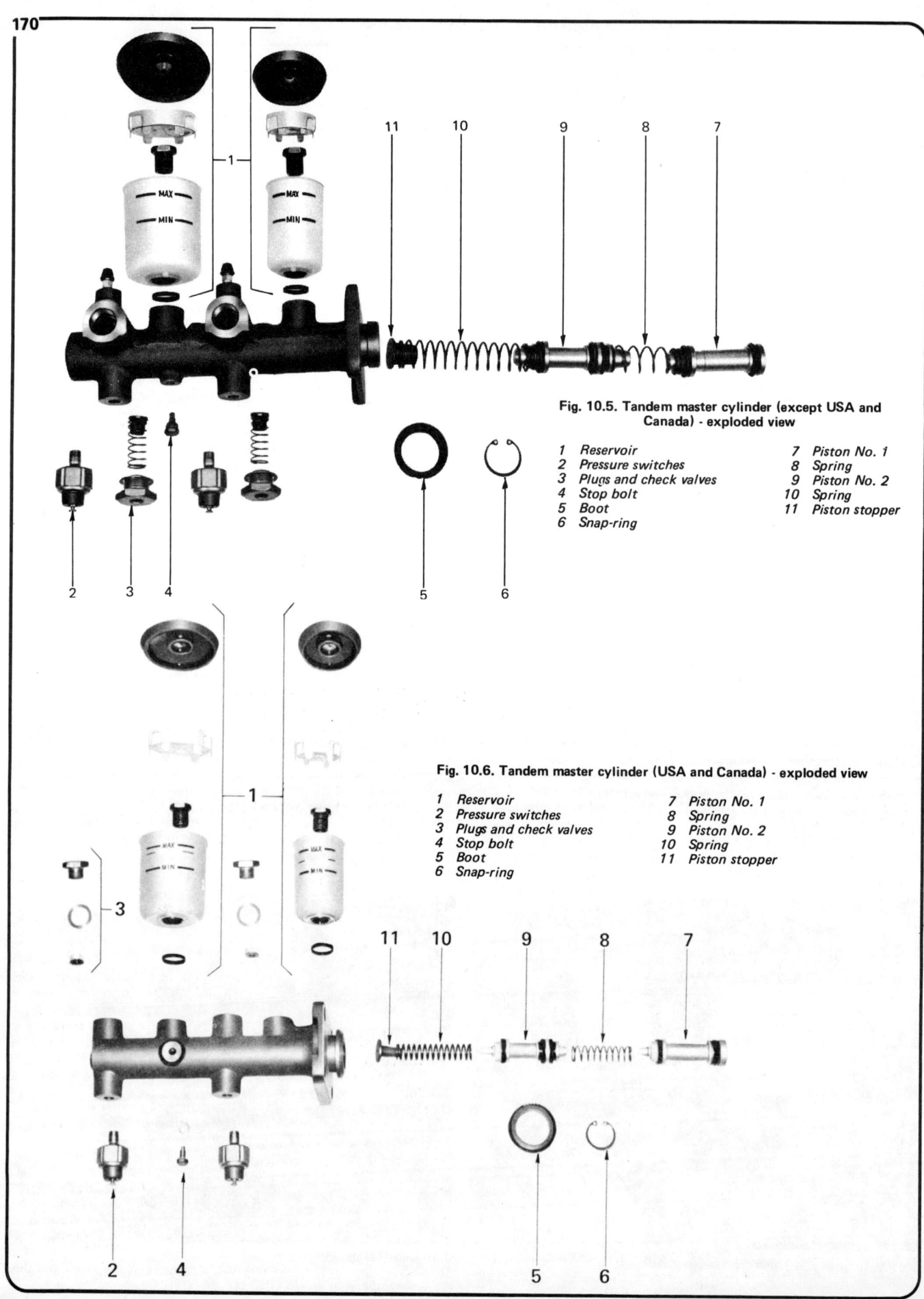

Fig. 10.5. Tandem master cylinder (except USA and Canada) - exploded view

1 Reservoir
2 Pressure switches
3 Plugs and check valves
4 Stop bolt
5 Boot
6 Snap-ring
7 Piston No. 1
8 Spring
9 Piston No. 2
10 Spring
11 Piston stopper

Fig. 10.6. Tandem master cylinder (USA and Canada) - exploded view

1 Reservoir
2 Pressure switches
3 Plugs and check valves
4 Stop bolt
5 Boot
6 Snap-ring
7 Piston No. 1
8 Spring
9 Piston No. 2
10 Spring
11 Piston stopper

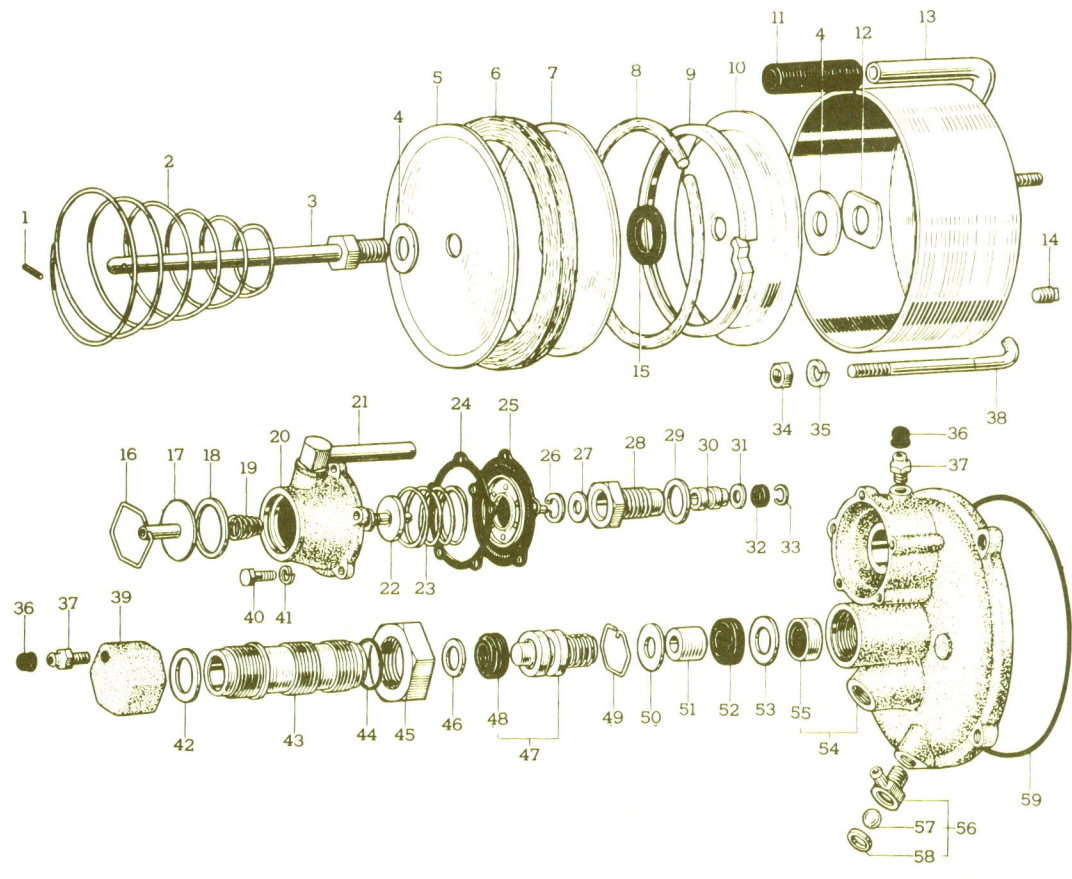

Fig. 10.7. Brake servo (early type) - exploded view

1 Pushrod pin	16 Snap-ring	31 Retainer washer
2 Piston return spring	17 Tube and cover	32 Piston cup No. 1
3 Pushrod	18 Gasket	33 Washer
4 Washer	19 Poppet valve spring	34 Nut
5 Piston front plate	20 Valve body	35 Lock washer
6 Piston gasket	21 Hose elbow	36 Bleed plug cap
7 Piston rear plate	22 Poppet valve	37 Bleed plug
8 Gasket wick	23 Diaphragm spring	38 Hook bolt
9 Piston gasket ring	24 Valve body gasket	39 Hydraulic cylinder plug
10 Piston wick retainer	25 Diaphragm assembly	40 Bolt
11 Vacuum hose	26 Retainer ring	41 Lock washer
12 Nut	27 Piston stop washer	42 Gasket
13 Shell	28 Valve fitting	43 Slave cylinder tube
14 Plug	29 Valve fitting seal	44 Slave cylinder seal
15 Piston rod seal	30 Relay valve piston	45 Slave cylinder lock nut
46 Seal		
47 Hydraulic piston assembly		
48 Hydraulic piston cup No. 2		
49 Snap-ring		
50 Piston stop washer		
51 Seal retainer		
52 Piston cup No. 2		
53 Pushrod washer		
54 End plate		
55 Pushrod seal		
56 Check valve assembly		
57 Check valve ball		
58 Check valve seal		
59 Cylinder seal		

6 Brake servo (booster) - general description

Three different types of brake servo have been used on Land Cruiser models and, although they differ considerably in design, they all function in a similar manner. The two later types are mounted between the brake pedal pushrod and the master cylinder, but the earlier type is remotely mounted and is connected to the outlet side of the master cylinder; pressure from the servo is then used to operate the brakes.

The servo is operated either by the brake pedal pushrod or by movement of the master cylinder piston, and uses the vacuum supply tapped from the intake manifold to provide additional braking effort. Should the vacuum supply fail or the servo suffer an internal fault, the brakes can be operated in the normal way, but a greater pedal load will be required.

7 Brake servo (early type) - removal, overhaul and installation

1 Depress the brake pedal several times to destroy any residual vacuum.

2 Plug the master cylinder reservoir to prevent excessive loss of fluid, then disconnect the vacuum line and two brake hydraulic lines from the servo.

3 Remove the servo and bracket (two bolts), then remove the single nut to detach the servo from the bracket. Take care that fluid does not spill on the vehicle paintwork or damage will occur.

4 Clamp the servo hydraulic cylinder plug in a vise and loosen the slave cylinder tube locknut. Now unscrew the slave cylinder tube.

5 Index mark the booster endplate and shell for correct alignment on reassembly, then remove the nuts and washers from the hook bolts. Separate the two major parts of the unit.

6 Remove the valve body from the endplate (five screws), then remove the diaphragm spring, diaphragm and gasket.

7 Remove the snap-ring to release the booster tube and cover, cover gasket and poppet valve spring from the valve body.

8 Press down on the endplate until the pushrod protrudes. Remove the pushrod pin to free the hydraulic piston. Remove the booster piston from the endplate.

9 Remove the retaining ring and piston stop washer, then pull out the relay valve piston from the valve fitting.

10 Using a suitable socket wrench, remove the valve fitting.
11 If necessary, the booster piston can be dismantled by clamping the pushrod nut in a vise and unscrewing the pushrod. The booster piston parts can then be separated.
12 Clean all metal parts in a suitable cleaning solvent and dry carefully; ensure that all internal passageways are clear. Parts in contact with hydraulic fluid may be cleaned with new hydraulic fluid. Examine all parts for wear, damage and corrosion, and renew as necessary. All piston cups, gaskets and seals should be renewed, but other parts may be re-used if serviceable.
13 Assembly is now the reverse of the dismantling procedure, but ensure that old parts on the hydraulic side of the unit are wet-assembled using clean hydraulic fluid. On completion, add 30 cc (0.06 US qt/0.05 Imp qt) of engine oil into the vacuum side of the unit thru the plug.
14 Installation is the reverse of the removal procedure, but do not forget to bleed the brakes as described in Section 3.

8 Brake servo (later types, single and dual master cylinders) - removal and installation

Note: Due to the special tool which would be required, overhaul of the later type servos is not considered worthwhile for the home mechanic. In the event of a fault occurring, it is recommended that the unit is repaired by a Toyota dealer, or an exchange item obtained.
1 Remove the master cylinder as described in Sections 4 or 5.
2 Pull off the vacuum hose from the check valve or remove the check valve from the servo, then remove the servo from its mounting on the bulkhead (photo).
3 Installation is basically the reverse of the removal procedure, but on completion bleed the brakes as described in Section 3 and adjust the pedal travel if necessary as described in Section 2.

9 Dual twin-leading shoe brakes - shoe renewal

Note: This procedure is applicable to the rear brakes of all models, and to the front brakes of later models which do not have disc brakes.
1 Jack-up the appropriate end or side of the vehicle, and remove the roadwheel.
2 Back off the brake adjuster, then remove the single retaining screw and remove the brake drum. Note: On some models there may be a gasket between the brake drum and hub flange (photo).
3 Remove the brake shoe hold-down springs and pins (photo).
4 Using a screwdriver for leverage, carefully pry the ends of the brake shoes out of the slots in the wheel cylinder pistons and adjusters.
5 Lift the brake shoes away. Note the way that the return springs are fitted, then remove them. To prevent the wheel cylinder pistons from accidentally coming out, they can be held in place with a rubber band or wire clip (photo).
6 Remove any dust and grease from inside the drum and backplate. If there is any evidence of oil leaking from the axle or hub, or hydraulic fluid leaking from the wheel cylinders, these faults should be rectified before commencing to reassemble. While the brake drum is off, check that it is not badly scored and is still within the specified diameter.
7 Installation of the brake shoes is now the reverse of the removal procedure. Apply a trace of high melting point grease to the backplate where the shoes rub. Attach the return spring to the rear ends of the shoes and place the shoe ends in the slots; the front side return spring can be installed once the shoes are in position. On completion, adjust the brakes as described in Section 2. If the wheel cylinder has been removed, or the pistons have accidentally come out of the cylinders in spite of the precautions taken, the brakes must be bled as described in Section 3.

10 Twin-leading shoe brakes - shoe renewal

Note: This procedure is applicable to the front brakes of early models.
1 Jack-up the appropriate side of the vehicle and remove the roadwheel.
2 Back off the brake adjuster, then remove the brake drum retaining screws and take off the drum.
3 Remove the brake shoe hold-down springs and pins.
4 Pull out the shoes from the slots in the wheel cylinder pistons and

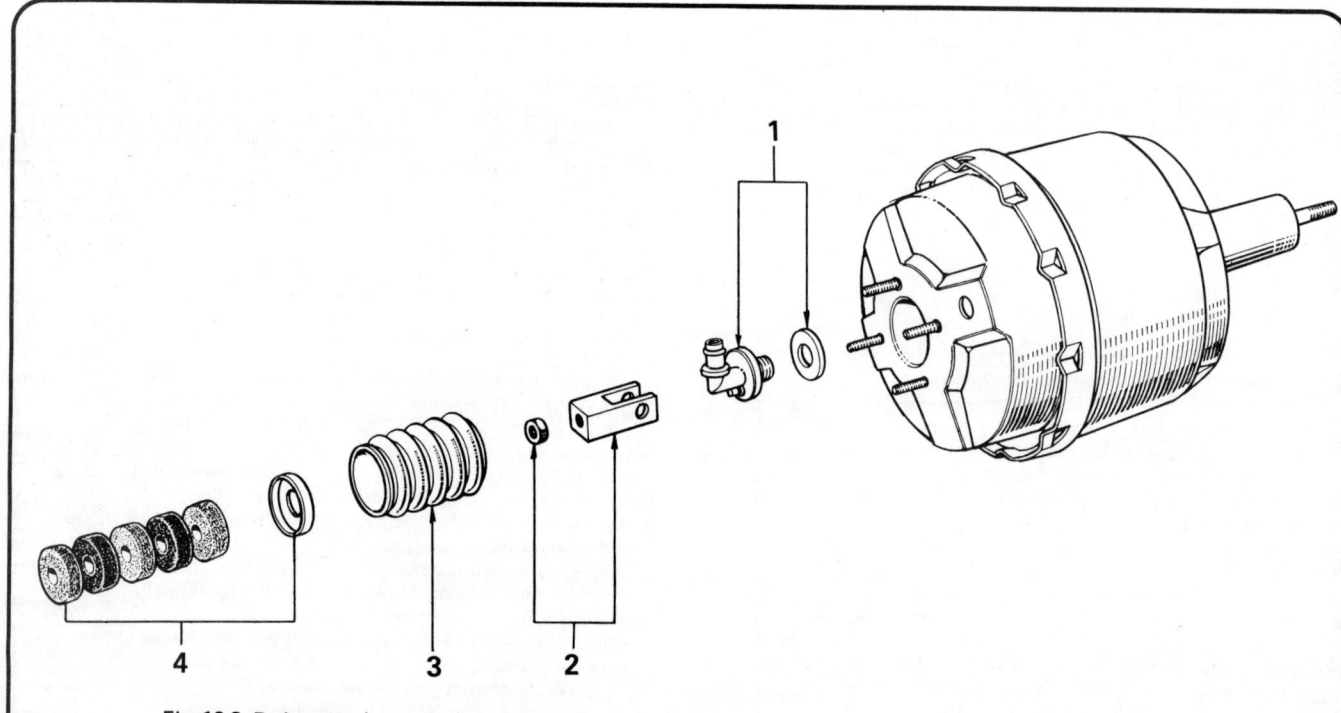

Fig. 10.8. Brake servo (later type), showing items which can readily be removed - dual master cylinder type shown

1 Check valve and grommet
2 Clevis and nut
3 Boot
4 Retainer, filter and silencer

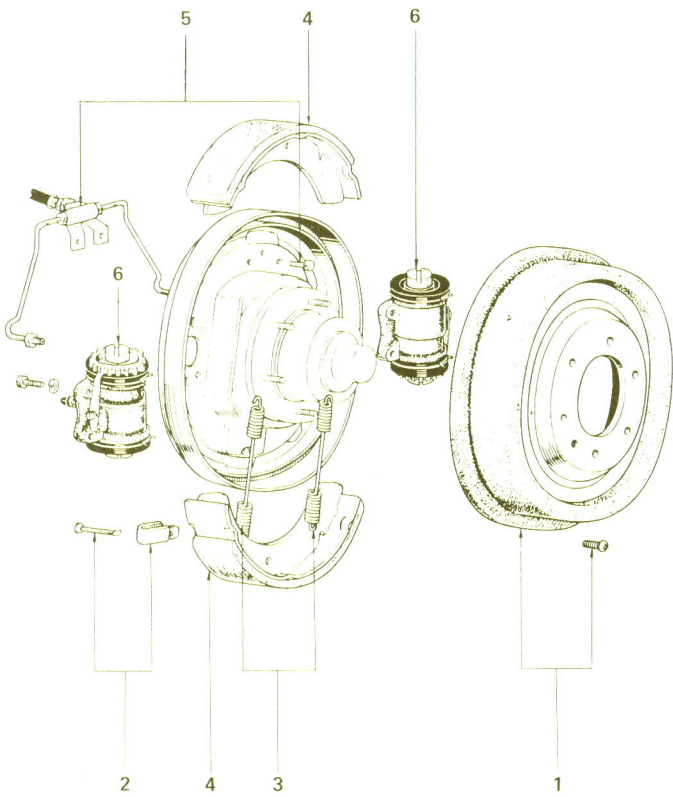

Fig. 10.9. Dual two-leading brake assembly (front brake shown, but rear is virtually identical)

1 Brake drum
2 Hold down spring and pins
3 Return springs
4 Shoes
5 Brake tube
6 Wheel cylinders

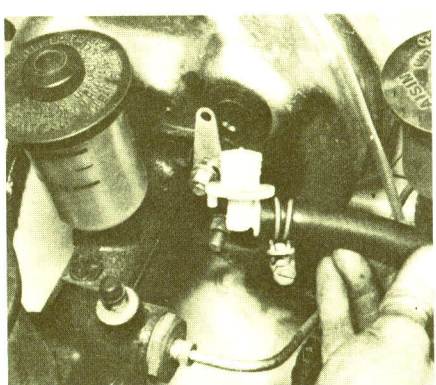

8.2 Servo check valve. The retainer is secured by one of the master cylinder nuts on this model

9.2 Removing a drum retaining screw

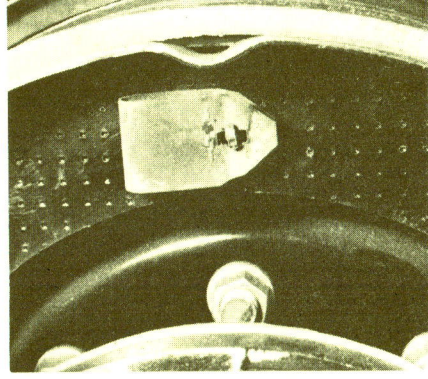

9.3 Hold-down spring and pin

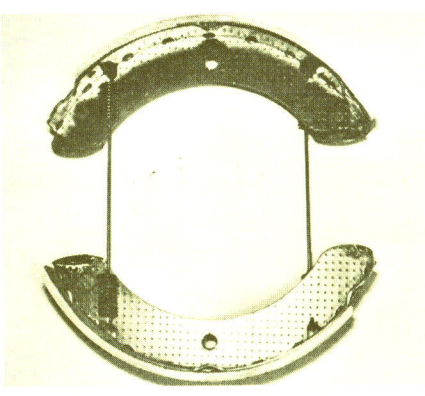

9.5 Note how the return springs are fitted. This is a right-hand rear brake; the right-hand side of the shoes face towards the front of the vehicle

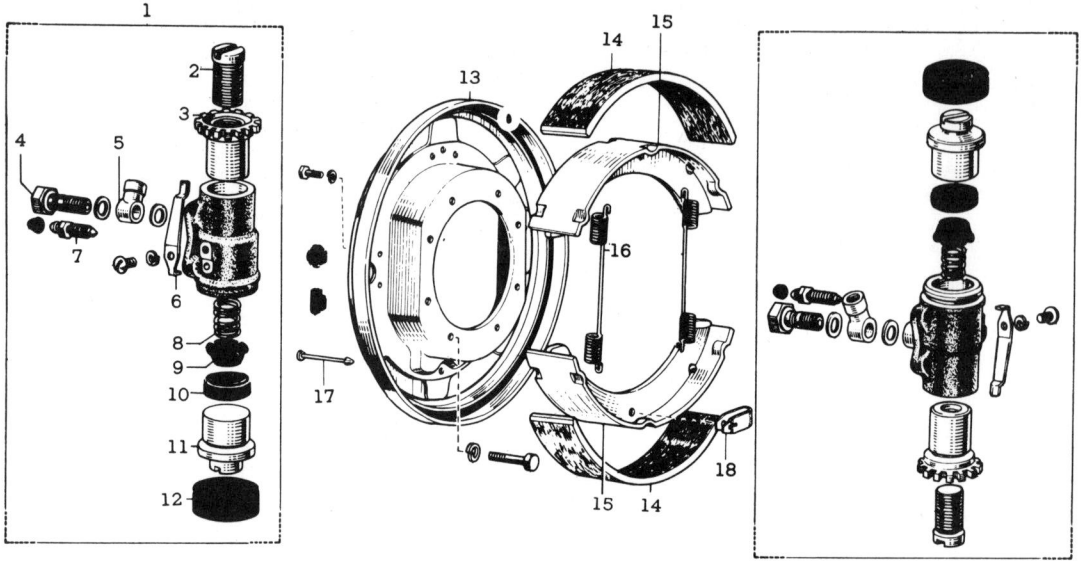

Fig. 10.10. Two-leading shoe front brake assembly - exploded view

1 Wheel cylinder assembly
2 Wheel cylinder adjusting bolt
3 Wheel cylinder adjusting nut
4 Union bolt
5 Union
6 Adjuster lock spring
7 Bleed plug
8 Compression spring
9 Spring seat
10 Cylinder cup
11 Cylinder piston
12 Wheel cylinder boot
13 Brake backplate
14 Brake lining
15 Brake shoe
16 Shoe return spring
17 Hold down spring pin
18 Hold down spring

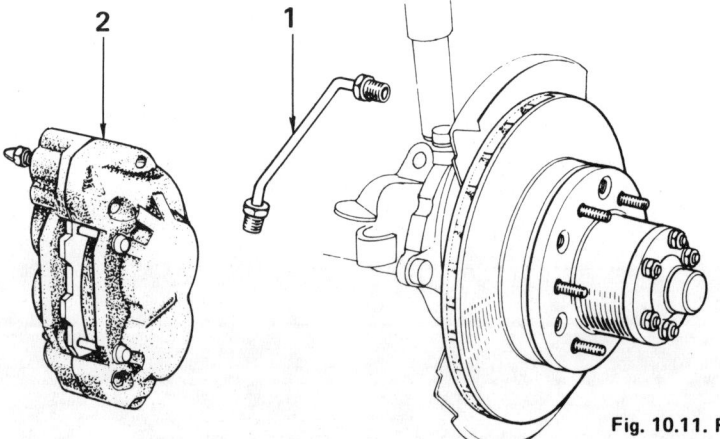

Fig. 10.11. Front disc brake assembly - exploded view

1 Brake tube
2 Disc brake caliper assembly
3 Clip, pin and anti-rust spring
4 Brake pad
5 Set ring
6 Cylinder boots and piston
7 Seal ring

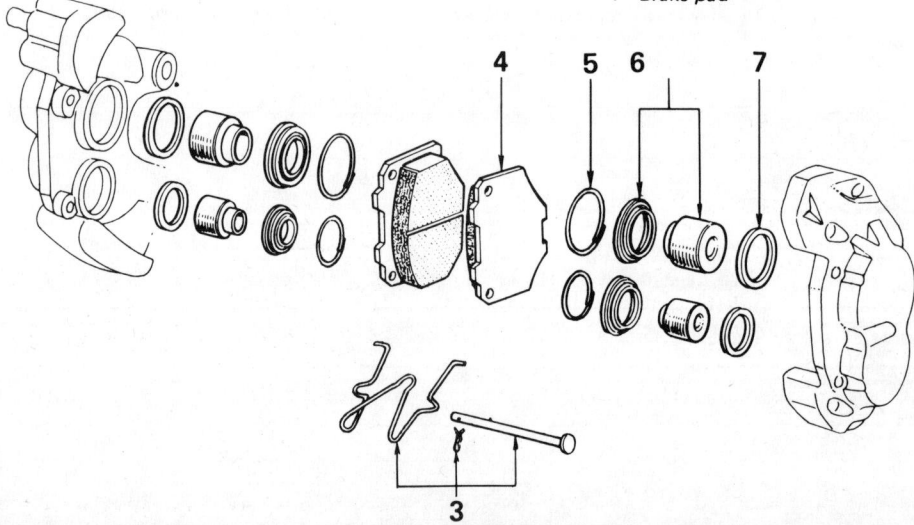

remove them from the brake backplate. **Note:** Provided that care is taken, it is permissible to pry against the ridge in the backplate to assist in removal of the shoes.
5 Detach the springs from the brake shoes.
6 To prevent the wheel cylinder pistons from accidentally coming out, they can be held in place with a rubber band or wire clip.
7 Remove any dust or grease from inside the drum and backplate. If there is any evidence of oil leaking from the axle or hub, or hydraulic fluid leaking from the wheel cylinders, these faults should be rectified before commencing the reassembly. While the brake drum is off, check that it is not badly scored and is still within the specified diameter.
8 Installation of the brake shoes is now the reverse of the removal procedure. Apply a trace of high melting point grease to the backplate where the shoes rub, and ensure that the front side return spring is hooked onto the inner sides of the shoes, and the rear side return spring is hooked onto the outer side. On completion, adjust the brakes as described in Section 2; if the wheel cylinder has been removed, or the pistons have accidentally come out of the cylinders in spite of the precautions taken, the brakes must be bled as described in Section 3.

11 Disc brakes - pad renewal

1 Jack-up the appropriate side of the vehicle and remove the roadwheel.
2 Remove the two small spring clips, then carefully drive out the brake pad retaining pins using a small drift.
3 Remove the anti-rattle spring.
4 Using a piece of stiff wire with a suitably hooked end, pull out the brake pads.
5 Blow out any dust from inside the caliper, and check for any evidence of brake fluid which may have leaked past the seals (if evident this leakage must be rectified before commencing reassembly - see Section 13).
6 Installation of the new pads is the reverse of the removal procedure. However, it will almost certainly be necessary to push the caliper pistons back into their bores a little way to accomodate the thicker pads. When doing this, the reservoir level will rise, so take care that it does not spill. If necessary, syphon a little off.

12 Drum brake wheel cylinders - overhaul

1 Although several different types of brake cylinders have been used on the Land Cruiser models, they can basically be described as the single or double piston type. The single piston type are used for the twin-leading shoe brakes whereas the double piston type are used for the dual twin-leading shoe brakes.
2 Regardless of the type, remove the brake shoes as described in Section 9 or 10.
3 Place a polythene film over the brake reservoir filler and install the cap. This will help to prevent excessive fluid loss.
4 Detach the hydraulic supply pipe and interconnecting pipe to the cylinders.
5 Remove the wheel cylinder mounting screws, then remove the cylinders from the backplate.
6 Remove the wheel cylinder boot(s) - on some models a spring clip needs to be removed first.
7 Remove the pistons, piston cups, springs and associated parts. The illustrations show the various components of the different types. Unscrew the adjusting nuts and bolts, noting that those used for right-hand wheels have left-hand threads and vice versa.
8 Discard all the rubber parts and clean the remaining parts in alcohol or clean brake fluid. Check the cylinder bore and piston(s) for scoring and corrosion, and renew parts as necessary.
9 Lubricate all the internal hydraulic parts with clean hydraulic fluid, and smear a little high melting point grease on the adjuster screw threads.
10 The wheel cylinder can now be assembled following the reverse of the removal procedure. Ensure the adjuster screw tapered slots are as shown in Fig. 10.13, and do not mix up the left (marked L) and right (marked R) cylinders when installing if both have been removed.
11 On completion, adjust the brakes and bleed the hydraulic system as described previously in this Chapter.

13 Disc brake calipers - overhaul

1 Jack-up the appropriate side of the car and remove the roadwheel.
2 Place a polythene film over the brake reservoir filler and install the

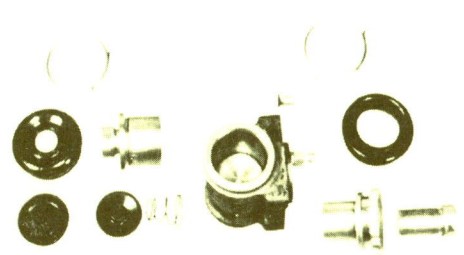

Fig. 10.12. Wheel cylinder component parts - dual two-leading shoes type

Fig. 10.13. Adjuster screw tapered slots - right-hand front brake shown

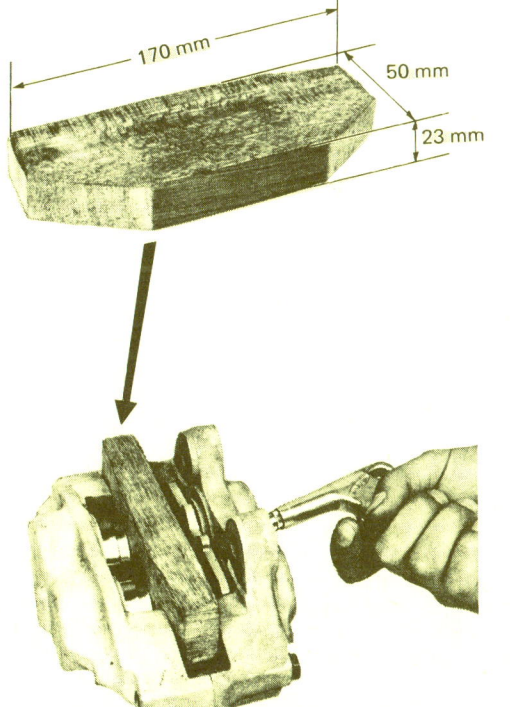

Fig. 10.14. Hardwood packer used when removing pistons

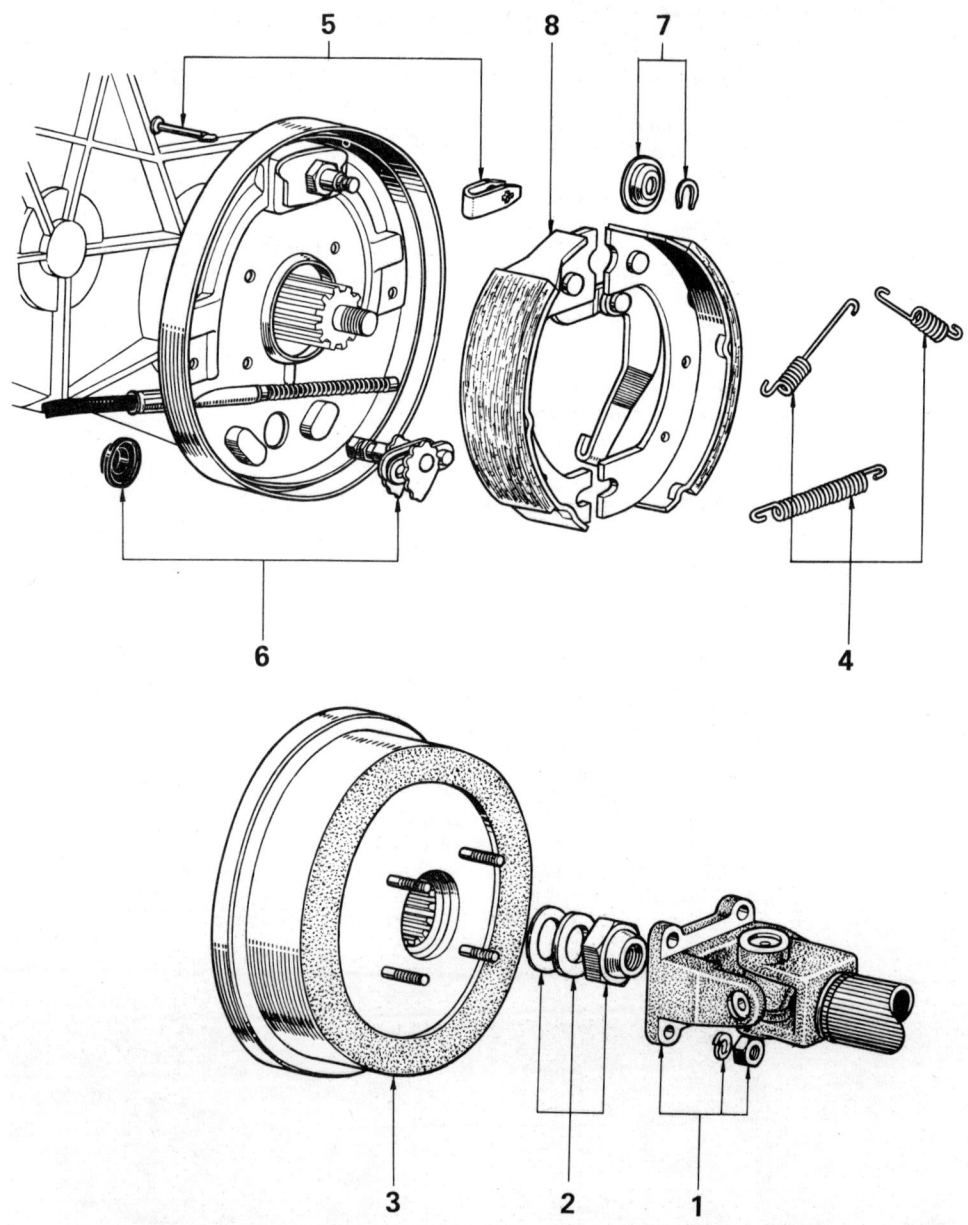

Fig. 10.15. Parking brake assembly - exploded view

1 Propeller shaft	3 Brake drum	5 Hold down springs and pins	7 'C' washer and washer
2 Nut, washer and shim	4 Tension springs	6 Cover and shoe adjuster	8 Shoes and levers

cap. This will help to prevent excessive loss of fluid.
3 Completely remove the rigid brake supply pipe to the caliper.
4 Remove the retaining bolts and detach the caliper from the hub assembly.
5 Remove the brake pads as described in Section 11.
6 Carefully prise out the set rings from the piston bores. It is very important that the bore surface is not scratched.
7 Place a suitable hardwood packer in the caliper slot as shown in Fig. 10.14, and insert a brake pad on one side.
8 Apply compressed air to the hydraulic port on that side to blow out the pistons and cylinder boots.
9 Repeat paragraph 8 for the opposite side pistons and cylinder boots.
10 This is the limit of any permitted dismantling it is essential that the bolts retaining the two caliper halves are **NOT** disturbed.
11 Check the caliper for damage to the exterior, and for scoring and corrosion of the piston bore. Discard all the rubber parts, and any others which are unserviceable.
12 Examine the disc for wear. Check for minimum thickness and run-out dimensions as given in the Specifications. If the disc is to be removed, pull off the front hub as described in Chapter 9, Section 2. Having done this, the disc can be removed by unscrewing the retaining bolts. When reassembling, tighten the disc/hub bolts to the specified torque; when installing, refer to the procedure in Chapter 9, not forgetting the hub adjustment.
13 Reassembly of the brake caliper is basically the reverse of the dismantling procedure. Ensure that all hydraulic parts are lubricated with clean hydraulic fluid, and take care that no dirt contaminates any of the internal parts. On completion, bleed the brakes as described in Section 3.

14 Hydraulic lines - inspection, removal and installation

1 Periodically, carefully examine all brake pipes, both rigid and flexible, for rusting, chafing and deterioration. Check the security of unions and connections.

2 First examine for signs of leakage where the pipe unions occur. Then examine the flexible hoses for signs of chafing and fraying and of course, leakage. This is only a preliminary part of the flexible hose inspection, as exterior condition does not necessarily indicate their interior condition which will be considered later in the Section.
3 The steel pipes must be examined equally carefully. They must be cleaned off and examined for any signs of dents, or other damage, and rust and corrosion. Rust and corrosion should be scraped off and if the depth of pitting in the pipes is significant, they will need replacement. This is particularly likely in those areas underneath the body and along the axle where the pipes are exposed to the full force of road and weather conditions.
4 If any section of pipe is to be taken off, first of all remove the fluid reservoir cap and line it with a piece of polythene film to make it air tight and replace it. This will minimise the amount of fluid dripping out of the system, when pipes are removed, by preventing the replacement of fluid by air in the reservoir.
5 Rigid pipe removal is usually quite straightforward. The unions at each end are undone and the pipe and union pulled out and the center sections of the pipe removed from the body clips where necessary. Underneath the vehicle, exposed unions can sometimes be very tight. As one can use only an open ended wrench and the unions are not large, burring of the flats is not uncommon when attempting to undo them. For this reason a self-locking grip wrench (mole) is often the only way to remove a stubborn union.
6 Flexible hoses are always mounted at both ends in a rigid bracket attached to the body or a sub-assembly. To remove them it is necessary first of all to unscrew the pipe unions of the rigid pipes which go into them. Then, with a wrench on the hexagonal end of the flexible pipe union, the locknut and washer on the other side of the mounting bracket need to be removed. Here again exposure to the elements often tends to seize the locknut and in this case the use of penetrating oil is necessary. The mounting brackets, particularly on the body frame, are not very heavy gauge and care must be taken not to wrench them off. A self-grip wrench is often of use here as well. Use it on the pipe union in this instance as one is unable to get a ring wrench on the locknut.
7 With the flexible hose removed, examine the internal bore. If it is blown thru first, it should be possible to see thru it. Any specks of rubber which come out, or signs of restriction in the bore, mean that the inner lining is breaking up and the pipe must be renewed.
8 Rigid pipes which need replacement can usually be purchased at any garage where they have the pipe, unions and special tools to make them up. All they need to know is the total length of the pipe and the type of flare used at each end with the union. This is very important as one can have a flare and a mushroom on the same pipe.
9 Installation of pipes is a straightforward reversal of the removal procedure. If the rigid pipes have been made up it is best to get all the sets (or bends) in them before trying to install them. Also if there are any acute bends, ask your supplier to put these in for you on a tube bender. Otherwise you may kink the pipe and thereby restrict the bore area and fluid flow.
10 With the pipes installed, remove the polythene film from the reservoir (paragraph 4) and bleed the system as described in Section 3.

15 Parking brakes shoes - removal and installation

1 Jack-up the vehicle to a suitable working height for access to the transfer case and rear propeller shaft.
2 Drain the oil from the transfer case into a container of suitable size (approx. 1.8 US qts/1.5 Imp qts/1.7 liters).
3 Detach the front end of the rear propeller shaft from the parking brake drum. Refer to Chapter 7, if necessary.
4 Apply the parking brake and engage a transmission gear.
5 As appropriate, remove the cotter pin or use a small punch to relieve the nut staking.
6 Unscrew the drum retaining nut, and remove the washer and shim (photo).
7 Release the parking brake and remove the brake drum. This may be tight; if necessary back-off the adjuster and apply blows from a lead mallet or similar item to the side of the drum to free it. As the drum is removed there may be a little oil spillage from around the shaft, but this will not contaminate the shoes. However, before installation, the backplate must be wiped dry as soon as the oil has stopped leaking out.
8 Carefully pry off the tension springs, noting their installed positions (photo).
9 Remove the hold down springs and pins.
10 Take out the adjuster assembly from the backplate.
11 Remove the C-washer and special washer from the pivot pin on the backplate, and pull out the shoes. Detach the parking brake cable as the shoes are removed.
12 The shoes can be separated, and the operating levers removed, by taking off the C-washers from the pivot pins. These can be prised open with a screwdriver or chisel. If damaged, new ones should be used for reassembly; after installing, crimp the ends together with pliers to retain them.
13 Examine the drum for scoring on the friction face end on the oil seal surface of the internally splined spigot. If oil has been leaking into the drum, the seal should be renewed; further information on this will be found in Chapter 6.
14 Installation is now the reverse of the removal procedure, but apply a little high melting point grease to the friction surfaces of the adjuster and shoe pivots, and to the raised parts of the backplate where the shoes rub. After tightening the drum nut to the specified torque, install a new split pin or stake the nut with a center punch, as appropriate.

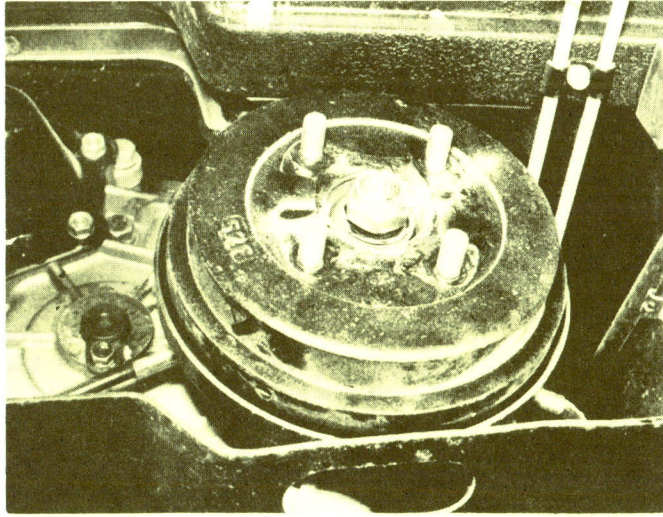

15.6 Remove the drum retaining nut

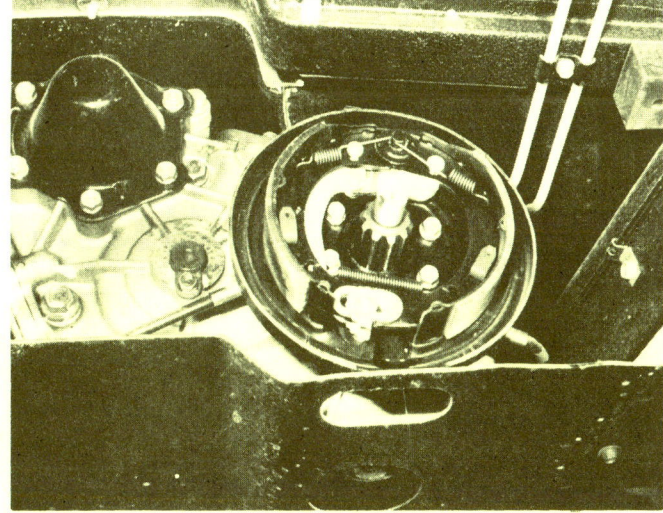

15.8 Note the positions of the parking brake shoe tension springs

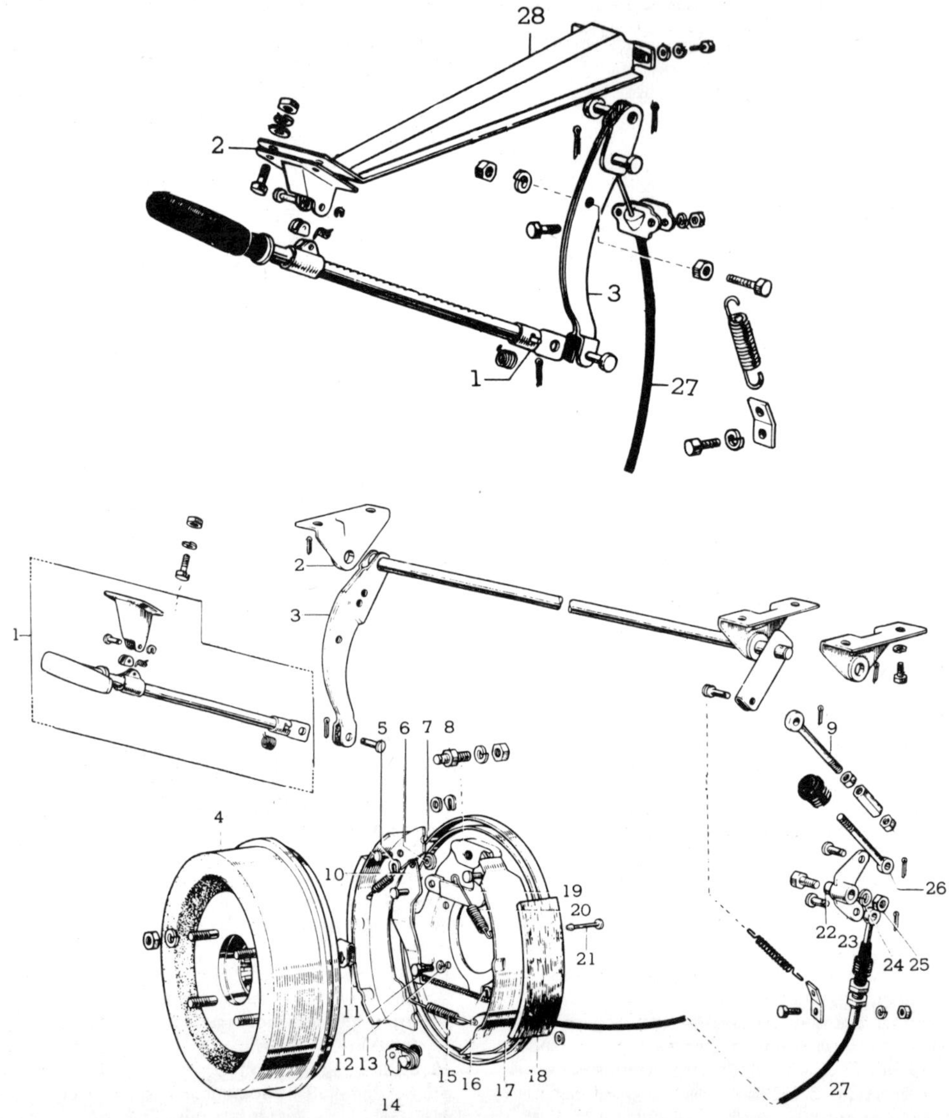

Fig. 10.16. Parking brake components

Upper – FJ40 models
1. Parking brake plunger assembly
2. Parking brake plunger bracket
3. Parking brake link lever
4. Brake drum
5. 'C' washer
6. Washer
7. Brake backing plate
8. Anchor
9. Intermediate lever pull rod (No. 1)
10. Brake shoe lever
11. Hold down spring
12. Bolt
13. Lockwasher
14. Adjuster

Lower – FJ55 models
15. Tension spring
16. 'C' washer
17. Brake shoe
18. Lining
19. Parking brake shoe lever strut
20. Tension spring
21. Hold down spring pin
22. Spacer
23. Parking brake link lever
24. Lockwasher
25. Nut
26. Intermediate lever pull rod (No. 2)
27. Parking brake cable
28. Bracket

Fig. 10.17. Cable retaining 'C' washer on backplate

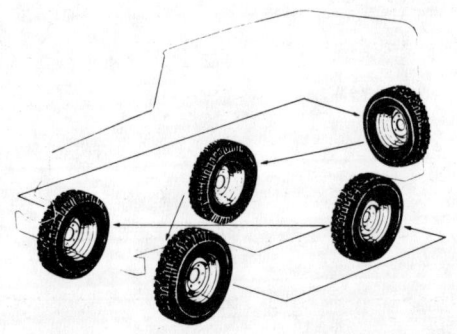

Fig. 10.18. Suggested rotation pattern to equalize tread wear of tires

Chapter 10/Brakes, wheels and tires

15 On completion, adjust the parking brake as described in Section 2, and add the correct grade and quantity of oil to the transfer case.

16 Parking brake linkage and cables - removal and installation

1 Disconnect the throttle and choke cables from the carburetor, and remove the controls from the instrument panel.
2 Remove the number 1 air duct from the heater.
3 Disconnect the parking brake link lever spring, then remove the cotter pins from the ends of the link lever shaft (photo).
4 Remove the link lever bracket bolts and the parking brake plunger bolts, so that the plunger and link lever can be withdrawn.
5 Working in the engine compartment, remove the cotter pin from the parking brake link lever, then remove the intermediate lever pull rod from inside the vehicle.
6 Detach the brake cable from the link lever, and loosen the locknut at the cable end.
7 It is now necessary to remove the brake shoes as described in the previous Section to detach the cable from the brake shoes.
8 Having removed the brake shoes, remove the C-washer retaining the cable to the backplate so that the cable can be withdrawn.
9 Installation is the reverse of the removal procedure. On completion, adjust the parking brake as described in Section 2, and add the correct grade and quantity of oil to the transfer case.

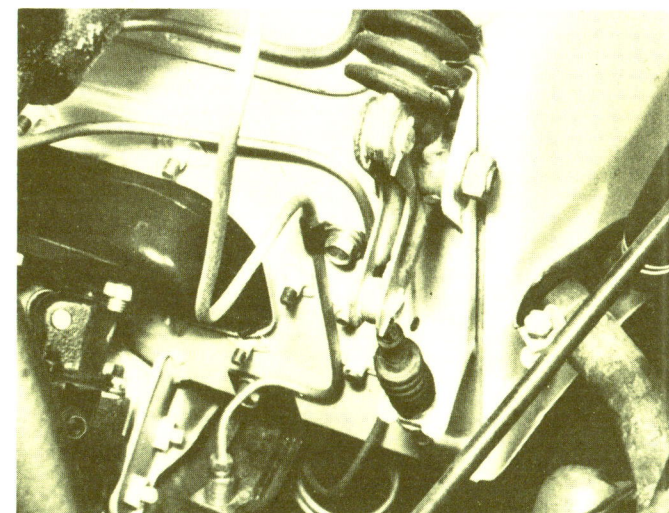

16.3 Parking brake link lever (FJ55 model)

17 Wheels and tires

1 Provided that they are not damaged during an accident or by striking the kerb, wheels can be expected to last the life of the vehicle with no maintenance other than cleaning and occasional painting.
2 Different types of wheels and tires are used, according to the vehicle model and usage. Where replacements are required the advice of a tire dealer or Toyota agent should be sought in order to obtain the most suitable types.
3 It may be preferred by the owner to change the wheels round at intervals to equalize the tire tread wear. Where this is done, they should be rotated as shown in the illustration, but it is advisable to take note of the wear pattern on each tire as this may give warning of the need for steering geometry adjustments or less severe driving habits.
4 In order to obtain the best tire wear, and at the same time to reduce the out-of-balance loads on the steering and suspension, the wheels should be balanced dynamically. This not only balances the wheel and tire, but also compensates for the smallest out-of-balance forces in the hubs and brake drums. Therefore, if a balanced wheel is removed from a hub, it should always be installed in the same hub-to-wheel relationship, and where it is fitted to another hub it may well need rebalancing for optimum service.
5 When a wheel has to be removed, it is recommended that the wheel nuts are each loosened about ¼ turn with the wheel on the ground. The vehicle can then be raised and the nuts removed. When installing, finally tighten the nuts with the wheel on the ground.
6 The spare wheel is held in a special carrier at the rear of the vehicle. To remove it, insert the vehicle starting handle and turn it counter-clockwise to lower the wheel carrier (photo).

17.6 Spare wheel location

18 Fault diagnosis - brakes

Before diagnosing faults from the following chart, check that any braking irregularities are not caused by:

1 Uneven and incorrect tire pressures
2 Incorrect 'mix' of radial and crossply tires
3 Wear in the steering mechanism
4 Defects in the suspension and dampers
5 Misalignment of the body frame

Symptoms	Reason/s
Spongy pedal action	Air in hydraulic system - needs bleeding.
Brakes dragging	Incorrect pedal or shoe adjustment. Faulty master cylinder.

	Air in hydraulic system - needs bleeding. Weak or broken shoe return spring. Faulty wheel cylinder.
Excessive pedal free travel	Incorrect adjustment. Air in hydraulic system - needs bleeding. Worn brake linings. Master cylinder reservoir fluid level low.
Excessive pedal effort required	Brake linings contaminated. Worn or incorrectly adjusted brakes. Wheel cylinder piston seized. One half of dual braking system not operating. Brake servo not operating - where applicable.
Vehicle pulls to one side	Loose or incorrectly adjusted wheel bearings. Worn or contaminated brake linings. Incorrectly adjusted brake shoes. Brake drum worn or distorted. Faulty wheel cylinder.

19 Fault diagnosis - tires

Symptoms	Reason/s
Excessive wear in centre of tread	Tire over-inflated.
Excessive wear at edges of tread	Tire under-inflated.
Flat spots on tire tread	Wheels out of balance. Brake drums out-of-round.

Chapter 11 Electrical system

Contents

Alternator - general description, maintenance and precautions ... 6	Fault diagnosis - electrical system ... 24
Alternator regulator - checking and adjusting ... 11	Fuses and fusible link ... 15
Alternator - removal and installation ... 8	General description ... 1
Alternator - testing in vehicle ... 7	Heaters (FJ 55 models) ... 22
Alternator (conventional type) - dismantling, servicing and reassembly ... 9	Heaters (FJ 40 series models) ... 23
	Horn - general ... 20
Alternator (heavy duty type) - dismantling, servicing and reassembly ... 10	Instrument panel combination metal - removal and installation ... 16
Battery - charging ... 5	Lighting system - servicing operations ... 14
Battery - electrolyte replenishment ... 4	Starter motor - dismantling, servicing and reassembly ... 13
Battery - maintenance ... 3	Starter motor - removal and installation ... 12
Battery - removal and installation ... 2	Switches and associated controls - general ... 18
Combination metal instruments and sender units - serviceability checks ... 17	Turn signal and hazard warning flashers - general ... 19
	Windshield wiper and washer ... 21

Specifications

System type ... 12 volt, negative ground

Alternator
Output current (max) ...	40 or 50 amp (conventional type)
	50 or 55 amp (heavy duty type)
Brush exposed length (conventional type) ...	0.49 in (12.5 mm) max
	0.35 in (9.0 mm) min
Brush length (heavy duty type) ...	0.73 in (18.5 mm) max
	0.31 in (8.0 mm) min
Rotor coil resistance ...	4.1 to 4.3 ohms (5 to 9 ohms measured between E & F terminals on assembled alternator)

Alternator control unit
Regulating voltage ...	13.6 to 14.6 volts (F engine)
	13.8 to 14.8 volts (2 F engine)
Relay coil resistance ...	25 ohms
Relay operating voltage ...	4.0 to 5.8 volts

Starter motor
Voltage ...	11 volts
Armature shaft/bush clearance ...	0.008 in (0.2 mm) max
Armature shaft thrust clearance ...	0.002/0.0138 in (0.05/0.35 mm)
Brush length (min) ...	0.51 in (13 mm)
Commutator diameter (min) ...	1.22 in (31 mm)
Insulation undercutting depth ...	0.020/0.031 in (0.5/0.8 mm)
Pinion end/stop collar clearance ...	0.008/0.16 in (0.2/4.0 mm)
Armature shaft thrust adjusting shim thickness ...	0.021 in (0.5 mm)

Fuses
Fuse box location ...	Beneath instrument panel
Rating and circuits ...	Refer to wiring diagram, fuse box lid and Section 15

Bulbs
	Wattage
Headlights ...	50/40 Except for Europe and Australia
	45/40 Europe and Australia
Front turn signal ...	21
Front parking light ...	5
Side turn signal light ...	5
Stop/tail light ...	23/28 Except FJ 55 models for Europe and Australia, and all FJ 40

Tail light ... ... 21/5 All other models
8 Australia only
Rear turn signal and back-up (reverse) light ... ... 23 Except FJ 55 models for Europe and Australia, and all FJ 40 series models
21 All other models
License plate light ... ... 7.5 Except FJ 55 models for Europe and Australia, and all FJ 40 series models
10 All other models
Interior light 10

Torque wrench settings

	lb f ft	kg f m
Alternator pulley nut	41	5.8

1 General description

The electrical system is of the 12 volt, negative earth type. The major components comprise a battery, alternator and starter motor, and the associated wiring and ancillaries.

The battery is charged by the alternator, and supplies a reserve of power for the ignition and electrical circuits.

2 Battery - removal and installation

1 The battery is mounted on a bracket attached to the engine compartment sidewall.
2 To remove it, disconnect the negative (ground) cable first, followed by the positive cable.
3 Remove the retaining nuts and lift off the clamp bar.
4 Lift the battery up and out of the engine compartment.
5 With the battery removed, wipe the top with a clean dry cloth to remove any dirt and grease deposits.
6 Installation is straightforward, but ensure that the lead polarities are not accidentally reversed or irreparable damage will occur to the alternator.
7 After tightening the terminals, smear them with a little petroleum jelly.

3 Battery - maintenance

1 Normal weekly battery maintenance consists of checking the electrolyte level of the cells to ensure that the separators are covered by ¼ inch of electrolyte. If the level has fallen, top up the battery using distilled or de-ionized water. Do not overfill. If the battery is overfilled or any electrolyte spilled, immediately wipe away the excess, as electrolyte attacks and corrodes any metal it comes into contact with very rapidly. In an emergency, where the electrolyte level is too low, it is permissible to use boiled drinking water which has been allowed to cool but this is not recommended as a regular practice.
2 If the battery terminals are showing signs of corrosion, brush or scrape off the worst taking care not to get the deposits on the vehicle paintwork or your hands. Prepare a solution of household ammonia, washing soda or bicarbonate of soda and water. Brush this onto all the corroded parts, taking care that none enters the battery. This will neutralize the corrosion, and when all the fizzing and bubbling has stopped the parts can be wiped clean with a dry, lint-free cloth. Do not forget to smear the terminals and clamps with petroleum jelly afterwards to prevent further corrosion.
3 Inspect the battery clamp and mounting tray and treat these in the same way. Where the paintwork has been damaged, after neutralizing, the area can be painted with a zinc based primer and the appropriate finishing color, or an underbody paint can be used..
4 At the same time inspect the battery case for cracks. If a crack is found, clean and plug it with one of the proprietary compounds marketed for this purpose. If leakage thru the crack has been excessive then it will be necessary to refill the appropriate cell with fresh electrolyte as described later. Cracks can be caused at the top of the battery case by pouring in distilled water in the middle of winter *after* instead of *before* a run. This gives the water no chance to mix with the electrolyte and so the former freezes and splits the battery case.
5 If topping-up becomes excessive and the case has been inspected for cracks that could cause leakage, but none are found, the battery is being overcharged and the voltage regulator will have to be checked and reset.
6 With the battery on the bench, measure the specific gravity with a hydrometer to determine the state of charge and condition of the electrolyte. There should be very little variation between the different cells and, if a variation in excess of 0.025 is present, it will be due to either:

   a) *Loss of electrolyte from the battery at some time caused by spillage or a leak, resulting in a drop in the specific gravity of the electrolyte when the deficiency was replaced with distilled water instead of fresh electrolyte.*
   b) *An internal short circuit caused by buckling of the plates or similar malady pointing to the likelihood of total battery failure in the near future.*

7 The specific gravity of the elctrolyte for fully charged conditions at the electrolyte temperature indicated, is listed in Table A. The specific gravity of a fully discharged battery at different temperatures of the electrolyte is given in Table B.

Table A

Specific gravity - battery fully charged

1.268 at 100°F or 38°C electrolyte temperature
1.272 at 90°F or 32°C electrolyte temperature
1.276 at 80°F or 27°C electrolyte temperature
1.280 at 70°F or 21°C electorlyte temperature
1.284 at 60°F or 16°C electrolyte temperature
1.288 at 50°F or 10°C electrolyte temperature
1.292 at 40°F or 4°C electrolyte temperature
1.296 at 30°F or -1.5°C electrolyte temperature

Table B

Specific gravity - battery fully discharged

1.098 at 100°F or 38°C electrolyte temperature
1.102 at 90°F or 32°C electrolyte temperature
1.106 at 80°F or 27°C electrolyte temperature
1.110 at 70°F or 21°C electrolyte temperature
1.114 at 60°F or 16°C electrolyte temperature
1.118 at 50°F or 10°C electrolyte temperature
1.122 at 40°F or 4°C electrolyte temperature
1.126 at 30°F or- 1.5°C electrolyte temperature

4 Battery - electrolyte replenishment

1 If the battery is in a fully charged state and one of the cells maintains a specific gravity reading which is 0.025 or lower, than the others, and a check of each cell has been made with a battery voltage meter to check for short circuits (a four to seven second test should give a steady reading of between 1.2 and 1.8 volts), then it is likely that electrolyte has been lost from the cell with the low reading at some time.
2 Top up the cell with a solution of 1 part sulphuric acid to 2.5 parts of distilled or de-ionized water, If the cell is already fully topped up

Chapter 11/Electrical system

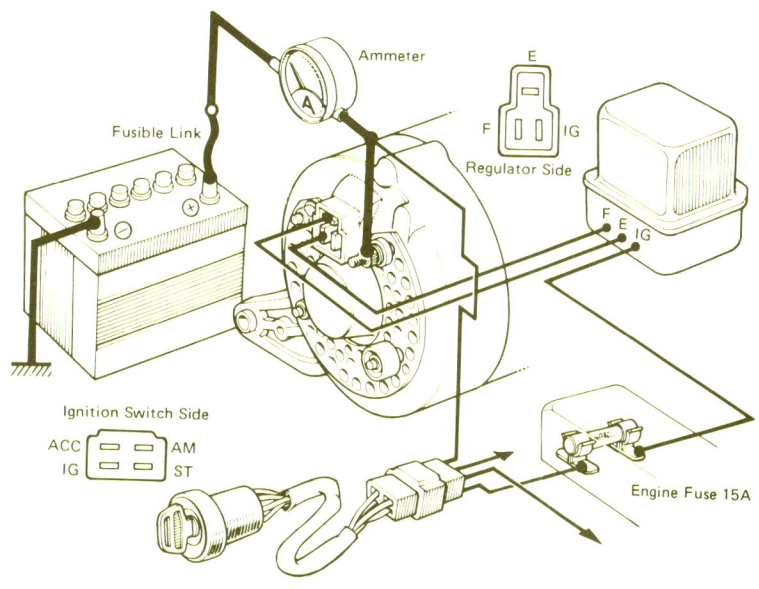

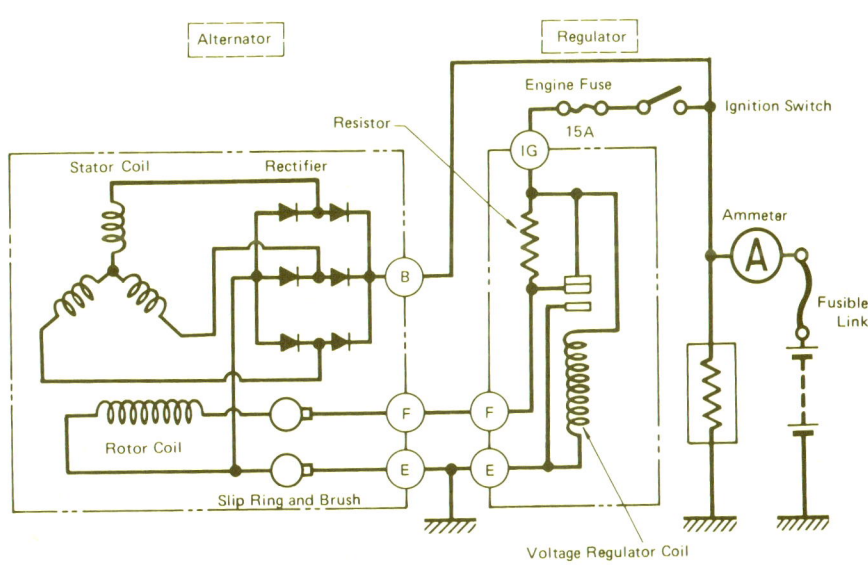

Fig. 11.1. Alternator connections - ammeter types

draw some electrolyte out of it with an hydrometer.
3 When mixing the sulphuric acid and water **never add water to sulphuric acid** - always pour acid slowly onto the water in a glass container. **If water is added to sulphuric acid it will explode.**
4 Continue to top up the cell with the freshly made electrolyte and recharge the battery and check the hydrometer readings.

5 Battery - charging

Note: If the battery is to remain in the vehicle when being charged always disconnect the battery leads.
1 In winter time when a heavy demand is placed on the battery, such as when starting from cold, and much electrical equipment is continually in use, it is a good idea to occasionally have the battery fully charged from an external source at a rate of approximately 4 amps.
2 Continue to charge the battery at this rate until no further rise in specific gravity is noted over a four hour period.
3 Alternatively, a trickle charger, charging at the rate of 1.5 amps, can be safely used overnight.
4 Special rapid 'boost' charges that are claimed to restore the power of the battery in 1 to 2 hours are not recommended unless they are thermostatically controlled as they can cause serious damage to the battery plates through overheating.
5 While charging the battery, note that the temperature of the electrolyte should never exceed 100°F (37.8°C).

6 Alternator - general description, maintenance and precautions

1 The alternator generates three-phase alternating current which is rectified into direct current by silicone diode rectifiers installed within the end frame of the alternator. The in-built characteristics of the unit obviate the need for a cut-out or current stabiliser.
2 A voltage regulator unit is incorporated in the charging circuit to control the exciting current and the current applied to the voltage coil.
3 Check the fan belt tension every 5,000 miles (8,000 km) and adjust as described in Section 8 by loosening the mounting bolts.
4 No lubrication is required as the bearings are grease-sealed for life.

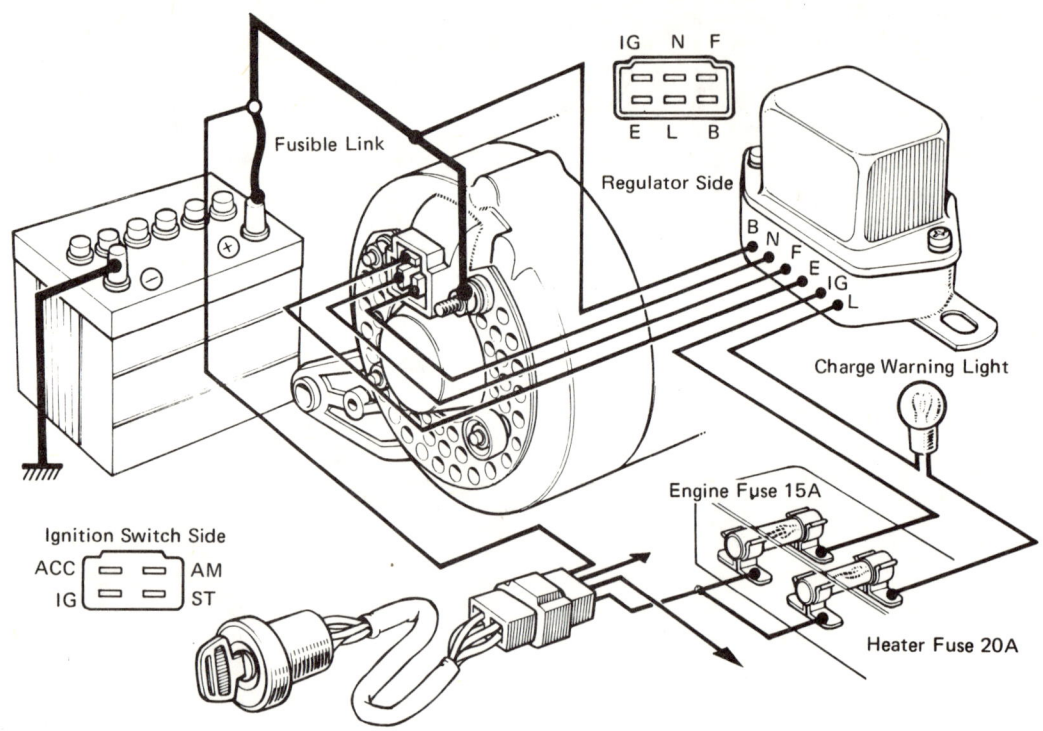

Fig. 11.2. Alternator connections - charge warning light types

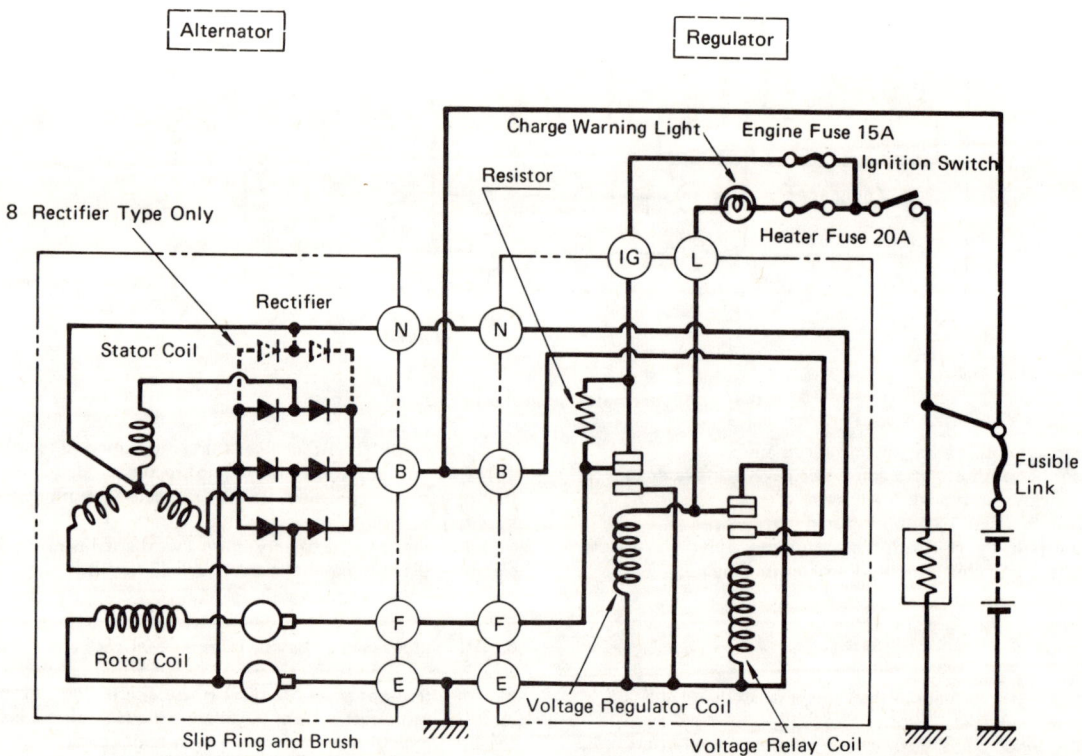

Chapter 11/Electrical system

5 Take extreme care when making circuit connections to a vehicle fitted with an alternator and observe the following:

When making connections to the alternator from a battery always match correct polarity.

Before using electric-arc welding equipment to repair any part of the vehicle, disconnect the connector from the alternator and disconnect the positive battery terminal.

Never start the car with a battery charger connected.

Always disconnect the battery leads before using a mains charger.

If boosting from another battery, always connect in parallel using heavy cable.

7 Alternator - testing in vehicle

1 In the event of failure of the normal performance of the alternator carry out the following test procedure paying particular attention to the possibility of damaging the charging and electrical system unless the notes (a) to (c) are observed.

  a) *The alternator output 'B' terminal is connected to the battery at all times. When the ignition switch is operated, the 'F' terminal is also at battery voltage.*
  b) *Never connect the battery leads incorrectly or the rectifiers will be damaged.*
  c) *Never run the engine at high revs, with the alternator 'B' terminal disconnected, otherwise the voltage at the 'N' terminal will rise abnormally and damage to the voltage relay will result.*

2 Check the security of the alternator mountings, the terminal leads and the drive belt tension (Section 8).
3 Check the fuses and renew them if any are blown.
4 Switch on the vehicle radio and tune into a local transmitter. Start the engine and increase its speed from idling to 200 rev/min. If a distinct humming sound is heard from the radio speaker then this indicates that the alternator rectifier is shorted or open.
5 Connect a voltmeter and ammeter to the alternator 'B' terminal. Start the engine and gradually increase its speed to 2,000 rev/min.

The voltmeter should read between 13.8 and 14.8 volts and the ammeter under 10 amps. If the current is greater than the specified figure, the battery is either discharged or there is an internal short circuit. If the voltmeter needle fluctuates the regular contacts may be dirty or arced or the alternator 'E' terminal may be loose.
6 If the voltage reading is too high then (i) the regulator contact gaps may be too wide (ii) there is an open circuit at the regulator and voltage relay coil, (iii) the 'N' and 'B' regulator terminals are open or (iv) the regulator has a defective earth connection.
7 Switch off the engine and disconnect the wiring harness connecting plug. Turn on the ignition switch and measure the voltage between the 'F' and 'E' sockets of the connecting plug. This should be 12 volts. If the reading is low or zero, check for (i) a faulty fuse connection (ii) open circuit between 'F' or 'IG' terminals or (iii) the regulator contact points are fused together.
8 Repeat the tests described in the preceding paragraphs 5 and 6 but run the engine at only 2,000 rev/min with all lights and accessories switched on, when the ammeter reading should be in excess of 30 amps. If the reading is less than 30 amps, it is indicative of open rectifiers, stator coil circuit or short circuited rectifiers.

8 Alternator - removal and installation

1 Disconnect the battery ground lead, then the alternator harness plug and lead (photo).
2 Remove the air cleaner assembly (refer to Chapter 3 if necessary).
3 Loosen the alternator mounting bolts and adjusting link bolts.
4 Move the alternator towards the engine and take off the drive bolt.
5 Remove the bolts and lift the alternator out of the engine compartment.
6 Installation is the reverse of the removal procedure.
7 Adjust the fan belt so that when it is depressed at the point shown in Figs. 11.3 or 11.4, with a load of approximately 22 lb (10 kg), the correct deflection is obtained. If a bar has to be used when moving the alternator to adjust the belt tension, pry at the drive end bracket only (photo).

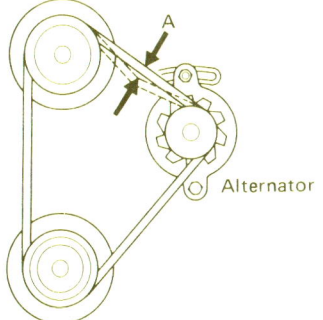

Fig. 11.3. Alternator drivebelt adjustment

A = 0.28 to 0.39 in (7 to 10 mm)

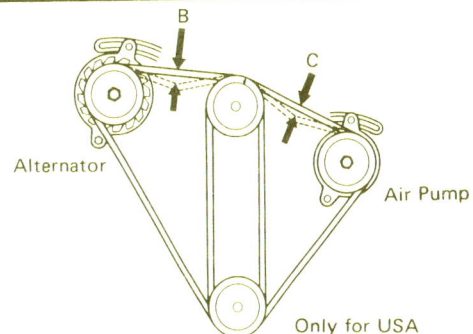

Fig. 11.4. Alternator (and air pump) drive belt adjustment

B = 0.51 to 0.59 in (13 to 15 mm)
C = 0.28 to 0.39 in (7 to 10 mm)

8.1 Alternator lead connections - typical

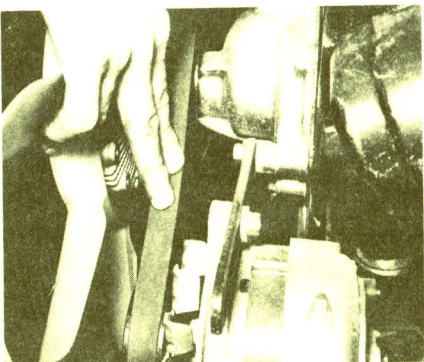

8.7 Checking alternator drivebelt tension - typical

9 Alternator (conventional type) - dismantling, servicing and reassembly

1 Before dismantling an alternator, make sure that your reasons for doing so are valid. More harm than good can result from this type of job if the person doing it is not suitably qualified or experienced. Also, check the spare part availability before commencing any work because it may be less time - consuming and expensive to obtain an exchange assembly.

2 To commence dismantling, remove the three through bolts and separate the front and rear frame assemblies. If necessary, a screwdriver can be used to pry apart the assemblies, but take care that damage does not occur.

3 Remove the nut and spring washer securing the pulley and fan.

4 Using a suitable press or drift, carefully drive the rotor out of the drive end frame.

5 Using a universal puller, draw off the bearing from the rear end of the shaft.

6 Remove the front bearing end associated parts from the drive end frame.

7 Remove the retaining nuts, washers and insulators, and remove the stator coil and rectifier holder.

8 Remove the brush holder and rectifier holder from the stator coil. Take care during this, and any subsequent soldering operation that the minimum possible amount of heat is used, or damage will occur to the semi-conductors.

9 Using a 10 mm (or similar size) socket and a vise, press out the brush holder assembly screws.

10 Detach the leads connecting the diode plates.

11 Using a suitable ohmmeter, check for a resistance of 4.1 to 4.3 ohms between the slip rings. Check for infinity between each slip ring and the rotor. Check the slip rings for scoring and contamination. Cleaning with gasoline, and careful polishing with very fine glass paper is permitted, but if the rotor is otherwise unserviceable, a replacement must be obtained.

12 Check for bearings for signs of rough-running; if evident, replacements must be obtained.

13 Using a suitable ohmmeter, check all four stator leads for continuity; also check each lead to the stator frame for infinity. If either test reading is unsatisfactory, a replacement stator assembly must be obtained.

14 Check the brush holder for damage, and for the amount of brush exposed. If less than 0.35 in (9.00 mm), new brushes must be installed (see Fig. 11.9).

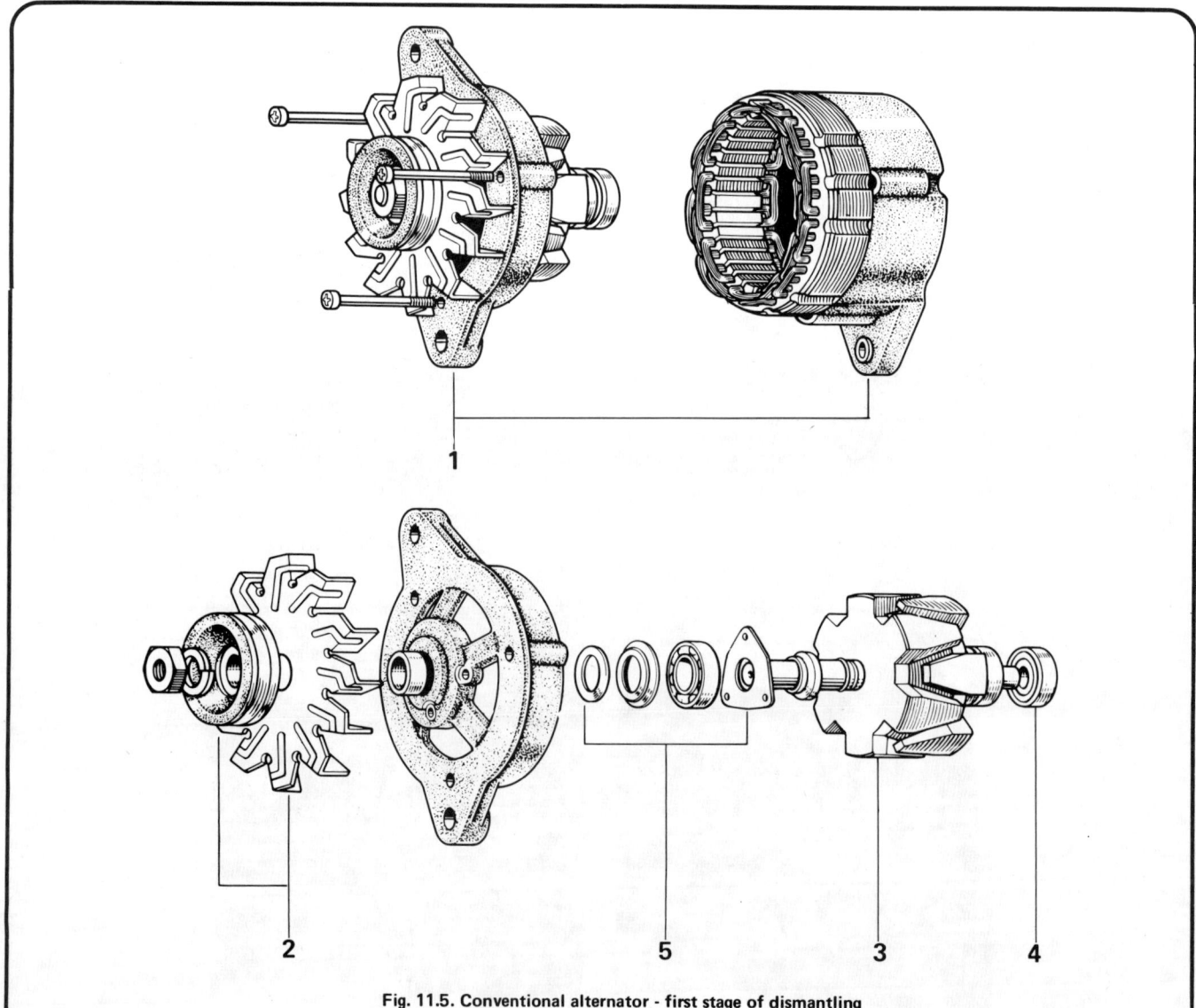

Fig. 11.5. Conventional alternator - first stage of dismantling

1 Front and rear frame assemblies 2 Pulley and fan 3 Rotor 4 Rear bearing 5 Front bearing

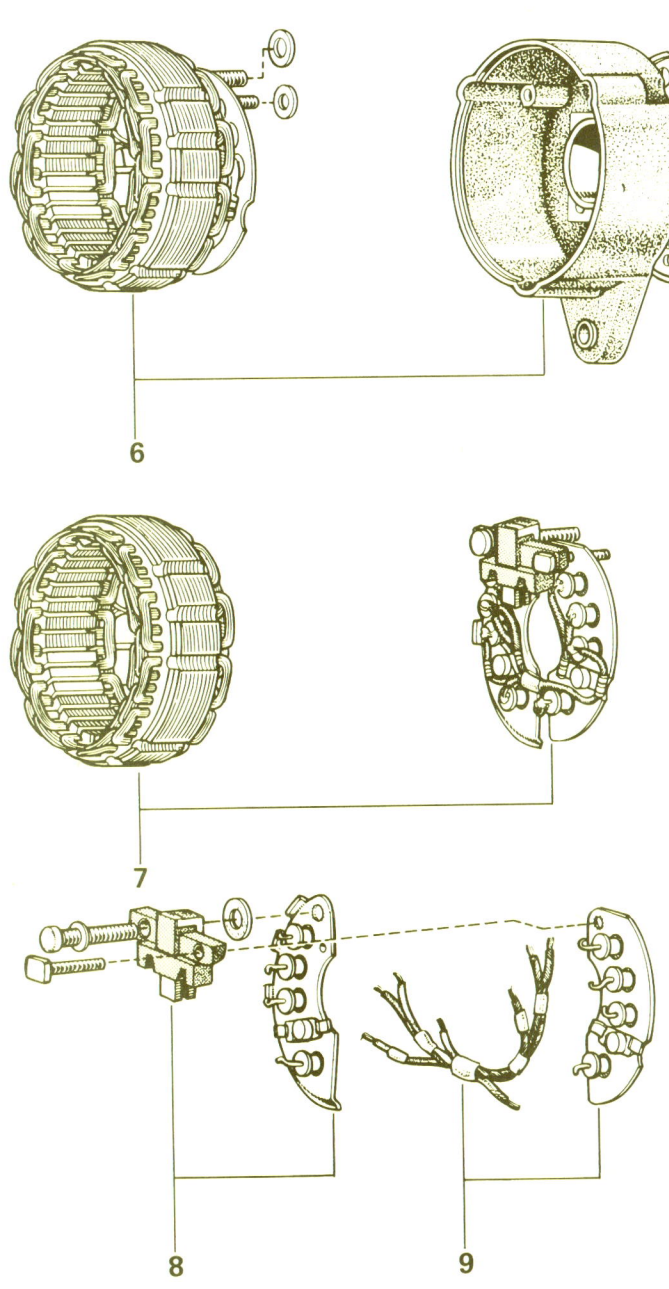

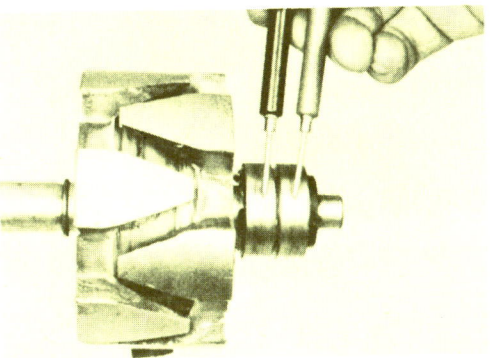

Fig. 11.7. Checking resistance between slip-rings

Fig. 11.8. Checking stator leads to frame

Fig. 11.6. Conventional alternator - second stage of dismantling

6 Stator coil and rectifier holder   8 Brush holder
7 Stator coil and rectifier holder   9 Lead wire

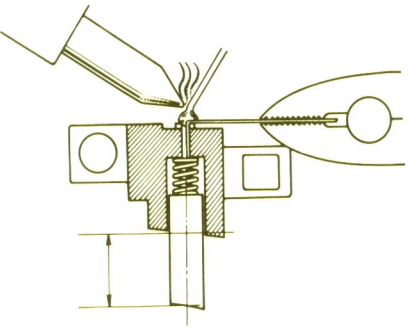

Fig. 11.9. Soldering in new brush leads

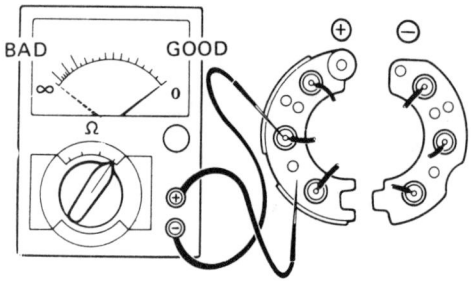

Fig. 11.10. Checking positive rectifiers

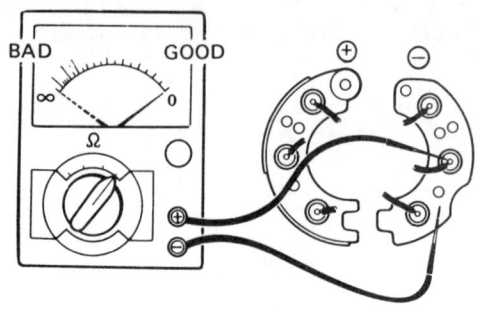

Fig. 11.11. Checking negative rectifiers

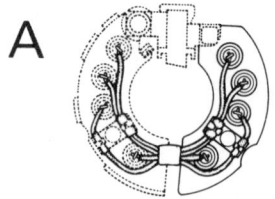

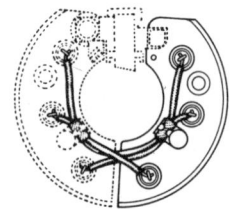

Fig. 11.12. Negative rectifier connections

    a) 8 Rectifier type   *b)* 6 Rectifier type

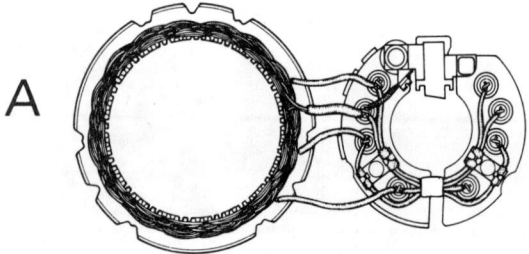

Fig. 11.13. Stator coil connections

    a) 8 Rectifier type   *b)* 6 Rectifier type

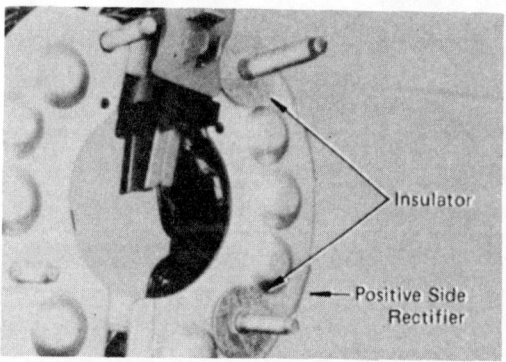

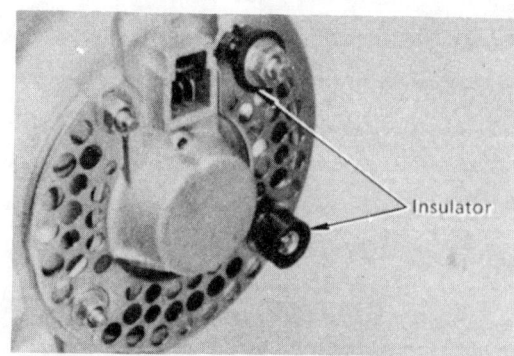

Fig. 11.14. End frame and rectifier holder insulators

15 Using a suitable ohmmeter, check the positive and negative rectifiers. Place the rectifiers on the bench, and connect the ohmmeter, as shown in Fig. 11.10. Continuity should be indicated; if there is no continuity, replace the positive rectifier holder. Reverse the polarity of the test leads and check that there is no continuity; if there is continuity, replace the positive rectifier holder.

16 Repeat the check for the negative rectifiers, connecting the meter initially as shown in Fig. 11.11. Continuity should be indicated; if there is no continuity, replace the negative rectifier holder.

17 Reassembly of the alternator is generally straightforward, following the reverse of the dismantling procedure. However, the following points should be noted:

a) When resoldering the rectifier leads, connect them as shown in Fig. 11.12
b) When reconnecting the stator coil, connect it as shown in Fig. 11.13.
c) Ensure that insulators are positioned as shown in Fig. 11.14.
d) Ensure that the bearings are installed with their sealed sides towards the rotor.
e) When installing the rotor assembly, insert a piece of stiff wire (eg, a straightened paper clip) through the hole in the end frame, to hold the brushes clear of the slip-rings.

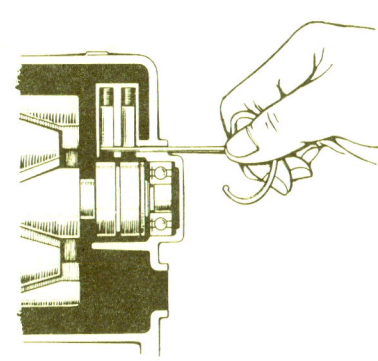

Fig. 11.15. Using a stiff wire to hold the brushes clear of the slip-rings

10 Alternator (heavy duty type) - dismantling, servicing and reassembly

1 Dismantling of this alternator is generally similar to that given for the conventional type alternator, the main differences being the brush assembly and the method of mounting the rectifiers. Figs. 11.16 and 11.17 show the parts in their breakdown order.

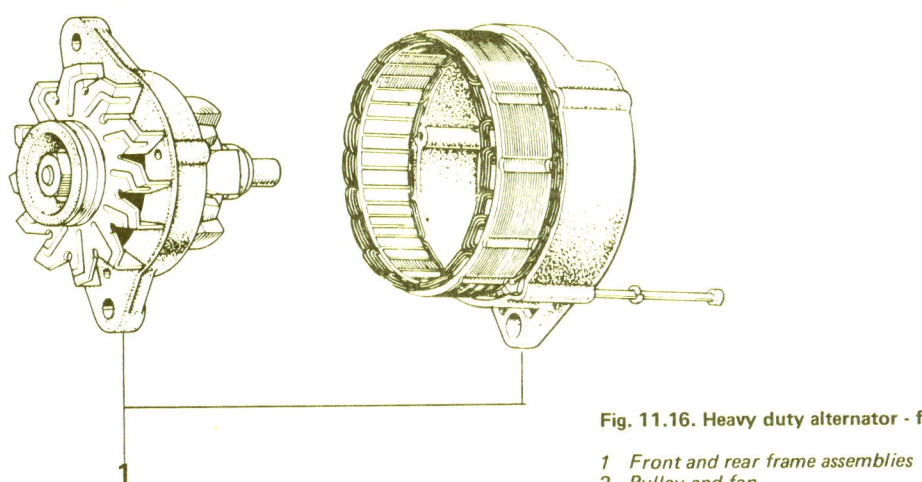

Fig. 11.16. Heavy duty alternator - first stage of dismantling

1 Front and rear frame assemblies 3 Rotor
2 Pulley and fan   4 Front bearing

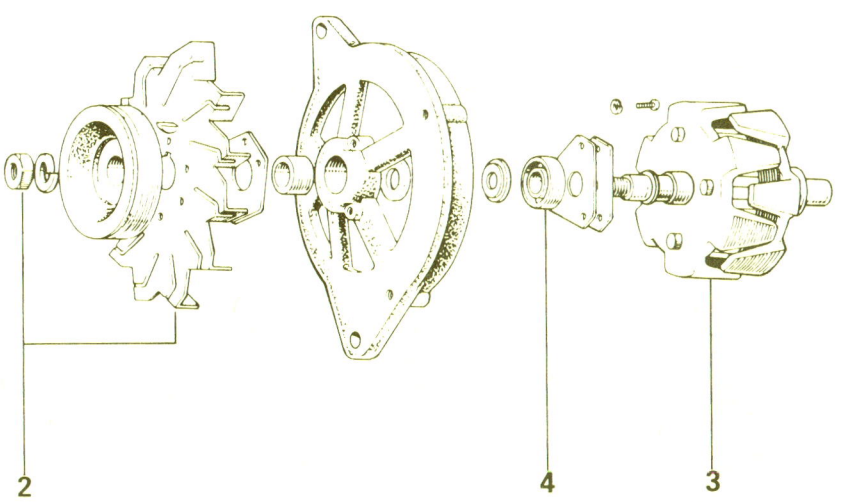

2 With the alternator dismantled, check the brush length, and renew if they are below that given in the Specifications.
3 When reassembling, follow the reverse of the dismantling procedure, taking care over the following points:

   a) Insert insulators between the positive rectifier holder and end frame (see Fig. 11.18).
   b) Assemble the brush holder and insulators onto the rear end frame as shown in Fig. 11.19, lifting the brushes as necessary to avoid damage.
   c) Insert the 'N', 'E' and 'F' lead terminals into the connector socket as shown in Fig. 11.20.
   d) Connect the stator coil leads to the rectifier terminals as shown in Fig. 11.21
   e) The cavity in the rear bearing housing should be half-filled with a general purpose grease.
   f) When installing the end cover, ensure that the brush springs are clear of the brushes. Once the cover is in position, release the springs so that the brushes contact the slip rings.
   g) Do not forget the insulator that is used on the 'B' terminal bolt.

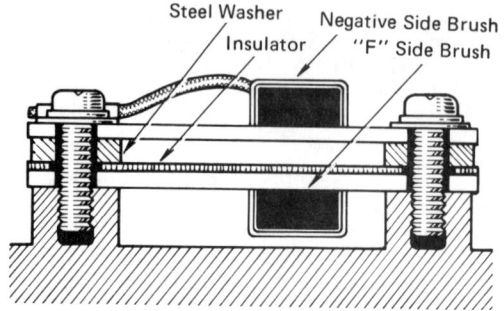

Fig. 11.19. Brush holder assembly - sectional view

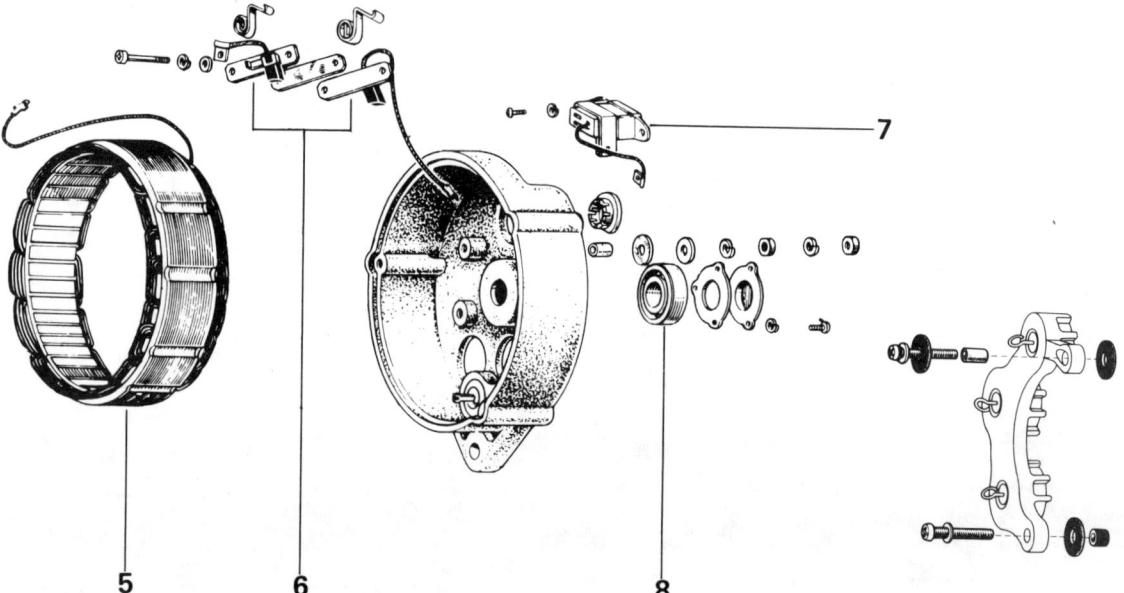

Fig. 11.18. Position of insulators

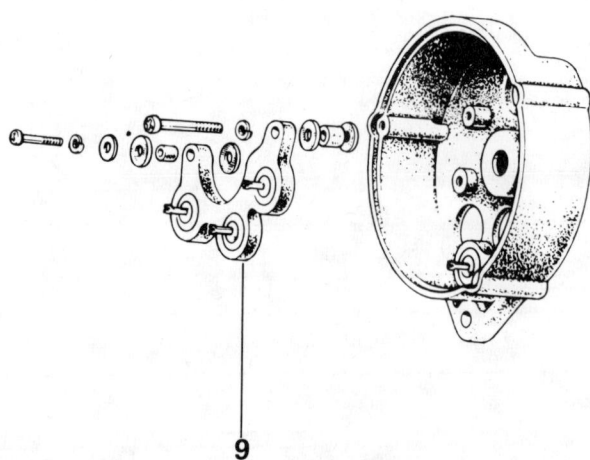

Fig. 11.17. Heavy duty alternator - second stage of dismantling

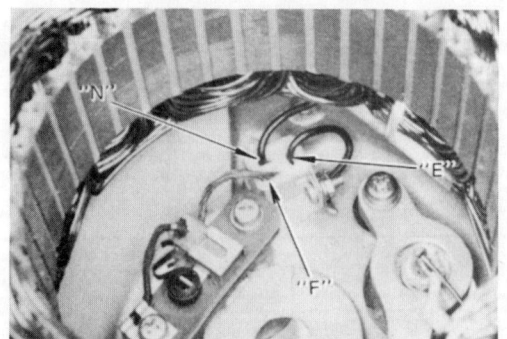

Fig. 11.20. 'N', 'E' and 'F' lead positions

5 Stator coil
6 Brush holder
7 Connector socket
8 Rear bearing
9 Positive rectifier

11 Alternator regulator - checking and adjusting

1 Alternator regulators are extremely reliable, and are unlikely to require any attention. If a fault is suspected, first ensure that the electrical connector pins are clean, and are making satisfactory contact.
2 If further investigation is required, separate the connector plug and socket, and remove the cover (two screws or two spring clips, according to type). Although it is possible to renew the contacts if badly burned, it is considered preferable to obtain a new regulator on an exchange basis.
3 Adjustment and/or checking of the voltage regulator and/or voltage relay should be entrusted to a car electrical specialist. If an ohmmeter is available, resistance checks can be carried out as follows:

Charge warning light type

Voltage regulator (Terminals 'IG' and 'F')	Armature released Armature pressed down	0 ohm 11 ohm approx.
Voltage relay (Terminals 'L' and 'E')	Armature released Armature pressed down	0 ohm 100 ohm approx.
Voltage relay (Terminals 'B' and 'E')	Armature released Armature pressed down	Infinity 100 ohm approx.
Voltage relay (Terminals 'B' and 'L')	Armature released Armature pressed down	Infinity 0 ohm
Voltage relay coil (Terminals 'N' and 'E')		25 ohm approx.

Ammeter type

Terminals 'IG' and 'F'	Armature released Armature pressed down	0 ohm 11 ohm approx.
Terminals 'IG' and 'E'	Armature released Armature pressed down	100 ohm approx. Infinity
Terminals 'F' and 'E'	Armature released Armature pressed down	100 ohm approx. 0 ohm

Fig. 11.21. Stator coil connections

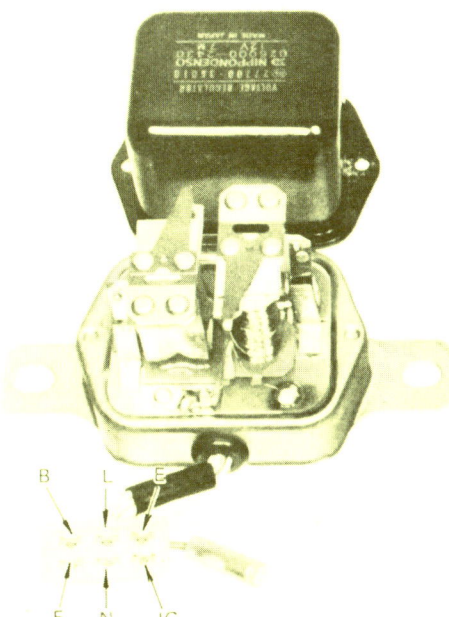

Fig. 11.22. Insulator on 'B' terminal bolt

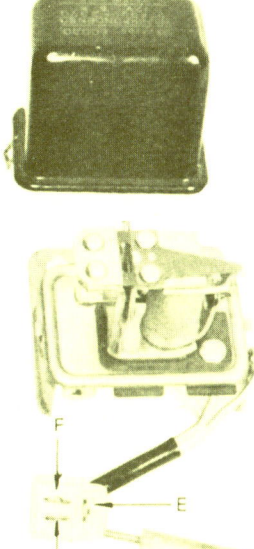

Fig. 11.23. Alternator regulators

12 Starter motor - removal and installation

1   Disconnect the battery ground cable.
2   Disconnect the wire(s) from the starter motor solenoid. If there is any possibility of a mix-up, tie a label on each one or make a sketch of the connections (photo).
3   Remove the retaining nuts, then draw the starter motor forward into the engine compartment to remove it.
4   Installation is the reverse of the removal.

13 Starter motor - dismantling, servicing and reassembly

1   Detach the field coil lead from the solenoid terminal.
2   Remove the two screws and washers, and detach the solenoid, lifting or turning the hook end of the armature out of engagement with the drive lever.
3   Remove the bearing cover (two screws and washers); where applicable remove the rubber seal.

12.2 Starter motor connections

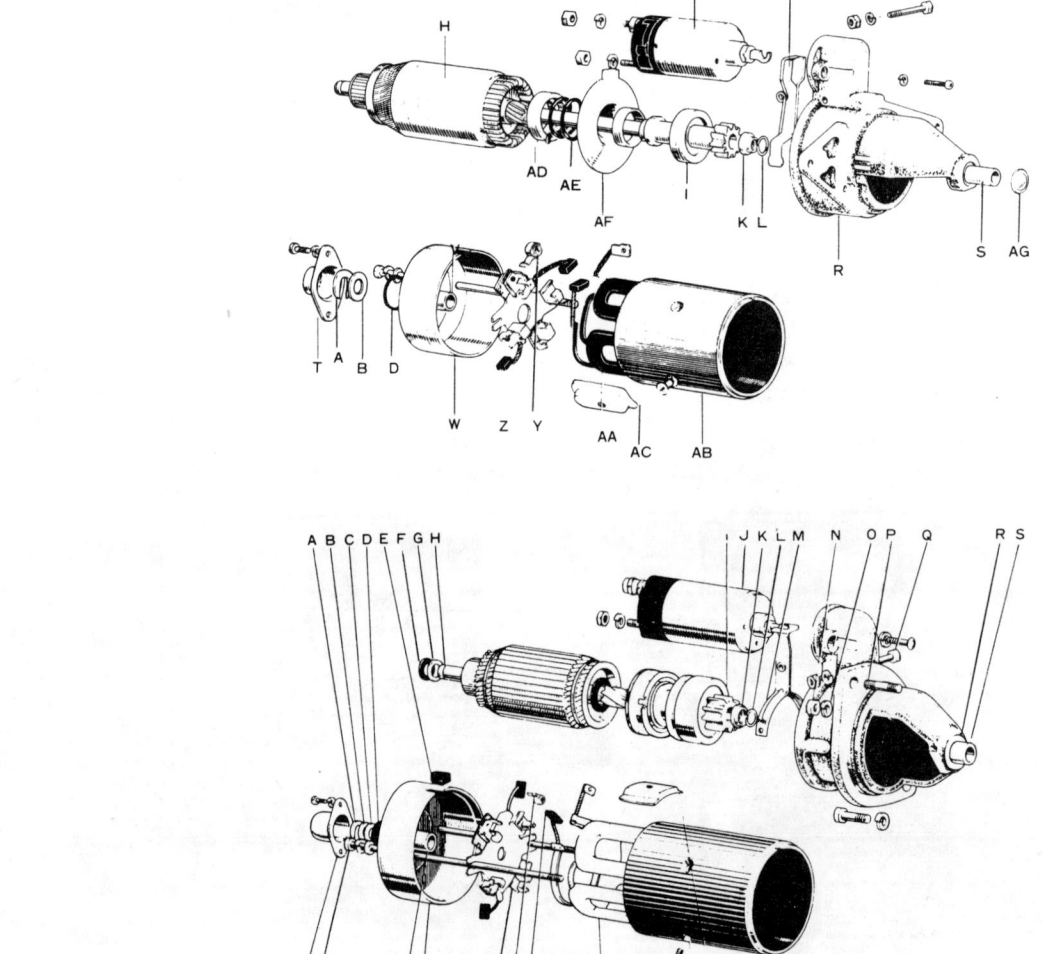

Fig. 11.24. Alternative types of earlier starter motors

A Lockplate	I Starter clutch	Q Drive lever set pin	Y Brush spring
B Washer	J Solenoid	R Starter drive housing	Z Starter brush
C Washer	K Pinion stop nut	S Bush	AA Field coil
D Rubber ring	L Jump ring	T Bearing cover	AB Starter yoke
E Rubber bush	M Pinion drive lever	U Through bolt	AC Pole core
F Bakelite washer	N Nut	V Bush	AD Spring holder
G Washer	O Lockwasher	W Commutator end frame	AE Starter clutch spring
H Starter armature	P Stud bolt	X Brush holder	AF Center bearing
			AG Expansion plug

Chapter 11/Electrical system

4 Using a feeler gauge, measure the armature thrust clearance at the non-drive end. This should be 0.002/0.0138 in (0.05/0.35 mm); record the value obtained.
5 Remove the lockplate and adjusting washers.
6 Remove the through-bolts so that the commutator end frame can be detached from the field coil and yoke assembly.
7 Remove the two brushes which connect to the field coil, from the brush holder.
8 Remove the brush holder complete with the two remaining brushes.
9 Remove the armature thrust washers, then tap the drive housing to free it from the yoke. Alternatively, use a screwdriver to pry the two parts apart.
10 Remove the drive lever set pin so that the armature, starter clutch and pinion drive lever can be removed.
11 Using a socket or piece of tube of suitable diameter, drive the pinion stop collar downwards towards the starter clutch to release the snap-ring (jump-ring) from the end of the armature shaft; remove the

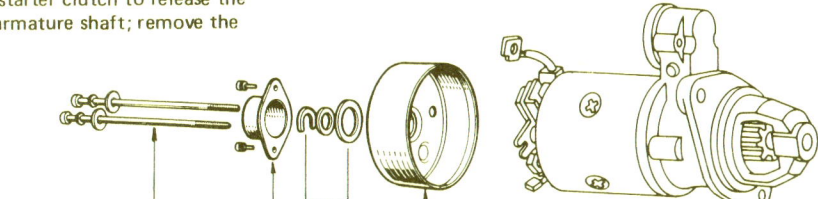

Fig. 11.25. Later starter motor

1 Solenoid
2 Bearing cover
3 Lockplate
4 Bolt
5 Commutator end frame
6 Yoke and brush holder
7 Drive lever bolt
8 Armature and drive lever
9 Jump ring
10 Stop collar
11 Clutch and pinion gear
12 Center bearing

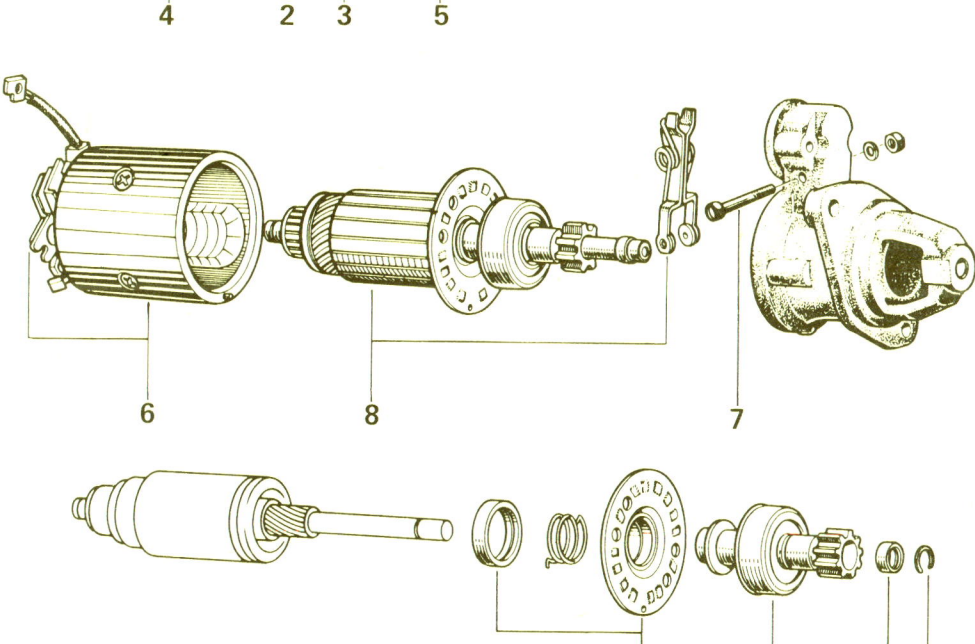

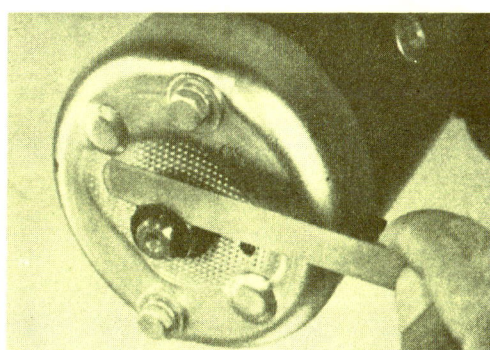

Fig. 11.26. Measuring armature thrust clearance

Fig. 11.27. Removing the jump ring (snap-ring)

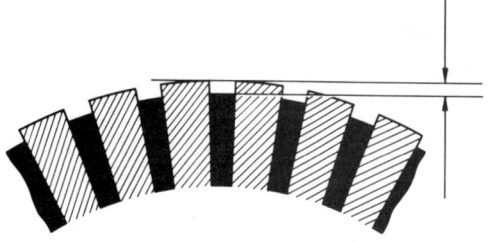

Fig. 11.28. Depth of segment insulation - see text

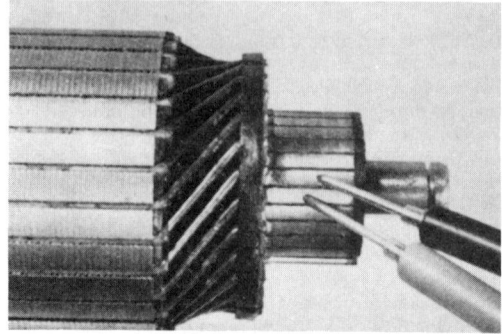

Fig. 11.29. Checking for continuity between segments

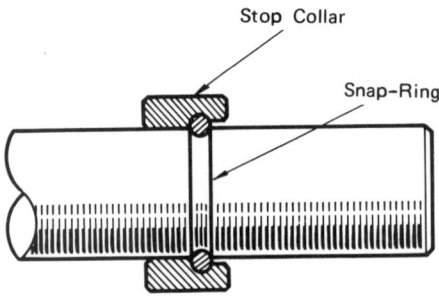

Fig. 11.30. Sectional view of the jump ring (snap-ring)

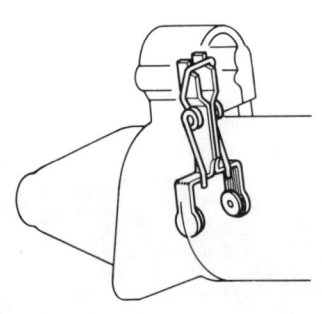

Fig. 11.31. Alternative types of drive lever

Fig. 11.32. The brush holder in position

Fig. 11.33. Starter clutch pinion clearance check - see text

snap-ring.
12 Remove the stop collar, clutch and pinion gear, and the center bearing.
13 Examine the armature and pole shoes for signs of rubbing, and for free play between the armature spindle and bushes. Free play up to 0.008 in (0.2 mm) is acceptable, but if more play exists the end cover must be pried out so that the bushing can be pressed or driven out. After installing a replacement bush it should be reamed to give a 0.002/0.004 in (0.05/0.10 mm) clearance.
14 Examine the commutator for burning. If necessary it may be skimmed in a lathe and polished with 400 grade sandpaper, provided that the diameter is not reduced below 1.22 in (31 mm). The insulation between the segments should be cut back if necessary to 0.008/0.031 in (0.2/0.8 mm) below the armature surface, but care must be taken to remove any burrs from the armature surface afterwards.
15 If more than 0.008 in (0.2 mm) clearance exists between the armature shaft and center bearing, a replacement bearing must be obtained.
16 Examine the starter clutch parts for wear and damage, and obtain replacements as necessary. When assembled, the pinion gear should rotate clockwise but not anticlockwise.
17 Using a suitable continuity tester, check that there is no electrical continuity between the armature core and the commutator; also check that there is continuity between each adjacent segment.
18 Using a suitable continuity tester, check for continuity between each brush connection and the field coil connection: also check that there is no continuity between the field coil connection and the field coil frame.
19 Obtain replacement brushes if the free length is less than 0.51 in (13 mm). Cut off the braided leads close to the original termination and solder replacement leads to the remaining braided part. Ensure that there is no electrical continuity between the positive and negative brush holders.
20 Examine the drive lever and spring for wear and damage, renewing if necessary.
21 Check that the solenoid armature has a good spring-return action when pressed in. If necessary, adjust the hooked end piece to obtain a measurement of 1.34 in (34 mm) from the solenoid and face to the extreme end of the hooked piece.

22 Check for continuity between the '50' terminal and the 'C' terminal (or 'F' terminal), and between the '50' terminal and the solenoid body. With the solenoid armature pushed fully in, check for continuity between the '30' terminal and the 'IG' lead wire (where applicable).
23 Reassembly is basically the reverse of the removal procedure, but the following points should be noted:

a) Apply a little multipurpose grease to the armature shaft splines, starter clutch drive ring, shaft bushes and solenoid armature stud and drive lever.
b) After assembling the starter clutch, pinion stop collar and snap-ring, lock the stop collar in position over the snap-ring by center punching in two places.
c) The method of installation and attachment of the pinion drive lever varies on some models, but the arrangements shown in Fig. 11.31 are typical.
d) When installing the brush holder, hold the brushes clear of the commutator, and position the holder as shown in Fig. 11.32.
e) When fitting the commutator end frame, ensure that the brush leads are not grounded. If the armature endfloat (measured at paragraph f) was outside the specified limit, re-shim as necessary before installing the lock plate. The grease cap should then be half-filled with a general purpose grease before installing.
f) After installing the solenoid, check the clearance between the starter clutch pinion and the pinion stop collar. This should be 0.008/0.16 in (0.2/4.0 mm) if the end piece is correctly adjusted (see paragraph 21), but readjustment is permitted in order to obtain the specified clearance.

14 Lighting system - servicing operations

1 A wide range of vehicle lights have been used on Land Cruiser models. In some cases it will be found that an alternative type of light has been introduced for one particular application during the production run of the vehicle; an example of this is the front turn signal/parking light on the FJ 55 models. In other cases, alternative

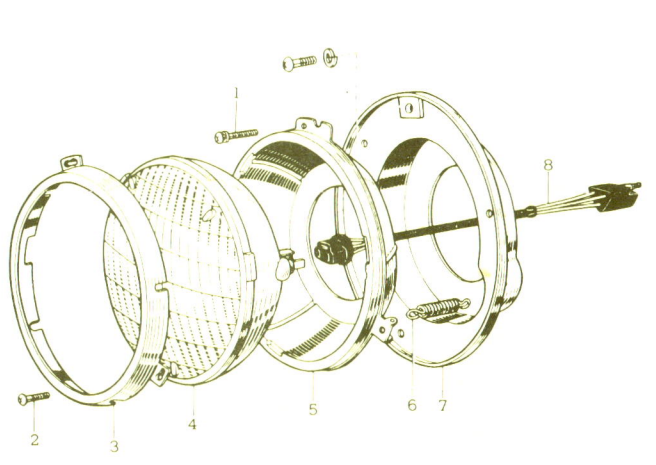

Fig. 11.34. Headlamp arrangement - FJ55 (typical)

1 Adjusting screw
2 Retaining screw
3 Retaining ring
4 Beam unit
5 Beam mounting ring
6 Spring
7 Housing
8 Connector

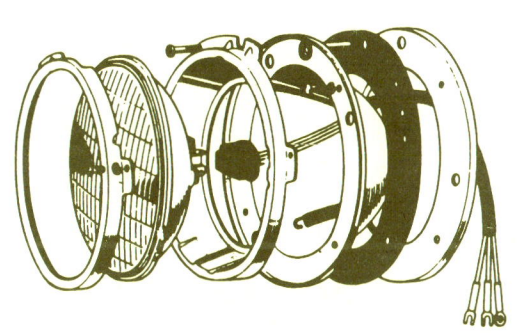

Fig. 11.35. Headlamp arrangement - FJ40 series (typical)

14.4a Removing a headlight lens

14.4b Headlight connector

14.5 Removing a headlight housing - note the retaining clip used on some models

14.10 Headlamp adjustment - vertical plane

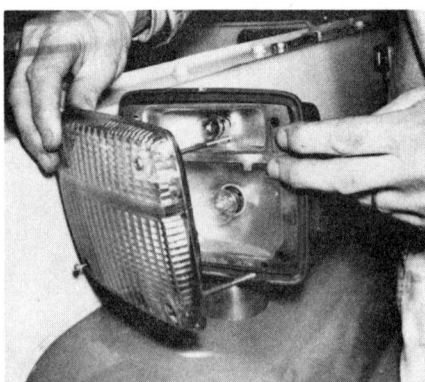
14.11a Typical arrangement for the front turn signal and sidelights (FJ 55 models)

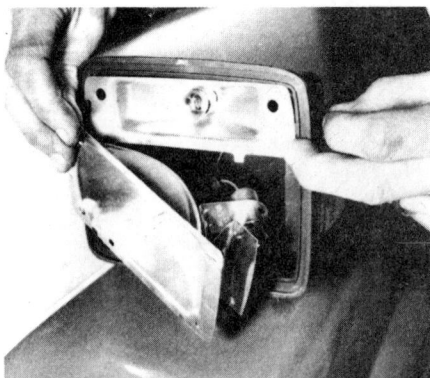
14.11b Typical arrangement for the front turn signal and sidelights (FJ 55 models)

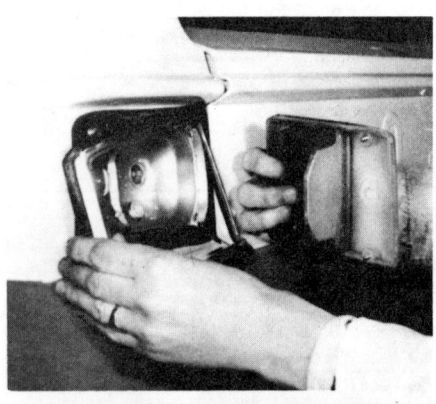

14.16a, 14.16b Typical arrangement for rear combination lamp (FJ55 models - the rear lamp bulb is missing on some models to comply with lighting regulations - see photo 14.17)

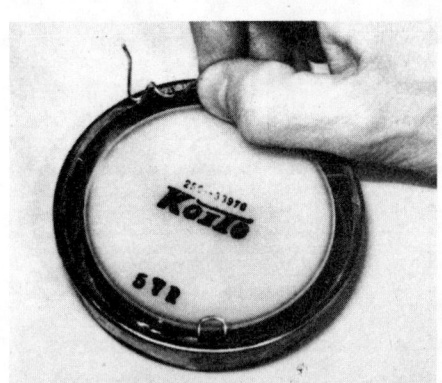
14.17 Alternative rear light used on some models

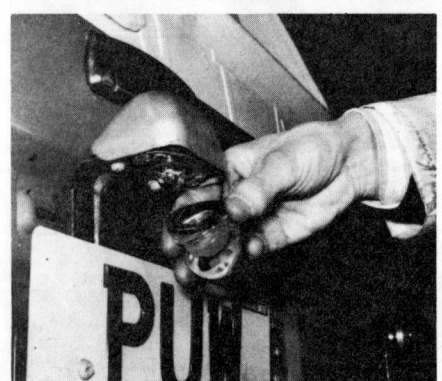
14.18 Typical license plate lamp (FJ 55 models)

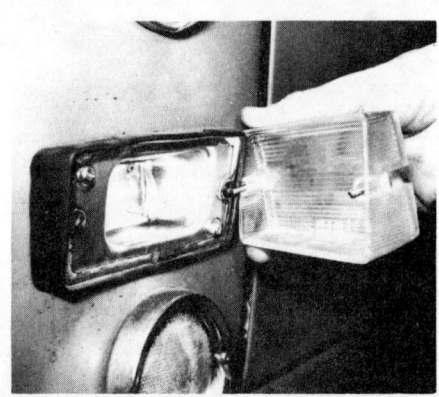
14.21 Typical back-up light (FJ 55 model)

14.23 Reflector lens retaining spring

types of light have been used to comply with lighting regulations in a particular country where, for example, the standard vehicle rear lights are too high from the ground.

Headlights
2 To remove the headlight, first remove the headlight bezel or radiator grille (as appropriate) for access to the retaining screws.
3 Loosen the screws and rotate the retaining ring counter-clockwise to remove it.
4 Pull out the light unit and disconnect the electrical connector. Note: on some models a rubber cover is fitted over the connector (photo).
5 If only the bulb or sealed beam unit is to be renewed, the assembly can be installed by following the reverse of the removal procedure. If further dismantling is required, the mounting ring and headlight housing can be removed also. Fig. 11.34 shows a typical arrangement (photo).
6 After any servicing operation on the headlight, the beam adjustment should be checked.

Headlight adjustment
7 To adjust the beam aim accurately, it will be necessary to contact a suitably equipped dealer who has a beam setting meter. However, the procedure outlined in this Section will provide a reasonably accurate setting, but it must be appreciated that lighting regulations for some markets stipulate that a beam setting meter must be used.
8 Place the vehicles on a level floor, 25 ft (7.6 m) from a vertical wall.
9 Draw a horizontal line on the wall at the height of the headlight center-line, then draw another line 2 in (50 mm) below it. Draw a vertical line on the wall at the center-line of each headlight.
10 Cover one headlight, and adjust the other so that when on high beam it is aimed at the vertical line and at the horizontal line 2 in (50 mm) below the headlight center-line. Repeat this for the other beam (photo).

Front turn signal lamps
11 For access to the lamp bulbs, remove the lens retaining screws, then remove the lamp rim (where applicable), lens and gasket. The bayonet fitting bulbs can then be removed.
12 The lamps are attached to the fenders or engine compartment sidewall. To remove them disconnect the in-line connector, then remove the nut, washer, gasket and associated parts.

Front parking lamps
13 Where separate front parking lights are installed, the bulb is accessible after the lamp rim and lens are removed (three screws).
14 The lamp is attached by two nuts and washers which screw onto studs on the lamp body. When removing and installing, do not forget the lamp base.

Rear combination lights
15 In all cases, the rear lamp bulbs are accessible after the lens has been removed. Typical arrangements are shown in the accompanying illustrations.
16 The lamps are attached to the body parts by nuts and washers which screw onto studs on the lamp body, or by screws (photos).
17 On some models there is no bulb behind the red lens of the combination lamp. On these models a separate lamp is installed but it is similar in principle to the other types of lamp (photo).

License plate lamps
18 For access to the bulbs, remove the cover or lens retaining screws, then take off the cover or lens and associated parts (photo).
19 On some models, once the lens or cover has been removed, the lamp body is free to be pulled away. On other models, the lamp is attached by nuts and washers, or screws. Removal is straightforward.

Side turn signal lamps
20 These are used on some models, and are generally similar to the other lamps described. It may be necessary to remove the rear interior trim panel for access to the retaining nuts if the complete lamp is to be removed.

Back-up lights (reverse lights)
21 For access to the bulbs, remove the lens (two screws) and associated

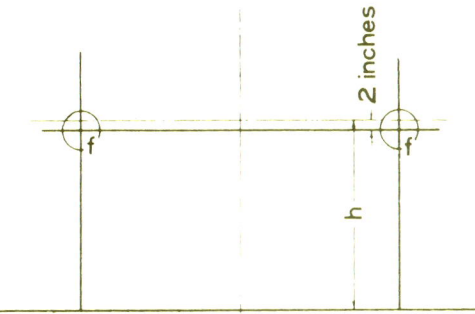

Fig. 11.36. Headlight adjustment scale

h = headlight center height
f = headlight center line

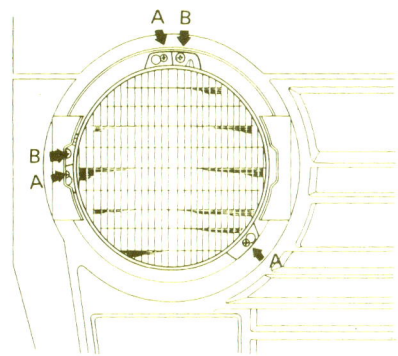

Fig. 11.37. Headlight retaining screws (A) and adjusting screws (B) - typical

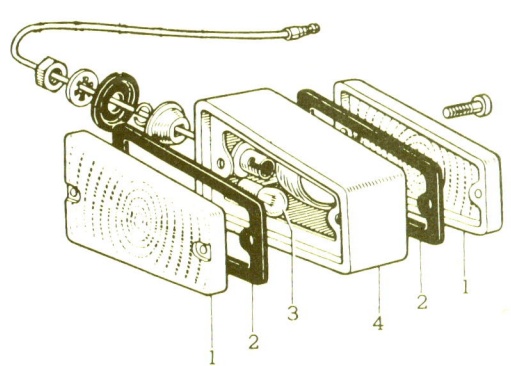

Fig. 11.38. Front turn signal light - FJ55 (typical for early models)

1 Lens   3 Bulb
2 Gasket   4 Light body

14.25 Dome type interior light

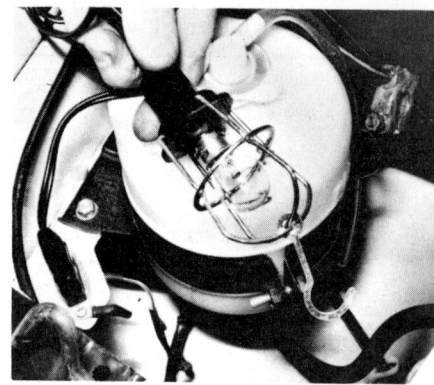
14.26 Inspection light

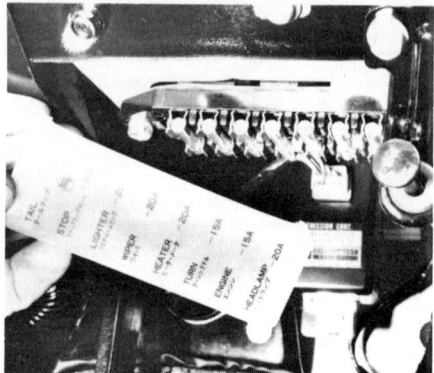
15.2 Fusebox location

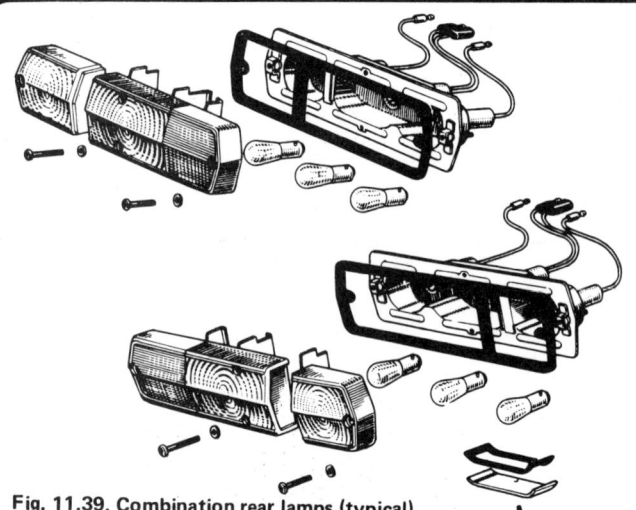

Fig. 11.39. Combination rear lamps (typical)

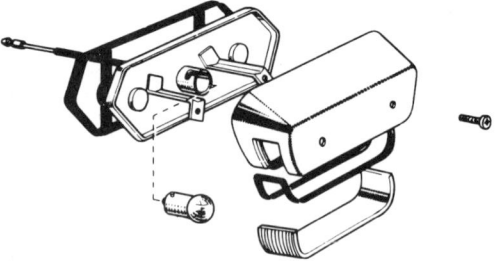

Fig. 11.40. License plate light (typical)

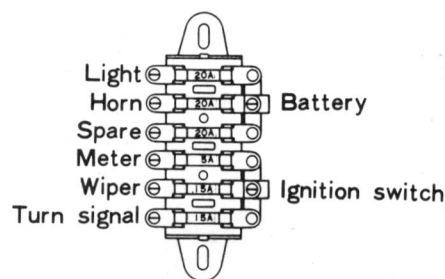

Fig. 11.41. Fuses - typical for 1968/72 models

20-A Lighting, combination meter light, and the interior light circuits (except the stoplights)
20-A Horn, cigarette lighter and stoplight circuits
20-A Spare
5-A   Fuel, temperature, and oil pressure gauge circuits
15-A Wiper and washer, and heater
15-A Turn signal lights, and charging circuits

Fig. 11.42. Fuses - typical for 1973/74 models

1973
1   Tail meter PL
15-A Instrument panel lights, parking lights, side marker lights, tail lights and license plate lights
2   Horn stop
20-A Stop lights, horns and hazard warning lights
3   Lighter room
20-A Cigarette lighter, interior light and inspection light socket
4   Wiper, radio
20-A Radio, windshield wiper and washer
5   Heater gauge
20-A Back-up lights, heater (air conditioner), blower and gauges
6   Turn gen.
15-A Alternator regulator (IG terminal), turn signal lights, vacuum switching valve and spark control computor
7   Ig. coil
15-A Ignition coil + terminal
8   Headlamp
20-A Headlights

1974
1   Tail meter PL
15-A Instrument panel lights, parking lights, side marker lights, tail lights and license plate lights
2   Horn stop
20-A Stop lights, horns and hazard warning lights
3   Lighter room
20-A Cigarette lighter, interior light and inspection light socket
4   Wiper, radio
20-A Radio, windshield wiper and washer
5   Heater gauge
20-A Back-up lights, heater (air conditioner), blower and gauges, vacuum switching valve and spark control computor
6   Turn gen.
15-A Alternator regulator (IG terminal), turn signal lights
7   IG. coil
15-A Ignition coil + terminal
8   Headlamp
20-A Headlights

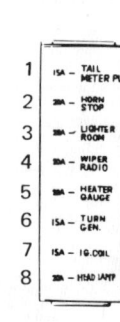
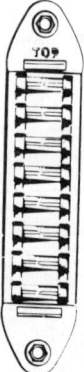

parts (where applicable) (photo).
22 The lamps are attached to the body by nuts and washers, or screws. Removal is straightforward.

Reflector lenses
23 On some models separate rear reflectors are used. To remove the reflector lens, remove the two screws, and take off the lens and bezel. If necessary, remove the spring clips to release the lens (photo).
24 If necessary, the reflector body can be removed after the nuts, spring washers and flat washers have been taken off.

Interior light
25 Some models have an interior light. this may be a dome type, where the lens is rotated counter-clockwise to remove it, or an oblong type. The lens of the oblong type is either retained by two screws, or can be removed by squeezing the sides of the lens and pulling (photo).

Inspection light
26 For certain models in the range, an inspection light is supplied. This has an extension lead which plugs into a socket at the front right-hand side of the engine compartment. (FJ 55 models) or in the glovebox (FJ 40 series models). Bulb renewal is straightforward after the wire bulb guard has been removed (photo).

15 Fuses and fusible link

1 A fusible link is installed on later models. This is an 'in-line' link and when installed will be found in the main supply lead (not starter motor lead) from the battery positive terminal.
2 The location of the fusebox varies according to the particular vehicle, but is normally beneath the instrument panel or on the sidewall of the footwell area. The fusebox has a transparent plastic cover, with the fuse ratings and protected circuits marked (photo).
3 Fuses normally last for many years and will only need replacing if blown (burned out). On rare occasions a fuse may blow for no apparent reason, and a replacement will be all that is required. However, it can normally be assumed that there is a fault in the circuit, and this must be rectified without delay. Never be tempted to install a fuse of a higher rating if one blows, as this may well cause the associated circuit or component(s) to be overlooked, which will then cause much more serious damage and possibly create a fire hazard.
4 Vehicles which have a power operated tail-gate window also have a circuit breaker which protects the vehicle wiring in the case of an electrical overload. The circuit breaker is mounted alongside the fusebox.

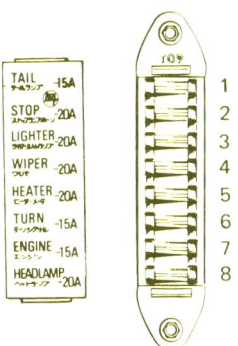

Fig. 11.43. Fuses - typical for 1975/76 models

1 (15-A) Instrument panel lights, parking lights, tail lights and license plate lights
2 (20-A) Stop lights, horns and hazard warning lights
3 (20-A) Cigarette lighter, interior light and inspection light socket
4 (20-A) Radio, windshield wiper and washer
5 (20-A) Back-up lights, heater blower, gauges and front drive system
6 (15-A) Turn signal lights
7 (15-A) Alternator regulator (IG terminal)
8 (20-A) Headlights (USA models)

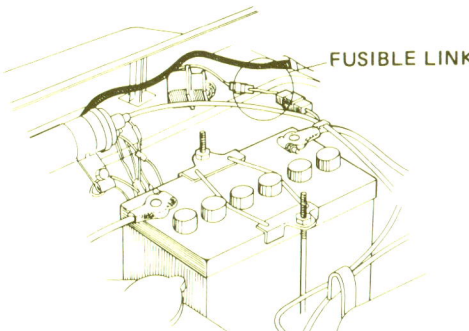

Fig. 11.44. Location of fusible link - typical

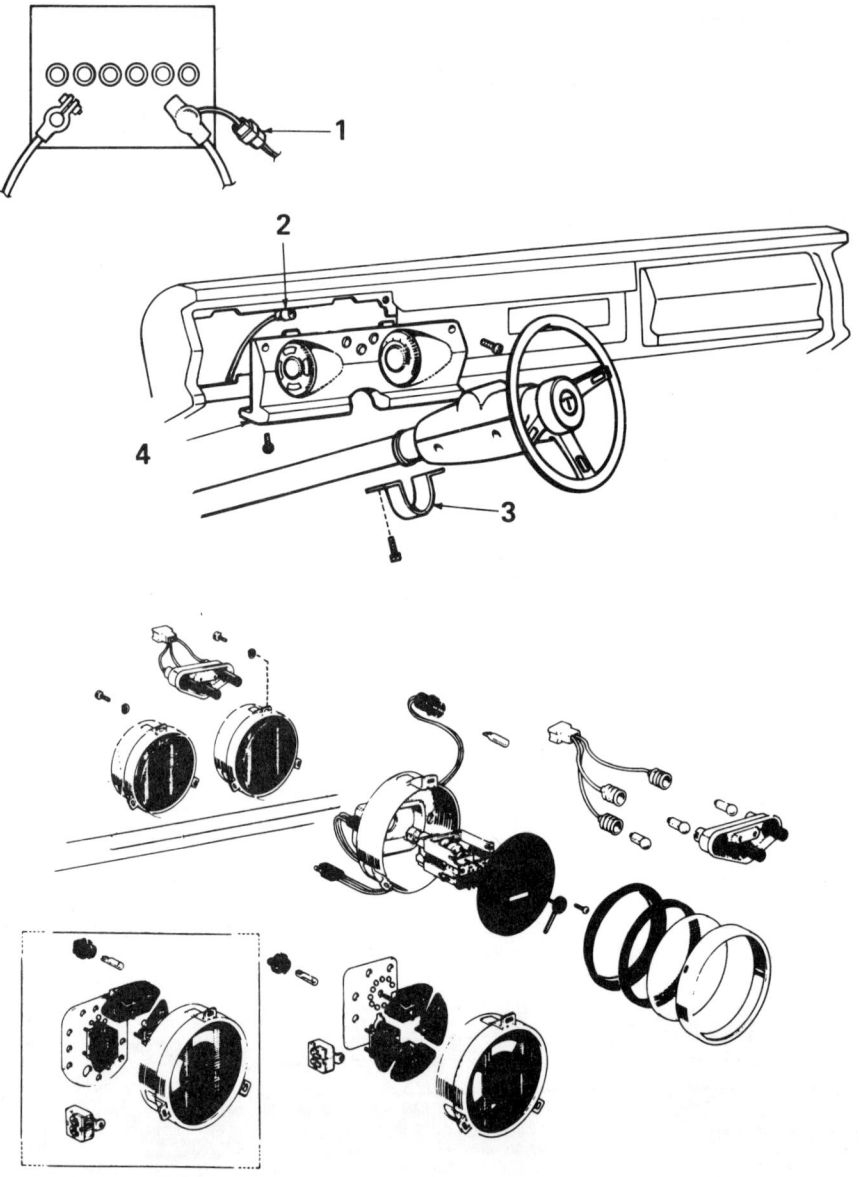

Fig. 11.45. Removal sequence for FJ55 instrument panel combination meter

1 Fusible link (disconnect, or detach lead)
2 Speedometer cable
3 Bracket
4 Combination meter

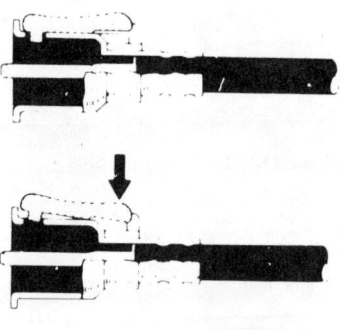

Fig. 11.46. Sectional view of speedometer cable and fittings

Chapter 11/Electrical system

16 Instrument panel combination meter: removal and installation

FJ 55 Series

1 Initially, remove the battery ground lead or disconnect the main feed line at the fusible link.
2 Either remove the steering column nacelle or loosen the steering column bracket bolts for additional clearances.
3 Remove the panel retaining screws and draw the combination meter forward so that the speedometer cable can be detached. This is retained by a plastic clip which is depressed to release (photo).
4 Draw the combination meter further away, and detach the electrical leads.
5 It will be noted that most of the panel bulbs are attached to the panel itself. These either pull out complete with the bulb holders, or can be pressed and turned to remove them. The remaining bulbs are connected to the instrument wiring loom and are not actually removed with the instrument (photos).
6 If the need ever arises, the two major instruments can be removed by taking out the attaching screws and/or nuts.
7 Installation is the reverse of the removal procedure, but take care that electrical leads are not trapped.

FJ40 Series

8 Initially, remove the battery ground lead or disconnect the main feed line at the fusible link.
9 From behind the instrument panel, press the retaining clip on the speedometer cable end fitting then detach the cable.
10 Remove the retaining screws and withdraw the combination meter so that the bulbs and wiring connectors can be detached.
11 If necessary, the instruments can be removed from the meter assembly after the screws have been removed. Where it is necessary to detach electrical leads, make a note of their positions before they are removed.
12 Installation is the reverse of the removal procedure, but take care that electrical leads are not trapped.

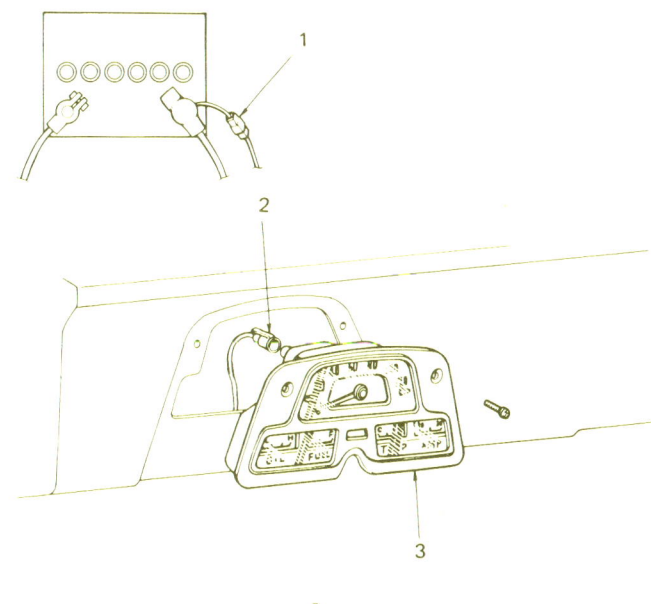

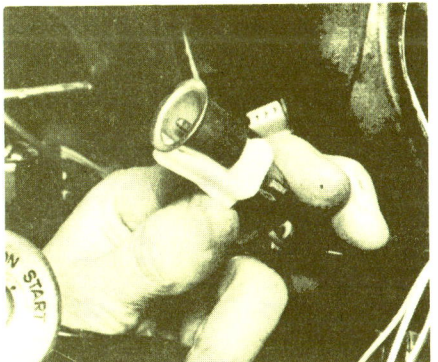

16.3 Speedometer cable retaining clip

Fig. 11.47. Removal sequence for FJ40 series instrument panel combination meter

1 Fusible link (disconnect, or detach lead
2 Speedometer cable
3 Combination meter

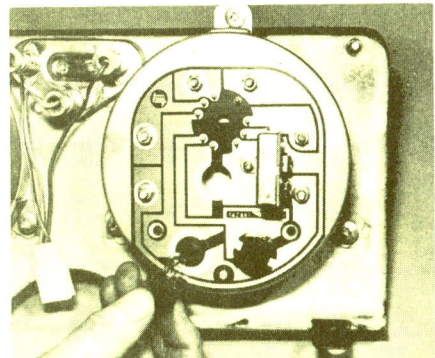

16.5a Typical panel light bulb arrangements

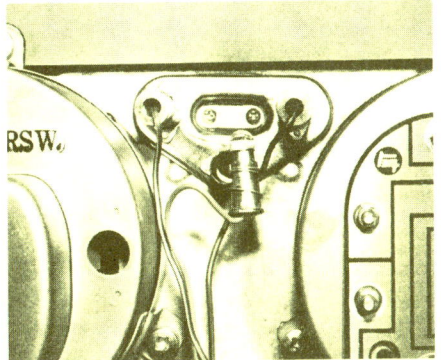

16.5b Typical panel light bulb arrangements

16.5c Instrument lights in wiring loom connectors

17 Combination meter instruments and sender units - serviceability checks

Fuel gauge

1 Detach the fuel gauge sender lead at the in-line connector, then ground the lead thru a 3.4W bulb. If the gauge is working satisfactorily, the bulb should light initially, then start to flash after a few seconds, and the gauge needle should deflect.

2 If the gauge is not operating satisfactorily, remove the combination meter as described in Section 16, then connect the multi-pin connector and turn on the ignition switch. Check that the battery voltage is reaching the instrument panel by measuring between terminal A (+) and ground (–) (See Fig. 11.50). If this is satisfactory, check that the voltage at terminal A is fluctuating between 2 and 7 volts after a few seconds of operation. If no fluctuating voltage is obtained, switch off the ignition and measure the resistance between terminals B and C; this should be 25 ohms approx.

Fuel gauge sender unit

3 To remove the sender unit, pull back the floor covering in the rear of the vehicle (where applicable) and remove the inspection panel.
4 Disconnect the wiring connector from the sender unit (photo).
5 Remove the retaining screws and lift out the sender unit. If the gasket is damaged, a replacement will be needed for installation.
6 Using an ohmmeter, check the resistance of the sender unit between the unit body and terminal. This should vary between 17 ± 2.1 ohms at the lowest float setting; the resistance change should be smooth thru-out the range of travel.
7 Installation of the sender unit is the reverse of the removal procedure.

Water temperature gauge

8 The procedure for checking the water temperature gauge is identical to that given previously in this Section for the fuel gauge, except that the lead is detached from the sender unit, which is on the engine cylinder head at the left-hand side towards the rear. (photo). Refer to Fig. 11.51 for the electrical connections.

Temperature gauge sender unit

9 Detach the sender unit lead, then use an ohmmeter connected between the sender unit terminal and body to check the resistance. Typical resistance values are as follows, according to the water temperature.

Temperature °C/°F	Resistance (ohms)
60/140	90
80/176	50
100/212	27
105/221	23

Oil pressure gauge

10 Detach the oil pressure gauge sender lead, then ground it thru a 3.4W bulb. If the gauge is working satisfactorily, the bulb should light and the gauge needle should deflect (photo).
11 If the gauge is not operating satisfactorily, remove the combination meter as described in Section 16, then connect the multi-pin connector and turn on the ignition switch. Check that the battery voltage is reaching the instrument panel by measuring between terminal A (+) and ground (–) (see Fig. 11.52). If no voltage is obtained, switch off the ignition and measure the resistance between terminals A and B, this should be 44 ohms approx.

Oil pressure gauge sender unit

12 Detach the lead from the sender unit, then connect a lead from the battery positive terminal thru a 3.4W bulb to the sender unit terminal. With the engine not running, the bulb should be extinguished, but should flash when the engine is running. The speed of flashing may alter a little with engine speed, and the bulb may illuminate momentarily after the engine has stopped.

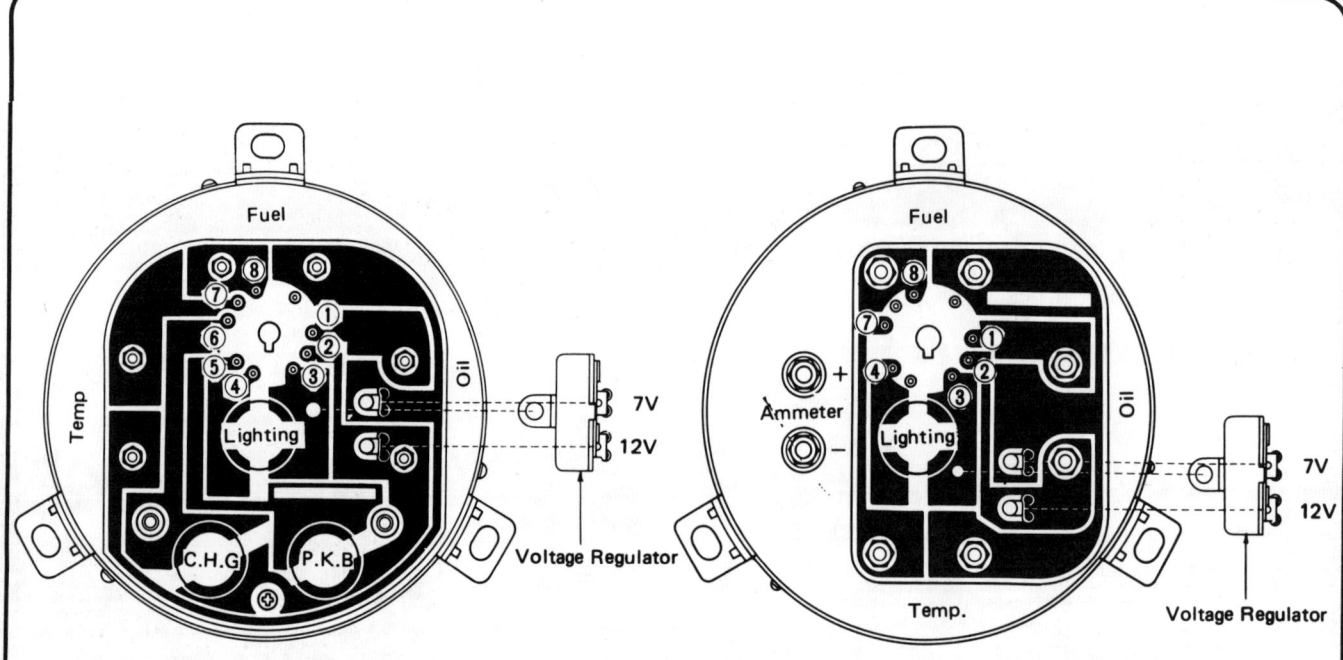

Fig. 11.48. Combination meter connections - FJ55 models

Left   Charge warning light type
1 Pressure gauge/sender unit
2 From ignition switch
3 Ground
4 Meter pilot light/light switch

Right   Ammeter type
5 Brake light/brake light switches
6 Charge light/alternator light
7 Temperature gauge/sender unit
8 Fuel gauge/sender unit

17.4 Fuel gauge sender unit

17.8 Water temperature gauge sender unit. Until February 1976, this was on the left side of the cylinder block, but later models had the sender unit on the oil filter housing

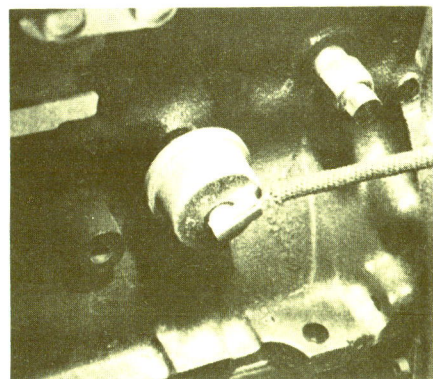

17.10 Oil pressure gauge sender unit

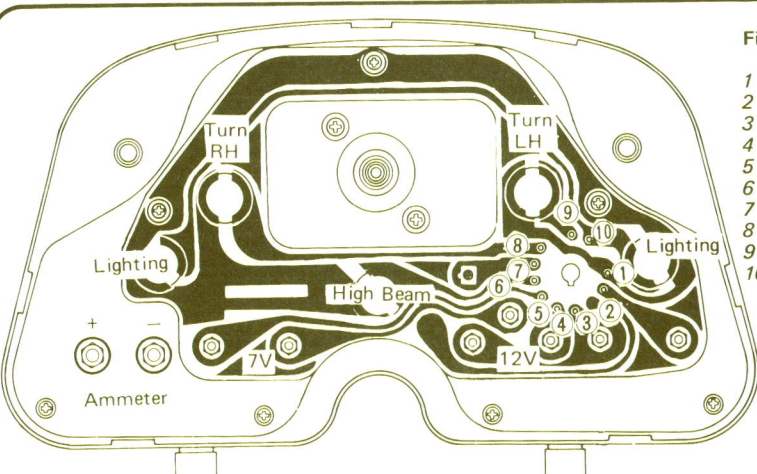

Fig. 11.49. Combination meter connections FJ40 series models

1. Ground
2. Oil pressure gauge/sender unit
3. From ignition switch
4. Fuel gauge/sender unit
5. Temperature gauge/sender unit
6. High beam indicator/dimmer switch
7. Reed switch/emission control computer (USA and ECE)
8. RH turn signal indicator/switch
9. LH turn signal indicator/switch
10. Meter pilot light/switch

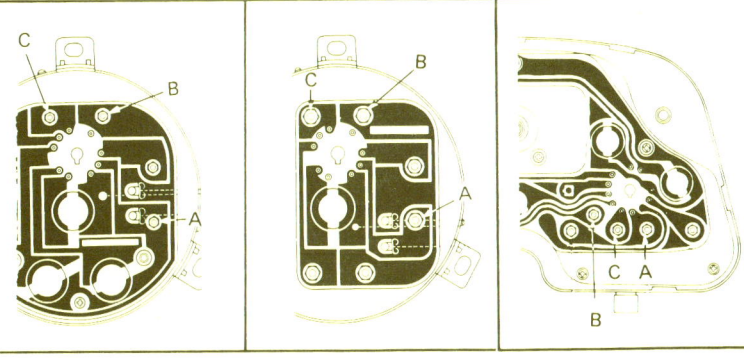

Fig. 11.50. Terminal connections for fuel gauge checks

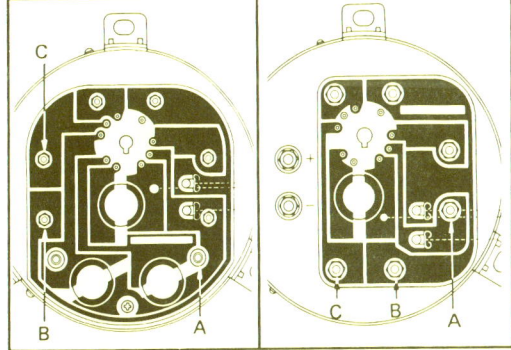

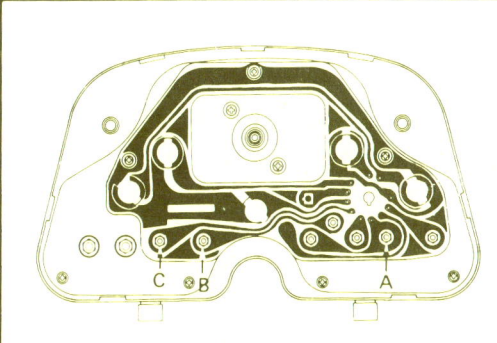

Fig. 11.51. Terminal connections for water temperature gauge checks

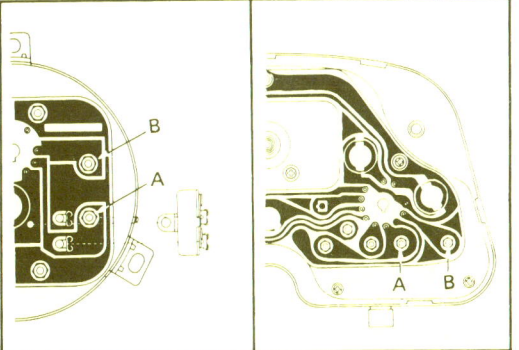

Fig. 11.52. Terminal connections for oil pressure gauge checks

18 Switches and associated controls - general

Ignition switch and steering lock (late models) - removal and installation

1 Remove the retaining screws, and detach the steering column bracket.
2 Remove the retaining screws, and detach the steering column contact ring upper housing (nacelle).
3 Remove the retaining screw, and detach the ignition switch assembly from the steering lock.
4 To remove the steering lock barrel, select the ACC position then, with the key still in position, use a stiff wire pushed thru the access hole in the lock housing. This will release the locking pin to allow the lock barrel to be pulled out.
5 Installation is the reverse of the removal procedure. Take care to align the locking pin with the access hole, and the concave and convex parts of the lock barrel and switch.

Ignition switch (early FJ 55 models) - removal and installation

6 Using a suitable small C-wrench or similar item, unscrew the switch locking ring from the instrument panel.
7 Remove the switch and detach the electrical connector.
8 Installation is the reverse of the removal procedure.

Ignition switch (early FJ 40 Series models) - removal and installation

9 Detach the wires from the switch terminals, noting their installed positions to prevent mix-up.
10 Unscrew the switch retaining ring using pliers, then withdraw the switch from behind the panel.
11 Installation is the reverse of the removal procedure.

Reverse light switch (remotely mounted type) - removal and installation

12 Disconnect the switch leads, then remove the retaining screw to release the switch.
13 Installation is the reverse of the removal procedure.

Reverse light switch (transmission mounted type) - removal and installation

14 Remove the retaining screws and lift out the flow panel from around the transmission.
15 Detach the switch leads and unscrew the switch from the rear of the transmission (photo).
16 Installation is the reverse of the removal procedure.

Steering column mounted switches (FJ55 models) - removal and installation

17 Remove the steering wheel (refer to Chapter 9 if necessary).
18 Detach the wiring connector, then remove the three screws to release the switch assembly.
19 Installation is the reverse of the removal procedure.

Steering column mounted switches (FJ 40 Series models) - removal and installation

20 Remove the plate from the instrument panel, then remove the screw from the clamp for the lower switch.
21 Open the clamp so that the lower switch and intermediate rod can be removed.
22 Remove the control lever pin, then the control lever halfway out of the control shaft.
23 Remove the steering wheel (refer to Chapter 9 if necessary).
24 Remove the upper switch clamp screw, then pull the upper part of the switch from the steering post and upper bracket shaft.
25 Turn the upper bracket shaft counter-clockwise to remove it from the upper bracket.
26 Installation is the reverse of the removal procedure

Windshield wiper and light switches (FJ 55 models) - removal and installation

27 Loosen the locking screw and take off the switch knob.
28 Using a suitable tool, unscrew the switch locking ring.
29 Disconnect the wiring connector and remove the switch.
30 Installation is the reverse of the removal procedure.

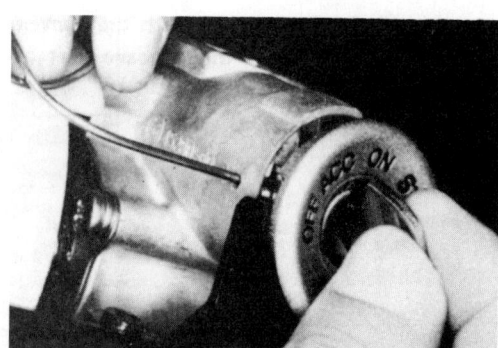

Fig. 11.53. Using a stiff wire to release the locking pin

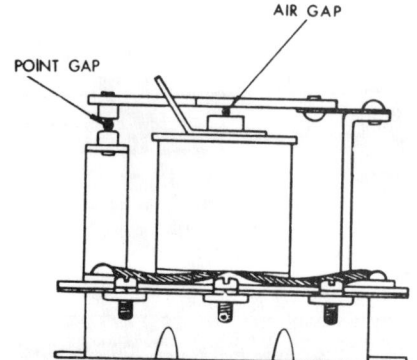

Fig. 11.54. Horn adjustment

18.15 Reverse light switch location

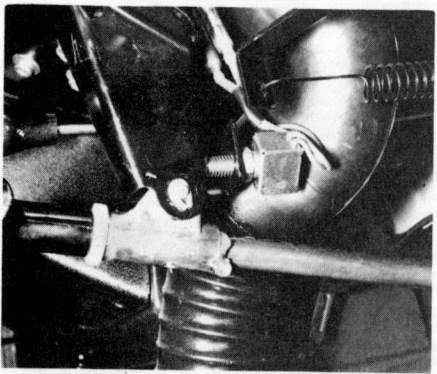

18.41 Parking brake light switch location

Windshield wiper and light switches (FJ 40 Series models) - removal and installation

31 Loosen the locking screw and remove the switch knob.
32 Unscrew the switch retaining ring, then withdraw the switch from the rear of the panel.
33 Detach the switch wires, noting their installed positions to avoid mix-up.
34 Installation is the reverse of the removal procedure.

Brake light (stop light) switch - removal and installation

35 Loosen the locknut, then unscrew the switch from the pedal bracket by turning it anticlockwise.
36 Disconnect the wires from the switch terminals.
37 Installation is the reverse of the removal procedure; adjust the switch so that it operates the brake lights as the brake pedal is depressed.

Floor mounted headlight dimmer (dip) switch - removal and installation

38 Remove the two switch attaching bolts, then remove the switch from the rear of the toe-board.
39 Detach the switch wires, noting their installed positions to prevent mix-up.
40 Installation is the reverse of the removal procedure.

Parking brake switch - removal and installation

41 This switch is generally similar to the brake light switch - see paragraph 35 thru 37 (photo).

Hazard switch - removal and installation

42 This switch is generally similar to the other fascia mounted switches - see paragraph 27 thru 34.

Front drive vacuum control switch - removal and installation

43 This switch is generally similar to the other fascia mounted switches - see paragraph 27 thru 34.

Front drive vacuum control indicator light switch - removal and installation

44 This switch is mounted on the diaphragm cylinder of the front drive vacuum control. For removal and installation details, refer to the procedure given in paragraphs 14 thru 16.

Front drive vacuum control transfer switch - removal and installation

45 This switch is mounted on the side of the transfer gear housing. For removal and installation details, refer to the procedure in paragraphs 14 thru 16.

19 Turn signal and hazard warning flashers - general

1 Refer to the previous Section for the switch removal procedures.
2 Several different arrangements have been used on the Land Cruiser models. The circuit connections can be seen on the wiring diagrams at the end of the Chapter.
3 The flasher unit is mounted behind the fascia panel, but the exact position varies with the different vehicle types.

20 Horn - general

Horn button(s) - removal and installation

1 Remove the three attaching screws from behind the steering wheel and take off the steering wheel pad.
2 Remove the horn button cover screw from behind the steering wheel and take off the button cover.
3 Remove the horn button attaching screw and take out the horn button.
4 Installation is the reverse of the removal procedure.

Horn - removal and installation

5 This is a straightforward procedure after the horn leads have been disconnected.
6 Different types of horn have been used on Land Cruiser models, but they are generally similar for the purpose of adjustment. For correct adjustment, an air gap of 0.016 in (0.4 mm) and a point gap of 0.032 in (0.8 mm) should be set.

Horn relay

7 In the event of malfunction of the horn, the most likely cause is the horn relay. The contact points can become burnt after a long period in service, and may be dressed with a fine file or sandpaper if necessary.

21 Windshield wiper and washer

Windshield wiper blades - renewal

1 On most models, the windshield wiper blades are retained by a small spring clip on the end of the wiper arm. When the spring clip is depressed, the wiper blade can be pulled off and a replacement installed (photo).
2 Some models may have wiper blades attached to the wiper arms by a simple screw fitting. Removal of the blades is straightforward.

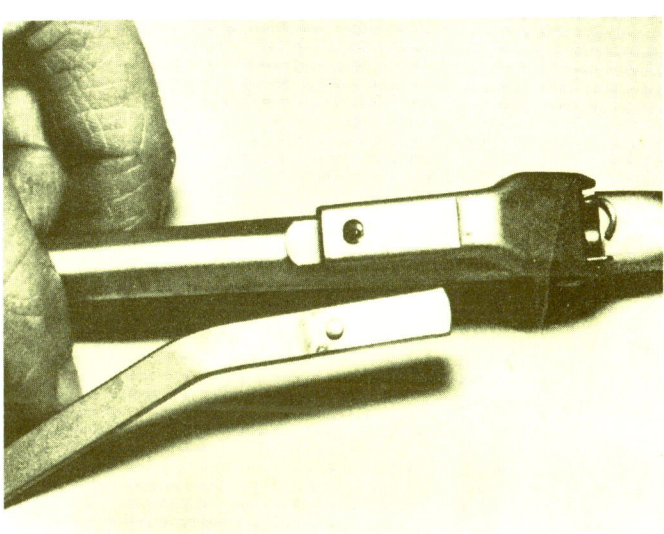

21.1 Wiper blade and arm attachment - typical

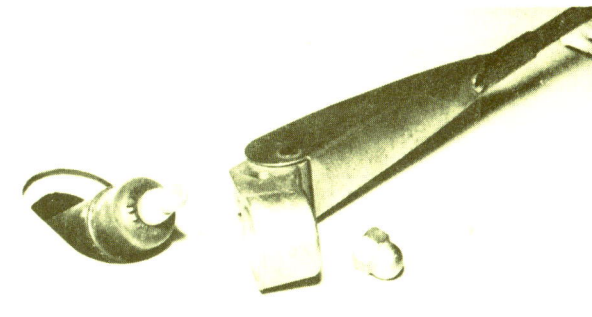

21.3 Wiper arm attachment - typical

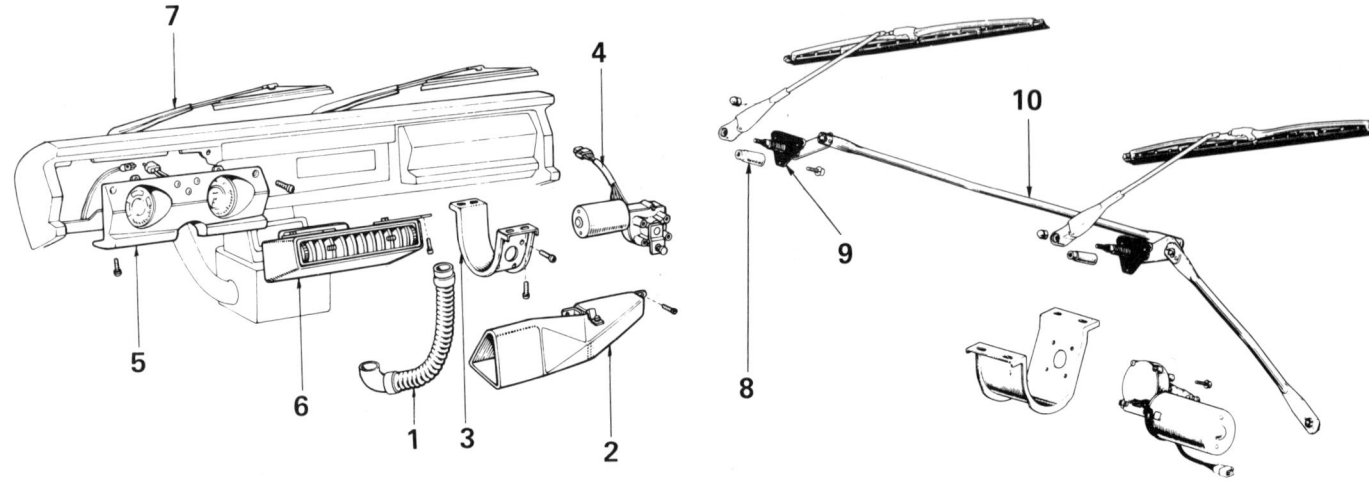

Fig. 11.55. Removal sequence for wiper motor and linkage (FJ55 models)

1 Defroster hose
2 Heater air duct
3 Wiper bracket
4 Wiper motor
5 Combination meter
6 Ventilation louver
7 Wiper blade
8 Wiper pivot cap
9 Wiper pivot (combination meter side)
10 Wiper link

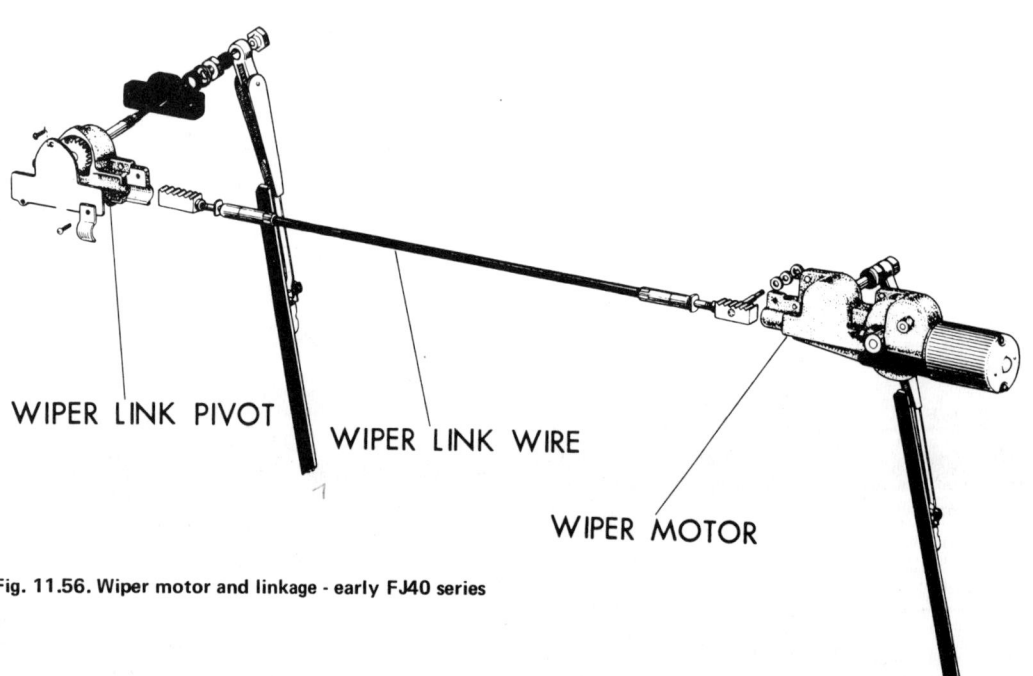

Fig. 11.56. Wiper motor and linkage - early FJ40 series

Windshield wiper arms - removal and installation

3 The wiper arms engage on splines on the pivots, which permit them to be repositioned, as necessary, to obtain the correct parking position. They are either retained by a nut, a spring clip, or are simply pulled off when the arm is pulled away from the windshield, according to the vehicle model (photo).

Wiper motor and linkage (FJ 55 models) - removal and installation

4 Detach the heater defrost hose and the heater air duct (where applicable).
5 Detach the wiper link from the motor, then remove the four retaining bolts and take off the wiper motor and bracket.
6 Where necessary, detach the motor from the bracket (four screws).
7 Remove the combination meter - refer to Section 16 for further information.
8 Remove the retaining screws and pull away the ventilation lever.
9 Remove the wiper arms (paragraph 3).
10 Remove the wiper pivot cap.

11 From inside the vehicle, remove the retaining screws and wiper pivot. The wiper link can now be detached.
12 Installation is the reverse of the removal procedure.

Wiper motor and linkage (early FJ 40 Series models) - removal and installation

13 Remove the wiper arm and blade (paragraph 3).
14 Remove the pivot housing and plate from the pivot housing, then detach the link wire.
15 Remove the link wire from the wiper motor, then remove the wiper motor drive shaft assembly.
16 Remove the wiper motor gear plate and wire clamp, then remove the link wire from the gear housing.
17 Installation is the reverse of the removal procedure.

Wiper motor and linkage (later FJ 40 Series models) - removal procedure

18 Remove the wiper motor cover from the base of the windshield (four screws).

Chapter 11/Electrical system

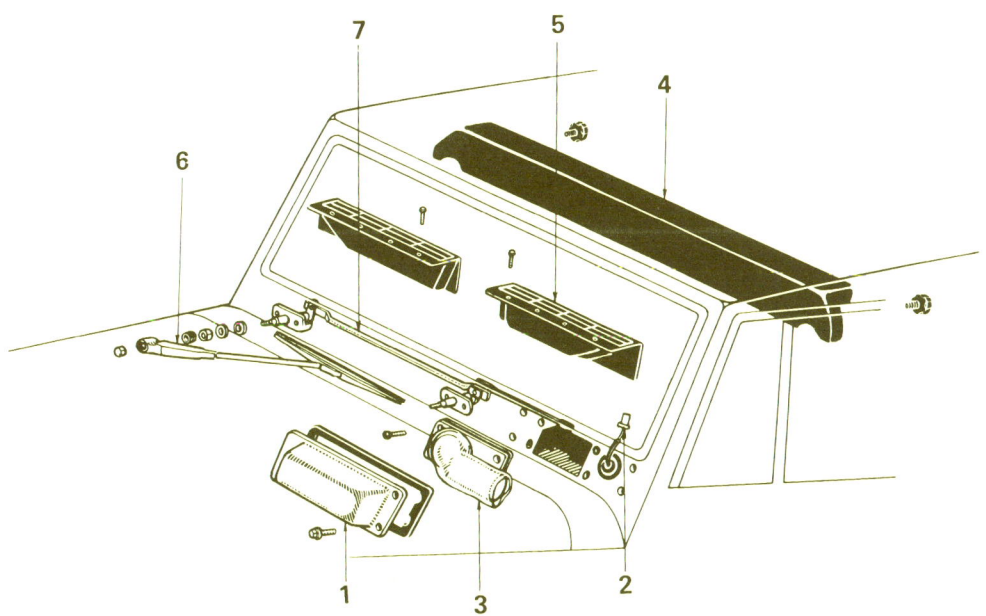

Fig. 11.57. Removal sequence for wiper motor and linkage (later FJ40 series)

1 Wiper motor cover
2 Wiring harness connector
3 Wiper motor
4 Safety pad
5 Defroster nozzle
6 Wiper arm
7 Wiper link

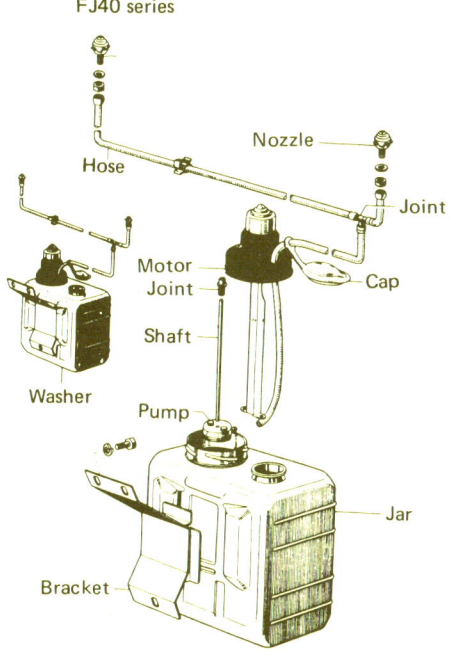 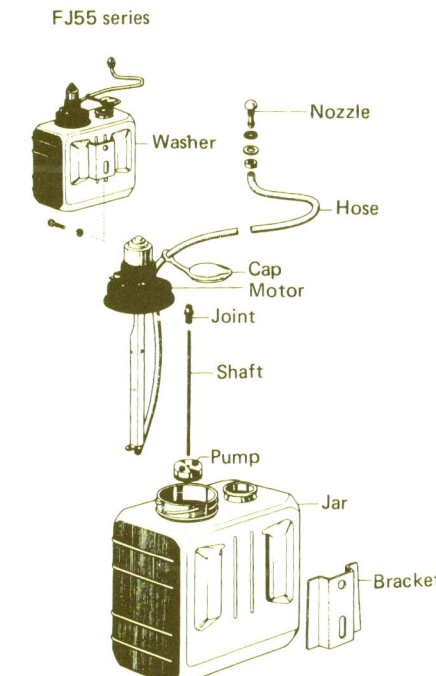

Fig. 11.58. Typical windshield washer arrangement

19 Disconnect the harness connector to the wiper motor.
20 Disconnect the wiper motor link and then remove the motor.
21 Remove the fascia safety pad.
22 Position the wiper arm upward, then lift the defroster nozzles upward and to the side of the vehicle to remove them.
23 Remove the wiper arms (see paragraph 3).
24 Remove the nuts and washers, and take out the wiper link.
25 Installation is the reverse of the removal procedure, ensure that the locating pips on the link pivot plates align with the indentations in the body panel.

Windshield washers
26 A windshield washer system is available as an accessory for early models, but later models have the system installed as standard equipment.
27 The components and system layout vary, but the illustrations show typical set-ups.
28 When installed as standard equipment, the system is operated by turning the wiper knob clockwise. **Note**: damage will occur if the washer is operated for longer than 30 seconds at a time, or where there is no fluid in the reservoir.

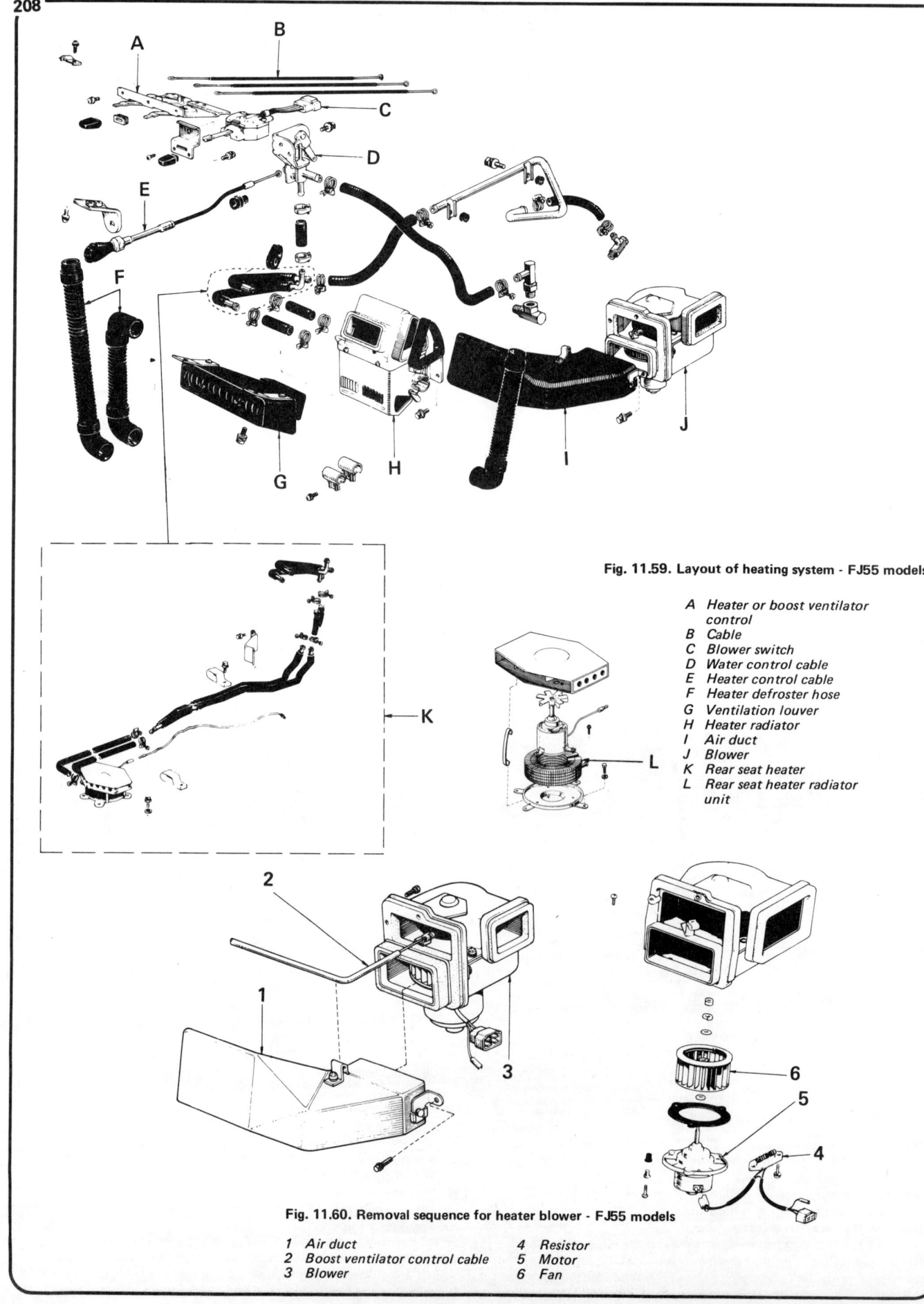

22 Heaters (FJ 55 models)

Main heater blower - removal and installation
1 Loosen the air duct clamp and remove the duct retaining bolts; remove the air duct.
2 Where applicable, detach the boost ventilator control cable at the heater blower end.
3 Disconnect the loom connector, then remove the three attaching bolts and lift away the blower assembly.
4 If necessary, the resistor, motor and fan can be separated; the parts are shown in Fig. 11.60.
5 Installation of the blower is the reverse of the removal procedure.

Heater radiator - removal and installation
6 Drain the cooling system (refer to Chapter 2 if necessary).
7 Remove the air duct (see paragraph 1).
8 Detach the defroster hoses.
9 Remove the two retaining bolts and take off the ventilation louver.
10 Place sheets of newspaper on the vehicle floor to catch any coolant, then remove the hoses from the heater radiator.
11 Detach the air inlet flap cable, then pry the defroster control cable from the bracket and detach it from the lever.
12 Remove the four retaining bolts and remove the heater radiator assembly.
13 If necessary, the radiator assembly can be dismantled by removing the top cover.
14 Installation is the reverse of the removal procedure. Refill the cooling system as described in Chapter 2.

Heater controls and switch
15 Remove the air duct (see paragraph 1).
16 Carefully pry off the retainers and detach the cables.
17 Remove the two retaining bolts and take off the ventilation louver.
18 Carefully pull off the heater control knobs; also remove the knob retaining clips.
19 Press upward the spring clip which retains the heater switch knob, then pull the knob off.
20 Remove the three screws, and remove the heater control complete with the control cable.
21 Remove the heater switch bracket (one screw from behind the bracket) and switch. If necessary remove the bracket from the switch.
22 Installation is the reverse of the removal procedure; check and adjust the cables if necessary for satisfactory operation.

Rear heater - removal and installation
23 Close the water valve to the heater.
24 Place sheets of newspaper around the heater to catch any coolant, then detach the hoses from the inlet and outlet.
25 Disconnect the wiring connector then remove the bolts and lift out the heater.
26 Installation is the reverse of the removal procedure. If necessary, top up the coolant system after running the engine and operating the rear heater for a short time.

23 Heaters (FJ 40 Series models)

1 Although the layout of the components is different, the general instructions given in the previous Section are applicable to these models.

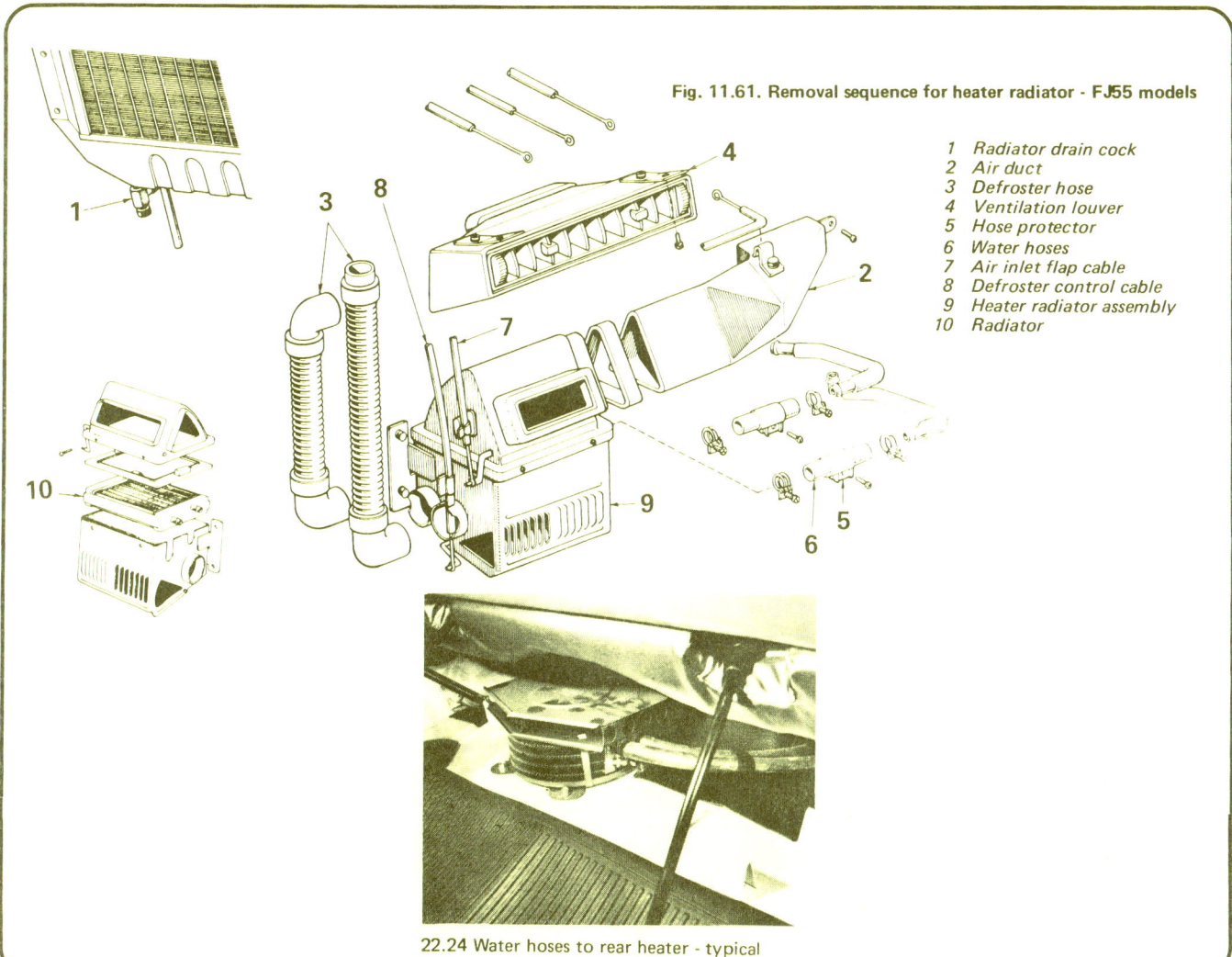

Fig. 11.61. Removal sequence for heater radiator - FJ55 models

1 Radiator drain cock
2 Air duct
3 Defroster hose
4 Ventilation louver
5 Hose protector
6 Water hoses
7 Air inlet flap cable
8 Defroster control cable
9 Heater radiator assembly
10 Radiator

22.24 Water hoses to rear heater - typical

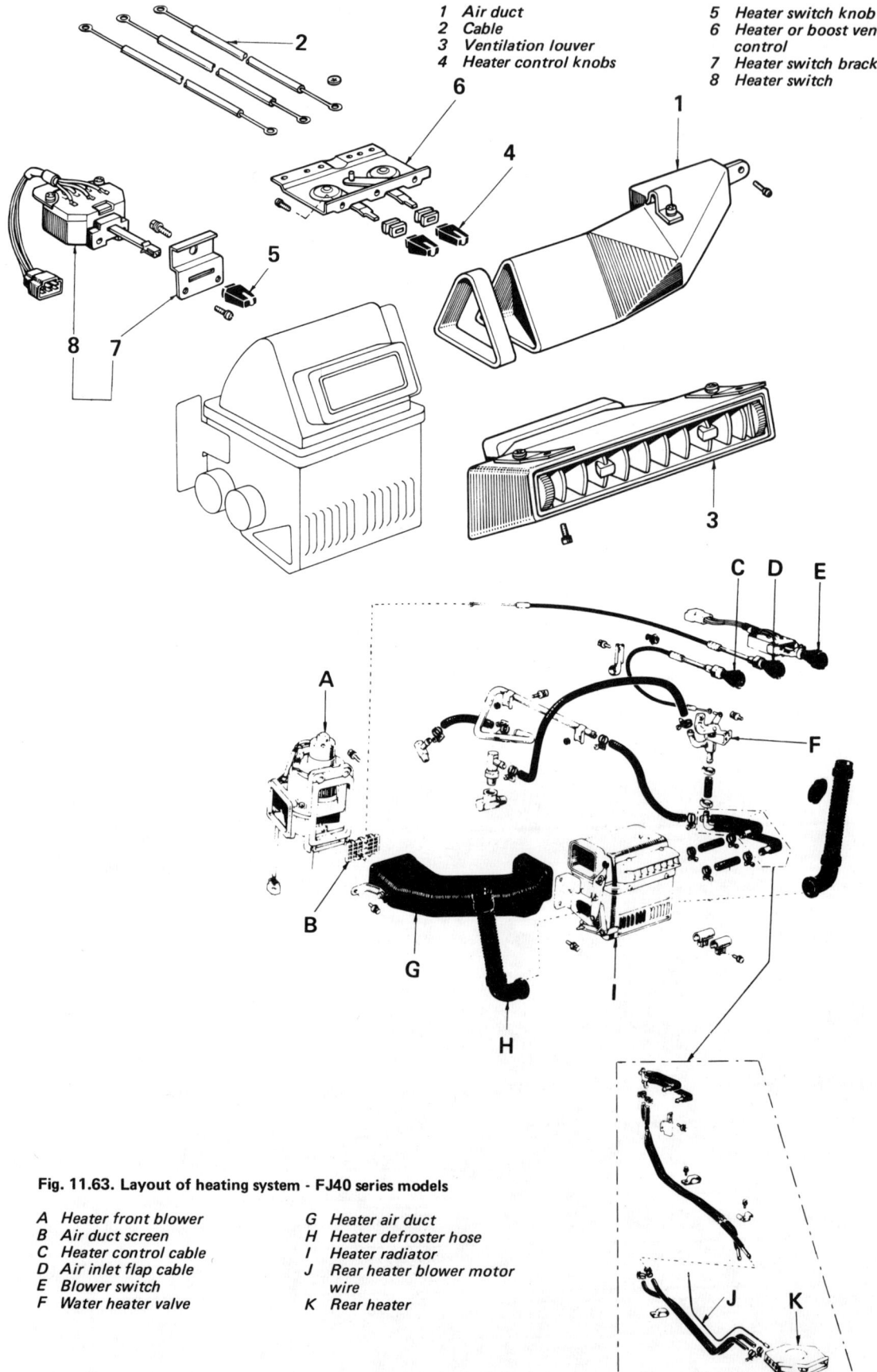

Fig. 11.62. Removal sequence for heater control and switch - FJ55 models

1 Air duct
2 Cable
3 Ventilation louver
4 Heater control knobs
5 Heater switch knob
6 Heater or boost ventilator control
7 Heater switch bracket
8 Heater switch

Fig. 11.63. Layout of heating system - FJ40 series models

A Heater front blower
B Air duct screen
C Heater control cable
D Air inlet flap cable
E Blower switch
F Water heater valve
G Heater air duct
H Heater defroster hose
I Heater radiator
J Rear heater blower motor wire
K Rear heater

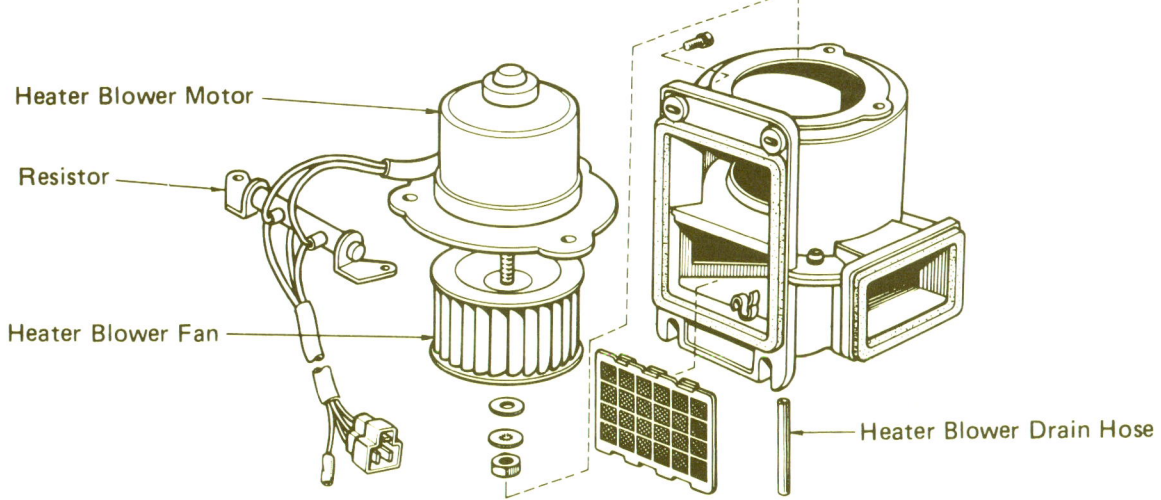

Fig. 11.64. Heater front blower - FJ40 series models

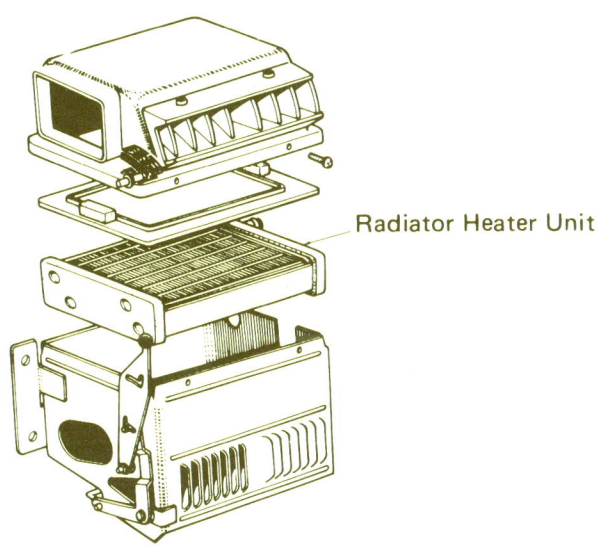

Fig. 11.65. Heater radiator - FJ40 series models

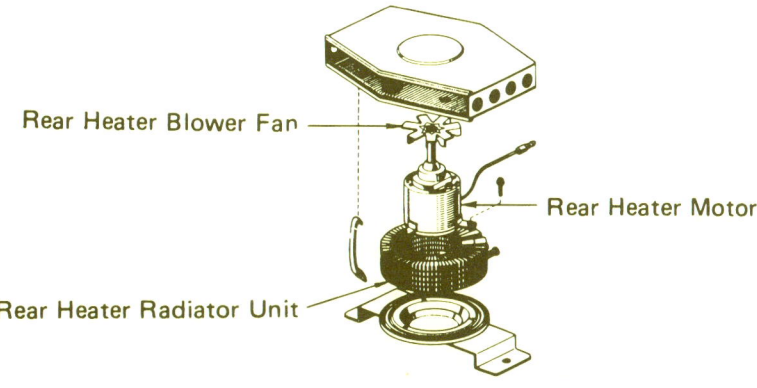

Fig. 11.66. Rear heater - FJ40 series models

212

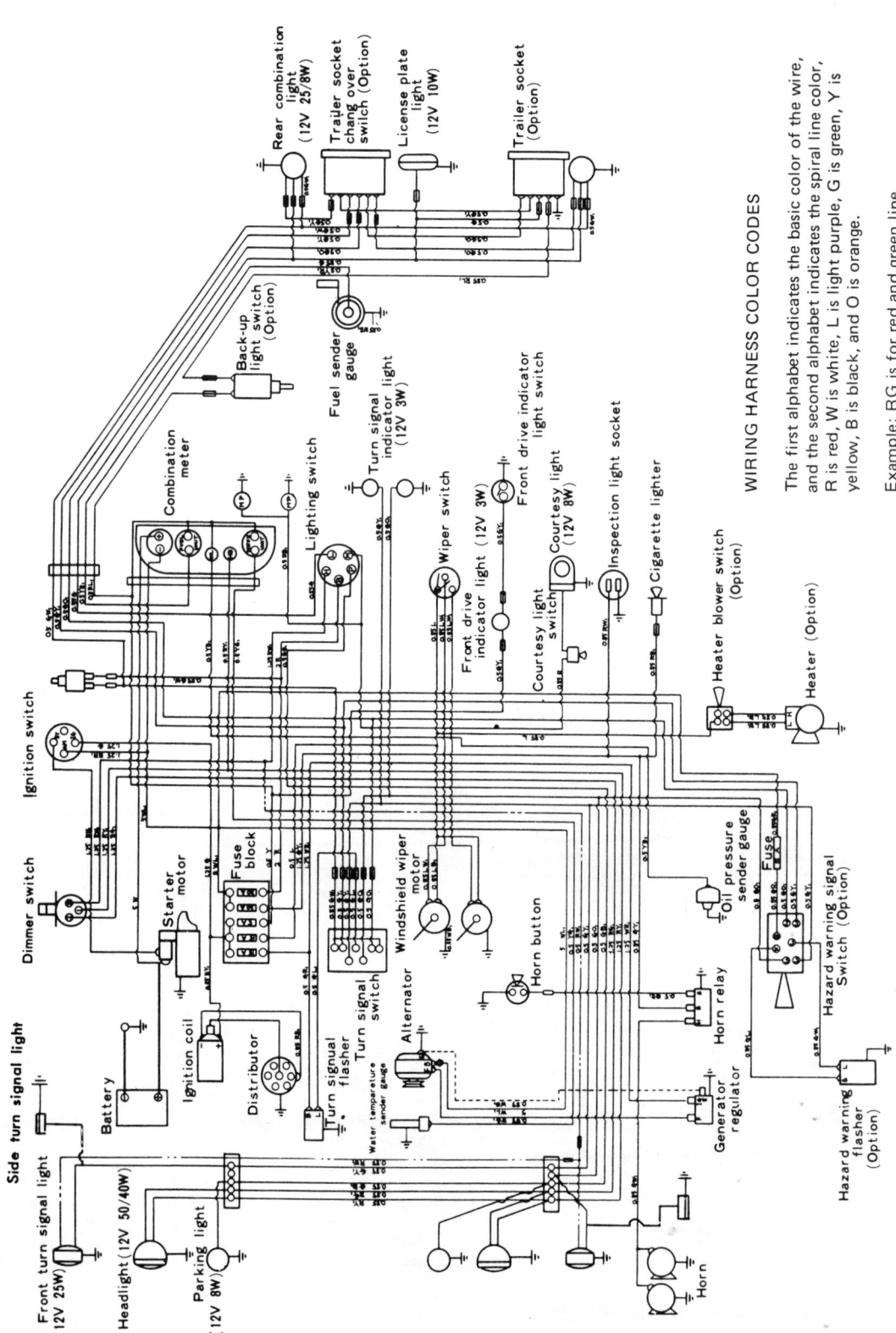

Fig. 11.67. Wiring diagram - FJ40 series, pre-1972

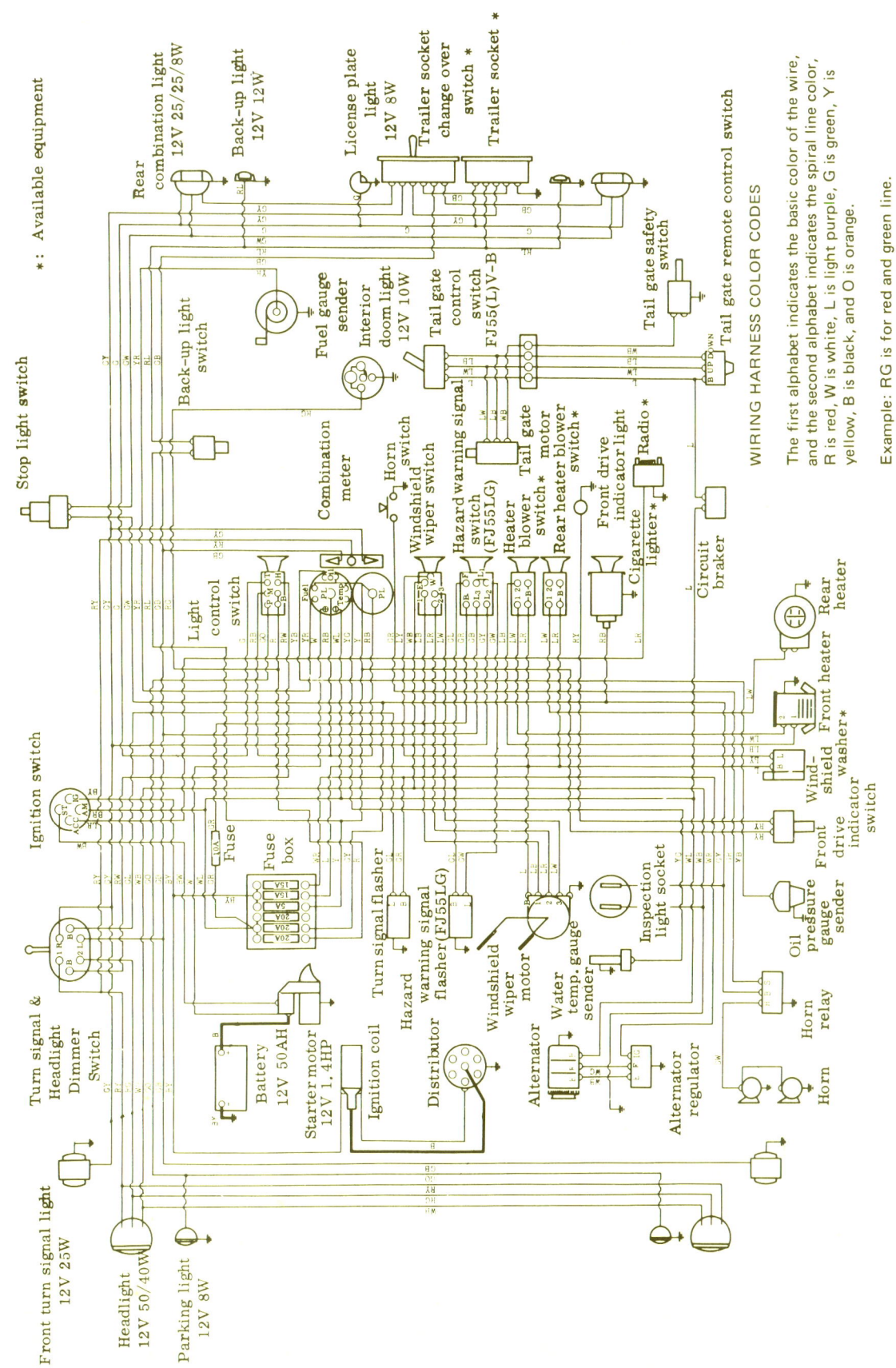

Fig. 11.68. Wiring diagram - FJ55 series, pre-1972 (early)

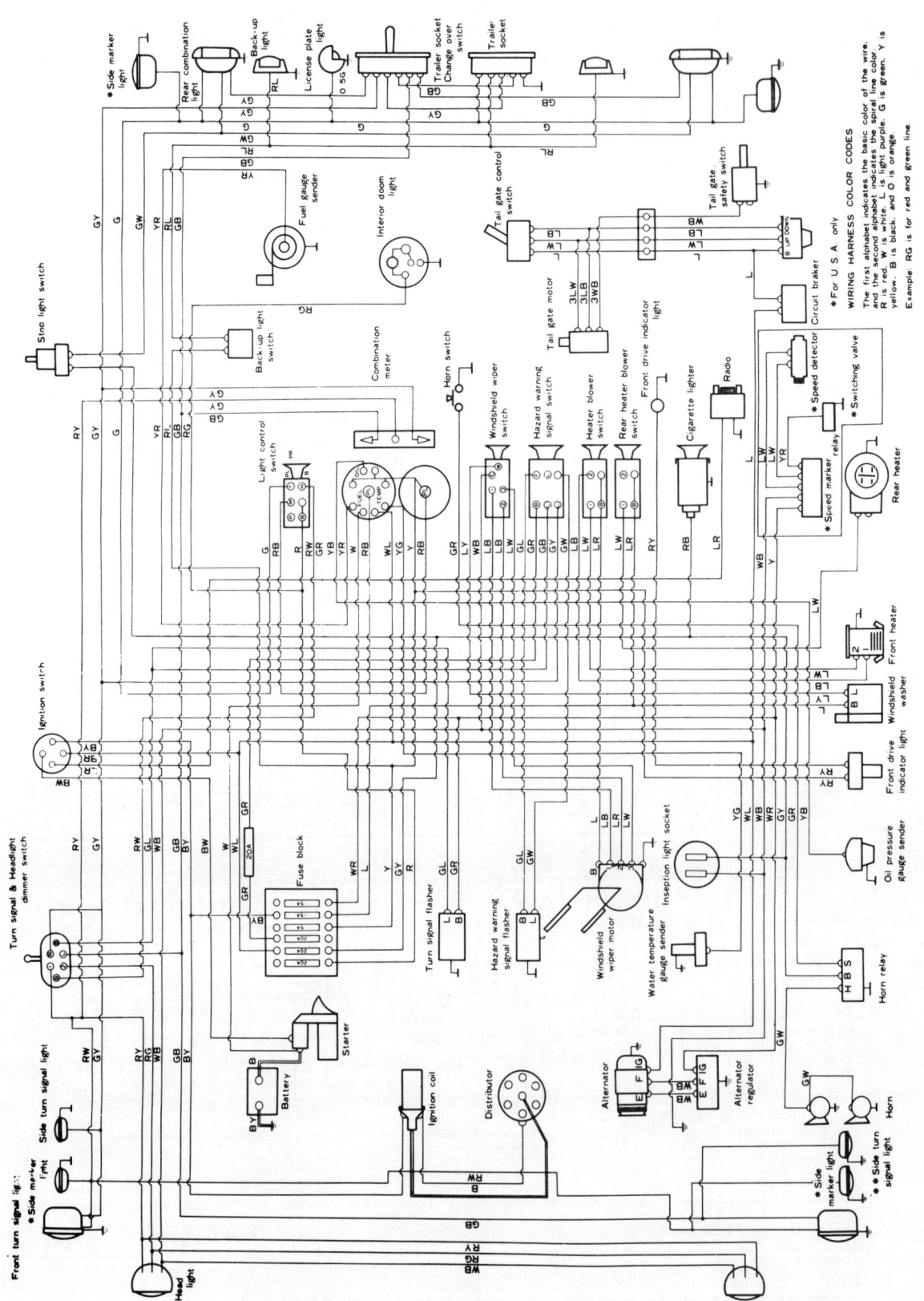

Fig. 11.69. Wiring diagram - FJ55 series, pre-1972 (late)

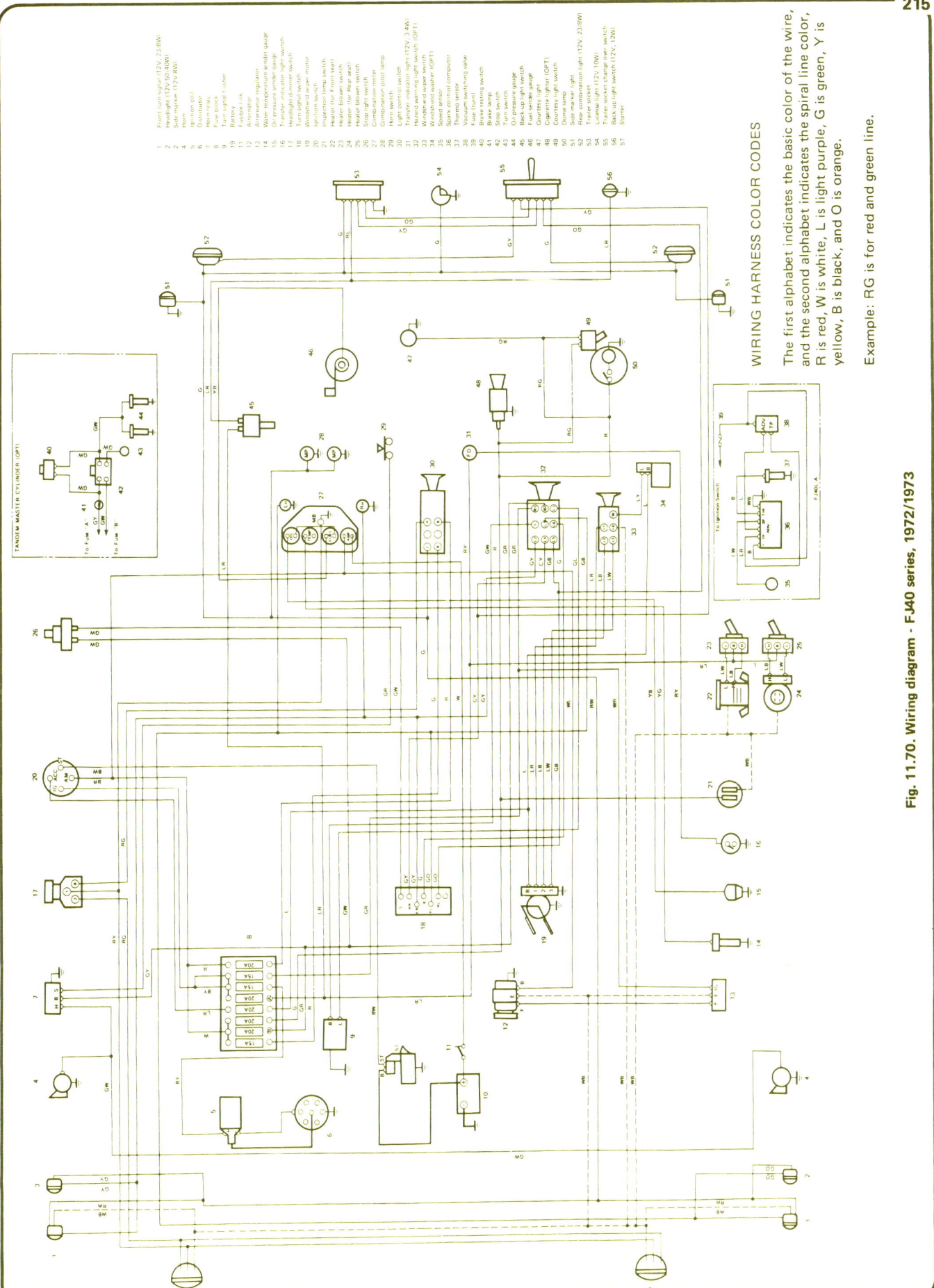

Fig. 11.70. Wiring diagram - FJ40 series, 1972/1973

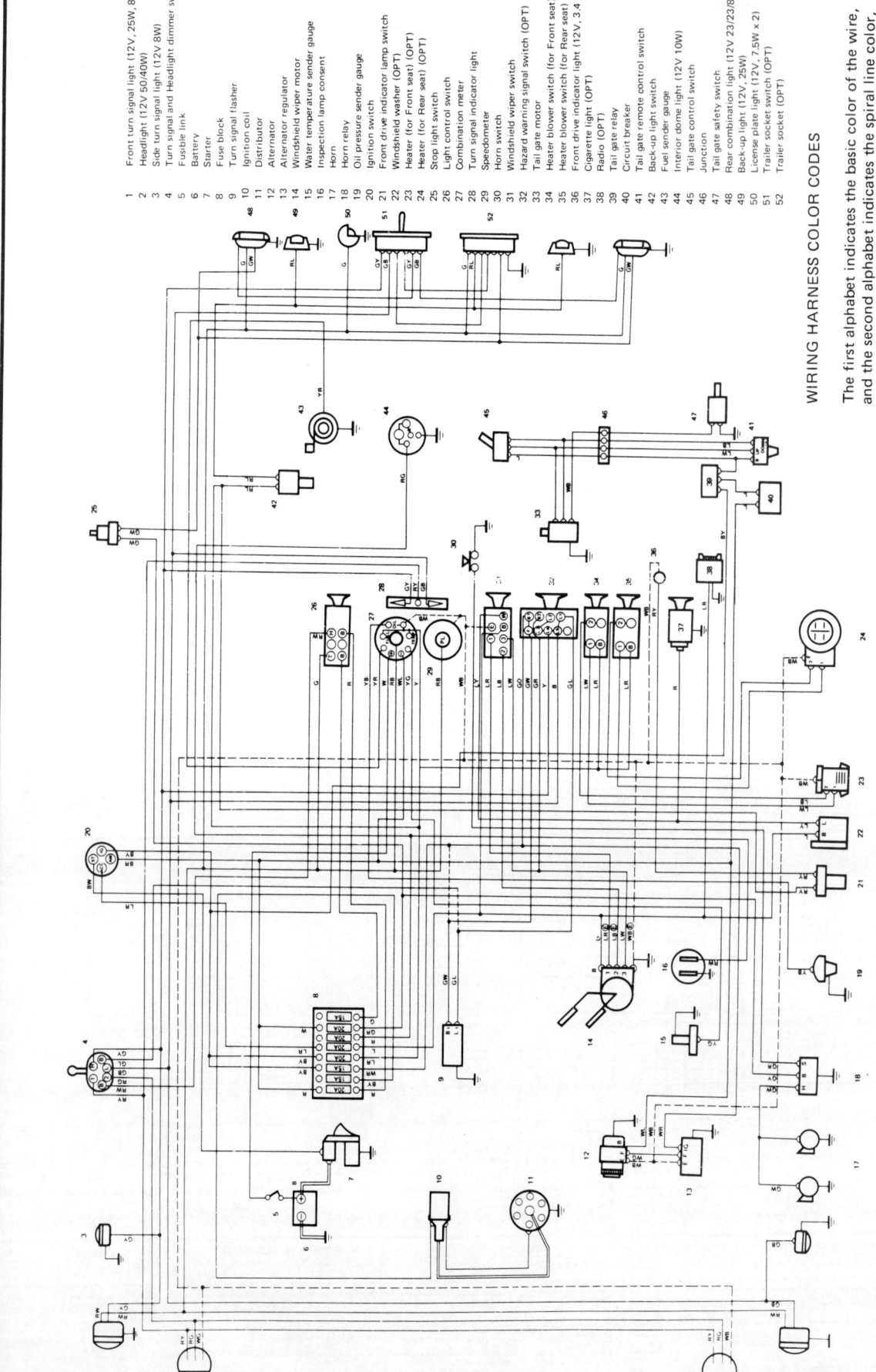

Fig. 11.71. Wiring diagram - FJ55(L)V, 1972/1973

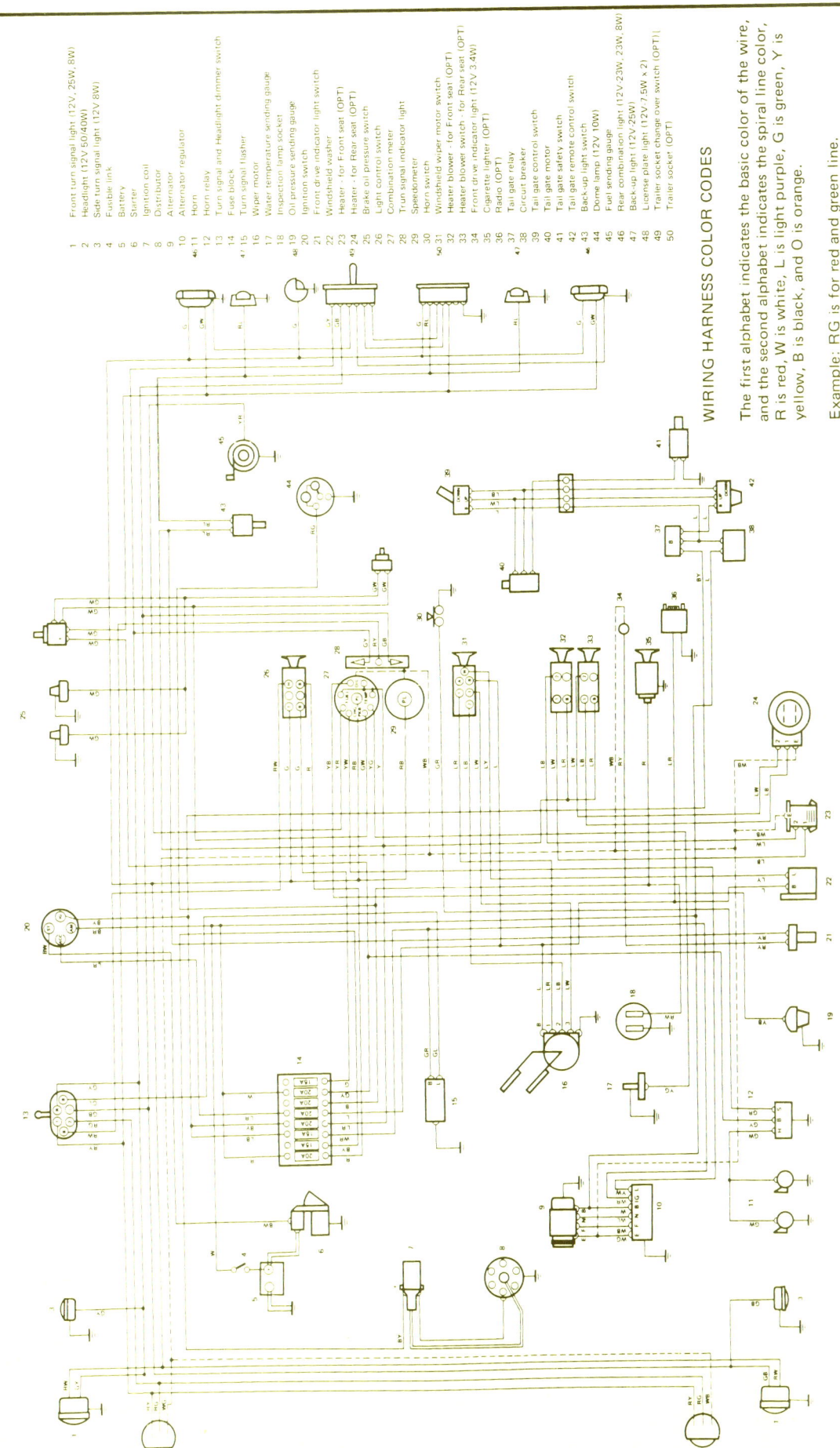

Fig. 11.72. Wiring diagram - FJ55V (Australia), 1972/1973

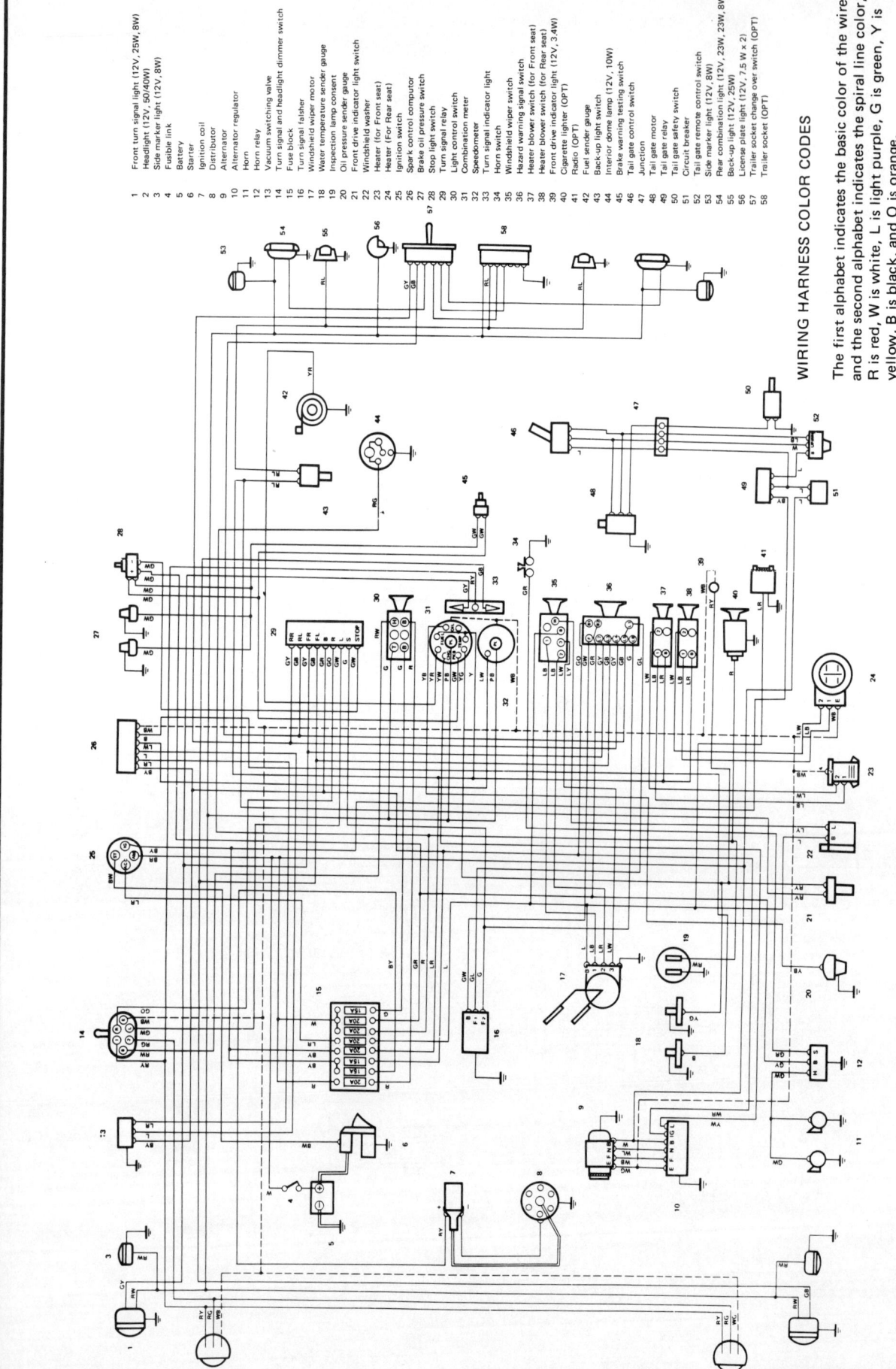

Fig. 11.73. Wiring diagram - FJ55LG, 1972/1973

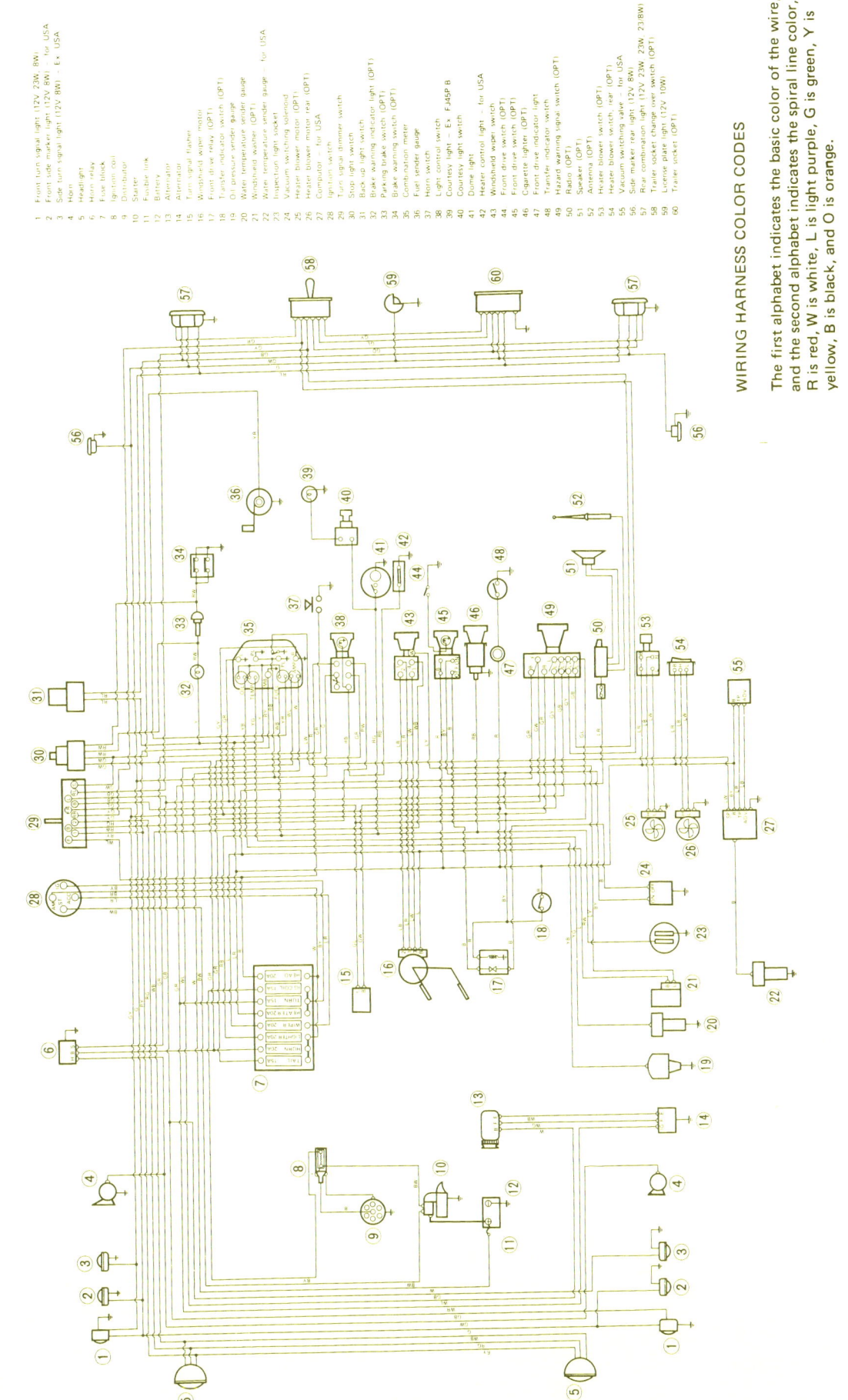

Fig. 11.74. Wiring diagram - FJ40 and 45P-B, 1974 models

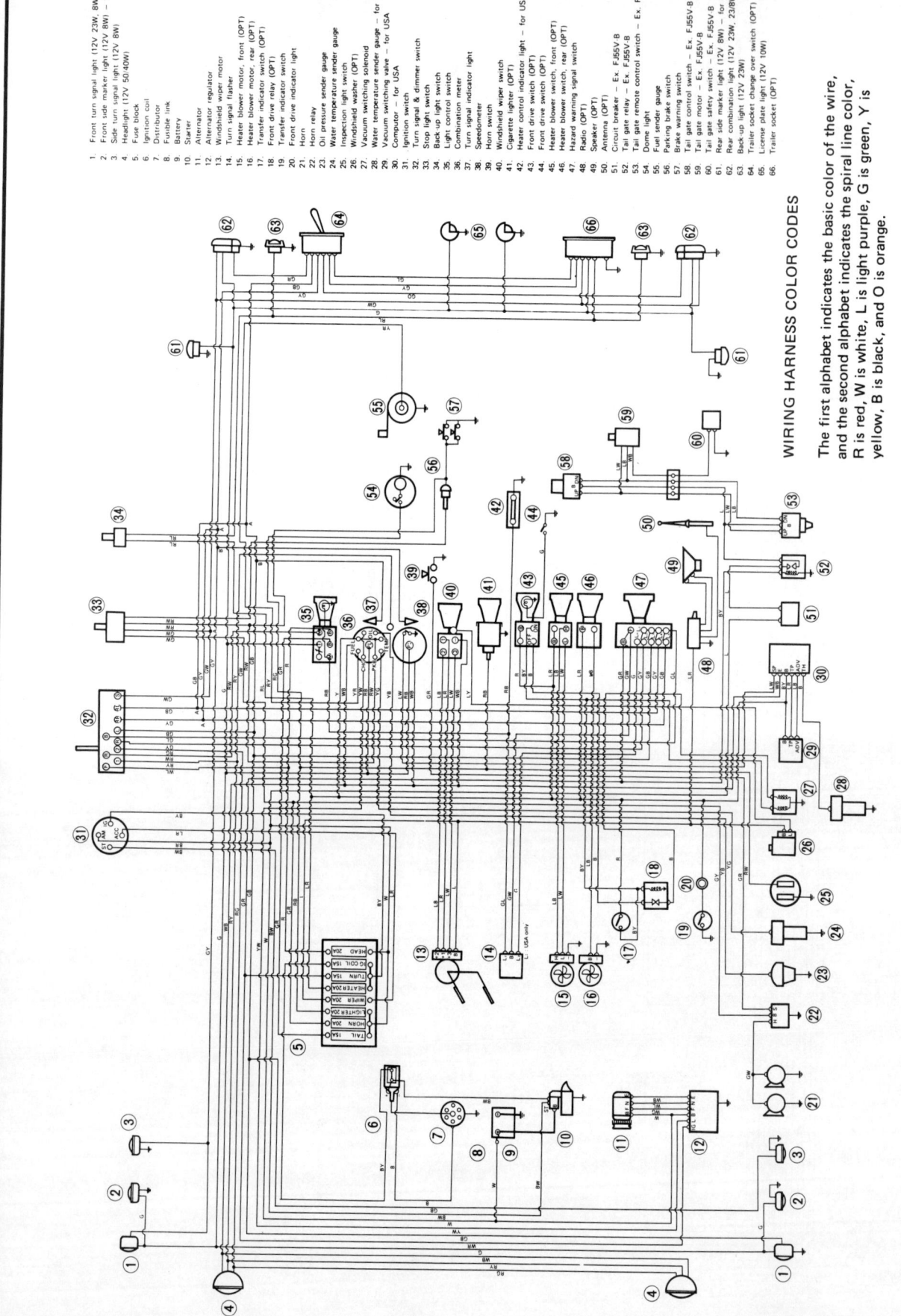

Fig. 11.75. Wiring diagram - FJ55LG and FJ55V with tandem master cylinder, 1974 models

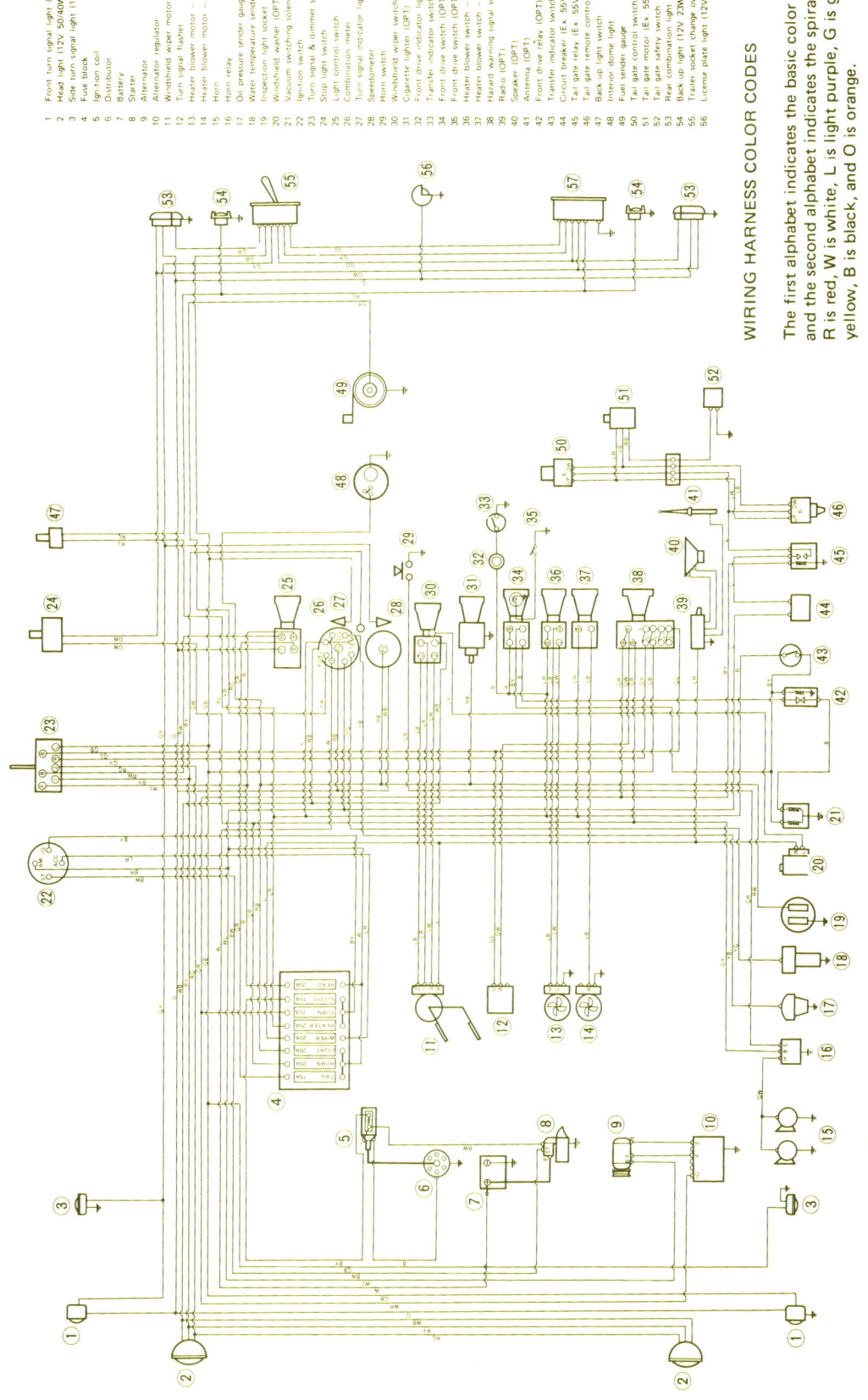

Fig. 11.76. Wiring diagram - FJ55(L)V series, 1974 models

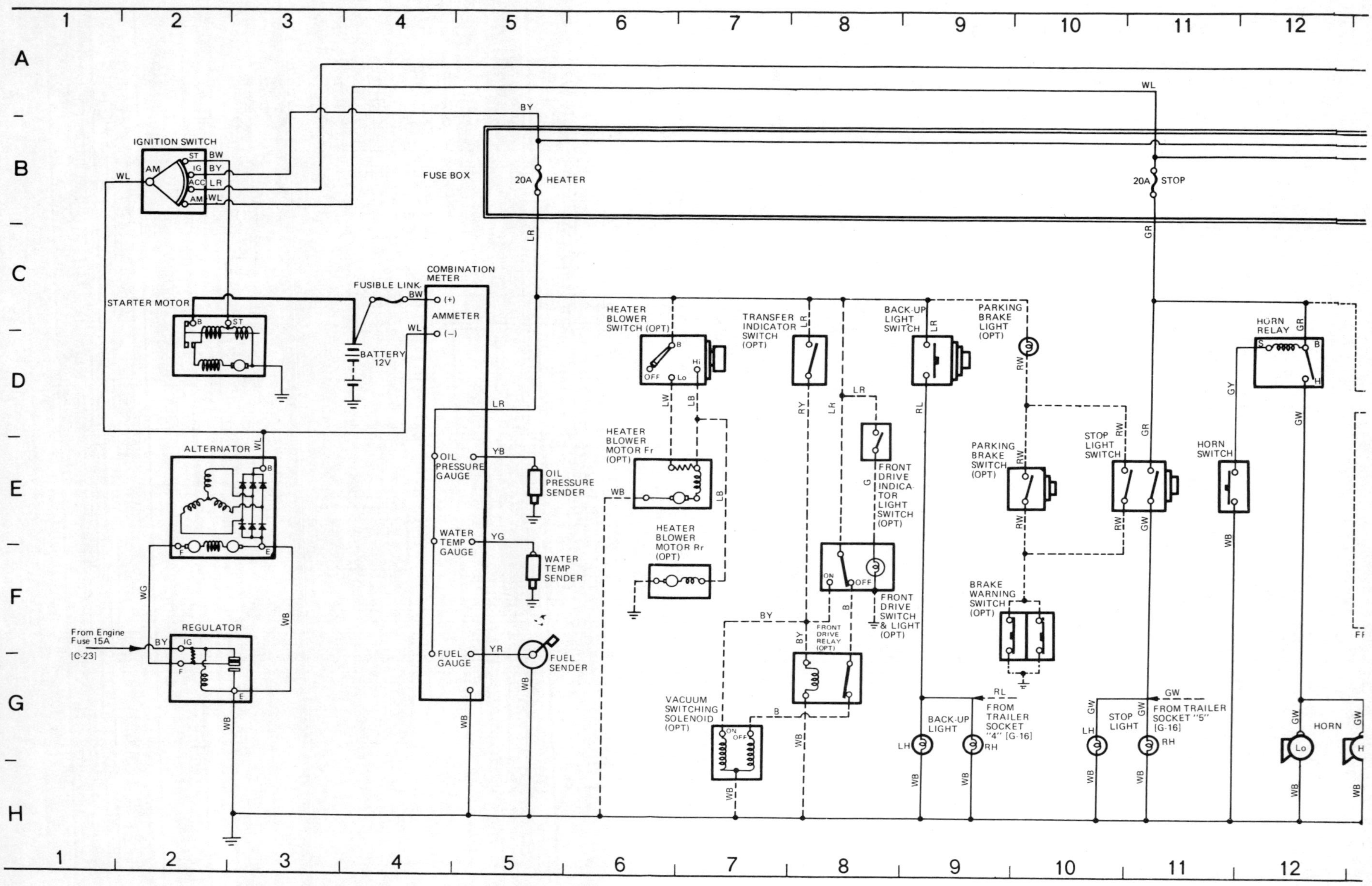

Fig. 11.77. Wiring diagram - FJ40, 43 and 45 (except USA and Canada), 1975 onwards (For color code, refer to page 221)

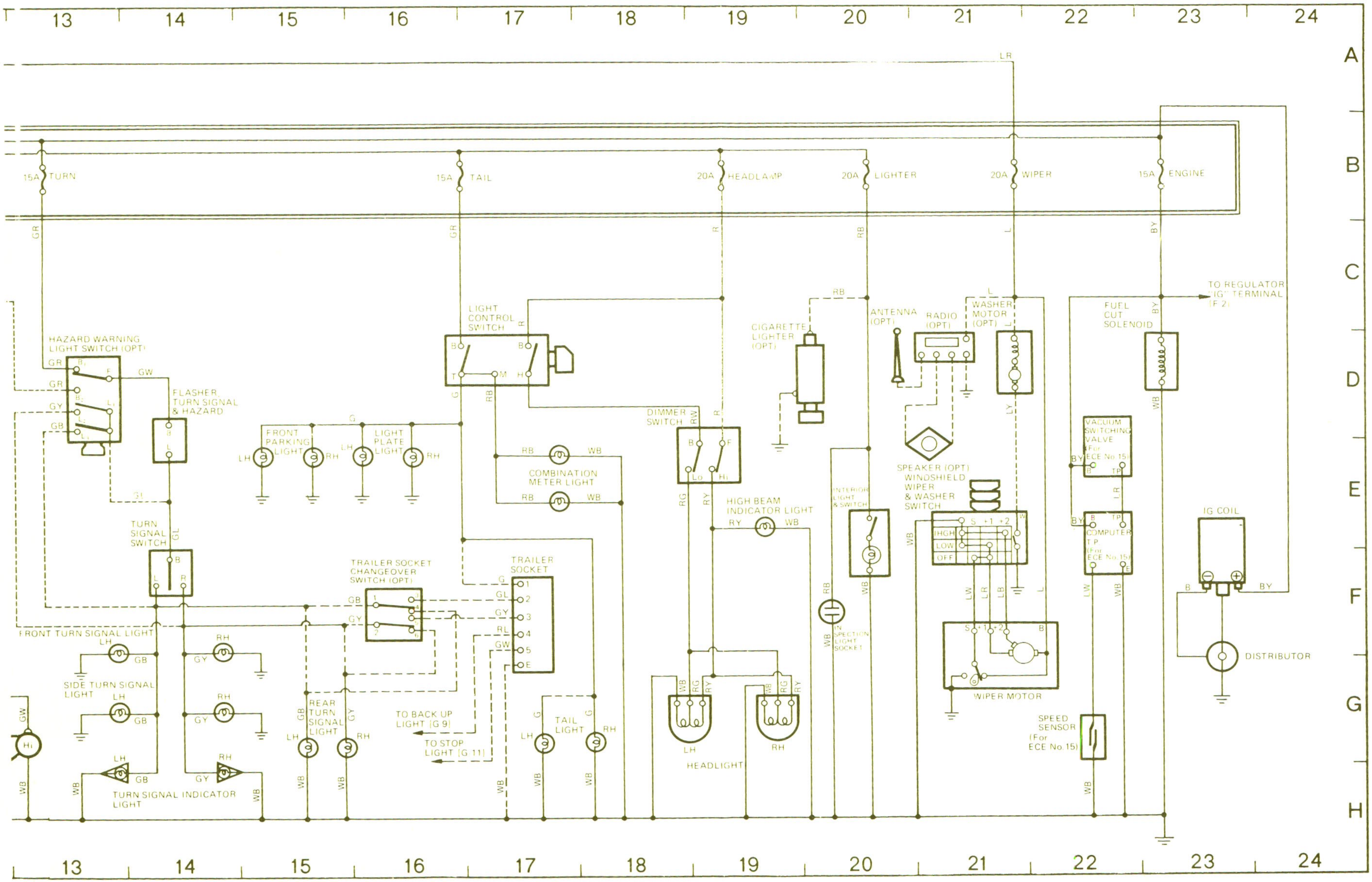

Fig. 11.77. Wiring diagram - FJ40, 43 and 45 (except USA and Canada), 1975 onwards (continued)

224

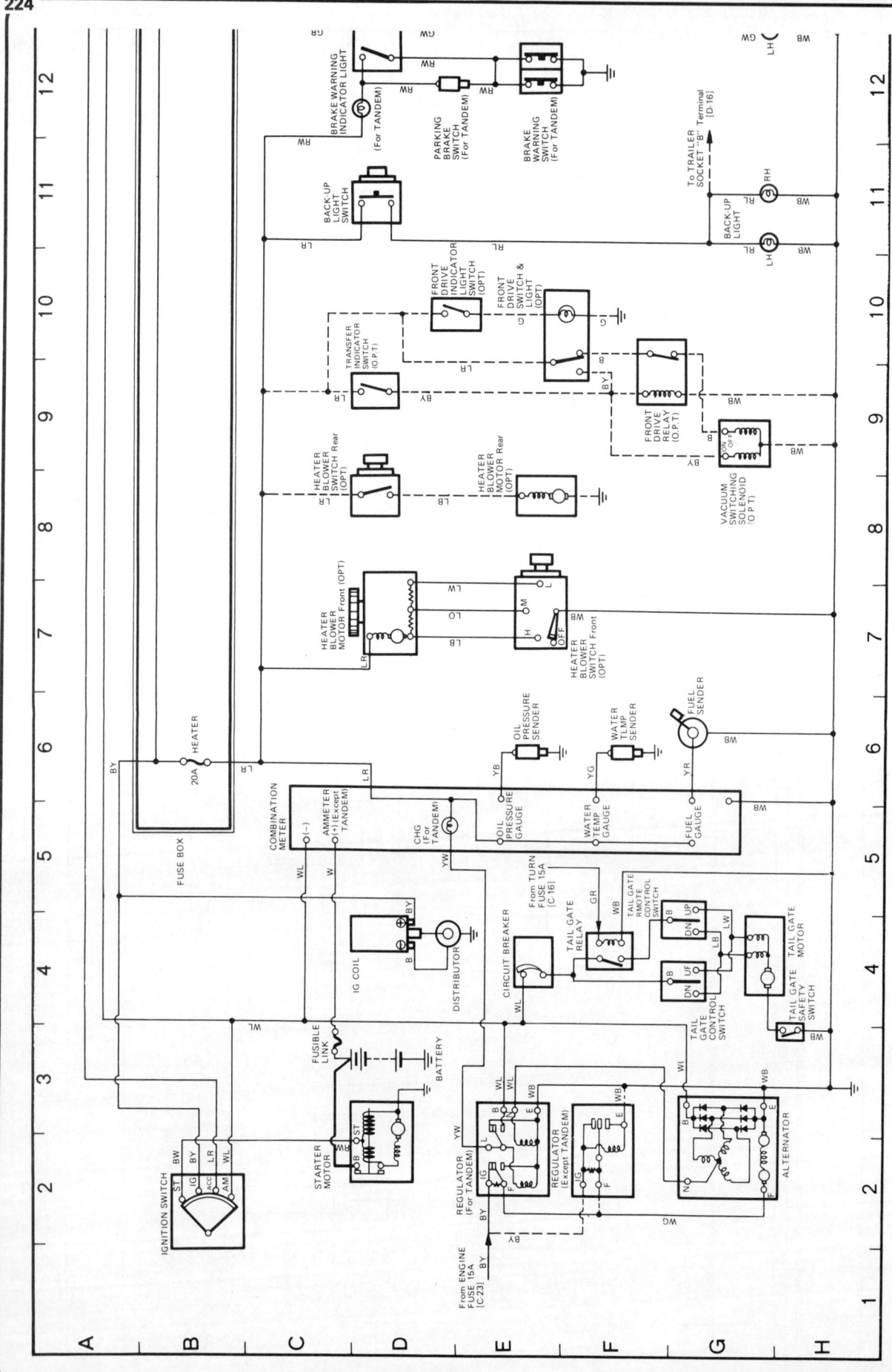

Fig. 11.78. Wiring diagram - FJ55 series (except USA and Canada), 1975 onwards (For color code, refer to page 221)

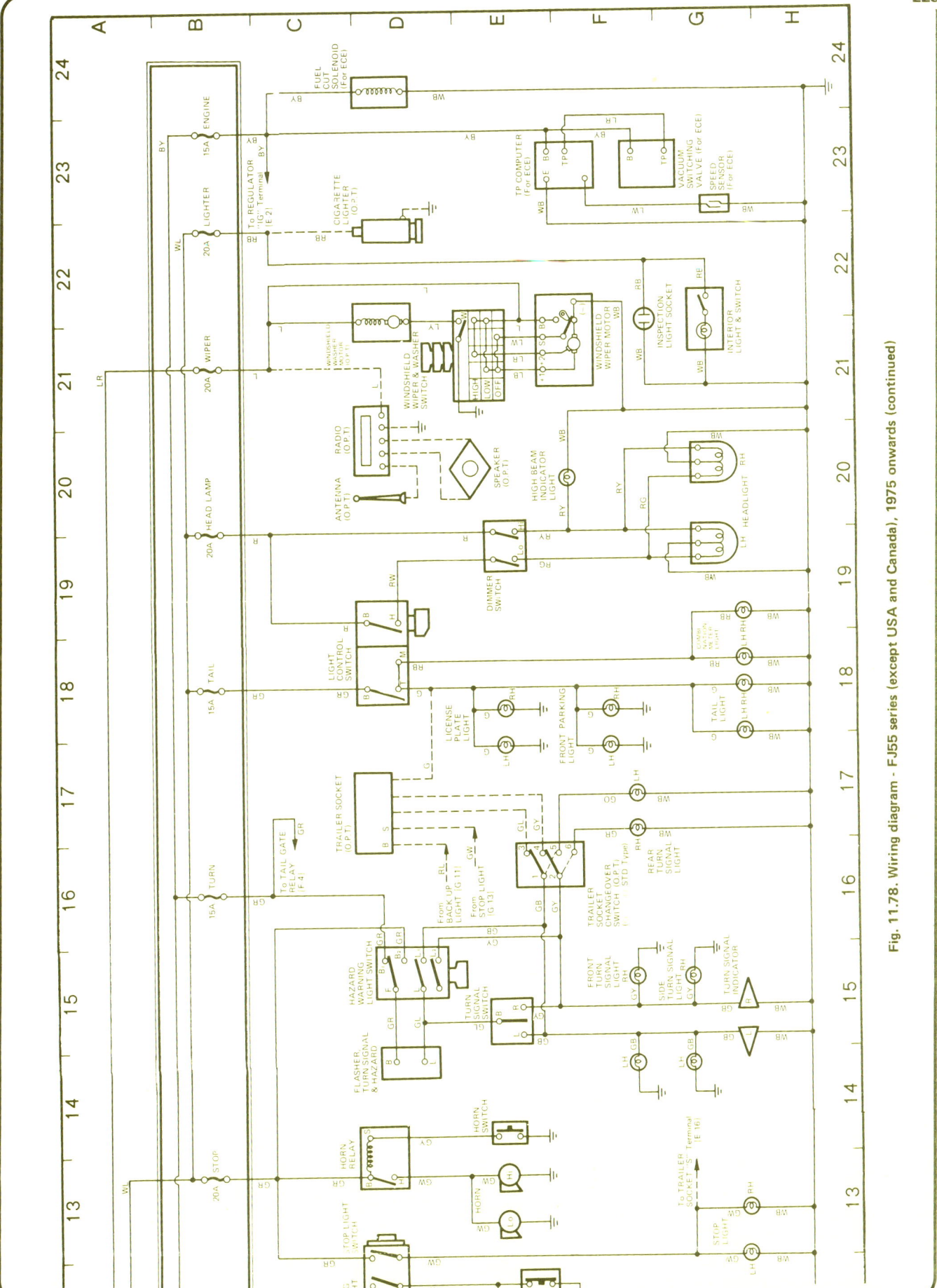

Fig. 11.78. Wiring diagram - FJ55 series (except USA and Canada), 1975 onwards (continued)

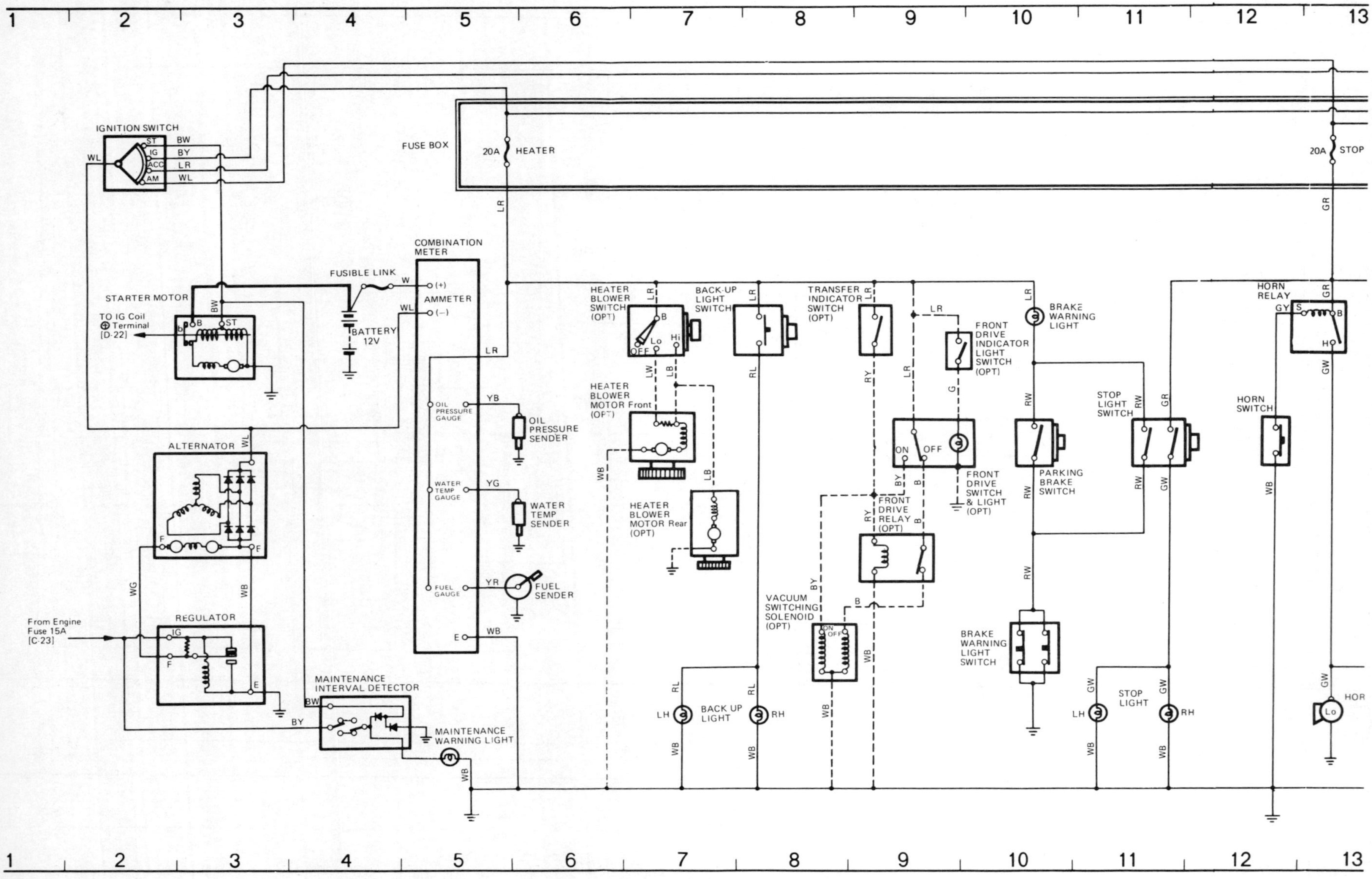

Fig. 11.79. Wiring diagram - FJ40 series (USA and Canada), 1975 (For color code, refer to page 221)

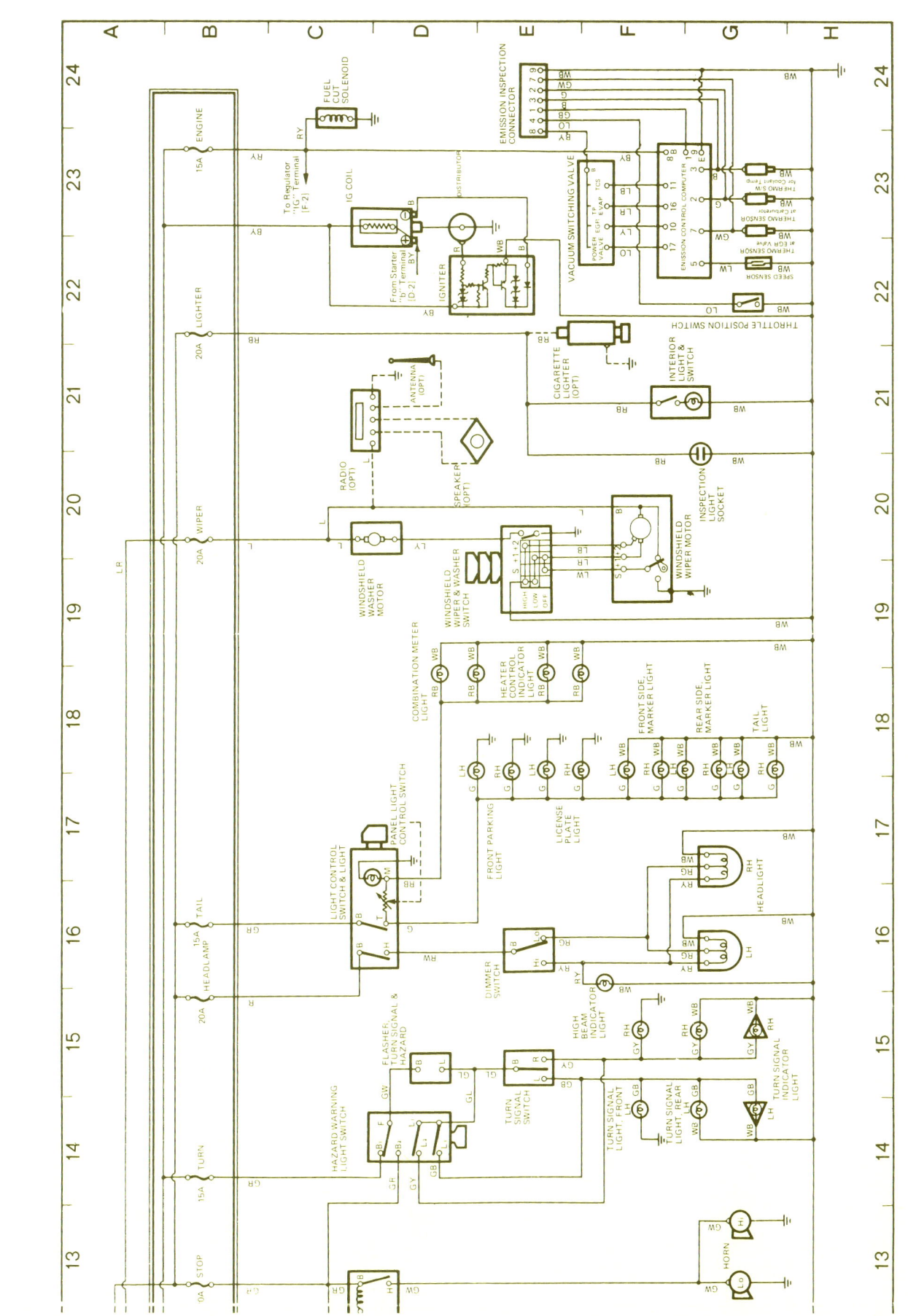

Fig. 11.79. Wiring diagram - FJ40 series (USA and Canada), 1975 (continued)

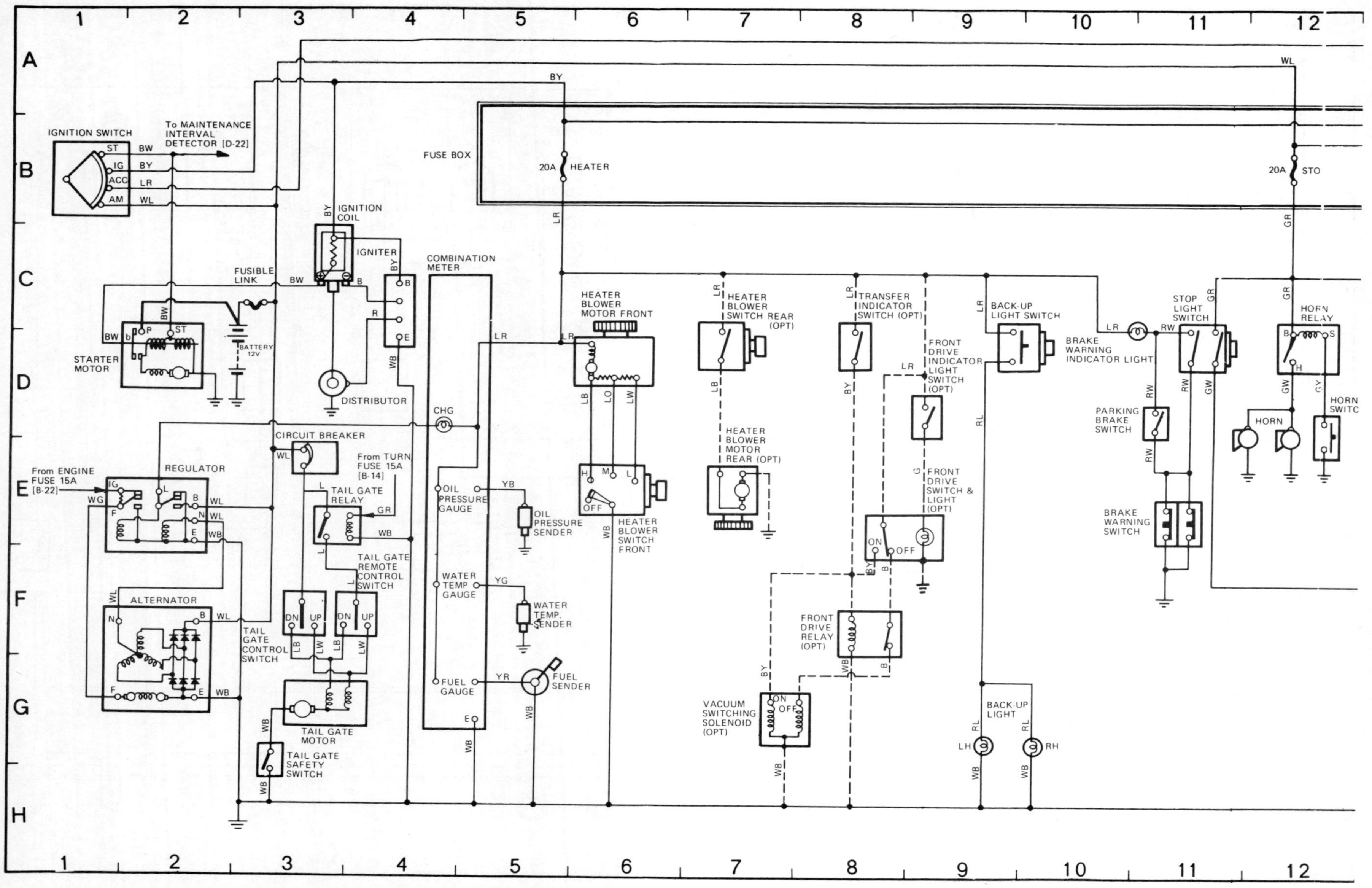

Fig. 11.80. Wiring diagram - FJ55LG (USA and Canada), 1975 (For color code, refer to page 221)

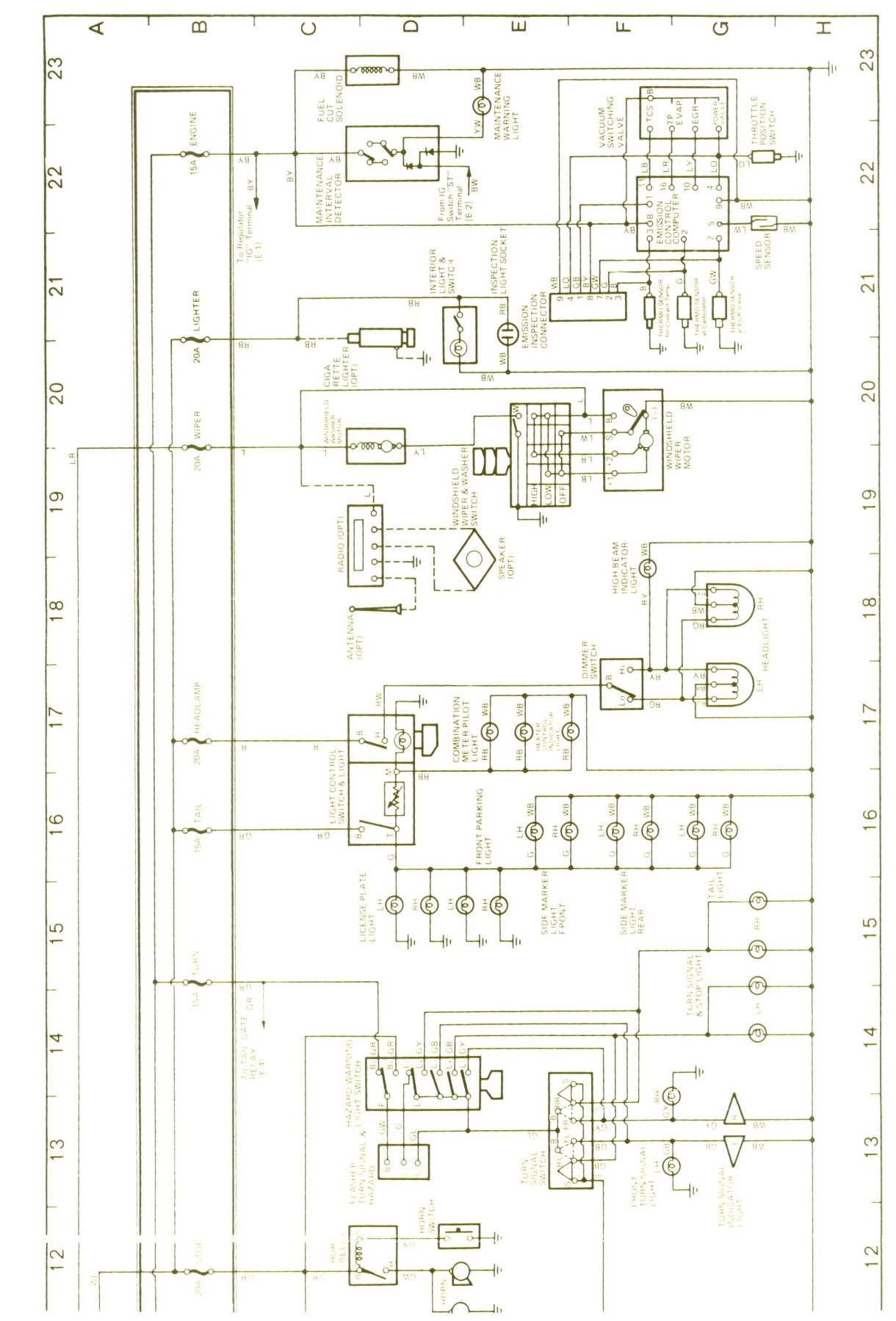

Fig. 11.80. Wiring diagram - FJ55LG (USA and Canada), 1975 (continued)

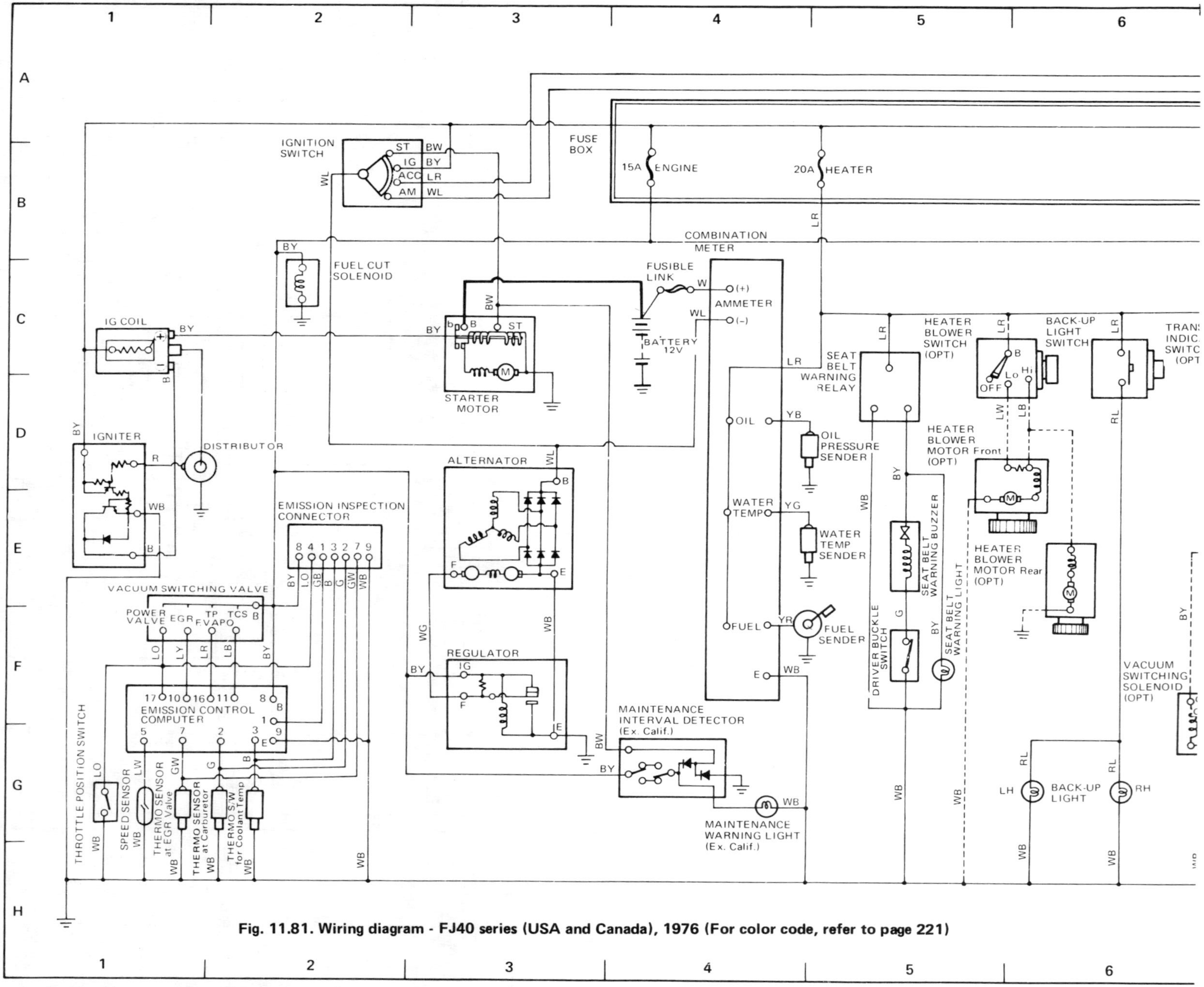

Fig. 11.81. Wiring diagram - FJ40 series (USA and Canada), 1976 (For color code, refer to page 221)

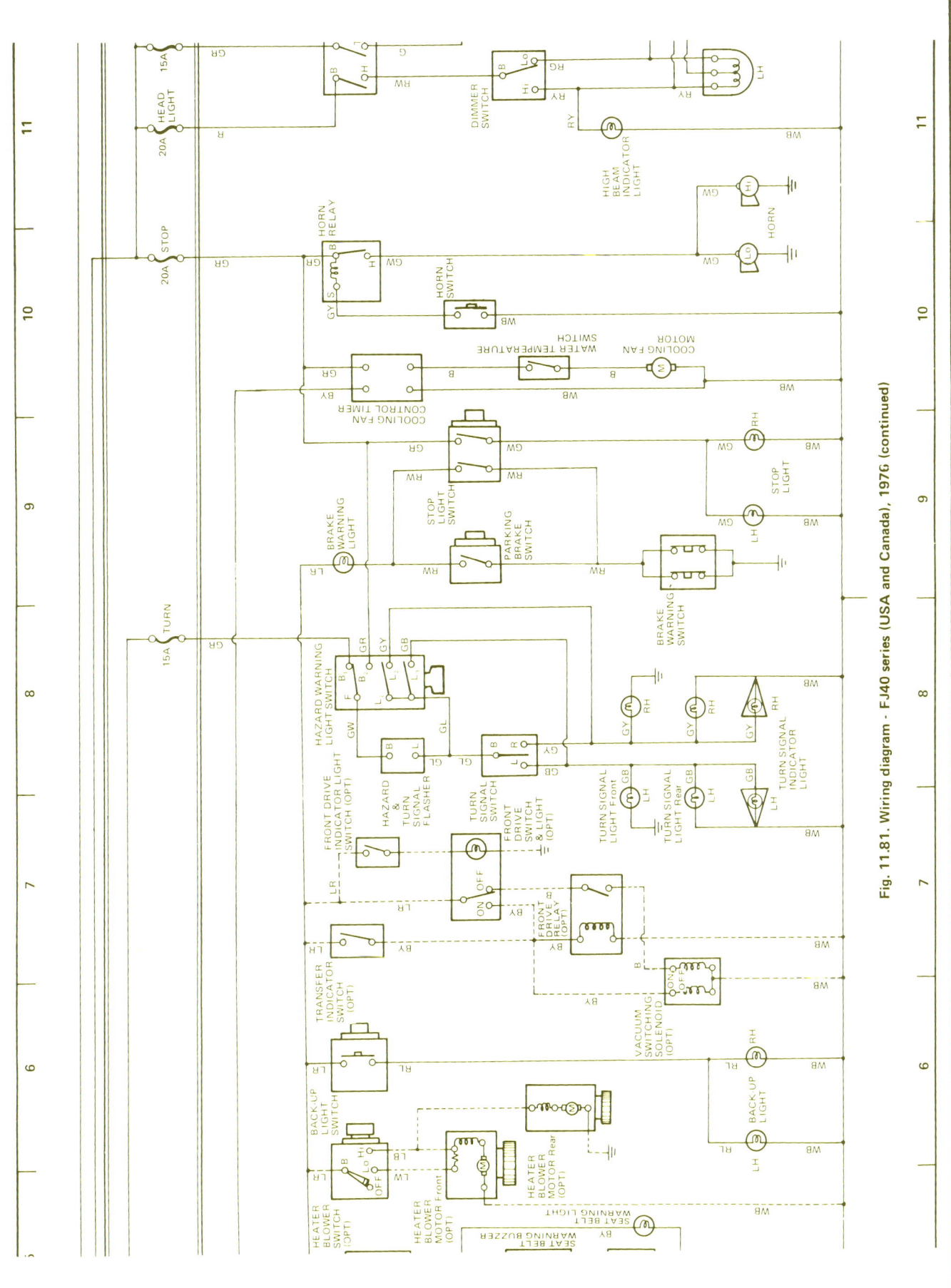

Fig. 11.81. Wiring diagram - FJ40 series (USA and Canada), 1976 (continued)

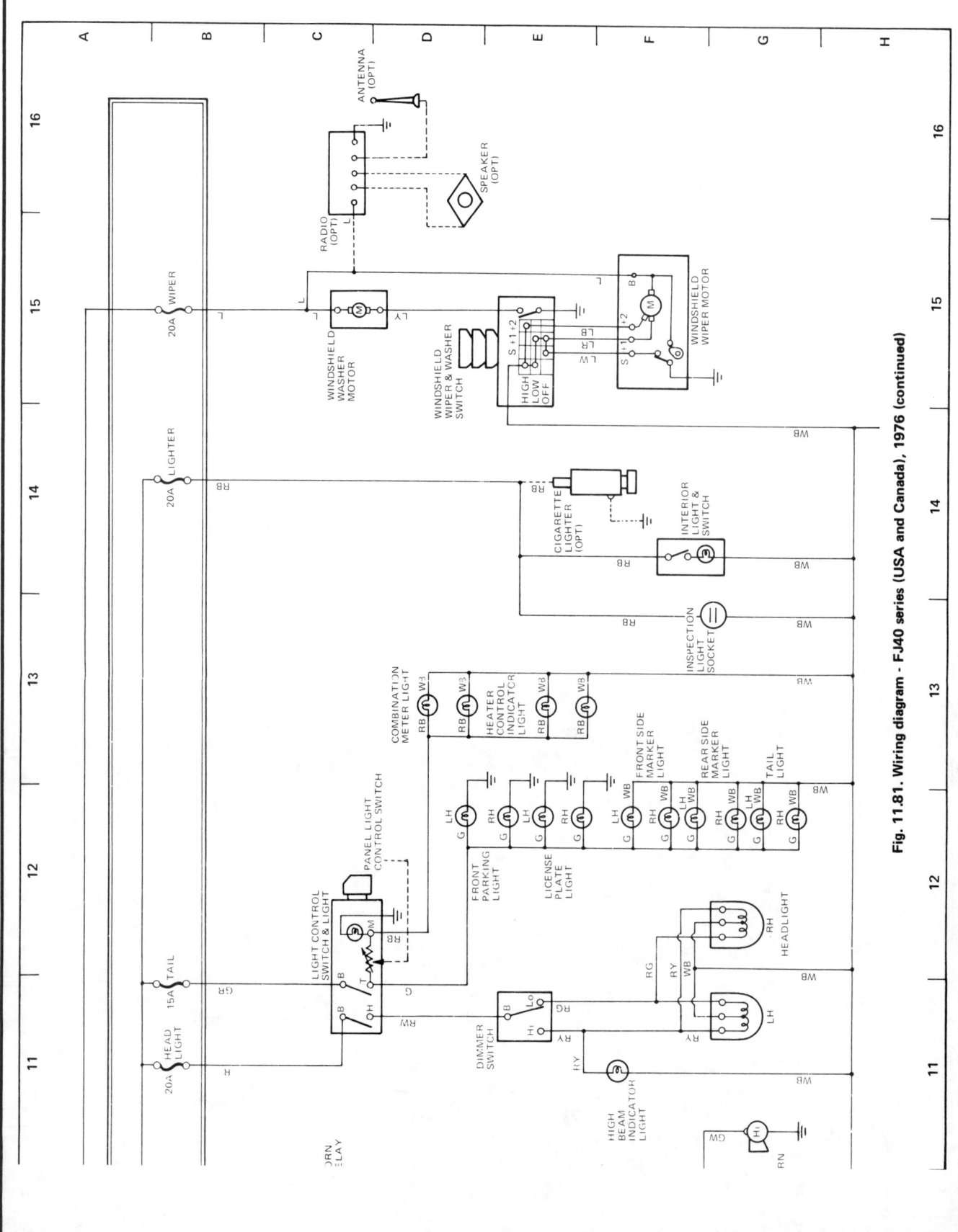

Fig. 11.81. Wiring diagram - FJ40 series (USA and Canada), 1976 (continued)

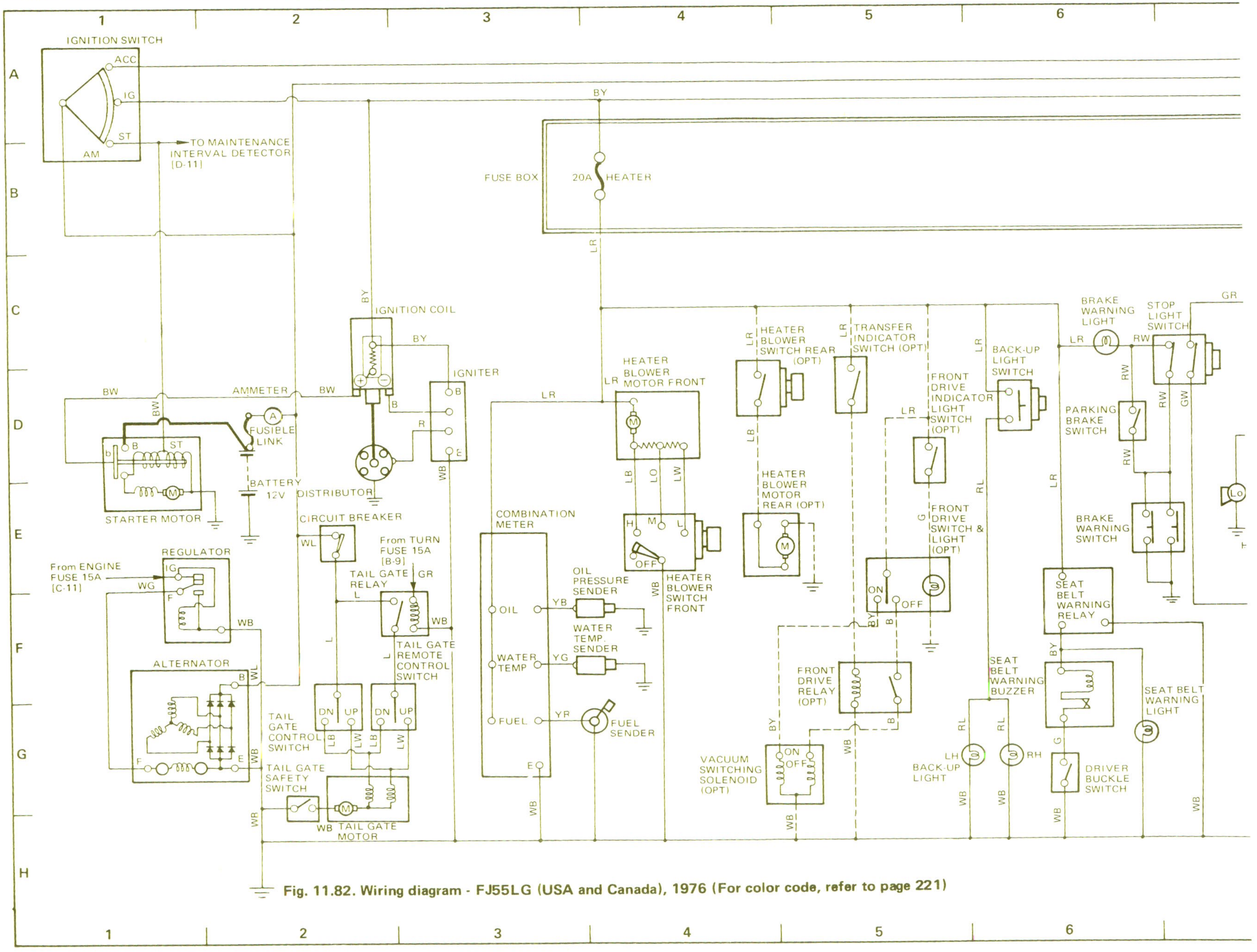

Fig. 11.82. Wiring diagram - FJ55LG (USA and Canada), 1976 (For color code, refer to page 221)

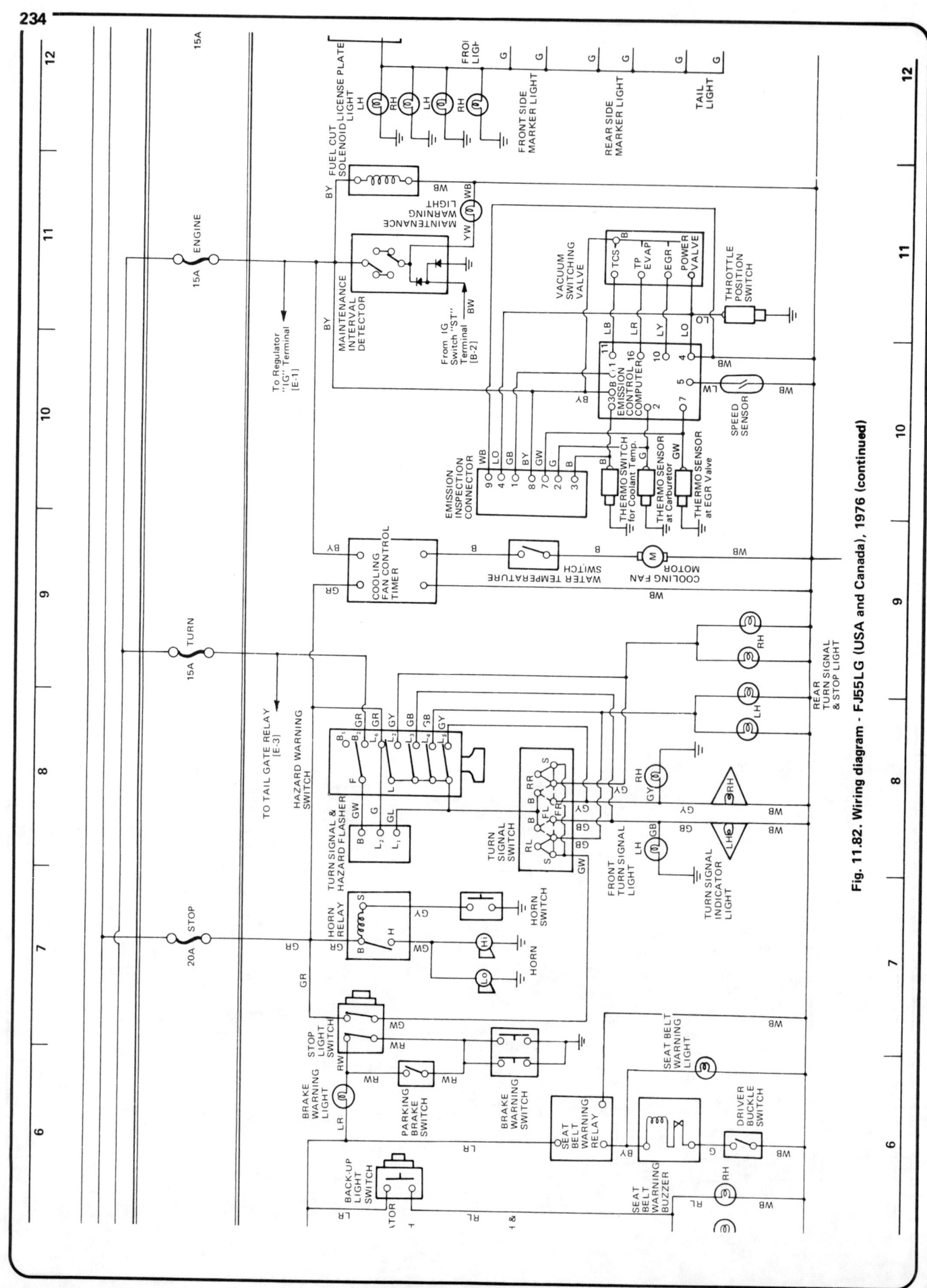

Fig. 11.82. Wiring diagram - FJ55LG (USA and Canada), 1976 (continued)

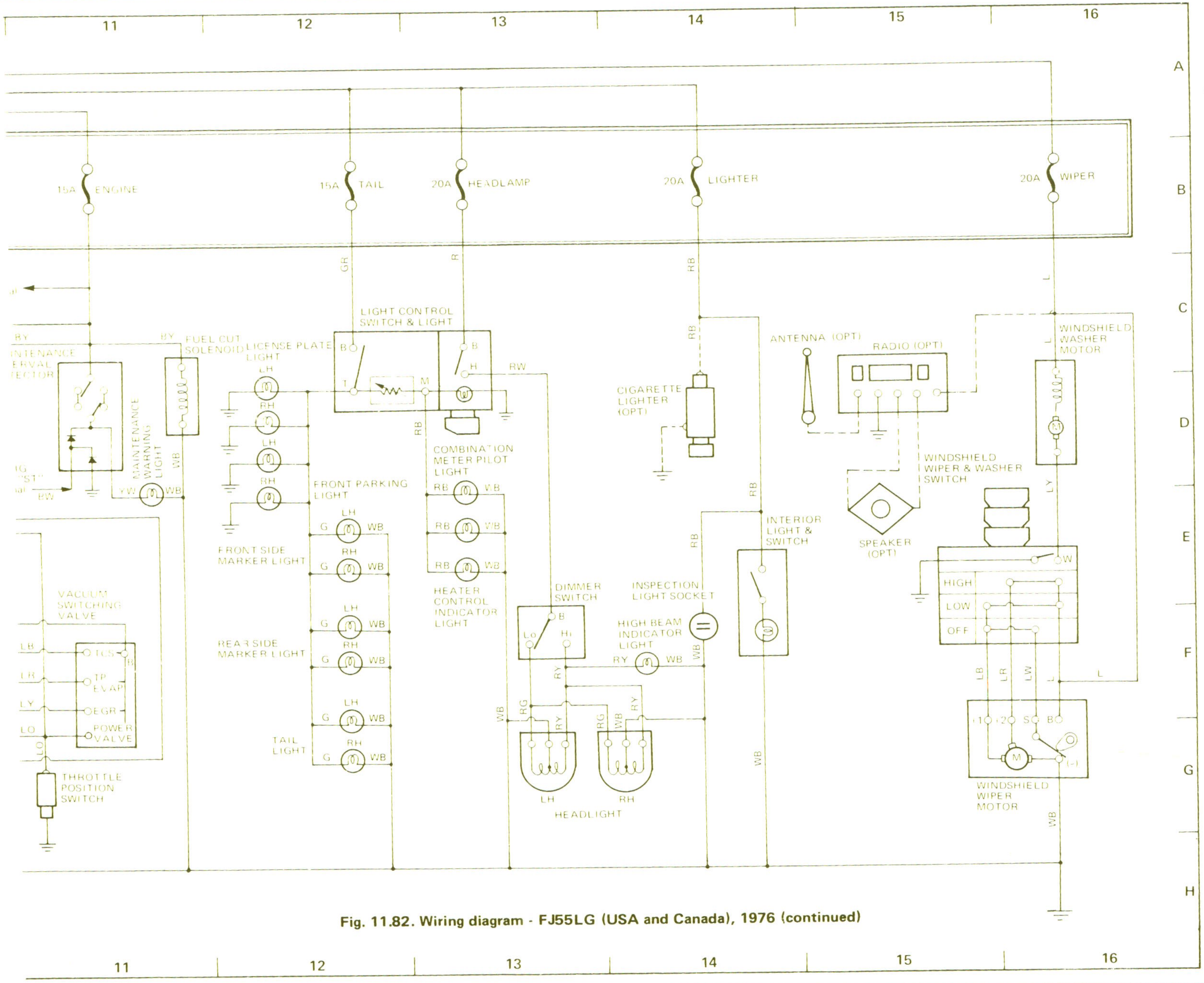

Fig. 11.82. Wiring diagram - FJ55LG (USA and Canada), 1976 (continued)

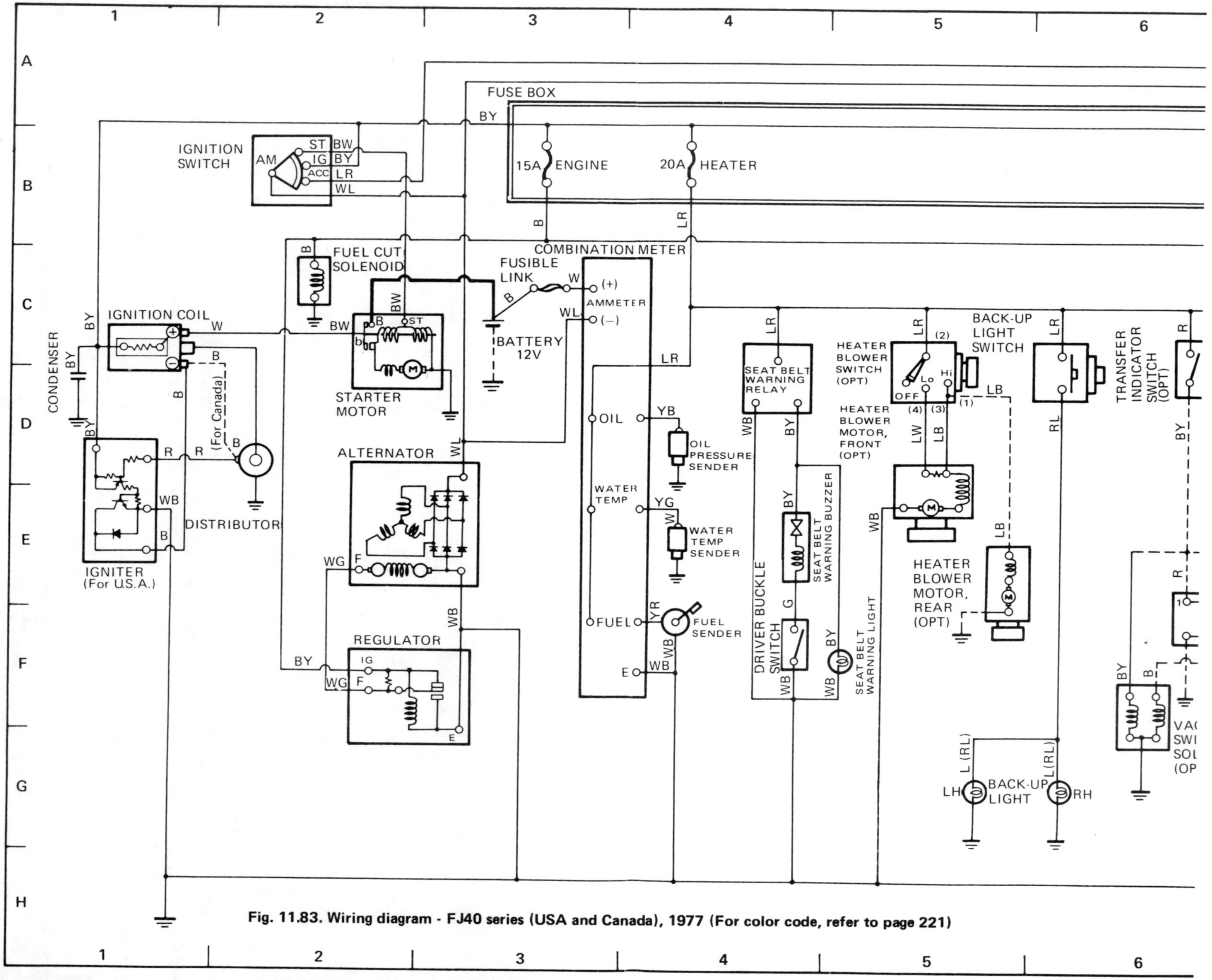

Fig. 11.83. Wiring diagram - FJ40 series (USA and Canada), 1977 (For color code, refer to page 221)

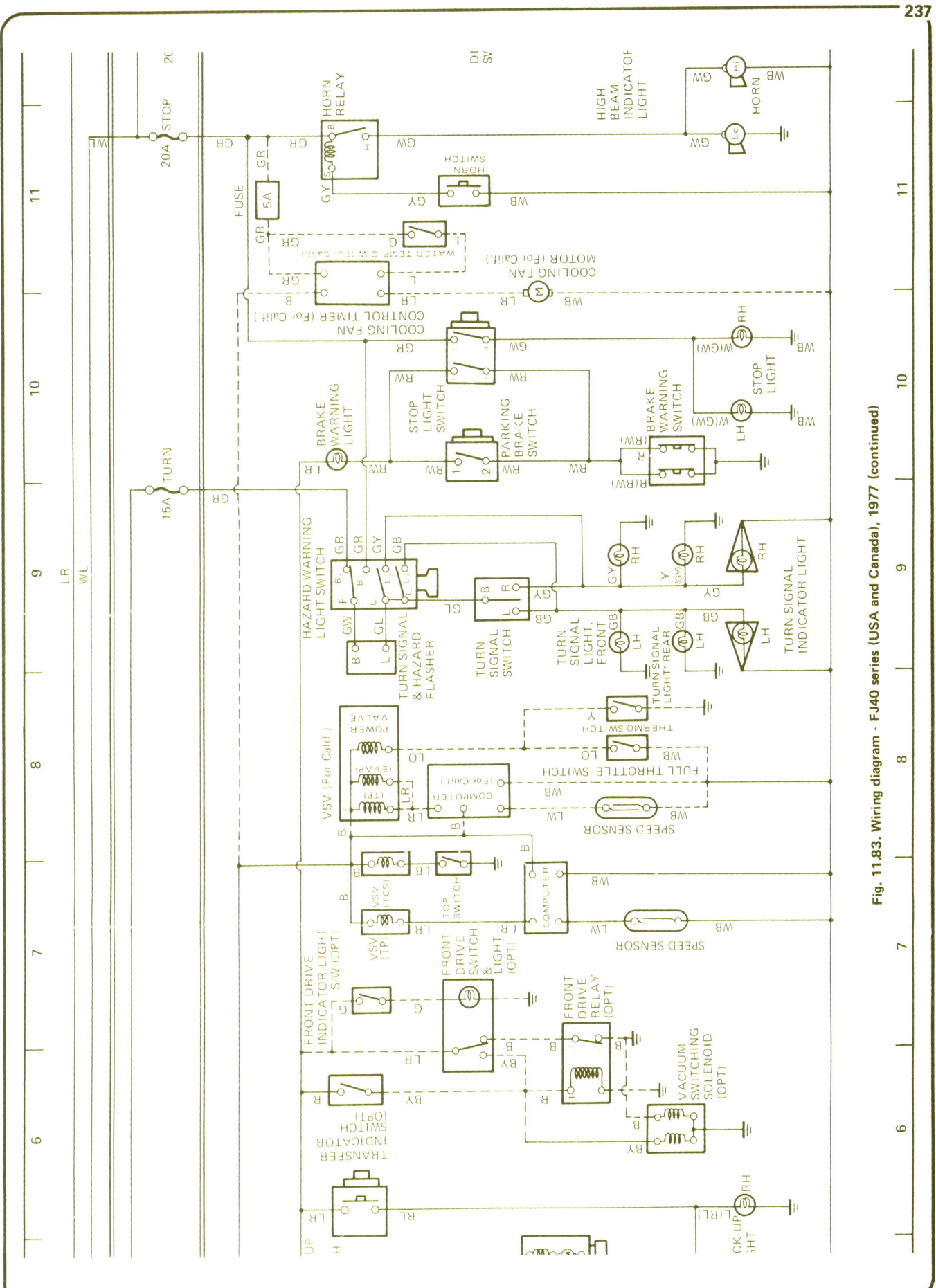

Fig. 11.83. Wiring diagram - FJ40 series (USA and Canada), 1977 (continued)

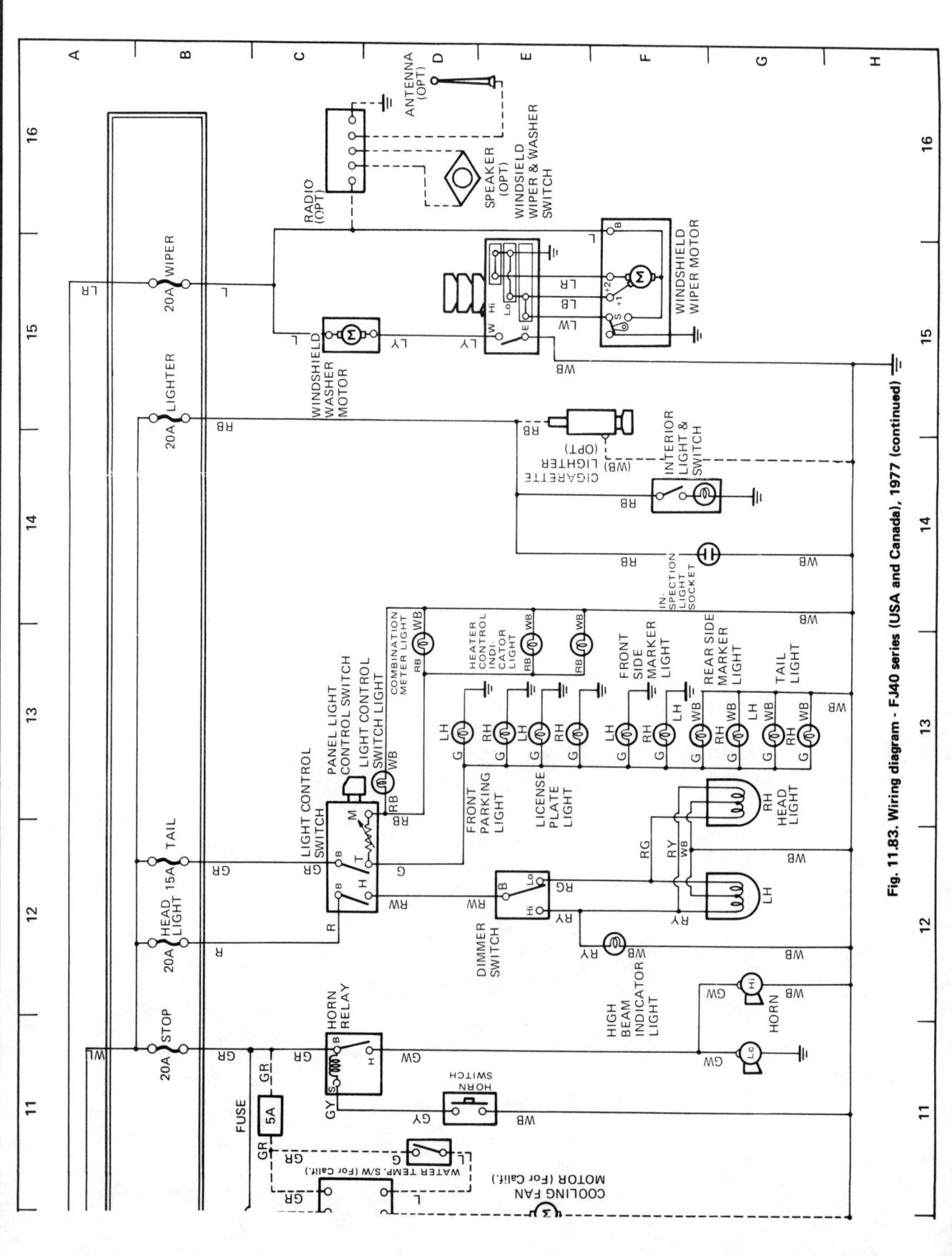

Fig. 11.83. Wiring diagram - FJ40 series (USA and Canada), 1977 (continued)

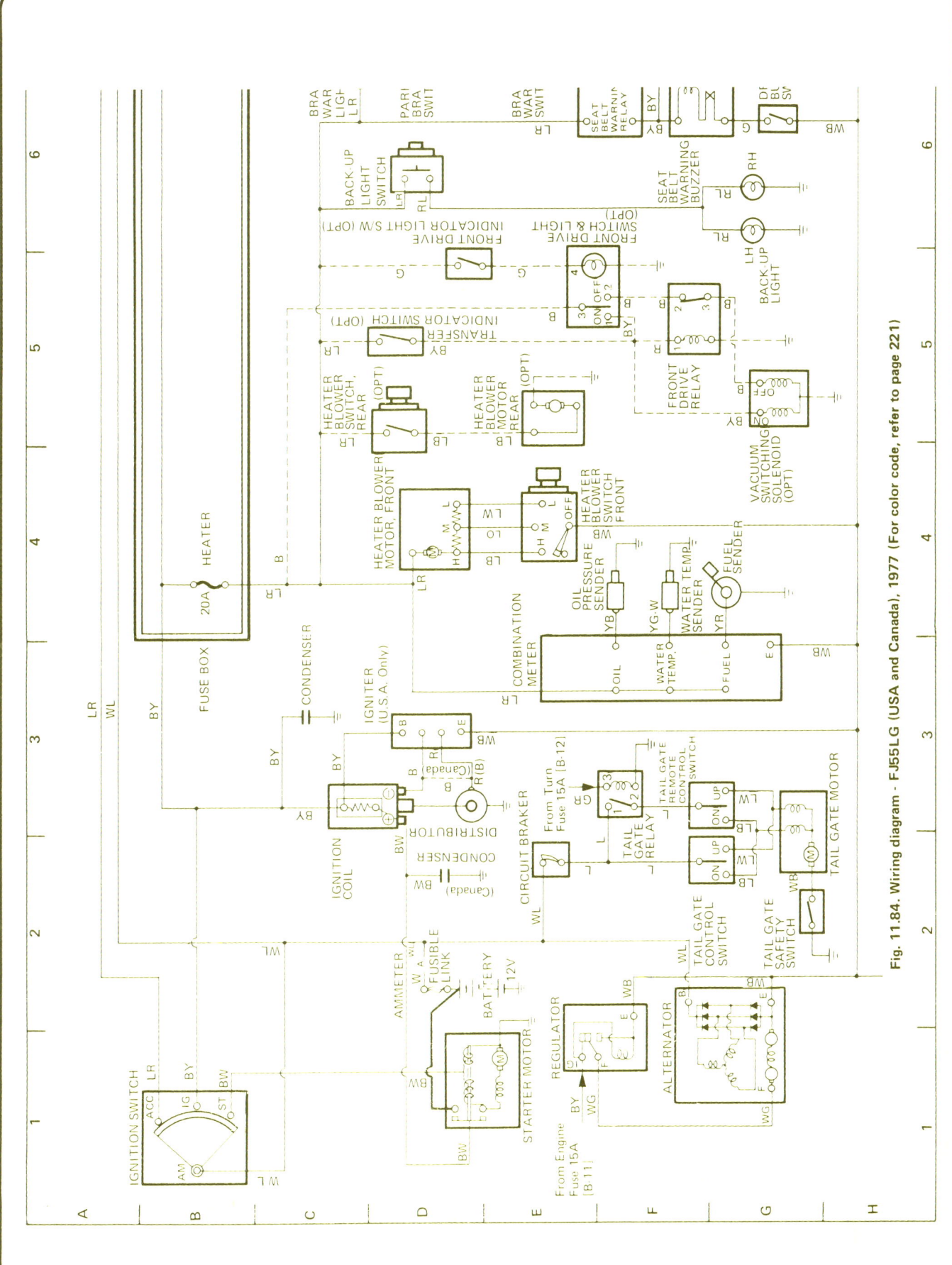

Fig. 11.84. Wiring diagram - FJ55LG (USA and Canada), 1977 (For color code, refer to page 221)

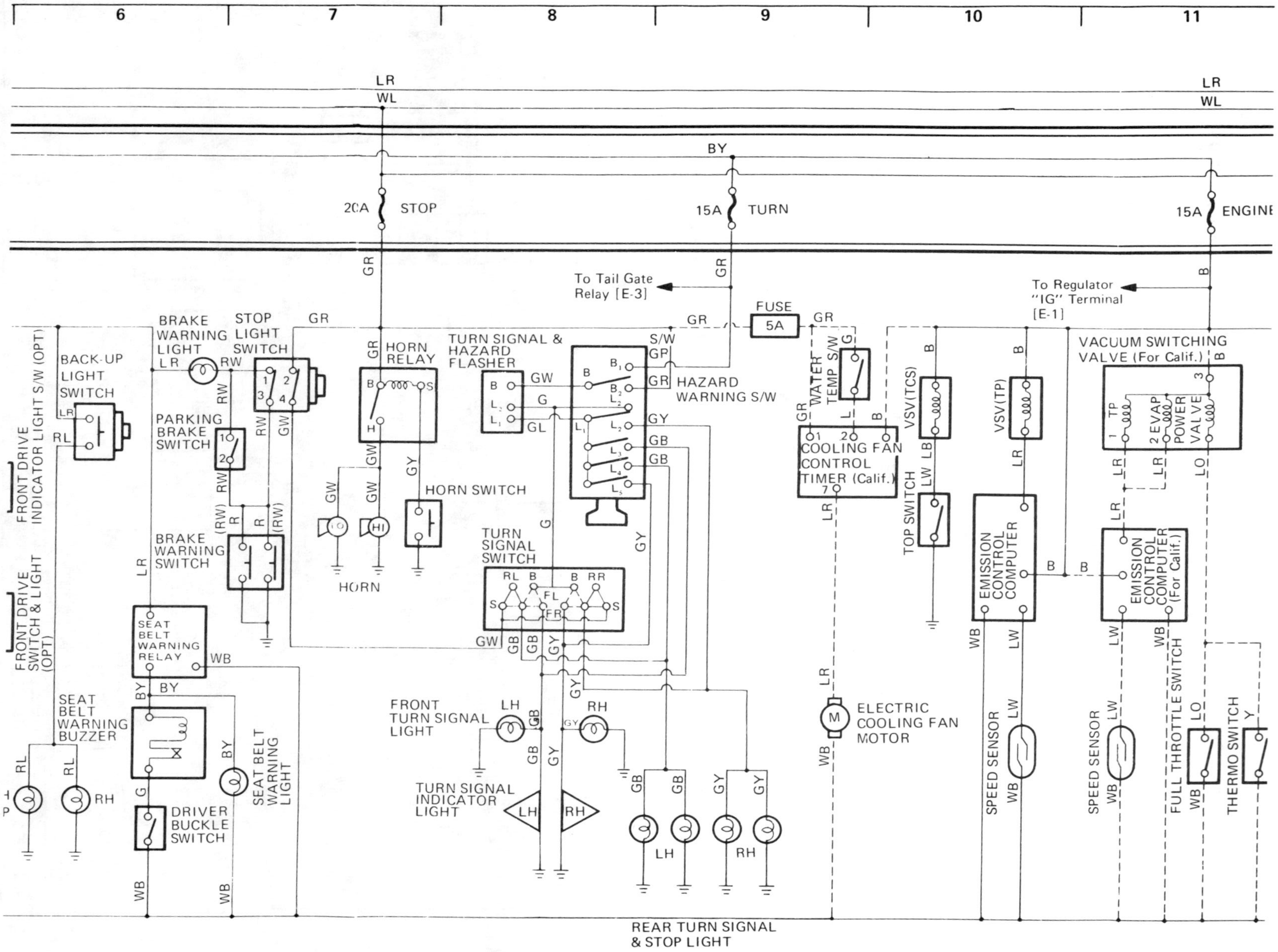

Fig. 11.84. Wiring diagram - FJ55LG (USA and Canada), 1977 (continued)

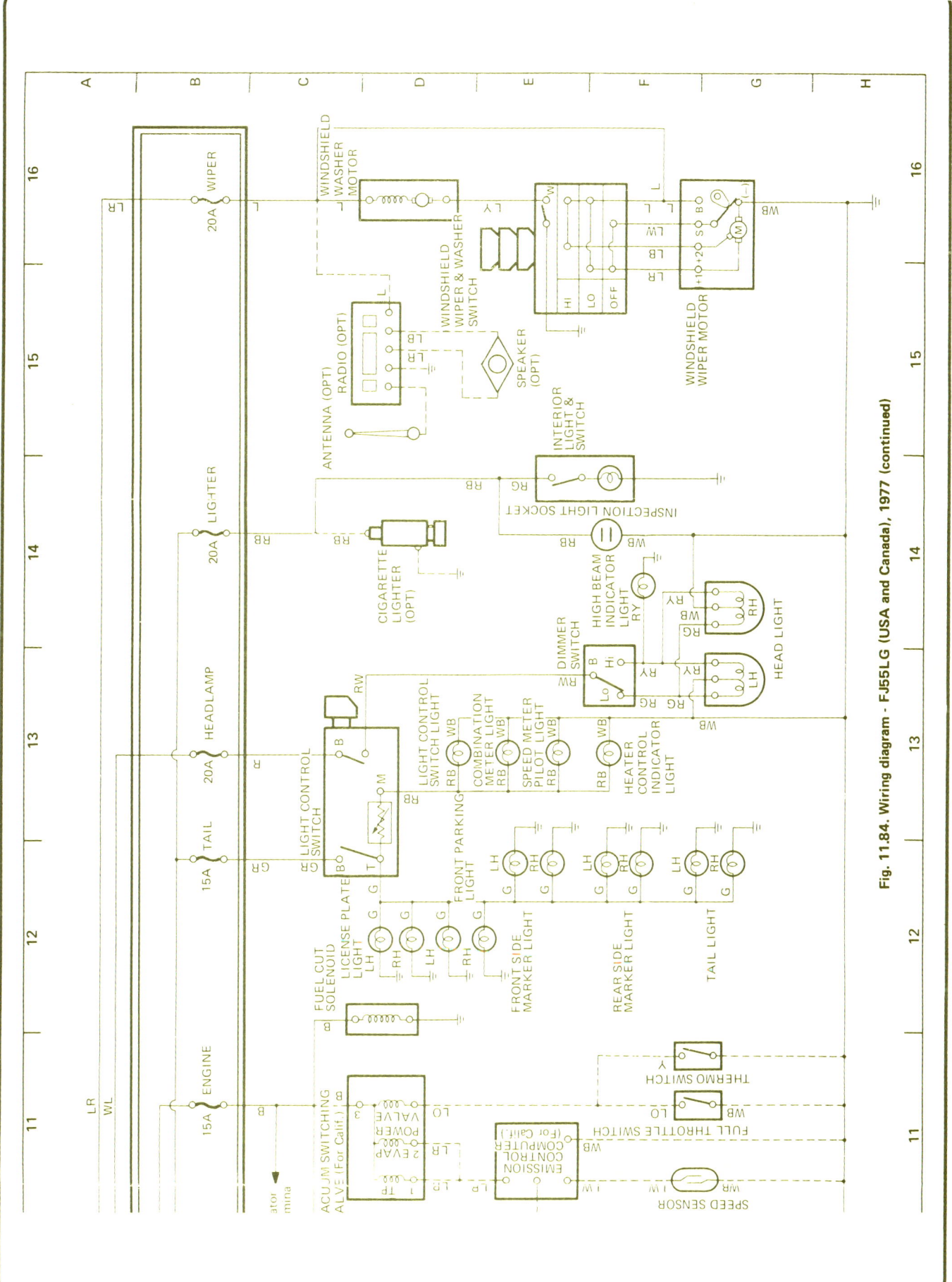

Fig. 11.84. Wiring diagram - FJ55LG (USA and Canada), 1977 (continued)

24 Fault diagnosis - electrical system

Symptom	Reason/s
Refer to Section 17 for instruments and sender units	
Starter motor fails to turn engine	Battery discharged. Battery defective internally. Battery terminal leads loose or ground lead not securely attached to body. Loose or broken connections in starter motor circuit. Starter motor solenoid switch faulty. Starter motor pinion jammed in mesh with flywheel gear ring. Starter brushes badly worn, sticking or brush wires loose. Commutator dirty, worn or burnt. Starter motor armature faulty. Field coils grounded.
Starter motor turns engine very slowly	Battery in discharged condition. Starter brushes badly worn, sticking or brush wires loose. Loose wires in starter motor circuit.
Starter motor operates without turning engine	Pinion or flywheel gear teeth broken or worn.
Starter motor noisy or engagement excessively rough	Pinion or flywheel teeth broken or worn. Starter motor retaining bolts loose.
Starter motor remains in operation after ignition key released	Faulty ignition switch. Faulty solenoid.
Charging system indicator on with ignition switch off	Faulty alternator rectifier.
Charging system indicator light on - engine speed above idling	Loose or broken drivebelt. Alternator rectifier grounded. No output from alternator.
Charge indicator light not on when ignition switched on but engine not running	Burnt out bulb. Field circuit open. Lamp circuit open.
Battery will not hold charge for more than a few days	Battery defective internally. Electrolyte level too weak or too low. Battery plates heavily sulphated.
Horn will not operate or operates intermittently	Loose connections. Defective switch. Defective relay. Defective horn.
Horns blow continually	Faulty relay. Relay wiring grounded. Horn button stuck (grounded).
Lights do not come on	If engine not running, battery discharged. Light bulb filament burnt out or bulbs broken. Wire connections loose, disconnected or broken. Light switch grounding or otherwise faulty.
Lights come on but fade out	If engine not running battery discharged. Light bulb filament burnt out, or bulbs or sealed beam units broken. Wire connections loose, disconnected or broken. Light switch shorting or otherwise faulty.
Lights give very poor illumination	Lamp glasses dirty. Lamps badly out of adjustment.
Lights work erratically - flashing on and off, especially over bumps	Battery terminals or ground connection loose. Lights not grounding properly. Contacts in light switch faulty.
Wiper motor fails to work	Blown fuse. Wire connections loose, disconnected, or broken. Brushes badly worn. Armature worn or faulty. Field coils faulty.

Wiper motor works very slowly and takes excessive current	Commutator dirty, greasy or burnt. Armature bearings dirty or unaligned. Armature badly worn or faulty.
Wiper motor works slowly and takes little current	Brushes badly worn. Commutator dirty, greasy or burnt. Armature badly worn or faulty.
Wiper motor works but wiper blades remain static	Wiper motor gearbox parts badly worn or teeth stripped.

Chapter 12 Bodywork and chassis

Contents

Air conditioning system - general description and maintenance ... 30	Instrument panel and glove compartment ... 26
Back doors and rear gates - general ... 18	Maintenance - bodywork and chassis ... 2
Bumpers - removal and installation ... 24	Maintenance - locks and hinges ... 6
Doors - rattles and their rectification ... 7	Maintenance - upholstery and carpets ... 3
Doors - removal and installation ... 8	Major bodywork damage - repair ... 5
Doors fixed window glass (FJ40 series) - removal and installation ... 15	Minor bodywork damage - repair ... 4
	Radiator grille - removal and installation ... 25
Door window glass and regulator (FJ40 series) - removal and installation ... 13	Rear door lock mechanism (FJ55) - removal and installation ... 12
	Rear door window glass and regulator (FJ55) - removal and installation ... 11
Door window glass, regulator and door lock (FJ45) - removal and installation ... 17	Rear trim panels (FJ55) - removal and installation ... 28
	Tailgate (FJ55) - general ... 19
Engine compartment hood - removal, installation and adjustment ... 23	Tailgate glass and regulator (FJ55) - removal and installation ... 20
	Tailgate lock (FJ55) - removal and installation ... 22
Front door lock mechanism (FJ40 series) - removal and installation ... 16	Tailgate regulator motor (FJ55) - removal, dismantling, reassembly and installation ... 21
Front door lock mechanism (FJ55) - removal and installation ... 10	Ventilator window (FJ40 series) - removal and installation ... 14
Front door window regulator and glass (FJ55) - removal and installation ... 9	Windshield, side window and back door fixed glass - removal and installation ... 29
Front window ventilator panel (FJ40 series) ... 27	
General description ... 1	

1 General description

All models in the Land Cruiser range utilize a ladder-type chassis frame, with box section side members and crossmembers.

The wagon version (FJ55) has a unitized body structure which is bolted to the chassis frame through vibration-absorbing rubber mounts. The front fenders and fender panels are detachable, as are the engine compartment hood, side doors and rear door.

The FJ40 model is manufactured as an open-top, hard-top or canvas-top vehicle. This also has a unitized body structure with detachable fenders and fender panels, hood, side doors and rear door(s). The FJ43 model is supplied as a canvas-top vehicle and is generally similar to the FJ40, but on a longer chassis. The FJ45 has an even longer chassis and is supplied as a pick-up or wagon model. The main body and rear cargo area on the wagon model can be detached from the chassis as separate items.

The standard of interior trim on the FJ40 series models is fairly basic, but the FJ55 models are fully equipped and are along the lines of a saloon car with twin bench seats.

An air-conditioning system is available as an optional item on Land Cruiser models. However, in view of the complexity of the system, no repair procedures are considered suitable for inclusion in this Manual. If this should become necessary, contact an air-conditioning specialist. On no account disconnect any of the refrigerant lines, as the refrigerant can cause serious skin irritation. Refer to Section 30 for a general description and maintenance information.

2 Maintenance - bodywork and underframe

1 The condition of your vehicle's bodywork is of considerable importance as it is on this that the secondhand value will mainly depend. It is very much more difficult to repair neglected bodywork than to renew mechanical assemblies. The hidden portions of the body, such as the wheel arches and the underframe and the engine compartment are equally important though obviously not requiring such frequent attention as the immediately visible paintwork.

2 Once a year or every 12,000 miles (19,000 km) it is a sound scheme to visit your local main agent and have the underside of the body steam cleaned. This will take about 1½ hours. All traces of dirt and oil will be removed and the underside can then be inspected carefully for rust, damaged hydraulic pipes, frayed electrical wiring and similar maladies.

3 At the same time the engine compartment should be cleaned in the same manner. If steam cleaning facilities are not available then brush a water soluble cleanser over the whole engine and engine compartment with a stiff paintbrush, working it well in where there is an

2.4 Door drain holes - these must be kept clear

Chapter 12/Bodywork and chassis

accumulation of oil and dirt. Do not paint the ignition system but protect it with oily rags when the cleanser is washed off. As the cleanser is washed away it will take with it all traces of oil and dirt, leaving the engine looking clean and bright.

4 The wheel arches should be given particular attention as undersealing can easily come away here and stones and dirt thrown up from the road wheels can soon cause the paint to chip and flake and so allow rust to set in. If rust is found, clean down to the bare metal with wet and dry paper, paint on an anticorrosive coating and renew the paintwork and undercoating.

5 The bodywork should be washed once a week or when dirty. Thoroughly wet the vehicle to soften the dirt and then wash the vehicle down with a soft sponge and plenty of clean water. If the surplus dirt is not washed off very gently, in time it will wear the paint down as surely as wet and dry paper. It is best to use a hose if this is available. Give the vehicle a final wash down and then dry with a soft chamois leather to prevent the formation of spots.

6 Spots of tar and grease thrown up from the road can be removed with a rag dampened with gasoline.

7 Once every six months, or every three months, if wished, give the bodywork and chromium trim a thoroughly good wax polish. If a chromium cleaner is used to remove rust on any of the vehicle's plated parts remember that the cleaner also removes part of the chromium so use sparingly.

3 Maintenance - upholstery and carpets

1 Remove the carpets and thoroughly vacuum clean the interior of the vehicle every three months or more frequently if necessary.

2 Beat out the carpets and vacuum clean them if they are very dirty. If the headlining or upholstery is soiled apply an upholstery cleaner with a damp sponge and wipe off with a clean dry cloth.

4 Minor body damage - repair

The photo sequence on pages 246 and 247 illustrates the operations detailed in the following sub-Sections.

Repair of minor scratches in the vehicle's bodywork

If the scratch is very superficial, and does not penetrate to the metal of the bodywork, repair is very simple. Lightly rub the area of the scratch with a paintwork renovator (eg: T-cut), or a very fine cutting paste, to remove loose paint from the scratch and to clear the surrounding bodywork of wax polish. Rinse the area with clean water.

Apply touch-up paint to the scratch using a thin paint brush, continue to apply thin layers of paint until the surface of the paint in the scratch is level with the surrounding paintwork. Allow the new paint at least two weeks to harden; then blend it into the surrounding paintwork by rubbing the paintwork in the scratch area with a paintwork renovator (eg: T-cut), or a very fine cutting paste. Finally, apply wax polish.

An alternative to painting over the scratch is to use Holts 'Scratch-Patch.' Use the same preparation for the affected area; then simply pick a patch of a suitable size to cover the scratch completely. Hold the patch against the scratch and burnish its backing paper; the patch will adhere to the paintwork, freeing itself from the backing paper at the same time. Polish the affected area to blend the patch into the surrounding paintwork. Where the scratch has penetrated through to the metal of the bodywork, causing the metal to rust, a different repair technique is required. Remove any loose rust from the bottom of the scratch with a penknife, then apply rust inhibiting paint (eg: Kurust) to prevent the formation of rust in the future. Using a rubber nylon applicator fill the scratch with bodystopper paste. If required, this paste can be mixed with cellulose thinners to provide a very thin paste which is ideal for filling narrow scratches. Before the stopper-paste in the scratch hardens, wrap a piece of smooth cotton rag around the top of a finger. Dip the finger in cellulose thinners and then quickly sweep it across the surface of the stopper-paste in the scratch; this will ensure that the surface of the stopper-paste is slightly hollowed. The scratch can now be painted over as described earlier in this Section.

Repair of dents in the vehicle's bodywork

When deep denting of the vehicle's bodywork has taken place, the first task is to pull the dent out, until the affected bodywork almost attains its original shape. There is little point in trying to restore the original shape completely, as the metal in the damaged area will have stretched on impact and cannot be reshaped fully to its original contour. It is better to bring the level of the dent up to a point which is about 1/8 in (3 mm) below the level of the surrounding bodywork. In cases where the dent is very shallow anyway, it is not worth trying to pull it out at all.

If the underside of the dent is accessible, it can be hammered out gently from behind, using a mallet with a wooden or plastic head. Whilst doing this, hold a suitable block of wood firmly against the impact from the hammer blows and thus prevent a large area of bodywork from being 'belled-out.'

Should the dent be in a section of the bodywork which has a double skin or some other factor making it inaccessible from behind, a different technique is called for. Drill several small holes thru the metal inside the dent area - particularly in the deeper sections. Then screw long self-tapping screws into the holes just sufficiently for them to gain a good purchase in the metal. Now the dent can be pulled out by pulling on the protruding heads of the screws with a pair of pliers.

The next stage of the repair is the removal of the paint from the damaged area, and from an inch or so of the surrounding 'sound' bodywork. This is accomplished most easily by using a wire brush or abrasive pad on a power drill, although it can be done just as effectively by hand using sheets of abrasive paper. To complete the preparations for filling, score the surface of the bare metal with a screwdriver or the tang of a file, or alternatively, drill small holes in the affected area. This will provide a really good 'key' for filler paste.

To complete the repair see the Section on filling and respraying.

Repair of rust holes or gashes in the vehicle's bodywork

Remove all paint from the affected area and from an inch or so of the surrounding 'sound' bodywork, using an abrasive pad or a wire brush on a power drill. If these are not available a few sheets of abrasive paper will do the job just as effectively. With the paint removed you will be able to gauge the severity of the corrosion and therefore decide whether to replace the whole panel (if this is possible) or to repair the affected area. Replacement body panels are not as expensive as most people think and it is often quicker and more satisfactory to fit a new panel than to attempt to repair large areas of corrosion.

Remove all fittings from the affected area except those which will act as a guide to the original shape of the damaged bodywork (eg: headlamp shells etc). Then, using tin snips or a hacksaw blade, remove all loose metal and any other metal badly affected by corrosion. Hammer the edges of the hole inwards in order to create a slight depression for the filler paste.

Wire brush the affected area to remove the powdery rust from the surface of the remaining metal. Paint the affected area with rust inhibiting paint (eg: Kurust); if the back of the rusted area is accessible treat this also.

Before filling can take place it will be necessary to block the hole in some way. This can be achieved by the use of one of the following materials: Zinc gauze, Aluminium tape or Polyurethane foam.

Zinc gauge is probably the best material to use for a large hole. Cut a piece to the approximate size and shape of the hole to be filled, then position it in the hole so that its edges are below the level of the surrounding bodywork. It can be retained in position by several blobs of filler paste around its periphery.

Aluminium tape should be used for small or very narrow holes. Pull a piece off the roll and trim it to the approximate size and shape required, then pull off the backing paper (if used) and stick the tape over the hole; it can be overlapped if the thickness of one piece is insufficient. Burnish down the edges of the tape with the handle of a screwdriver or similar, to ensure that the tape is securely attached to the metal underneath.

Polyurethane foam is best used where the hole is situated in a section of bodywork of complex shape, backed by a small box section (eg: where the sill panel meets the rear wheel arch - most vehicles). The unusual mixing procedure for this foam is as follows: Put equal amounts of fluid from each of the two cans provided in the kit, into one container. Stir until the mixture begins to thicken, then quickly pour the mixture into the hole, and hold a piece of cardboard over the larger apertures. Almost immediately the polyurethane will begin to expand, gushing frantically out of any small holes left unblocked. When the foam hardens it can be cut back to just below the level of the surrounding bodywork with a hacksaw blade.

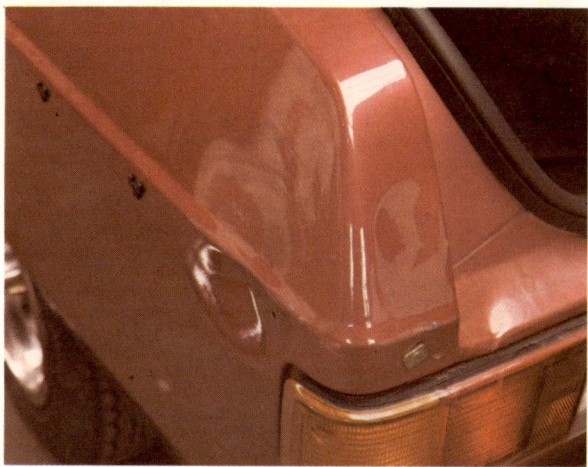

This sequence of photographs deals with the repair of the dent and scratch (above rear lamp) shown in this photo. The procedure will be similar for the repair of a hole. It should be noted that the procedures given here are simplified - more explicit instructions will be found in the text

In the case of a dent the first job - after removing surrounding trim - is to hammer out the dent where access is possible. This will minimise filling. Here, the large dent having been hammered out, the damaged area is being made slightly concave

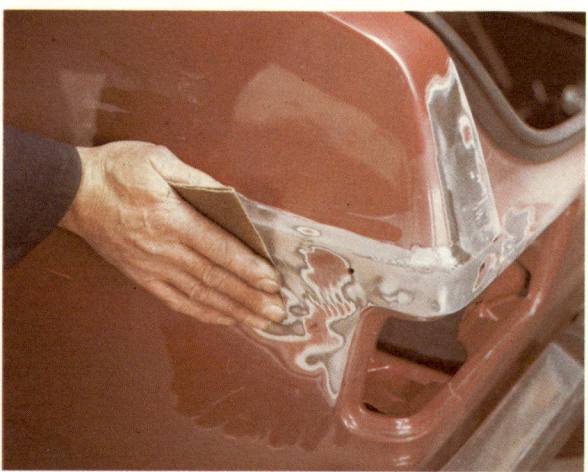

Now all paint must be removed from the damaged area, by rubbing with coarse abrasive paper. Alternatively, a wire brush or abrasive pad can be used in a power drill. Where the repair area meets good paintwork, the edge of the paintwork should be 'feathered', using a finer grade of abrasive paper

In the case of a hole caused by rusting, all damaged sheet-metal should be cut away before proceeding to this stage. Here, the damaged area is being treated with rust remover and inhibitor before being filled

Mix the body filler according to its manufacturer's instructions. In the case of corrosion damage, it will be necessary to block off any large holes before filling - this can be done with zinc gauze or aluminium tape. Make sure the area is absolutely clean before ...

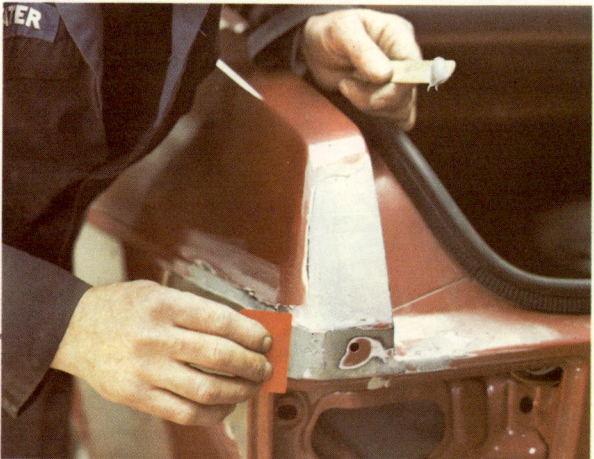

... applying the filler. Filler should be applied with a flexible applicator, as shown, for best results: the wooden spatula being used for confined areas. Apply thin layers of filler at 20-minute intervals, until the surface of the filler is slightly proud of the surrounding bodywork

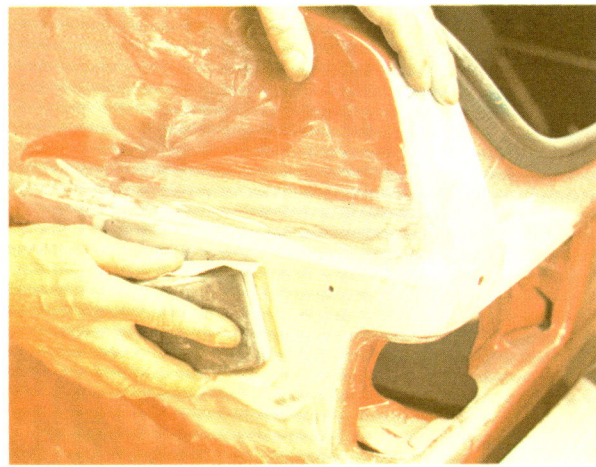
Initial shaping can be done with a Surform plane or Dreadnought file. Then, using progressively finer grades of wet-and-dry paper, wrapped around a sanding block, and copious amounts of clean water, rub-down the filler until really smooth and flat. Again, feather the edges of adjoining paintwork

The whole repair area can now be sprayed or brush-painted with primer. If spraying, ensure adjoining areas are protected from over-spray. Note that at least one-inch of the surrounding sound paintwork should be coated with primer. Primer has a 'thick' consistency, so will fill small imperfections

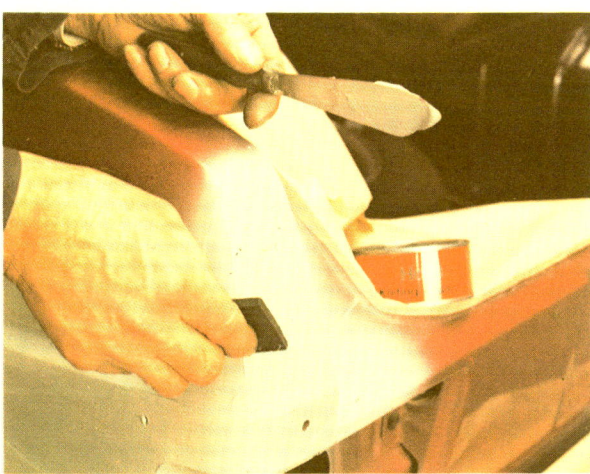
Again, using plenty of water, rub down the primer with a fine grade of wet-and-dry paper (400 grade is probably best) until it is really smooth and well blended into the surrounding paintwork. Any remaining imperfections can now be filled by carefully applied knifing stopper paste

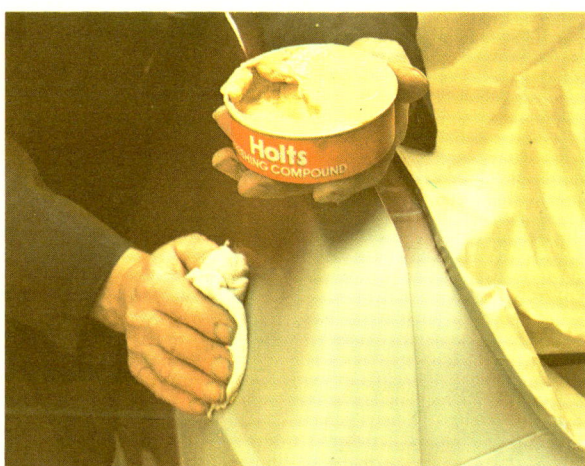
When the stopper has hardened, rub-down the repair area again before applying the final coat of primer. Before rubbing-down this last coat of primer, ensure the repair area is blemish-free - use more stopper if necessary. To ensure that the surface of the primer is really smooth use some finishing compound

The top coat can now be applied. When working out of doors, pick a dry, warm and wind-free day. Ensure surrounding areas are protected from over-spray. Agitate the aerosol thoroughly, then spray the centre of the repair area, working outwards with a circular motion. Apply the paint as several thin coats.

After a period of about two-weeks, which the paint needs to harden fully, the surface of the repaired area can be 'cut' with a mild cutting compound prior to wax polishing. When carrying out bodywork repairs, remember that the quality of the finished job is proportional to the time and effort expended

Chapter 12/Bodywork and chassis

Bodywork repairs - filling and re-spraying

Before using this Section, see the Sections on dent, deep scratch, rust hole and gash repairs.

Many types of bodyfiller are available, but generally speaking those proprietary kits which contain a tin of filler paste and a tube of resin hardener (eg; Holts Cataloy) are best for this type of repair. A wide, flexible plastic or nylon applicator will be found invaluable for imparting a smooth and well contoured finish to the surface of the filler.

Mix up a little filler on a clean piece of card or board - use the hardener sparingly (follow the maker's instructions on the packet) otherwise the filler will set very rapidly.

Using the applicator, apply the filler paste to the prepared area; draw the applicator across the surface of the filler to achieve the correct contour and to level the filler surface. As soon as a contour that approximates to the correct one is achieved, stop working the paste - if you carry on too long the paste will become sticky and begin to 'pick-up' on the applicator. Continue to add thin layers of filler paste at twenty minute intervals until the level of the filler is just 'proud' of the surrounding bodywork.

Once the filler has hardened, excess can be removed using a Surform plane or Dreadnought file. From then on, progressively finer grades of abrasive paper should be used, starting with a 40 grade production paper and finishing with 400 grade 'wet-and-dry' paper. Always wrap the abrasive paper around a flat rubber, cork or wooden block - otherwise the surface of the filler will not be completely flat. During the smoothing of the filler surface the 'wet-and-dry' paper should be periodically rinsed in water. This will ensure that a very smooth finish is imparted to the filler at the final stage.

At this stage the 'dent' should be surrounded by a ring of bare metal, which in turn should be encircled by the finely 'feathered' edge of the good paintwork. Rinse the repair area with clean water, until all of the dust produced by the rubbing-down operation is gone.

Spray the whole repair area with a light coat of grey primer - this will show up any imperfections in the surface of the filler. Repair these imperfections with fresh filler paste or bodystopper, and once more smooth the surface with abrasive paper. If bodystopper is used, it can be mixed with cellulose thinners to form a really thin paste which is ideal for filling small holes. Repeat this spray and repair procedure until you are satisfied that the surface of the filler and the feathered edge of the paintwork are perfect. Clean the repair area with clean water and allow it to dry fully.

The repair area is now ready for spraying. Paint spraying must be carried out in a warm, dry, windless and dust free atmosphere. This condition can be created artifically if you have access to a large indoor working area, but if you are forced to work in the open, you will have to pick your day very carefully. If you are working indoors, dousing the floor in the work area with water will 'lay' the dust which would otherwise be in the atmosphere. If the repair area is confined to one body panel, mask off the surrounding panels; this will help to minimise the effects of a slight mis-match in paint colors. Bodywork fittings (eg; chrome strips, door handles etc) will also need to be masked off. Use genuine masking tape and several thicknesses of newspaper for the masking operation.

Before commencing to spray, agitate the aerosol can thoroughly, then spray a test area (an old tin, or similar) until the technique is mastered. Cover the repair area with a thick coat of primer; the thickness should be built up using several thin layers of paint rather than one thick one. Using 400 grade 'wet-and-dry' paper, rub down the surface of the primer until it is really smooth. While doing this, the work area should be thoroughly doused with water, and the 'wet-and-dry' paper periodically rinsed in water. Allow to dry before spraying on more paint.

Spray on the top coat, again building up the thickness by using several thin layers of paint. Start spraying in the centre of the repair area and then, using a circular motion, work outwards until the whole area and about 2 inches of the surrounding original paintwork is covered. Remove all masking material 10 to 15 minutes after spraying on the final coat of paint.

Allow the new paint at least 2 weeks to harden fully; then, using a paintwork renovator (eg; T-Cut) or a very fine cutting paste, blend the edges of the new paint into the existing paintwork. Finally, apply wax polish.

5 Major bodywork damage - repair

Where serious body damage has occurred, or large areas need renewal due to neglect, it means that completely new sections or panels will be required. Where these are 'bolt-on' panels, the procedure is reasonably straightforward, but where welding is required it is best left to the professionals. If damage is due to impact, it will also be necessary to check the alignment of the chassis frame and bodyshell; in such cases the services of the official Toyota dealer or a bodywork repair specialist will be required, so that special alignment jigs can be used. If a body is left misaligned it is first of all dangerous as the vehicle will not handle properly, and secondly uneven stresses will be imposed on the steering, suspension and transmission causing abnormal wear or complete failure. Tire wear may also be uneven and excessive.

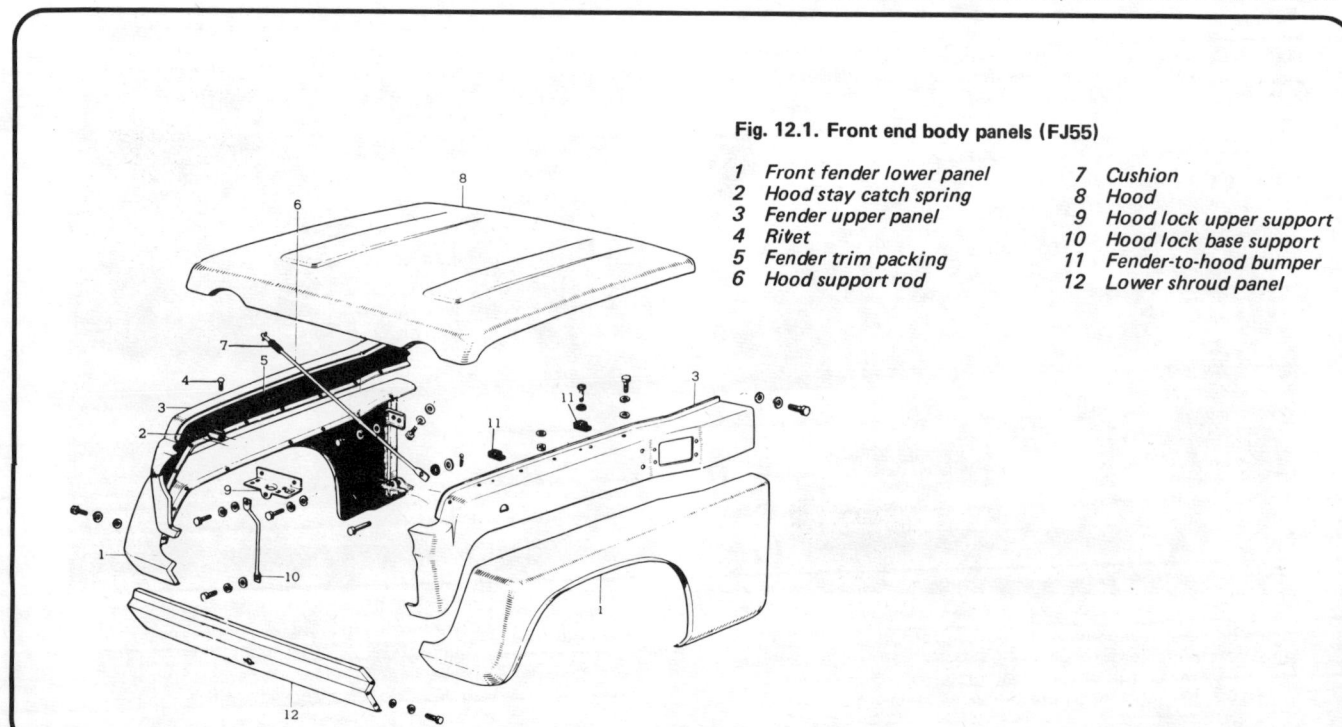

Fig. 12.1. Front end body panels (FJ55)

1. Front fender lower panel
2. Hood stay catch spring
3. Fender upper panel
4. Rivet
5. Fender trim packing
6. Hood support rod
7. Cushion
8. Hood
9. Hood lock upper support
10. Hood lock base support
11. Fender-to-hood bumper
12. Lower shroud panel

6 Maintenance - hinges and locks

1 Periodically, lubricate the hinges of the doors, hood, tailgate, etc. with a few drops of engine or light lubricating oil.
2 Similarly lubricate the hood release mechanism and door lock mechanism.
3 Apply a little general purpose grease to items such as door lock strikers and rear gate catches.

7 Doors - rattles and their rectification

1 Check first that the door is not loose at the hinges and that the latch is holding the door firmly in position. Check also that the door lines up with the aperture in the body.
2 If the hinges are loose, or the door is out of alignment, it will be necessary to reset the hinge positions. This is a straightforward matter after slackening the hinge retaining screws slightly, following which the door can be repositioned in/out or up/down.
3 If the latch is holding the door properly, it should hold the door tightly when fully latched and the door should line up with the body. If adjustment is required, slacken the striker plate screws slightly and reposition the plate in/out or up/down as necessary.
4 Other rattles from the door could be caused by wear or looseness in the window winder, or the glass channels, seal strips and interior lock mechanism.
5 With the passage of time, vehicles which have been subjected to rough usage will develop rattles in rear door/tailgate hinges and catches. Unless you are prepared to renew all these items, it will probably be very difficult to eliminate them entirely.

8 Doors - removal and installation

1 Several different types of door are used on Land Cruiser models, and the instructions given in this Section are necessarily of a general nature.
2 On models which have a canvas top, the door can generally be removed by pulling out the door hinge pins. During this operation it is best to obtain assistance to support the door, or to support the door on suitable jacks or blocks.
3 For other models, it will again be necessary to support the door weight, but the hinge retaining bolts can then be removed. If the same door is to be installed, it is a good idea to mark around the hinge first so that the door alignment is not altered.
4 Installation of doors is a straightforward operation. Adjustment can be made at the hinges and striker plates as necessary.

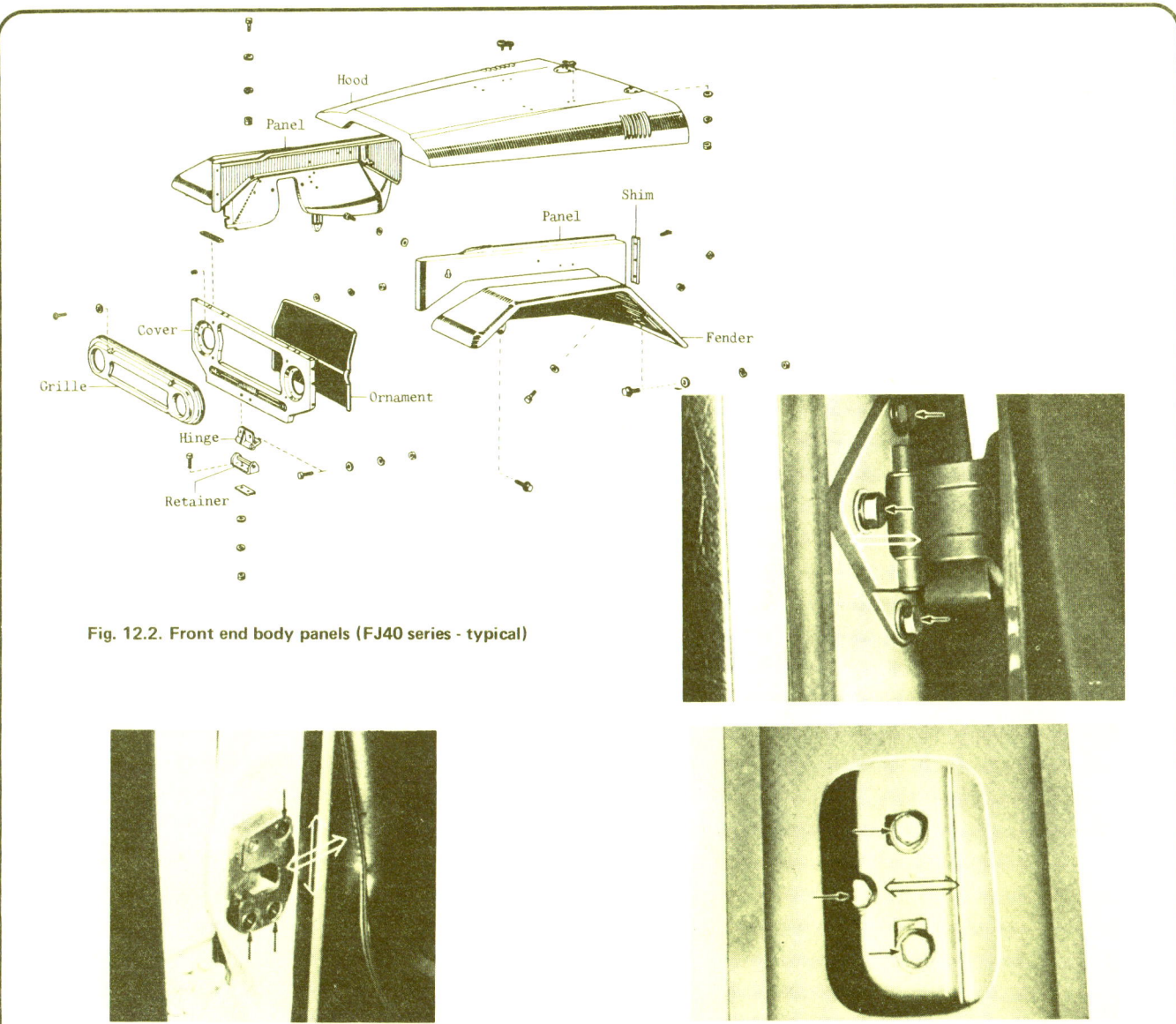

Fig. 12.2. Front end body panels (FJ40 series - typical)

Fig. 12.3. Door hinges and strikers, showing direction of adjustment - typical

9.2 Remove the screw from the trim plate

9.3 The regulator handle spring clip. It should be in this position when installing

9.4 One of the trim panel spring clips

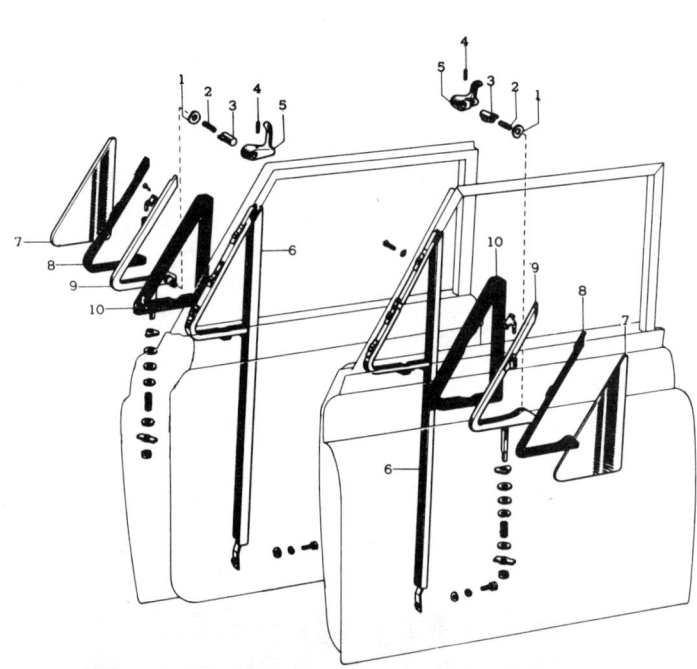

Fig. 12.4. Front door window glass - typical for early FJ55 models

1. Wave washer
2. Compression spring
3. Ventilating window lock handle push button
4. Pin
5. Door ventilating window lock handle
6. Division bar
7. Ventilating window glass
8. Ventilating window frame strip
9. Ventilating window glass frame
10. Ventilating window weatherstrip

9.6 Some of the regulator retaining bolts

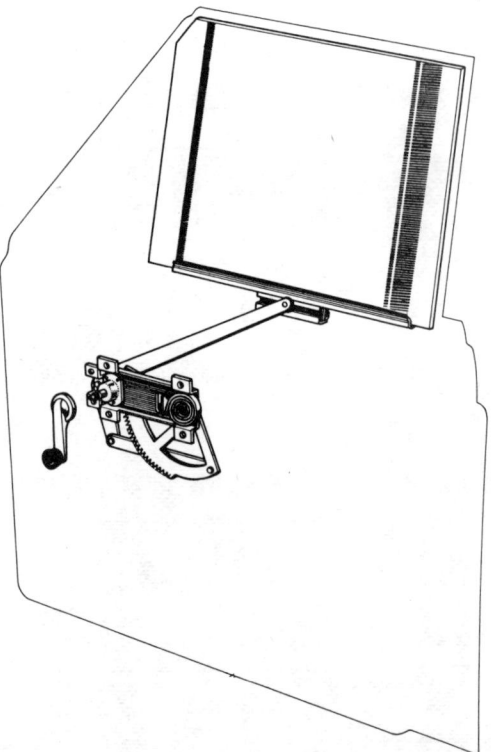

Fig. 12.5. Window regulator - early FJ55 models

9 Front door window regulator and glass (FJ55) - removal and installation

1 Remove the retaining screws and take off the armrest (where fitted).
2 Remove the screw and take off the trim plate for the inside door handle (photo).
3 Press in the door trim panel and plastic escutcheon so that the window regulator handle spring clip can be seen. Use a bent wire to pull the clip away, then remove the handle (photo).
4 Using a suitable flat tool, carefully pry out the trim panel clips from their sockets in the door panels. Remove the panel completely; also carefully remove the plastic sheeting, where applicable (photo).
5 Remove the two attaching bolts and disconnect the roller from the glass channel.
6 Remove the regulator retaining bolts (four on early models, eight on later models) and ease the regulator out of the service aperture (photo).
7 Carefully pry away the door window glass outer weatherstrip, taking care that paintwork is not damaged.
8 Where applicable, remove the division bar adjusting bolts, then remove the division bar glass run channel.
9 Where applicable, remove the three screws and remove the division bar rearwards from the door.
10 Raise the window glass upward and out of the door, turning it as necessary to permit removal.
11 Where a ventilator glass is installed, this can be removed by taking out the upper pivot bracket attaching screws and compression spring attaching nut.
12 Installation of the regulator and associated parts is a straightforward procedure, but apply a little general purpose grease to the various pivot points and sliding surfaces. Adjust the regulator for satisfactory operation before finally tightening the bolts.

10 Front door lock mechanism (FJ55) - removal and installation

Front door lock

1 Remove the trim panel as described in the previous Section.
2 Unscrew the door lock button (photo).
3 Raise the glass and disconnect the door lock remote control link, outside handle remote control lever and door lock cylinder.
4 Remove the attaching screws and take out the lock assembly.
5 Installation is a straightforward procedure, but first apply a little general purpose grease to the various pivot points and sliding surfaces. Ensure that the locking action is satisfactory before finally tightening the attaching screws.

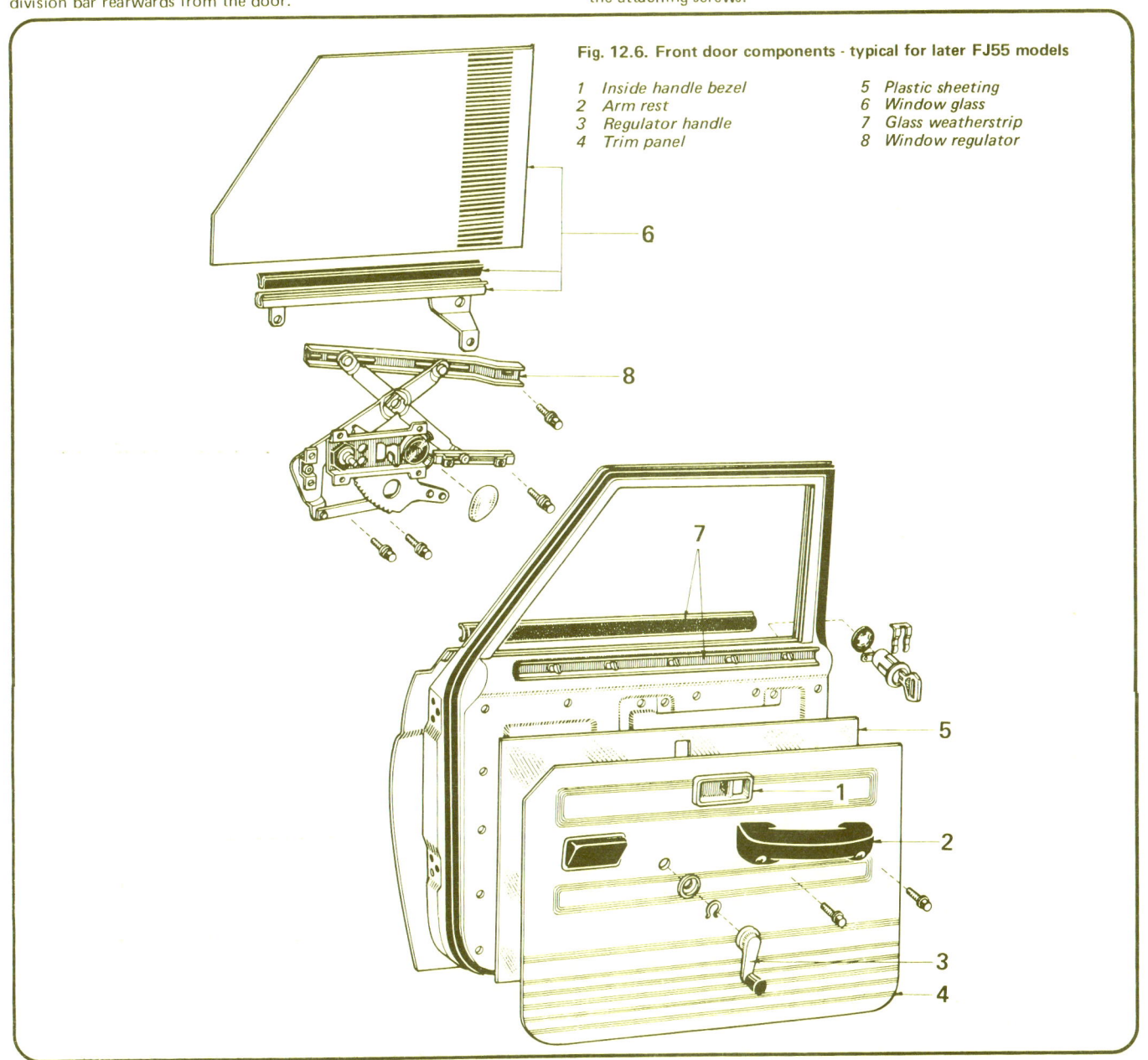

Fig. 12.6. Front door components - typical for later FJ55 models

1 Inside handle bezel
2 Arm rest
3 Regulator handle
4 Trim panel
5 Plastic sheeting
6 Window glass
7 Glass weatherstrip
8 Window regulator

Door lock cylinder

6 Remove the trim panel as described in the previous Section.
7 Raise the window glass and detach the lock mechanism from the lock cylinder lever.
8 Slide away the spring clip and remove the lock cylinder from the door (photo).
9 Apply a little general purpose grease to the lever pivot pin, then install the cylinder by following the reverse of the removal procedure.

Outside handle

10 Remove the trim panel as described in the previous Section.
11 Raise the window glass and remove the outside handle attaching nut and screw.
12 Withdraw the outside handle from the door.
13 Installation is the reverse of the removal procedure.

Door lock remote control

14 Remove the trim panel as described in the previous Section.
15 Raise the window glass and disconnect the remote control from the door lock.
16 Remove the attaching screw and bolts, and remove the remote control (photo).
17 Installation is the reverse of the removal procedure.

11 Rear door window glass and regulator (FJ55) - removal and installation

1 Remove the door trim panel. The procedure for this is virtually identical to that given for the front door trim panel - see Section 9.

Window glass

2 Lower the glass, then remove the two regulator attaching bolts. Disconnect the roller from the glass channel and lower the glass into the door.
3 Remove the glass inner and outer weatherstrips.
4 Remove the division bar (two or three attaching screws).
5 Remove the quarter window glass and the door window glass.
6 Installation is the reverse of the removal procedure, but first apply a little general purpose grease to the various pivot points and sliding surfaces. Adjust the regulator for satisfactory operation before finally tightening the bolts.

Regulator

7 Lower the window glass, then remove the two regulator attaching bolts. Disconnect the roller from the glass channel.
8 Remove the four regulator attaching bolts and ease the regulator out of the service aperture.
9 Installation is the reverse of the removal procedure, but first apply a little general purpose grease to the various pivot points and sliding surfaces. Adjust the regulator for satisfactory operation before finally tightening the bolts.

12 Rear door lock mechanism (FJ55) - removal and installation

Rear door lock

1 Remove the rear door trim panel - see paragraph 1 of the previous Section.
2 Disconnect the door opening control link and locking control link.
3 Remove the three screws and remove the lock assembly.
4 Installation is the reverse of the removal procedure.

Door lock remote control

5 Remove the rear door trim panel - see paragraph 1 of the previous Section.
6 Remove the remote control pushbutton, then disconnect the door locking control link from the locking control link assembly.
7 Remove the attaching screws, then disconnect the locking control link from the lock; remove the locking control link.
8 Remove the inside handle attaching screw, then disconnect the control link from the door knob. Remove the opening control link with the inside handle.
9 Installation is a straightforward procedure, but first apply a little general purpose grease to the various pivot points and sliding surfaces. Ensure that the locking action is satisfactory before finally tightening the attaching screws.

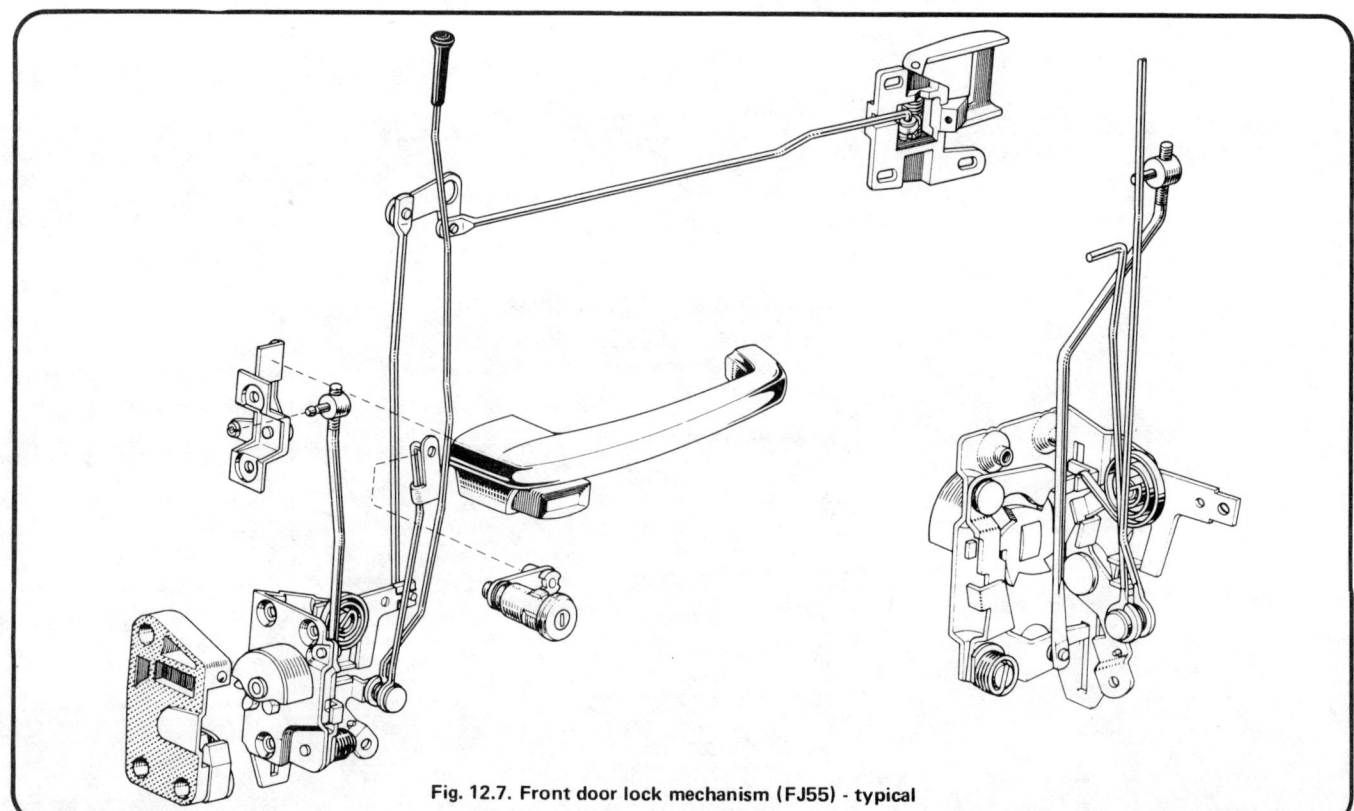

Fig. 12.7. Front door lock mechanism (FJ55) - typical

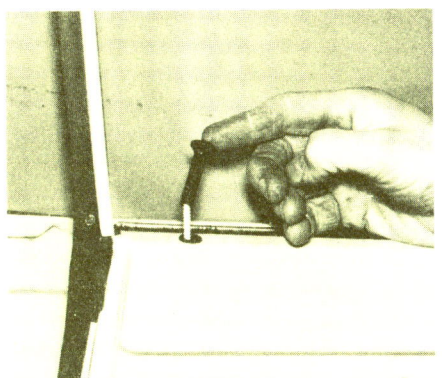

10.2 The door lock button

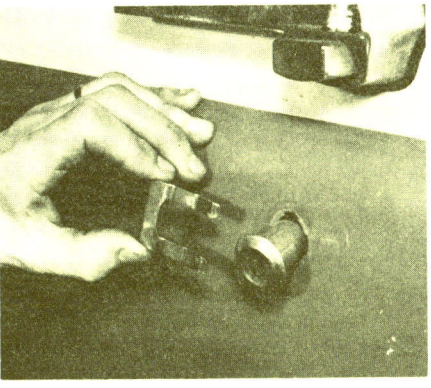

10.8 The door lock cylinder, showing the spring clip which is installed inside the door panel

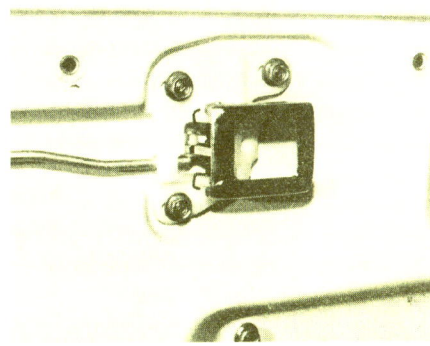

10.16 Door remote control handle

Fig. 12.8. Rear door window glass (FJ55) - typical

1 Arm rest
2 Regulator handle
3 Bezel
4 Trim board
5 Plastic sheeting
6 Division bar support
7 Window regulator
8 Division bar
9 Window glass
10 Quarter window glass

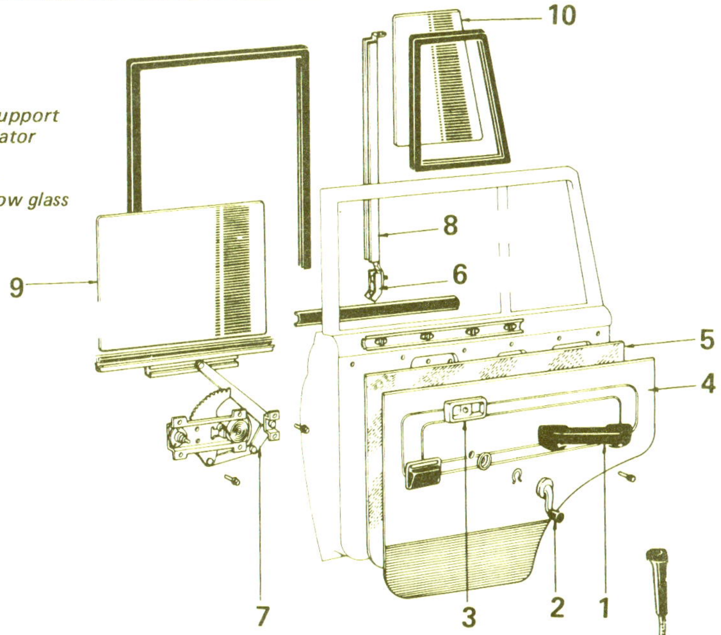

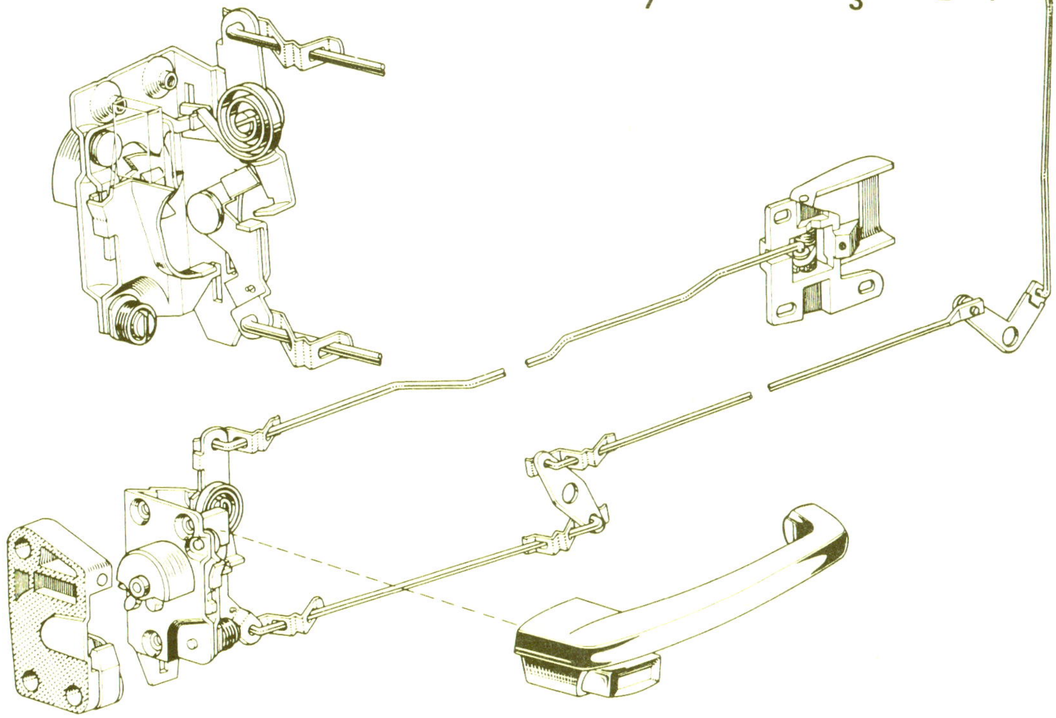

Fig. 12.9. Rear door lock mechanism (FJ55) - typical

13 Door window glass and regulator (FJ40 series) - removal and installation

Note: Refer to Section 17 for FJ45 models.

Early models
1 Carefully remove the weatherstrip from the door frame.
2 Remove the window frame retaining bolts, then lift the frame and window out of the door.
3 Remove the glass from the window frame.
4 Detach the glass channel from the window glass.
5 Remove the four attaching screws and detach the regulator assembly.
6 Take the regulator out of the door.
7 Installation is the reverse of the removal procedure, but first apply a little general purpose grease to the pivot points and friction surfaces of the assembly. Check the regulator action before finally tightening the bolts.

Later models
8 The doors on later models have a trim panel, and are very similar to those referred to in Section 9.

14 Ventilator window (FJ40 series) - removal and installation

1 Remove the ventilator window handle retaining pin.
2 Remove the ventilator window lock handle shaft nut, then remove the lock handle shaft from the glass frame.
3 If necessary, remove the glass from the frame.
4 Installation is the reverse of the removal procedure.

15 Door fixed window glass (FJ40 series) - removal and installation

1 Remove the door bumper rubbers at the bottom ends of the door glass channels.
2 Lift away the door window set channel.
3 Installation is the reverse of the removal procedure.

16 Front door lock mechanism (FJ40 series) - removal and installation

Note: Refer to Section 17 for FJ45 models.

Early models - hard-top
1 Remove the nuts and spring washers from the front door inside handle, then pull off the outside door handle.
2 Remove the four attaching screws and take off the door lock baseplate.
3 If necessary, the door lock mechanism can easily be dismantled.
4 Installation is the reverse of the removal procedure.

Early models - canvas top
5 Remove the door inside handle retaining nuts and detach the inside handle from the door lock spring. Detach the spring from the side channel.
6 Installation is the reverse of the removal procedure. Use adjusting washers as necessary to obtain a satisfactory latching action.

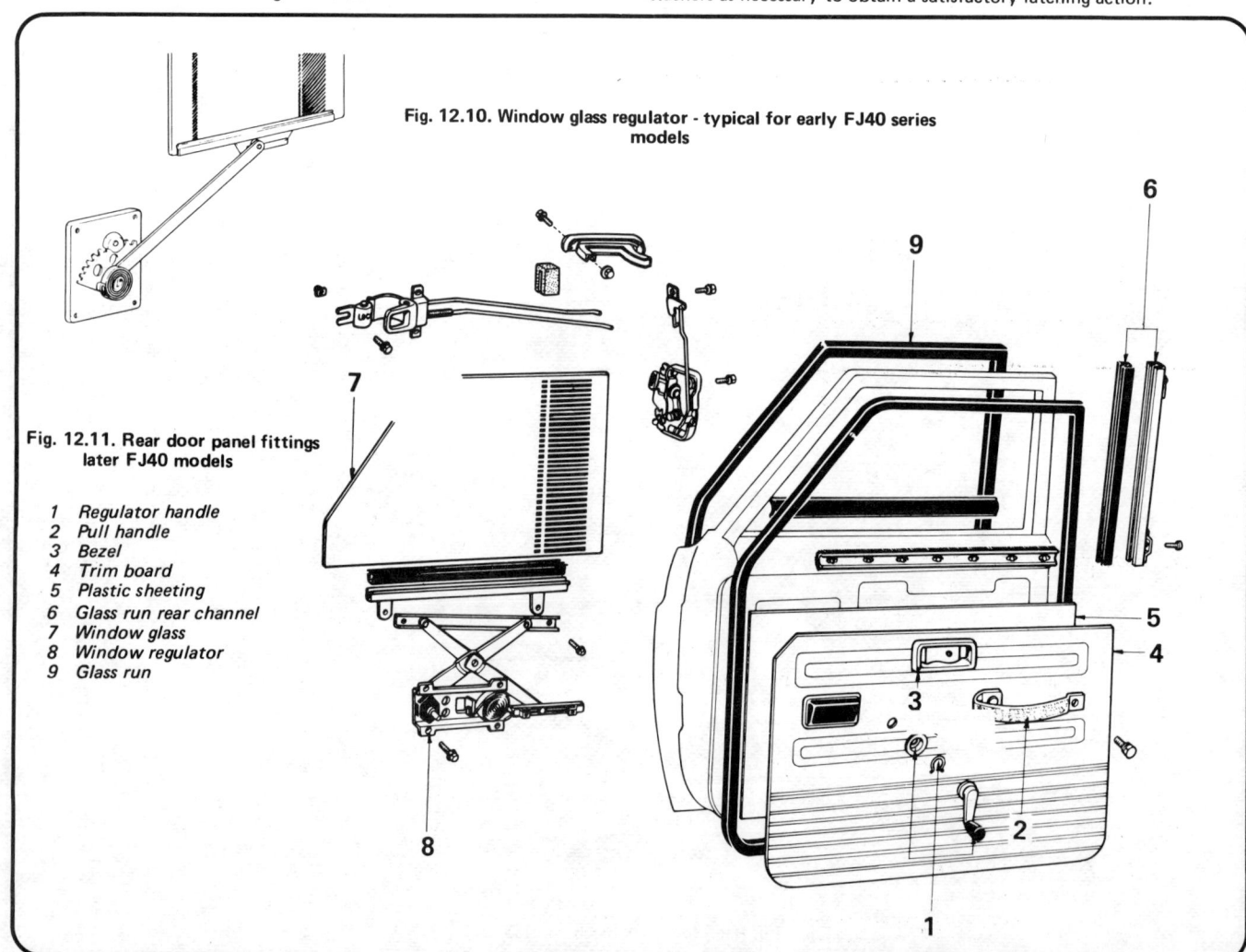

Fig. 12.10. Window glass regulator - typical for early FJ40 series models

Fig. 12.11. Rear door panel fittings later FJ40 models

1 Regulator handle
2 Pull handle
3 Bezel
4 Trim board
5 Plastic sheeting
6 Glass run rear channel
7 Window glass
8 Window regulator
9 Glass run

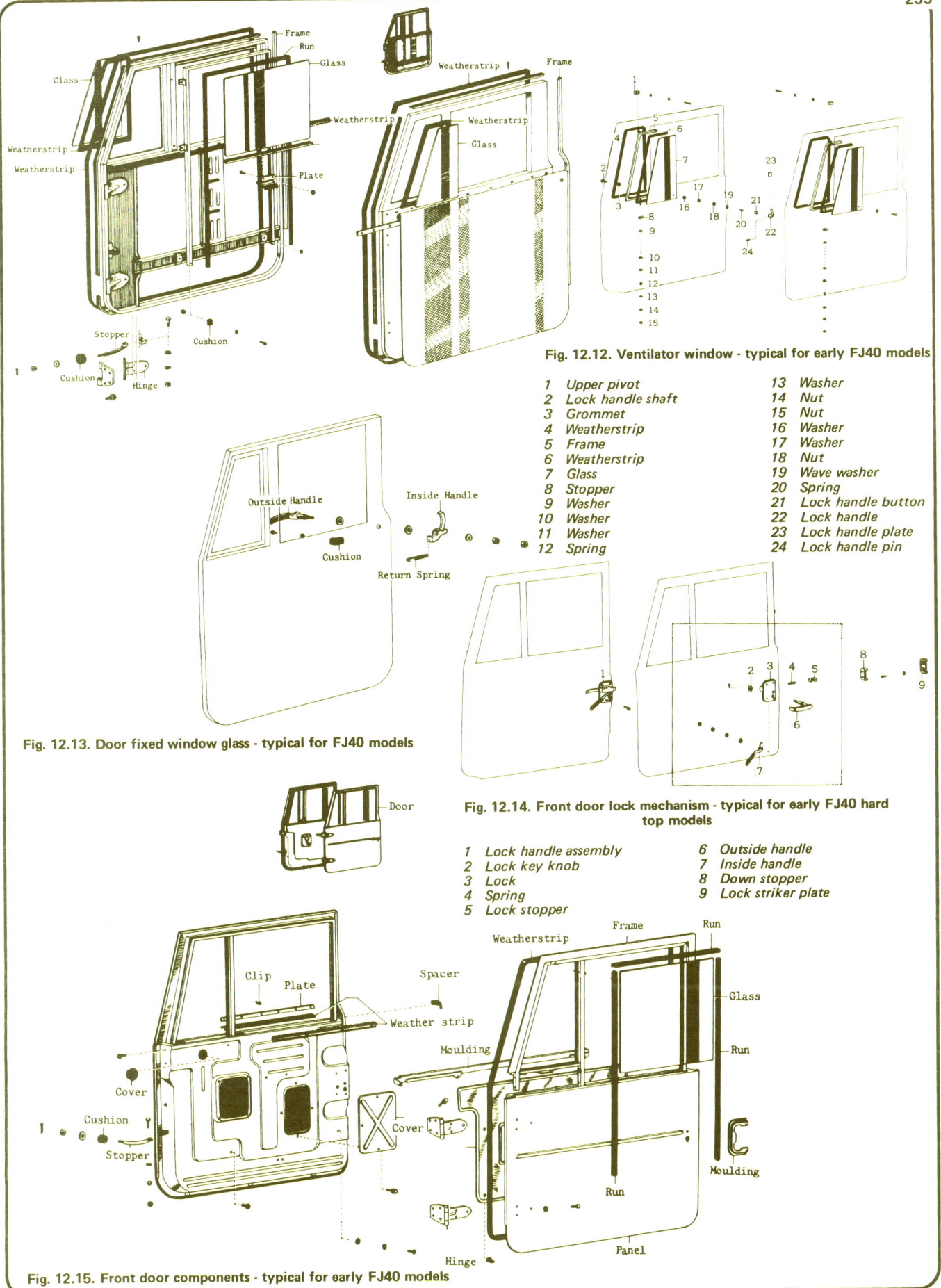

Fig. 12.12. Ventilator window - typical for early FJ40 models

1 Upper pivot
2 Lock handle shaft
3 Grommet
4 Weatherstrip
5 Frame
6 Weatherstrip
7 Glass
8 Stopper
9 Washer
10 Washer
11 Washer
12 Spring
13 Washer
14 Nut
15 Nut
16 Washer
17 Washer
18 Nut
19 Wave washer
20 Spring
21 Lock handle button
22 Lock handle
23 Lock handle plate
24 Lock handle pin

Fig. 12.13. Door fixed window glass - typical for FJ40 models

Fig. 12.14. Front door lock mechanism - typical for early FJ40 hard top models

1 Lock handle assembly
2 Lock key knob
3 Lock
4 Spring
5 Lock stopper
6 Outside handle
7 Inside handle
8 Down stopper
9 Lock striker plate

Fig. 12.15. Front door components - typical for early FJ40 models

17 Door window glass, regulator and door lock (FJ45) - removal and installation

1 Press out the retaining pins, and remove the window regulator handle and door inside handle.
2 Carefully detach the trim panel and plastic water shield.
3 Remove the set bolts and detach the door glass channel.
4 Disconnect and remove the window regulator from the door glass skirt holder.
5 Remove the skirt holder and door glass cleaner rubber; take out the door glass by pulling upward.
6 Remove the door lock and door lock remote control assembly, then remove the door lock outside handle.
7 Installation is the reverse of the removal procedure, but first apply a little general purpose grease to the various pivot points and sliding surfaces.

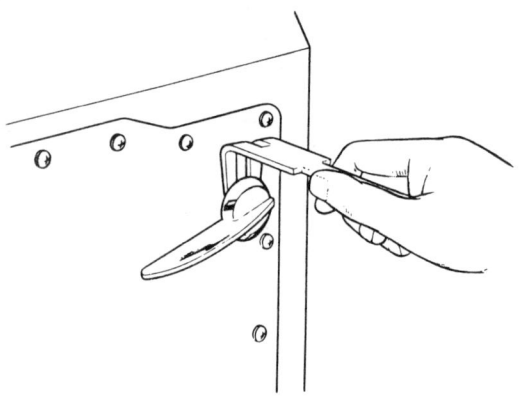

Fig. 12.16. Door inside handle removal - FJ45 models

18 Back doors and rear gates - general

1 Several different types of back door have been used, but the procedures for removal, and for removal of the lock mechanisms, are similar to those given for other doors in the model range. Refer to the illustrations which show the important components of the rear gates.

Fig. 12.17. Door window glass regulator arrangment - FJ45 models (front door illustrated)

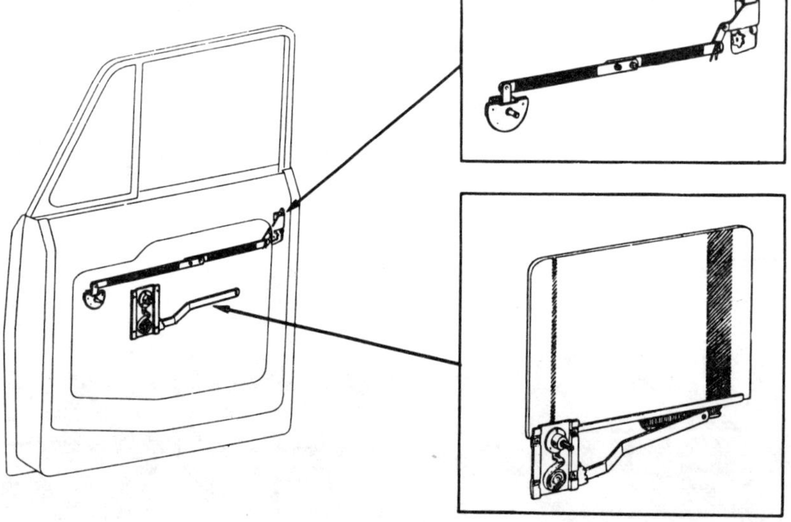

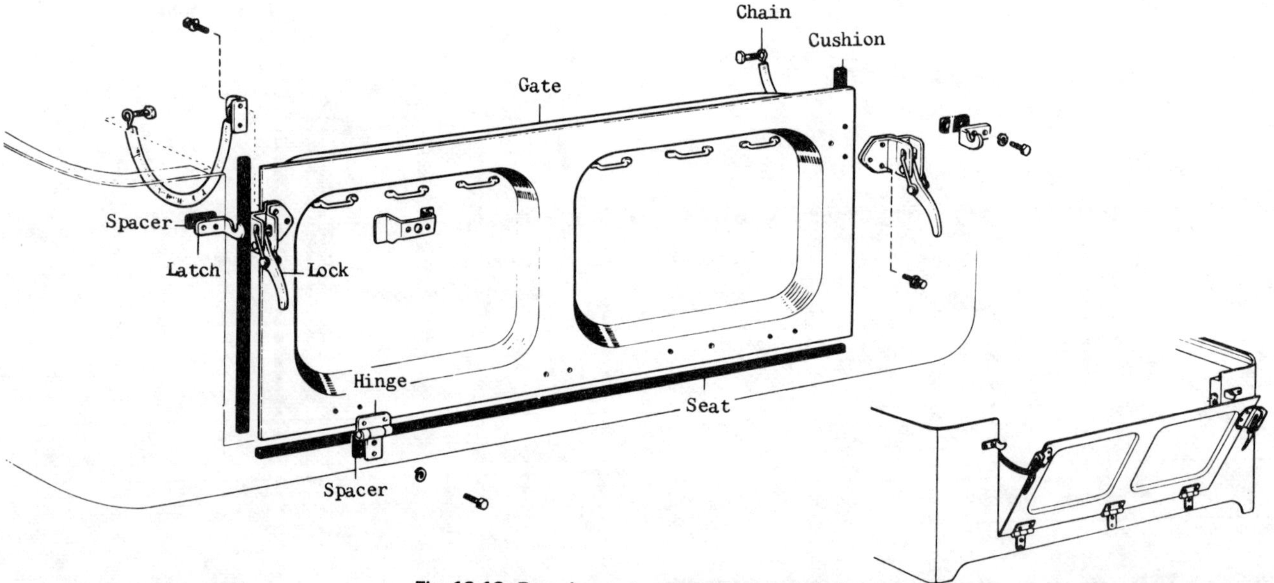

Fig. 12.18. Rear drop gate components - typical

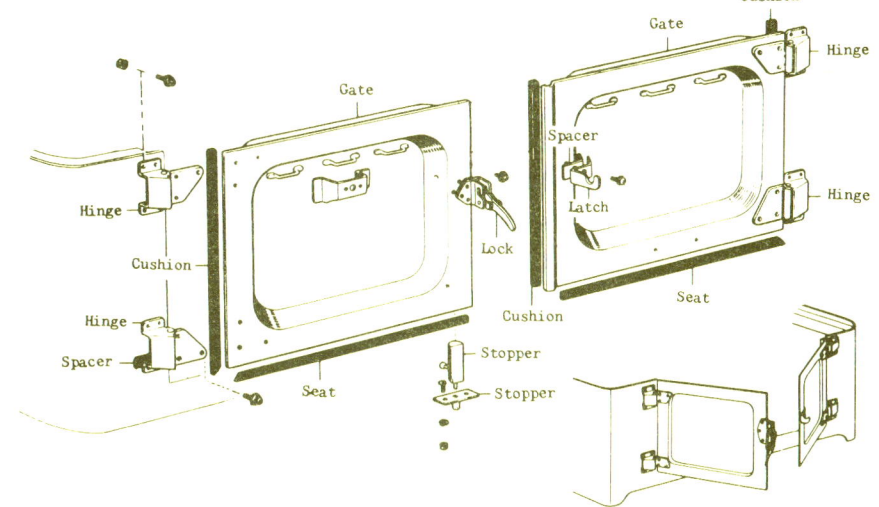

Fig. 12.19. Rear swing door components - typical

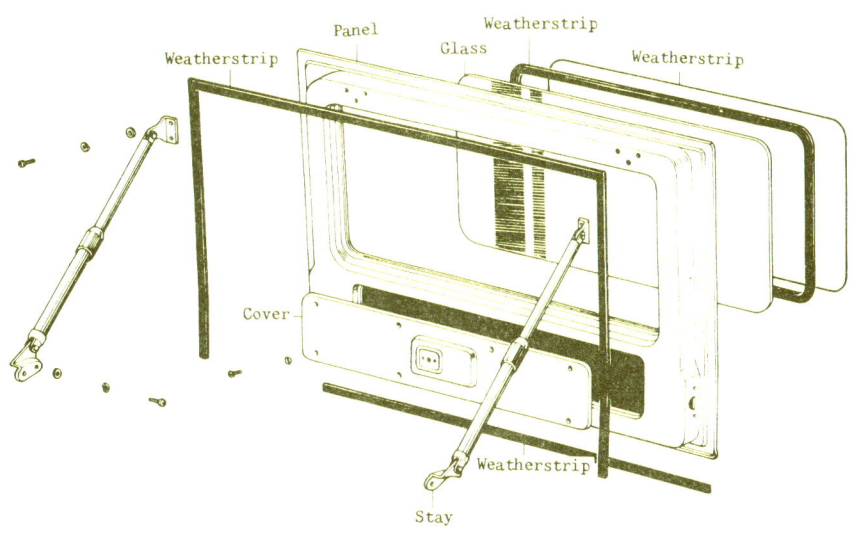

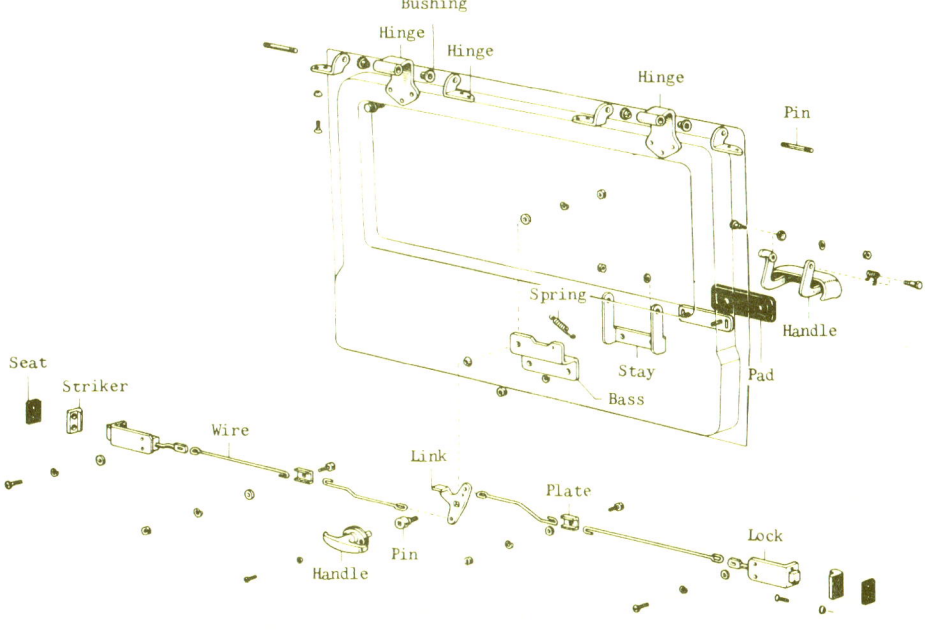

Fig. 12.20. Rear gate components - typical

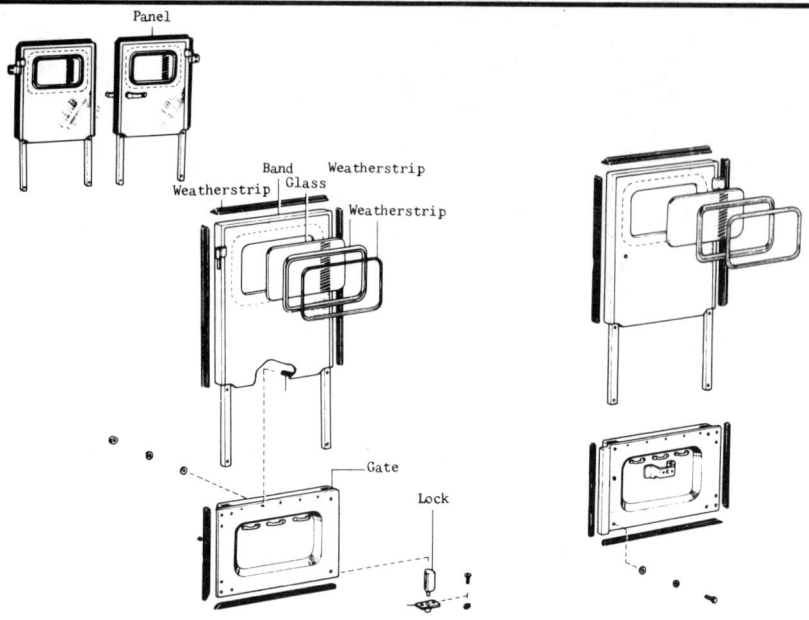

Fig. 12.21. Rear swing gate components - typical for early models

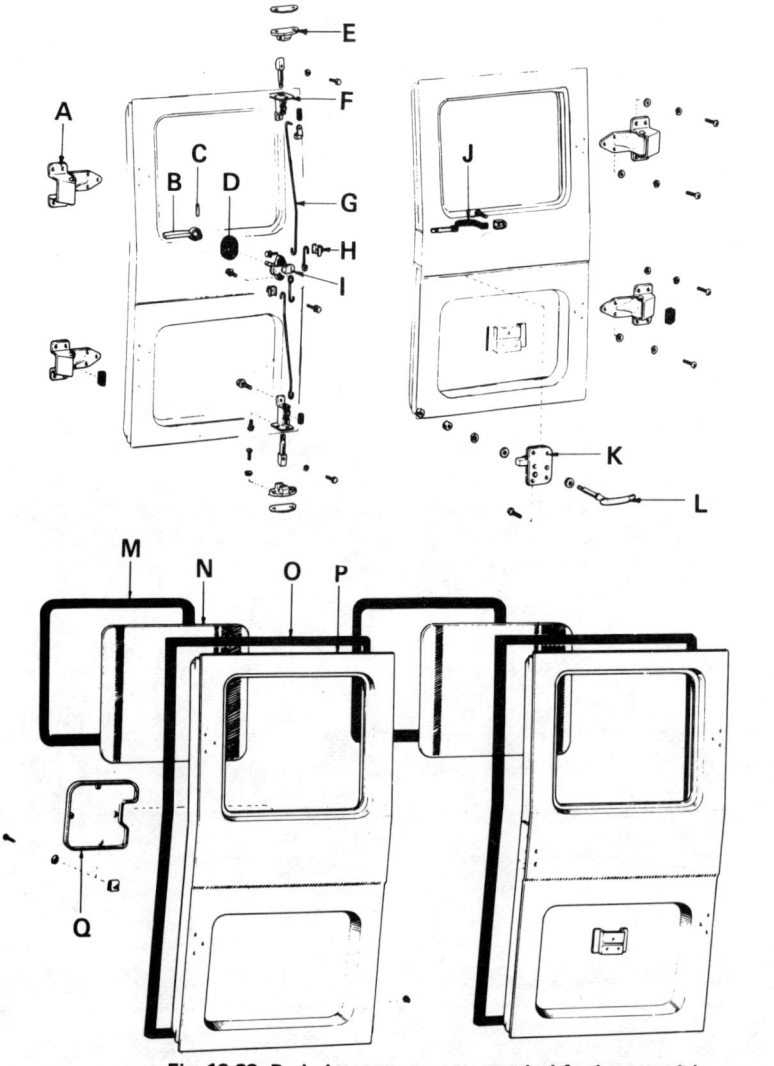

Fig. 12.22. Back door components - typical for later models

A Back door hinge	F Catch base	J Safety grip	N Glass
B Inside handle	G Lock control rod	K Lock assembly	O Weatherstrip
C Lock pin	H Control plate	L Lock handle	P Panel
D Inside handle seat	I Lock control assembly	M Weatherstrip	Q Cover
E Lock catch			

Chapter 12/Bodywork and chassis

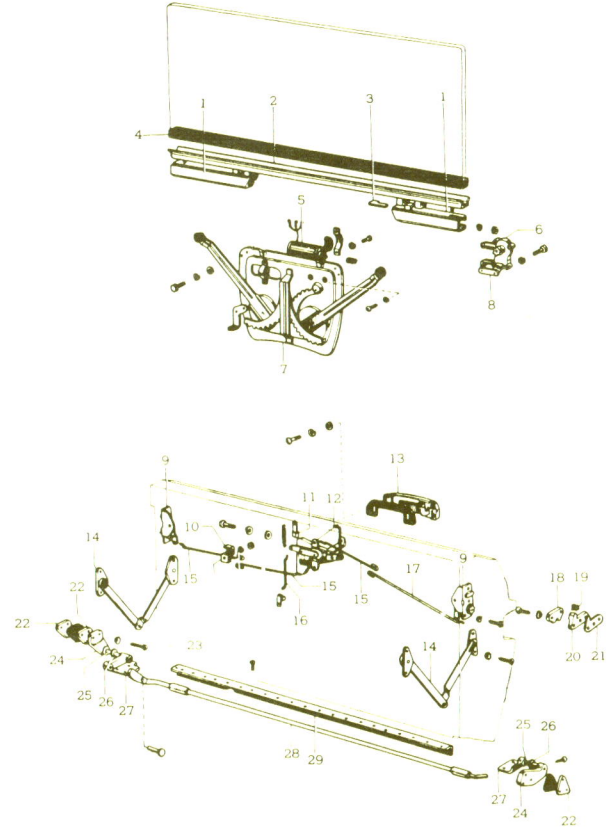

Fig. 12.23. Tailgate lock and regulator

1. Roller guide
2. Tailgate glass holder
3. Stop plate
4. Glass packing
5. Regulator motor
6. Regulator gearbox
7. Power regulator body
8. Gearbox retainer
9. Gate lock
10. Connecting plate
11. Lock snap
12. Tailgate remote control
13. Tailgate handle
14. Tailgate support stay
15. Connecting wire (No. 1)
16. Connecting wire (No. 3)
17. Connecting wire (No. 2)
18. Striker gear
19. Striker cushion
20. Striker
21. Striker plate
22. Hinge seat
23. Connecting plate
24. Pillar side hinge
25. Hinge shaft
26. Hinge bushing
27. Pillar side hinge
28. Torsion bar
29. Torsion bar cover

19 Tailgate (FJ55) - general

1 Many models have a power operated tailgate, the power being derived from an electric motor.
2 Where a crank handle operated tailgate is installed, the operating mechanism is generally similar to that for the power operated type with the exception of the motor (photo).

Tailgate - removal and installation

3 Lower the tailgate and remove the hinge attaching screws on the tailgate side.
4 Remove the support stay attaching screws.
5 Remove the torsion bar attaching screws.
6 Where applicable, detach the wiring to the tailgate window motor.
7 Remove the torsion bar cover and detach the torsion bar.
8 If necessary, remove the hinges from the side pillars.
9 Installation is the reverse of the removal procedure.
10 Adjust the tailgate hinges for satisfactory operation at the side pillar or on the tailgate sides. Adjust the torsion bar, if necessary, for satisfactory action of the tailgate.

20 Tailgate glass and regulator (FJ55) - removal and installation

Note: The procedure given is for the electrically operated type; the procedure for the crank handle type is generally similar.
1 Remove the inside cover and the plastic film (photo).

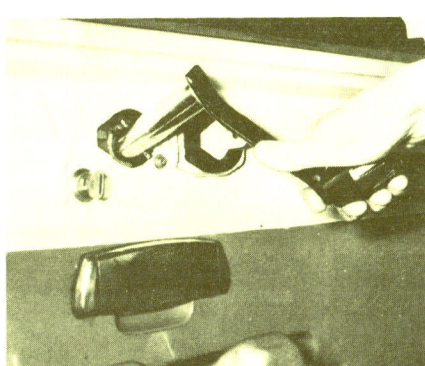

19.2 The crank handle for the manually operated tailgate

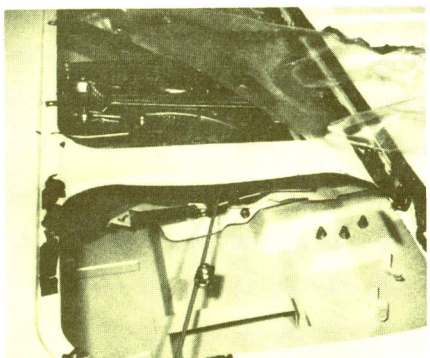

20.1 The plastic film folded back for access to the regulator

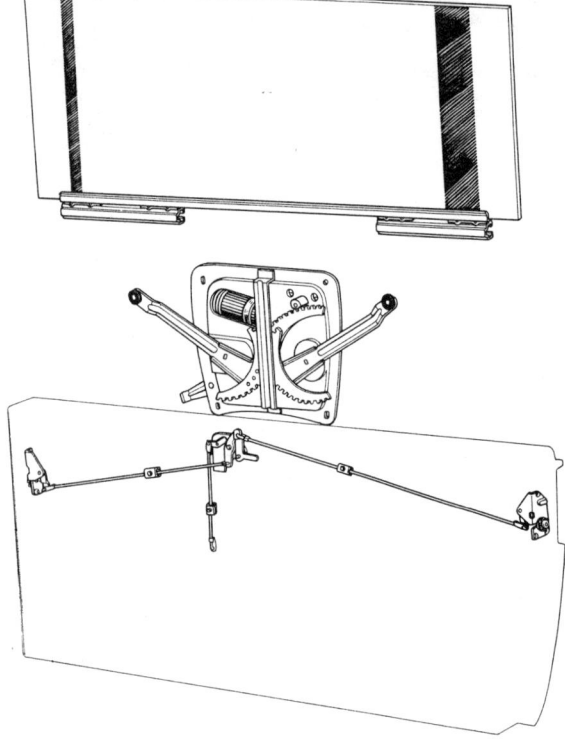

Fig. 12.24. Tailgate regulator assembly

2 Raise the tailgate window approximately half-way up, then remove the stop plate which connects the roller guide to the glass rubber.
3 Remove the roller guide from the glass holder, then lower the glass.
4 Remove the inner and outer weatherstrips, then remove the glass.
5 Detach the battery ground lead or disconnect the fusible link, then disconnect the junction block wiring. Note the relative connections to avoid mix-up during installation.
6 Disconnect the 'Lock-off' lever connecting wire, then remove the regulator assembly.
7 Installation is the reverse of the removal procedure, but ensure that the regulator is square before finally tightening the screws. Also apply a little general purpose grease to the pivot points and friction surfaces.

21 Tailgate regulator motor (FJ55) - removal, dismantling, reassembly and installation

1 Remove the regulator (see previous Section).
2 Remove the attaching nuts and screws, and take off the motor.
3 Remove the nuts and washers, and take out the motor through bolts.
4 Remove the bearing holder, thrust washer, armature, end frame and steel ball.
5 Where necessary, new brushes can be installed, their leads being soldered to the loom wiring.
6 Installation is the reverse of the removal procedure. Adjust the armature thrust gap to 0.002/0.008 in (0.05/0.2 mm) using two to four thrust washers; if a thrust set screw and nut are used on your particular motor, adjust the screw for 0.002/0.012 in (0.05/0.3 mm) thrust gap, then tighten the locknut afterwards.

22 Tailgate lock (FJ55) - removal and installation

1 Remove the tailgate regulator (see Section 20), then disconnect the three attaching screws to release the tailgate lock.
2 To remove the lock handle, remove the two attaching screws. Remove the two bolts securing the tailgate handle to the handle seat, then detach the remote control wire from the handle.
3 Installation is the reverse of the removal procedure, but apply a little general purpose grease to pivot points and sliding surfaces of the mechanism. Adjust the 'Lock off' lever, if necessary, by altering the connecting wire length; adjust the tailgate for a satisfactory locking action by means of the striker plate.

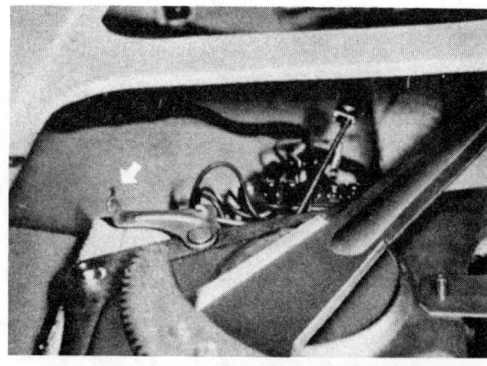

Fig. 12.25. Tailgate 'Lock-off' lever (arrowed)

23 Engine compartment hood - removal, installation and adjustment

1 Removal procedures for the engine compartment hoods are straightforward as will be seen by reference to the accompanying illustrations. To assist with alignment when installing, it is a good idea to mark around the hinge positions with a pencil or ballpoint pen. Also, because of the weight, it is necessary to have assistance from another person to support the hood while it is being disconnected.
2 Fore and aft adjustment of the hood is taken care of at the hinges on the hood. On FJ55 models lateral adjustment is possible where the hinges are attached to the body (photo).
3 The hood lock on FJ55 models can be adjusted at the mounting bolts. If necessary the dowel bolt can be adjusted using a screwdriver after the locknut has been loosened.

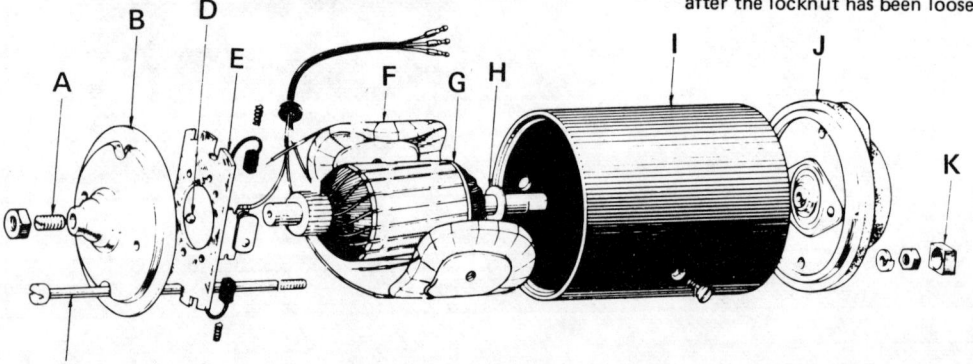

Fig. 12.26. Tailgate regulator motor - exploded view of later type

A Set screw
B End frame
C Bolt
D Steel ball
E Brush holder
F Field coil
G Armature
H Thrust washer
I Yoke
J Bearing holder
K Space collar

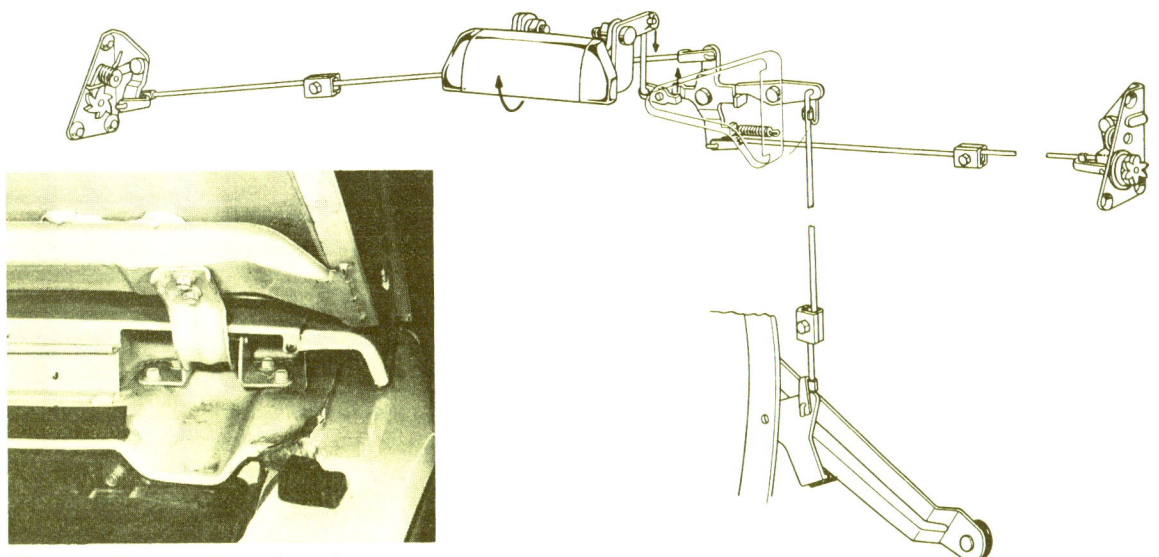

23.2 Hood hinge attachment (FJ55)

Fig. 12.27. Tailgate lock

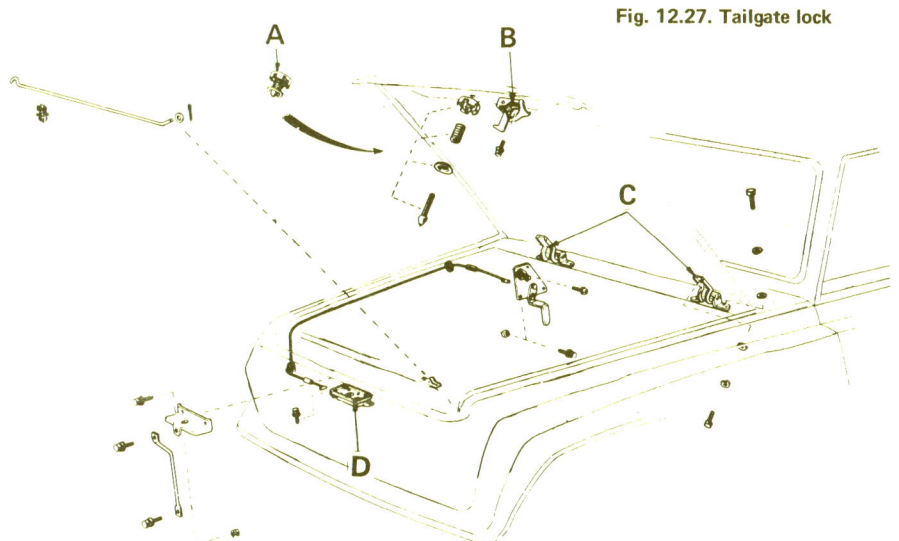

Fig. 12.28. Hood components - typical for FJ55 models

| A Hood lock hook assembly | B Auxiliary catch hook | C Hinge | D Hood lock |

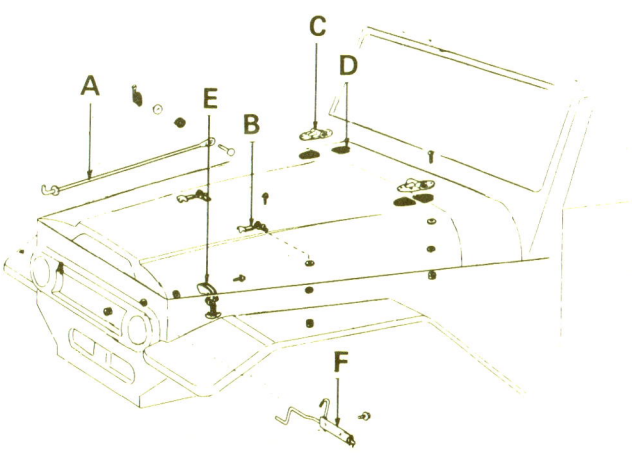

Fig. 12.29. Hood components - typical for FJ40 models

A Hood stopper
B Hood fastener
C Hinge
D Hinge seal
E Side auxiliary catch hook
F Front auxiliary catch hook

28.1 Air outlet duct escutcheon

24 Bumpers - removal and installation

1 Removal of the bumpers is a straightforward operation after the attaching nuts, bolts and washers have been removed. Take note of their relative positions when removing them.
2 When installing, ensure that they are correctly aligned for side-to-side and horizontal positioning.

25 Radiator grille - removal and installation

1 Remove the grille attaching nuts and screws, and ease the grille away.
2 Where applicable, detach the turn signal light wires.
3 If necessary, detach the turn signal light.
4 Installation is the reverse of the removal procedure.

26 Instrument panel and glove compartment

1 The instrument panel and glove compartment can be removed if necessary. The component parts are shown in Figs. 12.30 and 12.31.

27 Front window ventilator panel (FJ40 series)

1 Some models have a ventilator panel in front of the windshield. The component parts are shown in Fig. 12.32.

28 Rear trim panels (FJ55) - removal and installation

1 The method of fixing the side panels is similar to that used for the door trim panels - see Section 9. Additionally, it is necessary to remove the escutcheon screws so that the air outlet duct can be detached. On the left-hand side the retaining screws will also have to be removed to release the trim from around the fuel tank filler tube (photo).

29 Windshield, side window and back door fixed glass - removal and installation

Note: The procedure given in this Section is specifically for the windshield, but the procedure for the rest of the vehicle is similar except for the windshield mouldings which are used on some models.
1 Place a protective covering over the hood, side panels, fenders, instrument panel and front seats.

Fig. 12.30. Instrument panel and glove compartment parts - typical for FJ55 models

1 Glove compartment door lock cylinder housing
2 Glove compartment
3 Switch escutcheon
4 Instrument panel pad
5 Air control hole cover
6 Heater control escutcheon
7 Instrument panel upper cover
8 Glove compartment door pad
9 Inner panel
10 Glove compartment door hinge
11 Radio opening cover
12 Instrument center upper pad
13 Instrument center lower cover
14 Ash tray hole cover
15 Meter hood pad
16 Ash tray
17 Instrument panel

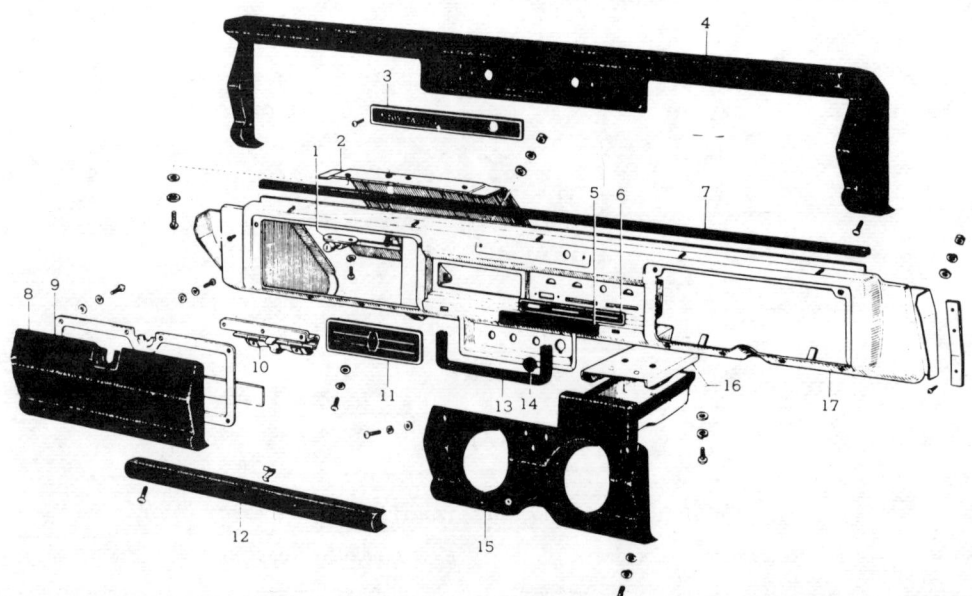

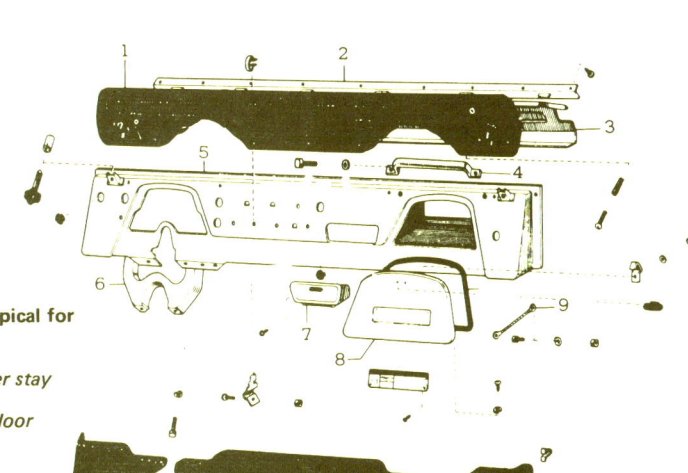

Fig. 12.31. Instrument panel and glove compartment parts - typical for FJ40 models

1 Upper safety pad
2 Safety pad retainer
3 Instrument impact panel
4 Handgrip
5 Instrument lower panel
6 Steering column upper stay
7 Ash receptacle
8 Glove compartment door
9 Stay
10 Lower safety pad
11 Lower safety pad

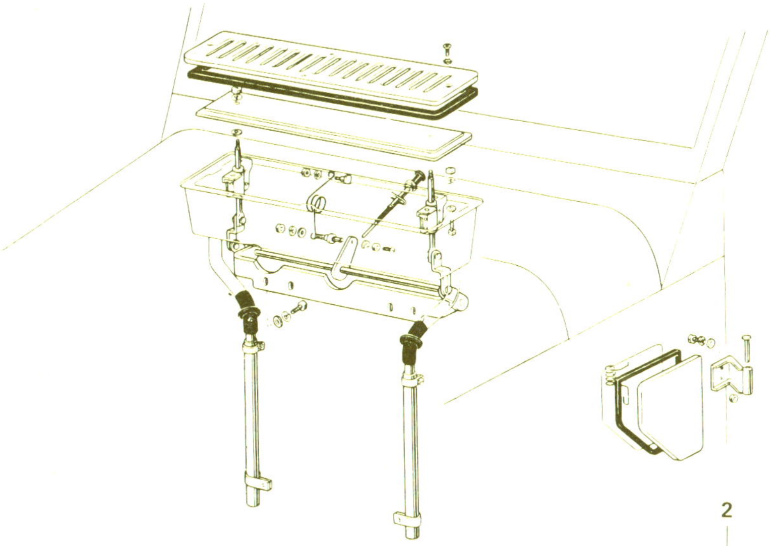

Fig. 12.32. Front window ventilator panel (FJ40)

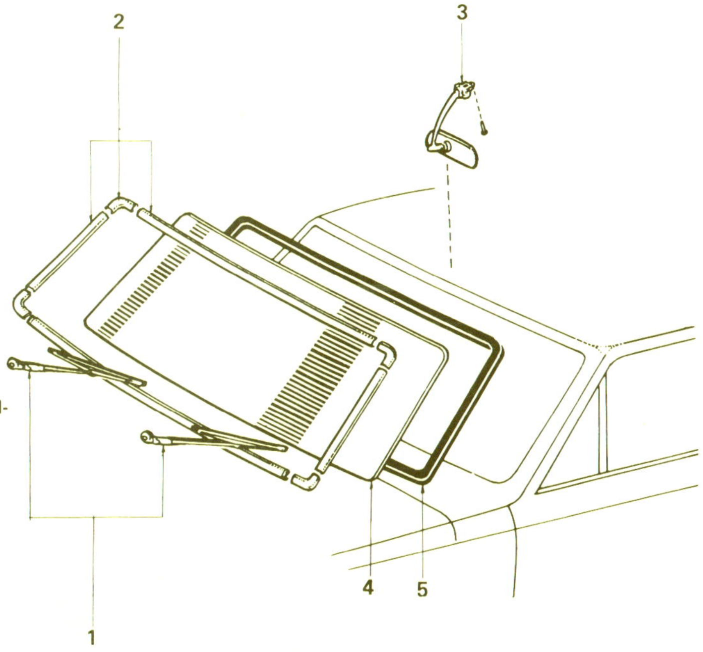

Fig. 12.33. Windshield arrangement - typical for vehicles with windshield mouldings

1 Wiper arm
2 Windshield moulding
3 Rear view mirror
4 Windshield glass
5 Windshield weatherstrip

2 Remove the interior rear view mirror.
3 Remove the windshield wiper arms (refer to Chapter 11 if necessary).
4 When applicable, remove the windshield mouldings.
5 From the inside of the vehicle, use a blunt putty knife or similar tool and ease the weatherstrip from the glass and body aperture. As this is being done, press on the windshield with the palm of the hand.
6 With help from an assistant, press out the windshield and lift it clear. Take care that it is not scratched whilst removed from the vehicle.
7 If the weatherstrip is in good condition and the old adhesive can be cleaned off, it can be re-used for installation. However, this is unlikely to be so, and it is recommended that a new one is used.
8 When installing, first clean off all the old adhesive around the body aperture, and check for irregularities, rust, etc. Treat these as necessary, or it will not be possible to obtain a satisfactory seal.
9 Install the weatherstrip onto the glass, then insert a strong cord into the body cavity of the weatherstrip around the complete length so that the ends overlap. Also leave a loop along the windshield top edge.
10 With help from an assistant, position the glass against the body aperture, with the ends of the cord inside the vehicle.
11 Apply a solution of soap and water around the body aperture and weatherstrip flange, then ensure that the glass is properly positioned.
12 Now slowly pull the ends of the cord at right angles to the windshield, starting at the bottom center, to seat the weatherstrip over the body flange. This should be done progressively at each side, with the assistant pressing on the glass from the outside.
13 When the weatherstrip is installed, apply a suitable black mastic adhesive between the weatherstrip and the body, and between the weatherstrip and the glass. **Note:** If masking tape is used around the weatherstrip, it will prevent the adhesive from smearing onto the body paintwork, and glass and will facilitate cleaning, which can be done with gasoline.
14 On completion, install the windshield mouldings (where applicable) windshield wiper arms and rear view mirror.

30 Air conditioning system - general description and maintenance

1 The optionally specified system comprises a heating and cooling unit, a belt driven compressor, a condenser and a receiver, together with the necessary temperature controls and stabilisers.
2 The oil filled compressor is driven from the crankshaft pulley and incorporates a magnetic-type clutch.
3 Servicing of the system is outside the scope of the home mechanic as special equipment is needed to purge or recharge the system with refrigerant gas, and dismantling of any part of the system must not be undertaken, in the interest of safety, without first having had the system pressure discharged.
4 To maintain optimum performance of the system, the owner should limit his operations to the following items.
   Check the tension of the compressor driving belt. This should have a deflection of 0.5 in (13 mm) when pressed at its mid-point, with a load of 20 lb (9 kg).
   Check the security of all hoses and unions.
   Always keep the ignition timing correctly set.
   Check adjustment of facia mounted control cable.
   Check security of system electrical leads.
   Remove, and wash if necessary, the air filter screen located in the cooling unit intake grille.
   Use a soft brush to regularly remove accumulations of dust and dirt from the condenser fins.
   During the winter months operate the air conditioning system for a few minutes each week to lubricate the compressor interior (normally disconnected by magnetic clutch non-engagement - facia control off).

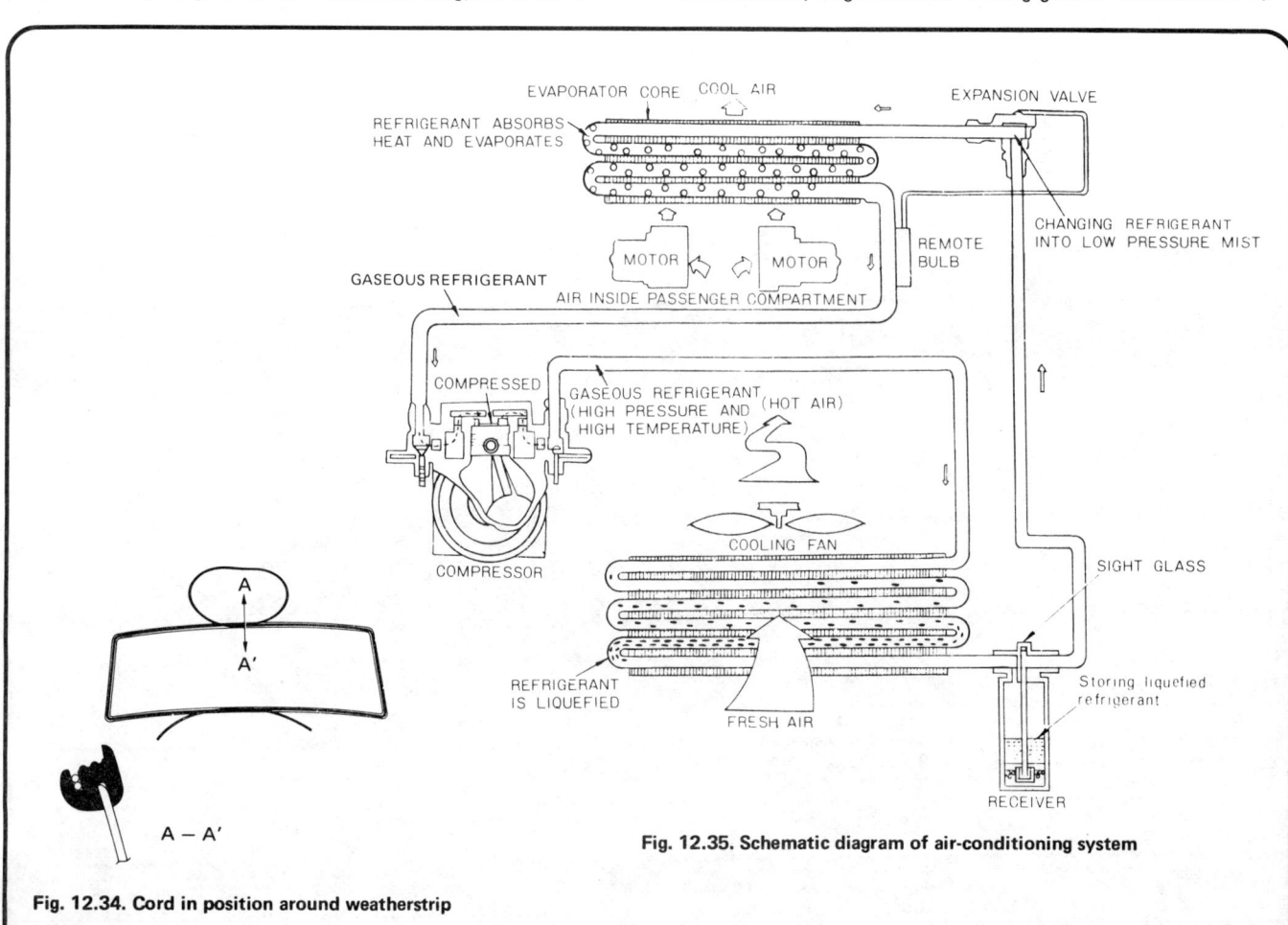

Fig. 12.34. Cord in position around weatherstrip

Fig. 12.35. Schematic diagram of air-conditioning system

Metric conversion tables

Inches	Decimals	Millimetres	Millimetres to Inches		Inches to Millimetres	
			mm	Inches	Inches	mm
1/64	0.015625	0.3969	0.01	0.00039	0.001	0.0254
1/32	0.03125	0.7937	0.02	0.00079	0.002	0.0508
3/64	0.046875	1.1906	0.03	0.00118	0.003	0.0762
1/16	0.0625	1.5875	0.04	0.00157	0.004	0.1016
5/64	0.078125	1.9844	0.05	0.00197	0.005	0.1270
3/32	0.09375	2.3812	0.06	0.00236	0.006	0.1524
7/64	0.109375	2.7781	0.07	0.00276	0.007	0.1778
1/8	0.125	3.1750	0.08	0.00315	0.008	0.2032
9/64	0.140625	3.5719	0.09	0.00354	0.009	0.2286
5/32	0.15625	3.9687	0.1	0.00394	0.01	0.254
11/64	0.171875	4.3656	0.2	0.00787	0.02	0.508
3/16	0.1875	4.7625	0.3	0.1181	0.03	0.762
13/64	0.203125	5.1594	0.4	0.01575	0.04	1.016
7/32	0.21875	5.5562	0.5	0.01969	0.05	1.270
15/64	0.234275	5.9531	0.6	0.02362	0.06	1.524
1/4	0.25	6.3500	0.7	0.02756	0.07	1.778
17/64	0.265625	6.7469	0.8	0.3150	0.08	2.032
9/32	0.28125	7.1437	0.9	0.03543	0.09	2.286
19/64	0.296875	7.5406	1	0.03937	0.1	2.54
5/16	0.3125	7.9375	2	0.07874	0.2	5.08
21/64	0.328125	8.3344	3	0.11811	0.3	7.62
11/32	0.34375	8.7312	4	0.15748	0.4	10.16
23/64	0.359375	9.1281	5	0.19685	0.5	12.70
3/8	0.375	9.5250	6	0.23622	0.6	15.24
25/64	0.390625	9.9219	7	0.27559	0.7	17.78
13/32	0.40625	10.3187	8	0.31496	0.8	20.32
27/64	0.421875	10.7156	9	0.35433	0.9	22.86
7/16	0.4375	11.1125	10	0.39270	1	25.4
29/64	0.453125	11.5094	11	0.43307	2	50.8
15/32	0.46875	11.9062	12	0.47244	3	76.2
31/64	0.484375	12.3031	13	0.51181	4	101.6
1/2	0.5	12.7000	14	0.55118	5	127.0
33/64	0.515625	13.0969	15	0.59055	6	152.4
17/32	0.53125	13.4937	16	0.62992	7	177.8
35/64	0.546875	13.8906	17	0.66929	8	203.2
9/16	0.5625	14.2875	18	0.70866	9	228.6
37/64	0.578125	14.6844	19	0.74803	10	254.0
19/32	0.59375	15.0812	20	0.78740	11	279.4
39/64	0.609375	15.4781	21	0.82677	12	304.8
5/8	0.625	15.8750	22	0.86614	13	330.2
41/64	0.640625	16.2719	23	0.90551	14	355.6
21/32	0.65625	16.6687	24	0.94488	15	381.0
43/64	0.671875	17.0656	25	0.98425	16	406.4
11/16	0.6875	17.4625	26	1.02362	17	431.8
45/64	0.703125	17.8594	27	1.06299	18	457.2
23/32	0.71875	18.2562	28	1.10236	19	482.6
47/64	0.734375	18.6531	29	1.14173	20	508.0
3/4	0.75	19.0500	30	1.18110	21	533.4
49/64	0.765625	19.4469	31	1.22047	22	558.8
25/32	0.78125	19.8437	32	1.25984	23	584.2
51/64	0.796875	20.2406	33	1.29921	24	609.6
13/16	0.8125	20.6375	34	1.33858	25	635.0
53/64	0.828125	21.0344	35	1.37795	26	660.4
27/32	0.84375	21.4312	36	1.41732	27	685.8
55/64	0.859375	21.8281	37	1.4567	28	711.2
7/8	0.875	22.2250	38	1.4961	29	736.6
57/64	0.890625	22.6219	39	1.5354	30	762.0
29/32	0.90625	23.0187	40	1.5748	31	787.4
59/64	0.921875	23.4156	41	1.6142	32	812.8
15/16	0.9375	23.8125	42	1.6535	33	838.2
61/64	0.953125	24.2094	43	1.6929	34	863.6
31/32	0.96875	24.6062	44	1.7323	35	889.0
63/64	0.984375	25.0031	45	1.7717	36	914.4

Index

A

Accelerator linkage - 64
Air cleaner - 60,61,63
Air injection system - 72
Alternator
    dismantling, servicing and reassembly - 186,189
    general description - 183
    removing and installation - 185
    testing - 185
Antifreeze - 40

B

Battery
    charging - 183
    electrolyte replenishment - 182
    maintenance - 182
    removal and installation - 182
Bodywork and fittings
    air conditioning - 264
    bonnet - 260
    bumper - 262
    description - 244
    doors - 249,251,252,254,256
    globe compartment - 262
    hinges and locks - 249
    instrument panel - 262
    interior trim - 262
    maintenance - 244
    repair - major damage - 248
             - minor damage - 245
    tailgate - 259
    upholstery - 245
    windows - 251,254,256
Braking system
    adjustment - 166
    bleeding hydraulic system - 169
    calipers - 175
    description - 166
    disc - 175
    drum - 175
    fault diagnosis - 179
    hydraulic lines - 176
    master cylinder - 169
    parking brake - 166,177,179
    pedal - 166
    servo unit - 171
    shoes - 166,172,177
    specifications - 165
    wheel cylinders - 169
Bumpers - 262
Buying spare parts - 6

C

Camshaft
    bearings - 30
    installation - 35
    removal - 23
    renovation - 30
Capacitors - 45
Carburetor
    adjustment - 47,50,54,58
    description - 47
    dismantling and reassembly - 47,53,55
    fault diagnosis - 91
    removal and installation - 47
    specifications - 45
Clutch
    description - 104
    faults - 110
    housing - 32
    installation - 110
    master cylinder - 107
    pedal - 107
    release bearings - 110
    release cylinder - 107
    release fork - 107
    removal - 108
    renovation - 110
    specifications - 104
Column shift linkage - 129
Condenser - 96
Connecting rods
    dismantling - 24
    reassembly - 33
    removal - 23
    renovation - 30
Contact breaker points
    adjustment - 96
    removal and installation - 96
Cooling fan - 42
Cooling system
    description - 39
    draining - 40
    fault diagnosis - 44
    filling - 40
    flushing - 40
    specifications - 39
Crankcase ventilation - 28
Crankshaft
    installation - 34
    removal - 23
    renovation - 30
Cylinder bores
    renovation - 30
Cylinder head
    decarbonisation - 32
    dismantling - 24
    installation - 36
    reassembly - 34
    removal - 22

D

Distributor
    dismantling and reassembly - 97
    removal and installation - 97
Doors
    handles - 252
    locks - 251
    removal and installation - 249
    rattles - 249
    window glass and regulator - 251
Driveshaft - 139

E

Electrical system
    alternator - 183,185,186,189

Index

battery - 182,183
  description - 182
  fault diagnosis - 242
  flashers - 205
  fuses and fusible link - 199
  headlamp - 195
  heater - 209
  horn - 205
  ignition switch - 204
  indicator switch - 204
  instrument panel combination meter - 201
  lighting switches - 204
  reverse light switch - 204
  specifications - 181
  starter motor - 192
  stop light switch - 205
  windshield wipers - 204,205
Emission control systems - 66
Engine
  ancillary components, installing - 37
  ancillary components, removal - 22
  dismantling - 20
  examination and renovation - 28
  fault diagnosis - 38
  general description - 18
  idle speed adjustment - 59
  modification system - 68
  reassembly - 33
  removal method - 18
  start-up after ovehaul - 37
  specifications - 15
Engine/transmission
  installation - 20
  removal - 20
Exhaust system and manifolds - 66,75

F

Flywheel
  removal - 20
  renovation - 32
Front axle
  description - 154
  fault diagnosis - 164
  removal and installation - 160
  specifications - 153
Fuel filter - 60
Fuel pump
  dismantling, inspection and reassembly - 60
  removal and installation - 60
Fuel system
  description - 47
  emission control system - 71
  fault diagnosis - 91
  specifications - 45
Fuel tank - 63
Fluid coupling - 42

H

Heat control valve - 79
Heaters - 209
High altitude compensation system - 79
Horn - 205
Hydraulic system - 108

I

Idle speed adjustment - 59
Ignition system
  description - 92
  fault finding - 102
  semi-transistorised - 106
  specifications - 92
  switch - 204
  timing 97
Instrument panel - 201, 262

J

Jacking points - 7

L

Lighting system - 195,197,199
Lubrication system - 24

M

Main bearings
  installation - 34
  removal - 23
  renovation - 30
Maintenance routine - 8
Manifolds - 66

O

Oil pan - 23
Oil pump
  dismantling, inspection and reassembly - 28
  removal - 23
Oil seals
  rear axle pinion 149,160
  timing cover - 33

P

Piston/connecting rod assemblies - 23
Piston rings
  reassembly and refitting - 33
  renovation - 30
Pistons
  dismantling - 24
  installation - 34
  reassembly and refitting - 33
  removal - 23
  renovation - 30
Positive crankcase ventilation - 28
Power take-off - 138
Power valve control system - 77
Propeller shaft
  description - 142
  fault diagnosis - 142
  removal and installation - 142
  specifications - 142
  universal joints - 142
Pushrods - 31

R

Radiator - 40
Radiator grille - 262
Rear axle
  axleshaft - 145
  description - 145
  differential assembly - 148
  fault diagnosis - 152
  pinion oil seal - 149,160
  removal and installation - 145,151
  specifications - 145
Rockers - 31

S

Spare parts buying - 6
Spark control system - 77
Spark plugs - 102
Starter motor
  dismantling, overhaul and reassembly - 192
  removal and installation - 192
Steering
  alignment - 164
  description - 154
  fault diagnosis - 164
  front wheel hubs - 158
  gear removal and installation - 162
  linkage - 163
  specifications - 153
  steering wheel - 161
Suspension (front)
  axleshaft - 154
  bearing - 158
  contact velocity point - 157

differential - 160
   general description - 154
   shock absorber - 160
   specifications - 153
   steering knuckle - 154
Suspension (rear)
   fault diagnosis - 152
   general description - 145
   removal and installation - 151
   Shock absorbers - 151
   specifications - 145

T

Tailgate - 259
Thermal reactor system - 79
Thermostat - 42
Throttle positioner - 71
Timing gear
   installation - 36
   removal - 23
Tires - 179,180
Tire pressures - 166
Tools - 11
Towing points - 7
Transfer front drive - 132, 135
Transfer gear
   dismantling, inspection and reassembly - 131
   removal - 115
   separation - 116
Transmission
   components - 123
   description - 115

   dismantling - 118,120,123
   fault diagnosis - 141
   reassembly - 125
   removal - 115
   specifications - 112
   top cover - 129

U

Universal joints - 142

V

Valves
   clearance adjustment - 36
   dismantling - 24
   installation - 36
   guides - 31
   renovation - 30
   rocker mechanism - 34
   seats - 30
   springs - 31
Vehicle identification numbers - 6

W

Water pump
   dismantling, overhaul and reassembly - 42
   removal - 42
Wheels - 179
Winch - 139
Windshield wipers - 204,205
Wiring diagrams - 212-241
Working facilities - 11

Printed by
Haynes Publishing Group
Sparkford Yeovil Somerset
England